Modelling Driver Behaviour in Automotive Environments

Carlo Cacciabue (Ed.)

Modelling Driver Behaviour in Automotive Environments

Critical Issues in Driver Interactions with Intelligent Transport Systems

Springer

P. Carlo Cacciabue, Ph.D.
EC JRC -IPSC, Italy

British Library Cataloguing in Publication Data
A catalogue record for this book is available from the British Library

ISBN-13: 978-1-84996-628-3 e-ISBN-10: 1-84628-618-2
e-ISBN-13: 978-1-84628-618-6

Printed on acid-free paper

9 8 7 6 5 4 3 2 1

Springer Science+Business Media
springer.com

Contents

Editorial

The implementation of information technology and automation has been the driving force of the development of technology in the last decades. At the same time the presence of humans in control of systems has been kept as the locus of design principles. Only more recently, fully unmanned technology is beginning to find its application, in a limited number of domains, such as urban guided transport systems and military aviation. However, even in the cases of totally automatic systems, it is not possible to avoid the assessment of the human-in-control principle, as the overall remote operator of the fully automatic systems remains to be accounted for in the design and development processes. For these reasons, the consideration of the user and controller of technologically advanced systems is one of the most relevant issues for design development, and during production and implementation processes.

The use of "intelligent" systems implies that the level of autonomy and the possibility to delegate control processes to technology and automation has improved enormously. The human being has been freed from performing a number of activities and has progressively been removed from the direct control loop of systems, in favour of high level decision making processes.

Therefore, in parallel to the development of technology, the need to account for the behaviour of the human being has progressively evolved from the consideration of the human-manual-controller to the human-supervisor of processes, procedures and performances of automatic control systems. The evaluation of behavioural performance has been replaced by the analysis of cognitive and mental processes. In other words, the demand for modelling manual and behavioural activities has been replaced and combined with the need for modelling cognition. This is the requirement that has mostly affected the development of new technologies and interfaces in modern control devices.

This feature of design and development of technological systems is common to many different domains, from energy production, chemical and process industry, transport and health care. In this scenario, the automotive transport is the domain mostly affected by the need to consider the multiplicity of human behaviour, as it presents the highest possible variety of operating environments, of human behaviours, and it offers many different technological solutions for all different control processes.

In reality, many automation controls currently applied to vehicles already contain models of a certain complexity of cognition and behaviour, based mostly on dynamic manifestation of control operations. The "automatic gearbox" of certain vehicles is a typical example of this type of control systems, which adapt dynamically and independently to different "driving styles", measured through intrinsic evaluation of behavioural variables, such as rate of accelerator pressure, overall speed, etc. Another example is the system that manages the availability of in vehicle information systems (IVIS), such as telephones or radios. In this case, certain IVIS managers adapt to the environmental situations, by inhibiting or discouraging the use of certain IVIS in risky situations.

The models of cognition and behaviour that are implemented in such types of vehicle control systems are naturally elementary from the cognitive point of view. However, this shows that this *industrial* field, both in terms of vehicle integrators and original equipment manufacturers, needs to apply at design level and integrate at implementation level adequate models of driver behaviour. These models are equally important for *academic* and *research* purposes, where more complex and varied solutions can be proposed and studied in relation to theoretical paradigms of different nature and targets. Another area where modelling of driver behaviour is essential is the *transport safety authorities* and *regulators*, where the consideration of driver performance becomes essential in setting standards and rules governing new and future regulations of vehicle control systems, road infrastructures and traffic management. Similarly, models of drivers are necessary for the study of accidents and investigation of root causes.

The availability of models and paradigms of driver behaviour at different levels of complexity and development is therefore quite obvious according to the field of application.

This book offers to the reader the possibility to assess different approaches and considerations in relation to driver behaviour modelling, resulting from different fields. Indeed, the authors of the different manuscripts come from the industrial area, both car and original equipment manufactures and integrators, from the research and academic fields and from national and international regulators and automotive transport authorities.

More in detail, Chapter 1 presents the ongoing activities in *International Projects and Actions on Driver Modelling*. In particular, the European sustained research Projects carried out over the last decades and presently under development are reviewed in the paper by Panou, Bekiaris, and Papakostopoulos. Similarly, the US research actions on driver models and a recently held workshop on these issues are discussed in the paper by Cody and Gordon. The last paper of this Chapter, by Inagaky, also revises the actions in Japan on driver modelling, focusing on monitoring and modelling situation-adaptive driver assistance systems.

After this initial review, more specific subjects are dealt with, beginning with the existing *Conceptual Frameworks and Modelling Architectures* (Chapter 2) that sustain the development of specific models of driver behaviour. In all three papers, a short historical review of paradigms and architectures for considering the human element in a Driver-Vehicle-Environment perspective is performed. The three papers then focus on a specific modelling architecture that enables the reader to consider very high level structures of interaction, primarily in the papers by Engström and Hollnagel, and by Peters and Nilsson, and more practical and field focused architectures in the paper by Carsten.

Chapter 3, contains a overall discussion and overview of one of the major issues that affect driver behaviour modelling: *Learning and Behavioural Adaptation.* This issue is dealt with from different perspectives, beginning with the view on Testing for Evaluation of driver information systems and driver assistance systems, by Bengler. The crucial issue of risk taking and risk perception is discussed in the work of Janssen. The Chapter is then completed by the paper of Saad, that offers a wide and distributed review of theoretical stands on adaptation and processes that affect driver performance.

In Chapter 4 another essential and widely debated aspect of driver behaviour is tackled: *Modelling Motivation and Psychological Mechanisms*. The three contributors to this Chapter offer different and, in some cases, controversial views on specific formulations and algorithms that can be applied to describe and account for these critical factors governing driver behaviour. In particular, Fuller concentrates on determinants of control in the driving task. Summala describes motivational and emotional factors through the concept of "satisfying". Vaa offers an overview of his long standing arguments on emotions and feelings.

Chapter 5 deals with *Modelling Risk and Errors.* The issue of risk management and risk perception, already dealt with in the Chapter about adaptation, is further developed here in the paper by Van der Horst, where the specific problem of time-related measures for modelling risk are discussed in detail. The other two papers focus more closely on aspects associated with human error. The paper of Baumann and Krems is dedicated to critical causes of human error. A model based on the evaluation of Situation Awareness for different driving situations is developed. The paper by Parker offers instead a wider overview and discussion on the human error making more correlated to classical and well established theories. The specific application to the automotive domain demonstrates the possibility to apply such theories to this domain as it has been done in other cases, e.g., aviation, nuclear energy etc.

Chapter 6, introduces the second part of the book, dedicated to the review of a number of numerical simulation and computerised implementation of the theories and paradigms described in the previous five chapters of the book. In particular, Chapter 6 discusses the *Control Theory Models of Driver Behaviour.* The paper by Jürgensohn offers a very comprehensive review of many Control Theory Models of the Driver that have been developed in the past and are still nowadays very valuable numerical approaches for describing human machine interactions. The paper by Weir and Chao also offers a review of control theory approaches, but then quite readily focuses on a specific control theory approach developed by the authors over a number of years for describing Directional and Speed Control over a certain period of time.

Chapter 7, concentrates on the problem of the overall *Simulation of Driver Behaviour* and representation of the interaction with the vehicle and environment. The paper by Bellet, Bailly, Mayenobe, and Georgeon describes a computational simulation of drivers mental activities called COSMODRIVE, based on several Artificial Intelligence approaches such as the Blackboard architecture and specific simulation languages that enable the fast and simple description of driver performance. The paper by Cacciabue, Re and Macchi offers a similar simulation approach, called SSDRIVE, which describes the driver behaviour by means of Object Oriented Languages and applies the theoretical paradigm described in Chapter 2 of the book and exploits the power of control theory to describe driver control actions.

Finally, Chapter 8 deals with the issue of *Simulation of Traffic and Real Situations.* The need to simulate the driving context is directly associated to the ability of modern simulations to predict behaviour and driver interactions with the vehicle in many driving situations. Consequently in order to make the simulation as realistic as possible, it is necessary that the models that are coupled to driver simulation are equally detailed and representative of real traffic situations. Two papers complete this chapter. The paper by Amditis, Polychronopoulos, and Bekiaris concentrates on real-time traffic and environment risk estimation, while the paper by Tango, Montanari, and Marzani describes a set of existing simulations of traffic and discusses the new orientation and perspectives of future models and simulations of traffic.

The above description of the Chapters demonstrates that the Book can be read as a whole in order to get a general perspective of the ongoing topics of development for present generation of automation and intelligent support systems. At the same time, it offers the overview on open issues characterising research into new areas of concern for future control perspectives. However, it is equally possible to consider selected readings of papers and chapters, when the needs of the reader focus on well defined and specific subjects, such as for example driver adaptation or simulation of DVE interactions.

The quality and completeness of this Book rests primarily on the excellence of the papers that are included. For this reason, the editor of this book is deeply grateful to all authors who have diligently, professionally and proficiently collaborated to its development. The editor has simply acted as catalyser and integrator of ideas and competences, ensuring that the pieces of this puzzle could come together in a consistent and coherent vision of the problems under scrutiny. The success of this endeavour rests eventually on the quality of its content and on the response of the scientific community to which it is addressed.

P. Carlo Cacciabue

List of Contributors

Angelos Amditis
I-SENSE Group,
Institute of Communications and Computer Systems,
Athens, Greece.

Béatrice Bailly
INRETS- LESCOT,
Bron cedex, France.

Martin Baumann
Chemnitz University of Technology,
Department of Psychology,
Chemnitz, Germany.

Evangelos Bekiaris
Hellenic Institute of Transport,
Athens, Greece.

Thierry Bellet
INRETS-LESCOT,
Bron cedex, France.

Klaus Bengler
BMW Group,
Forschung und Technik,
Munich, Germany.

P. Carlo Cacciabue
EC, Joint Research Centre,
Institute for the Protection and Security of the Citizen,
Ispra (VA), Italy.

Oliver Carsten
University of Leeds,
Institute for Transport Studies,
Leeds LS2 9JT, UK.

Kevin C. Chao
Dynamic Research, Inc.,
Torrance, CA, USA.

Delphine Cody
UC Berkeley,
California PATH,
Richmond, CA, USA.

Johan Engström
Volvo Technology Corporation,
Göteborg, Sweden.

Ray Fuller
Trinity College Dublin,
Department of Psychology,
Dublin 2, Ireland.

Olivier Georgeon
INRETS-LESCOT,
Bron cedex, France.

Timothy Gordon
University of Michigan,
Transportation Research Institute,
Ann Arbor, MI, USA.

Erik Hollnagel
École des Mines de Paris,
Pôle Cindyniques,
Sophia Antipolis Cedex, France.

Toshiyuki Inagaki
University of Tsukuba,
Department of Risk Engineering,
Tsukuba, Japan.

Wiel Janssen
TNO Defence, Security & Safety,
BU Human Factors,
Soesterberg, The Netherlands.

Thomas Jürgensohn
HFC Human-Factors-Consult GmbH,
Berlin, Germany.

Josef F. Krems
Chemnitz University of Technology,
Department of Psychology,
Chemnitz, Germany.

Luigi Macchi
EC, Joint Research Centre,
Institute for the Protection and Security of the Citizen,
Ispra (VA), Italy.

Stefano Marzani
University of Modena and Reggio Emilia,
Dipartimento di Scienze e Metodi dell'Ingegneria,
Reggio Emilia, Italy.

Pierre Mayenobe
INRETS-LESCOT,
Bron cedex, France.

Roberto Montanari
University of Modena and Reggio Emilia,
Dipartimento di Scienze e Metodi dell'Ingegneria,
Reggio Emilia, Italy.

Lena Nilsson
VTI,
Linköping, Sweden.

Maria Panou
Hellenic Institute of Transport,
Athens, Greece.

Vassilis Papakostopoulos
Hellenic Institute of Transport,
Athens, Greece.

Dianne Parker
University of Manchester,
School of Psychological Sciences,
Manchester M13 9PL, UK.

Björn Peters
VTI,
Linköping, Sweden.

Aris Polychronopoulos
I-SENSE Group,
Institute of Communications and Computer Systems,
Athens, Greece.

Cristina Re
EC, Joint Research Centre,
Institute for the Protection and Security of the Citizen,
Ispra (VA), Italy.

Farida Saad
INRETS-GARIG,
Champs-sur-Marne, France.

Heikki Summala
University of Helsinki, Department of Psychology,
Helsinki, Finland.

Fabio Tango
Centro Ricerche Fiat (C.R.F.)
Orbassano (TO), Italy.

Truls Vaa
Institute of Transport Economics (TØI),
OSLO, Norway.

Richard van der Horst
TNO Defence, Security & Safety,
BU Human Factors,
Soesterberg, The Netherlands.

David H. Weir
Dynamic Research, Inc.,
Torrance, CA, USA.

I
International Projects and Actions on Driver Modelling

1 Modelling Driver Behaviour in European Union and International Projects

M. PANOU, E. BEKIARIS AND V. PAPAKOSTOPOULOS

1.1 Introduction

Human (or operator) modelling has been an extensive area of research in many application areas, such as artificial intelligence, aviation, probabilistic risk assessments, system safety analysis and human performances in working contexts (Cacciabue et al., 1993; Baron et al., 1980). Still, human behaviour is fairly contextual and substantially different from one person to another. Thus, the initial linear models have been gradually replaced by nonlinear and even probabilistic models, based upon artificial intelligence (AI) principles, such as artificial neural networks or genetic algorithms. This becomes even more intrigued if we consider a complex behavioural task such as vehicle driving.

The traffic system as a whole can be seen as being composed of three interactive parts: vehicles, road users and the road environment. Any traffic situation is the result of the interaction between these three systems. Normally, the traffic situation develops as planned, but, in certain circumstances the resulting interaction will result in a critical situation or in a crash.

The driver is a critical component of the traffic system. Attempts have been made to estimate the importance of the driver as an accident cause (Evans, 1985). It has been estimated that road user factors are the sole or contributory factors in a great majority of road crashes.

There is no generally accepted model of the complete driving task. There are detailed descriptions focusing on perception and handling aspects and reporting what drivers really do in every possible ('normal') situation from the beginning to the end of a journey (see McKnight and Adams, 1970). There are also more analytical approaches focusing on driver behaviour in relation to task demands, with the purpose of trying to explain and understand the psychological mechanisms underlying human behaviour (Rasmussen, 1984; Michon, 1985).

Usually, car driving is described as a task containing three different levels of demands. At the strategic level, the general planning of a journey is handled. For example, the driver chooses the route and transportation mode and evaluates resulting costs and time consumption. At the tactical level, the driver has to exercise manoeuvres, allowing him/her to negotiate the 'right now' prevailing circumstances, for instance, turning at an intersection or accepting a gap. Finally, at the control (stabilisation) level the driver has to execute simple (automatic) action patterns, which together form a manoeuvre, for example, changing the gear and turning the wheel.

The demands imposed on the driver are met through his/her driving behaviour. Also, the performance of the driving task is usually assigned to three different levels: knowledge-based, rule-based and skill-based behaviour. Skill-based behaviour is described as data-driven, meaning that skills are performed without conscious control and use of attention resources. They are immediate and efficient. Rule-based behaviour on the other hand occurs under conscious control and requires attention. Therefore, it is less immediate and efficient. Knowledge-based behaviour involves problem solving and is relevant when it is not given how to act in a specific situation. Thus, an important aspect of knowledge-based behaviour is that reasoning is required.

1.2 Evaluation of Driver Behaviour Models

Analysing the driving task requires consideration of the dynamic interaction between drivers and the traffic system. Driver-specific factors include performance aspects, individual dispositions and transient driver states. Driver behaviour models attempt to formalise the complex relation between the driver and the traffic system.

1.2.1 Michon's Hierarchical Control Model

Michon (1985) proposed a simple two-way classification of driver behaviour models: One dimension distinguished between behaviour, i.e., input–output-oriented models and internal-state-oriented models. The second dimension differentiates between functional models and taxonomic models, where model components do or do not interact, respectively.

According to Michon (1985), all models lack in one or more respect: they are generally bottom-up controlled, internal models. Corresponding top–down processes are hardly specified or they tend to be too simplistic. Michon regards cognitive process models as the most encouraging step towards a valid model of driver behaviour because these types of models combine elements of driving task analysis with an information-processing approach. Therefore his Hierarchical Control Model subdivides the driving task into three coupled and hierarchically ordered levels, namely the strategic, the manoeuvring and the control levels. Adapting this model, to incorporate the GADGET fourth level (see next section), one more level is added, i.e., the 'behaviour level' (Fig. 1.1).

The strategical level includes trip planning, route choice and other general principles including time constraints. This level is little involved in actual driving. However, it sets criteria for factors at the lower levels, like speed control and associated subjective risk levels. At the manoeuvring level, drivers interact

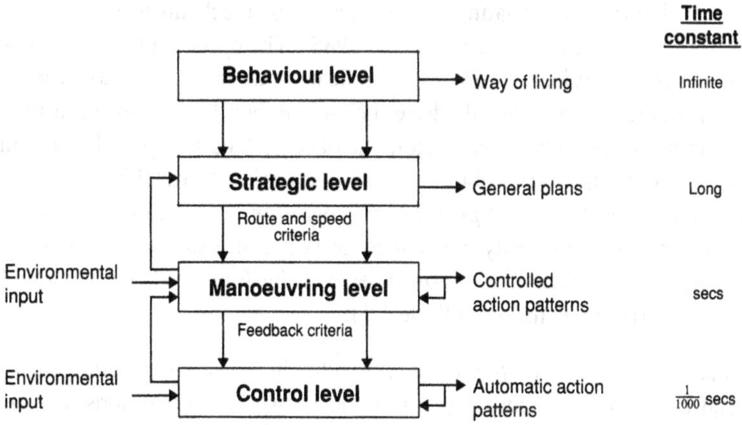

FIGURE 1.1. The hierarchical structure of the driving task (adapted from Michon, 1985).

with the traffic system. The control level, finally, refers to basal car control processes. Although a dynamic relationship between the concurrent activities is assumed, the different levels require different types of information: The strategical level is mainly top–down (knowledge) controlled. The manoeuvring and control levels require in addition bottom-up (data) input from the traffic environment.

Closely associated to Michon's hierarchical model of driver behaviour is Rasmussen's division of operative behaviour into three levels: skill-based behaviour refers to automatic procedures, rule-based behaviour to application of learned rules and knowledge-based behaviour to conscious problem solving (Rasmussen, 1984). Skill-based behaviour is applied in Michon's model mainly at the control level in the form of automatic action patterns. Ranney (1994) relates Michon's control hierarchy to Rasmussen's taxonomy of operative behaviour. Skill-based behaviour is applied in all familiar situations. Rule-based behaviour dominates during standard interactions with other road users as well as in some rare situations like driving a new car, where automatic routines have to be transferred to a new system. Knowledge is applied when driving in unfamiliar traffic networks, in difficult environmental conditions or when skills are not fully developed as in novice drivers.

1.2.2 The GADGET-Matrix: Integrating Hierarchical Control Models and Motivational Models of Driver Behaviour

Motivational models of driver behaviour 'propose a general compensatory mechanism whereby drivers adjust their driving (e.g. speed) to establish a balance between what happens on the road and their level of acceptable subjective risk (Ranney, 1994). An important assumption of motivational models is that drivers establish a constant level of risk by activating risk-compensation mechanisms when a subjective threshold is exceeded (e.g., Summala, 1988). The opportunity to compensate risks by adjusting subjective risk levels indicates that drivers' personal motives are as well a crucial factor for safe driver behaviour. For this reason, a fourth level corresponding to individual dispositions has been added to hierarchical control models of driver behaviour within the European project GADGET (Christ et al., 2000). The new level refers to *personal preconditions* and *ambitions in life,* and as such has the highest priority inside the matrix because such dispositions heavily influence driving decisions at lower levels. The four levels of the so-called GADGET-Matrix are as follows (Table 1.1):

(a) *Goals for life and skills for living:* An individual driver's attitudes, lifestyle, social background, gender, age and other personal preconditions that might influence driving behaviour and accident involvement.
(b) *Driving goals and context:* Strategical planning of a trip; the focus is on why, where, when and with whom one is driving.
(c) *Mastery of traffic situations:* Actual driving in a given context, resembles Michon's manoeuvring level.
(d) *Vehicle manoeuvring*: Overlaps despite a different terminology with Michon's car control level. The focus is on the vehicle, its construction and how it is operated.

A safe driver has, however, not only developed skills but also knowledge about his/her own abilities, preconditions and limits. Experienced drivers have, in addition, cognitive driving skills, such as anticipation and risk perception. In order to cover these higher-order aspects of driver behaviour, vertical columns are added to the so far horizontal structure of hierarchical control models (see Table 1.1). The columns of the GADGET-Matrix are as follows:

(a) *Knowledge and skills*: Routines and information required for driving under normal circumstances.
(b) *Risk-increasing factors*: Aspects of traffic and life associated with higher risk.
(c) *Self-assessment*: How good the driver reflects his/her own driving skills and motivations.

Levels and cells of the GADGET-Matrix are not mutually exclusive – there is large vertical as well as horizontal overlap due to the complex and cyclic nature of the driving task, where subtasks usually have to be carried out in parallel at different levels (e.g., routing, turning left, gap acceptance, speed control, steering, braking, etc.).

1.2.3 DRIVABILITY Model

The most recent evaluation in driver modelling concerns the notion that driver behaviour is not necessarily static, but evolves dynamically with time, as well as is context-related. It is subjected not only to permanent but also temporary

TABLE 1.1. The GADGET-matrix (adapted from Hatakka et al., 1999).

Hierarchical levels of driver behaviour	Knowledge and skills	Risk-increasing factors	Self-assessment
Goals for life and skills for living	Awareness about • relation between personal tendencies and driving skills • lifestyle/life situation • peer group norms • motives • personal values	Risky tendencies like • acceptance of risks • high level of sensation seeking • complying to social pressure • use of alcohol and drugs	Awareness of • impulse control • risky tendencies • dangerous motives • risky habits
Driving goals and context	Awareness about • effects of journey goals • planning and choosing routes • effects of social pressure by passengers inside the car	Risks associated with • physical condition (fitness, arousal, alcohol, etc.) • purpose of driving • driving environment (rural/urban/highway) • social context and company	Awareness of • personal planning skills • typical driving goals • alternative transport modes
Mastery of traffic situations	Knowledge about • traffic regulations • traffic signs • anticipation • communication • safety margins	Risks associated with • wrong expectations • vulnerable road users • violations • information overload • unusual conditions • inexperience	Awareness of • strong and weak points of manoeuvring skills • subjective risk level • subjective safety margins
Vehicle manoeuvring	Skills concerning • control of direction and position • vehicle properties • physical phenomena	Risks associated with • insufficient skills • environmental conditions (weather, friction, etc.) • car condition (tyres, engine, etc.)	Awareness of • strong and weak points of car control skills

contributors, which may or may not be independent. The DRIVABILITY model (Bekiaris, Amditis, Panou, 2003) introduced as most important the following ones:

1. *Individual resources*, namely physical, social, psychological and mental conditions of the specific driver. Physical conditions include motor, sensoric and coordination functions. Mental status depends also on the actual level of stress, concentration to the task and vigilance level.
2. *Knowledge/skills level*: This refers not only to actual driver training and experience, but also to generic knowledge, as basic education greatly influences motivations and behaviour of the driver. This level also considers the self-awareness of the own skills and it includes all the four levels of the GADGET model.

3. *Environmental factors:* This includes the vehicle status, the existence of traffic hazards, the weather, road and traffic conditions. The combinations of these may generate a risky situation, which certainly influences DRIVABILITY.
4. Two common denominators between driver resources and environmental status, namely *workload* and *risk awareness.*

The two intermediate factors between driver resources and the environment, namely workload and risk assessment, are among the key issues in order to understand and analyse driving performance. Risk awareness depends on three major contributors:

1. Risk perception, namely the ability to understand/recognise the specific risk at the specific time moment.
2. Level of attention, the ability to spot the risk in time.
3. Possible external support so as to spot the risk in time, i.e., by advanced driver assistance systems (ADAS).

In contrast to the risk awareness level, which is rather discrete and may change arbitrarily, the other factor, workload, is continuous and evolves with time. Even temporary input, i.e., use of mobile phone, may have high impact on workload for limited time periods. The major contributors to DRIVABILITY are depicted in Fig. 1.2.

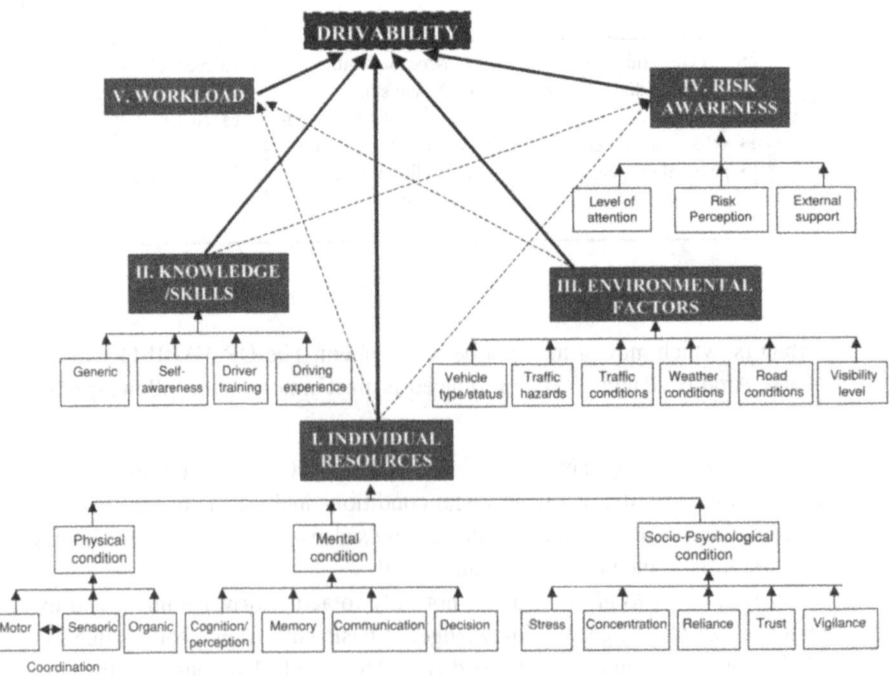

FIGURE 1.2. Contributors to DRIVABILITY.

The contributors shown in Fig. 1.2 are combined in a mathematical formula, which comprises the DRIVABILITY index (DI) of each individual driver at any given moment in time. Considering that the individual resources are the most significant contributor, the knowledge/skills and workload are of equal importance, while environment and risk awareness are third in importance, the overall DI is calculated through the following empirical formula:

$$\mathrm{DI} = \mathrm{IRI} \times \frac{\mathrm{KSI}}{2} \times \frac{\mathrm{WI}}{2} \times \frac{\mathrm{EFI} + \mathrm{RAI}}{6}$$

where IRI is the individual resources index, KSI the knowledge/skills index, WI the workload index, EFI the environmental factors index and RAI the risk awareness index.

The DRIVABILITY model contributors validity are being proved within the AIDE IP, where five modules are being developed, as components of one model, that monitor whether the driver is engaged and/or distracted by a secondary task and his/her availability/unavailability (related to the contributor V of Fig. 1.2), his/her inattention/fatigue (related to contributor IV of Fig. 1.2), his/her personal characteristics (related to the contributors I and II of Fig. 1.2) as well as the monitoring of the traffic and environment (related to the contributor III of Fig. 1.2). In a few words, the Cockpit Activity Assessment (CAA) module in AIDE is intended to monitor the activities of the driver to detect workload by visual distraction, cognitive distraction, and signs of lateral manoeuvring intent. Furthermore, the Driver Availability Estimator (DAE) module aims to assess the driver's 'level of availability/unavailability' to receive and process information, according to the requirements of the primary driving task (depending on the nature of the road infrastructure, the goal followed at this time, the current driving actions carried out, etc.). The Driver State Degradation (DSD) module intends to detect and to diagnose in real-time the driver hypo-vigilance state due to drowsiness and sleepiness situations, giving an indication about the driver's ability to execute the driving task. The Driver Characteristics (DC) module personalises the warning and/or information provision media, timing and intensity according to driver's profile (experience, reaction time, average headway, etc.), explicit and implicit preferences. The Traffic and Environment Risk Assessment (TERA) monitors and measures activities outside the vehicle in order to assess the external contributors to the environmental and traffic context and also to predict the driver's intention for lateral manoeuvre (Boverie et al., 2005).

1.3 Driver Behaviour Adaptation Models and Their Relation to ADAS

ADAS are currently being developed and installed within vehicles at an increasing rate. These systems aim to improve driving safety by automating aspects of the driving process, through information, warnings and support to the driver, hence reducing driver workload.

TABLE 1.2. Driver behaviour issues when introducing ACC (Bekiaris et al., 2001).

<table>
<tr><th>Short term</th><th>Long term</th></tr>
<tr><td>Mistrust: distrusting the ACC system</td><td>Spare capacity: using spare capacity for other in-vehicle tasks</td></tr>
<tr><td colspan="2">Over-reliance: relying too much on the ACC system</td></tr>
<tr><td>Brake pedal forces: increasing brake pedal forces
Imitation: unequipped vehicles imitate equipped vehicles
Reliance on vehicle in front: vehicle in front might have poor driving behaviour</td><td>Fatigue: ACC could take over too many driving tasks causing fatigue
Quick approach to vehicle in front: the development of new behaviour
Time-headway: driving with smaller time-headways
Indication for overtaking: use ACC as an indication of when to overtake</td></tr>
<tr><td colspan="2">Overtaking: difficulties with overtaking and being overtaken</td></tr>
</table>

Automation can reduce driver workload in areas of decision choice, information acquisition and information analysis. This reduction in workload should then reduce driver error and stress, thereby increasing road safety. However potential problems exist with the introduction of automated systems. The reduction of mental workload may not always occur under conditions of system failure or when a user is unfamiliar with the system. Under these conditions, workload may in fact increase rather than reduce (Stokes et al., 1990). Also, changes in driver skills, learning and behaviour, which may occur due to the shift in locus of control, may prove detrimental and therefore predictions as to how drivers will react when locus of control shifts between the driver and the vehicle are required. Short- and long-term driver behavioural changes with the use of an advanced cruise control (ACC) system, from six research projects are summarised in Table 1.2 (Bekiaris et al., 2001).

The introduction of ADAS, as with any changes to the driving environment, may lead to changes in driver behaviour. However, the nature of these behaviour changes in response to changes in the driving environment and has on occasions proved to be the opposite of that which was intended. Grayson (1996) pointed out that 'people can respond to innovation and change in ways that are unexpected, unpredictable, or even wilfully perverse'. For example, Adams (1985) claimed that the introduction of seat belts in vehicles leads to a perception of greater safety, in turn leading to drivers increasing their speed on the road.

It has been suggested that improved safety cannot be predicted directly from the efficiency resulting from improved technology, as people adapt to some kinds of improved efficiency by taking more risks (Howarth, 1993). The introduction of safety measures may lead to compensatory behaviours that may reduce the benefits of the measures being implemented. This phenomenon has most recently been described as 'behavioural adaptation' (OECD, 1990). However, previous models explaining the behaviour have termed it as 'risk compensation' and 'risk homeostasis'.

The most important relevant theories and issues related to driver behavioural adaptation because of an external stimuli (ADAS introduction in our case) are summarised below (Bekiaris etal., 2001)..

1.3.1 Automaticity

Automation refers to the mechanical or electrical accomplishment of work. Some of the automatic components provided by ADAS act as a substitution for tasks that humans would otherwise be capable of performing. In other cases, ADAS provides automatic components, which carry out additional tasks that humans would not have been capable of but will also assist in the overall driving task.

Introducing automation into the driving task offers several potential advantages in aspects of both efficiency and safety. For example, the use of dynamic route guidance systems will assist drivers in taking the most cost-effective route, in terms of fuel and time, for current traffic conditions. Furthermore, automation can reduce driver workload in areas of decision choice, information acquisition and information analysis. This reduction in workload should then reduce driver error and stress, thus increasing road safety.

Overtrust on a system also brings problems. Drivers may become complacent and may not detect when a system fails. Drivers are left with a false sense of security, thereby failing to monitor the system leading to the added disadvantage of loosing system awareness. Drivers may also lose the opportunity to learn and retain driving skills. Furthermore, the role of the driver may be reduced to such an extent that their manual driving skills may degrade. This concept has been termed 'out-of-the-loop familiarity'.

Bainbridge (1987) discusses what she terms the 'ironies of automation', which occur with the changing role of the human in the human–machine relationship when a system is automated. She points out that the more advanced a system is, the more crucial the contributions of the human operator become. Automation aims to eliminate the human factor; however, ironically, the human operator is required to carry out those tasks that cannot be automated. The human operator is therefore required to monitor the system and to take over and stabilise the system manually in situations of system failure. However, as previously discussed manual control skills deteriorate when using an automated system, leading an experienced user to become inexperienced.

Bainbridge points out the loss of cognitive skills that an operator using an automated system, such as ADAS, is likely to suffer. As the retrieval of knowledge from the long-term memory is dependent on the frequency of use, operators will loose the benefit of long-term knowledge concerning processes. This practical knowledge can be used to generate strategies in emergency or unusual situations. It is difficult to teach practical knowledge without experience; it is thus of great concern that when automating a system this practical experience and the reinforcement by frequency of use will be taken away from the operator.

1.3.2 Locus of Control

Locus of control is the location of control over a situation or system. The implementation of ADAS will, in many cases, move the locus of control away from the driver and instead will lie with the vehicle. It is therefore necessary to consider the impact of this change in locus of control both on driver behaviour and also in terms of safety. The level of control left to the driver must be carefully considered (e.g., will drivers be given the opportunity to override vehicle decisions and vice versa?).

Once level of control is decided upon, it is still important to consider the likely consequences of implementation. Several concerns exist, including those discussed in the previous section. First, drivers may feel mistrust in the system and experience problems in handing over control to the vehicle; this factor is dependent on the confidence a driver has in the capabilities of the system. Secondly, drivers may overtrust the system; drivers may become dependent on the system. This may be problematic both in cases where the system fails; the driver may not detect failure due to reduced monitoring. Also, in situations when the driver is handed back control, driver's skills and learning may have been diminished due to out-of-the-loop familiarity.

Finally, driver behaviour and safety during the handover of control between the driver and the vehicle needs to be considered. De Vos et al. (1997) investigated safety and performance when transferring control of the vehicle between the driver and an Automatic Vehicle Guidance (AVG) system. Drivers were found to be able to leave the automated lane even when high-speed differences and traffic-density differences between lanes were present. Unsafe interactions were observed in the scenario of a low-speed manual lane. As expected, increased trust in the reliability of the system increased driver comfort. However, as headway decreased drivers were observed to experience greater discomfort, implying that total trust in the system did not exist.

1.3.3 Risk Homeostasis

One of the most considered and debated models in the area is Wilde's risk homeostasis theory. The model bears similarities to earlier models such as that of Taylor, and Cownie and Calderwood's. Taylor's risk-speed compensation model (1964) claims simply that the larger the perceived risk, the lower the chosen speed will be. Cownie and Calderwood (1966) proposed that drivers drive in a way that will maintain a desired level of anxiety, leading to the self-regulation of accidents within a closed-loop; feedback from the consequences of driver decisions will affect future decisions.

In a like manner, Wilde's risk homeostasis theory holds that drivers have a target level of risk per unit time that they attempt to maintain. He proposed that drivers make adjustments that ensure perceived subjective risk is equal to an internalised target level of risk. The theory asserts that if a driver is provided with additional safety measures, such as information concerning traffic ahead or the installation of a seat belt, the driver will exhibit more risky behaviour to compensate and return to the target level of risk.

Wilde also posited what he named the 'principle of preservation of the accident rate'. This principle implies that the number of accidents within a given population is dependent solely on the number of accidents that population is willing to tolerate.

1.3.4 Risk Compensation

As with other risk compensation theories, Näätänen and Summala propose a zero-risk hypothesis, stating that drivers normally avoid behaviour that elicits fear or anticipation of fear. Avoidance behaviour is motivated by subjective risk, which according to the theorists is not high enough, thereby leading to accidents. The main addition to the theory is its focus on the drivers' desired action. The theory contends that driver behaviour is motivated not only by perception, expectancy and subjective risk, but also by the relative attractiveness and benefits of carrying out a behaviour in a given situation. Furthermore, Näätänen and Summala (1973) postulate that the motivation of desired action is the most important route leading to a driver's decision to take action. The model proposes that a decision-making process occurs, weighing up the motivating and inhibiting factors, before a decision is made for action, such as overtaking. According to the model, driver adaptation occurs when perceptions concerning motivations and subjective risk are altered, hence altering the balance of the decision-making process.

1.3.5 Threat Avoidance

Fuller's (1984) threat-avoidance theory is developed both from Wilde's theory of risk homeostasis and the zero-risk model of driver behaviour proposed by Näätänen and Summala. The theory presupposes that drivers opt for zero risk of accident and that they make avoidance, competing or delayed avoidance responses depending on a wide number of factors. These factors are the rewards and punishments associated with the response, the accuracy of discriminative stimuli recognition, the subjective probability of a threat, the effectiveness of avoidance responses and finally the driver's level of arousal. The theory differs from the other theories in that it is not based on a motivation variable. Instead it views the driving task as involving learned avoidance responses to potentially aversive stimuli.

Fuller argues against the presupposition that drivers are capable of monitoring the probability of an accident. Instead, he proposes that drivers consider the subjective probability (or likelihood) of an accident. He proposes that the discriminative stimulus for a potential aversive stimulus is a projection into the future formulated through the integration of drivers' perceptions of their speed, the road environment of the intended path and their ongoing capability. Their expectations of the threat posed by each of these factors combine, leading to either a discriminative stimulus or no discriminative stimulus. This model also considers the influence of rewards and punishments. He proposes that when a discriminative stimulus is detected, the anticipatory avoidance response is not only determined by the subjective probability of expected threat, but also by the rewards and punishments associated with the various response alternatives. The theory also differs from that of Wilde, and Näätänen and Summala in that it highlights the role of learned responses.

1.3.6 Utility Maximisation

The utility maximisation model proposed by O'Neill (1977) assumes that the driver has certain stable goals and makes decisions to maximise the expected value of these goals. Some of these goals are achievable more effectively through risk-taking behaviour, for example, speeding to save time or gain social status. These motivating factors are counteracted by the desire to avoid accidents as well as by fear of other penalties such as speeding tickets. Balancing goals with the desire to avoid accidents therefore derives driving behaviour choice. O'Neill claims that the balance, which affects the decision made, is shifted when a safety measure is introduced. An assumption made by the theory, which has been questioned (OECD, 1990), is that the driver is 'rational'. In other words, the driver is an accurate judge of the accident probability resulting from each mode of behaviour.

Blomquist (1986) also presented a utility maximisation model, which claimed to illustrate that risk compensation is a natural part of human behaviour when individuals pursue multiple goals with limited resources. He claimed that drivers choose target levels of accident risk, based on the perceived net benefits of safety effort. Again the model proposes that, under plausible conditions, a change in safety, which is beyond driver control, causes a compensatory change in driver effort in the opposite direction. Blomquist (1986) likens this theory to Wilde's theory of risk homeostasis in that utility maximisation focuses on the choice of safety goals and risk homeostasis focuses on maintenance of those goals.

1.3.7 Behavioural Adaptation Formula

Evans (1985) proposes a human behaviour feedback parameter by which the actual safety change in traffic systems is related to that which was expected. A mathematical representation of the process dictates that feedback can occur through physical changes to the system, adjustments in user behaviour for personal benefits and adjustments in behaviour to re-establish previous risk levels. Evans suggests that human behaviour feedback is a pervasive phenomenon in traffic systems, which may greatly influence the outcome of safety measures to the extent that in some cases the opposite effect to that which was intended may occur.

In a review of driving behaviour theories, Michon (1985) commented that although behavioural adaptation theories explain the behaviour, and the motivations, attitudes and factors affecting that behaviour are detailed, the actual processes by which the behaviour occurs are not explained. Similarly, an OECD report found the models to be vague. The report states that risk compensation theories do not explain how or which cognitions lead to the expected compensation of objective risk. The report also points out the problem of how the objective risk can be accurately assessed by the driver; again models fail to explain this process.

1.4 Use of Driver Behaviour Models in EU and International Projects

The field of application of such models in EU projects is vast and is gaining pace over the last decades. Rather than attempting to meticulously cover this extensive area, we will provide an in-depth overview of characteristic examples, showing the related difficulties as well as benefits in applying such models.

1.4.1 Driver Models Use for Driver Training and Assessment

Indeed, many of the driver models have been developed, not aiming at driver behaviour and support but at facilitating better, theory-based, driver training model. A characteristic example is the GADGET-Matrix developed with the EC project GADGET in order to structure post-license driver education.

This model as well as different extension of the Michon model have been used as basis in nearly all recent EC projects dealing with driver training. In TRAINER project (GRD1-1999-10024), the different layers of the GADGET-Matrix have been further detailed and correlated to the problems of novice drivers, following a relevant accident analysis end experts opinion survey. This work resulted in the adapted GADGET-Matrix that correlates key subtasks of the different GADGET layers to the needs of driver trainees, with support by multimedia tools and/or driver simulators (Table 1.3). Thus, the development of appropriate new training tools and scenario was based upon the relevant theoretical model of novice drivers' needs.

Another training (in fact re-training) and assessment application is that of AGILE project (QLRT-2001-00118), regarding the assessment of driving ability and eventual re-training of elderly drivers. In this project, a mapping has been attempted of the age-related deficits and benefits to the different levels and cells of the GADGET-Matrix (Breker S. et al., 2003). The second level of the adapted GADGET-Martix is presented in Table 1.4.

This resulted in the prioritisation of specific driving scenaria, where elderly drivers would need more thorough assessment and/or support (re-training or aiding).

1.4.2 Evaluation of Driver Models' Use for Safety Aids

1.4.2.1 Use of Seat Belts

Evans (1982) observed that unbelted drivers drive at higher speeds and with smaller headways in comparison to drivers wearing belts. This evidence supports the theory that an adaptation in behaviour has occurred; however, the reduction in risk-taking behaviour does not support the risk compensation hypothesis. In contrast, Streff and Geller (1988) found that go-kart drivers wearing seat belts drove faster than non-wearers, suggesting that the seat belt leads to a sense of security, enabling drivers to feel safe in increasing vehicle speed. The experimental validity is questionable

TABLE 1.3. Findings of the analyses made in TRAINER D2.1.

	Literature survey	Existing training	Experts' proposals	
			Multimedia	Simulator
Starting		O		X
Shifting gears		O		X
Accelerating/decelerating		O		X
Steering/lane following		O		X
Speed control		O		X
Braking/stopping		O		X
Use of new cars control aids (ABS, ACC, etc)	X	X		X
Insufficient skills and incomplete automation	X			
Realistic self-evaluation	X			
Following	X	O		X
Overtaking/Passing	X	O	X	X
Entering and leaving the traffic	X	O		X
Tailgating	X			X
Lane changing	X	O	X	X
Scanning the road (eye cues)	X	Ø	X	X
Reacting to other vehicles	X	Ø X		X
Reacting to pedestrians	X		X	X
Parking		O		
Negotiating intersections	X	O	X	X
Negotiating hills/slopes	X	O		X
Negotiating curves	X	O	X	X
Road surface (skid, obstacles)	X	Ø X		X
Approach/exit of motorways	X	O		X
Turning off/over		O		
Railroad crossings, bridges, tunnels		Ø		
Reacting to traffic signs and traffic lights	X	O	X	X
Reacting to direction signs (including in-car devices)	X			
Emergency brake		Ø X		
Urban driving		O	X	X
Rural driving		O		
Convoy driving		X		
Motorway driving		Ø X		X
Weather conditions	X	Ø X		X
Night driving	X	Ø X		X
Insufficient skills and incompletely automation	X		X	X
Information overload	X		X	X
Insufficient anticipating skills and wrong expectations	X		X	X
Risky driving style	X		X	X
Realistic self-evaluation	X		X	X
Awareness of personal driving style	X	X		X
Determination of trip goals, route and modal choice				
Preparation and technical check		O	X	
Safety issues	X	O	X	
Maintenance tasks		O	X	

TABLE 1.3. (*Continued*)

	Literature survey	Existing training	Experts' proposals	
			Multimedia	Simulator
International legislation		X		
First aid		Ø X		X
Economic driving	X	Ø	X	
Driver's condition (stress, mood, fatigue)	X	X		X
Motives for driving	X			
Awareness of personal planning skills				
Awareness of typical driving goals and risky driving motives	X			
Knowing about the general relations between lifestyle/age/gender and driving style	X			
Knowing the influence of personal values and social background	X			
Knowing about the influence of passengers	X			X
High level of sensation seeking	X			
Consequences of social pressure, use of alcohol and drugs	X	X		X
Awareness of own personal tendencies (risky habits, safety-negative motives)	X			

O: the task is trained in all or nearly all European countries as the analysis of the questionnaires showed; Ø: the task is trained only in few or at least one country; X: the driving authorities and driving instructors questioned indicate that the task is not trained, but should be trained in the particular country.

because of the generalisation of go-karting to real life driving, as well as due to the differences in overall behavioural patterns of drivers using seat belts versus those that do not.

1.4.2.2 Use of Motorcycle Helmet

The retraction of these laws in some states of the USA during the late 1970s made it possible to compare repeal and non-repeal conditions in a natural environment. However, results from accident studies suggested that wearing helmets provided a safety benefit; those states that had revoked laws requiring helmets to be worn suffered an increase in fatalities (Grayson, 1996). These findings were opposed by the analysis of Adams (1983), where higher fatality rates were found in those states that had retained helmet-wearing laws. Adams argued that these results support the risk compensation theory: motorcycle riders who wore helmets felt less vulnerable to injury, thereby exhibiting riskier driving behaviours. The findings of Adams in favour of the risk compensation theory have again been disputed by the work of Chenier and Evans (1987). In their re-analysis of the USA accident statistics, they found that fatalities were increased in the states that had retracted compulsory crash helmet wearing laws. Their results imply that any increase of caution due to

TABLE 1.4. GADGET-Matrix level 2 (Mastery of Traffic Situations): Situation of older drivers (Breker et al., 2003).

Knowledge and skills		Risk factors		Self-assessment	
Pro	Contra	Pro	Contra	Pro	Contra
Knowledge about traffic regulations/traffic signs/anticipation/communication/safety margins, etc.		Risks associated with wrong expectations/vulnerable road users/violations/information overload/unusual conditions/inexperience, etc.		Awareness of strong and weak points of manoeuvring skills/subjective risk level/subjective safety margins, etc.	
	–priority (esp. right before left, right-hand driving) –signalling –reduced perception of road signs –dementia –cataract –diabetes + associated –glaucoma –cardiac & cardiovascular condition –seizure disorders –back pain	–slower on motorways –uniform driving style on country roads –larger gaps, especially when turning left –less overtaking –less night driving –slower approach of junctions –early speed reduction at junctions –smooth slow down at junctions –less driving on low friction –early observation of situations –tolerance towards other road users	–interpreting movement of other drivers –judging other drivers movement –junctions/intersections –yield right of way –right-angle (side) collisions –left turns (right-hand driving) –right turns (left-hand driving) –multiple vehicle accidents –merging onto motorways –risky merging in traffic flow –running over red –railway crossings –too early observation of situations (it might changed) –situation complexity especially in urban settings –late detection of other road users –judgement of gaps –underestimation of speed of vehicles at higher speeds –problems with reappearing situations when new information becomes available –problems with interrupting actions when necessary –problems with situation complexity –skill decline by compensation –lateral safety margins –dementia –cataract –diabetes + associated –glaucoma –cardiac & cardiovascular condition –seizure disorders –back pain	–larger safety margins (headway etc.) –lower risk level –avoiding complex settings –avoiding give-way or stop junctions –avoiding heavy traffic –awareness of difficulties at intersections –general awareness of age-related skill declines	–over estimation of one's own driving abilities –less sensibility to changes in performance and capacities –insufficient awareness that oneself is subject to general age-related skill declines –dementia

the removal of helmets was not great enough to compensate for the loss of safety benefits that the helmets provide. Overall, research into motorcycle helmet wearing has been found to provide a safety benefit and offers little support to any of the behavioural adaptation theories. However, as Grayson (1996) pointed out these findings are not surprising and more relevant to the theories are those mechanisms which protect one part of the anatomy and lead to disregard for safety of other parts of the body.

1.4.2.3 Studded Tyres

Studded tyres have been developed to improve safety in icy and snowy conditions; they provide better track-holding properties and shorter breaking distances under these conditions. Evidence from studies investigating the behavioural effects of fitting vehicles with studded tyres have often been cited in support of both behavioural adaptation (OECD, 1990) and risk compensation (Adams, 1985). The most greatly cited study is that of Rumar (1976). Results from this study indicated that in icy (low friction) conditions drivers of vehicles equipped with studded tires drive at faster speeds when negotiating curves in the road. However, it was determined that this increase in speed does not lead to a reduction in safety. It should therefore be noted that the observation of higher speeds in itself is inconclusive. Lund and O'Neill (1986) argue that the increased feedback provided by studded tyres allows vehicles to be driven at higher speeds without reducing safety. The Rumar study therefore provides evidence that the behavioural effect of driving faster with studded tyres reduces the safety benefits; however, an overall increase in safety is still achieved through their implementation.

1.4.2.4 Antilock Braking Systems

Antilock braking systems (ABS) are a recent safety feature introduced to the vehicle, and studies concerning their effect on driver behaviour are cited to support some of the theories of behavioural adaptation. ABS are designed to make breaking distances shorter and to allow vehicles to be steered during breaking manoeuvres. Rompe (1987) conducted a series of tests to investigate the benefit of these systems. Results showed that when simulating high-risk manoeuvres drivers without ABS made 2.4 times more errors. Real life evidence does not support this sizeable predicted benefit and therefore support theories of behavioural adaptation. A study conducted by Aschenbrenner (1994) is one of the only studies designed to specifically investigate the risk compensation theory; their hypothesis being that ABS will fail to reduce accidents despite its technical benefits. The study looked at two fleets of taxis in Munich: one fitted with ABS and the control one without. Aschenbrenner concluded that since it was not possible to prove a universal increase in safety, the results indicated the occurrence of behavioural adaptation in the form of risk compensation. The overall accident rate was unchanged, but inconsistencies such as decreases in blameworthy accidents and increases in parking and reversing accidents for fitted vehicles were observed. These inconsistencies were described as indicating a tendency to riskier driving by drivers of fitted vehicles when reviewed in the OECD report.

More supporting evidence has been provided by a US study (HLDI, 1994). Findings from this study indicated that the introduction of ABS has failed to reduce the frequency or cost of insurance claims. However, this does not necessarily imply that ABS does not provide a safety benefit, as Grayson (1996) points out, the circumstances under which ABS could prevent accidents are quite rare. Kullgren (1994) supplied evidence that ABS is effective in reducing accidents. This analysis of Swedish accident statistics indicated an overall effectiveness of 15% for ABS vehicles under snowy or icy conditions. It was also found that fitted cars were more likely to be struck from behind in rear-end accidents.

Evidence for the occurrence of behavioural adaptation is both inconsistent and conflicting. The OECD report reviewed empirical evidence concerning behavioural adaptation. It was concluded that behavioural adaptation does occur although not consistently, and the magnitude and direction of its effects on safety cannot be precisely stated. The studies reviewed suggested that behavioural adaptation does not eliminate safety gains from programmes but tends to reduce the size of the expected benefits.

1.4.3 Driver Models Use for ADAS Design and Impact Assessment

Few studies have been carried out investigating behavioural effects of future automated systems, and many of these have revealed the occurrence of negative behavioural effects.

A study conducted by Winsum et al. (1989) provides support to the theory that drivers will exhibit behavioural adaptation in response to ADAS. Winsum et al. suggested that the use of a navigation system, in place of a map, leads to a reduction in workload, which in turn leads to drivers increasing vehicle speed, implying that drivers demonstrate behavioural adaptation in response to the implementation of automated navigation.

Similarly, Forward (1993) reviewed the evidence concerning the effects of dynamic route guidance (DRG) systems, concluding that benefits such as reduced workload and stress exist as do undesirable effects such as increased speed. However, Forward noted that the real effect of the system cannot be fully comprehended until its use becomes more extensive.

Focus mainly tends to concentrate on the negative effects of introducing automation to the vehicle. However automation benefits have also been observed during evaluation of future systems.

In the case of AWAKE (IST-2000-28062), the DRIVABILITY model has been employed to design its warning levels and strategy. AWAKE was a project aimed to develop an unobtrusive and personalized, real-time driver monitoring device, able to reliably predict driver hypovigilance and effectively and timely warn the driver. AWAKE has recognised the importance of actual traffic risk level as well as driver status, type and key environmental factors, and worked towards a

TABLE 1.5. Correlation of AWAKE (driver vigilance monitoring and warning system) use cases and warning strategy with overall DRIVABILITY Index (Bekiaris et al., 2003).

AWAKE use cases	Values of DRIVABILITY Indexes	Overall DRIVABILITY Index	AWAKE warning levels/strategy
• Driver is hypovigilant; • Rural environment, with sufficient traffic density (normal workload); • No major environmental risk identified; • Standard type of driver; • No sign that the driver missed any risk.	IRI = 3.5 WI = 2 EFI = 3 KSI = 2 RAI = 3 **Thus DI = 3.5**	4 (the system closely monitors the driver, without any action)	No action but monitoring system parameters are strengthened to cautionary case
• Driver is hypovigilant; • Urban environment, with normal traffic density (normal workload); • No major environmental risk identified; • Standard type of driver; • Driver seems to miss some risks (i.e. rather small TTC or headway).	IRI = 3.5 WI = 2 EFI = 3 KSI = 2 RAI = 2 **Thus DI = 2.9**	3 (the system provides warning)	Driver warning by audio and visual means (warning level 1)
• Driver is hypovigilant; • Highway environment, with low traffic density (low workload); • High speed, cautionary case; • Standard type of driver; • Driver seems to miss some risks (i.e. lane deviation or swerving).	IRI = 3.5 WI = 1.4 EFI = 2 KSI = 2 RAI = 2 **Thus DI = 1.75**	2 (the system intervenes)	Driver warning by audio and haptic means (warning level 2) (intervention is excluded from AWAKE, due to liability issues)

multi-stage driver monitoring and driver warning system that takes such parameters into account. Table 1.5 correlates the overall DI and the indexes of the DRIVABILITY contributors to the different AWAKE driver warning levels and media. It should be noticed that the sensors included in the AWAKE system (such as driver eyelid and steering grip force monitoring, frontal radar, lane recognition system, etc.) allow for sufficient, real-time estimation of all DRIVABILITY indexes (except KSI, which is however included in the system by the driver at its initiation as the system adapts itself to the driver profile). This is done by storing driver's, vehicle and environmental data on the system and automatically processing them. Further processing off-line is also feasible.

TABLE 1.6. Driver model and rules for implementation.

PIPE driver model	Type of process	Rules or governing assumptions
Perception of signals	Sensorial process	– Haptic – Visual – Aural
Interpretation	Cognitive process	– Similarity Matching – Frequency Gambling
Planning	Cognitive process	– Inference/reasoning
Execution	Behavioural process	– Performance of selected actions/iterations

This is indeed one of the very few cases where such a direct relation between a driver behaviour model and the development of the HMI of an ADAS has been attempted, and in fact with great success, as the final AWAKE HMI has been rated as adequate and useful by over 90% of its users.

Finally, within AIDE (IST-1-507674), a new driver model is being developed, attempting to model concurrently the driver, the vehicle and the environment (Panou et al., 2005). The basic assumption made for the development of the model of the driver is that the driver is essentially performing a set of actions that are familiar according to his/her experience. As the driving process is very dynamic, these actions are continuously selected from a vast repository of knowledge (knowledge base) by a diagnostic process. Consequently, the processes of diagnosis and interpretation of acquired information become crucial for the dynamic sequencing of driver's activity. The model of the driver adopted is based on a very simple approach that assumes that behaviour derives from a cyclical sequence of four cognitive functions: perception, interpretation, planning and execution (PIPE). This model is not sequential as the execution function, i.e., the manifested form of behaviour, may result from several iterations (cyclical) of the other functions. Moreover, in agreement with the initial hypothesis, the planning function, is usually bypassed by the 'automatic' selection of familiar frames of knowledge that are associated with procedures or sets of several actions aiming at the fulfilment of the goal of a frame. This function is important as it becomes effective in unknown situations or in the case of novice drivers, when 'simpler' frames, based on single actions or on a limited sequence of very simple/familiar actions, are called into play to deal with the situation. These four cognitive functions can be associated to either sensorial or cognitive processes and are activated according to certain rules or conditions (Table 1.6). This model will be utilised in personalising the multi-ADAS system HMI, in accordance to a particular driver's needs and preferences, and will also be used in the traffic environment.

1.5 Conclusions

Driving task modelling has started as simple task-layers representation for taxonomic use in driver training and has gradually evolved to dynamic models, which consider driver behaviour adaptation as well as the impact of the traffic environment and the driving context. The initial list of driver training and assessment projects that used driver models as their theoretical basis (GADGET, DAN, TRAINER, AGILE, CONSENSUS, etc.) have been followed by a new generation of projects that use driver models to assess the impacts of driver support systems (i.e., ADVISORS, TRAVELGUIDE) and, more recently, by those that attempt to use the model parameters for optimal HMI design (AWAKE, COMUNICAR, AIDE, etc.). Preliminary results have proven that such a correlation is feasible and beneficiary, but it is far from obvious. The model output has to be evaluated and even modified by empirical results. Thus, currently the model is being applied and tested in AIDE, SENSATION and PREVENT Integrated Projects through short- and long-term testing of drivers. Furthermore, the model can only be at the starting basis of the design and development process and only influence the actual ADAS HMI within predefined design boundaries. Nevertheless, we seem to be at the infancy of a new design principle for driver support training and assessment systems – the model-based modular and personalised design.

References

Adams, J.G.U. (1985). Smeed's Law, seat belts and the emperor's new clothes. In L. Evans and R.C. Schwing (Eds.). *Human Behaviour and Traffic Safety*. Plenum, New York.

Aschenbrenner, K.M. and Biehl, B. (1994). Empirical studies regarding risk compensation processes in relation to anti-lock braking systems. In R.M. Trimpop and G.J.S. Wilde (Eds.). *Challenges to Accident Prevention: The Issue of Risk Compensation Behaviour*. Styx Publ., Groningen, The Netherlands.

Bainbridge, L. (1987). Ironies of automation. In J. Rasmussen, K. Duncan and J. Leplat (Eds.). *New Technology and Human Error*. Wiley, New York.

Baron, S., Zacharias, G., Muralidharan, R. and Lancraft , R. (1980). *PROCRU: A Model for Analyzing Flight Crew Procedures in Approach to Landing*. NASA CR-152397.

Bekiaris, E., Papakonstantinou, C., Stevens, A., Parkes, A., Boverie, S., Nilsson, L., Brookhuis, K., Van Wees, K., Wiethoff, M., Damiani, S., Lilli, F., Ernst, A., Heino, A., Widlroither, H. and Heinrich, J. (2001). *ADVISORS Deliverable 3/8.1v4: Compendium of Existing Insurance Schemes and Laws, Risk Analysis of ADA Systems and Expected Driver Behavioural Changes*. User Awareness Enhancement, dissemination report and market analysis and ADAS marketing strategy. ADVISORS Consortium, Athens, Greece.

Bekiaris, E., Amditis, A. and Panou, M. (2003). DRIVABILITY: A new concept for modelling driving performance. *International Journal of Cognition Technology & Work*, 5(2), 152–161.

Blomquist, G. (1986). A utility maximization model of driver traffic safety behaviour. *Accident Analysis and Prevention*, 18, 371–375.

Boverie, S., Bolovinou, A., Polychronopoulos, A., Amditis, A., Bellet, T., Tattegrain-Veste, H., Manzano, J., Bekiaris, E., Panou, M., Portouli, E., Kutila, M., Markkula, G. and Angvall A. (2005). AIDE Deliverable 3.3.1: AIDE DVE monitoring module – Design and development. AIDE Consortium, Toulouse, France.

Breker, S., Henrikson, P., Falkmer, T., Bekiaris, E., Panou, M., Eeckhout, G., Siren, A., Hakamies-Blomqvist, L., Middleton, H. and Leue E. (2003). *AGILE deliverable 1.1: Problems of elderly in relation to the driving task and relevant critical scenarios*.

Cacciabue, P.C., Mauri, C. and Owen, D. (1993). Development of a model and simulation of aviation maintenance technician task performance. *International Journal of Cognition Technology & Work,* 5(4), 229–247.

Chenier, T.C. and Evans, L. (1987). Motorcyclist fatalities and the repeal of mandatory helmet wearing laws. *Accident Analysis and Prevention*, 19, 133–139.

Christ et al. (2000). *GADGET final report: Investigations on influences upon driver behaviour – Safety approaches in comparison and combination.* GADGET Consortium, Wien, Austria.

Cownie, A.R. and Calderwood, J.M. (1966). Feedback in accident control. *Operational Research Quarterly*, 17, 253–262.

De Vos, A.P., Hoekstra, W. and Hogema, J.H. (1997). Acceptance of automated vehicle guidance (AVG): System reliability and exit manoeuvres. Mobility for everyone. Presented at the *4th World Congress on Intelligent Transport Systems,* Berlin.

Evans, L. (1985). Human behaviour feedback and traffic safety. *Human Factors*, 27 (5), 555–576.

Evans, L. and Schwing, R.C. (Eds.) (1982). *Human Behaviour and Traffic Safety*. Plenum, New York.

Forward, S.E. (1993). Prospective methods applied to dynamic route guidance. In O.M.J. Carsten (Ed.). *Framework for Prospective Traffic Safety Analysis*. HOPES Project Deliverable 6.

Fuller, R. (1984). A conceptualization of driving behaviour as threat avoidance. *Ergonomics* 27, 1139–1155.

Grayson, G. (1996). Behavioural adaptation: A review of the literature. *TRL Report 254*. Transport Research Laboratory, Crowthorne.

Hatakka, M., Keskinen, E., Gregersen, N.P., Glad, A and Hernetkoski, K. (1999). Results of EU-project GADGET. In S. Siegrist (Ed.). *Driver Training, Testing and Licensing – Towards Theory Based Management of Young Drivers' Injury Risk in Road Traffic*. BFU-report 40, Berne.

HLDI. (1994). *Collision and property damage liability losses of passenger cars with and without antilock brakes*. Highway Loss Data Institute Report A-41. HLDI, Arlington, VA.

Howarth, I. (1993). Effective design: Ensuring human factors in design procedures. In A. Parkes and S. Franzen (Eds.). *Driving Future Vehicles*. Taylor and Francis, London.

Kullgren, A., Lie, A. and Tingvall, C. (1994). The effectiveness of ABS in real life accidents. Paper presented at the *Fourteenth International Technical Conference on the Enhanced Safety of Vehicles,* Munich.

Lund, A.K. and O'Neill, B. (1986). Perceived risks and drinking behaviour. *Accident Analysis and Prevention*, 18, 367–370.

McKnight, A.J. and Adams B.D. (1970). *Driver Education Task Analysis, Vol. 1: Task Descriptions*. Human Resources Research Organization, Alexandria, VA.

Michon, J.A. (1985). A critical view of driver behaviour models: What do we know, what should we do? In L. Evans and R.C. Schwing (Eds.). *Human Behaviour and Traffic Safety*. Plenum, New York.

Näätänen, R. and Summala, H. (1973). A model for the role of motivational factors in drivers' decision making. *Accident Analysis and Prevention*, 6, 243–261.

OECD. (1990). *Behavioural Adaptations to Changes in the Road Transport System*. OECD, Paris.

O'Neill, B. (1977). A decision-theory model of danger compensation. *Accident Analysis and Prevention*, 9, 157–165.

Panou, M., Cacciabue, N., Cacciabue, P.C. and Bekiaris, E. (2005). From driver modelling to human machine interface personalisation. Paper presented at the *IFAC World Congress*, Prague.

Ranney, T. (1994). Models of driving behaviour: A review of their evolution. *Accident Analysis and Prevention*, 26(6), 733–750.

Rasmussen, J. (1984). Information processing and human–machine interaction. In *An approach to cognitive engineering*. North Holland, New York.

Rompe, K., Schindler, A. and Wallrich, M. (1987). Advantages of an anti-wheel lock system (ABS) for the average driver in difficult driving situations. Paper presented at the *Eleventh International Technical Conference on Experimental Safety Vehicles*, Washington, DC.

Rumar, K., Berggrund, U., Jernberg, P. and Ytterbom, U. (1976). Driver reaction to a technical safety measure – Studded tyres. *Human Factors*, 18, 443–454.

Stokes, A., Wickens, C. and Kite, K. (1990). *Display Technology: Human Factors Concepts*. Society of Automotive Engineers, Inc., USA.

Streff, F.M. and Geller, E.S. (1988). An experimental test of risk compensation: Between-subject versus within-subject analyses. *Accident Analysis and Prevention*, 20, 277–287.

Summala, H, Lamble, D. and Laakso, M. (1988). Driving experience and perception of the lead cars braking when looking at in-car targets. *Accident Analysis and Prevention*, 30(4), 401–407.

Taylor, D.H. (1964). Drivers' galvanic skin response and the risk of accident. *Ergonomics*, 7, 439–451.

Van Winsum, W., Van Knippenberg, C. and Brookhuis, K. (1989). Effect of navigation support on driver's metnal workload. In *Current Issues in European Transport, Vol. I: Guided Transport in 2040 in Europe.* PTRC Education and Research Services, London.

2 TRB Workshop on Driver Models: A Step Towards a Comprehensive Model of Driving?

DELPHINE CODY AND TIMOTHY GORDON

2.1 Introduction

Various disciplines use the same or similar terminology for driver models – vehicle and traffic engineering, psychology, human factors, artificial intelligence to mention the most common; however, the definition of the term varies not only between disciplines but even between different researchers within any given discipline. Recent efforts in applied psychology and human factors have emphasised the need of developing models that can be implemented and used in computer simulation, hence representing a possible link between these disciplines, and also a chance to consider the broader picture of driver model within a transportation/traffic system. In order to discuss this link, the authors organised a workshop on driver modelling during the 84th annual meeting of the Transportation Research Board, Washington, DC. The workshop was attended by 25 researchers from the various fields listed above and lead researchers from the United States, Europe and Asia.

Three objectives were set for this workshop: (i) create a group of driver model developers and users, (ii) share common experience and reach common definitions and finally (iii) set a road map for the next generation of driver models. The topics that were more specifically dealt with were the design and application of cognitive and driver behaviour models and their integration within a broader simulation framework. This chapter is divided into three sections. In the first section, we present the workshop content in more detail and provide a summary of the speakers' contribution. In the second section, we present a synthesis of these models with the introduction of a set of dimensions allowing for visualisation of the different models on a similar scale. The final section presents what the authors believe to be the critical steps necessary to coordinate efforts towards a new generation of driving model – a framework where researchers from different fields contribute to create a comprehensive model of the driving activity.

2.2 Workshop Presentation and Speakers' Contribution

This section comprises two parts. We will first detail each of the themes around which the speakers organised their presentation and will present summaries of each of the presentations in the second part.

2.2.1 *Workshop Content*

The workshop was based on three themes: (i) driver model purpose and application, (ii) driver model architectures and implementations and (iii) driver model calibration and validation. We will now discuss each of these themes.

2.2.1.1 Driver Model Purpose and Application

From a general standpoint, generating driver models can be seen as equivalent to developing a comprehensive description of scientific knowledge about drivers. The first step towards making a hierarchy of scientific methods to approach a phenomenon such as the driving activity is to conduct specific studies to observe and understand the phenomena (e.g., drivers' glances, perception of speed, decision-making process, drivers' attention control) and the second step is to reconcile the results of the different studies into a comprehensive description – in other words a model dynamically linking the results of these different studies to reproduce the driving activity. Hence, one of the interests of building driver models is to validate the results of studies looking into specific aspects of driving and identify the aspects that need to be addressed to further the understanding of driving.

Another interest for developing such models resides in their application. Two types of applications were discussed during the workshop: (i) application to safety and driver assistance system design and (ii) prediction and evaluation of new systems on traffic flow. Three presentations fell under the first type, namely, 'In-Vehicle Information System (IVIS) Model' by Jon Hankey, 'ACT-R Driver Model' by Dario Salvucci and 'Workload in Driver Modelling' by Jeroen Hogema and Richard van der Horst. The two other presentations, 'ACME – Driver Model' by Daniel Krajzewicz and 'FLOWSIM' by Mark Brackstone, addressed the traffic assessment category.

2.2.1.2 Driver Model Architecture and Implementations

Model architecture can be seen as the blueprint of the model. In that sense, a simple description of a model (see Fig. 2.1) consists of three elements: inputs, information processing or behaviour and outputs. This simple architecture allows to generate parameters of factors that can be used to derive measures of effectiveness or evaluation.

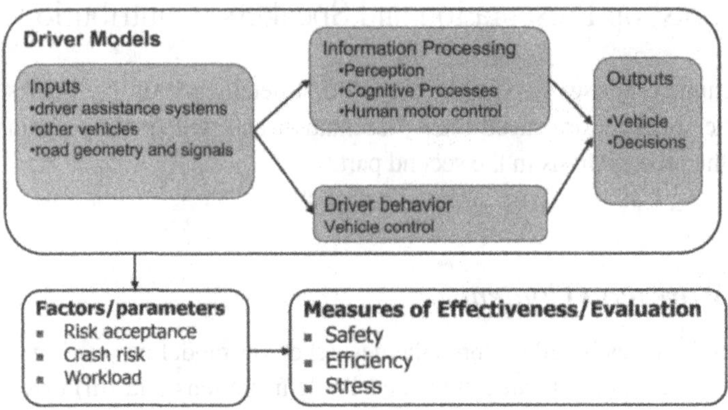

FIGURE 2.1. Modular high level representation of driver model structure.

2.2.1.3 Calibration and Validation

Model calibration consists of setting values for parameters which support the simulation. For example, when a model includes a gap regulation task, parameters that need to be calibrated are the gaps that the simulated drivers will maintain as well as conditions for variation of these gaps. The calibration addresses elements of the driving tasks as well as cognitive processes (e.g., memory decay) or other elements of the simulation (e.g., vehicle models). We distinguished two main methods for calibrating models. The first method consists of using data and results available in the scientific community, and the second consists of running specific data collection. This method can be subdivided into three more categories, depending on whether the data collected is driver centric (gaze, attention) or vehicle centric (steering, braking, speed control) or traffic centric (lane keeping, range, range rate). The use of the first method brings up the issue of standardisation in method to gather and measure data and the definition of parameters that are derived.

For model validation, there is one method of comparing the model output with data sets. The variation in the application of the method depends on the type of data used. For instance, the model output can be compared with collected data, with on-going behaviour, or with more general data. The comparison of model output with on-going behaviour raised an interesting question on the nature of the model output. Is a model providing a trend or should we expect to be able to predict real-time behaviour? The question was not answered directly during the workshop. Although some researchers present in the audience thought that a prediction of driver behaviour in real time would be a huge achievement for driver models, a lot of doubt about the possibility to reach such a level of accuracy was also expressed.

Clearly, there is fundamental issue resulting from the inherently stochastic nature of driving. On the one hand, a ‘real-time’ model should be capable of making precise and detailed predictions of driver actions as a function of time. On the other hand, real drivers display a range of decisions, driving styles, levels of attention, etc., and so should any realistic driving model; resolving these apparently conflicting viewpoints requires a somewhat deeper concept of what is required for model validation. At the very least, validation of real-time models must take account for a wide range of stochastic influences.

Out of the five models that were presented, four are proceeding with more or less extensive validation and one is still in the process of calibration.

2.2.2 *Summaries of the Speakers' Contributions*

Five speakers presented their research relative to each of the themes: Jon Hankey, Virginia Tech Transportation Institute; Dario Salvucci, Drexel University; Daniel Krajzewicz, Deutsches Zentrum für Luft - und Raumfahrt e.V. (DLR); Mark Brackstone, School of Engineering and the Environment, University of Southampton, and Richard van der Horst, TNO Human Factors. All the five summaries are divided into three parts: (i) model purpose description, (ii) architecture description and (iii) calibration and validation issues. The architectures that were presented are briefly explained for each of the model. The reader may refer speakers' publications on their model for more thorough descriptions. The models are also discussed based on the following factors: (i) simulation scale, along two dimensions, i.e., the unit simulated (e.g., one driver, groups of drivers or vehicle fleets) and the number of unit that can be simulated at once; (ii) visualisation, in terms of drivers' states, parameters that can be observed in simulation and traffic; (iii) the ease in using these models by other researchers.

2.2.2.1 In-Vehicle Information System – Jon Hankey

The purpose of in-vehicle information system (IVIS) is to provide a proof of concept design tool in order to assess and compare in-vehicle system concepts, prototypes and products for system designers and to provide insight into potential design improvements. The approach for the development of this model consists of compiling, analysing and using data from actual empirical research for creating 'micro-models' of performance prediction. The model predicts the visual and cognitive resources needed at a basic level. These predictions are made at the subtask level, because subtasks often require different resources and subtasks can be combined into tasks which can themselves be combined into system assessment. Therefore, the model accounts for a variety of information input, information processing and response output combinations.

The overview of the IVIS demand model is shown in Fig. 2.2. During the workshop, the emphasis was put on the software development of the tool and how users would manipulate the tool. In terms of driver model, if we observe Fig. 2.2, the component that most closely relates to the information processing is the one listing driver resources involved, i.e., visual demand, auditory demand, manual demand and speech demand. The assumption of the model is that the driver is a finite capacity, with a single-channel processor of visual information. The driver can 'share' cognitive resources to differing degrees and the resources needed to

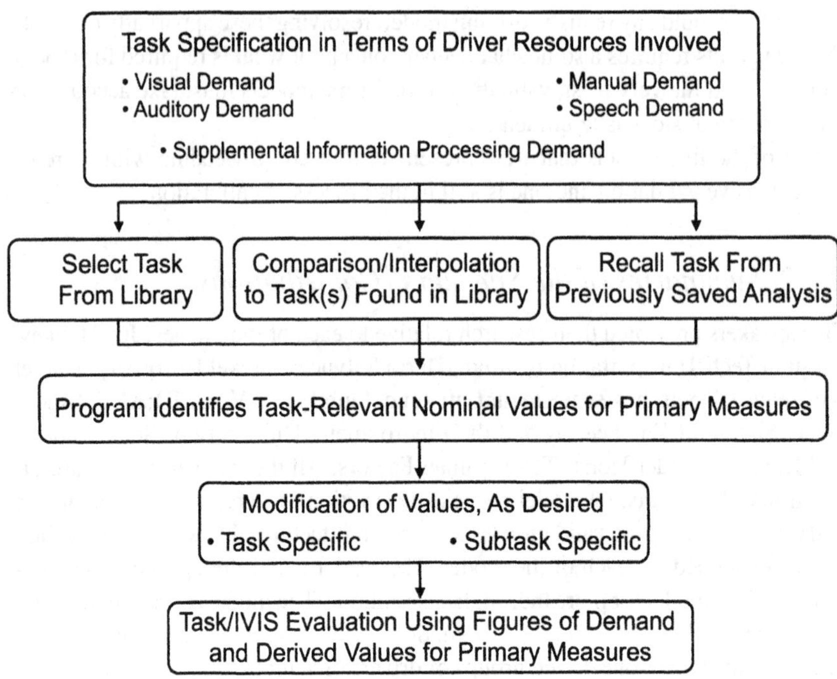

FIGURE 2.2. Overview of IVIS demand model.

perform IVIS tasks compete with the resources needed to drive the vehicle. In order to avoid reducing the driving performance to unacceptable levels, only limited resources can be required by IVIS. The different resource components and/or magnitudes can be used to perform the same task and are required for different tasks. The combination of the demand of these specific components determines the required resources to perform a task. The required resource demand can be used to estimate the potential of a decrement in driving performance. The principle of IVIS is that nominal values for measures are derived that can be modified to match a task or design specification; for example, a subtask modifier is the message length and a task modifier is the roadway complexity.

The scale of simulation is one driver within one of the three age groups. The software allows visualising the behaviour change outcome and the modifiers that can be selected to adjust. Finally, the source code and a user manual are available from FHWA. The software is still in a proof of concept stage. The model is used and designed to be used in the industry, which can make the feedback to the scientific community a slower process. For a review of the validation carried out at VTTI, the reader can consult Jackson and Bhise (2002).

2.2.2.2 ACT-R Driver Model – Dario Salvucci

The theoretical endeavour of the ACT-R driver model is to provide a psychologically plausible model of an individual driver and combine cognitive, perceptual

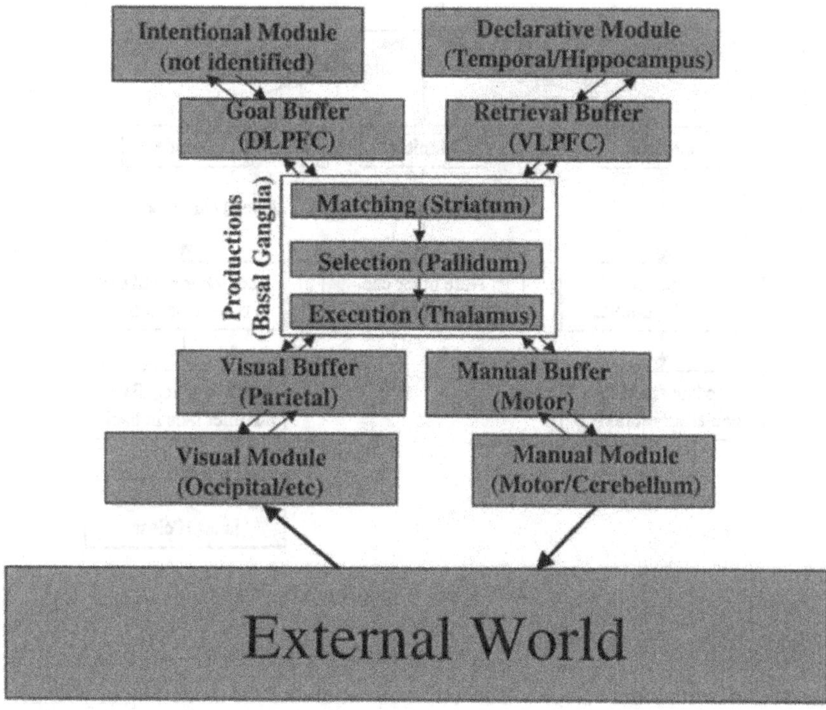

FIGURE 2.3. ACT-R architecture.

and motor dimensions (Salvucci et al., 2001). The approach involves applying a cognitive architecture, ACT-R associated to a computational framework. The advantage of this approach is the possibility to re-use theories and mechanisms already integrated within the cognitive architecture. This approach currently focuses on highway driving involving moderate traffic. The two current practical applications are (i) the prediction of driver distraction, for which models of typical secondary tasks (e.g., phone dialling) are integrated into the model in order to predict real-world observables measures and (ii) the recognition of driver intentions, where many models are run simultaneously, each trying to accomplish a different goal and the method consist of tracking which model best matches the observed data.

Figures 2.3 and 2.4 depict two diagrams: one for ACT-R and the other for ACT-R driver model. Figure 2.3 shows (Anderson et al., 2004) ACT-R architecture and details the overlap between brain structures and information processing steps. Figure 2.4 describes (Salvucci et al., 2001) the component involved in the ACT-R driver model. ACT-R provides a framework and specific rules are developed for the driving model. The model also integrates cognitive models for other tasks, such as using a cell phone or a navigation system. The current scale of simulation for the ACT-R driver model is focused on one driver in an environment that provides

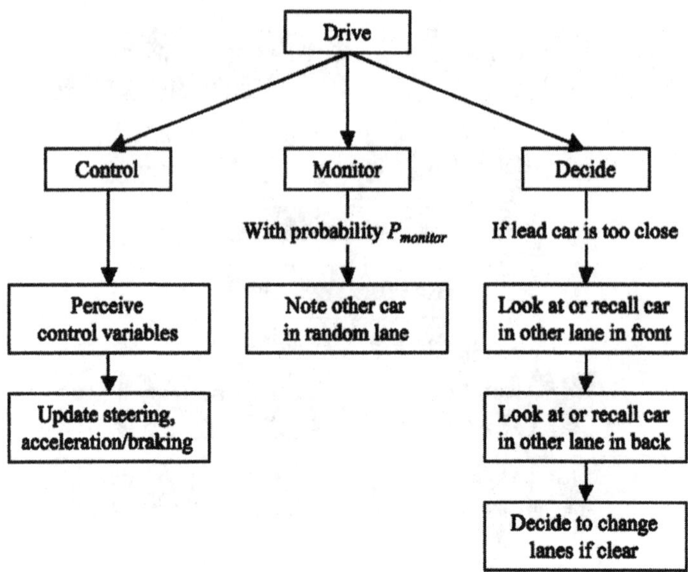

FIGURE 2.4. ACT-R driver model representation.

interactions with other vehicles. This effort also includes the modelling of younger versus older drivers. The visualisation allows observing driver's eye view and mirror and in a new system currently under development, graphs will provide measure of behaviour. Regarding the ease in using a model, the current version of the ACT-R driver model cannot be used easily by other researchers, but a new version is under development that should be easy to use (Salvucci et al., 2005).

In terms of calibration and validation, the approach applied for the ACT-R driver model is the comparison of model and human data sets recorded similarly in terms of real-world measures. The data sets that have been collected so far are highway driving, phone dialling and distraction, radio tuning and distraction and the age effects. Examples of measures are lane change steering profiles, gaze distribution on highway, lateral deviation during phone dialling.

2.2.2.3 Optimal Control Model – Richard van der Horst

The driver modelling effort at TNO aims at evaluating driver behaviour, performance and workload and at providing inputs for traffic flow model, such as MIXIC driver model and human-kinetic traffic flow model. This approach focuses on individual driver and vehicle units and is based on experimental research. The framework applied for this modelling effort is the one of 'optimal control', i.e., the use of a linear system theory, where the assumption is that the driver is well trained and well motivated to behave optimally. The model also integrates inherent limitations and constraints. The resulting model is a realistic description of driver behaviour in terms of driver performance, workload and total system performance measures.

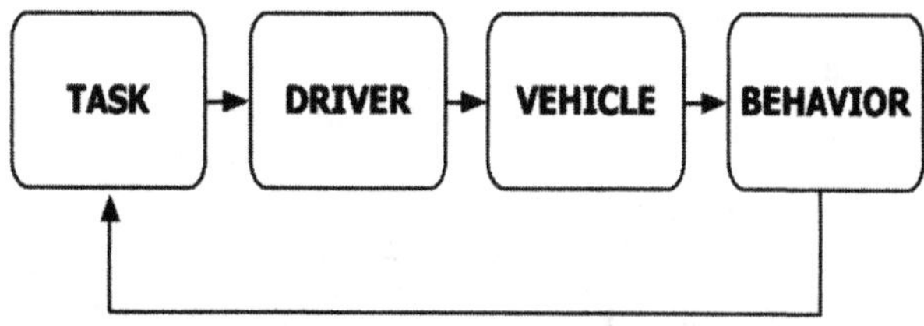

FIGURE 2.5. Block diagram for driver/vehicle/system and driver/model.

Two figures support the model architecture. Figure 2.5 is a block diagram of the driver vehicle system. In this figure, the concept of task covers elements such as lane keeping, car following or speed control, while the behaviour is described as measures of performance and workload. Figure 2.6 illustrates a 3 × 3 × 3 description of driver behaviour (Theeuwes, 2001) relative to the task hierarchy, task performance and information processing. The shaded area denotes the part of the behaviour that is currently modelled, i.e., the control of the vehicle at a skilled-based level. For this part of the behaviour, all of the information process is integrated, from perception to action. Figure 2.6 provoked a lot of interest from the audience, as it is commonly considered that strategic equals knowledge-based level, manoeuvring equals rule-based level and control equals skill-based level. A question was raised about how to transition within this 3× 3 × 3 representation. For example, how can a driver be simulated at the skill-based control and then simulated at the knowledge-based level? Is it only by learning? Can it also be due to other factors? The answer pointed to situations such as degraded driving conditions. For example, an experienced driver mobilises skills (Task performance) at the control level (Task hierarchy), but while driving another vehicle will move the vehicle control one level up to the rule level. Another example given was the case of a novice driver, for whom the control of the vehicle can be associated to a knowledge-level performance.

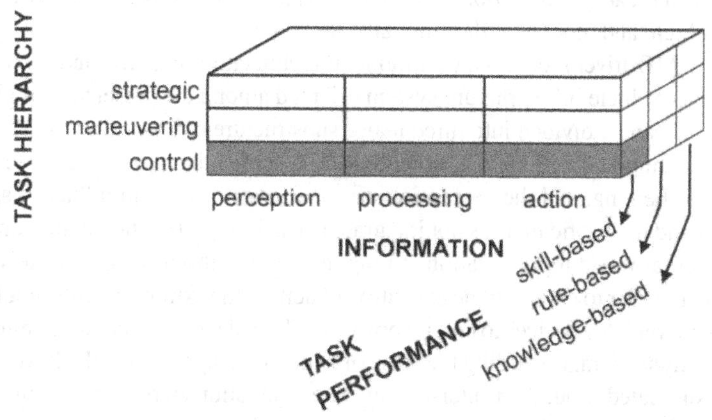

FIGURE 2.6. Driver model.

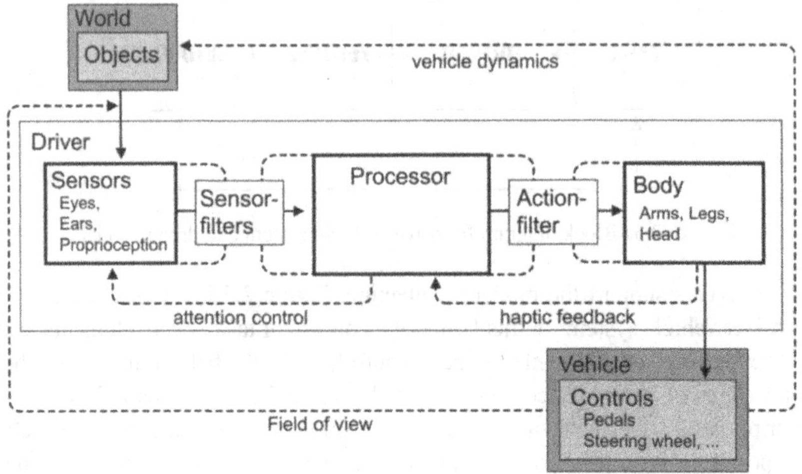

FIGURE 2.7. ACME driver model.

The outputs generated by the OCM are time simulation results, performance and workload measures and a workload index. The example of validation provided during the workshop was a comparison of data collected on a driving simulator and of model prediction on the lane-keeping task. The agreement between the model and experimental results indicates a useful predictive capability.

2.2.2.4 ACME

The purpose of the ACME driver model it to develop a combined view on car-following and lane-changing as well as describe and evaluate the mental processes needed for driving. It is a man in the loop simulation of a 'car-driver' unit composed of three sub-models: model of human sensors, model for information processing and a model for action execution. The simulation integrates models of the dynamics of the vehicle and models of the simulated area.

The ACME driver model is a very modular architecture (Fig. 2.7) and one of the most driver vehicle infrastructure system oriented among the presentations given. The model can be divided into three major substructures: (i) senses, (ii) information processing and (iii) actions execution. The senses that are implemented are vision and hearing, and the perception of acceleration is used to influence speed decision and the haptic input is not integrated. The information processor consists of an internal world representation storing, a planning instance and an execution instance. In order to carry out the execution of action, the extremities are simulated to move in-vehicles devices to certain position. These devices in turn determine the vehicle's dynamism. Regarding the scale of simulation, approximately 20 vehicles can be simulated around an intersection. The simulation step ranges from 10 to 100 ms. The visualisation represents the states within the driver's cognition and includes timelines of measures. Regarding the ease of using the model, it would

While driving, you are...

 Watching	 Thinking	 Responding

In Fuzzy Logic, this becomes

Fuzzy Input	**Fuzzy Firing**	**Defuzzification**
x (relative speed) = A′ y (headway divergence) = B′	If x = A and y = B then z = C	Because x = A′ and y = B′ z (acceleration rate) = C′

FIGURE 2.8. FLOWSIM driver model.

still require time for the user to become familiar with the model and its implementation. The ACME model is still in the process of development and hence has not been validated yet.

2.2.2.5 Fuzzy Logic Based Motorway Simulation

The development of Fuzzy LOgic based motorWay SIMulation (FLOWSIM) started in 1997. The model was initially focused on highway traffic, but now covers all type of roadway. This framework was first used for advanced driver assistance system (ADAS) and infrastructure speed control applications. Recent urban applications include network travel time prediction. It is now the object of an intensive enhancement program in China and has been chosen as the traffic simulation tool for supporting the city of Tianjin's transportation planning and management.

FLOWSIM driver model (Brackstone, 2000; ;rackstone et al., 1997; Wu et al., 2000) representation (Fig. 2.8) presents the three basic steps of watching, thinking and responding and how these basic steps can be associated to fuzzy logic. The example used for the description of the model focused on speed and gap control. It showed how the relative speed and distance divergence influence the driver's action in terms of acceleration rate. This model allows most units to be simulated during one simulation, with the possibility of simulating up to a 1000 vehicles. Different behaviours are simulated by using distributions. The speaker found little empirical evidence about the existence of groups such as young or old or aggressive drivers and therefore uses the distribution without labels tying the driver/vehicle unit to specific groups. The visualisation mainly displays individual vehicles and the road geometries. In order to use the system, it would be necessary to receive training.

The validation of FLOWSIM (Wu et al., 2003) concentrated on the comparison of simulated and measured traffic flows and showed a very satisfying fit.

2.3 Synthesis of Presented Models

This section presents two sub-sections. In the first one, we introduce a set of dimension and visualisation methods to understand the scopes of the different models that were presented above, their commonalities as well as their differences. In the second section, we will discuss briefly the notion of driver model as a tool used for the development or evaluation by users who are not necessarily human sciences scientists and, although they need to manipulate driver model, should not have to create all of the elements going into a driver model.

2.3.1 Understanding Models' Scope

We consider that the basic architecture of a simulation involving a driver model is constituted of at least three main components: (i) a driver model, (ii) a vehicle model and (iii) an infrastructure model. This hierarchy (Fig. 2.9) can be further expanded into increasing the levels of detail. For example, the driver model can be expanded in more modules or dimensions, such as driving tasks classification (strategic, tactical and operational) or psycho-motor dimension, which is constituted of perception, cognition and motor control. For the workshop, we defined a number of dimensions for each of these three main components and asked the speakers to rate their models on these dimensions.

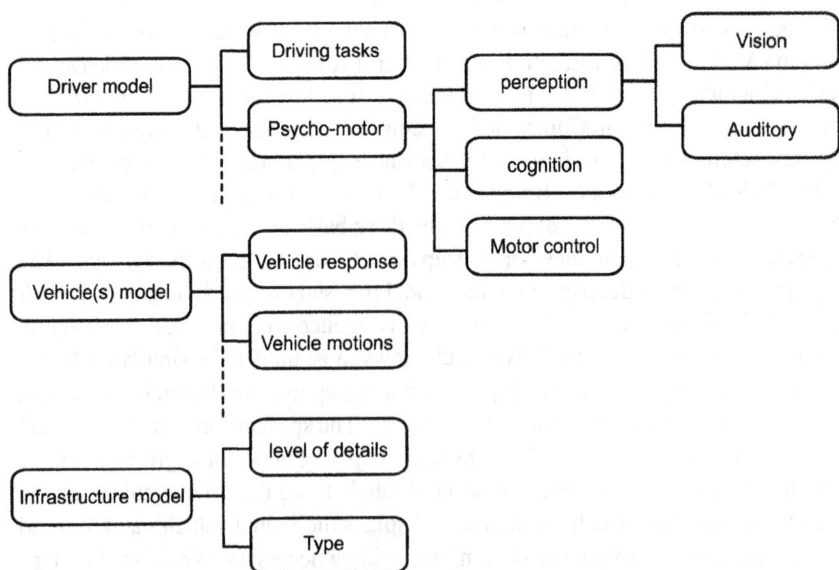

FIGURE 2.9. Hierarchy of model components.

For the driver component, the proposed dimensions were:

- psycho-motor
- driving tasks
- control level
- model capacities
- simulated phenomena
- simulation control

For the vehicle component, the proposed dimensions were

- control variables
- vehicle motions
- vehicle subsystems
- vehicle response

And, for the infrastructure component, the two main proposed categories were

- level of details (lane, signalisation)
- environment type (highway, urban ....)

As the workshop was limited in time, we focused the scope of the description to the three main components and on the details of the psycho-motor dimensions. The rating was as follows:

0: not represented
1: indirectly represented (there is a related parameter)
2: basic inclusion (there is a specific parameter in the model that indicates relevant trends)
3: included (the parameter or state is directly represented via a simple sub-model)
4: modelled (a sub-model represents the process)
5: represented in detail (the process is a core aspect of the model and be related in some detail to experiments or theories)

This rating was then integrated in a 'radar web' graph. Each speaker presented a graph for each of the three components and then a more detailed graph of the psycho-motor level. The ratings for all the models were then integrated on a same graph (see Figs. 2.10 and 2.11).

The purpose of representing the models presented at the workshop via a common graph was to identify synergies and limitations. In order to categorise synergistic dimensions, it was proposed that when a dimension was ranked three or above by at least three models, then a synergy between the three models is possible. As shown in Fig. 2.10, the dimensions that fit this category are perception, cognition, operational, rule, reaction and static input. A second category is one where dimensions could clearly be further developed, where at least one model ranks three or above. The dimensions in this category are motor control, strategic, tactical, skill, non-driving activities, knowledge, anticipation, distraction and driver characteristics. Another interesting category is one where none of the models ranked

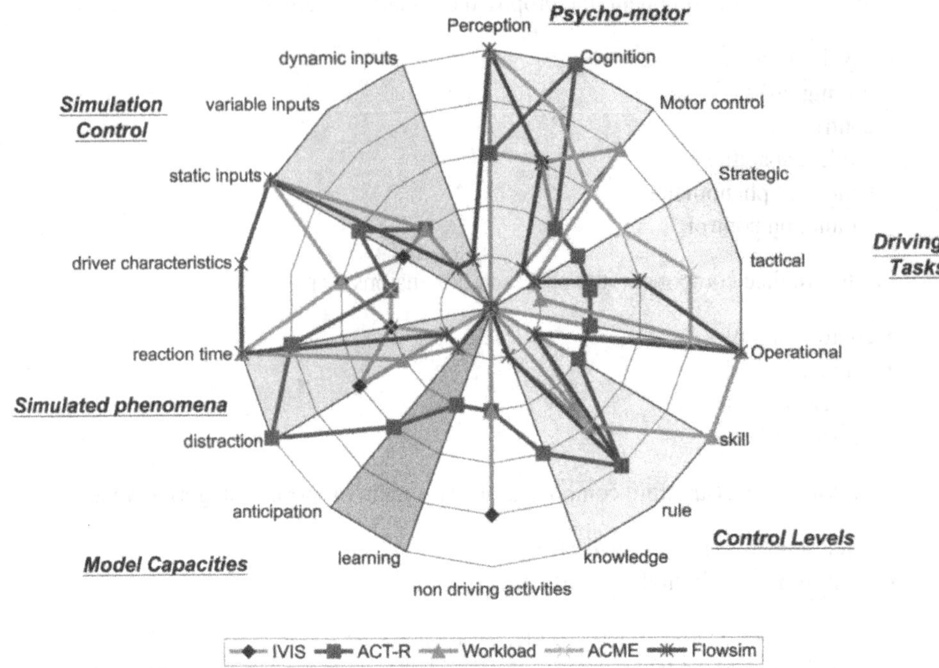

FIGURE 2.10. Representation of driver model dimensions.

three or above with the following three dimensions: learning, variable and dynamic inputs.

The same method was applied for the description of the psycho-motor dimensions (Fig. 2.11), and the areas for which we identified synergies are vision, decision making, memories, steering control and velocity control. The areas that need to be developed are haptic, auditory, recognition, anticipation, rules/knowledge and attentional resources. Finally, the areas still to be covered are tactile and other vehicle control.

This categorization of the dimensions led to a question about researchers implementation strategy and what dictates the choice of what to implement first. Are the dimensions from the first category receiving so much attention because they are easier to implement than the low ranking ones or because they are more important to the concept of driver model and its current applications?

2.3.2 Driver Model Toolbox

The notion of a driver model toolbox came up during the workshop discussion. A parallel was drawn with tools such as Matlab and Simulink, which allow the use of pre-existing tools to create simulations; for driver models, researchers have yet to start developing such a simulation environment. The two main aspects covered were how the toolbox should be developed and how to identify potential user groups.

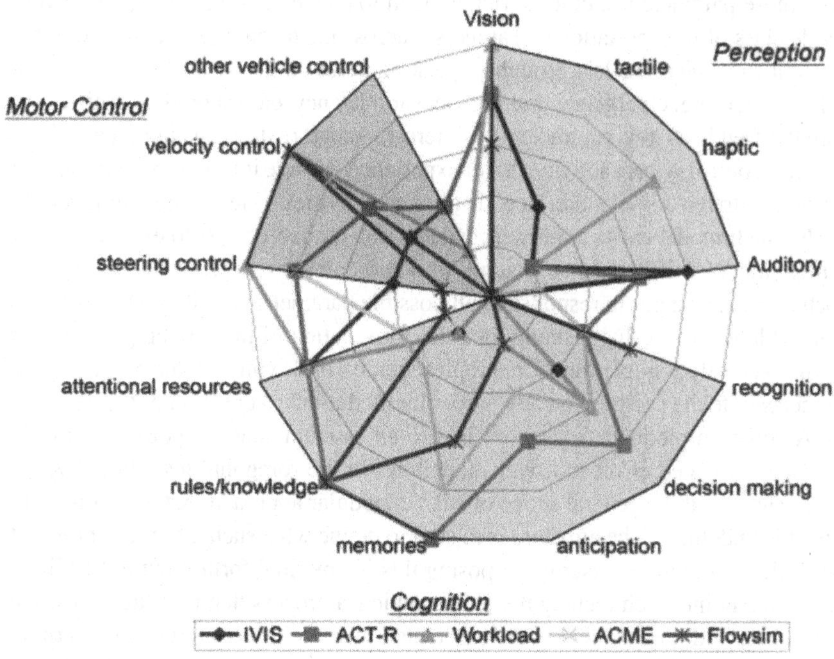

FIGURE 2.11. Representation of psycho-motor dimensions.

Matlab is a commercial software package supporting simulations from most engineering disciplines, and it is difficult to aim at a completely similar product. The equivalent would be a commercial software supporting simulation of intelligent systems or of the human mind. One of the open suggestions was to create a publicly available tool, based on the contributions of an international consortium of researchers. Such a tool would be a 'driver simulator' software, which would allow to observe as a simulation is conducted the different components of the model activity.

The two key groups – yet to be identified – are a scientist/researcher group, who would design and develop the toolbox, and a parallel user group, who would test, develop and help validate the resulting models. It is anticipated that whilst these two groups would have a range of differing requirements and interests, their activities could be complementary and lead to a new general level of driver modelling capability.

In some respect, the models closest to achieving this role are the IVIS and ACT-R driver model. The limitations of these models are their limited scope, ongoing calibration and validation and for the ACT-R driver model, the step of going towards a more user friendly platform and interface.

2.4 Towards a Comprehensive Model of Driving

Any comprehensive model of driving should be capable of reproducing statistically verifiable trends in response to changes made to its constitutive parameters, and those parameters should be rich enough to encompass the interests of a very wide class of transportation researchers – across the disciplines mentioned in the Introduction (Section 2.1). Roughly speaking, relevant time-based responses (eye glance, steering, emergency braking, decision latency, etc.) should be available to predict trends as key parameters of interest change (external vehicle behaviour, vehicle control system activity, driver experience, vehicle information and warning systems, driver–vehicle interface, distracting activities, external signalling, etc.).

No such model exists at present; indeed, it is probably naive to expect that any single model will ever be sufficiently full and complete to represent all possible behavioural changes in response to all possible parametric changes. However it is plausible to expect that a single modular formulation of the driving process – or more precisely a single functional representation of driving – could be developed to accelerate the progress on any particular model-based question of this type.

A common modular framework is also an essential starting point for any serious coordinated effort in driver modelling. In the foregoing text (Fig. 2.9) we have suggested the general scope of such a modular approach, but the framework itself is undefined. The aim here is to start to define what such a framework might look like, without necessarily proposing this in any final form. Figure 2.12 illustrates the point. Each rectangular shape depicts a process that is at the same time stochastic and predictable. Those associated with the driver are open to learning and adaptation. Note that in this representation, the driver appears as a distributed set of processes! Indeed, the structure embodies a whole range of assumptions and hypotheses. For example, it suggests that some form of 'vision-based' driving is possible without the involvement of higher cognitive function, but that manoeuvring decisions are not possible without (at least occasional) strategic input. The diagram is not intended to be complete (e.g., there is no auditory information channel) or even correct; indeed the correctness of this or other functional maps of its kind ultimately depends on its ability to match experiments.

2.5 Conclusions

The models presented at the workshop varied based on the goal for which they are designed and the methods applied to implement, calibrate and validate them. However, they do share commonalities in the processes that they manipulate. The authors' intention when convening the speakers was to illustrate the variety of driver models and to convey the point that the aim of developing driver models is not to create 'the' driver model or a driver model representing the right approach. Actually, the level of detail to integrate in a driver model really depends on the goal of the developer. For instance, in order to predict driver behaviour, how necessary is it to describe the psycho-motor processes underlying the driving activity or is a data analysis of data patterns and trends sufficient?

The intent of the workshop was to open up the discussion on modelling issues and exchange, move from a 'researcher centric' to a community-directed approach in order to take driver model development further. The other goal was to discuss the

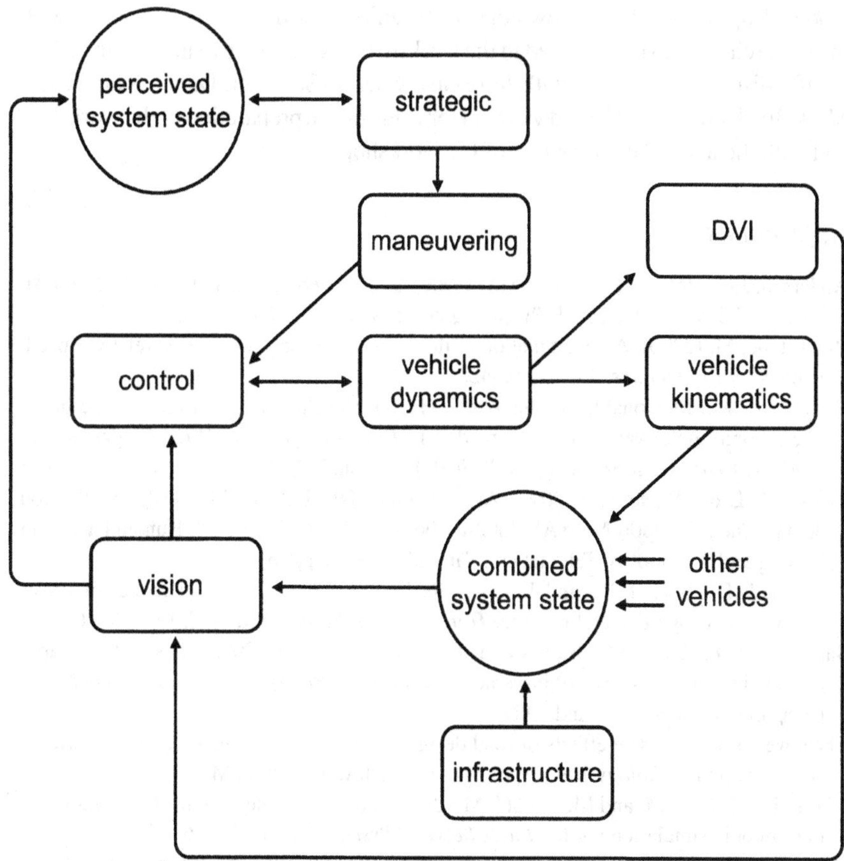

FIGURE 2.12. Possible functional representation of the driving process.

idea of extending the notion of driver model towards the concept of comprehensive driving model, where the driver becomes one the component of a system and could become a tool used in order to support ITS development or other safety application for which it is necessary to know more about the driver behaviour or information-processing characteristics. In this sense, this concept differs from classical traffic simulation tool by the scale at which it is envisaged, although simplified versions could eventually be coupled with more conventional traffic simulation tools. In this regard, the aim is to take the concept of driver model out of the research community and bring it to a wider range of users, who can be engineers designing in-vehicle systems and needing to understand the impact of their systems on driving or traffic engineers needing to use driver models when changing a roadway design without systematically having to conduct lengthy data collection.

The next step to pursue the development of a comprehensive driving model will be to continue to take advantage of conferences to bring together model developers and users in order to discuss about the elements to include on a driving model and methods for exchanging the results of their research.

Acknowledgments. We acknowledge the benefits we had from our exchanges with the researchers who participated in the workshop. We also give thanks for the many fruitful discussions we had with Jon Hankey, Dario Salvucci, Daniel Krajzewicz, Mark Brackstone and Richard van der Horst during the preparation of the workshop and with the audience on the day of the workshop.

References

Anderson, J.R., Bothell, D., Byrne, M.D., Douglass, S., Lebiere, C. and Qin, Y. (2004) An integrated theory of the mind. *Psychological Review*, 111, 1036–1060.

Brackstone, M. (2000). An examination of the use of fuzzy sets to describe relative speed. *Perception Ergonomics*, 43(4), 528–42.

Brackstone, M., McDonald, M. and Wu, J. (1997). Development of a fuzzy logic based microscopic motorway simulation model. In *Proceedings of the IEEE Conference on Intelligent Transportation Systems* (ITSC97). Boston, MA.

Jackson, D.L. and Bhise, V.D. (2002). An evaluation of the IVIS-DEMAnD driver attention demand model. Report No. SAE 2002-01-0092, UMTRI-95608 A08. Human Factors in Seating and Automotive Telematics, Warrendale, SAE, pp. 61–70.

Salvucci, D.D., Boer, E.R., and Liu, A. (2001). Toward an integrated model of driver behavior in a cognitive architecture. *Transportation Research Record*, 1779, 9–16.

Salvucci, D.D., Zuber, M., Beregovaia, E., and Markley, D. (2005). Distract-R: Rapid prototyping and evaluation of in-vehicle interfaces. In *Proceedings of Human Factors in Computing Systems*. Portland, OR.

Theeuwes, J. (2001). The effects of road design on driving. In Pierre-Emmanuel Barjonet (Ed.). *Traffic Psychology Today* (pp. 241–263). Kluwer, Boston, MA.

Wu, J., Brackstone, M. and McDonald, M. (2000). Fuzzy sets and systems for a motorway microscopic simulation model. *Fuzzy Sets and Systems* 116(1), 65–76.

Wu, J., Brackstone, M. and McDonald, M. (2003). The validation of a microscopic simulation model: A methodological case study. *Transportation Research C*, 11(6), 463–479.

3
Towards Monitoring and Modelling for Situation-Adaptive Driver Assist Systems

TOSHIYUKI INAGAKI

3.1 Introduction

In the classic tri-level study of the causes of traffic accidents, Treat et al. (1979) ascribe 92.6% of car accidents to human error, where human errors include improper lookout (known as 'looking but not seeing'), inattention, internal distraction and external distraction. Green (2003) reports that other studies have found similar results that a human error is involved in 90% of car accidents. Human errors, such as those listed in the above, can happen for everybody and may not be eradicated. However, if there were some technology to detect driver's possibly risky behaviour or state in a real-time manner, car accidents may be reduced effectively. *Proactive safety technology* that detects driver's non-normative behaviour or state and provides the driver with appropriate support functions plays a key role in automotive safety improvement. Various research projects have been conducted worldwide to develop such technologies (see, e.g. Witt, 2003; Panou et al., 2005; Saad, 2005; Amditis et al., 2005; Tango and Montanari, 2005; Cacciabue and Hollnagel, 2005).

This paper gives an overview on two of research projects in Japan, which aim to develop technologies to detect driver's behaviour or state that is inappropriate to a given traffic environment so that the driver may be provided with support for enhancing his or her situation awareness or for reducing risk in the environment. The first project is the 'Behaviour-Based Human Environment Creation Technology', which was conducted during the period of 1999 to 2003, with the support of the Ministry of Economy, Trade and Industry (METI), Government of Japan, and the New Energy and Industrial Technology Development Organization (NEDO). The other project is the 'Situation and Intention Recognition for Risk Finding and Avoidance' which has been proceeding since 2004, with the support of the Ministry of Education, Culture, Sports, Science and Technology (MEXT), Government of Japan.

This paper tries to focus on the modelling-related aspects of the projects, and picks up a model from each project. From the first project, is the Bayesian network model for detecting non-normative behaviour of the driver, in which the model has been constructed based on driving behavioural data collected in the real traffic environment. From the second project, is the discrete-event model of dynamical changes of driver's psychological state, which has been developed to analyse and determine how decision authority should be distributed between the driver and automation under possibility of the driver's overtrust in 'smart and reliable' automation. The models are still in their early stages; however, they are expanding description capabilities and applicabilities in the real world.

3.2 Behaviour-Based Human Environment Creation Technology Project

3.2.1 Aims of the Project

When a driver's performance is suitable to task demands determined by traffic situations (such as vehicle performance, vehicle speed, road structure, weather, other traffic), the driver can enjoy safe driving. However, if the driver's performance fails to adapt to the task demands, his or her behaviour may increase risk to the situation (see Fig. 3.1). In order to evaluate the level of risk, traffic situations as well as driving performance need to be sensed and monitored.

The Behaviour-Based Human Environment Creation Technology project was conducted during the period of 1999 to 2003, with the support of METI and NEDO. The project had four aspects, and one of the aspects was to create behaviour-based driving assist technologies that determine whether a driver's performance is deviated from the normative one in a given traffic situation as well as provide the driver with a warning or advice, when appropriate. A driver's normative (or baseline) behaviour was defined as his or her usual behaviour. The project took as an object of study a driver who usually bears safe driving in mind and used SAS 592, a self-rating scale of driving attitude, developed by the National Research Institute of Police Science, Japan, to exclude inherently unsafe drivers from the data collection phase.

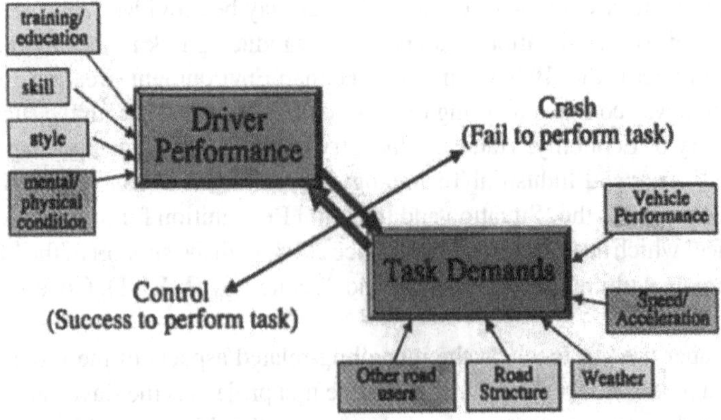

FIGURE 3.1. Driving performance and task demand (Akamatsu and Sakaguchi, 2003); originally from Fuller and Santos (2002).

3.2.2 Measurement of Driving Behaviour

In order to detect a driver's deviation from his or her normative performance, good knowledge on the driver's usual performance is necessary. Vehicles with a driving recorder system were developed, for the project, to record and collect behavioural data in real road environments. The system consists of sensors, small CCD cameras, a signal-processing device and a laptop on-board computer. The recorded data include steering wheel angle, turn signal, wiper activation, strokes of the brake and gas pedals, position of the right foot of the driver, geographical position of the vehicle, velocity and state of the vehicle, and relative distance and speed to the lead and following vehicles.

Eight different driving routes were chosen for investigation as 30-min trips with several right and left turns. Subjects were recruited and asked to drive a specified route once a day on weekdays for 2 months. Forty sets of behavioural data were collected for each subject per route (Akamatsu et al., 2003). At the end of data-collection phase, each subject was given the Driving Style Questionnaire developed for quantifying driver's attitudes, that may be related to or may affect his or her driving behaviour (Akamatsu, 2003). The total number of participants was 92 (59 male and 33 female). The age ranged from 21 to 71 years for males and from 20 to 66 years for females.

3.2.3 Driving Behaviour Modelling

A Bayesian network approach has been applied to driving behaviour modelling. Bayesian networks (often called belief networks) are directed graph models, in which an arc from a node, say A, to another, say B, represents a causal relation – 'A causes B'. The conditional probability distribution is specified at each node in the network to represent how a child node is affected by its parent nodes.

For each situation of interest, a Bayesian network model can be developed. Consider a case, for instance, in which a driver approaches an intersection with the STOP sign. Behavioural events needed for describing the case include (a) release of the gas pedal, (b) moving the foot to the brake pedal, (c) onset of braking, (d) reaching the maximum deceleration and (e) full stop. Figure 3.2 depicts the resulting Bayesian network model, obtained based on the collected behavioural data. In the Bayesian network modelling, the data analysis results used were those claiming that the weather conditions and the driver's score for the methodical scale in the Driving Style Questionnaire can be regarded as performance-shaping factors (Akamatsu and Sakaguchi, 2003).

3.2.4 Detection of Non-Normative Behaviour

Once a Bayesian network model has been obtained for a driver's normative behaviour, it then becomes possible to compute the probability distribution for each node in the network. Consider a case, as an example, in which some node, say Z, denotes a random variable related to a safety-critical action for avoiding an accident. Suppose Z has two nodes, X and Y, as its parents. Based on probability

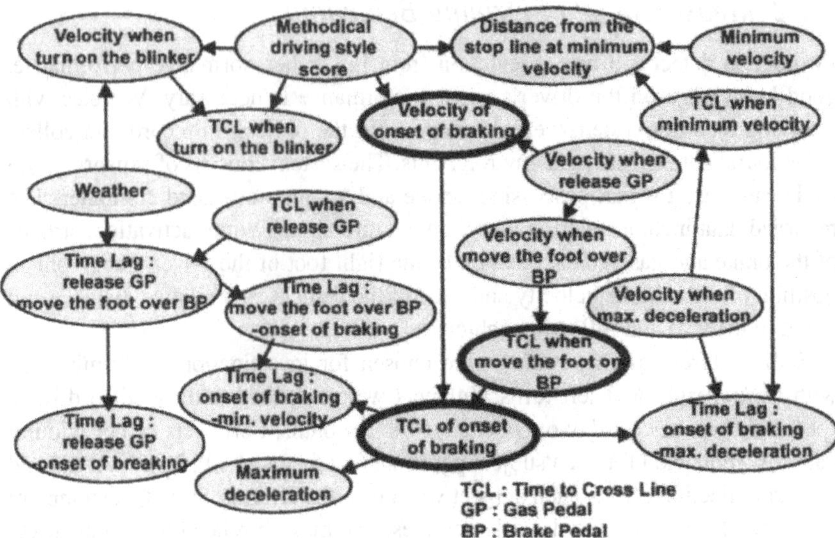

FIGURE 3.2. Bayesian network model for the behavioural events when approaching an intersection with the STOP sign (Akamatsu and Sakaguchi, 2003).

distributions for X and Y and the knowledge of probabilistic causal relation among the nodes, one can derive the conditional probability distribution, $P(Z|X, Y)$ for each combination of values of X and Y. The conditional probability distribution $P(Z|X, Y)$ describes how Z can take different values when the driver behaves in a normative manner.

Suppose an on-board sensor has observed that the random variable Z took a value z at some time point. Hypothesis testing is then performed to determine whether 'z may be regarded as a sample from the distribution $P(Z|X, Y)$'. If the hypothesis was rejected at some level of significance, it is then concluded that the driver's behaviour may be deviated from his or her normative performance. Akamatsu et al. (2003) defined the 'level of normality' and have developed a method to give a warning to the driver when the calculated level of normality becomes less than a specified threshold value.

3.2.5 *Estimation of Driver's State*

In the Behaviour-Based Human Environment Creation Technology project, methods for estimating driver's mental tension and fatigue were also investigated, because driver's status needs to be estimated to provide a driver with support functions suitable to his or her operational capability.

3.2.5.1 Estimation of Driver's Mental Tension

Mental tension is one of driver's internal factors affecting driving ability. Investigators in the project have found that chromogranin A (CgA) in saliva is a biochemical index of driver's mental strain (Sakakibara and Taguchi, 2003). The index was not convenient for real-time sensing of driver's mental tension. They found, however, that the steering operation and the head motion of a driver can replace salivary CgA in estimating a level of driver's mental tension. Taguchi and his colleagues argued that the steering operations at a frequency lower than 0.5 Hz may reflect a driver's reduced activation state in a monotonous driving environment and that the driver's intentional behaviour, such as a lane change, does not usually have influence on operational performance at such low frequencies (Sakakibara and Taguchi, 2005; Taguchi and Sakakibara, 2005). They also considered that while concentrating on driving, a driver generally puts power into various muscles to control body in response to vibrations from road surface, acceleration and/or deceleration of vehicle, which may create stiffness in the shoulders. Experiments were conducted to investigate relations between the two indices for tension. It has been observed that the steering operation and the head motions are complementary to each other. They have also found that a real-time estimation method can be implemented to distinguish the four grades of driver's tension (viz. reduced activation, neutral, moderate tension and hypertension).

3.2.5.2 Estimation of Driver's Fatigue

Fatigue is also one of the contributing factors affecting driving ability. Investigators in the project have tried to develop a non-invasive sensing method for real-time estimation of a driver's fatigue level (Furugori et al., 2003, 2005; Miura et al., 2002). With sensor sheets, Furugori and his colleagues measured the pressure distribution on the seat and found a relationship between changes in the load centre position (LCP) calculated from the pressure distribution and driver-indicated subjective fatigue. It was also found that the LCP contains information about 'prolonged changes' in posture with time (e.g. bending forward or backward) as well as 'momentary changes' in posture (e.g. shifting weight). A 'postural change parameter' and a 'weight-shifting parameter' were defined for the seatback and the seat cushion. However, individual differences were observed in direction of postural changes and weight shifting. A robust algorithm was thus required to estimate fatigue level for each individual. Based on the ratios that indicate the degree to which each parameter range deviates from those in normal driving, the 'fatigue index' was calculated to estimate a driver's fatigue level. It was found that in around 90% cases the calculated fatigue index agreed with subjective fatigue (Furugori et al., 2005).

3.3 Situation and Intention Recognition for Risk Finding and Avoidance Project

3.3.1 Aims of the Project

Driving requires a continuous process of perception, decision and action. Understanding of the current situation determines what action needs to be done (Hollnagel

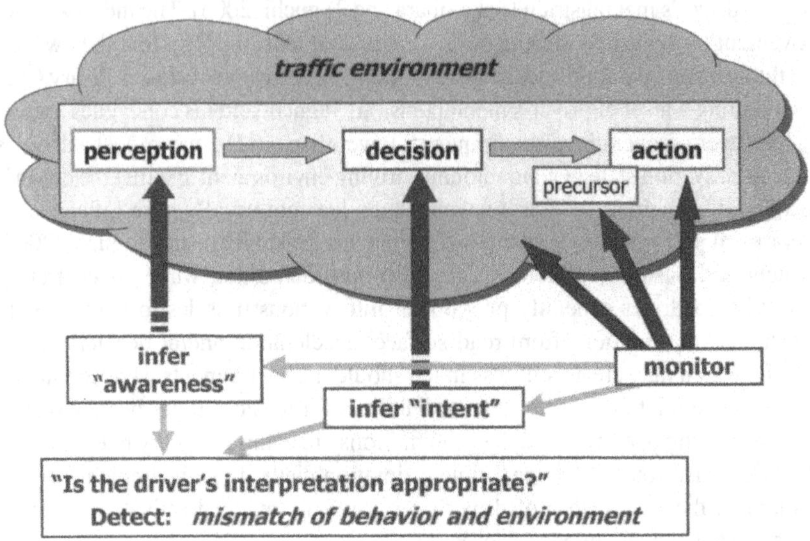

FIGURE 3.3. Assessing appropriateness of a driver's situation recognition.

and Bye, 2000). In reality, however, drivers' situation recognition may not always be perfect. Decisions and actions that follow poor or imperfect situation recognition can never be appropriate to given situations. It is not possible to 'see' directly whether a driver's situation recognition is correct or not. However, monitoring the driver's action (or its precursor) and traffic environment may make it be possible to estimate (a) whether the driver may have lost situation awareness, (b) whether the driver's interpretation of the traffic environment is appropriate and (c) whether the driver is inactive psychologically, e.g. due to complacency, or physiologically, e.g. due to fatigue, (see Fig. 3.3).

Since 2005, the author has been conducting a 3-year research project, entitled 'Situation and Intention Recognition for Risk Finding and Avoidance', with the support of the MEXT. The aim of the project is to develop proactive safety technologies to (a) monitor driver behaviour for assessing his or her intention, (b) detect mismatches of traffic environment and driver's interpretation of it, (c) assess the driver state and (d) provide the driver with appropriate assist functions in a situation-adaptive and context-dependent manner (see Fig. 3.4).

The research topics in the project are categorised as follows: (1) estimation of driver's psychological and physiological state, (2) driver behaviour modelling, (3) intelligent information processing for situation recognition and visual enhancement and (4) adaptive function allocation between drivers and automation. In (1), real-time methods are under development for detecting the driver's inattentiveness, hypo-vigilance, and complacency, through monitoring parameters, such as body movement, dynamical changes of the LCP on the back, eye and head movements, blinks, instep position of the right leg, operation of the steering wheel and movements of gas and brake pedals (Itoh et al., 2006). In (1), levels of

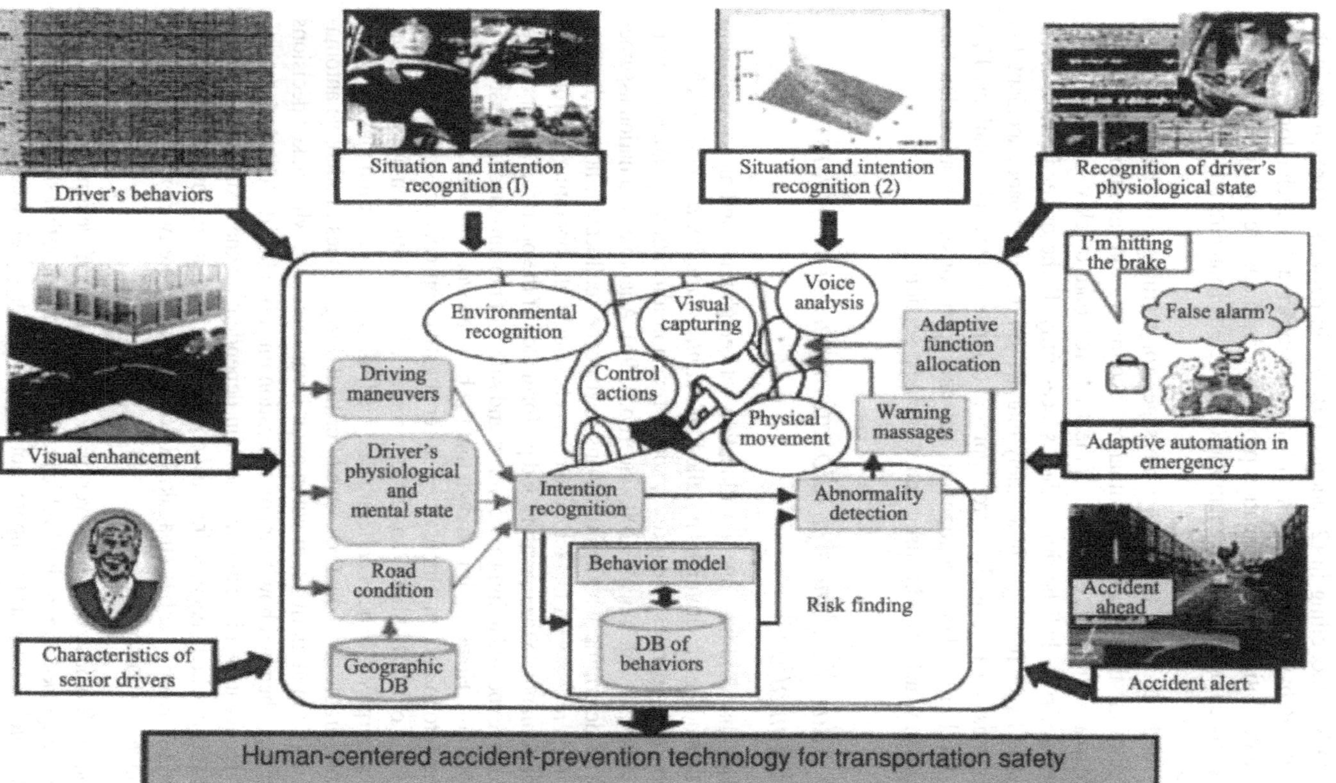

FIGURE 3.4. Situation and intention recognition for risk finding and avoidance project.

driver's fatigue and drowsiness are also estimated by applying a chaos theoretic method (Shiomi and Hirose, 2000) to a driver's voice during verbal communication. Driver modelling in (2) adopts a Bayesian network approach, as in the case of the Behaviour-Based Human Environment Creation Technology project. Some mathematical and information processing methods are under development in (3) for machine learning, recognition of traffic environments and human vision enhancement.

The methods in (1) to (3) give messages (or warnings) to the driver, when they determine that the driver's situation recognition and intention may not be suitable to a given traffic condition. If the driver responds quickly to the messages, the potential risk shall be diminished successfully. If the driver fails to accept or respond to the messages in a timely manner, on the other hand, accidental or incidental risks may grow. Research topics in (4) investigate such situations. They aim to develop an adaptive automation that can support drivers at various levels of automation, which shall be discussed in the next section.

3.3.2 Adaptive Function Allocation Between Drivers and Automation

A scheme that modifies function allocation between human and machine dynamically depending on situations is called an *adaptive function allocation*. The automation that operates under an adaptive function allocation is called *adaptive automation* (see e.g. Inagaki, 2003; Scerbo, 1996). Adaptive automation assumes criteria to determine whether functions have to be reallocated, how and when. The criteria reflect various factors, such as changes in the operating environment, loads or demands to the operators and performance of the operators. Adaptive automation is expected to improve comfort and safety of human–machine systems in transportation. However, it is known that the humans working with highly intelligent and autonomous machines often suffer negative consequences of automation, such as the out-of-the-loop familiarity problem, loss of situation awareness, automation surprises. When carelessly designed, adaptive automation may face with such undesirable consequences. One of critical design issues in adaptive automation is decision authority over automation invocation (viz. who makes decisions concerning when and how function allocation must be altered). The decision authority issue can be discussed in a domain-dependent manner. Automobile is one of domains in which machine-initiated control over automation invocation may be allowed for assuring safety (Inagaki, 2006). Following are two examples that are under investigation in the project.

Example 1: Suppose that the driver of the host vehicle H determines to make a lane change because the lead vehicle A has been driving rather slowly. When the host vehicle's on-board computer noticed that the driver glanced the side mirror several times, it inferred that the driver had formed an intention of changing lane, where the computer regarded 'glancing the side mirror several times in a short period of time' as precursor to the action of changing lane (see Fig. 3.3). The computer, monitoring backward with a camera, also noticed that a faster vehicle

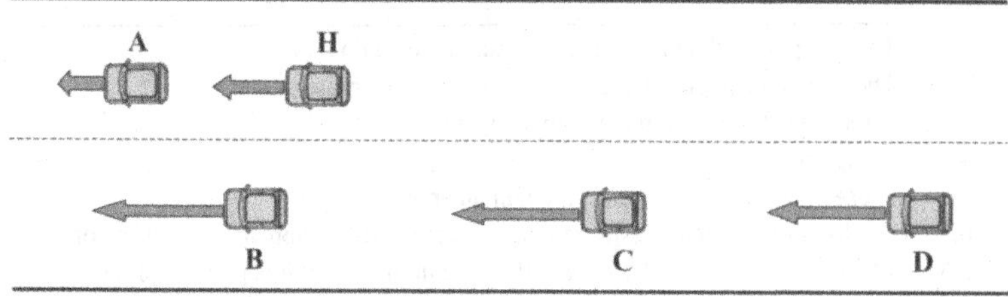

FIGURE 3.5. An example in which machine intelligence is given decision authority.

C is coming from behind on the left lane. Based on the understanding of driver's intention and the approach of vehicle *C*, the computer puts its safety control function into its armed position in preparation for a case when the driver chooses a wrong timing to execute an action (viz. steering the wheel) due to improper interpretation of the traffic environment. Now the driver, who has seen that a very fast vehicle *B* almost passed him on the left, begins to steer the wheel to the left, failing to notice vehicle *C* (Fig. 3.5). The computer immediately activates the safety control function to make the wheel either slightly heavy to steer (*soft protection*) or extremely heavy to steer (*hard protection*). The soft protection is for correcting the driver's interpretation of the traffic environment, and the hard protection is for preventing a collision from occurring. The computer takes the steering authority from the driver partially in cases of soft protection and fully in cases of hard protection.

Example 2: Suppose that the driver of the host vehicle *H* wants to make a lane change to the left, because the lead vehicle *A* drives rather slowly. When glancing at the rear view mirror, the driver noticed that faster vehicles, *C* and *D*, are coming from behind on the left lane (Fig. 3.5). By taking several looks at the side mirror, the driver tries to find a precise timing to cut in. In the meantime, based on the observation that the driver looked away many times in a short period of time, the on-board computer determined that the driver has formed an intention of changing lane and that he might not be able to pay full attention to the lead vehicle *A*. The computer then puts its safety control function into its armed position in preparation for a deceleration of the lead vehicle *A*. If the lead vehicle *A* did not make any deceleration before the host vehicle's driver completes a lane change, the computer will never activate the safety control function and will put it back into a normal standby position. On the other hand, if the computer detected a rapid deceleration of the lead vehicle *A* while the driver is still looking for a timing to make a lane change, it immediately activates its safety control function, such as an automatic emergency brake.

3.3.3 Decision Authority and the Levels of Automation

For the discussion of decision authority, the notion of the *level of automation* (LOA) is useful. Table 3.1 gives an expanded version in which an LOA comes between levels 6 and 7 in the original list by Sheridan (1992). The added level, called

TABLE 3.1. Scales of levels of automation.

1.	The computer offers no assistance; human must do it all.
2.	The computer offers a complete set of action alternatives and
3.	narrows the selection down to a few, or
4.	suggests one and
5.	executes that suggestion if the human approves, or
6.	allows the human a restricted time to veto before automatic execution, or
6.5	executes automatically upon telling the human what it is going to do, or
7.	executes automatically, then necessarily informs humans,
8.	informs him after execution only if he asks,
9.	informs him after execution if it, the computer, decides to.
10.	The computer decides everything and acts autonomously, ignoring the human.

After Sheridan (1992), Inagaki et al. (1998) and Inagaki and Furukawa (2004).

level 6.5, was first introduced in Inagaki et al. (1998) with twofold objectives: (1) to avoid automation surprises possibly induced by automatic actions and (2) to implement actions indispensable to assure systems safety in emergency. When the LOA is positioned at level 6 or higher, the human may not be in command. Generally speaking, it would be desirable, philosophically and practically, that human is maintained as the final authority over the automation. However, as can be seen in Examples 1 and 2, there are cases in which automation may be given decision authority (Inagaki, 2006).

3.3.4 Model-Based Evaluation of Levels of Automation

This section gives a driver model for evaluating design of interactions between a driver and automation under the possibility of the driver's overtrust in the automation. Let us take a case, as an example, in which an adaptive cruise control (ACC) system is available on the host vehicle. The ACC system is a partial automation for longitudinal control, designed to reduce the driver's workload by freeing the driver from frequent acceleration and deceleration. It controls the host vehicle so that it can follow a vehicle ahead (the target vehicle) at a specified distance. When the ACC system detects the deceleration of the target vehicle, it slows down the host vehicle at some deceleration rate. As long as the deceleration of the target vehicle stays within a certain range, the ACC system can control the speed of the host vehicle perfectly and no rear-end collision into the target vehicle occurs. It would be natural for the driver to trust in the ACC system while observing it behaves correctly and appropriately. Sometimes the driver may place excessive trust in the automation and may fail to allocate his or her attention to the traffic environment. If the target vehicle makes a rapid deceleration at a high rate, the ordinary brake by the ACC system may not be powerful enough to avoid a collision into the target vehicle. In such cases, the automation issues an 'emergency-braking alert', which tells the driver to hit the brake himself or herself hard enough to avoid a collision. If the driver has been in a hypovigilant state, however, he or she may fail to respond quickly to the situation.

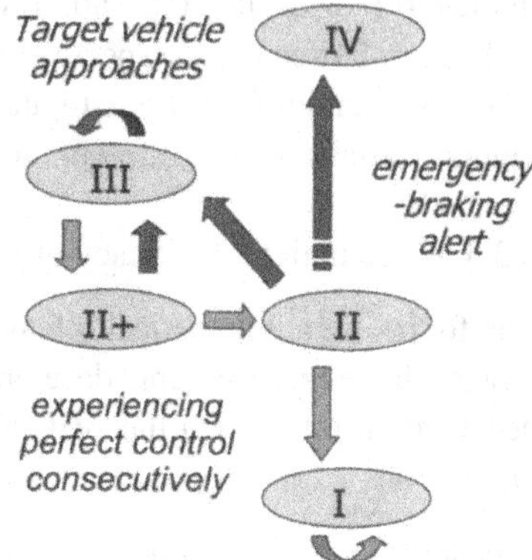

FIGURE 3.6. Drivers' psychological state and their dynamic transitions.

3.3.4.1 Drivers' Psychological States and Their Transitions

Inagaki and Furukawa (2004) have distinguished five psychological states for drivers, by modifying the original model by Hashimoto (1984):

State I: Subnormal and inactive state.
State II: Normal and relaxed state, with complete faith in the automation.
State II+: Normal and relaxed state with moderate level of trust in the automation.
State III: Normal and vigilant state, which is the best state for safe driving.
State IV: Hyper-normal and excited state.

State transitions occur dynamically in time as time passes by. Suppose a driver's psychological state was positioned initially at State III, when he or she started driving. If the driver has observed a certain number of the ACC system's perfect longitudinal controls in response to decelerations of the lead vehicle, the driver's psychological state goes from III to II+. Observing some more consecutive perfect controls by the ACC system, the driver's psychological state may change further from State II+ to II. If the driver felt alarm, while observing the host vehicle came close to the lead vehicle, his or her trust in the ACC system goes down a bit, and a state transition occurs, say, from State II to II+ or from State II+ to III (see Fig. 3.6).

3.3.4.2 Driver's Response to an Alert

Each psychological state is characterised by a corresponding driver performance in situation recognition and swiftness of response to an emergency-braking alert. A model for the driver's response to an emergency-braking alert may be given as follows: (1) If the driver was in State I when the alert was set off, he or she does not respond to the alert at all. (2) If the driver was in State II, he or she stays in the same state with probability p and hits the brake pedal in T2 seconds. With probability $1 - p$, the driver state jumps into State IV. (3) If the driver was either in State II+ or III, he or she applies the emergency brake himself or herself either in T2+ or T3 seconds, respectively. (4) In State IV, the driver panics and fails to take any meaningful actions to attain car safety. T2, T2+ and T3 are treated as random variables with different means.

3.3.4.3 Evaluation of Efficacy of Levels of Automation

The following are realistically feasible design alternatives for cases in which the target vehicle makes a rapid deceleration at a rate much greater than the maximum deceleration rate which the ACC system can handle with its ordinary automatic brake:

Scheme 1: Upon recognition of a rapid deceleration of the target vehicle, the ACC system gives an *emergency-braking alert*, where the LOA is positioned at 4.
Scheme 2: Upon recognition of a rapid deceleration of the target vehicle, the ACC system gives an emergency-braking alert. If the driver does not respond within a pre-specified time (due to inattentiveness or delay in situational recognition), it applies an automatic emergency brake, where the LOA is positioned at 6.
Scheme 3: Upon recognition of a rapid deceleration of the target vehicle, the ACC system applies its automatic emergency brake simultaneously when it issues an emergency-braking alert, where the LOA of this scheme is positioned at 6.5.

With the models of driver's psychological state and response time for each state, Monte Carlo simulations can be performed to evaluate efficacy of the LOAs under possibility of driver's overtrust in the ACC system. The following are some of observations obtained (Inagaki and Furukawa, 2004):

(1) A safety control scheme with LOA-6 may not be effective, compared to one with LOA-4, if the driver trusts in the automation excessively. In order to mitigate the drawback of the LOA-6, some measures are needed to keep the driver alert.
(2) The drawback of LOA-6 is partially due to the time delay of the automatic safety control action. The LOA-6.5 scheme may be more effective than LOA-6 or LOA-4 in order to assure systems safety in time – criticality under possibility of driver's complacency.

3.4 Concluding Remarks

This paper has given brief descriptions on two driver behaviour modelling related research projects in Japan the aims of which are to develop proactive safety technologies to detect mismatches between driver's behaviours and the traffic environment. This paper discussed two models in the projects: one is the Bayesian network model for detecting non-normative behaviour of the driver and the other is the discrete-event model for analysing driver interactions with 'smart and reliable' automation. These models may still be in their early stages of development, compared to control theoretic models such as those discussed by Weir and Chao (2005) and Juergensohn (2005). However, the models are expanding their description capabilities and applicability.

Drivers must be provided with necessary and sufficient supports by machine or automation. Intention understanding and communication play important roles in realising such meaningful support functions. If the driver fails to understand the intention of machine intelligence, an automation surprise may happen. If the machine does not recognise the driver's intention, its 'good support' may be annoying to the driver. The topic of intent inference attracts keen interests in Japan as well as the rest of the world. Although no discussion could be made in this paper, a fuzzy association system model with case-based reasoning has been developed for recognising human intention through monitoring his or her behaviour in the 'Humatronics' project in Japan for the safety of drivers and pedestrians (Umeda et al., 2005; Yamaguchi et al., 2004).

In spite of its usefulness, an intention understanding approach may have some limitations, at least at the present time. The second project described in this paper, for instance, sometimes found difficulty in understanding the intention of the driver from his or her behaviour. Norman (1988) has distinguished *seven stages of action*, in which the first-four stages are (1) forming the goal, (2) forming the intention, (3) specifying an action and (4) executing the action. The project tries to infer the intention of the driver by catching some 'precursor' to the action (recall, Fig. 3.3) that may come between stages (3) and (4). Some of problems observed in the project are as follows: (a) No useful precursor may exist for some intended actions, which might also be individual-dependent. (b) The driver may form a goal for a very immediate future in dynamically changing environment, which makes it hard either to infer its associated intention or to identify in a timely manner a driver support that is appropriate for the intention. (c) When the driver's action was corrected by the machine, the driver is likely to perceive that the machine did not understand his or her intention at all, although the action needed to be corrected because its execution timing did not match the traffic environment. Proactive safety technologies usually assume machine intelligence. Failure in mutual understanding of intentions between the driver and the machine intelligence may bring various inconveniences, such as automation surprises, distrust and overtrust. The second project is now trying to challenge these problems via a context-dependent adjustment of LOA as well as designing human interface that enables the driver to (a) understand the rationale why the automation thinks so, (2) recognise intention of the automation, (3) share the situation recognition with the automation and (4) perceive limitations of automation's functional abilities (Inagaki, 2006).

Acknowledgments. This study was conducted as part of the government project, 'Situation and Intention Recognition for Risk Finding and Avoidance' with the support of the Ministry of Education, Culture, Sports, Science and Technology,

Government of Japan. The author expresses his appreciation to Dr. Cacciabue and anonymous referees for their constructive comments and suggestions. They helped a lot in improving the quality and clarity of the paper.

References

Akamatsu, M. (2003). Measurement technologies for driver and driving behavior. In *Proceedings of IEA2003* (CD-ROM).

Akamatsu, M. and Sakaguchi, Y. (2003). Personal fitting driver assistance system based on driving behavior model. In *Proceedings of the IEA2003* (CD-ROM).

Akamatsu, M., Sakaguchi, Y. and Okuwa, M. (2003). Modeling of driving behavior when approaching an intersection based on measured behavioral data on an actual road. In *Proceedings of the Human Factors and Ergonomics Society 47th Annual Meeting* (CD-ROM).

Amiditis, A., Lentziou, Z., Polychronopoulos, A., Bolovinou, A. and Bekiaris, E. (2005). Real time traffic and environment monitoring for automotive applications. In L. Macchi, C. Re and P.C. Cacciabue (Eds.). *Proceedings of the International Workshop on Modelling Driver Behaviour in Automotive Environments* (pp. 125–131).

Cacciabue, P.C. and Hollnagel, E. (2005). Modelling driving performance: A review of criteria, variables and parameters. In L. Macchi, C. Re and P.C. Cacciabue (Eds.). *Proceedings of the International Workshop on Modelling Driver Behaviour in Automotive Environments* (pp. 185–196).

Fuller, R. and Santos, J. (2002). Psychology and the highway engineer. In R. Fuller and J. Santos (Eds.). *Human Factors for Highway Engineers* (pp. 1–10). Pergamon, Amsterdam.

Furugori, S., Yoshizawa, N., Iname, C. and Miura, Y. (2003). Measurement of driver's fatigue based on driver's postural change. In *Proceedings of the SICE Annual Conference* (pp. 1138–1143).

Furugori, S., Yoshizawa, N., Iname, C. and Miura, Y. (2005). Estimation of driver fatigue by pressure distribution on seat in long term driving. *Review of Automotive Engineering*, 26(1), 53–58.

Green, M. (2003). *What causes 90% of all automobile accidents?* Available at http://www.visualexpert. com/accidentcause.html.

Hashimoto, K. (1984). *Safe Human Engineering*. Chuo Rodo Saigai Boushi Kyokai (in Japanese).

Hollnagel, E. and Bye, A. (2000). Principles for modeling function allocation. *International Journal of Human–Computer Studies*, 52, 253–265.

Inagaki, T. (2003). Adaptive automation: Sharing and trading of control. In E. Hollnagel (Ed.). *Handbook of Cognitive Task Design* (pp. 147–169). Lawrence Erlbaum, Mahwah, NJ.

Inagaki, T. (2006). Design of human–machine interactions in light of domain-dependence of human-centered automation. *Cognition, Technology and Work*, 8, 161–167.

Inagaki, T. and Furukawa, H. (2004). Computer simulation for the design of authority in the adaptive cruise control systems under possibility of driver's over-trust in automation. In *Proceedings of the IEEE SMC Conference* (pp. 3932–3937).

Inagaki, T., Moray, N. and Itoh, M. (1998). Trust self-confidence and authority in human–machine systems. In *Proceedings of the IFAC Man–Machine Systems* (pp. 431–436).

Itoh, M., Akiyama, T. and Inagaki, T. (2006). Driver behavior modeling. Part II: Detection of driver's inattentiveness under distracting conditions. In *Proceedings of the DSC-Asia/Pacific* (CD-ROM).

Juergensohn, T. (2005). Control theory models of the driver. In L. Macchi, C. Re and P.C. Cacciabue (Eds.). *Proceedings of the International Workshop on Modelling Driver Behaviour in Automotive Environments* (pp. 37–42).

Miura, Y., Yoshizawa, N. and Furugori, S. (2002). Individual variation analysis of body pressure distribution for long term driving simulation task. *The Japanese Journal of Ergonomics*, 38(Suppl), 70–72.

Norman, D.A. (1988). *The Psychology of Everyday Things*. Basic Books, New York.

Panou, M., Bekiaris, E. and Papakostopoulos, V. (2005). Modeling driver behavior in EU and international projects. In L. Macchi, C. Re and P.C. Cacciabue (Eds.). In *Proceedings of the International Workshop on Modelling Driver Behaviour in Automotive Environments* (pp. 5–21).

Saad, F. (2005). Studying behavioural adaptations to new driver support systems. In L. Macchi, C. Re and P.C. Cacciabue (Eds.). *Proceedings of the International Workshop on Modelling Driver Behaviour in Automotive Environments* (pp. 63–73).

Sakakibara, K. and Taguchi, T. (2003). Biochemical measurement for driver's state based on salivary components. In *Proceedings of the IEA2003* (CD-ROM).

Sakakibara, K. and Taguchi, T. (2005). Evaluation of driver's state of tension. In *Proceedings of the HCI International* (CD-ROM).

Scerbo, M.W. (1996). Theoretical perspectives on adaptive automation. In R. Parasuraman and M. Mouloua (Eds.). *Automation and Human Performance* (pp. 37–63). Lawrence Erlbaum, Mahwah, NJ.

Sheridan, T.B. (1992). *Telerobotics, Automation, and Human Supervisory Control*. MIT Press, Cambridge, MA.

Shiomi, K. and Hirose, S. (2000). Fatigue and drowsiness predictor for pilots and air traffic controllers. In *Proceedings of the 45th Annual ACTA Conference* (pp. 1–4).

Taguchi, T. and Sakakibara, K. (2005). Evaluation of driver's state of tension. *Review of Automotive Engineering*, 26(2), 201–206.

Tango, F. and Montanari, R. (2005). Modeling traffic and real situations. In L. Macchi, C. Re and P.C. Cacciabue (Eds.). *Proceedings of the International Workshop on Modelling Driver Behaviour in Automotive Environments* (pp. 133–147).

Treat, J.R., Tumbas, N.S., McDonald, S.T., Shinar, D., Hume, R.D., Mayer, R.E., Stansifer, R.L. and Castellan, N.J. (1979). Tri-level study of the causes of traffic accidents: Final report volume 1. Technical report, Federal Highway Administration, US DOT.

Umeda, M., Yamaguchi, T. and Ohashi, K. (2005). Intention recognition system using case-based reasoning. In *Proceedings of the RISP International Workshop on Nonlinear Circuit and Signal Processing* (pp. 243–246).

Weir, D.H. and Chao, K.C. (2005). Review of control theory models for directional and speed control. In L. Macchi, C. Re and P.C. Cacciabue (Eds.). *Proceedings of the International Workshop on Modelling Driver Behaviour in Automotive Environments* (pp. 25–36).

Witt, G.J. (2003). *SAfety VEhicle(s) Using Adaptive Interface Technology (SAVE-IT) Program*, DTRS57-02-R-20003. U.S. Department of Transportation.

Yamaguchi, T., Matsuda, S., Ohashi, K., Ayama, M. and Harashima, F. (2004). Humane automotive system using driver and pedestrian intention recognition. In *Proceedings of the World Congress on Intelligent Transport Systems* (CD-ROM).

II
Conceptual Framework and Modelling Architectures

4 A General Conceptual Framework for Modelling Behavioural Effects of Driver Support Functions

JOHAN ENGSTRÖM AND ERIK HOLLNAGEL

4.1 Introduction

In recent years, the number of in-vehicle functions interacting with the driver has increased rapidly. This includes both driving support functions (e.g. anti-lock brakes, collision warning systems, adaptive cruise control) and functions supporting non-driving tasks, e.g. communication and entertainment functions. Today, many of these functions are also featured on portable computing systems, commonly referred to as *nomadic devices*. Moreover, in order to handle this growth in diversity and complexity of in-vehicle functionality, several types of meta functions for human–machine interface integration and adaptation have been proposed. Such functions, often referred to as *workload management functions*, are intended to resolve potential conflicts between individual functions with respect to their interaction with the driver (see Engström et al., 2004; Broström et al., 2006). The term *driver support functions* will henceforth be used to refer to in-vehicle functions that support what drivers do, whether related to driving or not.

The proliferation of driver support functions naturally changes the nature of driving and the different types of functions may induce a variety of behavioural effects. One general reaction to new driver support functions is that drivers change their behaviour in various ways to incorporate the functions into the driving task, an effect commonly referred to as *behavioural adaptation* (Smiley, 2000; Saad et al., 2004). Another issue that has received much recent attention is the effects of multitasking while driving, e.g. driver distraction due to interaction with in-vehicle functions, passengers or other objects in the vehicle.

While a wide range of driver models exists, addressing different aspects of driver behaviour, a generally agreed conceptual framework for describing behavioural effects of driver support functions is still lacking. Technological and methodological development in this area is therefore generally made without a common conceptual basis. The objective of this paper is to outline some basic requirements for such a conceptual framework as well as to propose a specific candidate. The main starting point will be models based on the cognitive systems engineering tradition, specifically the COCOM/ECOM framework (Hollnagel et al., 2003; Hollnagel and Woods, 2005). It should be stressed that the aim here is not to present a validated model of driver behaviour but rather to propose a general conceptual framework that can be used to describe behavioural effects of driver support functions, and how these effects relate to accident risk. A principal motivation for this work was the need for a common conceptual framework in the AIDE (Adaptive Integrated Driver–vehicle Interface) EU-funded project, which deals with technical and human factor issues related to driver behaviour and automotive human–machine interface development (see Engström et al. (2004) for an overview of the AIDE project).

The chapter is organised as follows: In the next section, the general intended application areas and the key requirements for the framework are outlined. Section 4.3 provides a review of existing driver behaviour models that are relevant for present purposes. In Section 4.4, the key elements of the proposed framework are described. In Section 4.5, some specific example applications are described. Finally, Section 4.6 provides a general discussion and conclusions.

4.2 Intended Application Areas and Requirements

In order to derive the basic requirements for the intended conceptual framework, it is necessary to first consider how it is intended to be used. As mentioned above, the main purpose of the framework is not a validated model of driver behaviour. Rather, the idea is that the framework should provide a common language to describe key issues related to behavioural effects of in-vehicle functions. More specifically, the framework should be applicable to (at least) the following problems:

4.2.1 Functional Characterisation of Driver Support Functions

As in many other fields, the development of driver support functions is still to a large extent driven by technological possibilities rather than the actual needs of the users. This often results in 'solutions that are looking for a problem' (Hollnagel, 2006). As a result, driver support functions are often described in terms of the underlying technology, e.g. 'driver monitoring' and 'vehicle-to-vehicle communication', while it is not always entirely clear what driver goals or task they are intended to support. In order to link driver support functions to their potential behavioural effects, it is useful to be able to characterise the different functions with respect to their intended purpose, i.e. which goal(s) they support (including driving- as well as non-driving-related goals). The present framework should be able to provide such a functional taxonomy.

4.2.2 Coherent Description of Expected Behavioural Effects of Driver Support Functions

The framework should be applicable as a coherent conceptual basis to describe all different types of behavioural effects of driver support functions, from the effect of multitasking while driving to short- and long-term behavioural adaptations such as risk compensation and over-reliance on the support function.

4.2.3 Conceptualising Relations Between Behavioural Effects and Road Safety

While a basic understanding of behavioural effects of driver support functions is an important goal in itself, a further critical issue concerns the relation between such effects and actual road safety, e.g. changes in incident and accident risk (see Dingus (1995) for a good discussion on this topic). While not intended as a general accident model, the framework proposed here should be applicable to these problems as well.

4.2.4 Specific Requirements

From these three general intended application areas, some more specific requirements for the framework can be outlined. First, since different functions support different aspects of driving, from low-level vehicle handling to high-level navigation and route planning, the framework must be able to account for behaviour on all levels and, equally important, the *relation* between the different levels. Second, related to the previous requirement, it is important that the same principles of analysis are applied on all levels of description, i.e. the model should be *recursive* (Cacciabue and Hollnagel, 2005). Finally, the framework must be able to account for time, i.e. the dynamics of behaviour. This is particularly important to capture the self-paced, adaptive, nature of driving.

4.3 Existing Models of Driver Behaviour

Driver behaviour modelling has a long history and a wide range of existing models address different aspects of driving. However, models specifically targeting behavioural effects of driver support functions are rare. According to Michon (1985), a general distinction could be made between taxonomic and functional models. The former refers to descriptive models, or 'inventory of facts', without an account of the interaction between the model components, including trait models (for example of driver accident proneness) and task analysis. The latter refers to models that account for processes and/or interactions within the modelled system. The focus of this review is on functional models.

4.3.1 Manual Control Models

The early driver modelling efforts focused mainly on control-theoretic models of vehicle handling (e.g. Weir and McRuer, 1968). In these models, vehicle control was generally modelled in terms of feedback control mechanisms with the goal of minimising the difference between a reference (or target) state (e.g. the desired heading angle) and the actual state. Later developments of these models included elements of feed forward control (McRuer et al., 1977; Donges, 1978). While these types of models are useful for modelling manual lateral and longitudinal vehicle control in constrained situations, they do not capture higher level aspects of driving such as decision making, planning or motivation.

4.3.2 Information Processing Models

During the past 40 years, the information processing paradigm, based on the digital computer as the main metaphor, has dominated human factors and cognitive science. The basic idea behind this paradigm is that human cognition can be modelled as sequences of logically separated computational steps, including perception, decision and response selection. Human attention and performance limitations are then modelled in terms of limited capacity at these different stages (Moray, 1967; Kahneman, 1973). The information processing paradigm has had a great influence on theories of multiple task sharing, which are often used to understand the effects of interacting with a driver support system while driving. In particular, the concept of mental workload, defined by de Ward (1996) as 'the specification of the amount of information processing capacity that is used for task performance' (p. 15), is directly based on the limited capacity metaphor. Most experimental work in this area also involved dual task studies to investigate the level of interference between different types of tasks, leading to the influential *multiple resource theory* (Wickens, 2002). However, with a few exceptions (e.g. Shinar, 1992; Salvucci, 2001) information processing models have not been incorporated in more general driver behaviour models. Whether this should be considered as a failure of the automotive human factors trade, as proposed by Michon (1985), or as due to the fact that 'early information processing models and their associated experimental techniques were incompatible with the requirements of complex tasks such as driving' (Ranney, 1994), could be discussed. In any case, one shortcoming of information processing models when applied in the driving domain is the basic notion of the human as primarily a passive receiver of information, which makes it difficult to account for drivers' active management of traffic situations, e.g. by means of self-pacing and dynamic task allocation.

4.3.3 Motivational Models

Many existing models characterise driver behaviour in terms of dynamic regulation of *risk*. These types of models are often referred to as *motivational models* (Ranney, 1994). By contrast to information processing models, motivational models emphasise the self-paced nature of driving and attempt to understand the dynamical adaptation to varying driving conditions. The main differences among existing motivational models concern the criteria proposed to govern the adaptation. For example, the risk-homeostasis theory (Wilde, 1982) hypothesises that drivers strive to maintain a constant level of accepted risk. By contrast, the zero-risk theory (Summala, 1985; 1988) states that the driver aims to keep the subjectively perceived risk at zero-level. A related account has been offered by Fuller (1984), who suggests that drivers' behaviour is guided by threat avoidance.

In more recent model, the same author proposes that the driver attempts to maintain a certain level of task difficulty rather than a level of risk (Fuller, 2005; see also Chapter 10 in this book). Finally, based on Damasio's concept of somatic markers (Damasio, 1994), Vaa (Chapter 12 in this book) proposes that driver behaviour is largely driven by emotional responses to risky situations.

Motivational models have been criticised for being too unspecific regarding internal mechanisms and, as a result, being unable to generate testable hypotheses (Michon, 1985). It could also be argued that the need to include motivational or emotional aspects partly is an artefact of the limitations of information processing models. Since 'cold' cognition automatically excluded 'hot' cognition (Abelson, 1963), something important was missing from these models. This is, however, not an issue in models that pre-dates information processing models, such as Gibson and Crooks (1938, see below).

4.3.4 Safety Margins

As described in the previous section, a key issue in understanding driver behaviour concerns the criteria that drivers use as the reference for adaptation. While the motivational models use qualitative criteria such as risk or task difficulty, other models have attempted a more quantitative approach based on *safety margins*. A key starting point here is that humans, in most situations, tend to act as *satisfiers* (rather than optimisers), i.e. they generally do not put more effort into a task than needed (Simon, 1955). Many driver models incorporate the concept of subjectively chosen safety margins as key criteria for guiding driver behaviour. Probably the first account of safety margins in driving was offered by Gibson and Crooks (1938), who proposed that drivers aim to stay within a 'field of safe travel', which can be conceptualised as 'tongues' stretching out in front of the vehicle, with their size and form being determined by the time-to-contact to surrounding obstacles. More recently, this concept has been developed into more concrete time-based safety margins parameters. There is abundant evidence that *time-to-object* information is used by humans and animals for guiding locomotion (Gibson, 1979). Lee (1976) used the perceptual variable *tau*, representing time-to-contact in terms of optically specified parameters, to model drivers' braking behaviour. In traffic research, time-to-collision is often used as a driving performance metric (van der Horst, 1990; van der Horst and Godthelp, 1989; Minderhoud and Bovy, 2001). The corresponding metric for lateral control is time-to-line-crossing (TLC). Godthelp et al. (1984) demonstrated that TLC correlates strongly with driver's self-chosen occlusion time. Too small TLC values are thus strong indicators of violations of the driver's subjectively chosen safety margins. For a general account of safety margins in driving, see Nilsson (2001).

Summarising the models reviewed in the present and the previous section, there seems to be a strong convergence towards the general idea that driver performance could be understood in terms of adaptation governed by some type of safety margins, although these are conceptualised differently by different authors, e.g. in terms of objective quantitative parameters such as TTC and TLC, or more concepts such as perceived risk or task difficulty.

4.3.5 Hierarchical Models

A common approach is to model the driving task as a set of hierarchically organised sub-tasks. A general hierarchical account of *human performance* is Rasmussen's three-level model, which proposes a distinction between knowledge-based, rule-based and skill-based performance (Rasmussen, 1983). Knowledge-based performance is mainly needed in situations that have not been encountered before and thus requires conscious deliberation, while rule-based performance refers to the application of learned rules. Finally, skill-based performance refers to automated skills that do not require any cognitive processing.

There are also several examples of hierarchical models that describe the *driving task*, e.g. Alexander and Lunenfeld (1986) who characterise the driving tasks in terms of three levels: navigation, guidance and control. Another example is Michon's influential description of the driving task in terms of strategic, tactical and operational levels (Michon, 1985). These models, which have been called 'second generation motivational models' (Ranney, 1994), describe goals and motives on different levels, from general trip planning (strategic), via obstacle avoidance (tactical) to immediate vehicle control (operational). It is assumed that activities on the different levels interact dynamically but none of these models say much about how this is actually accomplished. Hale et al. (1990) proposed to combine Michon's and Rasmussen's levels into a two-dimensional matrix where (Rasmussen's) driving performance levels are mapped onto (Michon's) driving task levels. Such a representation is useful to describe differences between experts and novices in terms of the degree to which different tasks in the hierarchy are automated (Ranney, 1994). In most of these hierarchical driving models the different levels are (more or less explicitly) intended to represent levels of information processing. A different type of hierarchical driver model is the Extended Control Model (ECOM) proposed by Hollnagel et al. (2003), which puts a hierarchical description of driving-related goals (similar to Michon's model) into a control theoretic framework. ECOM provides a representation of the *performance* (rather than information processing) on different levels of the driving task and also offers an account of the dynamic interactions between concurrent activities on the different levels. In the current version, four layers are proposed: targeting, monitoring, regulating and tracking. The model is an extension of the Contextual Control Model (COCOM; Hollnagel, 1993; Hollnagel and Woods, 2005), which provides a general account of the dynamical coupling between perception (or, more generally, situation assessment), decision and action. The COCOM and ECOM models are further described in the following section.

4.4 A Conceptual Framework

In this section, the proposed conceptual framework is outlined. The section starts with a short discussion on the key concept of behaviour and a description of how concepts from control theory can be used to model the dynamics of behaviour.

The key elements of the proposed framework, the COCOM and ECOM models, are then presented.

4.4.1 Driver Behaviour as Goal-Directed Activity

Interaction between the driver and vehicle functions can be viewed as an instance of the more general notion of driver *behaviour*. Thus, it is important to define more precisely what we mean by behaviour. As suggested, e.g. by Dennett (1987), behaviour, as opposed to mere bodily movement, can be defined as *goal-directed* activity. According to Dennett, we understand the activity of other people by adopting what he calls the *intentional stance*. This entails ascribing intentions and goals to other agents, which enables us to make predictions about their behaviour (naturally, these ascriptions may not always correspond to actual intentions of people).

Based on this notion, *driver* behaviour can be understood in terms of what is required to accomplish a number of different goals while driving. In addition to driving related goals (such as keeping within the lane or reaching a destination), drivers may also be occupied with other goals that are only vaguely related, or entirely unrelated, to vehicle operation (such as finding a track on an MP3 player). Thus, *driver behaviour* could be defined as the general pursuit of driving- and non-driving-related goals while driving. Consequently, the general role of *driver support functions* is to support the driver in accomplishing these goals. *Driving* can further be defined as the subset of driver behaviours aimed towards goals associated with vehicle operation. The role of *driving* support functions (a subset of driver support functions) is thus to support driving-related goals.

A distinction can also be made between goals that are *permanent* (such as avoiding accidents, complying with the traffic code and avoiding risk) hence applicable to more than one journey, *persistent* (i.e., valid for the duration of a single journey, such as reaching the destination) and *transient* in the sense that they may come and go during a journey (e.g., overtaking the car in front, reaching a cafeteria before noon).

4.4.2 Dynamical Representation of Driver Behaviour

In order to understand driver behaviour in terms of goal-directed activity, we need a way to describe how drivers' goals are dynamically achieved and maintained. *Control* is a useful concept for describing the dynamics of goal-directed behaviour, in man as well as in machines. In general, control can be understood as the ability to direct and manage the development of events (Hollnagel and Woods, 2005). Controlling a process means that actions are determined by the aim to achieve a consistent goal state (often called the *reference* or *target* value), e.g. by means of countering effects of external disturbances. Control is thus closely related to orderliness or predictability, i.e. a controlled system is orderly, stable and predictable while a system that is out-of-control is disorderly, unstable and unpredictable.

There are two basic forms of control: In *feedback* (or compensatory) control, the controller performs corrective actions based on the deviation between a desired outcome (the goal) and the actual state. The prototypical example of a feedback control system is the thermostat. Another type of control is *feed forward* (or anticipatory) control. In this case, control actions are based on predictions of future states and, hence, proactive rather than reactive. Driving behaviour is generally a mixture of feedback and feed forward control.

In engineering control applications, such as a thermostat or an Adaptive Cruise Control system, the target values (i.e. the desired temperature and time gap respectively) are generally determined beforehand by the engineer or set by the user. However, when analysing human controlled behaviour, identifying the target, or *controlled variable*, is often viewed as *the* key issue (Powers, 1998; Marken, 1986). The indentification of the controlled variable is complicated by the fact that the human controller, as mentioned above, seldom operates as an optimiser but rather acts as a satisfier (Simon, 1955), thus tolerating a certain deviation from the target value. In driving, time based safety margins (e.g. van der Horst and Godthelp, 1989) or risk thresholds (Summala, 1988) could be thought of as reference values for the vehicle control loop (although this idea has not yet, to our knowledge, been exploited in extisting models).

As described in the previous section, control theory has been widely applied to the modelling of vehicle handling, in automotive and other domains (e.g. Weir and McRuer, 1968; Donges, 1978). Control theory has also been applied to the modelling of higher-level aspects of driving. For instance, many of the motivational models reviewed above, especially the risk homeostasis model (Wilde, 1982), are based on control theoretical concepts. However, few existing models allow for a unified representation of controlled behaviour at different levels of the driving task. One existing modelling framework able to provide such descriptions is the COCOM/ECOM model (Hollnagel and Woods, 2005), which thus has been selected as the main starting point for the proposed conceptual framework. The next two sections describe the COCOM and ECOM models in more detail.

4.4.3 The Contextual Control Model (COCOM)

The contextual control model (COCOM), described in Hollnagel (1993) and Hollnagel and Woods (2005), provides a general account for modelling human control of a process or plant, based on Neisser's (1976) perceptual cycle concept. An important starting point for COCOM is that the controller and controlled system is viewed as a *joint cognitive system* (JCS). The central object of study is then the JCS rather than the controller or the controlled system in isolation. This approach offers a perspective that differs from traditional information processing models where the human operator and the machine are normally treated as logically separate entities. The boundaries between the JCS and its environment are generally determined by the objective of the analysis. Pragmatically speaking, an object is considered part of the JCS if (1) it is considered important for the ability of the JCS to maintain control and (2) it can be controlled by the JCS. Moreover, objects satisfying (2) but not (1) may be included in the JCS if this facilitates the purpose of the analysis (Hollnagel and Woods, 2005). For present purposes, the JCS of interest is in most cases the *joint driver–vehicle system* (JDVS).

COCOM is a general model of how control is maintained by a JCS and is applicable across a range of different JCS types on different levels of description. This type of analysis makes minimal assumptions about internal cognitive processes and focuses on behaviour and the dynamical interactions between the components in the JCS, in particular on how the JCS maintains, or loses, control of a situation.

A central concept in COCOM is the construct-action-event cycle. The *construct* refers to what the controller knows or assumes about the situation in which the action takes place. The construct is the basis for selecting actions and interpreting information. The selected actions affect the process/application to be controlled. This generates events that provide feedback on the effects of the action which, together with external disturbances, modifies the construct and, hence, the future action selection. An important property of this model is thus that it accounts for both the feedback and feedforward aspects of control, i.e. action selection is a function of both direct feedback and the predictions of future events.

The main factors determining the level of control maintained by a JCS is *predictability* and *available time*. A key property of COCOM is that it offers an explicit account of time. Figure 4.1 gives an illustration of the three main temporal parameters involved: (1) Time to *evaluate* events (T_E), (2) time to *select* an action or response (T_S) and (3) time to *perform* an action (T_P; see Hollnagel and Woods,

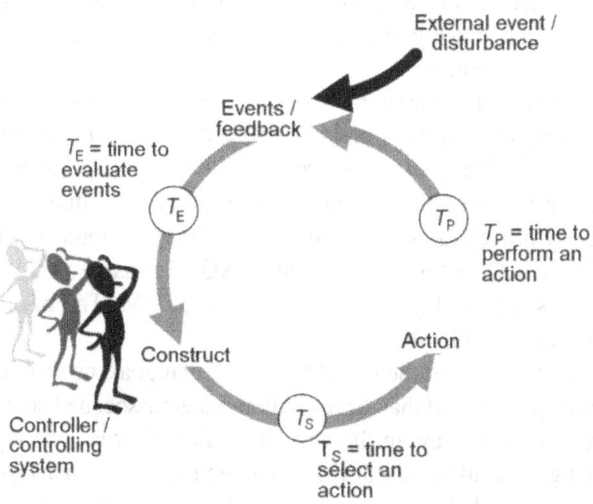

FIGURE 4.1. The contextual control model (Hollnagel and Woods, 2005).

2005, for a more elaborate description of the timing relations in COCOM). As in any control system, the relations between these time parameters determine the performance of the JCS. The relation between the time needed to evaluate, select and perform an action (T_E, T_S and T_P) and the time available (T_A) is of special importance. In order to maintain control, the time needed to perform one cycle ($T_E + T_S + T_P$) must, in the long run, be less than the total time available. If the available time becomes too small, it may be increased by slowing down the pace of the task, e.g. by reducing speed in the case of driving (as long as the task is self-paced). It is in many cases uncertain how much time is available, due to the dynamics of the environment, including the unpredictability of other drivers. In such cases humans tend to sacrifice thoroughness in order to maintain efficiency, as described by the efficiency-thoroughness trade-off (ETTO) strategy (Hollnagel, 2004).

4.4.4 The Extended Control Model (ECOM)

While COCOM only describes a single control process (i.e. pursuit of a single goal), the driving task generally involves the pursuit of several simultaneous sub-goals with different time frames. A long-term goal could be to reach a destination in time. An example of a medium-term scale goal is to overtake a vehicle ahead, while short-term goals include staying in lane and avoiding obstacles. Note that the temporal characteristics of goals is different from whether they are permanent, persistent, or transient. A goal may also subsume goals on shorter time frames. For example, in order to reach a destination in time, it may be necessary to overtake a number of vehicles. This, in turn, requires safe vehicle handling in order to avoid collisions. Thus, the driving task can be described as a set of simultaneous, interrelated and layered control processes. In addition, drivers generally also pursue goals that are unrelated to driving, e.g. talking to a passenger, using the cell phone, looking for a place to eat, etc.

As reviewed above, this hierarchical organisation is reflected in many models of driving, e.g. Alexander and Lunenfeld (1986) and Michon (1985). However, none of these models provide a sufficient account of the dynamical aspects of driving (i.e. the relation between performance and time), or the simultaneous relations *between* control processes on different layers. This is offered by the Extended Control Model (ECOM) (Hollnagel et al., 2003; Hollnagel and Woods, 2005), which represents a multi-layered extension to COCOM. The basic structure of ECOM is illustrated in Fig. 4.2.

A key assumption behind the ECOM model is that goals on different layers are pursued simultaneously and that these goals and their associated control processes interact in a non-trivial way. In the current version, four control layers are proposed: Tracking, regulating, monitoring and targeting, where each layer potentially contains multiple parallel control processes (it should be noted that these particular layers are not fixed and may be revised and adapted to different application domains).

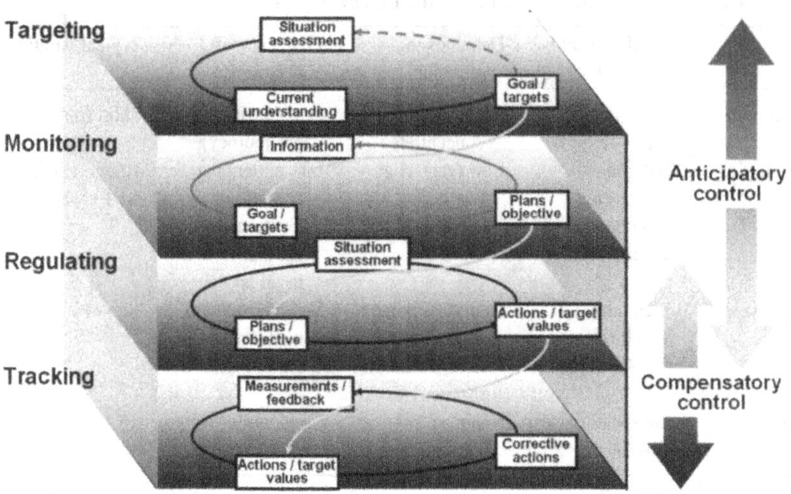

FIGURE 4.2. The extended control model (ECOM).

A key property of the model is that during normal (controlled) task performance, the goals/targets for the control processes on a given layer are determined by the control processes one layer up. In the driving domain, the *tracking* control refers to the momentary, automated, corrections to disturbances, e.g. wind gusts. *Regulating* refers to more conscious processes of keeping desired safety margins to other traffic elements. This determines the target values for the tracking control loops. *Monitoring* refers to the control of the state of the joint vehicle-driver system relative to the driving environment. It involves monitoring the location and condition of the vehicle, as well as different properties of the traffic environment, e.g. speed limits. This generates the situation assessment that determines the reference for the regulating layer. Finally, the *targeting* control level sets the general goals of the driving task, which determines the objectives for the monitoring layer. The functional characteristics of the four layers, in the context of driving, are described in Table 4.1.

As illustrated in Fig. 4.2, tracking control is typically based on feedback (compensatory control) while monitoring and targeting are mainly of the feed-forward (anticipatory) type. The regulating layer may involve a mix of feedback and feed forward control. The ECOM model provides an account of how goals at different layers interact and how higher goals propagate all the way down to moment-to-moment vehicle handling. Control tasks on different layers may also interfere with each other and disturbances on lower layers may propagate upwards. For example, looking for directions (monitoring) may disrupt visual feedback, which may affect regulating and tracking control; a sudden experience of slipperiness due to ice on the road, manifested on the tracking level may modify higher-level goals (e.g. increasing safety margins on regulating level) and even change the targets for driving (e.g. choosing a different route).

TABLE 4.1. Functional characteristics of the ECOM layers.

	Type of control involved	Demands to attention	Frequency of occurrence	Typical duration
Targeting	Goal setting (feedforward)	High, concentrated	Low (mostly pre-journey)	Short (minutes)
Monitoring	Condition monitoring (feedback + feedforward)	Low (car). High (traffic, hazards)	Intermittent but regular (car). Continuous (traffic, hazards)	10 min to duration of voyage
Regulating	Anticipatory (feedback + feedforward)	High (uncommon manoeuvres), Low (common manoeuvres)	Very high (town), medium (country)	1 s – 1 min
Tracking	Compensatory (feedback)	None (pre-attentive)	Continuous	<1 s

4.5 Application

This section gives some examples of how the proposed framework can be applied in the three problem domains stated in Section 2: (1) Characterisation of driver support functions, (2) description of their behavioural effects and (3) reasoning about the relation between behaviour/performance and road safety.

4.5.1 Characterising Driver Support Functions

In terms of the proposed framework, driver support functions are characterised with respect to the goal(s) they are intended to support (where some functions support non driving-related goals). Based on this, a tentative taxonomy of in-vehicle functions could be outlined. The sub-set of *driving* support functions (with 'driving' defined as in Section 4.1) can be categorised with respect to the ECOM layers described in the previous section. In addition, *driver* support functions include non-driving related functions as well as workload management 'meta' functions with the purpose to manage the different driving and non-driving related functions with respect to their interaction with the driver. These function categories are further described below, and illustrated in Fig. 4.3.

4.5.1.1 Support for Tracking

This category includes functions which support driving by (partly) automating tracking control actions of speed and direction, e.g. antilock brakes (ABS), dynamic stability and traction control (DSTC), adaptive cruise control (ACC) and lane keeping aid (LKA). For some functions, such as ACC, this means that human involvement is to a large extent re-allocated to the regulating control layer. In fully

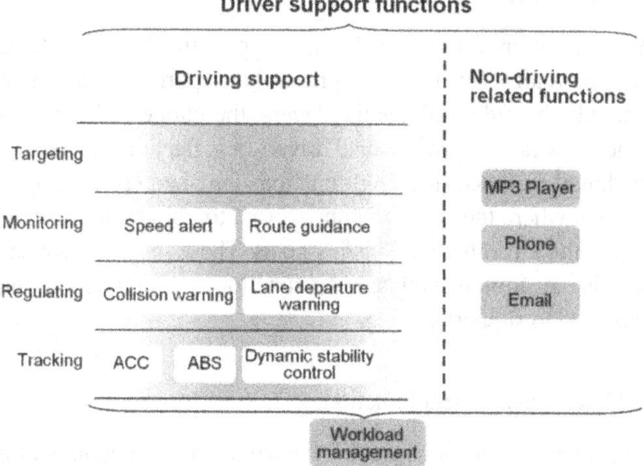

FIGURE 4.3. Examples of driver support functions mapped onto the ECOM layers. Workload management can be viewed as a meta function that arbitrates between different control tasks. (See the text for further explanation.)

automated driving, the driver's task would be limited to targeting, e.g. setting the destination, perhaps supported by monitoring of non-instrumented information sources.

4.5.1.2 Support for Regulating

These are functions with the purpose to support regulatory control, for instance helping the driver maintain adequate safety margins. This can be done, e.g. by providing warnings when safety margins are about to be violated or otherwise enhancing the perception of safety margins. Examples include forward collision warning (FCW), lane departure warning (LDW) and night vision systems.

4.5.1.3 Support for Monitoring

In-vehicle functions belonging to this category support the monitoring of higher level aspects related to the driver-vehicle-environment state. Examples include vehicle state monitoring functions (e.g. fuel and oil level indication), route guidance and traffic information functions. Importantly, activities on the monitoring level may interfere with tracking and regulatory control, as further discussed below.

4.5.1.4 Support for Targeting

Targeting is in driving, as well as in most other domains, predominantly a human activity. To some extent a smart navigation system can be seen as impinging on that, but on the whole, targeting goals are set by humans and not by machines.

4.5.1.5 Non-Driving-Related Functions

In addition to the different types of driving support functions mentioned above, there are many in-vehicle functions that primarily support other tasks than driving. Examples include the radio, the media players, the phone and various functions supporting the work task of professional drivers, e.g. fleet management functions. However, it should be noted that such functions *may* be used to support driving, e.g. in a situation where the mobile phone is used to obtain directions or a traffic broadcast forces the driver to revise his/her goals. These functions are nevertheless conceptually distinct from driving support functions by the fact that they are not *primarily intended* to support driving.

4.5.1.6 Workload Management Functions

Workload management functions can be viewed as 'meta-functions', responsible for coordinating individual functions, e.g. by means of information prioritisation or by putting non-critical information on hold in demanding driving situations. So far only a few systems of this type have entered the market (e.g. Volvo cars' intelligent driver information system (IDIS) and Saab's dialogue manager), but more advanced functions are being developed in different research efforts, both in-house at the companies (see Broström et al., 2006, for a description of the next generation IDIS) and in collaborative efforts such as COMUNICAR (Amditis et al., 2002), AIDE (Engström et al., 2004) and SAVE-IT (SAVE-IT, 2001). By contrast to the individual functions described above, the workload management meta-functions do not directly support specific driver goals. Rather, in terms of the proposed framework, these functions could be conceptualised as indirectly supporting the driver by resolving conflicts between different (driving- or non-driving related) goals. One key objective is to promote safe driving by means of supporting the driver in prioritising the tracking and regulating control tasks in demanding driving situations. It should be noted that the adaptivity provided by workload management functions, e.g. changing presentation format to resolve conflicts with other functions or the driving situation, potentially reduces the predictability of system behaviour. Since, as mentioned above, predictability is of key importance for the JCS to maintain control, great care must be taken in the design of such functions in order to avoid unexpected usability and/or safety problems.

4.5.2 Characterising Behavioural Effects of Driver Support Functions

The behavioural effects of a specific driver support function is the result of a complex dynamic interaction between individual driver characteristics (motivation for driving, subjectively chosen safety margins, driving skills, personality, effort etc.), vehicle parameters (e.g. steering and braking dynamics) and the driving environment (road type, curvature, lane width, traffic density etc.). It is useful to make a general distinction between *direct* and *indirect* (side) behavioural effects.

Direct effects are those that are intended by the system designers and implied by the system's functional specification. For driving support functions, direct effects are normally the intended performance enhancements on one or more control layers (e.g. increased lane keeping performance for LDW and increased route-finding ability for navigation support). By contrast, indirect effects are not intended by the designers (and thus not implied by the functional specification). It should be noted that indirect effects are not necessarily bad. For example, a potential positive indirect behavioural effect of a lane departure warning system could be an increased use of the turn signal.

In the following sections, some of the main types of behavioural effects found in the literature are discussed from the perspective of the proposed framework.

4.5.2.1 Behavioural Adaptation to Driving Support Functions

The ability to adapt to changing circumstances is central to human (and animal) behaviour. The term behavioural adaptation (BA) generally refers to 'the whole set of behaviour changes that are designed to ensure a balance in relations between the (human) organism and his surroundings and at the same time the mechanisms and processes that underlie this phenomenon' (Bloch et al., 1999). However, in traffic research, behavioural adaptation is often used to refer to a more specific type of adaptation, as defined by OECD (1990): 'Those behaviours which may occur following the introduction of changes to the road-vehicle-user system and which were not intended by the initiators of the change.' (p. 23). Hence, according to this definition, BA only refers to indirect effects, e.g. compensatory behaviours that may reduce, or even cancel out, the expected benefits of a safety measure.

BA has been demonstrated for many different types of driver support functions (see Smiley, 2000 and Saad et al, 2004, for examples). According to the proposed framework, such changes can be more precisely described in terms of performance on the ECOM control layers and the relation between them. For example, in one of the most cited studies on BA, it was found that taxi drivers with ABS- (anti-lock braking system) equipped-vehicles tended to drive with higher speed and adopt shorter headways than drivers of vehicles without ABS (Fosser et al., 1997). (This particular effect was actually predicted almost 60 years earlier by Gibson and Crooks (1938)). According to the proposed framework, this phenomenon can be described in terms of a change of goals and criteria on the regulating layer, caused by changing conditions on the tracking layer. When ABS is activated, drivers experience that the improved braking (i.e. longitudinal tracking) performance increases their safety margins due to the shorter stopping distance. Thus, if there is a high-level motivation (on the targeting level) for arriving quickly at the destination (as is often the case for taxi drivers), the drivers can reduce headway and increase speed while still keeping within their subjective safety margin. (Whether the actual risk remains constant is, however, another issue). This safety margin threshold could thus be viewed as the reference value for the tracking loop. This example shows how the dynamical interaction between high- and low level driving goals can be conceptualised by the present framework.

4.5.2.2 Effects of Multitasking While Driving

An important issue that has attracted much recent attention is how the time sharing between driving and other tasks affects driving performance and safety. A typical case of such multitasking is the use of different in-vehicle information functions while driving. These tasks are often referred to as *secondary tasks* while driving is considered the primary task. The effects of secondary tasks are often conceptualised in terms of *distraction*, which has been defined as 'attention given to a non-driving related activity, typically to the detriment of driving performance' (ISO TC22/SC13/WG8 CD 16673). However, this type of terminology creates conceptual difficulties because 'driving-related activity' and 'driving performance' are not further defined. For instance, reading a map on the navigation system display should clearly be regarded as a 'driving related activity'. On the other hand, it could at the same time distract the driver and cause degraded driving performance. Related problems have also been noted in analysis of naturalistic driving data in the recent 100 car study. As pointed out by Neale et al. (2005):

'Historically, driver distraction has been typically discussed as a secondary task engagement. Fatigue, has also been described as relating to driver inattention. In this study, it became clear that the definition of driver distraction needed to be expanded to a more encompassing 'driver inattention' construct that includes *secondary task engagement* and *fatigue* as well as two new categories, 'Driving-related inattention to the forward roadway' and 'non-specific eye glance'. 'Driving-related inattention to the forward roadway' involves the driver checking rear-view mirrors or their blind spots. This new category was added after viewing multiple crashes, near crashes and incidents for which the driver was clearly paying attention to the driving task, but was not paying attention to the *critical aspect* of the driving task (i.e. forward roadway) at an inopportune moment involving a precipitating factor.' (p. 6).

The proposed framework reconciles these conceptual difficulties in a quite straightforward way. As suggested above, the driving task should not be seen as a single activity, but rather as a set of multiple simultaneous and layered control tasks. Thus, driving *performance* could be defined with respect to any of these control tasks. For example, driving performance on the tracking level is associated with the ability to keep the vehicle within acceptable safety margins. Similarly, performance on the regulating level would be related to the ability to select appropriate safety margins based on a general situation assessment at the monitoring level. This situation assessment may induce inattention to the forward roadway (e.g. when checking mirrors), and could hence be described as a distraction on the tracking and/or regulating layers. In general, *distraction* with respect to a given control process (e.g. tracking) could thus be viewed in terms of interference by another (*driving- or non-driving related*) control process, typically resulting in degraded performance on the given control task. Historically, 'driver distraction' often implicitly refers to interference with the tracking and/or regulating control tasks (and this is probably the intended meaning of the definition cited above). However, the present framework enables a more precise conceptualisation and makes it possible to describe in more detail which tasks/control processes that are affected in a given distraction scenario.

Another commonly used concept is *mental workload*. While distraction is defined on the basis of attention allocation, driver mental workload refers to the amount of resources that the driver needs to perform one or more tasks, relative to a limited subjectively defined resource pool. As mentioned in section 4.3.2, the concept has strong roots in the information processing paradigm (e.g. Moray, 1967). It should be noted that mental workload is not a necessary precondition for distraction, since inappropriate attention allocation may be caused by low-workload tasks as well, e.g. daydreaming, checking mirrors and looking at road signs. One limitation of the traditional workload concept, based on the limited capacity metaphor, is that it does not account well for the dynamics of self-paced driving. Based on the COCOM/ECOM model, a more dynamic view of workload, viewing the driver as an active agent, can be outlined where the spare resources for a control process can be viewed in terms of the difference between total time available and the total time needed to perform the control loop (see Fig. 4.1). Thus, for example, if the available time for the tracking control loop is reduced, e.g. due to time sharing with another visually demanding task (e.g. entering a mobile phone number) the driver can gain time by reducing speed. The mechanisms that drive this type of adaptive behaviour can, again, be understood in terms of the balance between higher-level goals (e.g. the desire to arrive in time, i.e. targeting) and lower level goals (e.g. to keep acceptable safety margins, i.e. regulating).

In order to further illustrate the potential benefits of the proposed framework compared to traditional information processing models, it is useful to take a closer look at some empirical data from the HASTE EU-funded project. As part of the project, a set of parallel experiments were conducted in different sites across Europe, with the specific objective to investigate systematically the effects of visual and cognitive load on driving *performance* and state (see, e.g. Engström et al., 2005a; Victor et al., 2005; Jamson and Merat, 2005; Markkula and Engström, 2006; Östlund et al., 2004). In short, the HASTE results showed that visual time sharing induced increased lane position variation, increased number of large steering wheel reversals, reduced speed and increased headway to lead vehicles. By contrast, time sharing with purely cognitive tasks (i.e. tasks that require no visual interaction) did not interfere with tracking control at all, a result consistent with the meta-analysis of mobile-phone studies made by Horrey and Wickens (2004). Rather, results from HASTE indicate that cognitively loading tasks lead to significantly *improved* tracking control in terms of reduced lane keeping variation compared to baseline driving (e.g. Engström et al., 2005a; Jamson and Merat, 2005), an effect that has also been documented in other studies (e.g. Brookhuis et al., 1991). This increased lane keeping performance for cognitive tasks was also accompanied by a concentration of gaze towards the road centre (Victor et al., 2005), an effect also found in previous studies (e.g. Harbluk and Noy, 2002; Recarte and Nunes, 2003) and an increased number of steering micro corrections (Markkula and Engström, 2006). Other studies have also found that cognitive load impairs signal detection performance (e.g. Greenberg et al., 2003; Engström et al., 2005b). Finally, speed adaptation is seldom observed for cognitive tasks (Östlund et al., 2004) and some of the HASTE experiments found that the longitudinal safety margin, in terms of time-headway to a lead vehicle, was even reduced during cognitive load (Jamson and Merat, 2005).

A limited capacity model, viewing workload as the single factor that modifies behaviour (i.e. 'high workload leads to worse performance'), is of limited use for understanding these behavioural patterns. For instance, it would be hard to make sense of the fact that lane keeping variation is increased for visual tasks but reduced for cognitive tasks. In terms of the present framework, the effects of the visual task can be understood as a degradation of lateral tracking control due to reduced visual input during gazes away from the road. However, this is compensated for, at least to some extent, on the regulating layer, by means of speed reduction. By contrast, cognitive load does not interfere with tracking, but rather seems to reinforce the lateral tracking performance (for possible explanations for this peculiar phenomenon, see Engström et al., 2005a and Victor, 2005). In terms of ECOM, the main interference of cognitive tasks seems to be on the regulating and monitoring layers, as evidenced by the reduced detection performance, the inability to adapt speed and the reduced time headway. It should be stressed that the COCOM/ECOM framework, as applied here, does not offer a detailed explanation of the mechanisms underlying these phenomena. Rather, its main role is to provide a suitable common language for describing the effects. The development of more detailed explanations and models of multitasking while driving, and other behavioural effets, is an important area for further research.

4.5.3 Driver Behaviour and Accident Risk

Understanding the relation between behavioural effects and actual accident risk is one of the most important, and difficult, issues in current traffic safety research. The difficulties are due to a lack of sufficiently detailed behavioural data in existing accident databases as well as the lack of appropriate behavioural models. A further problem is that the usual interpretation of risks assumes both decomposability and linearity. Yet both of these qualities are absent in dynamic, complex environments such as traffic.

Based on the proposed framework, the relation between driving performance and risk (for an individual driver) can be thought of as a complex function involving (at least) the following factors:

1. The current complexity/difficulty of the driving task.
2. The driver's vehicle handling skills (performance on the tracking layer).
3. The ability to make a correct situation assessment (performance on the monitoring layer).

4. The ability to adopt safety margins that are appropriate to (1) and (2), based on (3) (determines performance on the regulation layer).
5. The effort spent on the control tasks on the different layers (2–4).

Based on this view, it is clear that performance degradation on one control layer does not automatically increase accident risk. For example, reduced tracking performance (e.g. due to visual distraction) is most risky if not properly compensated for on the regulating layer (e.g. by reducing speed). Thus, risk (as a function of performance) must be understood in terms of the *relation* between performance on the different layers, where *inadequate adaptation* to the current driving conditions and ones own driving skills could be hypothesised to be a critical factor. A typical example of this is drunk driving, where alcohol is well known to induce overestimation of the own performance driving capability. Thus, in this case, the erroneous safety margin setting (on the regulation layer) is due to the cognitive impairment induced by the drug. This line of reasoning also applies to individual differences with respect to risk taking. For example, the over-involvement of young male drivers in accidents could be understood as in terms of overestimation of driving performance combined with a higher propensity for sensation seeking (i.e. different goals on the targeting level), leading to inadequate safety margin settings. Yet another example is run-off-road accidents due to slippery roads. In this case, the erroneous safety margin setting (reflected, e.g. in too high speed in a curve) is due to an erroneous situation assessment on the monitoring layer, which affects the regulatory level and finally induces instability and breakdown of the tracking control. As discussed in the previous section, there is evidence that cognitively loading tasks, such as phone conversation, impairs the ability to set appropriate safety margins and adapt accordingly. However, the safety consequences of this are still unknown.

It is very difficult to determine whether adequate adaptation has been achieved in a particular situation, especially in terms of quantitative driving performance metrics. One potential approach is to look for *violations of safety margins*. Possible metrics of such violations include the amount of involuntary lane departures, minimum TLC/TTC value, the amount of TLC/TTC values below some critical value (van der Horst, 1990), or the total time spent below the critical value (time-exposed TTC—TET; Minderhoud and Bovy, 2001). However, a basic problem with this is that the accepted safety margins generally differ substantially between drivers (and possibly also varies over time for an individual driver). Moreover, there is yet no hard empirical data showing how these metrics relate to actual accidents. Other key factors related to accident risk are expectancy and predictability (Victor, 2005). The ability to predict is central to remain in control and the occurrence of unexpected events increases the risk for losing control. An issue of key importance is the ability of the driver to regain control. This is more difficult if the loss of control also involves the loss of goals (e.g. on the regulating level).

While the COCOM/ECOM framework is suitable for describing and reasoning about these issues, it is clear that accident causation cannot be explained only in terms of inadequate adaptation, or reduced predictability, but rather in terms of the interaction of multiple (behavioural, technological or organisational) precipitating factors. This requires models that deal specifically with accident causation, e.g. models based on Human Reliability Analysis (e.g. Hollnagel, 1993, 1998). However, the COCOM/ECOM framework is a useful starting point for describing and analysing the behavioural factors involved in accident causation.

4.6 Discussion and Conclusions

The objective of the present paper was to outline a conceptual framework for describing behavioural effects of driver support functions. A key starting point was the view of behaviour as a goal-directed, situated and dynamic activity. Driver behaviour involves the simultaneous pursuit of multiple goals that may be more or less related to driving itself. The COCOM/ECOM hierarchical control model (Hollnagel and Woods, 2005) was proposed as the basis for the framework.

It was shown that the framework offers a coherent taxonomy for categorising a wide range of driver support functions with respect to their functional purpose (rather than the underlying technology). This could be very useful, e.g. for clearly defining the scopes of different development and evaluation methodologies and standards (such as, e.g. the European Statement of Principles on Human Machine Interface; Commission of the European Communities, 2000) in terms of the types of functions that they apply to.

The second intended application area was the conceptualisation of behavioural effects of driver support functions. It was demonstrated that the framework yields coherent descriptions of a range of different effects, from behavioural adaptation to the effects of multitasking. Moreover, it was argued that the COCOM/ECOM framework accounts for many aspects that are missed when a traditional information processing/workload-based perspective is adopted, for example the radically different effects of visual and cognitive secondary task load on driving performance.

The third intended application area concerned the understanding of accident causation. It was illustrated how the framework could provide a useful starting point for addressing the difficult question of how driving behaviour/performance is related to risk. A main conclusion was that accident risk cannot generally be explained by a single aspect of driving performance. According to the proposed framework, risk needs to be understood in terms of the *relation* between different levels of performance. Thus, for example, a certain amount of weaving in the lane may not be too risky as long as it is appropriately compensated for by slowing down or increasing headway. It should also be noted that a *lack* of behavioural change, e.g. a failure to reduce speed when entering a slippery road segment, may be safety critical as well. Thus, *inadequate adaptation* can be proposed as one key behavioural factor related to risk.

The present framework is based on the view of the human driver as an *active* agent that, in most situations, is able to maintain control of the vehicle. A key advantage of the framework is that it is well suited to describe adaptive behaviour, which is a prevalent effect of all types of driver support functions. This contrasts to the traditional information processing models, which tend to view the human as a passive receiver of information, subject to overload if the limited capacity is exceeded. Another key property of the framework is the characterisation of driving performance in terms of hierarchical control. The idea of hierarchical driver models is certainly not new and the ECOM does not contradict existing models such as, e.g. Alexander and Lunenfeld (1986) and Michon (1985). However, the added value brought by ECOM is that it offers an account for how the different layers are related, e.g. how a change in a high-level goal (such as realising that one is late to the airport) can change performance on lower control layers (such as reducing the accepted safety margins).

As stressed throughout this paper, COCOM/ECOM are functional models that make very few assumptions about internal cognitive structures and processes. For present purposes, these models provide the starting point for a general conceptual framework, based on which more specific models can be developed. Such models should include both functional models as well as more detailed structural models of the cognitive/neural mechanisms underlying behavioural effects of driver support functions (see, e.g. Victor, 2005 for a comprehensive review of models of the latter type). Hence, functional and structural cognitive models should be viewed as complementary and useful for different purposes. In addition to the further development of more detailed driver models, the proposed conceptual framework is a suitable starting point for framing hypotheses for empirical work on behavioural effects of driving support functions. It is also useful as a common language in industrial development of driver support functions, which helps maintaining the focus on the *purpose* of the functions (e.g. how they should change driver behaviour), rather than their technological implementation (e.g. what type of sensors are used).

References

Abelson, R.P. (1963). Computer simulation of "hot" cognition. In S.S. Tomkins & S Messick (Eds.). *Computer simulation of personality*. John Wiley and Sons, New York.

Alexander, G.J. and Lunenfeld, H. (1986). *Driver expectancy in highway design and traffic operations. US Department of Transportation*. Report No: FHWA-TO-86-1.

Amditis, A., Polychronopoulos, A., Belotti, F. and Montanari, R. (2002). Strategy plan definition for the management of the information flow through an HMI unit inside a car. *e-Safety Conference Proceedings*, Lyon.

Bloch, H., Chemama, R., Gallo, A., Leconte, P., Le Ny, J.-F. and Postel, J. et al., (Eds.) (1999). *Grand Dictionnaire de la Psychologie*. Larousse, Paris.

Brookhuis, K.A., de Vries, G. and de Ward, D. (1991). The effects of mobile telephoning on driving performance. *Accident Analysis and Prevention*, 23(4), 309–316.

Broström, R., Engström, J., Agnvall, A. and Markkula, G. (2006). Towards the next generation intelligent driver information system (IDIS): The Volvo Cars Interaction Manager concept. In *Proceedings of the 2006 ITS World Congress, London*.

Cacciabue, P.C. and Hollnagel, E. (2005). Modelling driving performance: A review of criteria, variables and parameters. In L. Macchi, C. Re and P.C. Cacciabue (Eds.). *Proceedings of the International Workshop on Modelling Driver Behaviour in Automotive Environments*. Ispra, Italy.

Commission of the European Communities (2000). Annex to Commission Recommendation of 21 December 1999 on safe and efficient in-vehicle information and communication systems: A European statement of principles on human machine interface. *Official Journal of the European Communities L19, 25.1.2000*, p. 64 ff, Brussels, Belgium: European Union.

Damasio, A. (1994). *Descarte's error: Emotion, reason, and the human brain*. G.P. Putnam's and Sons, New York.

Dennett, D.C. (1987). *The intentional stance*. MIT Press, Cambridge, MA.

de Waard, D. (1996). *The measurement of drivers' mental workload. ISBN 90-6807-308-7*. Traffic Research Centre. University of Groningen.

Dingus, T.A. (1995). Moving from measures of performance to measures of effectiveness in the safety evaluation of ITS products or demonstrations. *Paper presented at the safety evaluation workshop*. University of Iowa.

Donges, E. (1978). A two-level model of driver steering behaviour. *Human Factors*, 20(6), 691–707.

Engström, J., Arfwidsson, J., Amditis, A., Andreone, L., Bengler, K. and Cacciabue, P.C. et al., (2004). Meeting the challenges of future automotive HMI design: Overview of the AIDE integrated project. *In Proceedings, ITS in Europe*. Budapest.

Engström, J., Johansson, E. and Östlund, J. (2005a). Effects of visual and cognitive load in real and simulated motorway driving. *Transportation Research Part F*, 8, 97–120.

Engström, J., Åberg, N., Johansson, E. and Hammarbäck, J. (2005b). Comparison between visual and tactile signal detection tasks applied to the safety assessment of in-vehicle information systems. *In Proceedings of the Third International Driving Symposium on Human Factors in Driver Assessment, Training and Vehicle Design*. Rockport, Maine.

Fosser, S., Saetermo, I.F. and Sagberg, F. (1997). An investigation of behavioural adaptation to airbags and antilock brakes among taxi drivers. *Accident Analyis and Prevention*, 29(3).

Fuller, R.G.C. (1984). A conceptualisation of driving behaviour as threat avoidance. *Ergonomics*, 27, 1139–1155.

Fuller, R.C.G. (2005). Towards a general theory of driver behaviour. *Accident Analysis and Prevention*, 37, 461–472.

Gibson, J.J. (1979). *The ecological approach to visual perception*. Houghton Mifflin, Boston.

Gibson, J.J. and Crooks, L.E. (1938). A theoretical field-analysis of automobile-driving. *The American Journal of Psychology*, 51(3), 453–471.

Godthelp, H., Milgram, P. and Blaauw, J. (1984). The development of a time-related measure to describe driving strategy. *Human Factors*, 26(3), 257–268.

Greenberg, J., Tijerina, L., Curry, R., Artz, B., Cathey, L. and Grant, P. et al. (2003). Evaluation of driver distraction using an event detection paradigm. *Journal of the Transportation Research Board*, 1843. TRB, Washington DC.

Hale, A.R., Stoop, J. and Hommels, J. (1990). Human error models as predictors of accident scenarios for designers in road transport systems. *Ergonomics*, 33, 1377–1388.

Harbluk, J.L. and Noy, Y.I. (2002). The impact of cognitive distraction on visual behaviour and vehicle control. Report no. TP 13889E. Transport Canada, Ontario.

Hollnagel, E. (1993). *Human reliability analysis: Context and control*. Academic Press, London.

Hollnagel, E. (1998). *Cognitive reliability and error analysis method*. Elsevier Science, Oxford, UK.

Hollnagel, E. (2004). *Barriers and accident prevention*. Ashgate Publishing Limited, Aldershot.

Hollnagel, E. (2006). Outline of a function-centred approach to joint driver-vehicle system design. *Cognition, Technology & Work* (in print).

Hollnagel, E., Nåbo, A. and Lau, I. (2003). A systemic model for driver-in-control. *Proceedings of the 2nd International Driving Symposium on Human Factors in Driver Assessment, Training, and Vehicle Design.*, Park City, UT. Public Policy Center, University of Iowa.

Hollnagel, E. and Woods, D.D. (2005). *Joint cognitive systems: Foundations of cognitive systems engineering*. Taylor and Francis/CRC Press, Boca Raton, FL.

Horrey, W.J. and Wickens, C.D. (2004). *The impact of cell phone conversations on driving: A meta-analytic approach.* Technical Report AHFD-04-2/GM-04-1, General Motors Cooperation, Warren, MI.

Jamson, A.H. and Merat, N. (2005). Surrogate in-vehicle information systems and driver behaviour: Effects of visual and cognitive load in simulated rural driving. *Transportation Research Part F*, 8, 79–96.

Kahneman, D. (1973). *Attention and effort.* Prentice Hall, Englewood Cliffs, NJ.

Lee, D.N. (1976). A theory of visual control of braking based on information about time-to-collision. *Perception*, 5, 437–459.

Marken, R.S. (1986). Perceptual organisation of behaviour: A hierarchical control model of coordinated action. *Journal of Experimental Psychology: Human Perception and Performance*, 12, 267–276.

Markkula, G. and Engström, J. (2006). *A steering wheel reversal rate metric for assessing effects of visual and cognitive secondary task load.* In *Proceedings of the 2006 ITS World Congress*, London.

McRuer, D.T., Allen, R.W., Weir, D.H. and Klein, R.H. (1977). New results in driver steering control models. *Human Factors*, 19, 381–397.

Michon, J.A. (1985). A critical review of driver behaviour models: What do we know? What should we do? In Evans L.A. and Schwing R.C. (Eds.). *Human Behaviour and Traffic Safety*. Plenum Press, NY, pp. 487–525.

Minderhoud, M.M. and Bovy, P.H.L. (2001). Extended time-to-collision measures for road traffic safety assessment. *Accident Analysis and Prevention*, 33, 89–97.

Moray, N. (1967). Where is attention limited? A survey and a model. *Acta Psychologica*, 27, 84–92.

OECD (1990). *Behavioural adaptations to changes in the road transport system.* Report Prepared by an OECD Expert Group. Road Transport Research Programme.

Neale, V.L., Dingus, T.A., Klauer, S.G., Sudweeks, J. and Goodman, M. (2005). An overview of the 100-car naturalistic study and findings. *Paper presented at the 19th International Technical Conference on Enhanced Safety of Vehicles (ESV).* Washington DC, June 6–9.

Neisser, U. (1976). Cognition and reality. Freeman, San Francisco.

Nilsson, R. (2001). *Safety margins in the driver.* PhD Thesis. Uppsala University, Sweden.

Östlund, J., Nilsson, L., Carsten, O., Merat, N., Jamson, H. and Jamson, S. et al., (2004). *Deliverable 2 – HMI and Safety-Related Driver Performance (No. GRD1/2000/25361 S12.319626).* Human Machine Interface and the Safety of Traffic in Europe (HASTE) Project.

Powers, W.T. (1998). *Making sense of behavior—the meaning of control.* Benchmark, New Canaan, CT.

Ranney, T. (1994). Models of driving behaviour. A review of their evolution. *Accident Analysis and Prevention*, 26(6), 733–750.

Rasmussen, J. (1983). Skills, rules, and knowledge: Signals, signs, and symbols, and other distinctions in human performance models. *IEEE Transactions on Systems, Man, and Cybernetics*, SMC13, 257–266.

Recarte, M.A.and Nunes, L.M. (2003). Mental workload while driving: Effects on visual search, discrimination, and decision making. *Journal of Experimental Psychology*, 9.

Saad, F., Hjälmdahl, M., Canas, J., Alonso, M., Garayo, P. and Macchi, L. et al., (2004). *Literature review of behavioural effects*. Deliverable 1.2.1, AIDE Integrated Project, Sub-project 1. IST-1-507674-IP.

SAVE-IT (2002). *Safety vehicle(s) using adaptive interface technology (SAVE-IT) Program, DTRS57-02-20003*. US DOT, RSPS/Volpe National Transportation Systems Center (Public Release of Project Proposal), www.volpe.dot.gov/opsad/saveit/index.html.

Salvucci, D.D. (2001). Predicting the effects of in-car interface use on driver performance: An integrated model approach. *International Journal of Human-Computer Studies*, 55, 85–107.

Shinar, D. (1993). Traffic safety and individual differences in drivers' attention and information processing capacity. *Alcohol, Drugs and Driving*, 9, 219–237.

Smiley, A. (2000). Behavioural adaptation. *Safety and Transportation Systems Research Record*, 1724, 47–51.

Simon, H.A. (1955). A behavioural model of rational choice. *The Quarterly Journal of Economics*, LXIX, 99–118.

Summala, H. (1985). Modeling driver behavior: A pessimistic prediction? In Evans L,A,, Schwing R.C. (Eds.). *Human Behaviour and Traffic Safety*. Plenum Press, New York, pp. 487–525.

Summala, H. (1988). Risk control is not risk adjustment: The zero-risk theory of driver behaviour and its implications. *Ergonomics*, 31(4), 491–506.

van der Horst, R. (1990). *A time based analysis of road user behaviour in normal and critical encounters*. PhD Thesis. Delft University of Technology, The Netherlands.

van der Horst, R., Godthelp, H. (1989). *Measuring road user behaviour with an instrumented car and an outside-the-vehicle video observation technique*. Transportation Research Record # 1213, Washington DC: Transportation Research Board, 72–81.

Weir, D.H., McRuer, T.M. (1968). A theory of driver steering control of motor vehicles. *Highway Research Record*, 247, 7–39.

Wickens, C.D. (2002). Multiple resources and performance prediction. Theoretical Issues in Ergonomics Science, 3(2), 159–177.

Victor, T.W. (2005). *Keeping eye and mind on the road*. PhD Thesis. Uppsala University, Sweden.

Victor, T.W., Harbluk, J.L. and Engström, J. (2005). Sensitivity of eye-movement measures to in-vehicle task difficulty. *Transportation Research Part F*, 8, 167–190.

Wilde, G.J.S. (1982). The theory of risk homeostasis: Implications for traffic safety and health. *Risk Analysis*, 2, 209–225.

5
Modelling the Driver in Control

BJÖRN PETERS AND LENA NILSSON

5.1 Introduction

Modelling driver behaviour can be done with different purposes. One obvious aim could be to provide a model of what drivers actually do and explain observed behaviour with or without support systems. Other objectives can be to discriminate between safe and unsafe driving. Furthermore, a model can be used to implement a dynamic real-time control of driver support functions (see Chapter 6). The following text is written in line with the first objective.

Safe driving requires that the driver is in control of the vehicle and the driving situation. Driver support systems aim to help the driver and facilitate driving in one way or the other. Support systems should be a response to identified existing or potential problems related to the driving task. New technology like ADAS and IVIS can facilitate driving but it could, on the other hand, make driving even more complex and demanding. Solving one problem could be done at the cost of introducing another. Thus, we need to understand driving task demands, driver behaviour and how support systems can influence the driver's control and safety. Here a broad overview of different theoretical approaches is given with focus on control and safety. The use of a cognitive systems engineering approach is advocated to investigate pros and cons of driver support systems. In the end, an example is given on how findings from an experiment with a joystick controlled car can be interpreted.

5.2 A Cognitive View of Driving

Driving is one of the most complex and safety critical everyday tasks in modern society (Groeger, 2000). Driving a car is complex in the sense that it requires the driver to employ a wide range of abilities in order to interact with a complex environment and to manage the driving task demands. Driving is dynamic as the demands can change back and forth from very low to extremely high, sometimes within fractions of a second. When demands are high, driving is carried out in a force-paced fashion; while as the demands are low, it can be performed in a more self-paced manner. Normal driving can be considered as a cognitively motivated and controlled task. Cognition is here used in the pragmatic sense as defined by Neisser (1976), that is, cognition in context. A motive for this cognitive stance can be found in Michon's (1985) visionary talk on driver behaviour modelling '... the distinctly hierarchical cognitive structure of human behaviour in the traffic environment...'. However, a cognitive approach does not imply that the driver's perceptual and psychomotor abilities are to be neglected. Thus, driving can be viewed as a cognitive task of control in a context perceived through the senses and manipulated with control actions based on unconscious (automated) or conscious decisions. This cognitive approach has been applied, for example, in adaptive control models, control theory and cognitive systems engineering in order to model driver behaviour.

5.3 Human Abilities

The human controller can be described in functional terms. In order to carry out the driving task, the driver utilises three, tentatively different, functional abilities: *Cognitive, perceptual* and *motor* abilities (see Fig. 5.1). Cognitive abilities include, for example, memory, decision, attention and supervision. Perceptual abilities can be, for example, visual, auditory, tactile and proprioceptive. Finally, motor abilities relate to physical dimension, motion and force, for example, reach, force and endurance. These human abilities can be developed into very efficient functions by training and experience. The abilities should not be considered as separate entities but as highly interactive and even more so as they develop into skilled behaviour. This functional description of the driver can be utilised to depict the driver from a cognitive systems engineering view.

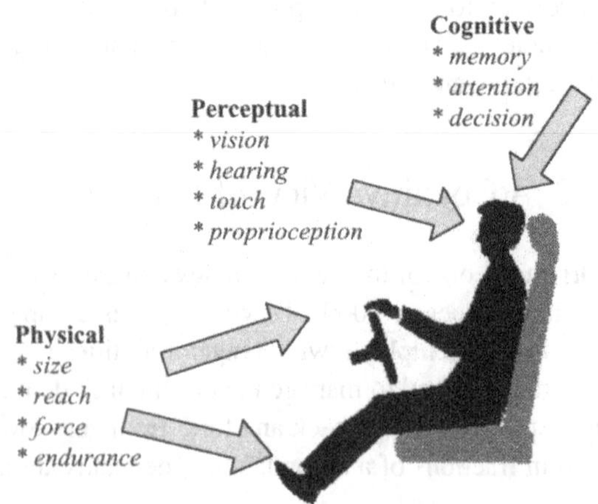

FIGURE 5.1. Human abilities employed by the driver.

TABLE 5.1. Classification of driver behaviour models (adapted from Michon, 1985).

	Taxonomic	Functional
Behavioural (input–output)	Task analyses	Adaptive control models
Internal state (psychological)	Trait models	Motivational models

5.4 Classifying Driver Behaviour Models

Several theories and models of driver behaviour have been presented, applied, analysed, criticised and abandoned. So far, no all-purpose, generic, comprehensive and verifiable model of driver behaviour has been presented (Ranney, 1994). Different models often emphasise specific and sometimes different aspects of driver behaviour, for example, accident causation, education and training, behavioural adaptation. Instead of searching for the ultimate model, it seems more feasible to use a generic framework in order to get a structured view of existing driver behaviour models. Two different modelling approaches can be distinguished. The first is to model what drivers actually do when driving. The second is to describe what the drivers should do by modelling the driving task itself. The first can be called a behavioural approach and the second a normative approach. Michon (1985) proposed a generic classification of driver behaviour models, using a two-dimensional classification (see Table 5.1). Firstly, he distinguished between behavioural or input–output oriented models and internal state or psychological models. Secondly, he differentiated between functional and taxonomic models. Taxonomic models are inventories of isolated facts, while functional models specify components of driver behaviour and their dynamic relations. In this way he distinguished between four types of models: task analysis models, trait models, adaptive control models and motivational models. Task analysis models decompose driving into tasks and subtasks and relate them to driver requirements and abilities. Trait models are based on the idea that it is possible to identify the accident-prone driver with the use of well-designed tests. Functional models differ from taxonomic in that they connect model components in order to consider the dynamics of driver behaviour, for example, hierarchical structures. Adaptive control models apply functional approach to capture behavioural changes. Finally, motivational models consider internal states as attitudes, subjective risk and insight as controlling factors. The models that will be discussed in the following can be mostly categorised as adaptive control models. For a discussion on other types of models, see Carsten (2005, Chapter 6).

5.5 Hierarchical Control Models

Most models can offer only post hoc explanations of observed behaviour or possibly explain aggregated accident data (Rumar, 1988). Early cognitive models focused on information processing, and driving was considered as a problem-solving task. Accidents were attributed to incorrect information processing, and Rumar concluded that there was an urgent need to develop models and hypothesis that can predict actual driver behaviour. Michon (1985) claimed that the lack of progress emerged from the failure to consider results from cognitive psychology. Later models incorporate developments from cognitive psychology, for example, hierarchical control structures and automaticity (Ranney, 1994). Rumar (1988) pointed out that an important behavioural uniqueness of driving can be its combination of consciously controlled (cognitive) and unconsciously, automatic (perceptual) behaviour. Hierarchical control models became more accepted when Michon (1985) advocated the idea that such an approach would resolve some of the identified shortcomings with earlier models. However, this was not a new idea, for example, Allen et al. (1971), McRuer et al. (1977) and Janssen (1979) described driving as a hierarchical structured task with strategic, tactical and operational components demanding different levels of driver control much earlier. At the strategic level, the driver is concerned with tasks such as planning the journey, selecting the mode of transport and choosing a route. At the manoeuvring level, the tasks concerned include overtaking, giving way to other vehicles and obeying traffic rules. At the control level, the driver is concerned with controlling the vehicle, for example, controlling speed, following the road and quite simply keeping the car on the road. The model assumes an interaction between the three levels in which goals and criteria are defined at a higher level and the outcome of lower levels modifies goals at a higher level. Finally, Michon (1985) meant that a comprehensive model of driver behaviour should not just identify different levels of control but also provide a control structure that enables control to shift from one level to another in a timely manner.

The hierarchical structure of the driving task can be matched to actual driver behaviour. Human control structures are highly flexible and highly dependent on practice and experience. These structural aspects of human performance were addressed in the hierarchical skill-, rule- and knowledge-based behaviour (SRK) model developed by Rasmussen (1986). Rasmussen identified a number of cognitive functional elements organised in a three-layered structure. The model discriminates between skill-based, rule-based and knowledge-based controls. The main issue in Rasmussen's framework is the hierarchical nature of human control replacing the serial model used in early models of human information processing. The SRK model has been extensively used to model driver behaviour. The hierarchical control model takes into account both the hierarchical structure of the driving task and the driver behaviour by combing the two frameworks mentioned above (Ranney, 1994). Thus, Michon (1985) compiled a two-dimensional matrix that has been used to explain driver behaviour and to identify driver support needs (Michon, 1993; Ranney, 1994; Nilsson et al., 2001) with driving task demand and driver behaviour as the two dimensions (see Fig. 5.2). New driver support systems might force the driver to learn new skills and forget old skills. As a consequence, the driver might have to shift from skill-based behaviour to knowledge-based behaviour in order change to new skill-based behaviour, for example, learning to use an ADAS type of system like ABS.

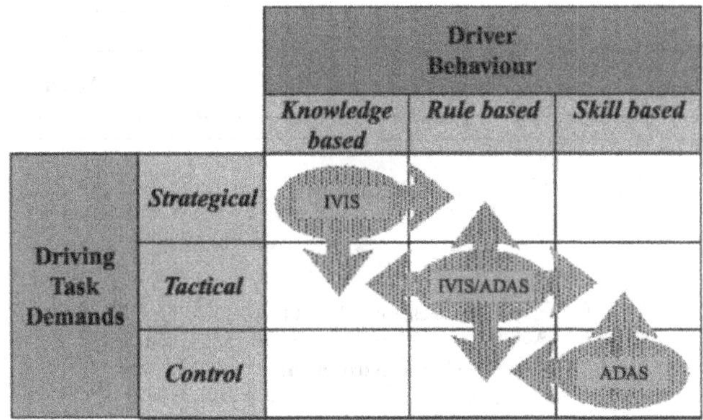

FIGURE 5.2. IVIS and ADAS can influence both driving task demands and driver behaviour (from Nilsson et al., 2001).

With the hierarchical structuring of both task and behaviour, it becomes evident that time is an aspect of driving that should be considered. Time constraints are implicitly different for the three task levels, even if time is not specifically addressed in the hierarchical control model. The following approximate time frames apply: 10 s or more for tasks at strategic level, between 1 and 10 s at tactical level and less than 1 s at control level. Finally, it should be noted that more complicated driver tasks, for example, performing route planning while driving or mobile phoning during driving may require knowledge-, rule- and skill-based actions in combination. It is not simply the time requirements that distinguish the different levels of tasks, but also the requirements of attention, workload and the consequences of mistakes, etc. The hierarchical control models are functional models, which do not specifically include motivational aspects and should be classified as adaptive control models. Furthermore, they do not explicitly consider the context, for example, controller's influence on the system to be controlled (Hollnagel, 2000).

5.6 Control Theory

Control theory or cybernetics is a general theory aimed at understanding self-regulating systems (Wiener, 1954; Ashby, 1956; Carver and Schreier, 1982). The systems view approach applied in cybernetics distinguishes itself from the more traditional analytic approach by emphasising the interactions and connectedness of the different components of a system. The basic control theory idea is simply based on a stimulus-response loop. The system current status is compared to a reference value and the deviation between system current status and reference determine the control action. However, the definitions of system boundaries and the relation between cause and effect are different from, for example, information-processing models. Control theory has been used to describe and study a wide range of systems from 'pure' technical to biological and social systems. Adaptive control models are also based on control theory.

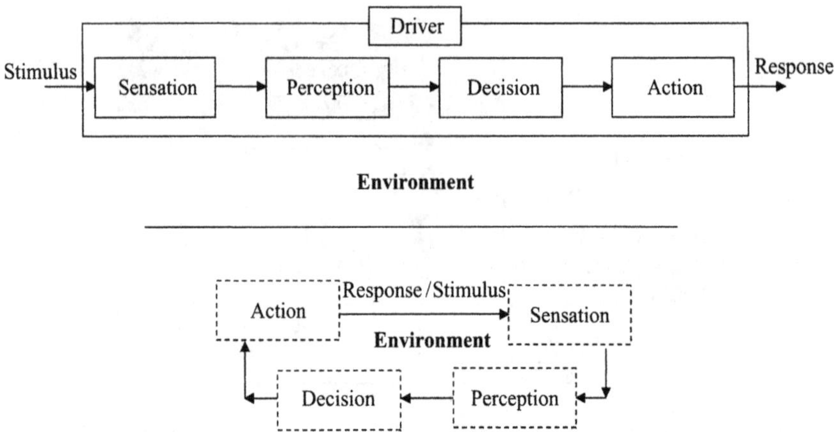

FIGURE 5.3. Open loop – closed system versus closed loop – open system adapted from Jagacinski and Flach (2003).

A system is an abstract construct, used to identify the focus of interest (Jagacinski and Flach, 2003). The system is also sometimes contrasted to the environment. A system typically refers to the phenomenon of interest and the environment to everything else. When there is a sharp boundary between the system and the environment, the system is considered as a *closed system*. The environment does not influence the system and can be disregarded. In a closed system, control is well defined and deterministic. Such a closed systems view is applied in human information-processing (HIP) models (e.g., Wickens, 1992) when the controller (e.g. driver) is considered as a closed system and the controlled object (e.g. car) belongs to the environment. The rationale for this approach was to divide human behaviour into isolated entities (e.g., sensation, perception, decision and action) which could be studied independently (see Fig. 5.3, top). As can be seen, it is a closed system (detached from the environment) and the control is an *open-loop*; that is, there is no feedback depicted from the controller's output to system input.

However, the demarcation between a system and the environment is often not that sharp. Or rather there are phenomena that cannot be explained with a closed systems view. This is specifically true when concerned with behavioural science where the relationship between, for example, a controller and the environment seems to be of prime importance in order to understand complex phenomena like behavioural adaptation. When the demarcation between a system and the environment is diffuse, the system can be considered an *open system*. All socio-technical systems can be viewed as open systems (Flach, 1999). The primary difference with other SR models is that control theory considers the operator's influence on the controlled object and the system boundaries are defined so that both the operator and the controlled object are included. This open system view is more consistent with an ecological view (Gibson, 1966). System boundaries can be very tight to all embracing depending on the focus. This open system view can be depicted by closing the loop and position the environment in the centre (see Fig. 5.3, bottom).

By closing the loop, the cause – effect relation between stimulus and response loses its meaning. In a closed-loop system the stimulus and response are tightly linked and there is no clear distinction between what is cause and what is effect. This restructuring was done to illustrate that the stimuli are as much determined by the actions as the actions are determined by the stimuli (Jagacinski and Flach, 2003). In this way we have a closed-loop open system, as the environment is included and the interdependencies between the controller and the environment are considered. This view can be useful when modelling driver behaviour and, in particular, driver behaviour adaptation and driver support systems.

Cognitive Systems Engineering (CSE) put cognition in context by applying an overall systems view. CSE decomposes complex tasks along two dimensions abstract – concrete and whole – part (Jagacinski and Flach, 2003). In this way the focus is shifted from internal functions of either humans or machines to the external function making up a joint cognitive system including both the controller and the controlled system (Hollnagel and Woods, 2005). The driver will be viewed as a controlling system and the car as a technical system to be controlled. In this perspective the car will constitute the primary context for the driver. As more of the context is included, the system will expand as a multi-layered functional description. The system boundaries have to be defined according to the purpose of the analysis. The two most important concepts in Control Theory are the open/closed system and the open/closed loop control. Jagacinski and Flach (2003), among others (e.g. Hollnagel and Woods, 2005; Hollnagel 2002), have further developed the concepts of control theory. Jagacinski and Flach have also provided some quantitative tools based on control theory that can be used to capture and understand also qualitative aspects of human performance, for example, driving behaviour and driver support systems.

5.7 Adaptive Control Models

Adaptive control models are concerned with issues of how the driver adapts his or her control to the characteristics of the system to be controlled (driver–vehicle–environment). Two categories of adaptive control models can be distinguished servo-control models addressing continuous tracking and information flow control models addressing discrete decision making (Michon, 1985). However, both views can be used in a complementary manner to understand some aspects of manual control. For example, firing the motor neurons is a set of discrete all-or-none response. However, the motion of an arm depends on the integration over many neurons and can best be described as continuous at a coarse time scale. Early servo-control models were mostly used to study compensatory (feedback) steering control performance on roads with varying curvature and for evasive manoeuvres. McRuer et al. (1977) questioned this way of modelling steering behaviour, as it did not consider the anticipatory control that seems to be a behaviour needed in order to understand skilled driving behaviour.

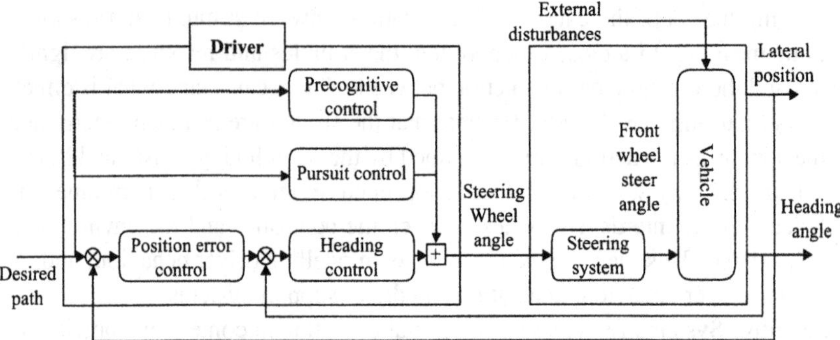

FIGURE 5.4. A three-level servo-control model of steering (from McRuer et al., 1977).

McRuer et al. (1977) proposed a three-level servo-control model of drivers' steering behaviour. First of all, they described driving as consisting of a hierarchy of navigation, guidance and control phases conducted simultaneously with visual search, recognition and monitoring operations. They also distinguished between closed-loop (*compensatory*) control and open-loop (*anticipatory*) control. Compensatory steering was described as two feedback loops (see Fig. 5.4). Firstly, the lateral position is fed back and compared to the desired path, and if there is a deviation it will result in an error-correcting action, which is compared to current heading angle and, if needed, a steering wheel correction will be made. The perceived road curvature derived from visual input guides the pursuit control. Secondly, pursuit control is an open-loop feed-forward control element that permits the driver to follow the anticipated road curvature. An interesting third concept is the precognitive control that in practice is a first phase of dual-mode control, that is, both open- and closed-loop controls. Precognitive control consists of previously learned control actions, which are triggered by situation and vehicle motion but work as pure open-loop control.

In view of this model, steering can be considered in terms of output as a position, velocity or acceleration control system (Jagacinski and Flach, 2003). If tyre angle is considered to be the output, then the steering system can be approximated as a position control system with a gain given by the steering linkage. While, if heading angle is viewed as the output, then steering can be considered a rate control system. In this case the gain is proportional to the velocity of the front wheels. Finally, if lateral position is considered the output, then steering should be viewed as an acceleration control system. If so, then the effective gain between steering wheel angle and lateral position is proportional to the square of the velocity. This shows that lateral and longitudinal control of the car is not independent but very much entwined. For a further discussion on control theory modelling, see also Wier and Chao (2005, Chapters 16 and 17).

Even if McRuer and his colleagues (1977) described driving as a hierarchical task, they concentrated very much on steering control. They largely considered driving as a closed system and disregarded the environment except road geometry. Michon (1985) cited Reid (1983), who concluded that the servo-control model described above cannot successfully cope with driver tasks other than following straight and smoothly curved roads. The model needs to be better integrated with the guiding visual environment as described by, for example, Gibson (1966). Michon concluded that 'The two fields – perception and vehicle control – are still lacking a theoretical integration. Combining them would constitute a major breakthrough, ... '.

5.8 Cognition in Control

Most of the models discussed so far are basically mechanistic, as they do not recognise the need of higher order cognitive abilities. The interaction between the driver and the environment is not explicitly included in the model but rather seems to be an implicit presumption. A useful model needs to be better connected with the context. The lack of context in cognition was addressed by Neisser. Neisser (1976) criticised the concept of direct perception (Gibson, 1966) by stating that to see is not just to perceive but also to interpret and understand on a conscious level. Neisser (1976) proposed a cognitively driven model of perception called the perceptual cycle, which includes the interaction between the observer and the environment. He introduced what he called anticipatory schemata that prepare and control our perception. Neisser (1976) further meant that human control works in a way similar to the perceptual cycle. Thus, to control a system, the controller has to have a model of the system to be controlled. The importance of a control-guiding model can also be understood in the light of 'The law of requisite variety' (Ashby, 1956), which states in principle that the variety of the controller should match the variety of the system to be controlled. Thus, the controller's understanding of the system that is being controlled will determine the actual control actions. In other words the driver's mental model of the vehicle, other drivers, road condition, etc., will determine the driver's control behaviour.

Hollnagel and Woods (2005) described a cyclical model of control, the basis of on the principles of Neisser's perceptual cycle. Hollnagel's cyclical control model was used as the basis for the Contextual Control Model, which describes in general terms how performance depends on perceiving feedback events, interpreting and modification of current understanding, selection and execution of actions. Driver control behaviour can be described as shown in Fig. 5.5, which is based on Hollnagel's cyclical model of control (Chapter 4).

The control cycle is divided into three phases: perception, decision and action. The control cycle is cognitively initiated by the driver depicted with the arrow coming out of the driver's head. The driver's mental model of the system to be controlled and the environment will guide the search for information during the perceptual phase. The perceived situation is compared to a reference value defined by the driver. The comparison is followed by a cognitive phase. During this phase a decision will be made on the basis of the difference between reference value and current situation, that is, the error. The aim will usually be to minimise the error. This cognitive phase is followed by an action phase during which an appropriate

FIGURE 5.5. The cognitive control cycle adapted from Hollnagel's (Hollnagel and Woods, 2005) contextual control model.

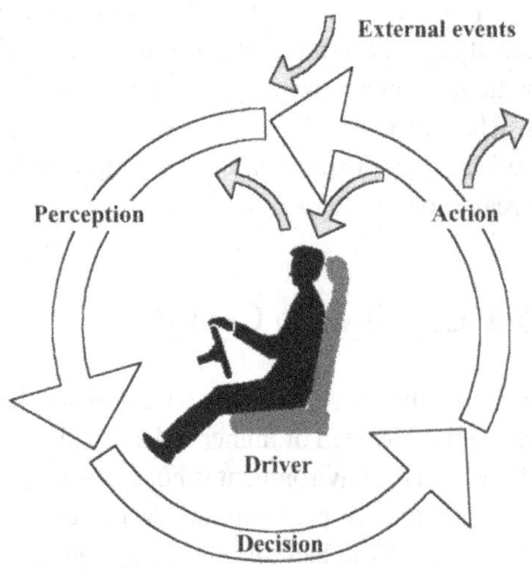

action is selected and carried out. This action influences the environment depicted by the outward arrow. Once the action is carried out, the driver searches and perceives the effect of the action together with possible external events and the circle is closed. The result of the action phase is also fed back to the driver and will change the driver's mental model of the control loop and the system under control. In other words it is previous experience and outcome of the driver's actions on the controlled system that will form and develop his or her mental models. The three phases are described as three distinct entities but in reality the phases might be overlapping and not separated as might appear from the figure. However, in principle the three phases are different in character. This model of driver control provides a foundation to capture the dynamics in driving, for example, compensatory closed-loop and anticipatory open-loop driving.

In relation to the discussed control model it can be interesting to consider the dual control problem: The driver should both determine the system status and at the same time control it (Jagacinski and Flach, 2003). The driver occasionally has to get out of control in order to maintain control. This was described by Weinberg and Weinberg (1979) as the fundamental regulator paradox: *The lesson is easiest to see in terms of an experience common to anyone who has ever driven on an icy road. The driver is trying to keep the car from skidding. To know how much steering is required, she must have some inkling of the road's slickness. But if she succeeds in completely preventing skids, she has no idea how slippery the road really is. Good drivers, experienced on icy roads, will intentionally test the steering from time to time by 'jiggling' to cause a small amount of skidding. By this technique they intentionally sacrifice the perfect regulation they know they cannot attain in any case. In return, they receive information that will enable them to do a more reliable, though less perfect job.* Unintentional skidding will, of course, provide sufficient information to the driver on how to adapt the driving behaviour in order to overcome the slippery road condition.

5.9 Goals for Control

The control theory model discussed above assumes that there is a goal or a reference value, which is used to determine appropriate actions. Different goals for safe driving behaviour have been proposed, for example, zero risk, threat avoidance, safety margins, response to risk (Näätänen and Summala, 1974; Fuller, 1984; Summala, 1985, 1988; Groeger, 2000). However, one of the first models aiming to describe safe (normal) driving behaviour was presented by Gibson and Crooks (1938). They meant that driving is a task that is carried out in time and space and described driving as a task of controlling the car within the field of safe travel. They defined the *field of safe travel* as 'an indefinite bounded field consisting, at any moment, of the field of possible paths which the car may take unimpeded'. It is an imaginary dynamic area in front of the vehicle with a shape of an outstretched tongue (see Fig. 5.6). Obstacles in the terrain mainly determine the boundaries in the field. Gibson and Crooks' model provides a foundation for the concept of safety margins and a guiding mechanism for normal safe driving behaviour.

Driving within safety margins is a concept that has been explored by several researchers. As an example, the concept of the longitudinal safety margins was explored by van der Hulst (1999). Van der Hulst meant that experienced drivers have a mental model of the driving task and expectations about what will occur in which situation. As a consequence, the driver can effectively scan the traffic environment. The mental model and the expectations will allow the driver to build up and preserve situation awareness and also to take advantage of a precognitive control as described by McRuer et al. (1977). Furthermore, driving is a task that can be carried out in many ways and will provide opportunities for behaviour

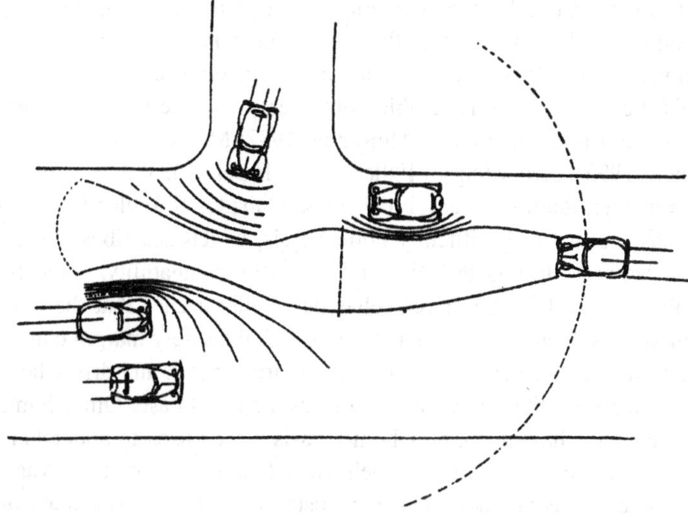

FIGURE 5.6. The concept of field of safe travel (from Gibson and Crooks [1938] published with permission of *The American Journal of Psychology*).

adaptation. The driver can choose from several driving strategies. This is a view that can help to better understand the mechanism behind the anticipatory behaviour. Van der Hulst (1999) also meant that driving is a task that allows for pace adjustments by means of adjustments in speed and other safety margin. The driver's choice of speed and safety margins will determine the time available to react to relevant changes in the environment. Van der Hulst thereby connected Gibson and Crooks's 'field of safe travel' with the Ashby's 'law of requisite variety'. Summala (1985, 1988) proposed that safety margins could be operationally defined as distance- or time-related measures like Time-to-line-crossing (TLC) and Time-to-collision (TTC). The concept of safety margins can also be used to explain, at least partly, accident causation. In-depth accident studies have shown that late detection is a very common explanation given for collisions (Rumar, 1988). Late detection can be described as violation of safety margins. Thus, time is critical for safe driving, which will be discussed later.

However, driver behaviour is most likely determined by a set of concurrent goals. The goals might also shift during a drive. Given the hierarchical structure of the driving task and driver behaviour as described above, it seems likely that the driver applies different goals for different levels of control. Thus, the driver can at the same time drive to reach a destination in time, stick to the traffic rules and avoid accidents. Goals for driving behaviour can also differ between drivers and situations. Furthermore, goals for driving can be extended to incorporate, for example, goals for life, skill for living, sensation seeking, pleasure, etc. (Hatakka et al., 2002). Thus, it seems likely that the driver has to find a balance between different goals. The idea of balancing between different goals was applied by Wilde (1982) in the risk homeostasis theory. Homeostasis is originally a term used to describe a complex mechanism for maintaining metabolic equilibrium in biological systems. Wilde meant that driver behaviour is guided by a target risk level that is determined by a combination of subjective and objective risk. An implication of Wilde's approach is that all actions taken to improve safety will be neutralised by the driver – at least on an aggregated level. The consequences of Wilde's theory led to considerable controversy and the theory has been rejected by several researchers (e.g. McKenna, 1982; Michon, 1985; Sanders and McCormick, 1993). According to Fuller (2005, Paper 10), Wilde based his theory on a misinterpretation of empirical findings made by Taylor (1964). Fuller proposed instead that task difficulty homeostasis, which describes the dynamic interaction between driving task demands and driver capability, could be used as key-sub goals to describe driver behaviour. Fuller argues that the task difficulty homeostasis overcomes some problems with the safety margin concept and conforms to the hierarchical structuring of the driving task and driver behaviour and risk homeostasis theory can be viewed as a special case. Other human behaviour researchers has shown how homeostasis can be used to understand how, for example, emotions can influence behaviour (Damasio, 1999; see Vaa, 2005, Paper 12). Thus, it seems likely that homeostasis is a mechanism that could be explored further to understand how different goals interact and determine driver behaviour.

5.10 Time and Time Again

Time considerations are crucial for the cognitive control cycle described above. Hollnagel and Woods (2005) divided the control cycle in three different phases: perception, decision and action. Time constraints can be incorporated into the cognitive control cycle (see Fig. 5.7), slightly adapted from Hollnagel. Thus, speed, road geometry, obstacles in the field of travel, sight conditions among a range of other factors determine the time available for the control cycle. This time is labelled T_u (usable time). The times needed to carry out the three phases (perceive, decide and act) are labelled T_p, T_d and T_a, respectively. In 'normal' driving $T_p + T_d + T_a$ is less than T_u.

Depending on the situation, normal driving constitutes a combination of compensatory and anticipatory control. The driver usually strives to balance between compensatory and anticipatory driving. Anticipatory driving requires T_u to be longer than $(T_p + T_d + T_a)$ but as the time required comes close to what is available driving becomes more compensatory. If the total usable time is not sufficient, performance will start to degrade. The control becomes more erroneous or sluggish and oscillatory (Jagacinski, 1977). Reducing speed is one way to gain time and control. The model also depicts that the reason for deteriorated performance can be attributed to prolonged perception, prolonged decision, prolonged action or some combination of the three. In any case, the result will be that the used time will be more than the usable time. All three phases are connected, meaning that if one part requires less time than expected then there will be more time for the remaining two phases. When traffic demands are low and the driver is experienced, evaluation, selection and even action require little time and there will be plenty of time available. Time pressure is in this view a critical component of driving behaviour when determining the driver's safety margins. Closely related to this is the concept of uncertainty. The driver will try to keep uncertainty at an acceptable level to maintain pace control and safety margins (Godthelp,

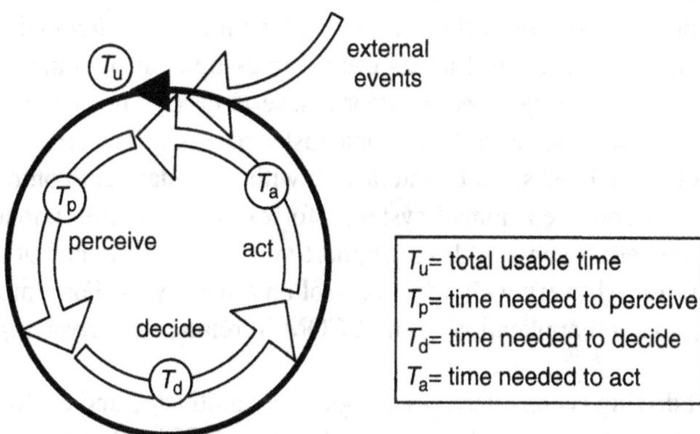

FIGURE 5.7. Time and control in the cyclic control model (adapted from Hollnagel, 2002).

Milgram and Blauw, 1984; Wierwille, 1993). The driver can apply an intermittent sampling strategy to cope with lack of time for the control loop. However, this strategy can, if maintained, increase the level of uncertainty, depending on the situation (Lee, 2006). Increased uncertainty and lack of anticipation will make drivers vulnerable to accidents. The time concept in the control cycle described above can also be applied to driver support systems. If the driver's mental model of a support system is incorrect or incomplete, this misunderstanding can prolong the time needed to complete the control loop. If the support system provides delayed or contradictory feedback and the driver is not guided to the right action, then the driver might eventually lose control. Lost control can also be due to a situation when the driver requires a long time to perceive what the system is doing.

5.11 Multiple Layers of Control

The driving task can be structured in hierarchical levels as discussed earlier. So far we have mostly been concerned with low levels of control. To get a more holistic view of driver behaviour, we need to expand the cognitive control loop to incorporate more of the context and apply a joint systems view (driver–vehicle–road–traffic etc.). The extended control model (ECOM) was developed by Hollnagel and Woods (2005) to consider aspects of joint system control. Hollnagel distinguished four hierarchical layers of control: tracking, regulating, monitoring and targeting, with targeting as top level and controlling at the bottom level. These four layers correspond to the levels distinguished in a generic decision model. Hollnagel pointed out that there is no absolute reference that can be used to determine the number of layers needed for all cases. Rather, the purpose determines the number of layers needed; for example, Powers (1998) identified 11 levels in his perceptual control theory. The layers in Hollnagel's model should not be considered as distinctive but more as continuous and overlapping. The control layers are connected in such a way that goals for control at lower layers are determined at higher layers and feedback is provided from lower to higher layers. The primary control of the car, that is, lateral and longitudinal motion of the vehicle, involves all control layers even if tracking control is the most obvious. Furthermore, the driver has to perform several tasks – not just the primary control of the car but also several additional tasks that are often carried out in parallel. Such additional tasks can be interaction with secondary car controls, driver support systems and even nomad systems, for example, mobile phones, handheld computers, etc. Even if a driver support system can be aimed at a specific control layer, it might very well affect control on other layers. For a more elaborated description and application of the ECOM in relation to driver support, see Paper 4.

Given that driving is considered as a cognitively motivated and controlled task, it is possible to reorganise the four control layers in ECOM starting with the top level of control targeting as an inner control loop and the monitoring, regulating

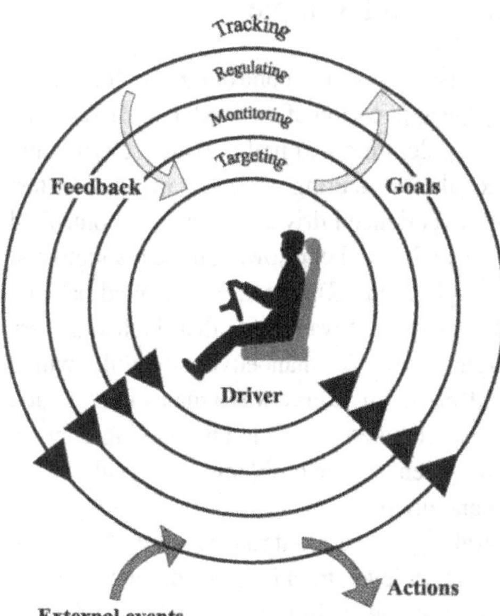

FIGURE 5.8. An extended control model adapted from Hollnagel's extended control model (Hollnagel and Woods, 2005).

and targeting loops as concentric circles with increasing diameters (see Fig. 5.8). Thus, what Hollnagel described as the lowest level of control tracking will be the outer circle representing the physical interaction with the interface to the vehicle's physical controls (e.g. steering wheel, pedals or various driver support systems). Control goals are determined in the inner control loops and applied in the outer control loops. That is to say that, for example in the targeting control loop the goals are determined for the monitoring control loop. This flow is represented by the outward-bound arrow-labelled goals at the top of Fig. 5.8. Feedback used to modify and supervise the control is fed back from outer circles to inner control circles represented by the in-bound arrow-labelled feedback at the top of Fig. 5.8. The interaction between the driver and the physical environment is represented by the two arrows-labelled external events and actions at the bottom of Fig. 5.8.

The driver can conduct an imaginary drive without physical interaction on the targeting level. The driver can also, while driving, anticipate the possible outcome of possible actions and let that determine the choice of action. However, even if the cognitive skills are important, it is the lower level psychomotor skills that are the foundation for safe driving (Ranney, 1997). Thus both cognitive and psychomotor skills are needed for safe driving and furthermore the integrations and interaction between the skills. The driver's mental model is, to a large extent, formed by the experiences from driving – 'learning by doing'. Driver support can be provided at different layers or levels of control and it seems likely that the ECOM can be used to analyse and better understand how different driver support systems can influence driving behaviour.

5.12 Joystick Controlled Cars – An Example

Experiences from experiments with four-way joystick controlled cars for drivers with severe disabilities will exemplify the application of the model discussed. The joysticks were used to control speed (accelerating and braking) and steering and thus replaced the standard controls (pedals and steering wheel). A manoeuvre test on a closed track was performed with experienced drivers of joystick-controlled cars (Östlund and Peters, 1999). The test included the following three manoeuvres: (1) firm and controlled braking on straight road, (2) firm and controlled braking in a narrow curve, and (3) double-lane change. It was found that the test drivers found it difficult to perform the straight road brake manoeuvre smoothly, which was attributed to the lack of feedback. Braking in a curve was a manoeuvre, which revealed problems of control interference between steering and braking control. Finally, time lags in the steering control system caused problems, specifically when performing the double lane-change manoeuvre.

The lack of tactile feedback when braking on a straight road was something that mainly influenced the activities at the lowest level, tracking. The drivers were not able to adjust the force applied on the brake lever in order to make a soft stop. It can be speculated that the feedback they experienced, as whole-body g-forces together with the visual cues, was not sufficient for the brake control function. However, it is probably a delicate task to implement feedback forces to suit the category of drivers who participated in the test, for example, drivers with sever muscular dystrophy. Adaptation companies installing these systems often claim that these drivers are extremely weak that active force feedback cannot be used. However, this is probably not true because all manual control depends on some form of tactile feedback. Whether it is technically feasible is another issue. In that case it might be possible to investigate other sources of feedback, for example, auditory feedback. However, such feedback will be artificial and not intuitive in the same way as force feedback would probably be.

The interference problem observed during curve braking mainly affected the activities on the regulating and monitoring levels. The drivers probably had a mental model of how their joysticks worked in terms of steering and braking but it was not sufficient to know what direction to move the lever in order to brake without affecting steering control. They had to regulate and monitor their control actions closely in order to adjust the joystick motion. This type of manoeuvre needs to be carried out at least partly as anticipatory control. With increased experience the drivers are likely to develop motor control schemata comparable to the precognitive control proposed by McRuer et al. (1977). It was also observed that the drivers compensated for performance decrements by driving slowly in the curve.

Finally, the time lag problem observed in the double-lane change had to be handled as anticipatory control. The drivers initially had to plan (target) in advance how to move the lever in order to compensate for the time lags and maintain control in the double lane change. It seems very difficult to develop a mental model of time lags and requires a lot of experience and training. It also turned out that the double lane change manoeuvre was the most difficult task to carry out correctly (i.e., without hitting any cones). The joystick drivers performed worse than a group of drivers matched with respect to age and driving experience. These drivers drove a standard car. The joystick drivers hit more cones and produced higher lateral acceleration forces despite driving their own individually adapted cars. All of the identified problems with these joystick systems can be described and analysed in terms of time-based safety margins.

Practical experiences have shown that it is a tedious task to learn to drive with this type of control system (often implemented as a electro-hydraulic system). Thus, in a follow-up simulator experiment an alternative joystick design was tested (Peters and Östlund, 2005). Time lags had been made similar to what is found in ordinary car controls (steering wheel and pedals), steering and speed control had been made more independent and active feedback was provided in the joystick lever. It was found that the reduced time lag contributed substantially to make it easy to learn to drive with this joystick. The separation of steering and speed control did not as clearly improve performance but contributed somewhat to improved control. The active feedback was not sufficiently tuned according to the individual drivers. Thus, it was only drivers with unimpaired upper limb functions who could benefit from the feedback.

In the example above it is obvious that the drivers were in need of support as they could not drive a standard production car due to their physical impairment (i.e., they were paralysed in their lower limbs and had impaired function in their upper limbs). However, it can well serve as an example on how to understand potential problems related to specifically ADAS and guide on how to resolve them. What becomes obvious is that a driver in control depends on timely, sufficient and intuitive feedback. Furthermore, integrated control functions with a high risk of interference should be avoided. The human controller can often learn how to compensate even badly designed support systems but a well-designed system will both facilitate learning and ensure that the driver stays in control even in a critical situation.

5.13 Summary and Conclusion

Driving task and driver behaviour modelling can be valuable to determine driver support needs. Modelling can also be useful to determine whether the objectives with a support system have been reached or to look for possible aversive consequences. A driver support system can have different purposes and a range of different consequences for driver behaviour. However, the main focus in this Paper is on driver support and safety. It has been argued that driving should be considered a cognitive task of control in context. Furthermore, the hierarchical structure of both the driving task and driver behaviour has to be considered. The principles of control theory can be used to understand the driver as an active controller. Context has to be included and system boundaries have to be determined. To understand complex phenomena like behaviour adaptation, it was proposed to apply a closed loop open system view. Thus, the cognitive control cycle that can be linked to basic human abilities needed for the driving task was proposed as a useful model of driver behaviour. Driver behaviour is also guided by a set of concurrent goals. The homeostasis principle seems to be useful to understand the interrelationship between different goals and driver behaviour. Human control seems to be very sensitive to time. Time determines the margins for action. The cognitive control cycle was described in terms of time. Finally the control cycle was expanded to also consider hierarchical layers of control and the interaction with the system to be controlled. The overall aim should be to ensure that the driver is in full control even when driver support systems are installed. Well-designed support systems are easier to learn and safer to use.

References

Allen, T.M., Lunenfeld, H. and Alexander, G.J. (1971). Driver information needs. *Highway Research Record*, 366, 102–115.

Ashby, W.R. (1956). *An introduction to cybernetics*. Chapman and Hall Ltd., London.

Carsten, O. (2005). From driver models to modelling the driver: What do we really know about the driver? In L. Macchi, C. Re and P.C. Cacciabue (Eds.). *Modelling driver behaviour in automotive environments*. Office of Official Publiations of the European Communities, Ispra, Italy.

Carver, C.S. and Schreier, M.F. (1982). Control theory: A useful conceptual framework for personality – social, clinical and health psychology. *Psychological Bulletin*, 92, 111–135.

Damasio, A.R. (1999). *The feeling of what happens: Body and emotion in the making of consciousness*. Harvest Book Harcourt Inc., San Diego, CA.

Engström, J. and Hollnagel, E. (2005). Towards a conceptual framework for modelling driver' interaction with in-vehicle systems. In L. Macchi, C. Re and P.C. Cacciabue (Eds.). *Modelling driver behaviour in automotive environments*. Office of Official Publications of the European Communities, Ispra, Italy.

Flach, J.M. (1999). Beyond error: The language of coordination and stability. In P.A. Hancock (Ed.). *Handbook of perception and cognition: Human performance and ergonomics*. Academic Press, New York.

Fuller, R.G.C. (1984). A conceptualisation of driving behaviour as threat avoidance. *Ergonomics*, 27, 1139–1155.

Fuller, R. (2005a). Control and affect: Motivational aspects of driver decision-making. In L. Macchi, C. Re and P.C. Cacciabue (Eds.). *Modelling driver behaviour in automotive environments*. Office of Official Publications of the European Communities, Ispra, Italy.

Fuller, R. (2005b). Towards a general theory of driver behaviour. *Accident Analysis and Prevention*, 37, 461–472.

Gibson, J.J. (1966). *The senses considered as perceptual systems*. Houghton Mifflin, Bostan.

Gibson, J.J. and Crooks, L.E. (1938). A theoretical field-analysis of automobile-driving. *The American Journal of Psychology*, 51, 453–471.

Godthelp, H., Milgram, P. and Blaauw, G.J. (1984). The development of a time-related measure to describe driving strategy. *Human Factors*, 26, 257–268.

Groeger, J.A. (2000). *Understanding driving – Applying cognitive psychology to a complex everyday task*. Psychology Press, Taylor and Francis, Hove, UK.

Hatakka, M., Kesikinen, E., Gregersen, N.P., Glad, A. and Hernetkoski, K. (2002). From control of vehicle to personal self-control; broadening the perspectives to driver education. *Transport Research Part F, Traffic Psychology and Behaviour*, 201–215.

Hollnage, E. and Woods, D.D. (2005). *Joint cognitive systems: Foundations of cognitive systems engineering*. Taylor and Francis, Boca Raton, FL.

Hollnagel, E. (2002). Time and time again. *Theoretical Issues in Ergonomics Science*, 3, 143–158.

Jagacinski, R.J. (1977). A qualitative look at feedback control theory as a style of describing behavior. *Human Factors*, 19(4), 331–347.

Jagacinski, R.J. and Flach, J.M. (2003). *Control theory for humans—Quantitative approaches to modelling performance.* Lawrence Erlbaum, Mahwah, NJ.

Janssen, W.H. (1979). *Routeplanning en geleiding: Een litteratuurstudie*. Institute for perception TNO, Soesterberg.

Lee, J.D. (2006). Driving safety. In R.S. Nickerson (Ed.). *Reviews of human factors and ergonomics*. Human Factors and Ergonomics Society, St. Monica, CA.

Mckenna, F.P. (1982). The human factor in driving accidents. An overview of approaches and problems. *Ergonomics*, 25, 867–877.

Mcruer, D.T., Allen, R.W., Weir, D.H. and Klein, R.H. (1977). New results in driver steering control models. *Human Factors*, 19, 381–397.

Michon, J.A. (1985). A critical view of driver behavior models: What do we know, what should we do? In L.A. Evans and R.C. Schwing (Eds.). *Human behavior and traffic safety* (pp. 487–525). New York: Plenum, New York.

Michon, J.A. (Ed.) (1993). *Generic intelligent driver support—A comprehensive report on GIDS*. Taylor and Francis, London.

Neisser, U. (1976). *Cognition and reality: Principles and implications of cognitive psychology*. W.H. Freeman and Company, New York.

Nilsson, L., Harms, L. and Peters, B. (2001). The effect of road transport telematics. In P.-E. Barjonet (Ed.). *Traffic psychology today* (1st ed., Vol. 1, pp. 265–285). Norwell: Kluwer Academic Publishers.

Näätänen, R. and Summala, H. (1974). A model for the role of motivational factors in driver' decision making. *Accident Analysis and Prevention*, 6, 243–261.

Östlund, J. and Peters, B. (1999). *Joystick Equipped Cars' Maneuverability*. VTI Meddelande No. 860A.

Peters, B. and Östlund, J. (2005). *Joystick controlled driving for drivers with disabilities – A driving simulator experiment*. Statens Väg och transportforskningsinstitut, Linköping.

Powers, W.T. (1998). *Making sense of behavior – The meaning of control*. Benchmark, New Canaan, CT.

Ranney, T.A. (1994). Models of driving behaviour: A review of their evolution. *Accident Analysis and Prevention*, 26, 733–750.

Ranney, T.A. (1997). Good driving skills: Implications for assessment and training. *Work*, 8, 253–259.

Rasmussen, J. (1986). *Information processing and human–machine interaction: An approach to cognitive engineering*. North-Holland, New York.

Reid, L.D. (1983). Survey of recent driving steering behaviour models suited to accident investigations. *Accident Analysis and Prevention*, 15, 23–40.

Rumar, K. (1988). Collective risk but individual safety. *Ergonomics*, 31, 507–518.

Sanders, M.S. and Mccormick, E.J. (1993). Human factors and the automobile. In M.S. Sanders and E.J. Mccormick (Eds.). *Human Factors in engineering and design* (7th ed.). McGraw-Hill, New York.

Summala, H. (1985). Modeling driver behavior: A pessimistic prediction? In L. Evans and R.C. Schwing (Eds.). *Human behavior and traffic safety* (pp. 43–65). New York: Plenum.

Summala, H. (1988). Risk control is not risk adjustment: The zero-risk theory of driver behaviour and its implications. *Ergonomics*, 31, 491–506.

Taylor, D.H. (1964). Drivers' galvanic skin response and the risk of accident. *Ergonomics*, 7, 439–451.

Vaa, T. (2005). Modelling driver behaviour on basis of emotions and feelings: Intelligent transport systems and behavioural adaptations. In L. Macchi, C. Re and P.C. Cacciabue (Eds.). *Modelling driver behaviour in automotive environments*. Office of Official Publications of the European Communities, Ispra, Italy.

Van Der Hulst, M. (1999). Adaptive control of safety margins in driving. *Department of Psychology.* University of Groningen, Groningen, The Netherlands.

Weinberg, G.M. and Weinberg, D. (1979). *On the design of stable systems.* Wiley, New York.

Weir, D.H. and Chao, K.C. (2005). Review of control theory models for directional and speed control. In L. Macchi, C. Re and P.C. Cacciabue (Eds.). *Modelling driver behaviour in automotive environments*. Office of Official Publications of the European Communities, Ispra, Italy.

Wickens, C.D. (1992). *Engineering psychology and human performance*. New York, Harper Collins.

Wiener, N. (1954). *The human use of human beings. Da Capo Series in Science*. Pergamon Press, Oxford.

Wierwille, W.W. (1993). Visual and manual demands of in-car controls and displays. In B. Peacock and W. Karwowski (Eds.). *Automotive ergonomics* (pp. 229–320). London: Taylor and Francis.

Wilde, G.J.S. (1982). The theory of risk homeostasis: Implications for safety and health. *Risk Analysis*, 2, 209–225.

6
From Driver Models to Modelling the Driver: What Do We Really Need to Know About the Driver?

OLIVER CARSTEN

6.1 Introduction

The variety of models of the driving task is almost as numerous as the number of authors who have contributed the models. Part of this variety is due to the different applications for which the models are intended and another part is due to the part of the driving task they are intended to describe. Since driving encompasses so many tasks and subtasks at different levels, often performed by the driver simultaneously, it is perhaps no surprise that it is hard to find any consensus in the literature on how the process of driving should be modelled.

Here the focus is on creating a structured model that can be used in real time, in particular by a driver assistance system to monitor driver state and performance, predict how momentary risk is changing, anticipate problem situations and in response to adjust the behaviour of in-vehicle information systems and driver assistance systems and also adjust feedback to the driver. The driver model would therefore be the major component of a larger model supervising the interaction among driver, vehicle and the traffic and road environment. The starting point is a review of existing models to identify elements that can be used to predict momentary risk.

The literature on models of the driving task is very extensive, going back at least as far as Gibson and Crooks' Field of Safe Travel Model (Gibson and Crooks, 1938). Yet, in spite of the considerable effort put into producing such models, few of them have been validated as predictive tools, apart from specific and limited aspects of the driving task, where for example mathematical representations of car following are used in microsimulation models of traffic. Still less is it the case that any generalised model has been used in a driving assistance system to guide the operation of the system as it supports the driver. Yet the potential of an assistance system that 'understood' the driver is huge: it could give feedback to novices, assist elderly drivers in difficult situations, inform a driver when he or she is fatigued and adapt the operation of the vehicle to the needs of each individual driver.

6.2 A Typology of Models

Two broad types of driver model can be distinguished in the literature. The first type is *descriptive models*. These models attempt to describe parts or the whole of the driving task in terms of what the driver has to do. The second major type is *motivational models*, which aim to describe how the driver manages risk or task difficulty. The first type can be further subdivided into a number of categories – there are task models, adaptive control models and production models.

6.3 Descriptive Models

These models attempt to describe either the whole of the driving task or some element of it. A major feature of such models is that they are not predictive, but are instead analytical. It is not possible to conclude from such models how changes in driver motivation, capability or decision would affect the quality of the performance of the driving task or situational risk.

6.3.1 Task Models

One major type of descriptive model of the driving process is the hierarchical task model of Michon (1985). This model is shown in Fig. 6.1. The only conclusions that can be drawn about performance or risk from this model is that a breakdown of input, for example, environmental input at the control level or of feedback will lead to a failure in the driving task.

Other more detailed task descriptions, such as the famous compilation of tasks and sub-tasks by McKnight and Adams (1970), have similar qualities. They

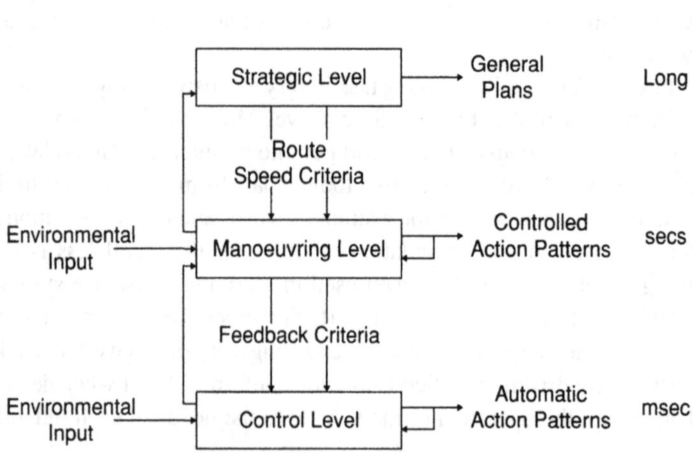

FIGURE 6.1. Michon's hierarchical structure of the road user task.

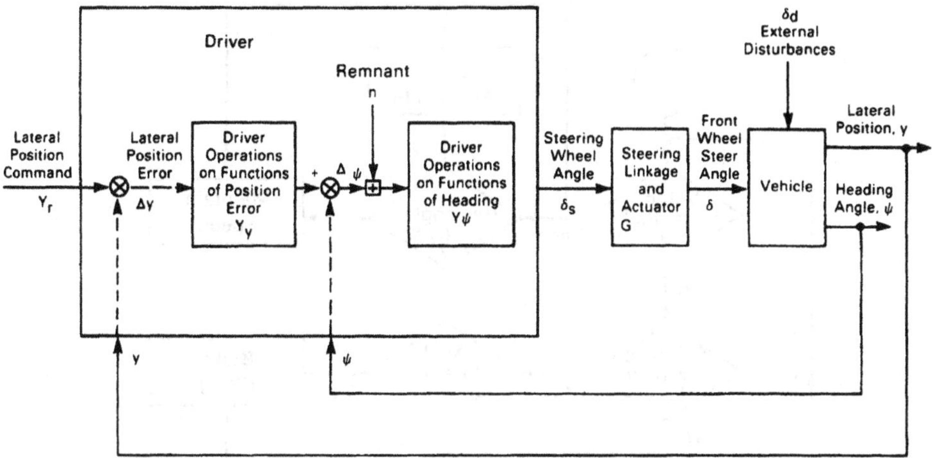

FIGURE 6.2. Compensatory model of driver steering (McRuer et al., 1977).

describe what the driver has to do in order to drive but they do not state explicitly how the *quality* of the driving performance is affected by the nature of driver performing the tasks or by the nature of the driving being carried out. Risk is only addressed implicitly in that a failure in performing a task is likely to lead to a problem, but no guidance is afforded on what might cause such failure.

6.3.2 Adaptive Control Models

Another type of descriptive model describes the operation of the driving task in terms of inputs, outputs and feedback. An example is the driver steering model of McRuer et al. (1977) as shown in Fig. 6.2, where steering inputs are described as compensation for errors in lateral position and heading angle. It can be noted that this model does not account for non-deliberate errors in lateral position. Similar models have been created for manoeuvring tasks. An example is shown in Fig. 6.3, which is intended to describe the process of a driver approaching a T junction and making a judgement about what speed to adopt in order to avoid collision with a vehicle approaching from the right.

A more complex adaptive control model has recently been proposed by Hollnagel et al. (2003). This model covers both manoeuvring and control, as shown in Fig. 6.4. Interestingly and presumably intentionally, this model covers only the driver in control and not the driver who is losing or who has lost control.

6.3.3 Production Models

Tasks can also be described in terms of a formal set of rules, that is, as a production system. Michon (1985) produced a formal set of such rules for changing gear in a

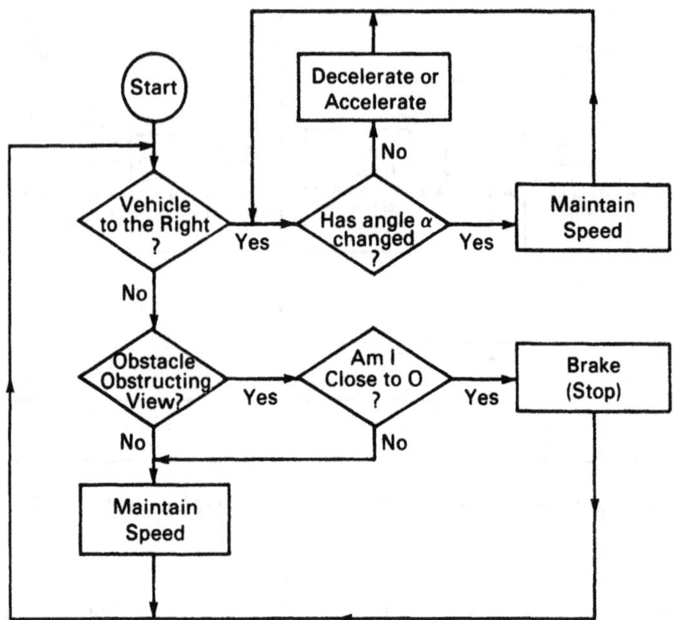

FIGURE 6.3. Driver decision making on approach to an intersection (Kidd and Laughery, 1964).

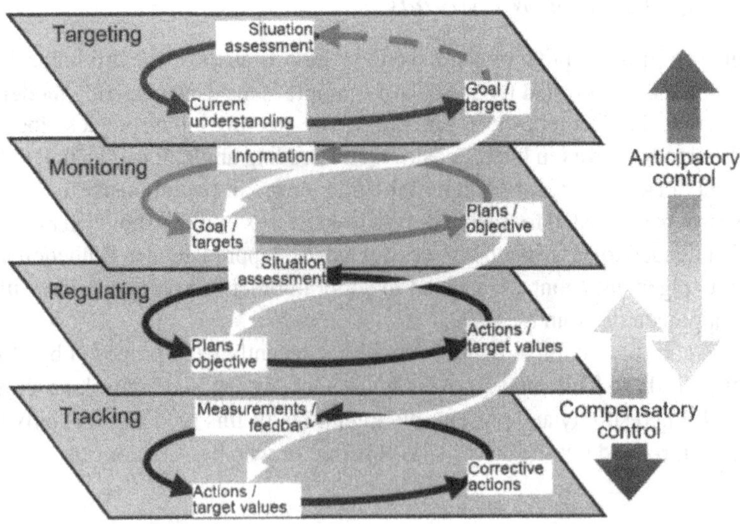

FIGURE 6.4. Driver in control model (Hollnagel et al., 2003).

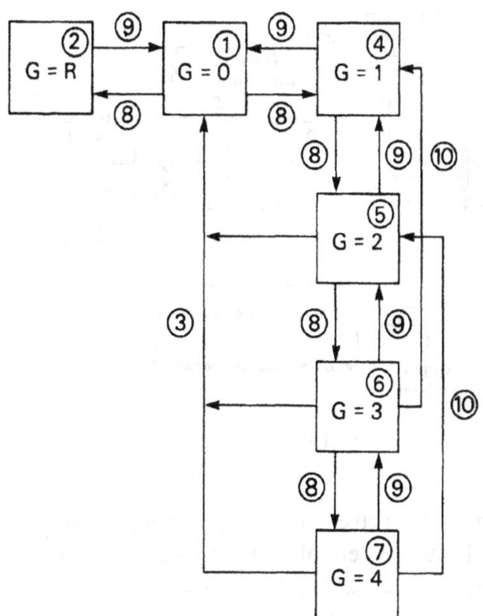

FIGURE 6.5. Action goal structure for changing gear (Michon, 1985).

four-speed car. The action goals structure for changing gear is shown in Fig. 6.5. Here Action Goal 3, for example, shows the process of shifting into neutral on stopping.

But once again such a model, while perhaps serving a purpose as a detailed description of the purposes for which a driver changes gear, does not help to explain why one driver may choose a higher gear than another in identical traffic circumstances. So it does not tell us in full *why* a driver changes gear at a particular moment. Car manufacturers know that motivation affects gear selection and therefore have produced cars that feature automatic gearboxes that can change style from sedate and economical to aggressive and sporty.

6.4 Motivational Models

Motivational models attempt to describe why drivers choose one alternative over another in terms of utilities and trade-offs. In all probability, the most famous motivation model of the driving task is the risk homeostasis model of Wilde (1982) as shown in Fig 6.6. It is not the purpose here to provide a detailed critique of this model – the literature is full of such critiques. More to the point is that Wilde introduces the notion of driver capability affecting risk: perceptual skills, decision skills and vehicle handling skills all feature in the model.

Other models introduce different aspects of driver motivation and capacity. Näätänen and Summala (1974) add personality, experiences, motivation and vigilance (see Fig. 6.7). Fuller (1984) adds capability and driver perception of rewards and punishment (see Fig. 6.8). A more recent model by Fuller (2004) concentrates

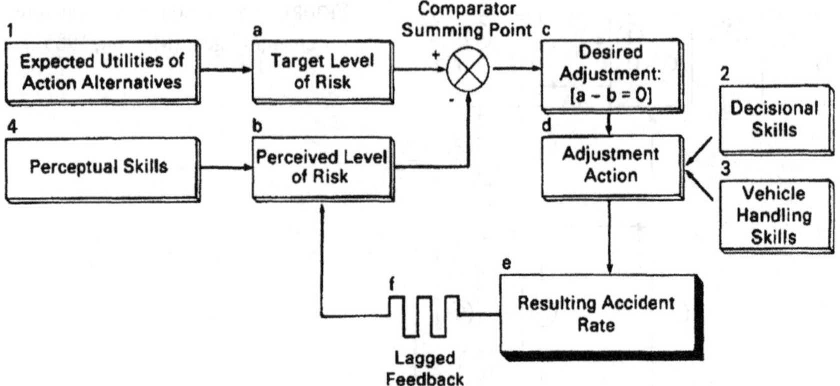

FIGURE 6.6. Risk homeostasis model of Wilde (1982).

on the interaction between task demands and driver capability, arguing that speed choice in one major mechanism for the adjustment of task demands so that they remain within capability. This latter model does not seek, however, to develop an explanation of the major factors that determine capability; rather they are identified in terms of broad groupings such as 'constitutional features', that is, biological factors and 'human factors'. Focusing in particular on human factors, Rumar (1985) describes the driving task in terms of information processing and introduces a number of filters (physical, perceptual and cognitive) that can introduce errors. He also incorporates such factors as motivation, experience, attention and expectation in his model (see Fig. 6.9).

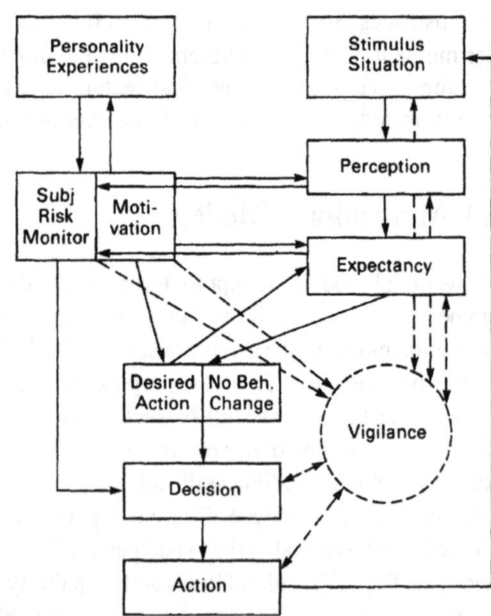

FIGURE 6.7. Risk threshold model (Näätänen and Summala, 1974).

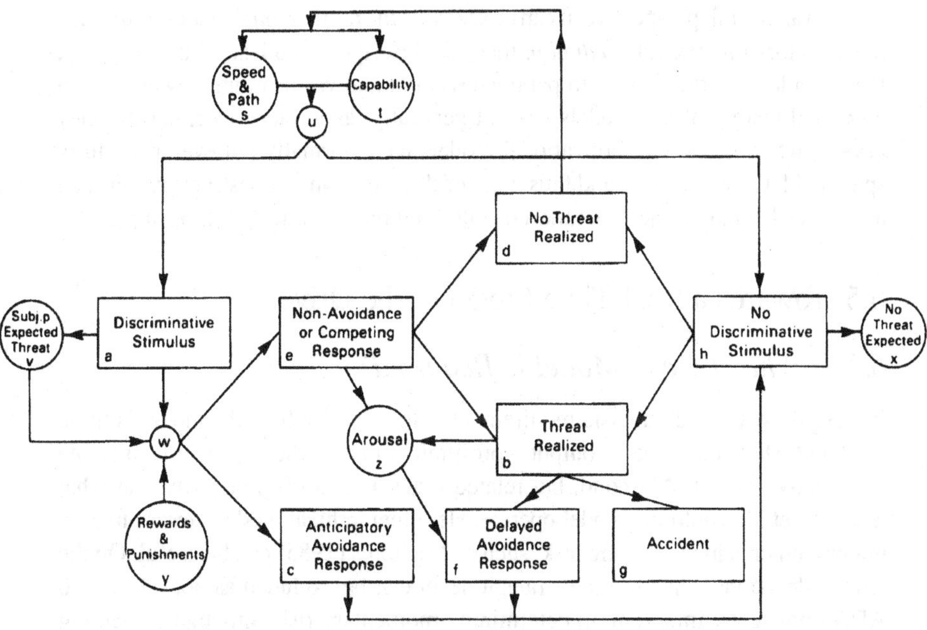

FIGURE 6.8. Risk avoidance model (Fuller, 1984).

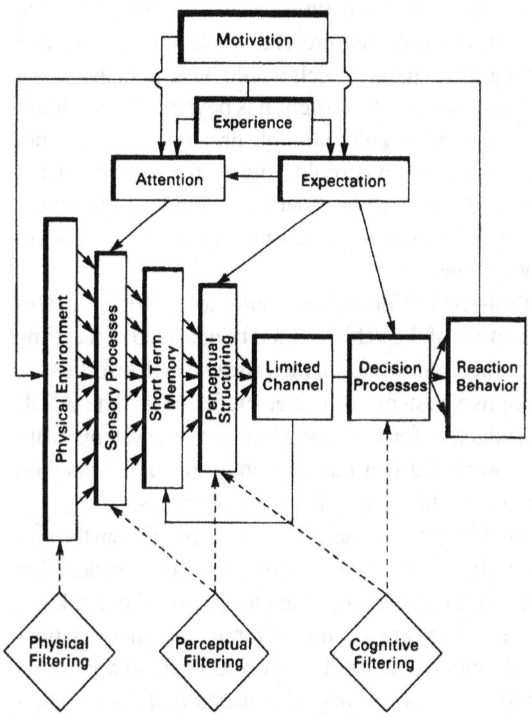

FIGURE 6.9. Model of driving as information processing (Rumar, 1985).

From an overall perspective, it can be seen that the motivational models introduce more factors that permit *prediction* than the descriptive models. Thus, in theory, they should be more subject to parameterisation and verification. However, such empirical testing of the models has not generally taken place (see, e.g. Ranney (1994), who argues that motivational models have normally not even been fully specified let alone tested), and thus most of them remain as constructs rather than as entities leading to the generation of rules and mathematical relationships.

6.5 Towards a Real-Time Model of the Driver

6.5.1 What Type of Model Is Required?

In designing a model, a basic requirement is to establish how the model is to be used and what should be its output – presuming, that is, the objective is to create a predictive model. A second, but related issue, is that of granularity – at what level of detail should the model operate. Here hierarchical models describing the major elements in the driving task, such as Michon's (1985) can be useful. On the whole, decisions related to the strategic level can be excluded as not relevant to ADAS nor really important in determining momentary risk, although preventing an impaired driver from setting out on a journey or even general trip suppression or modal shift can reduce risk (see, e.g. Rumar, 1999). At the most detailed and automated level of operation, namely vehicle control, we are faced with virtual impossibility of predicting from one very small time step to the next what the driver is likely to do. Such prediction would require almost absolute knowledge about how the driver is controlling the vehicle, which would have to be based on interpretation of physiological responses. Such prediction is beyond the capability of today's cognitive science and may well be an impossible dream: humans are not automatons whose precise reaction to a given complex situation can be predicted with any certainty. A misinterpretation of a driver's decision could lead to severe problems, for example preventing a lane change when the driver in the adjacent lane has signalled consent to the manoeuvre.

This does not mean that control-level information would not provide a useful input to the model. Thus, driver control of the vehicle could be analysed in real time to provide the model with a depiction of a driver's characteristics. Such information would be useful in 'tuning' adaptive systems to driver preferences. The AIDE project has recently investigated adaptive forward collision warning systems, with one type of adaptation being to observed driver reaction time, so that drivers who habitually reacted quickly got later and hence less irritating warnings.

There is a strong argument, then, for focusing mainly (but not entirely) on the manoeuvring level of driving. This is where many of the major risks occur – in decision making at junctions, interactions with pedestrians, lane changing and overtaking, etc. Errors in performing such manoeuvres are a major factor in accident causation, so that in Great Britain 59% of all injury road traffic accidents occur at a junction (Department for Transport, 2005). But this still begs the question of what should be predicted. There are strong arguments for a probabilistic approach as opposed to a deterministic approach. Rather than predicting precisely and reliably what a driver will do at any moment – an endeavour almost certainly doomed to failure because of the variability of human response both between and within individuals – a model should attempt to predict the probability of error or failure and thus current and future risk. For example, there may be strong indications that a driver is about to undertake an overtaking manoeuvre that, given the road layout and traffic situation, may be highly risky. Feedback to the driver in advance of actually starting the manoeuvre (so that the manoeuvre can be discouraged or prevented) may well be more useful than feedback once the manoeuvre is already under way (in the hope that it can be safely aborted). Control-level behaviour could be used to trigger such warnings. A driver intending to overtake is likely to position the vehicle close to or even slightly over the centreline.

6.5.2 Grouping the Factors

Thus it can be argued that an intelligent driver assistance system does not need to fully comprehend all aspects of how a driver performs the driving task; it merely needs to know about those driver factors that can affect the risk of vehicle operation. This, of course, presumes that the major goal of such a system is to reduce risk, but that seems a fairly reasonable constraint. The task of creating a model then becomes one of identifying those driver factors that can be used to predict safety-related performance or behaviour and of combining those factors into a structured 'model' that can be filled with rules and parameters, that is, a model that can be empirically tested.

For this purpose, the various factors proposed in the motivational models discussed above can be identified as follows:

- From Näätänen and Summala (1974)
  - Personality
  - Experiences
  - Motivation
  - Perception
  - Vigilance
  - Desired action
- From Fuller (1984)
  - Capability
  - Arousal
- From Rumar (1985)
  - Motivation
  - Experience
  - Attention
  - Expectation
  - Perception and cognition
- From Hollnagel et al. (2003)
  - Goals/targets/plans

  - Situation assessment
- From Fuller (2004)
  - Constitutional features (this model is somewhat unique in including biological characteristics such as physical strength and reaction time)
  - Training and education
  - Experience

These factors can be grouped into categories as follows:

- Attitudes/ personality
  - Näätänen and Summala: Personality
  - Rumar: Motivation
- Experience
  - Näätänen and Summala: Experiences
  - Rumar: Experience
  - Fuller (2004): Training and education
  - Fuller (2004): Experience
- Driver state (impairment level)
  - Näätänen and Summala: Vigilance
  - Fuller: Capability
- Task demand
  - Fuller (1984): Arousal
  - Fuller (2004): Task demands
- Situation awareness
  - Näätänen and Summala: Perception
  - Näätänen and Summala: Vigilance
  - Rumar: Attention
  - Rumar: Perception and cognition
  - Rumar: Expectation
  - Hollnagel: Situation assessment
- Intention
  - Hollnagel: Goals/targets/plans
  - Näätänen and Summala: Desired action

We thus end up with five major categories of driver capability, performance and behaviour that are related to risk. They are as follows:

1. Attitudes/personality
2. Experience
3. Driver state (impairment level)
4. Task demand (workload)
5. Situation awareness

Biological capability will be omitted on the grounds that permanent incapacity relates to only a small proportion of drivers (although there may be empirical arguments for including some aspects of age-related incapacity).

As regards intention, this is simply a requirement by the model to predict the driver's desired decision at a given moment. For example, we might infer from lane position and closing towards the lead vehicle that a driver is intending to perform an overtaking manoeuvre. The intention at one time step will then inform the model at the next time step. The precise granularity of the model operation will need to be defined, but it would seem sensible to start with fairly coarse time steps to reduce the precision required.

For each of these categories, it is possible to verify from the accident literature that they have a major role in terms of accident risk. For example, in terms of the first category, Stradling and Meadows (2000) have cited the role of the propensity to commit aggressive violations as a predictor of accident risk. For experience, the models developed by Maycock et al. (1991) relating age and experience to accident risk can be used as evidence. For driver state, there is the literature relating alcohol impairment to accident risk, including the most recent reanalysis of the Grand Rapids data (Hurst et al., 1994). For workload, we can look at the literature relating demands from road layout to driver performance. For the impact of situation awareness, we can go to the studies of the impact of mobile phone use on driving (e.g., Burns et al., 2002).

6.5.3 A Proposed Structure

A verifiable model requires a structure so that relationships can be proposed and tested. A proposed structure, with the various categories grouped into long term (years, months and days), medium term (hours and minutes) and short term (seconds and milliseconds), is shown in Fig. 6.10.

Creating a predictive model still begs the question of what is to be predicted. Any model created with today's knowledge must, of necessity, be probabilistic rather than deterministic. It is not possible to create a reliable prediction of an individual drivers decisions – after all even a drunk drive makes some correct

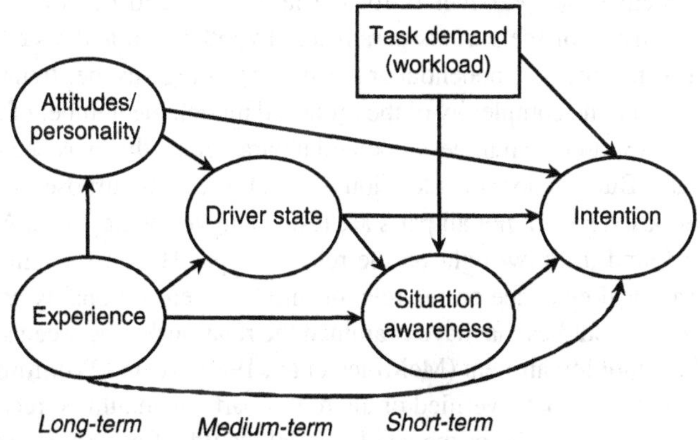

FIGURE 6.10. A causal structure for the categories of the driver model.

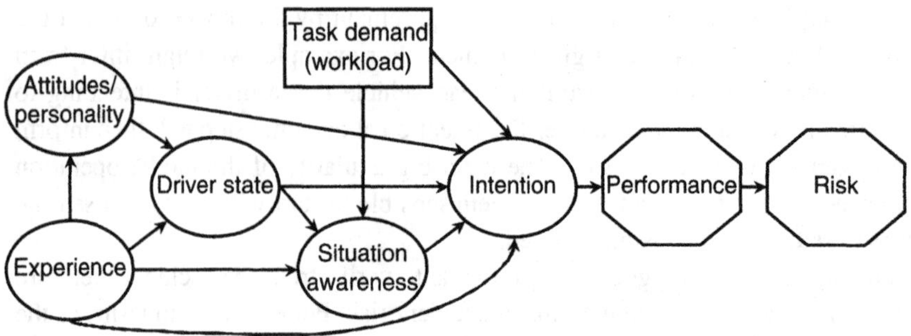

FIGURE 6.11. Relationship between categories of driver factors and risk.

decisions. In addition, given sensor technology, a model running in real time cannot be omniscient about the environmental situation and may indeed make errors in interpreting driver actions and capabilities. So it is sensible in using some kind of risk factor, that is, the risk of a serious error or the risk of crashing as the dependent variable. The risk factor could be used in real time to identify when a driver assistance system might need to warn the driver or to intervene in order to keep prevent performance from deteriorating drastically with consequent impact on risk. A relationship with performance and risk is suggested in Fig. 6.11.

6.5.4 Verifying the Model

Merely proposing a model does not justify it; still less does it demonstrate that the model is useful. Thus, Grayson (1997) has stated, 'Although it would be uncharitable to suggest that many psychological models [of driving] are little more than the current buzz-words enclosed in boxes and joined by lines with arrowheads, it is nevertheless difficult to avoid feeling that the term "model" has become devalued in recent times'. The model proposed here is framework and not yet a usable, validated predictive tool. Parameters for the factors need to be developed, and the inter-relationship of the various parameters hypothesised and tested both as regards their form (linear, exponential or power) and as regards the strength of the relationship. Given the complexity of the proposed model, the number of relationships within it (13) and the number of potential parameters, this may seem like an impossible task. But a major consideration is that, for testing purposes, the model can be decomposed so that not all parts are tested and verified at once. And prior work can be found to throw light on the relationships. Thus, for example there is already empirical evidence on the relationship between personality and driver state in the form of studies that have examined the relationship between sensation seeking and alcohol impairment (McMillen et al., 1989; Yu and Williford, 1993).

Once the model has been verified or altered in parts, it should be recomposed and tested in full. Such a test of the whole model would, of course, be a substantial task requiring large numbers of drivers to be observed over a considerable amount of driving. But the payoff would be the delivery of a truly intelligent co-driver.

A major step in model development and verification is identifying candidate parameters to be included in each of the categories. Here one can conceive of a two-stage process in which first of all the model is developed as an offline tool and then at a second stage an online, real-time version of the model is created to run on board the vehicle as an intelligent co-driver, supervisor of interaction with IVIS and ADAS systems and manager of those systems to adapt to the current driver state and current situation.

The second stage is clearly quite ambitious: care would have to be taken to ensure that such a model did not create safety risks by going into unanticipated states or unstable loops. One approach to minimise this would be setting boundaries on system flexibility. Another, more straightforward alternative for an on-board version is the creation of a simple rule-based structure that echoes the 'full' model but does not emulate it.

However, the potential ambition of the second stage does not negate the usefulness of the first stage. It could have wide application and utility as an offline design tool for new in-vehicle systems (creating 'what if?' scenarios, i.e. a kind of failure mode and effects analysis), as a tool for evaluating road designs (e.g. in safety audit) and even as a component in microsimulation models. In the last role, it could replace the current rather crude practice of representing driver behaviours by means of sampling from a set of built-in distributions, so as to represent for example desired speed, typical headway or reaction time.

The model can initially be populated with relationships derived from the literature. Thus, since Maycock et al. (1991) have quantified the relationship between, on the one hand, experience and age and, on the other hand, risk, it may be feasible to introduce some rules derived from that study into the model. However, what is really required is the confirmation of parameters, conditional relationships and interactions from empirical studies designed to test the hypothesised relationships.

6.6 Developing an Online Model

A further implication of the categories is that if they are to used by a real-time on-board system, then appropriate sensors will be required to generate information about the current conditions, that is, the 'ifs' of the various rules. Some of that information, for example, about driver age and experience could come from a smart driving licence. But most of the required information will need to be observed by the vehicle itself from how that vehicle is being driven. Thus, driver state and appropriate methods for capturing it in real time has been investigated in a host of European projects. However, Karel Brookhuis, one of the prime movers in this research, has recently observed that 'a valid framework for the evaluation of driver impairment is still lacking' (Brookhuis and de Waard, 2003). Steering movements, with an increase in amplitude and a reduction in frequency indicating impairment, are promising but to date a sufficiently reliable algorithm is lacking.

Estimating task demand in real time in order to manage driver workload has been the focus of such projects as COMUNICAR (Amditis et al., 2002) and CEMVOCAS (Bellet et al., 2002). Map-based information on road type and layout can provide basic essential information, for example on the frequency of intersections. The fact that a driving is manoeuvring can be interpreted from vehicle yaw. Traffic density can be provided from radar or image processing. Secondary task demand, as opposed to driving task demand, can be inferred from interaction with entertainment systems, navigation systems and other in-vehicle devices. Usage of the mobile phone by the driver can be identified provided that there is an interface between vehicle and mobile phone.

As regards situation awareness, the results of the HASTE project suggest that it may be feasible to capture situation awareness from vehicle control parameters. HASTE has been examining the impact of distraction from the use of in-vehicle information systems on the driving task, and has identified very different impacts from visual distraction as opposed to cognitive distraction (Carsten, 2004). Visual distraction leads to increased lateral deviation, whereas cognitive distraction leads to an apparent improvement in steering performance accompanied by an increase in gaze concentration to the road straight ahead and loss of general situation awareness. Thus a combination of eye movement cameras and steering sensors may be able to provide sufficient indication of distraction and hence of loss of situation awareness.

Steering behaviour can also potentially be used as an indicator of driving experience. Novice drivers have a generally reactive steering behaviour, whereas experienced drivers have a more feed-forward strategy in which steering adapts to road layout and obstacles (Jamson, 1999).

This leads to another problem that needs to be addressed. Steering behaviour is clearly highly diagnostic, but we cannot use the same indicator, e.g. standard deviation of lateral position, simultaneously to identify both visual distraction and drink-driving. There is a need to investigate steering behaviour at a very microscopic level to create unambiguous indicators. More refined indicators such as steering reversal rate (the number of changes in steering wheel direction per minute with a specific minimum threshold of movement) and steering entropy (Boer, 2001) will be needed.

Finally, there is a need to identify driver intention. Salvucci and Liu (2002) have shown how hard it is to identify a lane change that is about to be performed from steering patterns and/or eye movements. They conclude that there is too much variability in the data to be able to apply such methods reliably. However, there are simpler methods for achieving this, and one that may well be effective as a signal of a lane change is the use of the indicators by the driver. Furthermore, it could be argued that, as in the overtaking case discussed earlier, intention need only be known in a general rather than a precise sense. It may be more important and more useful to know in sufficient time to deter the actual manoeuvre that a driver is highly likely to overtake than to detect the overtaking manoeuvre once it has started and is too late to prevent. Here a system forearmed may mean a driver forewarned.

6.7 Conclusions

There are many driver models that are purely descriptive as opposed to being predictive. Even the motivational models tend to be incomplete, addressing only some of the driver factors that can elevate risk. A new structure has been proposed here for a model that can be both verified and, if confirmed, applied in the long run to monitor in real time the risk associated with the behaviour and performance of the driver and to adjust feedback to the driver and tune the response of driver assistance systems accordingly. It can be argued that, in order to produce a well-designed advanced driver assistance system, particularly a complex multi-functional one, such modelling is not only feasible but maybe even necessary. Otherwise, users may reject such systems because they are not adapted to their needs.

References

Amditis, A., Polychronopoulos, A., Belotti, F. and Montanari, R. (2002). Strategy plan definition for the management of the information flow through an HMI unit inside a car. In *Proceedings of the e-Safety Conference*. Lyon.

Bellet, T., Bruyas, M.P., Tattegrain-Veste, H., Forzy, J.F., Simoes, A., Carvalhais, J., Lockwood, P., Boudy, J., Baligand, B., Damiani, S. and Opitz, M. (2002). "Real-time" analysis of the driving situation in order to manage on-board information. In *Proceedings of the e-Safety Conference*. Lyon.

Brookhuis, K.A. and De Waard, D. (2003). On the assessment of criteria for driver impairment: In search of the golden yardstick for driving performance. In *Proceedings of Driving Assessment 2003, the 2nd International Driving Symposium on Human Factors in Driver Assessment, Training and Vehicle Design*. Park City, Utah.

Boer, E. (2001). Behavioral entropy as a measure of driving performance. In *Proceedings of Driving Assessment 2001, International Driving Symposium on Human Factors in Driver Assessment, Training and Vehicle Design*. Aspen, Colorado.

Burns., P.C., Parkes, A., Burton, S., Smith, R.K. and Burch, D. (2002). How dangerous is driving with a mobile phone? Benchmarking the impairment to alcohol. *TRL Report 547*. TRL, Crowthorne, UK.

Carsten, O. (2004). Implications of the first set of HASTE results on driver distraction. In *Behavioural Research in Road Safety 2004: Fourteenth Seminar* (pp. 100–109). Department for Transport, London.

Department for Transport. (2005). *Road casualties Great Britain 2004*. The Stationery Office, London.

Fuller, R. (1984). A conceptualization of driving behaviour as threat avoidance. *Ergonomics*, 27, 1139–1155.

Fuller, R. (2004). Towards a general theory of driver behaviour. *Accident Analysis and Prevention*, 37, 461–472.

Gibson, J.J. and Crooks, L.E. (1938). A theoretical field-analysis of automobile driving. *American Journal of Psychology*, 51, 453–471.

Grayson, G.B. (1997). Theories and models in traffic psychology – A contrary view. In T. Rothengatter and E. Carbonell Vaya (Eds.). *Traffic and transport psychology: Theory and application*. Pergamon, Amsterdam.

Hollnagel, E., Nåbo, A. and Lau, I.V. (2003). A systemic model for driver-in-control. In *Proceedings of Driving Assessment 2003, the 2nd International Driving Symposium on Human Factors in Driver Assessment, Training and Vehicle Design* (pp. 87–91). Park City, Utah.

Hurst, P.M., Harte, D. and Frith, W.J. (1994). The Grand Rapids dip revisited. *Accident Analysis and Prevention*, 26, 647–654.

Jamson, A.H. (1999). Curve negotiation in the Leeds driving simulator: The role of driver experience. In D. Harris (Ed.). *Engineering psychology and cognitive engineering* (Vol. 3, pp. 351–358). Ashgate, London.

Kidd, E.A. and Laughery, K.R. (1964). A computer model of driving behaviour: The Highway Intersection Situation. Report VI-1843-V-1, Cornell Aeronautical Laboratories, Buffalo, New York.

Maycock, G., Lockwood, C.R. and Lester, J.F. (1991). The accident liability of car drivers. *Research Report 315*. Transport and Road Research Laboratory, Crowthorne, UK.

Michon, J.A. (1985). A critical review of driver behaviour models. In L. Evans and R.G. Schwing (Eds.). *Human behavior and traffic safety* (pp. 485–520). Plenum Press, New York.

McKnight, A.J. and Adams, B.B. (1970). *Driver education task analysis. Vol. I: Task descriptions*. Human Resources Research Organization, Alexandria, Virginia. Final Report, Contract No. FH 11-7336.

McMillen, D.L., Smith, S.M. and Wells-Parker, E. (1989). Brief report: The effects of alcohol, expectancy, and sensation on risk-taking. *Addictive Behaviors*, 14, 477–483.

McRuer, D.T., Allen, R.W., Weir, D.H. and Klein, R.H. (1977). New results in driver steering control models. *Human Factors*, 19, 381–397.

Näätänen, R. and Summala, H. (1974). A model for the role of motivational factors in drivers' decision-making. *Accident Analysis and Prevention*, 6, 243–261.

Ranney, T.A. (1994). Models of driving behaviour: A review of their evolution. *Accident Analysis and Prevention*, 26, 733–750.

Rumar, K. (1985). The role of perceptual and cognitive filters in observed behavior. In L. Evans and R.G. Schwing (Eds.). *Human behavior and traffic safety* (pp. 151–165). Plenum Press, New York.

Rumar, K. (1999). *Transport safety visions, strategies and targets: Beyond 2000*. European Transport Safety Council, Brussels.

Salvucci, D.D. and Liu, A. (2002). The time course of a lane change: Driver control and eye-movement behaviour. *Transportation Research Part F*, 5, 123–132.

Stradling, S.G. and Meadows, M.L. (2000). Highway code and aggressive violations in UK drivers. In *Global Web Conference on Aggressive Driving*. http://www.aggressive.drivers.com/papers/stradling-meadows/stradling-meadows.pdf.

Wilde, G.J.S (1982). The theory of risk homeostasis: Implications for safety and health. *Risk Analysis*, 2, 209–225.

Yu, J. and Williford, W.R. (1993). Alcohol and risk/sensation seeking: Specifying a causal model on high-risk driving. *Journal of Addictive Diseases*, 12(1), 79–96.

III
Learning and Behavioural Adaptation

7
Subject Testing for Evaluation of Driver Information Systems and Driver Assistance Systems – Learning Effects and Methodological Solutions

KLAUS BENGLER

SUMMARY

Nowadays, subject testing represents a well-established methodology to evaluate different properties of driver information systems and driver assistance systems. Among several criteria, learnability is one important system property. User and usage strategies are dependent on the subject's learning state, for example, to switch attendance between driving task and operation of a driver information system. Therefore it is wishful that the user acquires a model of the system, for example learns as quickly as possible. Also, the intended usage of driver assistance systems in given driving situations is influenced by the user's experience. A suitable way to investigate related questions is to conduct a typical learning experiment and to analyse data with the given methodology. In this type of experiment, the familiarity and training state of the subject are set as independent variable. Beside learnablity, other properties of human–machine interaction are to be investigated and evaluated. In this case, however, the learning effectuated by a subject is an important dependent variable or even noise in sense of measurement theory that might cover a given main effect. After some empirical examples, possible solutions will be discussed that help to manage this problem with justifiable expense.

7.1 Introduction

Following the idea of user-centered system design, subject testing is an established and frequently used procedure to evaluate and ensure quality of human–machine interface (HMI) concepts. Appropriate methods are applied in areas of In-vehicle information systems (IVIS)[1] and advanced driver assistance systems (ADAS[2]) (Mayser, 2002). A good overview of different methodologies and of

[1] Also called driver information systems (DIS).
[2] Also called driver assistance systems (DAS).

their interaction with possible product development processes is given in the proceedings of Bundesanstalt für Straßenwesen (2000).

Documents like DIN 66234 Part 8 (DIN66234 1986) and the European Statement of Principles (2000/53/EC 2000) make clear that beneath properties like 'error robustness', 'interruptability' or 'visual demand', learnability of a system is also an important system property. More and more questions are raised concerning the quality of subject testing in the sense of test theory and methodology (Kanis, 2000; Haigney 2001). This paper discusses the conditions under which an independent evaluation of dialogue quality and assistance characteristics can be conducted. An evaluation that accounts for the fact that learnabilty and learning state should not influence the results erroneously.

Frank and Reichelt (2001) also mention that learnability is one criterion that can be tested during the development of an ADAS by expert judgement and experimental testing to ensure high product quality and system acceptance.

In general, *learning* is defined as a 'permanent change of behaviour based on experience' (Hilgard and Bower, 1966) and therefore parameters for the learning process were modelled for given tasks. More specifically, Woods (1999) states that the user is building up heuristics and simplified models to structure the interaction with a given system.

In addition, Reeves (1999) introduces the concept of 'cognitive complexity' as quality for an HMI based on models for cognitive processes. Cognitive complexity describes the property of a system that enhances or prohibits the user's learning process. This process includes elements of perception, model building and categorisation. Following this, Reeves (1999) gives recommendations for system interaction concepts and information presentation to increase the usability of an HMI concept. These include guidelines for a learner-oriented design process that targets interaction concepts that support perception, visualisation, model building, categorisation and problem solving (cf. also Groeger, 1991).

This emphasises that learnability of a system is a predominant feature of an interaction concept besides other properties that contribute to usability and utility of the system. Therefore, in the following, learning experiments as one type of experiment will be distinguished from system evaluations.

A learning experiment typically focuses on questions about acquisition of knowledge on the system and users' mental models. Questionnaires and interviews are used as dependent variables as well as performance measures (e.g. driving performance, user errors). In case of a system evaluation, properties like visual or motoric demand are analysed as well as additional performance measures and user errors – that is observable behaviour (Woods 1999) describes the idea of so-called built in or designed system diseases as one of the most important source for human errors in contrast to the mostly stated human error and give more information on error analysis as a further evaluation method. Thus, in both types of experiments, the analysis is based on similar measurements. If a subject was learning how to operate the system during a system evaluation, the learning process will produce variability and cover the main effect and item of interest of this investigation.

In this context, subjects' learning capabilities and inter-individual differences play a very important part of the learnability of the system. One must not oversee that in most cases experiments and data gathering take place in an automotive environment (vehicle or driving simulator) that is not familiar for the subject. Some examples shall help to get a better understanding of the quality and range of learning effects after some methodological discussions.

7.2 Methodological Issues

In general the in-car usage situation that is the learning context for a given in-car HMI is described with the following model: The driver has to fulfil the primary driving task that can be subdivided in stabilisation, manoeuvring and navigation. While stabilisation includes highly automated activities on the skill level, manoeuvring and navigation afford more rule- and knowledge-based user behaviour. Also these three subtasks and the acquisition of skills, rules and knowledge are subject to learning experiments. But the focus of the given publication is secondary and tertiary tasks include the operation of driver information and driver assistance systems like audio, navigation, HVAC and ACC.

Obviously primary, secondary and tertiary tasks use the same limited motoric, sensory and cognitive resources of the driver. The design of in-car HMI therefore requires that the primary task does not crucially interfere with a secondary or tertiary task. Apparently all these tasks underly learning processes that contribute to increasing driver performance. In the case of the primary task this is pointed out by a decrease in accident risk with an increase of driving experience. The content learnt by the driver is very complex as it includes procedural knowledge, semantic knowledge as well as knowledge on system behaviour and system limits. The systems that construct these learning 'items' range from the traffic system in general over traffic situations, the vehicle in its static and dynamic properties up to devices and functionalities.

To acquire this knowledge, drivers apply strategies that are well known from other domains: especially, rules on the traffic system and basic interaction with the vehicle. Learning strategies are learnt by education and observation and after this refined by training/exercise. Operation of in-car functionalities is, to a high degree, based on the application of transfer of trial-and-error strategies. Manuals might also play a minor role.

Manstetten (2005) emphasises the concept of learnability of driver assistance systems:

- With reference to the project RESPONSE, 'a system is learnable, if accurate assimilation of information by the driver occurs, evidenced in the driver's understanding of system function, system handling and situational limits'.
- A 'self-explanatory' support system is defined as a 'driver assistance system leaving a minimal amount of learning demand to the driver and eliminating learnability issues which can result in safety-critical traffic situations'.

This makes clear that learning processes expand the range of the driver especially by the establishment of highly automatised expert behaviour. Vehicle stabilisation (distance and lane keeping) and the more efficient usage of in-car devices based on usage strategies are an example. An example for such a strategy is to use a given device not in any but a suitable traffic situation or to interrupt the operation and continue afterwards (Sayer et al., 2005).

Learnability is therefore a beneficial system property that is to be tested ('Learnability' DIN 66234/8) like other ergonomic qualities during product development. A problematic fact in this context is that only few models exist, that describe the learning behaviour described in the section above. This fact makes it difficult to plan and conduct learning experiments during system development.

On the other hand, learning is also a potential source of 'noise' in empirical testing to other values describing HMI qualities like visual demand or interruptability. Therefore, learning processes have to be taken into account either as a main effect or as a side effect at the different steps of the evaluation process:

- planning (sample construction, subject selection, procedure, scenarios);
- conduction (training procedure, training criterion, measurements);
- analysis (data qualification, interpretation, explanation).

This is now the point to stress the lack of detailed learning models that could help the experimenter to decide on the above questions.

Especially the model of Rasmussen (1983) is suited and used to describe learning in the context of the driving task.

In relation to the driving task, learning is described as a staged process Rasmussen (1983), however, the transition between skill-based – rule-based – knowledge-based stages are not described very concisely. Therefore, the stages are difficult to handle for planning and experimental procedures. But they can be used post hoc to reduce variability, in most cases, as a covariate.

The learning processes in relation to in-car HMI are mostly modelled using the power law. This shall also help to deal with these effects within experimental procedures. As different system types and usage scenarios might require a very differentiated discussion, mostly the necessary parameters to describe the power law function are missing.

7.3 Experimental Examples

The following section will give examples for learning experiments and show that there is a possibility to describe in-car learning behaviour. Established methods can be used for this purpose. The description and modelling of these specific learning processes could then help to plan and conduct future evaluations of comparable functionalities.

7.3.1 Evaluation of a Multimodal HMI

Strategies to switch between secondary task and driving task are highly dependent on the learning state. Therefore, learning processes are an important factor during the evaluation of driver information systems. This can be seen looking at the evaluation of multimodal HMI demonstrator and error analyses on interaction data (cf. Bengler, 2002).

Within a field test, learning of a multimodal HMI that allowed to operate a navigation system and an in-car phone was investigated. Subjects could change anytime during operation between input modalities (speech vs manual turn/push knob). The study investigates user behaviour as well as driving behaviour in different traffic situations. Specific interest is put on learning process and effects that are correlated with learning.

The questions were as follows:

- Is the user able to operate typical driver information systems multimodally while driving?
- Is it possible to acquire necessary knowledge in appropriate time (i.e. to learn an efficient way of multimodal interaction)?

The study was conducted as a 2 × 2 within-subject design with independent variables *secondary task* (telephone/navigation) and primary *driving task* (simple/complex). The telephone task included to dial an instructed phone number while driving. The navigation task required to enter a destination (city and street) while driving. Subjects had free choice of the input modality (manual, voice). The simple driving condition was driving on a straight one or two/lane road, with right of way and only few traffic lights (the complex section was on narrow curvy urban roads without lane markers including yield/pass situations).

To negotiate the complete test track (12 km) required about 25 min. All subjects (N = 11) had a valid driving license, continuous driving experience and no or only minimal experience with speech recognition systems.

After a very short introduction and a very short training using the speech recognition system, each subject had to go through the test course three times: once without and twice with secondary task operations, following the instructions of the experimenter.

Data during voice dialling at the beginning and at the end of the experiment were used to analyse learning effects.

Driving performance and in-car operations of the subjects were videotaped.

Considering the first question, all subjects safely negotiated the secondary tasks, and compared to other studies, speed was not significantly reduced during secondary task operation.

The videotaped data were analysed following an error taxonomy that differentiates the following:

Timing errors: (user speaks to early):
User speaks to non-active ASR
User speaks while system's speech output

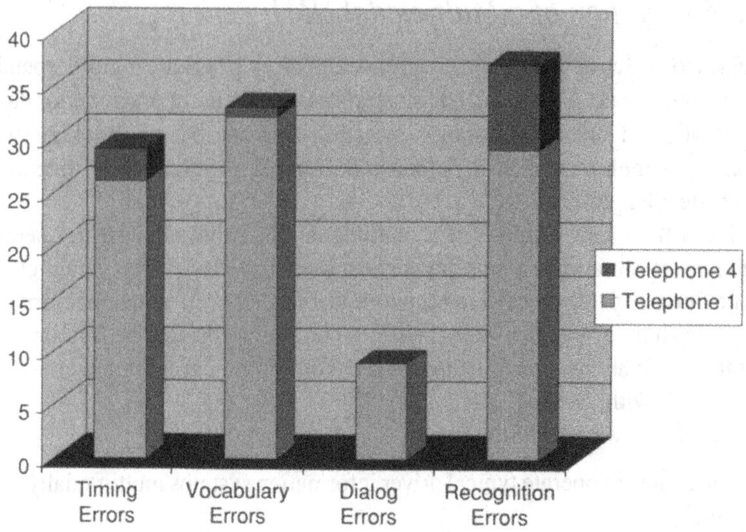

FIGURE 7.1. Frequency of different error types during first and last phases of experiment (all subjects and traffic situations).

Vocabulary errors: Non-valid/available command word used; Irrelevant item used (e.g. thinking aloud, laughing, hesitations 'aahm'); Inadequate command (e.g. 'DELETE' deletes all digits, instead 'ERROR' deletes only last digit).

Dialog errors: User ignores system prompt; User interprets system prompt in the wrong way.

Recognition errors: ASR recognises a correct user input in the wrong way; ASR 'ignores' a correct user input.

The error analysis shows that there is a well-known but remarkably fast learning effect that can be seen in the subjects' error behaviour (cf. Fig. 7.1).

A significant error reduction in all error categories can be seen. This effect is not based on a changed mode of operation of the speech system under test, but rather on a changed usage and speech behavior of subjects. This means that appropriate command words are spoken at the right point of time. Within the dialogue, questions from the system are answered correctly by subjects. The reduction of recognition errors refers to the fact that subjects corrected their level of speech volume. It can be shown that on the one hand the number of successfully finished dialogues increases due to a change of behavior, and on the other hand, a very strong learning effect using speech-operated systems can be observed. In case of a system evaluation using a treatment$_A$ – treatment$_B$ design – comparing a speech-operated HMI$_A$ to a second speech-operated HMI$_B$ – the second treatment under test would profit the subjects' experience with the first treatment. Assuming that both speech-operated systems would 'behave' the same way regarding vocabulary, timing and dialogue.

Analysis of total task times presents a similar result. During the experiment, total task times are remarkably reduced (Table 7.1). A more detailed analysis shows that a reliable estimation of total task time is possible after the second run.

TABLE 7.1. Total task times (mean and standard deviation) telephone and navigation tasks in four subsequent runs during the experiment ($N = 11$).

	Telephone tasks				Navigation tasks			
	1	2	3	4	1	2	3	4
Mean	104.4	40.7	38.9	41.0	56.7	35.6	40.2	36.0
SD	98.06	21.48	18.31	21.00	34.13	7.45	16.23	14.46

7.3.2 Destination Entry While Driving

A second experiment shall outline that learning effects have to be taken into account if dialogue properties like workload or demand that are often based on total task time, total glance time or single glance time are evaluated. For these variables, precise criteria values are formulated for evaluation. The critical question is whether only the 'worst case' of an novice user should be tested or also the efficiency potential of a given dialogue performed by a trained user. Because the goal should be that a dialogue is performed in the beginning, but performance increase is given with increasing user experience and practice.

Destination entry shall serve as a secondary in-car task and an example for a dialogue of long total task time. Within a learning experiment, Jahn (2002) compared total task times of destination entry dialogues, using different navigation systems. Of interest is whether a learning process takes place and which parameters describe the learning process of this specific dialogue in the best way.

Driving on a test track, subjects were instructed to enter a destination consisting of city and street. The system was operated using a turn push button.

- Twelve subjects participated in the experiment (aging 35–55 years) having more than 100,000-km driving experience.
- In sum, 100 destination entries were negotiated at speeds of 40–50 km/h.
- Two route complexities are distinguished.

  Easy: 1.5 km, straight
  Winding: 1.2 km; turning into narrow roads

The resulting data set gives insight into the learning process of this very specific task.

At first, a learning process can be seen with a clear performance improvement between Blocks 1 and 2 for the winding route. In addition, there is a significant influence of route complexity on mean duration for destination entry and the level of the learning process in general (see Fig. 7.2).

Comparison of different subjects shows two further effects. Learning processes of subjects 1 to 5 start at significant different levels and are hardly comparable in their shape. This means that either the mean value computed of this sample would go along with a high standard deviation. This is especially problematic if the data would be used for comparison with another sample using a different system. Or, the experimenter would have to decide to extract subgroups of subjects due to their difference in learning behaviour.

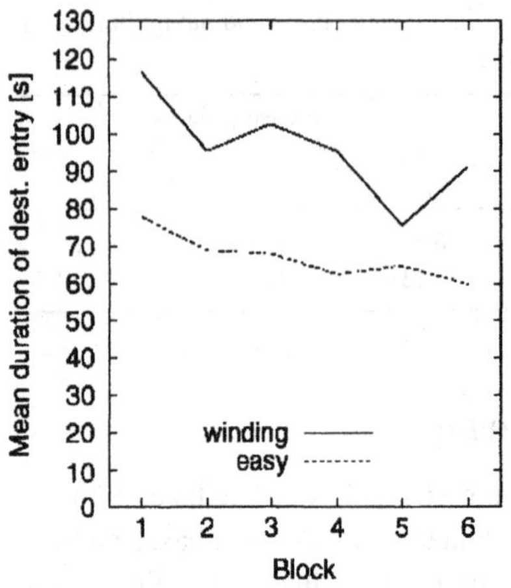

FIGURE 7.2. Mean duration of a destination entry depending on the experimental session and route characteristic. Block 1 = 20 destination entries. Block 2–6 = at times 16 destination entries.

Figures 7.2 and 7.3 show that both effects – learning process and inter-individual differences – result in a high level of variance of the data set. Therefore, they should be treated as error variance in system evaluation experiment.

7.3.3 Evaluation of Driver Assistance Systems

In the area of empirical evaluation of driver assistance systems, learnability and learning effects are an important parameter. Simon and Kopf (2001) emphasise this vividly in the context of automatic cruise control (ACC) systems. The study conducted was a long-term field trial to investigate learning effects. Five subjects who participated used an experimental car equipped with ACC for 3 weeks for their everyday trips. Data show that system experience increases with usage time. But also that subjects dealing with the limits of the ACC system establish different strategies.

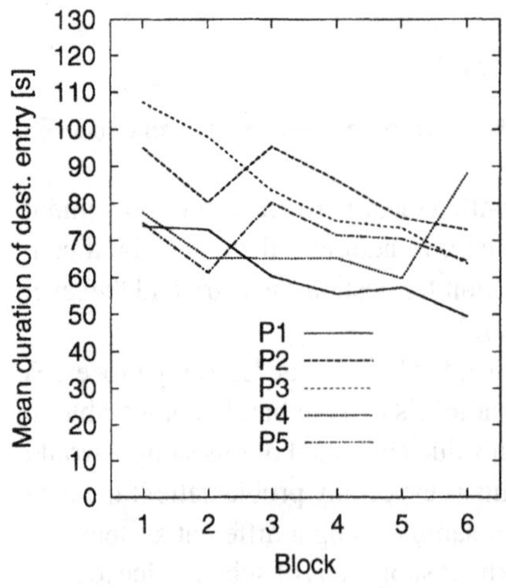

FIGURE 7.3. Mean duration of a destination entry depending on experimental run per subject (P1 to P5). Block 1 = 20 destination entries. Block 2–6 = at times 16 destination entries.

The authors distinguish 'eager testers' and 'careful approachers'. Obviously, different usage strategies again lead to a remarkable variance within this small sample. This variance can be used to describe different learning strategies. But driving performance and other effects – especially at the beginning of the experiment – have to be interpreted by taking account of these individual learning strategies.

An attempt to present a model on skill acquisition of an ACC system is given by Hoedemaeker (1999). She proposes the idea that the adaptation of the ACC mental model results of two processes that operate at different abstraction levels within the mental model. The first process is based on the difference of expected system behaviour provided by the user's mental model of the ACC and the observed system behaviour. Depending on the degree of wrong predictions, the ACC mental model is updated to arrive at a more accurate account of the ACC's operational domain. The second process dealing with the adaptation of the mental model takes place at a higher abstraction level. The intensity of ACC usage then is highly correlated with the degree of perceived inconsistencies between ACC behaviour and user expectation based on his or her mental model. The less inconsistencies the more system usage and vice versa.

A very sophisticated long-term field operational test using an ADAS was conducted by Weinberger (2001). The experiment gathered more information about the learning process for the usage of controls and display and the judgement of take-over situations. Participants used an ACC-equipped car for a period of 4 weeks per person. Data were analysed with respect to the duration of the learning phase. The change in behaviour was investigated using drivers' self-assessment of the length of learning and observed driving behaviour during take-over situations. The results suggest that 2 or 3 weeks are needed to learn the operation of ACC and the assessment of take-over situations for a goal-directed system usage. Interesting is the methodological advice given by the authors that other ACC users might need a different learning time as the participants in the study drove much more than the average driver.

Kostka et al. (2004) recommend the analysis of driver errors by expert observation as a practical empirical method to evaluate workload and distraction but might serve as well as a tool to investigate the learnability of the concept and especially erroneous user expectations on system functionality.

Results from this study and that of Weisse (2002) give the impression that the investigation of learning processes and individual behaviour in the context of driver assistance systems demands considerably more effort than driver information systems.

7.4 Solutions

The discussion of the 'learning problem' and the selected experiments show that on the one hand learning processes and learnability in the in-car domain can be investigated using classical methodologies. Due to this method, the effort is remarkable.

On the other hand it is also true that learning processes can lead to considerable data variablity in evaluation experiments:

- learning and carry-over effects;
- positive or negative transfer in within-subjects designs treatment A, which precedes treatment B in the experiment, will have influence on the variability of values in the second measurement; and
- everyday knowledge and experience will interact with subjects' performance.

Unfortunately, it is not possible to compute or estimate error variance as experience and concise models for these effects are still missing. This procedure might become feasible if the characteristic learning curve was known for a given system. After the citations of learning experiments and related problems, some approaches shall be presented to control learning effects in system evaluations.

Inter-individual differences should be covered most efficiently using a within-subjects design. A systematic distribution of subjects on experimental treatments using a Latin Square can avoid or at least balance positive and negative transfer effects over the whole experimental data set. Using this approach, the resulting number of subjects must not be underestimated (Bortz, 1999).

The most reliable solution of the learning problem is to use highly trained subjects combined with the application of a standardised performance criterion before measurement begins. This approach, however, requires a substantial effort for training and testing. The study of Jahn et al. (2002) gives an impression of the necessary training effort for a destination entry example.

A further possibility is to use so-called 'expert users' as subjects, for example, for conduction of a destination entry study, a sample of experienced users who have everyday experience with the given system, however, in this case also, a performance test should be conducted. But especially for the investigation of novel usage concepts this approach is no alternative.

A general recommendation on the conduction of learning experiments with driver information systems is given by Rauch et al. (2004). They recommend that learning experiments that investigate in-car systems for use while driving should be conducted in a dual-task setting to increase the validity of the method.

7.5 Conclusions

The examples give an impression of learning effects that have to be expected in connection with subject tests evaluating driver information systems and driver assistance systems. It turns out that learning experiments that investigate technologies such as voice recognition and future driver assistance systems would ease the planning and conduction of system evaluation and raise their quality.

In addition, one can state that the investigation of total task time and other performance measures is only reliable and makes sense if learning is finished and subjects are in a stable state.

Suitable models are still missing that would describe learning of driver information systems and driver assistance systems in detail. Therefore, the experimenter has to reduce high variances that are based on learning effects by carefully selecting experimental procedures that do not exceed manageable effort.

References

2000/53/EC (2000). 2000/53/EC: Commission recommendation of 21 December 1999 on safe and efficient in-vehicle information and communication systems: A European statement of principles on human machine interface. *Official Journal of the European Communities L19 43 (25.01.2000)*, 64–68.

Bengler, K., Noszko, Th. and Neuss, R. (2002). Usability of multimodal human–machine-interaction while driving. In *Proceedings of the 9-th World Congress on ITS, CD-Rom, 9th World Congress on Intelligent Transport Systems*, ITS America, October 2002.

Bortz, J. (1999). *Statistik für Sozialwissenschaftler* (5th ed.). Springer-Verlag, Berlin-Heidelberg.

Bundesanstalt für Straßenwesen (2000). Informations- und Assistenzsysteme im Auto benutzergerecht gestalten. Methoden für den Entwicklungsprozeß. Bd. Heft 152. Bergisch Gladbach: Bundesanstalt für Straßenwesen, 2000.

Norm DIN66234 8 8 (1986). Bildschirmarbeitsplätze: Grundsätze der Dialoggestaltung.

Frank, P. and Reichelt, W. (2001). Fahrerassistenzsysteme im Entwicklungsprozess. In Th. Jürgensohn and K.-P. Timpe (Hrsg.) (2001). Kraftfahrzeugführung. Springer, Berlin, Heidelberg, New York, pp. 71–80.

Groeger, J.A. (1991). Learning from learning: Principles for supporting drivers. In *International Symposium on Automotive Technology & Automation (24th: 1991: Florence, Italy)*. Croydon, UK: Automotive Automation, pp. 703–709.

Haigney, D. and Westerman, S.J. (2001). Mobile (cellular) phone use and driving: A critical review of research methodology. *Ergonomics*, 44(2), 132–143.

Hilgard, E.R. and Bower, G.H. (1966). *Theories of learning* (3rd ed.). Appleton-Century-Crofts, New York.

Hoedemaeker, M. (1999). *Driving Behaviour with Adaptative Cruise Control and the Acceptance by Individual Drivers*. Delft University Press, Delf.

Jahn, G., Krems, J.F. and Gelau, C. (2002). Skill-development when interacting with in-vehicle information systems: A training study on the learnability of different MMI concepts. In D. de Waard, K.A. Brookhuis, J. Moraal and A. Toffetti (Eds.). *Human factors in transportation, communication, health, and the workplace*. Shaker Publishing, Maastricht, The Netherlands.

Kanis, H. (2000). Questioning validity in the area of ergonomics/human factors. *Ergonomics*, 43(12), 1947–1965.

Kostka, M., Dahmen-Zimmer, K., Scheufler, I., Piechulla, W. and Zimmer, A. (2004). Fahrfehlerbeobachtung durch Experten. Eine Methode zur Evaluierung von Belastung und Ablenkung des Fahrers. In A.C. Zimmer, K. Lange, et al. (Hrsg.). *Experimentelle Psychologie im Spannungsfeld von Grundlagenforschung und Anwendung. Proceedings 43. Tagung experimentell arbeitender Psychologen (CD-ROM)*. Regensburg.

Manstetten (2005). Evaluating the traffic safety effects of driver assistance systems. *AAET 2005, Automation, Assistance and Embedded Real Time Platforms for Transportation: Airplanes, Vehicles, Trains, 6th Braunschweig Conference*. (Vol. 1). Braunschweig, DE.

Mayser, C. (2002). An advanced concept for integrated driver assistence systems (S.A.N.T.O.S.-Projekt). *Proceedings of the 9-th World Congress on ITS, CD-Rom, 9th World Congress on Intelligent Transport Systems*. ITS America, October 2002.

Rasmussen, J. (1983). Skills, rules and knowledge; signals, signs and symbols and other districtions in human performance models. *IEEE Transactions on Systems, Man and Cybernetics*, SMC 13(3).

Rauch, N., Totzke, I. and Krüger, H.-P. (2004). Kompetenzerwerb für Fahrerinformationssysteme: Bedeutung von Bedienkontext und Menüstruktur. In *VDI-Berichte Nr. 1864. Integrierte Sciherheit und Fahrerassistenzsysteme*. VDI-Verlag, Düsseldorf.

Reeves, W. (1999). *Learner centered design*. Sage Publications, Thousand Oaks, CA.

Sayer, J.R., Devonshire, J.M. and Flannagan, C.A. (2005). The effects of secondary tasks on naturalistic driving performance. *Report No. UMTRI-2005-29*. The University of Michigan Transportation Research Institute, Ann Arbor, Michigan, 48109-2150.

Simon, J. and Kopf, M. (2001). A concept for a learn-adaptive advanced driver assistance system. In *CSAPC 2001, 8th Conference on Cognitive Science Approaches to Process Control, The Cognitive Work Process: Automation and Interaction*, Universität der Bundeswehr, Neubiberg, Germany, 2001, pp. 1–11.

Weinberger, M. (2001). *Der Einfluß von Adaptive Cruise Control Systemen auf das Fahrerverhalten*. Shaker Verlag, Aachen.

Weisse, J., Landau, K., Mayser, C and König, W. (2002). A user-adaptive assistance system. In *Proceedings, ORP2002 – 2nd International Conference on Occupational Risk Prevention*, February 2002.

Woods, D.D. and Cook, R.I. (1999). Perspectives on human error. Hindsight biases and local rationality. In F.T. Durso (Ed.). *Handbook of applied cognition*. John Wiley and Sons, Riverton, NJ.

8
Modelling Driver's Risk Taking Behaviour

WIEL JANSSEN

8.1 Introduction

A realistic estimate of the risk-reducing effects that will be gained by the introduction of advanced driver supports (ADAS) requires knowledge of a number of elements, of which user behaviour is the least understood. This paper focuses on some of the most essential knowledge that is already available, in particular on the mechanisms by which users could possibly change their behaviour once they start using the support.

8.2 Expected Risk Reductions from New Technology on the Road

The safety effects resulting from the introduction of new technology in vehicles or – for that matter – in the road infrastructure follow from the interaction of four components:

1. The so-called 'engineering estimate' or intrinsic effectiveness estimate of a device's expected safety effect, that is, the accident reduction to be expected on the basis of purely statistical or mechanical considerations. For example, the seat belt's effectivity in increasing the probability of surviving a vehicle crash is estimated to be around 40% to 50%. This would then be the initial estimate of the reduction in fatalities if the entire population would use the belt.
2. The degree of penetration or use rate of the device in the relevant population. For devices which rely, for their effectiveness, on the acceptance by the population, there is the issue of selective recruitment, which means that the use rate per se and/or the effect a measure achieves is affected by self-selective processes in the population. The hypothesis is that those who opt for the device differ from those who do not in respects that are essential to measure the effectiveness, the particular assumption being that those who are least inclined to accept a safety device would profit the most from it (e.g. Evans, 1985).

3. Effects on and changes in the user's behaviour that may be brought about by the device, in particular the so-called behavioural adaptation processes.
4. The functional relationships linking behavioural parameters (e.g. driving speed and its variability) to resultant accident probability and severity.

We need to know more on all of these, but this paper focuses on the last two and on behavioural adaptation in particular. From the behavioural point of view, selective recruitment is an almost equally important issue, but it deserves more space than could be devoted here.

8.3 Behaviour When Driving with Supports

A number of behavioural factors are critical to the success of a support system (Janssen, 2001).

8.3.1 The Importance of Plain Old Ergonomics

The first factor is the badly designed in-vehicle (or roadside) supports, which may cause mental over- or under load of drivers, both of which may lead to a decrease in situational awareness and to increased risks. Even recent, on-the-market, systems sometimes suffer from this (Janssen et al., 1999). This should no longer be acceptable, given the extensive knowledge on display and handling characteristics, colour use, lettering, etc., that is contained in ergonomic handbooks.

8.3.2 The Loss of Potentially Useful Skills

When drivers are relieved from executing certain elements of the driving task, they may lose the ability to perform the associated skills. This is the equivalent of certain everyday phenomena, like younger people in Western societies supposedly no longer being able to do even simple additions without the help of a calculator. That skills are lost may not matter at all in some cases and it is certainly not necessary to retain each and every antique skill for some doomsday to come; however, sometimes the skill that is gone could well have been a safety asset in some situations.

8.3.3 Opportunities for New Errors

While advanced supports may take the opportunity away for drivers to make errors, the design and the required maintenance of these systems may themselves constitute new sources of errors. This also needs to be taken into account when estimating net safety effects in, at least, a qualitative sense.

8.3.4 Problematic Transitions

It is generally recognised that the introduction of (partially) automated supports will require a solution for problems associated with the ensuing mix of vehicles that have the support and those that have not. This is the problem of a transition taking place in *time*.

Less attention has been directed to the problems a driver may experience when he or she has to make a transition in *space*, that is, from non-automated to automated parts of a road network and vice versa. In particular, adaptation and take-over effects from the automated environment may play a negative role when getting adjusted to the non-supported environment again.

On a more general level, the driver may actually have to learn dealing with advanced supports. This may require fundamental changes in training curricula, as they presently exist.

8.3.5 Risk and Risk Perception: My Risk and Yours

People accept less risk that is imposed on them by others than when they make the choice themselves. Slightly exaggerating, mountaineers may be more afraid during the flight to the Himalayas than when climbing Everest itself. Thus, extra safety has to be provided whenever drivers feel an automatic device takes the process of determining what is risky out of their hands. This is a somewhat self-defeating process from the point of view of introducing an automated environment.

8.4 Behavioural Adaptation

'Behavioural adaptation' is a summary descriptive term that stands for a number of phenomena that may occur as a consequence of drivers interacting with the newly introduced element in their task environment. The general connotation of the concept is that it is detrimental to the positive effects originally foreseen to result from the new support system. Two forms may be distinguished, direct and higher-order behavioural adaptation.

8.4.1 Direct Changes in Behaviour

It has been established that drivers do indeed show riskier behaviours in several important cases in which risk-attenuating devices were provided. One of these is ABS, which was studied in the famous Munich taxi driver experiment (Aschenbrenner et al., 1994). This study had both a retrospective and a prospective part, and in neither could it be shown that ABS-vehicles were involved in less accidents than standard vehicles. The other case is the one involving seat belts (Janssen, 1994a). Table 8.1 shows the results of an instrumented-vehicle study with subjects

TABLE 8.1. Increase in average driving speed on motorway and in amount of car-following at very short headways, over three consecutive measurements at about 4-month interval in first year of belted driving, compared to previously unbelted driving (baseline).

	1st	2nd	3rd
Increase in driving speed (km/h; baseline: 112.3 km/h)	+ 2.2	+ 2.6	+ 2.8
Increase in occurrence of following headways < 0.5 s (%; baseline: 5.5 %)	+ 0.5	+ 6.3	+ 7.9

who originally were non-wearers of the belt and who became wearers for the purpose of the study. This long-term study could apply an almost ideal experimental design in that it had an alternating own vehicle/instrumented vehicle design; that is, subjects started wearing the belt all the time in their own vehicle and came to the laboratory for measurements in an instrumented vehicle at regular (4-months) intervals after an initial beltless baseline measurement. Their driving performance was compared to a control group of non-wearers who remained so for at least the duration of the study.

While ABS and seat belts are apparently demonstrations of the existence of the phenomenon, it is not yet clear (a) whether this will always happens or what would distinguish cases in which they do from cases in which they do not and (b) whether the compensation is complete and will totally eliminate the safety effect that should follow from the engineering estimate.

To come to terms with these questions, we would need valid and quantitative models of road user decision making. Elementary utility models (O'Neill, 1977; Janssen and Tenkink, 1988) have already paid some services in this respect. In the Janssen and Tenkink model (see Fig. 8.1), the road user is assumed to balance the (dis)utilities of time loss during the trip, plus the possible accident risk, against the utility of being at the destination. From this a choice of optimal speed, and possibly of other driving behaviour parameters, then follows so as to be at the optimum of that balance.

It has been derived, for example, from this type of consideration that a device having an expected effectiveness (i.e. an engineering estimate) ε will not reduce accident risk with that same factor but with a factor that happens to be

$$\hat{\varepsilon} = 1 - (1 - \varepsilon)^{-1/(c+1)}, \tag{1}$$

where c is Nilsson's (Nilsson, 1984) parameter in his speed-risk function, with values between 3 and 7 for different types of accidents. For fatalities, $c = 7$. It is clear that the safety effect to be realised will always be less than the expected effectiveness (see Fig. 8.2). For example, if we take the commonly used value of $\varepsilon = 0.43$ for the seat belt, the estimated effect to be achieved for the fatality rate per km would be in the order of 7% rather than 43% (at 100% use rate).

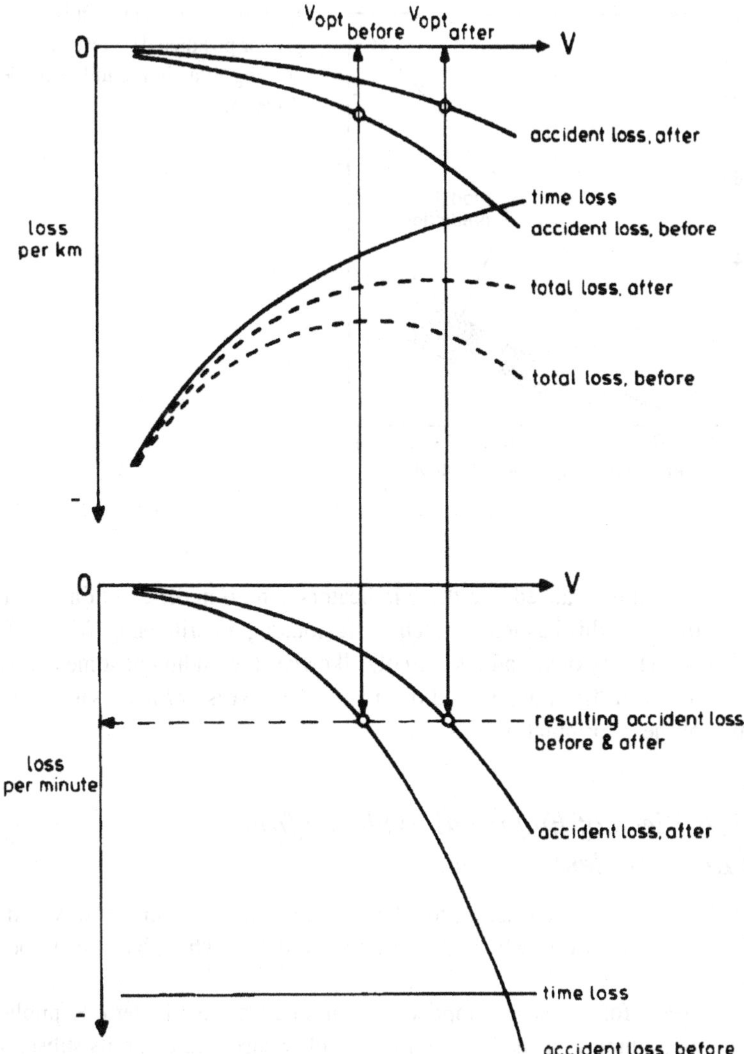

FIGURE 8.1. Utility model (Janssen and Tenkink, 1988) shows how drivers select optimum speed as a function of time (opportunity) losses and accident risk so as to make the resulting total expected loss minimal. It appears to be generally true that whenever accident risk is objectively reduced ('after' situation) the optimum speed that is selected will move towards the higher end of the scale.

8.4.2 A Word of Caution About Working with Risk Measures in Traffic Safety Studies

In the risk sciences, it is good to remind ourselves from time to time what is the 'risk' that we are dealing with. In traffic safety, for example, risk can be expressed per kilometre travelled, per capita/vehicle (per year) or per unit of time spent in

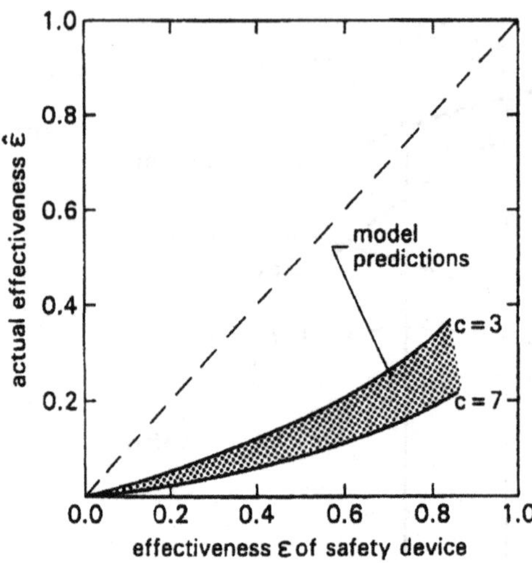

FIGURE 8.2. Expected and actual (i.e. pre- or postdicted) safety benefit, according to a simple utility model of driver behaviour.

traffic. It should be realised that these indicators can go in different directions at the same time and this has led to much confusion, e.g. in criticising Wilde's Risk Homeostasis Theory or variations thereof. Likewise, the finding of some risk level being *not* constant from one period of time to the next is *not* necessarily a valid criticism of these formulations.

8.4.3 A Piece of Empirical Evidence from Seat Belt Accident Statistics

Hardly does one ever have access to all components in the chain. However, there appears to be one case in which almost all is available, which happens to be the safety belt.

The statistics for this case comprise a set of data from the Federal Republic of Germany pertaining to a sudden rise in seat belt wearing rate and its subsequent effect on passenger car driver fatalities (Brühning et al., 1986).

From 1 August 1984, onward German road authorities exerted a strict enforcement of seat belt legislation by setting a fine of 40 Deutschmark ('Verwarnungsgeld') for being apprehended as a non-wearer passenger car driver. Almost overnight, the overall wearing rate in the country rose from 58 to 92%. This makes the German data as close as coming from an ideal 'natural' experiment as possible and it makes it feasible to postdict fatalities after the increase in wearing rates, given the availability of an engineering estimate of the belt's effectiveness in preventing a fatality when a crash happens.

Obviously, the spectacular increase in wearing rate should be reflected in an immediate downward step in passenger car fatalities. As a matter of fact, depending on the engineering estimate used for the seat belt's intrinsic effect the reduction in fatalities should have been between 24% and 31% (that is, the increase in use rate multiplied by the engineering estimate). On the other hand the utility model, on the basis of Equation (1), would have predicted a reduction of between 3% and 4%. The actual reduction was 6.7%. The readers may draw their own conclusions as to which of the two was the best prediction (or rather, postdiction): Janssen, (1994b), has further discussion[1].

8.4.4 Higher-Order Forms of Adaptation

Following are the other forms of adaptation that may occur as the result of having a new support available:

- *The generation of extra mobility (VMT).* For example, navigation systems may not so much reduce excess mileage as generate extra mileage into areas that were formerly avoided. Or entrepreneurs who formerly 'lost' 5% or 6% of the mileage driven by their fleet because drivers selected non-optimal routes to their destination may now plan an extra trip a day because navigation performance has become flawless.
- *Road use by less qualified segments of the driving population.* It is to be expected that some categories of users that did not dare to venture out in traffic, realising their own imperfections, will do so if offered an extra amount of 'built-in' safety.
- *Driving under more difficult conditions.* Similarly, the extra safety offered will tempt road users to move to places they formerly avoided.

All these effects lend themselves to modelling by elementary utility considerations, as discussed earlier.

On the level of aggregate accident statistics, a negative correlation between fatal accident rates and VMT is predicted by utility considerations and has often been observed. For example, a British investigation (Shannon, 1986) showed that for the period from 1973 to 1983, there was a correlation of −0.88 between the annual fatal accident rates (per mile) and VMT on British motorways. Exactly the same value can be calculated from that paper for US Interstate data. Finally, in Japan the death rate per km driven fell on average by a factor of 1.12 per year between 1966 and 1982, while the motorised mileage rose by an average of 1.08 from year to year in that same period. The correlation between these two rates amounted to −0.97. Thus, those years that were marked by relatively large decreases in the death rate per km were also marked by relatively large increases in kilometre per capita.

On a still higher level, many authors have noted that what is good for macro-economy is bad for traffic safety and vice versa and that this is not just because of economy-induced fluctuations in VMT (Joksch, 1984; Partyka, 1984; Wagenaar, 1984; Wilde, 1991). Table 8.2 lists correlations between annual unemployment

[1] In which it is shown that selective recruitment is not an explanation of the less-than expected safety effect in the German data.

TABLE 8.2. Correlation between annual unemployment rates and same-year per capita traffic death rates (from Wilde, 1991).

United States, 1948–1987	−0.68
Sweden, 1962–1987	−0.69
West Germany, 1960–1983	−0.83
Finland, 1965–1983	−0.86
Canada, 1960–1986	−0.86
United Kingdom, 1960–1985	−0.88
The Netherlands, 1968–1986	−0.88

rates and same-year per capita traffic death rates in seven Western countries. Taken together, the data do appear to confirm the basic assumption that safety and utility are related to each other, i.e. safety is a factor in the utility considerations associated with undertaking a trip.

8.5 The Link Between Behaviour and Risk

It would be of great help to the prediction of net safety effects if, given certain engineering estimates, use rates, behavioural changes, etc., the relationships between parameters conventionally used to describe driving behaviour and accident risk are known. This would then permit the translation of effects observed in behavioural studies in simulators and instrumented vehicles into safety effects to be expected in the population. While the issues are still not resolved, progress has indeed been made recently with respect to several important parameters.

8.5.1 Average Speed, Speed Variability and Risk

There presently exist several models that relate average speed and/or speed variability to accident risk. The most pragmatic and useful one is the one by Nilsson (1984), who distinguishes between different types of accident (fatal; killed + seriously injured; material damage). The functions are power functions of average driving speed, with powers ranging from three (material damage only) to seven (fatal). With respect to speed variability and risk functions, useful and ready-to-use expressions have been derived by Salusjärvi (1990).

8.5.2 Lane-Keeping Performance and Risk

The situation is somewhat less clear-cut for lateral performance indicators. It seems that for the time being we have to be satisfied with proxies like TLC and the frequency with which lane exceedances occur.

8.5.3 Car-Following and Risk

In the seminal work of Farber (1993, 1994), a set of car-following data measured in actual traffic was used to assess the impact of a collision-avoidance system that would effectively reduce the following driver's reaction time to a sudden braking action by the preceding vehicle. This can be generalised to calculating the risk attached to a given situation per se. The algorithm has the following steps (Janssen, 2000):

- For a given headway it is calculated whether, for a given range of reaction times, a collision would follow if the preceding vehicle were to brake vehemently, i.e. at full braking power.
- The total probability of a collision is then computed by integration over a log-normal distribution (which has a tail towards the longer reaction times) of driver reaction times.
- The mean and the standard deviation of the distribution are, moreover, adapted to headway itself. This procedure was introduced by Farber so as to indicate that drivers follow more attentively at shorter headways.
- In case of a rear-end collision, the speed difference at the moment of impact is computed. The overall risk of the car-following situation is then computed by multiplying accident probability by the squared speed difference at impact.

Fig. 8.3 illustrates results for a few everyday car-following situations. As has been observed by other authors, there is a 'worst' headway to follow, which is not at the shortest range. This is intuitively clear when it is realised that although the probability of the collision itself happening becomes higher at shorter headways, its severity will be less because at a short headway the speed difference between the two vehicles at the moment of impact will be less.

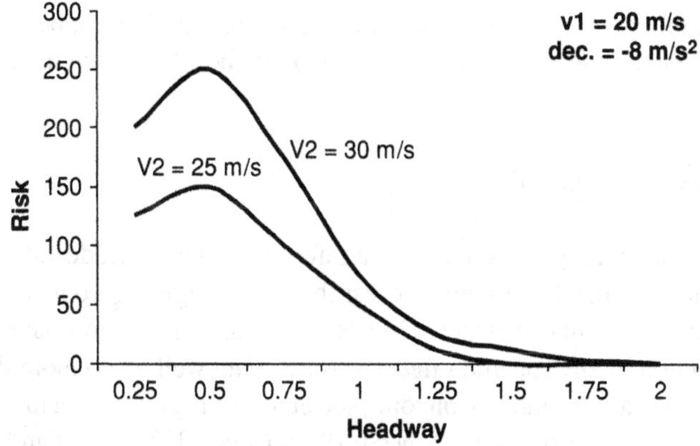

FIGURE 8.3. Rear-end collision risk when following a vehicle at a certain headway that drives at 20 m/s and brakes suddenly (for two speeds of the following vehicle). Risk units are arbitrary, i.e. defined as 100 at one of the configurations.

8.6 Countermeasures Against Behavioural Adaptation

8.6.1 Should There Be Any?

The first thing to be kept in mind when pondering the question of what to do against behavioural adaptation is that there is a good side to it as well. One has better primary performance at a somewhat decreased accident risk. Likewise, the extra mobility that is generated (grandmother gets out on the road again) is an asset, i.e. a social gain.

8.6.2 Incentive Schemes and Their Expected Results

To move the optimal speed that drivers select, according to the utility model, in one direction or the other, costs and benefits of driving in a more or less risky way should be changed. This is the theoretical way out and empirical evidence from lab studies and others indicates that this approach can work. The model then permits to predict what safety effects to expect from these so-called incentive schemes (e.g. Janssen, 1990).

8.7 Conclusions

There is now at least some useful knowledge available on the behavioural effects of driver supports, which permits more than an educated guess on what safety effects will follow from the provision of these supports. This derives both from a more advanced insight into the behaviour itself and from the availability of procedures to translate behavioural effects into safety effects. Thus

- behavioural adaptation is definitely here to stay;
- we better start modelling it, preferably in a quantitative way;
- we should forget our prejudices against econometric principles, because people are not mental cripples, as many (cognitive) psychologists want us to believe.

8.8 An Afterthought

When driver support systems that offer a safety benefit are introduced on the road their benefits will, in all likelihood, be less than what originally could be expected. This is, by itself, an important fact of life. However, as some authors have surmised, the introduction of any specific safety measure could well be no more than a tiny bubble on top of a continuously ongoing societal learning curve of a much broader nature. Although Smeed's ideas (Smeed, 1949, 1968, 1972; Smeed and Jeffcoate, 1970) about the learning process that comes along with a society's increasing level of motorisation are no longer popular today, they may well reflect what is the more significant permanent background against which all incidental safety measures become relatively minor. Modelling that background process is maybe really what we should aim for in the long term.

References

Aschenbrenner, K., Biehl, B. and Wurm, G. (1994). Mehr Verkehrssicherheit durch bessere Technik? Felduntersuchungen zur Risikokompensation am Beispiel des Antiblockiersystems (ABS). Bast, Bergisch Gladbach, Bericht 8323.

Brühning, E., Ernst, R., Glaeser, H.P., Hundhausen, G., Klöckner, J.H. and Pfafferott, I. (1986). Zum Rückgang der Getötetenzahlen im Straßenverkehr—Entwicklung in der Bundesrepublik Deutschland von 1970 bis 1984. *Zeitschrift für Verkehrssicherheit*, 32, 154–163.

Evans, L. (1985). Human behaviour feedback and traffic safety. *Human Factors*, 27, 555–576.

Farber, E. (1993). Using freeway traffic data to estimate the effectiveness of rear-end collision countermeasures. *Proceedings of the Third Annual Meeting of the Intelligent Vehicle Society of America*, Washington, DC.

Farber, E. (1994). Using the Reamacs model to compare the effectiveness of alternative rear end collision warning algorithms. *XIVth International Technical Conference on Enhanced Safety of Vehicles*, München. Paper Nr. 94 S3 O 03.

Janssen, W.H. (1988). Gurtanlegequoten und Kfz-Insassen-Sicherheit: eine Anmerkung zu jüngsten deutschen Erkentnissen. *Zeitschrift für Verkehrssicherheit*, 34, 65–67.

Janssen, W.H. (1990). The economy of risk; or, what do I get for my error? *Ergonomics*, 33, 1333–1348.

Janssen, W.H. (1994a). Seat-belt wearing and driving behaviour: An instrumented-vehicle study. *Accident Analysis and Prevention*, 26, 249–261.

Janssen, W.H. (1994b). Behavioural adaptation to road safety measures: A framework and an illustration. In R.M. Trimpop and G.J.S. Wilde (Eds.). *Challenges to Accident Prevention*. Styx, Groningen, pp. 91–100.

Janssen, W.H. (2000). Functions relating driver behaviour and accident risk. Report TM-00-D004. TNO Human Factors, Soesterberg, The Netherlands.

Janssen, W.H. (2001). Advanced driver supports, driver behaviour, and road safety. *Proceedings of the 8th World Congress on Intelligent Transport Systems*, Sydney. (CD-ROM)

Janssen, W.H., Kaptein, N. and Claessens, M. (1999). Behaviour and safety when driving with in-vehicle devices that provide real-time traffic information. *Proceedings of the 6th World Congress on Intelligent Transport Systems*, Toronto. (CD-ROM)

Janssen, W.H. and Tenkink, E. (1988). Considerations on speed selection and risk homeostasis in driving. *Accident Analysis and Prevention*, 20, 137–143.

Joksch, H.C. (1984). The relation between motor vehicle accidents deaths and economic activity. *Accident Analysis and Prevention*, 16, 207–210.

Nilsson ,G. (1984). Speeds, accident rates and personal injury consequences for different road types. Report number 277VTI, Linköping, Sweden.

O'Neill, B. (1977). A decision-theory model of danger compensation. *Accident Analysis and Prevention*, 9, 157–165.

Partyka, S.C. (1984). Simple models of fatality trends using employment and population data. *Accident Analysis and Prevention*, 16, 211–222.

Salusjärvi, M. (1990). Finland. In G. Nilsson (Ed.). *Speed and Safety: Research Results from the Nordic Countries*. Linköping.

Shannon, H.S. (1986). Road-accident data: Interpreting the British experience with particular reference to the risk homeostasis theory. *Ergonomics*, 29(8), 1005–1015.

Smeed, R.J. (1949). Some statistical aspects of road safety research. *Journal of the Royal Statistical Society*, Series A, Part I, 1–34.

Smeed, R.J. (1968). Variation in the pattern of accident rates in different countries and their causes. *Traffic Engineering and Control*, 364–371.

Smeed, R.J. (1972). The usefulness of formulae in traffic engineering and road safety. *Accident Analysis and Prevention*, 4, 303–312.

Smeed, R.J. and Jeffcoate, G.O. (1970). Effects of changes in motorisation in various countries on the number of road fatalities. *Traffic Engineering and Control*, 150–151.

Wagenaar, A.C. (1984). Effects of macro-economic conditions on the incidence of motor vehicle accidents.*Accident Analysis and Prevention*, 16, 191–205.

Wilde,G.J.S. (1991). Economics and accidents: A commentary. *Journal of Applied Behaviour Analysis*, 24, 81–84.

9 Dealing with Behavioural Adaptations to Advanced Driver Support Systems

FARIDA SAAD

9.1 Introduction

Over the past 15 years major technological advances have been made in the field of automotive technology. Many research and development programmes (in Europe, Japan and the United States) have been devoted to the design and implementation of new driver support systems and information management systems (for route planning, obstacle detection, car-following situations, speed control and so on).

The development of these systems raises crucial issues at a technical level as well as in terms of their consequences on driver activity (for an overview, see, e.g., Michon, 1993; Parkes and Franzen, 1993; Noy, 1997). Some of these issues deal, in particular, with the conditions of use of the systems, their effects on driver behaviour and strategies and their impact on the operation and safety of the traffic system. A major concern is about the 'behavioural adaptations' that may occur in response to the introduction of these systems in the driving task and their impacts on road safety (Smiley, 2000).

These new support systems will mediate drivers' interactions with their driving environment (vehicle, road infrastructure, traffic rules, other road users) by creating new sources of information and/or offering new modes of vehicle control. They will thus alter the conditions in which the driving task is currently performed and can thus be expected to engender changes in drivers' activity. Changes may occur (1) within the very activity of 'supported' drivers (in terms of divided attention between the new internal sources of information and direct monitoring of the road environment, changes of driving strategies, delegation of control to the driving support system and so on); (2) within their interactions with other road users (effect on the behaviour of other road users, 'readability' of assisted drivers' behaviour for other drivers, etc.). It is then important to specify the nature, direction and extent of the changes likely to occur at these different levels, since they will determine the ultimate impact on road safety (Evans, 1985; OCDE, 1990).

The changes associated with the use of these new support systems and their acceptance by drivers will depend (1) on the types of task they are designed to support (navigation, guidance or control tasks; Allen et al., 1971); (2) their functions and the type of mediation they provide ('description' as regards the state of the driving environment, 'prescription' as regards the regulating action the driver has to take; 'intervention' or 'taking over' part of the driving task in the event of deliberate driver delegation or of driver failure).

Up to now, most support systems are dedicated to specific driving tasks. Their competence is by definition limited to the area of that task (or a subset of conditions in which that task is performed, such as conditions of good visibility for instance). The mediation offered is thus only partial, the driver's direct control over the driving environment is always necessary and he remains responsible for the overall management of his journey.

Studying the integration of the systems into the overall driving task and identifying behavioural changes when using them are thus critical aspects that need to be carefully studied and analysed. This entails (Saad and Villame, 1999) the following:

- Taking account of the essential dimensions of the road environment in which that activity takes place (nature of the interactions at work, regulatory, structural and dynamic constraints, etc.). This reference to the context (Suchman, 1987) is particularly important in view of the diversity and variability of the road situations that drivers may encounter during a journey.
- Choosing functional units of analysis making it possible to examine not only the impact on the performance of the specific task to which the support system is dedicated (compliance with safety margins or speed limits, for instance), but also its compatibility with the performance of other driving tasks (overtaking, interacting with other users, etc.).
- Selecting the relevant indicators for revealing the changes likely to take place in driver's activity.

These issues make direct demands on our knowledge of the driving task and of the psychological processes (cognitive and motivational) that govern drivers' activity.

9.2 'Behavioural Adaptation' in Road Safety Research

In road safety research, the term 'behavioural adaptation' is mainly associated with unintended or unexpected behavioural changes that may appear in response to the introduction of a change in the traffic system and which may (more or less) jeopardise road safety. Thus, the emphasis is placed primarily on the negative aspects of the phenomenon.

For example, an OECD expert group (1990) defined *behavioural adaptations* as 'those behaviours which may occur following the introduction of changes to the road–vehicle–user system and which were not intended by the initiators of the change'. On the basis of a review of a large number of empirical studies, the expert group concluded that 'behavioural adaptation does occur, although not consistently'. Behavioural adaptation may be an immediate response to the change introduced in the traffic system or may only appear after a long time. Generally, behavioural adaptation does not eliminate safety gains from measures, but tends to reduce the size of the expected safety effects. Different elements are assumed to influence the occurrence of behavioural adaptation such as the nature and the 'perceptibility' of the changes introduced in the traffic system (changes that directly influence the way the driving task is performed or changes that alter the driver's subjective safety, for instance), the degree of freedom that the change allows drivers (changes that give the driver an opportunity for adapting his behaviour) or the presence of competitive motives (safety versus mobility or productivity motives, for instance).

Although behavioural adaptation is a widely acknowledged phenomenon, the factors likely to explain it and the processes underlying its occurrence are not clearly established. Numerous processes may in fact come into play between the introduction of an 'innovation' in the traffic system and its 'adoption' by drivers, its 'translation' into behaviour (whether 'safe' or 'risky') and its longer term consequences on the operation and safety of the traffic system (Brown, 1985).

These processes should be analysed in greater depth, in particular those influencing the way drivers interact with their driving environment (vehicle, road infrastructure, traffic rules, other road users, etc.). Such analyses should help to formulate hypotheses about the changes in behaviour that may occur, identify the conditions in which a 'negative' compensation for safety might appear and direct thoughts on the means of minimising the extent of such negative changes.

Within the European project adaptive integrated driver–vehicle interface (AIDE[1]), which aims to develop an harmonised interface that integrates all in-vehicle support and information systems, a research activity is devoted specifically to identifying crucial behavioural adaptation issues associated with the use of new support systems and determining the most relevant parameters that can be implemented in models for supporting design and safety assessment processes.

The aim of this paper is to present the main phases of this research activity and the results obtained so far. We begin by outlining the main results of a literature review on 'behavioural adaptation' to new driver support systems (Saad et al., 2004), especially advanced driver assistance systems (ADAS), which intervene more or less directly in the performance of the driving task, such as adaptive cruise control (ACC) or intelligent speed adaptation (ISA). We then describe the ongoing activity associated with the conduct of experimental studies in order to improve our knowledge on short and long term behavioural adaptation (Saad et al., 2005) and to develop models that can act as a reference for the design of an adaptive, integrated in-vehicle interface supporting the multiple tasks drivers have to perform in modern vehicles (Cacciabue and Hollnagel, 2005).

9.3 Behavioural Adaptation to Advanced Driver Support Systems

In most research on 'behavioural adaptation' to new support systems, one of the major concerns is the *identification of 'adverse behavioural consequences'* (Grayson,

[1] AIDE is an EC Funded Project of the 6th Framework Programme – Project N. IST-1-507674-IP

1996) *or negative side effects* associated with their use and which may reduce the expected (safety) benefits of the assistance provided to the driver. In many research studies, it is assumed that driving with systems which take over some elements of the driving task (such as speed and time headway control) may reduce drivers' workload and provide them with an opportunity for devoting less attention to the (primary) driving task. Another concern relates to the drivers' ability to cope with the limitation of support systems and to resume control in 'safety critical' traffic scenarios, either because of drivers' misconceptions about the functioning of the system and over-reliance on the system or as a consequence of drivers' reduced attention to the driving task. In some studies, particular emphasis is placed on the possible deterioration of drivers' interactions with other road users.

These research orientations guide the choice of the driving performance indicators taken into account for assessing behavioural changes (such as driving speed, safety margins in car-following situations and lateral control of the vehicle, performance to a secondary task or subjective assessment of workload). They also guide the choice of the driving situations or scenarios examined ('normal' driving situations, 'safety critical' driving situations such as take-over situations in which the driver has to regain control of his vehicle because of the limitations themselves of the systems or a technical failure).

The second major concern relates to *drivers' opinions and their acceptance* of the assistance provided. In most research studies, perceived usefulness of and satisfaction about the systems are assessed either through standardised questionnaires (see, e.g., Van der Laan et al., 1997) or through drivers' verbal reports and in-depth interviews. In some studies, drivers' acceptance of the support system is more precisely assessed through the very usage of the system (in terms of drivers' decision to engage the systems in various situational contexts and the overall duration of system engagement, for instance).

Several empirical studies have been carried out, focusing mainly on the impact of individual support systems, such as collision avoidance systems (CAS), speed limiters, ISA or ACC systems, either in the 'controlled' context of driving simulator or in the complexity of real driving situations. Most of these studies have been short-term studies and 'the effects (of support systems) on traffic safety and driver behaviour are still uncertain in many respects' (Nilsson et al., 2002), especially their long-term effects. Nevertheless, some critical issues have already been identified. These issues are presented and discussed below.

9.3.1 The Diversity of Behavioural Changes Studied and Observed

The first critical issue encountered when examining the impact of a given support system concerns the *diversity of behavioural changes* studied and observed, as well as the *magnitude and direction* of these changes.

For example, the main behavioural changes observed when studying the behavioural impact of ACC are changes in speed, in the safety margins (time headway or time-to-collision) adopted in various car-following situations (such as steady car-following, catching up a slower vehicle, etc.) and in the lateral control of the vehicle, as well as changes in lane occupancy and in the frequency of lane change manoeuvres. *The results obtained are sometimes contradictory*. For example, in some studies, the average driving speed increased when using ACC (Ward et al., 1995; Hoedemaeker and Brookhuis, 1998), whereas in others this was not the case (Hogema and Janssen, 1996; Stanton et al., 1997; Törnos et al., 2002). The same divergent tendencies were observed when it came to the frequency of unsafe safety margins adopted in car-following situations and the lateral position of the vehicle when using ACC. For example, Fancher et al. (1998) and Saad and Villame (1996) observed that the use of ACC reduced the frequency of short-time headway, Stanton et al. (1997) and Hoedemaeker and Kopf (2001) found no differences between manual and ACC driving and Ward et al. (1995) observed a tendency to drive with shorter time headways with ACC. *Sometimes the results are more convergent*. For example, when driving with ACC on motorways, one observes a general tendency for drivers to spend more time in the left lane (Hoedemaeker and Brookhuis, 1998; Nilsson, 1995; Saad and Villame, 1996; Törnros et al., 2002). In 'safety critical' scenarios, which require the drivers to reduce their speed or to brake, drivers generally react later and/or with reduced safety margins when driving with ACC (Nilsson and Nåbo, 1996; Hoedemaeker and Brookhuis, 1998; Rudin-Brown and Parker, 2004).

The same divergent trends are observed when studying the behavioural impact of ISA. For example, changes in car-following behaviour were observed when driving with ISA and the direction and magnitude of these changes varied from one study to another. In urban areas, Várhelyi and Mäkinen (2001) and Hjälmdahl and Várhelyi (2004) found that, when driving with ISA, the time headway in car-following situations increased, whereas Carsten and Fowkes (2000) observed an increase in close following (time headway less than 1 s). On rural roads, the results are more convergent and suggest that there is an increase in close following.

As regards the workload associated with the use of the systems, the results also reveal some variations. Nilsson (1995) and Ward et al. (1995) found no difference in subjective workload between usual driving and ACC driving, while Hoedemaeker and Brookhuis (1998) and Törnros et al. (2002) found that the subjective workload was lower in ACC driving. Stanton et al. (1997) and Rudin-Brown and Parker (2004) found that a secondary task was better performed when driving with ACC, while this was not the case in the study of Young and Stanton (2002). Some studies suggest that workload depends on the characteristics of the systems studied and/or the task to be carried out (Nilsson and Nåbo, 1996; Hoedemaker and Kopf, 2002; Young and Stanton, 2004). Other studies suggest that workload also depends on drivers' degree of familiarisation with the system (Kopf and Nirschl, 1997).

Thus, part of the observed diversity may be due to the functional characteristics of the systems studied (for ACC, control algorithm, time headway targets available, deceleration level used, etc.) and to the degree of drivers' experience with them.

More generally, the diversity of the results obtained raises questions about the methods used, the type and number of variables selected for assessing the impact of the system, and finally the (implicit or explicit) models governing their choice. When examining the results, attention should be paid to these theoretical and methodological issues. In particular, the context in which the studies have been carried out (driving simulator, closed tracks or real driving situations) should be specified as well as the various scenarios and driving tasks in which the behavioural changes have been identified. The diversity of the results obtained could then be examined and discussed in the light of the characteristics of these various contexts and scenarios. Such analysis is particularly relevant insofar as the situational context plays an important role in the behavioural changes observed when driving with a support system and more generally in drivers' activity (Saad, 2002).

9.3.2 *The Importance of the Situational Context and the Interactive Dimension of Driving*

The second critical issue when studying behavioural changes when driving with ADAS is related to *the diversity and variability of the road situations* that drivers may encounter during a journey.

Many systems are designed to support drivers in maintaining some safety thresholds or ensuring compliance with some formal driving rules (such as maintaining safe time headways in car-following situations or adhering to legal speed limits), independently of the characteristics of road situations (infrastructure and traffic related) and the task planned or being performed, which determine the driver's current regulating actions.

Several studies reveal *the influence of the road infrastructure and traffic conditions* on the driver's decision to use the support systems (decision to engage ACC and ISA systems or a speed limiter; Comte, 2000; Fancher et al., 1998; Saad and Malaterre, 1982) and his willingness to follow the systems' 'advices' (Malaterre and Saad, 1986) as well as on the magnitude of the behavioural changes observed when using them (for instance, increased safety margins before overtaking only in light traffic conditions when receiving time headway feedback – Fairclough et al. (1997) or when driving with an ACC – Saad and Villame (1996).

These results suggest that drivers' use and acceptance of the systems closely depend on the way they integrate (safety) formal rules in their driving and the tolerances they deem admissible, according to the situational context (infrastructure and/or traffic related) and the task planned or carried out ('stable' car-following, pulling in or pulling out manoeuvres, etc.).

Drivers' use and acceptance of the assistance provided also depend on its impact on *the way they usually manage their interactions with other drivers* (on the basis of more or less informal rules or behavioural norms; Saad et al., 1999). In many interaction situations, such as driving in dense or unstable traffic conditions, drivers seem reluctant to use the systems when doing so would require a significant deviation from their usual strategies. For example, in a field trial with a 'Driver Select' ISA (one which the driver can choose to engage or not), Carsten and Fowkes (2000) observed that drivers were prone to disengage the system in areas where speeding was the norm for the surrounding traffic. In such traffic conditions, drivers prefer to be in control of their speed and turn the system off when they feel under pressure from other drivers. Furthermore, drivers are concerned about the way other drivers might interpret their own behaviour (Saad and Malaterre, 1982). Certain aggressive reactions on the part of other drivers (close-following behind, cutting-in manoeuvres, flashing headlights, etc.) are perceived as *negative social feedback* and often lead them to give up the use of the support system.

Finally, some studies have shown that driving with ISA may also influence the driver's interaction with other road-users (at junctions or at pedestrian crossings in urban areas), either negatively (Persson et al., 1993) or positively (Almqvist and Nygard. 1997) in the short term, but with the probability of improvement after longer experience with the system (Hjälmdahl and Várhelyi, 2004).

These studies highlight *the circumstantial requirements* of driving assistance according to the dynamics of various environmental conditions and to the drivers' motives, objectives and intentions in these conditions. They also confirm *the need to adopt a multi-level approach* when assessing behavioural adaptation to new driver support system, which is to say to study possible changes within the activity of 'assisted' drivers as well as within their interactions with other road users.

9.3.3 The Potential Differential Impact of Driver Support Systems

The third critical issue encountered when studying behavioural adaptation is related to the potential differential impact of support systems. The question at issue here is to find out whether some categories of drivers are more prone to adapt their behaviour than others when driving with new support systems (see, e.g., Jonah, 2001).

Because of the great diversity of the driver population (in terms of both car usage and individual characteristics), many driver characteristics may be considered relevant for dealing with this issue, such as drivers' age and gender, their degree of driving experience and practice, their degree of familiarity with new technologies, their attitudes towards driving and traffic rules and so on. Choosing a set of individual characteristics to take into account depends primarily on the objectives of the research study and the processes under investigation.

In some studies, the concept of 'driving style' has received particular attention. It is not in the scope of this short presentation to discuss either the various dimensions characterising 'driving style' or the different behavioural indicators used to render this variable operational. Basically, 'driving style' is described as a relatively stable characteristic of the driver, which typifies his or her personal way of driving, the way he or she chooses to drive (for instance, the level of speed or the safety margins most frequently adopted, the level of attention devoted to the driving task and so on; French et al., 1993). Several studies have taken into account this variable when studying the impact of ACC, whether by design (Hoedemaeker and Brookhuis, 1998, who selected the participants on the basis of two dimensions of the driving style questionnaire established by French et al. op.cit., namely 'speed' and 'focus') or a posteriori, on the basis of the identification of some manifest behaviour patterns (such as the driver's propensity to change lane frequently on the motorway – Saad and Villame, 1996 – or the driver's tendency to drive faster or slower than the surrounding traffic and to adopt short-time headways in car-following situations; Fancher et al., 1998). The results suggest that the various dimensions of 'driving style' taken into account in these studies may play an important role in the use and acceptance of new driver support systems and in the occurrence of behavioural changes when using them. For example, some behavioural changes observed in ACC driving, such as a reduction in the number of lane change manoeuvres and a higher rate of left-lane occupancy, were primarily observed within the group of drivers who usually tend to change lane frequently when driving on motorways, while no significant changes were observed for the other " rather less mobile " group (Saad and Villame, op. cit.). Fancher et al. (1998) also suggest that driving style may account for the differences in the overall use of ACC. A particular finding was that drivers who are described as " hunter/Tailgater " because they drive fast and are inclined to adopt short-time headways used ACC less often than the other groups. Hoedemaeker and Brookhuis (1998) also identified some differences as regards (self-reported) driving styles, depending on the variable taken into consideration. For instance, while all drivers increase their driving speed with ACC, irrespective of their driving style, in a critical scenario (in this case a situation in which the driver has to brake in response to the full stop of a lead vehicle) 'low speed' drivers braked harder when driving with ACC while 'high speed' drivers braked the same as when driving without ACC. Differences in driving styles have also an effect on drivers' acceptance of the assistance provided: 'high speed' drivers are less positive about ACC than 'low speed' drivers.

Other authors (Rudin-Brown and Parker, 2004; Ward et al., 1995) took into account some general personality traits, namely 'Sensation Seeking' and/or 'Locus of Control' (LOC) when studying the effect of ACC on driver behaviour. These personality traits are assumed to influence, more or less directly, the occurrence of behavioural adaptation either through a general propensity for 'risk compensation' (for 'high sensation seekers') or a tendency to manifest over-reliance on automation (for 'external LOC'). Their results suggest that these individual characteristics tend to *amplify some behavioural changes* observed when driving with ACC, such as impaired lane keeping, slower reaction to the activation of the brake lights of a lead vehicle (more pronounced for 'high sensation seekers' than for 'low sensation seekers') or slower reaction to a (simulated) failure of ACC (more pronounced for drivers with external LOC than for drivers with internal LOC). Individual characteristics also influence drivers' subjective assessments of the impact of the system on their driving (for instance, 'high sensation seekers' reported lower level of arousal and effort when driving with ACC than 'low sensation seekers').

The results suggest that individual driver characteristics, such as 'driving style', 'sensation seeking' or 'locus of control', seem to play a role in the overall frequency of ACC usage, in the occurrence and/or the magnitude of some behavioural changes when using it and in the acceptance of the assistance provided. It should be noted, however, that the relationship between general personality traits and other individual characteristics such as 'driving style' are not quite clear and should be more precisely established.

9.3.4 Learning to Drive with New Driver Support Systems

As emphasised in the introduction, most support systems are dedicated to a specific driving task and their function is by definition limited to the area of that task. It is important therefore to determine whether drivers can easily learn the scope and limits of the support system's competence. This issue is of vital importance for support systems that intervene directly in vehicle control.

The learning process is certainly crucial for helping drivers to build an appropriate representation of the assistance provided by the system and for 'calibrating' their trust in it. Appropriate mental models of and confidence in new driver support systems should promote their optimal (and safe) use by drivers (Muir, 1987; Amalberti, 1996). However, to our knowledge, these aspects have received little attention up to now and only a few research studies dealing directly with this issue have been identified. These studies dealt primarily with the learning process of ACC systems.

Some research has covered the learning issue by using questionnaires and interviews to try and gauge the ease with which drivers think they have learned to use ACC and the elements that facilitated the learning process. Nilsson (1995) indicates that the drivers rated the ACC system very easy to learn and to manoeuvre. According to Faucher et al. (1998), ACC was found to be 'rather easy to use, quick to learn, satisfying in its use and more or less straightforward to supervise in the hands of most lay drivers'. An interesting point emphasised in their study is that the kinaesthetic feedback provided by the action of ACC seems to be a primary factor determining the driver's relative ease in learning to use the system.

Other studies have investigated the learning process of ACC systems in greater detail and especially in 'take-over' situations, where the driver has to decide whether to regain control over his speed or not. Kopf and Nirschl (1997) studied the learning of three versions of ACC (differing mainly in the maximum deceleration which could be applied by the system – soft, medium and hard – and the set values for the time headway). The participants performed five 130-km journeys with ACC. The findings indicate that the frequency of drivers' interventions and the (subjective) workload decrease as drivers become more experienced. They also reveal that a different layout of ACC parameters influences driver behaviour with respect to learning and workload. An in-depth analysis of long-term driver interactions with an ACC was carried out by Kopf and Simon (2001). The participants drove with ACC for 2.5 weeks. The results indicate that ACC usage evolves through different stages: a preliminary stage of getting to know the system (learning to operate it); a testing stage (learning the system limits); and a familiarisation stage (learning to use the system appropriately according to the situational context). An analysis of changes over time in drivers intervention in 'take-over' situations suggests that there was a trend towards testing the limits of the system at the beginning, followed by a certain apprehension of the system's capabilities and then a more personalised 'steady use' of the system. Weinberger et al. (2001) conducted a long-term operational field test to obtain more information about the learning process as regards both the usage of controls and display and the judgement applied in take-over situations. The participants used an ACC-equipped car over a period of 4 weeks each. Both drivers' self-assessment of the length of the learning process and drivers' behaviour during 'take-over' situations suggest that 2 or 3 weeks are needed to learn the operation of ACC and the assessment of take-over situations. However, as the participants in the study drove much more than the average driver, the authors suggest that other ACC users might need a longer learning time.

These studies provide some useful insights into the duration of the learning process of ACC and its different stages and into the way in which drivers' interactions with the system change and develop over time. They also suggest that it is important to find *means to accelerate the learning process*, by supporting drivers' predictive activities about the behaviour of ACC and more generally by helping drivers develop appropriate conceptions of the systems' behaviour and limits. More generally, these studies highlight an important dimension to take into account when dealing with behavioural adaptation, the *temporal dimension of behavioural changes*.

It should be noted that the issue of learning to use new support systems is attracting more attention, as indicated by the development of projects such as the INVENT FVM project (Manstetten et al., 2003) or the TAC Safecar project (Regan et al., 2001) and more recently by the research activity planned within the HUMANIST Noe (EC funded network of excellence within the sixth framework programme). The research planned in the AIDE project will also contribute to this effort of understanding learning processes and their impact on short- and long-term behavioural adaptations.

Some interesting concepts have been introduced, such as the concept of 'learnability' and of 'self-explanatory' support systems. With reference to the RESPONSE project (Beker et al., 2001), 'a system is learnable, if accurate assimilation of information by the driver occurs, evidenced in the driver's understanding of system function, system handling and situational limits'. A 'self-explanatory ADAS' is defined as a 'driver assistance system leaving a minimal amount of learning demand to the driver and eliminating learnability issues which can result in safety-critical traffic situations'.

These concepts are interesting inasmuch as they extend the number of criteria for assessing the usability of support systems and emphasise the need to take account of learning issues in the design of driver support systems. These issues are likely to be particularly crucial in the future development of support systems, as the systems will become more complex and integrate multiple driver support and information functions.

9.4 Behavioural Adaptation in the AIDE Project

As emphasised in the Introduction, most studies of behavioural adaptation have been short-term studies and the effects of longer practice and experience with the system are unknown. Furthermore, these studies have mainly dealt with the use of a single support system. Studying long-term behavioural adaptations and developing an integrated management of driver support remains a challenge for research.

This issue is one of the major goals of the AIDE project. In particular, AIDE aims at generating knowledge and methodologies and developing human–machine interface technologies for safe and efficient integration into the driving environment of ADAS and in-vehicle information systems (IVIS), as well as nomad devices (such as 'personal digital assistants' – PDA – or 'communicators').

Within the AIDE project, a specific research activity is dedicated to deepening the analysis of short- and long-term behavioural adaptation associated with the use of various support systems (Saad et al., 2005) and to determining the most relevant parameters that can be implemented in models for supporting design and safety assessment processes (Cacciabue and Hollnagel, 2005).

The planning of the research activity with respect to the issue of behavioural adaptation deals firstly with the problem of the *circumstantial* and *temporal* management of the assistance provided by various systems in the driving process. The systems studied are ADAS dedicated to the main safety critical driving tasks, that is, time-headway, speed and lateral control tasks. The systems varied according to their modes of action (warning or direct intervention) and their degree of adaptability to the situational context or to the drivers' characteristics. Furthermore, the planned studies provide an opportunity for examining the effects of combining several ADAS during the driving process.

With respect to the *circumstantial* conditions that affect processes of behavioural change, the following aspects are studied:

- The nature and extent of behavioural changes associated with the use of various driver support systems;
- The conditions in which these changes take place;
- The 'reasons' why these changes occur; and
- The characteristics of the drivers more likely to present these behavioural changes.

This entails in particular (1) gauging the occurrence, nature and magnitude of the behavioural changes as a function of the type of support system being studied (informative, prescriptive or intervening system); (2) then examining to what extent these changes are observed in relation to analogous driving situations or tasks and/or in relation to drivers' common characteristics.

With respect to the *temporal* factors affecting behavioural adaptation, two main phases are considered, namely:

- *Learning and appropriation phase*. During this phase, drivers discover the systems, learn how they operate, identify the precise limits of their competence and delimit their domains of utility. This learning phase is assumed to be crucial for drivers to build an appropriate model of the operation of the systems and for 'calibrating' their trust in them. It is also assumed that the learning process is oriented by the way the systems are presented to the driver (instruction for use in the manuals, for instance) as well as by the information and feedbacks they received on-line when interacting with them.
- *Integration phase*. It is assumed that, through experience gained with the systems in various driving situations, the drivers are able to assess whether or not, how and in which situational context, it is possible to integrate them in the management of the overall driving task.

This involves examining whether, when and how behaviour associated with the use of support systems changes with training and experience. It has to be pointed out that, because of the scarcity of research carried out into the learning process and the long-term effects, it is hard to determine the temporal span of the different phases distinguished above. Different support systems will probably require different learning and integration times. The research planned in the AIDE project has been developed in such a way as to optimise the opportunities for identifying the main 'stabilisation phases' of the learning and integration process for different support systems.

This research activity will lead to the identification of the relevant variables to be used to assess behavioural adaptation effects. The correlation between these variables and adequate taxonomies and classification of road situations and driving tasks (scenarios of dynamic situation) will be devised to associate the variables with realistic conditions. On this basis, it will be possible to develop a model of driver behaviour that can act as reference for the design of an adaptive-integrated in vehicle interface supporting the multiple tasks of drivers in modern vehicles (Cacciabue and Hollnagel, 2005).

References

Allen, T., Lunenfeld, H. and Alexander, G. (1971). Driver information needs. *Highway Research Record*, 366, 102–115.

Almqvist, S. and Nygard, M. (1997). Dynamic speed adaptation: A field trial with automatic speed adaptation in an urban area. *Bulletin 154*. Lund Institute of Technology, Department of Traffic Planning and Engineering, University of Lund, Sweden.

Amalberti, R. (1996). *La conduite des systèmes à risques*. Presses Universitaires de France, Paris.

Becker, S., Johanning, T., Feldges, J. and Kopf, M. (2001). *RESPONSE. The integrated approach of user, system, and legal perspective.* Final report on recommendations for testing and market introduction of ADAS. Commission of the European Communities, DG XIII, Project TR4022, Deliverable No. D2.2.

Brown, I.D. (1985). Concepts and definitions in road safety. In M.B. Biecheler, C. Lacombe and M. Mulhrad (Eds.). Evaluation 85. *Proceedings of the International Meeting on the Evaluation of Local Traffic Safety Measures*. Paris, France, pp. 413–422.

Cacciabue, P.C. and Hollnagel, E. (2005). Mental model of drivers: A review of criteria, variables, and parameters. In L. Macchi, C. Re and P.C. Cacciabue (Eds.). Modelling driver behaviour in automotive environments. *Proceedings of HUMANIST Workshop*. Ispra, Italy, pp. 185–196.

Carsten, O. and Fowkes, M. (2000). External vehicle speed control. *Executive summary of project results*. University of Leeds, Leeds, UK.

Comte, S. (2000). New systems: New behaviour? *Transport Research, Part F*, 3, 95–111.

Evans, L. (1985). Human behavior feedback and traffic safety. *Human Factors*, 27(5), 555–576.

Fairclough, S.H., May, A.J. and Carter, C. (1997). The effect of time headway feedback on following behaviour. *Accident Analysis and Prevention*, 29(3), 387–397.

Fancher, F., Ervin, R., Sayer, J., Hagan, M., Bogard, S., Bareket, Z., Mefford, M. and Haugen, J. (1998). *Intelligent cruise control field operation test*. Final Report. NHTSA Report No. DOT HS 808849.

French, D.J., West, R.J., Elander, J. and Wilding, J.M. (1993). Decision-making, driving style, and self reported involvement in road traffic accidents. *Ergonomics*, 36(6), 627–644.

Grayson, G.B. (1996). Behavioural adaptation: A review of the literature. *TRL Report 254*, Transport Research Laboratory, Crowthorne, England.

Hjälmdahl, M. and Varhelyi, A. (2004). Effects of an active accelerator pedal on driver behaviour and traffic safety after long-term use in urban areas. *Accident Analysis and Prevention*, 36, 729–737.

Hoedemaeker, M. and Brookhuis, K. (1998). Behavioural adaptation to driving with an adaptive cruise control (ACC). *Transport Research, Part F*, 1, 95–106.

Hoedemaeker, M and Kopf, M. (2001). Visual sampling behaviour when driving with adaptive cruise control. In *Proceedings of the 9th International Conference on Vision in Vehicles*. Australia.

Hogema, J.H. and Janssen, W.H. (1996). *Effects of intelligent cruise control on driving behaviour: A simulator study*. TNO report TM-96-C012. TNO Human Factors Research Institute, Soesterberg, The Netherlands.

Jonah, B.A., Thiessen, R. and Au-Yeung, E. (2001). Sensation-seeking, risky driving and behavioral adaptation. *Accident Analysis and Prevention*, 33, 679–684.

Kopf, M. and Nirschl, G. (1997). Driver–vehicle interaction while driving with ACC in borderline situations. In *Proceedings of the 4th World Congress on Intelligent Transport Systems*. Berlin, Germany.

Kopf, M. and Simon, J. (2001). A concept for a learn-adaptive advanced driver assistance system. In *Proceedings of the Conference on Cognitive Science Approaches 2001*. Neubiberg.

Malaterre, G. and Saad, F. (1986). Les aides à la conduite: définitions et évaluation. Exemple du radar anti-collision. *Le Travail Humain*, 49(4), 333–346.

Manstetten, D., Krautter, W., Engeln, A., Zahn, P., Simon, J., Kuhn, F., Frank, P., Junge, M., Lehrach, K. and Buld, S. (2003). Learnability of driver assistance systems – Invent FVM- driver behavior and human machine interaction. In *Proceedings of the 10th World Congress on Intelligent Transport systems*. Madrid, Spain.

Michon, J.A. (1993). *Generic intelligent driver support, a comprehensive report on GIDS.* Taylor and Francis, London.

Muir, B.M. (1987). Trust between humans and machines, and the design of decision aids. *International Journal of Aviation Psychology*, 8, 47–63.

Nilsson, L. (1995). Safety effects of adaptive cruise controls in critical traffic situations. In *Proceedings of the 2nd World Congress on Intelligent Transport Systems.* Yokohama, Japan, pp. 1254–1259.

Nilsson, L., Harms, L. and Peters, B. (2002). The effect of road transport telematics. In P Barjonnet (Ed.). *Traffic psychology today.* Kluwer Academic Publishers, Boston, pp. 265–285.

Noy, I. (1997). *Ergonomics and safety of intelligent driver interfaces.* Lawrence Erlbaum Associates, Mahwah.

OECD (1990). *Behavioural adaptations to changes in the road transport system.* Organization for Economic Co-operation and Development, Paris.

Parkes, A.M. and Franzen, S.F. (1993). *Driving future vehicles.* Taylor and Francis, London.

Regan, M.A., Mitsopoulos, E., Tomasevic, N., Healy, D., Connelly, K. and Williams, L. (2001). Behavioural adaptation to in-car ITS technologies: Update on the Australian TAC safecar project. In *Proceedings of the 8th World Congress on Intelligent Transport Systems.* Sydney, Australia.

Persson, H., Towliat, M., Almqvist, S., Risser, R. and Magdeburg (1993). Speed limiters for cars. In *A field study of driving speeds, driver behaviour, traffic conflicts and comments drivers in town and city traffic.* Report of Department of Traffic Planning and Engineering, University of Lund, Sweden.

Rudin-Brown, C.M. and Parker, H.A. (2004). Behavioural adaptation to adaptive cruise control (ACC): Implications for preventive strategies. *Transport Research, Part F*, 7, 59–76.

Saad, F. and Malaterre, G. (1982). Régulation de la vitesse: aide au contrôle de la vitesse. *Synthèse.* Rapport ONSER.

Saad, F. and Villame, T. (1996). Assessing new driving support systems – Contribution of an analysis of drivers' activity in real situations. In *Proceedings of the Third Annual World Congress on Intelligent Transport Systems.* Orlando, USA.

Saad, F. and Villame, T. (1999). Intégration d'un nouveau système d'assistance dans l'activité des conducteurs d'automobile. In J.-G. Ganascia (Ed.). *Sécurité et cognition. Editions Hermes.* Paris, pp. 105–114.

Saad, F., Mundutéguy, C. and Darses, F. (1999). Managing interactions between car drivers: An essential dimension of reliable driving. In *Proceedings of Seventh European Conference on Cognitive Science Approaches to Process Control (CSAPC'99).* Villeneuve d'Ascq, France. Presses Universitaires de Valenciennes, pp. 99–104.

Saad, F. (2002). Ergonomics of the driver's interface with the road environment – The contribution of psychological research. In R. Fuller, and J.A. Santos, (Eds.). *Human factors for highway engineers.* Pergamon, Oxford, pp. 23–41.

Saad, F., Hjälmdahl, M., Cañas, J., Alonso, M., Garayo, P., Macchi, L., Nathan, F., Ojeda, L., Papakostopoulos, V., Panou, M. and Bekiaris, A. (2004). *Literature review – Analysis of behavioural changes induced by ADAS and IVIS.* AIDE Project, Deliverable D1_2_1.

Saad, F., Bekiaris, A., Brouwer, R., Carsten, O., Hjälmdahl, Hoedemaker, M., Ojeda, L., Papakostopoulos, V., Nathan, F. and Vezier, B.(2005). *General experimental plan for short and long term behavioural assessment.* AIDE project IST-1–507674-IP, Deliverable D1_2_2.

Smiley, A. (2000). Behavioural adaptation, safety and intelligent transportation systems. *Transport Research Record*, 1724, 47–51.

Stanton, N.A., Young, M. and McCaulder, B. (1997). Drive-by-wire: The case of driver workload and reclaiming control with adaptive cruise control. *Safety Science*, 27(2/3), 149–159.

Suchman, L.A. (1987). Plans and situated actions. *The problem of human–machine communication*. Cambridge University Press, Cambridge.

Törnros, J., Nilsson, L., Östlund, J. and Kircher, A. (2002). Effects of ACC on driver behaviour, workload and acceptance in relation to minimum time headway. In *Proceedings of the 9th World Congress on Intelligent Transport Systems*. Chicago, IL, USA.

Van der Laan, J.D., Heino, A. and De Waard, D. (1997). A simple procedure for the assessment of acceptance of advanced transport telematics. *Transport Research, Part C*, 5(1), 1–10.

Várhelyi, A. and Mäkinen, T. (2001). The effects of in-car speed limiters: Field studies. *Transport Research, Part C*, 9(3), 191–211.

Ward, N.J., Fairclough, S. and Humphreys, M. (1995). The effect of task automatisation in the automotive context: A field study of an autonomous intelligent cruise control system. In D.J. Garland and M.R. Endsley (Eds.). *Experimental analysis and measurements of situational awareness*. Embry-Riddle Aeronautical University Press, Daytona Beach, pp. 369–374.

Weinberger, M., Winner, H. and Bubb, H. (2001). Adaptive cruise control field operational test – The learning phase. *JSAE Review*, 22, 487–494.

Young, M. and Stanton, N.A. (1997). Automotive automation: Investigating the impact on drivers' mental workload. *International Journal of Cognitive Ergonomics*, 1, 325–336.

Young, M.S. and Stanton, N.A. (2004). Taking the load off: Investigations of how adaptive cruise control affects mental workload. *Ergonomics*, 47(9), 1014–1035.

IV
Modelling Motivation and Psychological Mechanisms

10
Motivational Determinants of Control in the Driving Task

RAY FULLER

10.1 Introduction

Road transport is mainly about moving people and goods in motorised vehicles. Since the introduction of such vehicles in the nineteenth century, people have had the task of controlling them, although developments in technology today are moving rapidly towards the possibility of displacing the human element. For the time being, however, a human driver is in control and is faced at each moment on a journey with two fundamental choices, the direction in which to steer the vehicle (i.e., path choice) and the speed at which to move. In trying to understand how drivers make these choices, this paper will focus primarily on the choice of speed. Choice of speed is not only a much less constrained choice than choice of path (except in congested traffic) but it is choice of an *inappropriate* speed which contributes significantly to a very large proportion of collisions and road run-offs. As has frequently been written and perhaps all too frequently forgotten, driving is a self-paced task and it is the freedom of this self-pacing that underlies so much of what can go wrong. Despite the focus on speed choice here, however, choice of path or direction is not entirely neglected: The emerging understanding of the fundamental determinant of speed choice will be seen to apply equally well to choice of direction.

10.2 Understanding Speed Choice

10.2.1 Behaviour Analysis

So how might we begin to understand drivers' choices about speed? One explanatory framework that is potentially useful as a starting point is that of behaviour analysis and the fundamental processes of operant conditioning. In its simplest form, this theoretical approach eschews consideration of what might be going on in the driver's head (except, perhaps, observable parallel processes of neural activity) and confines itself to describing systematic relationships amongst observable events. The basic paradigm of this approach is represented by a three-term contingency of stimulus condition (or more specifically, discriminative stimulus), the behaviour of interest and the consequences of the behaviour.

Under particular stimulus conditions, behaviour that is followed by rewarding consequences becomes reinforced or strengthened relative to alternative behaviours which could occur under those conditions. Thus, in a particular road environment (stimulus condition), the speed 'choice' (behaviour) that is followed by rewarding consequences (e.g., maintenance of control of vehicle while continuing to attain travel goals) becomes strengthened relative to other speed 'choices'. Over time, particular stimulus conditions (discriminative stimuli) come to signal this behaviour–consequences relationship. These contingencies can then be described as an implicit internalised rule which tells the driver what to do under particular conditions (e.g., 'if it's raining, drive more slowly'). Through this process, particular speed 'choices' are gradually learned, initially through a kind of 'trial-and-error' stage (in which the error might be experienced as unpleasantly high *g* forces, the beginnings of a skid, a near miss or even a complete loss of control). Eventually particular speeds for particular conditions become established, habitual behaviours. Through the further process of stimulus generalisation, what is learned in one specific context, such as a speed that is rewarding on a bend of a particular radius, transfers to other similar contexts, without the need for additional trial-and-error learning and conditioning.

This way of thinking about drivers' speed 'choices' was earlier articulated by the author in the threat-avoidance model (Fuller, 1984), which focused on the rewarding consequence of the avoidance of collision. This emphasis was preferred for two reasons. First, there is the inescapable observation that as soon as a driver sets the vehicle in motion the probability of collision is one – unless, of course, frequent actions are taken to avoid this outcome. Thus driving may be considered to be, in the main, an avoidance task. The second reason was that there was a reasonably extensive empirical literature on the conditions under which avoidance responses might be delayed and it was possible in principle to translate the extent of delay of an avoidance response into a level of statistical risk of collision. Thus the opportunity presented itself to build on previous work on avoidance learning in various contexts (admittedly mainly undertaken with species other than humans) in attempting to understand drivers' speed behaviour. However, this approach suffered from its very emphasis, namely avoidance learning, and ignored motivation to make progress. This shortcoming was subsequently dealt with by recasting the analysis within the broader framework of instrumental learning which encompassed both types of rewarding consequence: Avoidance of threat and making progress (see Fuller, 1991a, 1991b).

In parallel with this development and to a large extent converging with it, was the seminal work of Näätänen and Summala (1976), subsequently developed by Summala (1986, 1997) and which is sometimes referred to as the zero-risk model. Summala argues that for most situations drivers have learned what they should or should not do to avoid a certain or almost certain collision. Driver behaviour, including speed choice, is determined by the maintenance of safety margins. These are learned through experience and so most of driving becomes a 'habitual activity which is based on largely automatised control of safety margins in partial tasks' (Summala, 1986, p. 10). Thus this model may be seen to be firmly situated in the well-established instrumental learning paradigm, as described above. The model further argues that what undermines the maintenance of safety margins, however, are motivating conditions which push drivers to higher speeds, insensitivity to low probability events on the roadway and desensitisation to potential threats because these are not realised.

Although driver behaviour research which makes explicit use of a behaviour analysis paradigm is not frequently published, there are some notable exceptions (see, e.g., the work of Geller, 1998; Ludvig and Geller, 2000; Reinhardt-Rutland, 2001; Hutton et al., 2001; Harrison, 2005). Furthermore, it is rather difficult to escape the paradigm if one wishes to understand from a psychological perspective the effects of enforcement on driver behaviour, including effects on speed choice. The implementation of enforcement in relation to traffic regulations, such as a speed limit, changes the consequences of not complying with the regulations by making the consequences more punishing. Regulation-compliant behaviour is thus strengthened to avoid the additional punishment (Fuller and Farrell, 2001). The effectiveness of this strategy when implemented with sufficient intensity is testament to the effectiveness of manipulating consequences to achieve changes in behaviour (Mäkinen et al., 1999).

There is clear merit in the parsimony of the conceptual framework of behaviour analysis and it successfully avoids reliance on hypothetical constructs (see MacCorquodale and Meehl, 1948). Nevertheless, using the driver's conditioning history of learned relations amongst discriminative stimuli, responses and consequences to explain the driver's choice of speed are not without serious problems. This strict behavioural approach is vulnerable to the somewhat implausible requirement that drivers learn through a prolonged conditioning process how to respond safely to what is virtually an infinite number of road and traffic scenarios. There is a huge burden on the process of learning to explain sustained mobility at a particular speed while avoiding collision. There is no question that experience contributes significantly to the development of driver competence but, as has been argued before (Fuller, 2002), the learning of contingencies in the road and traffic system is challenged by a low frequency of opportunities for learning about infrequent hazards and by uncertain relationships amongst the events being experienced. Ranney (1994) has also criticised the behaviour-analytic approach for its theoretical difficulty in handling embedded contingencies. As Michon has so succinctly put it (Michon, 1989), there is no place in the model for 'meanwhile'.

10.2.2 The Theory of Planned Behaviour

The cognitive revolution beginning in the early 1960s created a new climate for the study of internal mental processes as causes of overt behaviour, expressed in its simplest form as 'what we think determines what we do' (Bem and de Jong, 2006). An example of this kind of approach is the theory of planned behaviour (Ajzen, 1991). Although it is not usually explicitly recognised, this theory forms a clear link with the behavioural approach discussed above, because its implicit fundamental feature is an internalisation of the behavioural paradigm as a set of beliefs about each specific behaviour that might be emitted.

In the theory of planned behaviour (TPB), any specific behaviour is determined by intention. This term does *not* appear to mean intention in the conventional sense (i.e., a conscious representation of a plan or purpose) but rather is assumed 'to capture the motivational factors that influence a behaviour; they (intentions) are indications of how hard people are willing to try, of how much effort they are planning to exert, in order to perform the behavior' (Ajzen, 1991, p. 181). Thus the stronger the intention, the more likely the behaviour (assuming it is under volitional control). Intention is in turn determined by three other constructs or variables, respectively labelled 'attitude toward the behaviour', 'subjective norm' and 'perceived behavioural control' (see Fig. 10.1).

The variable 'attitude toward the behaviour' is influenced by beliefs which link the behaviour to certain outcomes or some other attribute such as the cost incurred in performing the behaviour (both are types of consequence). Thus beliefs about behaviours internalise consequences as important determinants of what behaviour is learned: 'We learn to favour behaviours we believe have largely desirable consequences and we form unfavourable attitudes toward behaviours we associate with mostly undesirable consequences (op. cit. p. 191).'

The variable 'subjective norm' represents a specific kind of social consequence, expressed as perceived social pressure to perform or not to perform the behaviour in question. This social pressure is determined by the degree of approval or disapproval (i.e., rewarding or punishing social consequences) of the behaviour by important referent individuals or groups.

Finally in Ajzen's theory, 'perceived behavioural control' is based on beliefs about the availability of opportunities and resources for performing the behaviour of interest. This aspect of the belief structure in the theory may be regarded as an internal representation of the discriminative stimulus which, as described earlier, plays a key role in behaviour analysis – specifying the conditions which signal the behaviour-consequences contingency. Interestingly in behaviour analysis it is argued that over time a discriminative stimulus can come to exert direct control over behaviour, the concept of stimulus control. In the same way, this notion is reflected in TPB by the assertion that there can be a direct determining link between 'perceived behavioural control' and the behaviour itself (see Fig. 10.1).

So the step in the direction of a cognitive explanation characterised by TPB essentially provides for a mental representation of the contingencies of the behaviour analysis paradigm, but with an added emphasis on social consequences of behaviour. How does it fare? According to Ajzen (1991), the theory is designed to predict human behaviour in specific contexts. If the theory successfully includes all of the determinants of behaviour, then all variance in behavioural outcome should be predicted, except for any residual arising out of measurement error. Each individual behaviour should have associated with it a particular pattern showing the relative contribution of each variable in the theory in the determination of that particular behaviour and it may be noted that in the individual case it is not

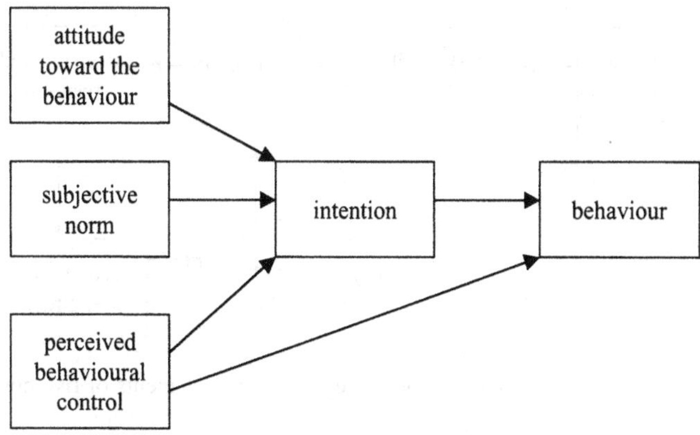

FIGURE 10.1. A simplified representation of the constructs of the theory of planned behaviour (arrows identify potential determining relationships).

necessary that all variables should have an equal or indeed any influence. In a relatively recent meta-analysis performed by Armitage and Connor (2001), it was found that the TPB model accounted for only about 27% of the variance in actual behaviour. Furthermore, if reinforcement history is included as an additional predictor, operationalised as frequency of the behaviour in the past, the increase in explained variance can be anything from 5% to 32% (Ajzen, 1991). Thus, although one published study has demonstrated that the TPB can provide some account of actual speeding behaviour (Elliott et al., 2003), the outlook for the theory in this respect does not look very promising. Perhaps its real strength for the moment is in its potential for separately identifying key beliefs which are strongly related to a particular behaviour, beliefs which might then provide the focus for interventions to change that behaviour.

10.2.3 Risk Homeostasis Theory

An alternative cognition-situated solution to the question of what determines a driver's choice of speed is the suggestion that drivers carry out a risk evaluation of speed (and other) response alternatives and settle on the level of risk that optimises net benefit. This approach is represented in its most developed form in Risk Homeostasis theory and the concept of Target risk (e.g., Wilde, 2001), but a similar utility model is also entertained by other researchers such as Janssen and Tenkink (1988) and Deery (1999). A simplified version of the key components of Wilde's model is presented in Fig. 10.2.

In Wilde's model, drivers weigh up the costs and benefits of alternative actions and this results in an accepted level of risk which they actively target (target risk). On a continuous basis, this target level of risk is compared with the perceived level of risk arising from the driver's actions in relation to the road and traffic environment. Drivers then adjust their behaviour as discrepancies between target and perceived risk arise. The decision-making process is thus characterised as a

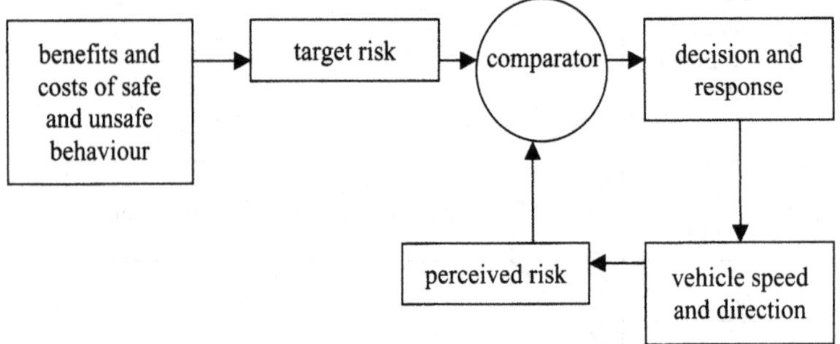

FIGURE 10.2. A simplified representation of key functional elements of risk homeostasis theory.

closed-loop homeostatic system. Thus if a driver perceives that current speed on a particular bend is at a risk level that exceeds the target risk level, then the driver will slow down until the perceived and target levels converge. In the same manner, if current speed is perceived to be at a risk level lower than target risk, then the driver will speed up until, again, perceived and target levels converge (it may be noted that this example simplifies drivers' options somewhat – alternative ways of modifying risk may also be employed, such as engaging in a secondary task – however the speed manipulation is clearly the dominant one in typical driving).

Wilde argues that the aggregation of individuals' target risk levels produces the accident toll in the drivers' jurisdiction over a period of time. Thus target risk and accident rates covary. An important implication of this conceptualisation is that safety interventions such as safer vehicle design, improved roadway design and improved driver training and assessment are all doomed to failure. Their safety impact is by and large traded for increased speed. The only way to reduce accidents on the road (and in general), therefore, is to reduce the target level of risk aimed for by drivers.

However the validity of this conceptualisation founders on certain kinds of evidence. The probabilities associated with collisions on the roadway are extremely low, with the average risk for a US driver, for example, being approximately equivalent to one crash every 5 years (Evans, 1991). If such a risk level is distributed over each and every decision made by a driver over that length of driving period, the distributed risk estimation emerges as being completely beyond human computational capability (Slovic et al., 1977). Furthermore, drivers show *incomplete* compensation for various safety interventions. For example, Rumar et al. (1976) found that drivers with studded tyres on snow compared with drivers without such tyres did indeed drive faster. However, they did not drive so much faster that they cancelled out the added safety benefit of the studded tyres; there remained a significant decrease in risk of loss of traction. Similarly, as published in an OECD review of evidence for adaptation by drivers to safety measures, increases in lane width cause increases in average speed (1 to 2 mph per foot) – but there is also a reduction in accidents; the addition of a paved shoulder to two-lane rural roads increases speeds by up to 10% – but decreases accidents by up to 40%, and the addition of edge-lines to two-lane rural roads increases average speeds, but decreases accident frequency and severity (OECD, 1990). The report concluded that although there was some evidence of risk *compensation* under certain conditions – there was little to support the concept of risk homeostasis. Drivers are clearly able to adapt their behaviour in varying ways, to varying extents and to varying conditions. However until relatively recently, there has been no account to explain the conditions under which behavioural adaptation may occur. An attempt to do this and to describe the components that influence driver decision making in a comprehensive way is the task–capability interface model (Fuller, 2000; Fuller and Santos, 2002).

10.2.4 The Task–Capability Interface Model

The task–capability interface (TCI) model starts with the self-evident truth that a loss of control by the driver necessarily arises when the demands of the driving task exceed the available capability of the driver and that control is maintained when those task demands are less than the driver's available capability. When loss of control occurs, this may lead to a collision (or road run-off). On some occasions, however, the driver may be able to regain control without further mishap or the task may abruptly change by a potential collision-object changing course at the last moment, thereby getting out of the way of the approaching vehicle (see Fig. 10.3). One implication of this is that it makes more sense to refer to loss of control of the driving task as the key marker of safety in driving. There has been a consensual move to drop reference to the term 'accident' as the key marker, with collision

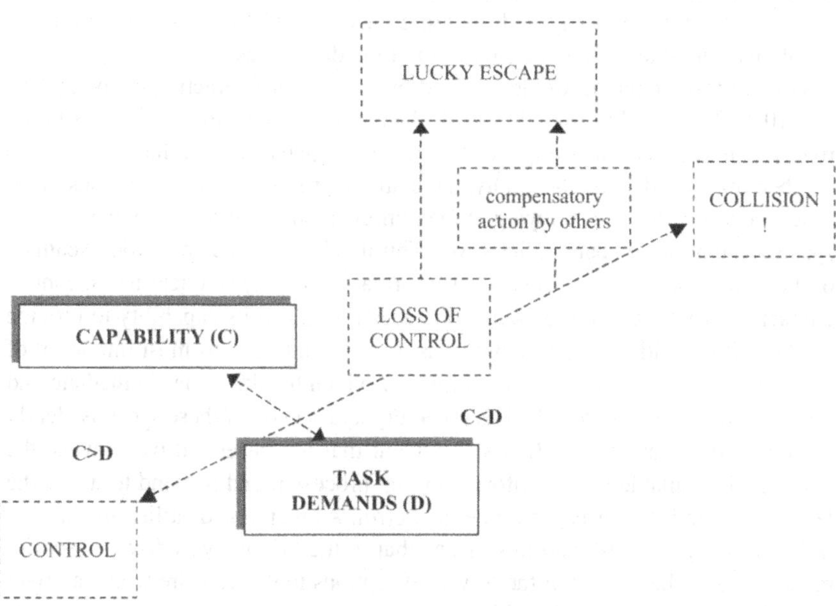

FIGURE 10.3. The basic conditions for control of the driving task.

being the current preferred term. In principle, however, although collisions are frequently the outcome of failed driver performance and are the significant events from a safety perspective, they are nevertheless not a necessary outcome.

We can explore the TCI model further by unpacking the elements of driver capability on the one hand and driving task demands on the other. Driver capability is bounded by the constraints imposed by the biological characteristics of the driver, constraints associated with for example the effectiveness and efficiency of sensory and perceptual processes, information processing capacity and speed, speed of motor response, motor coordination, flexibility, strength and physical reach. Starting with these constitutional biological characteristics, education, training and experience each contribute to the development of knowledge and skills. Such knowledge includes formal elements such as rules of the road, procedural knowledge defining what to do under what circumstances (conditional rules) and a representation of the dynamics of road and traffic scenarios which enable prediction of how those scenarios will develop (like an internalised mental video which runs on ahead of the immediately-observed situation). Skills include basic vehicle control skills as well as handling skills in challenging circumstances (such as skidding). Together these biological characteristics and acquired characteristics through education, training and experience determine the upper limit of competence of the driver. However, this competence is not necessarily available at every moment. Performance is vulnerable to a host of variables which include motivation, fatigue, drowsiness, time of day, drugs, distraction, emotion (such as fear, anger and aggression), stress and level of effort. Any of these can undermine driver competence to yield a level of capability at a somewhat lower level (see Fig. 10.4). We might label these variables collectively as human factor variables. A further set of human factor variables relate to motivation for speed and therefore have an effect not so much on driver capability but rather on the demand level of the driving task.

Driving task demands are determined by a range of interacting elements (see Fig. 10.4). These include first the physical environmental factors such as visibility, road alignment, road marking, road signs and signals, road surfaces and curve camber angles and so on. Secondly, there are other road users with various properties including that of occupying or the imminent potential of occupying, critical space in the projected path of the driver. Thirdly, there are the operational features of the vehicle being driven, such as its information display characteristics, control characteristics of steering, braking and accelerating and its capability to provide roadway illumination in dark conditions. Finally and perhaps most important of all, there are elements of task difficulty over which the driver has immediate and direct control, namely the vehicle's trajectory and speed. Of these speed is clearly the most significant factor: It is self-evident that the faster a driver travels, the less time is available to take information in, process it and respond to it and the less time there is to correct any emergent error. As mentioned earlier, the driving task is a self-paced task and this means that in the last analysis driving task demand is under the control of the driver (exceptions to this rule are where a driver complies with a speed limit which is slower than the driver's preferred speed; where a driver is under pressure to comply with a schedule or where a minimum

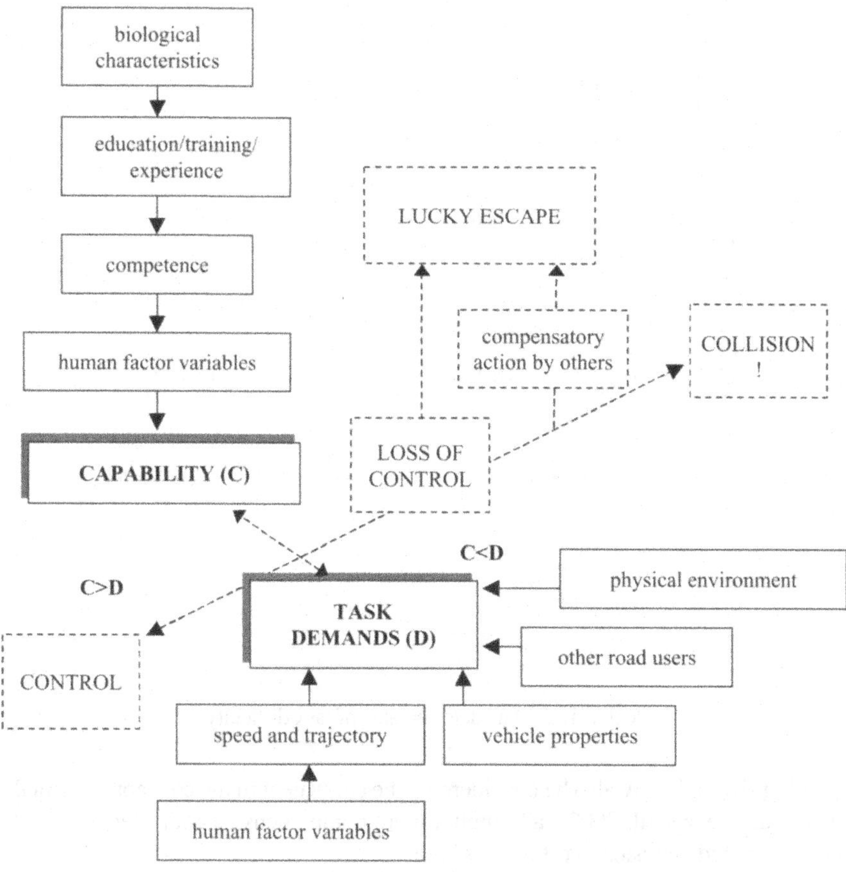

FIGURE 10.4. Elements of the task–capability interface model.

speed is required over a road section). Each of these task demand variables may independently contribute to the level of task demand and they may also interact in generating that demand. Furthermore, human factor variables may influence speed choice, which in turn may influence other human factor variables such as arousal level (see Fuller, 2005a). These determinants of task demand and the determinants of driver capability described above are brought together in the representation of the task–capability interface model presented in Fig. 10.4.

Thus far, what we have is a descriptive model of classes of variable which interact at the interface between capability and task demand to determine the outcome for the driver in terms of maintenance of control. We can now conceptualise and define the difficulty of the driving task in terms of the degree of separation of task demand and capability, with high difficulty where there is little separation and low difficulty where there is large separation. Difficulty level as here defined is proportional to the inverse of spare capacity, with spare capacity shrinking as difficulty level rises

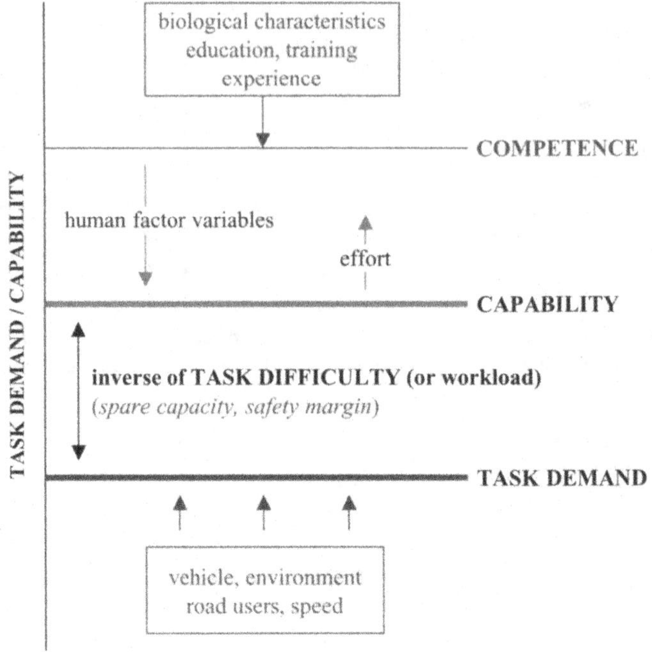

FIGURE 10.5. The determinants of task difficulty.

(see Fig. 10.5). It may also be considered to be equivalent to the concept of mental workload (de Waard, 2002), although a more comprehensive equivalence would need to include physical workload as well.

As a model, the TCI model provides a conceptual framework for organizing the critical variables which generate potential hazard scenarios and the conditions under which the driver will lose control of the driving task and become vulnerable to the range of possible disastrous consequences which might ensue. At this level of description the model is mainly behavioural in the sense that it is largely confined to describing observable phenomena (driver performance characteristics, history of learning, training and experience and human factor variables on one side of the key interface between capability and task demand and the characteristics of the road and road–user environment, the vehicle, vehicle trajectory and speed on the other). Note that this approach avoids a difficulty which is not addressed in some other formulations (e.g., Deery, 1999) namely the important question of how to define a hazard: This is determined in the model as the outcome of the interface or transaction between capability and task demand.

10.2.4.1 The Determination of Task-Difficulty Level: Task-Difficulty Homeostasis

Thus far, recourse to a cognitive level of description has not been invoked. However as it stands, the TCI model simply provides a snapshot of key interacting elements

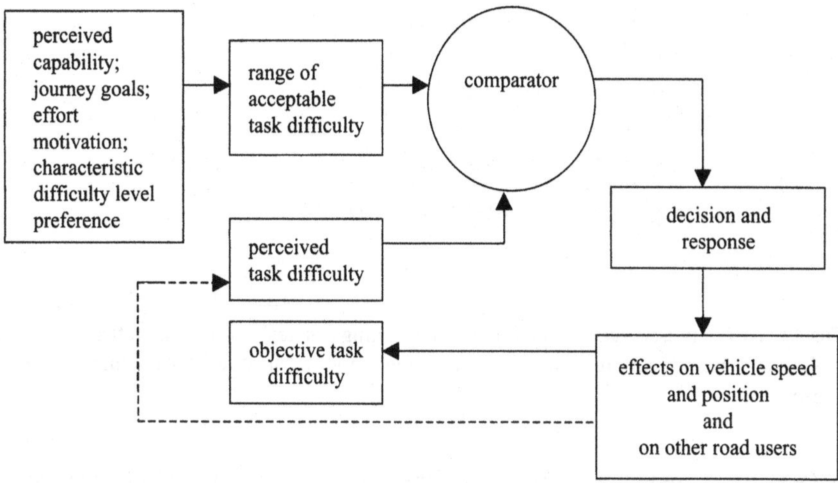

FIGURE 10.6. Representation of the process of task-difficulty homeostasis.

in the complex dynamic of a driver engaging with the road and traffic system. One important question then arises from a safety perspective and that is the question of what determines the level of task difficulty that pertains at any moment of time. It is self-evident that this is clearly not a random state that emerges quite independently of driver determination. As stated earlier, driving is a self-paced task and by manipulating the speed of the vehicle the driver has direct control over the most important single determinant of task demand. The TCI model thus specifies one key hypothesis, namely that drivers drive in such a way as to maintain level of driving task difficulty within a preferred range. This hypothesis amounts to one of task-difficulty (or workload) homeostasis, as represented in Fig. 10.6. Based on the goals of a particular journey, self-appraisal of capability, effort motivation and perhaps a reasonably stable preferred level of difficulty characteristic of the individual, a driver 'selects' a range of difficulty within which she or he is prepared to operate and drives in such a way as to maintain experienced difficulty within that range. Manipulation of speed is the primary mechanism for achieving this, although undertaking or dumping other tasks secondary to the primary driving task may be used on occasion (see, e.g., Hart and Wickens, 1990). This hypothesis of task-difficulty homeostasis provides an intriguing explanation for why inexperienced drivers are so vulnerable to loss of control and collision: They are liable to underestimate task difficulty by (a) overestimating capability on the one hand and (b) underestimating task demand on the other (some relevant evidence is reviewed in Fuller, 2000). The hypothesis also provides a theoretical basis for the design of safety interventions, for example by making the driving task appear more difficult than it really is in situations where a reduction in driving speed is warranted. However what is more important for this discussion is to examine next the evidence for the hypothesis of task-difficulty homeostasis.

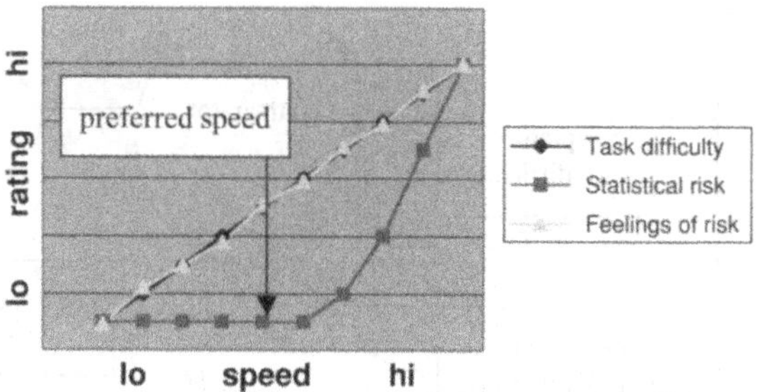

FIGURE 10.7. Stylised representation of driver ratings of task difficulty, statistical risk, feelings of risk and preferred speed for road segments viewed at systematically incremented speeds.

One strong prediction from the hypothesis is that, if all else is held constant, task difficulty should correlate with speed. A second prediction is that estimates of statistical risk should be zero until task demand begins to approach capability, that is when difficulty level exceeds some criterion value. This point would correspond with the driver's perception of a real hazard emerging in the road and traffic situation. A third prediction is that a driver's preferred level of difficulty should be at a speed lower than that at which estimates of the statistical risk of loss-of-control and crashing rise above zero. This last provides a further test of Wilde's target risk hypothesis. We have examined these predictions by soliciting drivers' ratings of task difficulty and preferred speed as they viewed video-tapes of the same segment of roadway travelled at different speeds. We also got the drivers to provide an estimate of statistical risk by imagining travelling each segment at a particular speed on 30 separate occasions and indicating how many times they thought they would lose control. This technique was devised to enable drivers to avoid the difficulty associated with providing a probability estimate of a single rare event, at the same time enabling use of a meaningful estimate (e.g., 2 times out of 30; 0.1 times out of 30, etc.).

The results confirmed both predictions one and two (see Fig. 10.7). Task difficulty correlated very highly with speed (speed accounted for over 98% of the variance in ratings of difficulty) and over a range of slow to moderate speeds, statistical risk ratings remained at zero and did not begin to rise until speeds were very much faster. We obtained the same pattern for different types of roadway and repeated the results in a subsequent replication (see Fuller et al., 2006, in press). In relation to the test of Wilde's Target risk hypothesis, as can be seen from the vertical line in Fig. 10.7, the driver's preferred speed was lower than the point at which statistical risk exceeded zero, providing further evidence against the Target risk concept. However the simulation studies threw up an unexpected discovery.

Along with ratings of task difficulty and ratings of statistical risk, we also asked drivers to rate their feelings of risk, fully expecting those ratings to track their statistical risk ratings. There seemed to be no *a priori* reason why feelings of risk should be dissociated from ratings of statistical risk and there seemed to be no reported evidence in the literature to suggest such dissociation. But our expectations were confounded. Ratings of feelings of risk did not track statistical risk: What they did track were the ratings of task difficulty (see Fig. 10.7). The correlation between the two variables was of the order of 0.97 (Fuller et al., 2006, in press). This finding raises an intriguing question. Why should task difficulty and feelings of risk be so strongly associated? Is it through a feeling of risk, which has been shown to be different from an estimate of statistical risk, that drivers sense task difficulty? Taylor (1964) concluded from a study of the relationships between driver arousal (operationalised as GSR level), speed and road segment characteristics that 'drivers adopt a level of anxiety that they wish to experience when driving and drive so as to maintain it'. Similarly, Näätänen and Summala (1976) have long advocated the concept of a subjective risk (or more recently 'fear') monitor in driver decision making, although Summala (1986) has argued that zero-risk experience of road and traffic leads to a desensitisation to emotional feedback. In the last decade, one researcher who has strongly advocated the role of feelings in decision making is Damasio (1994, 2003). Vaa (2003) has subsequently developed his own driver behaviour model predicated on this viewpoint (see also this volume).

10.2.4.2 The Representation of Task-Difficulty

Before considering the possibility of feelings of risk as the determinant of driver speed choice, let us take a step back to consider the more general problem. If the Task-difficulty homeostasis hypothesis is correct, then the question of how drivers represent and determine task difficulty or workload is fundamental to developing our understanding further. This question may be re-phrased as 'how is task difficulty represented in the 'comparator' element of the process depicted in Fig. 10.6?'

If the analysis of task-difficulty here was restricted to physical workload in dynamic work, then the answer to this question would be reasonably straightforward (see, e.g., Oborne, 1995). As physical workload increases, there is an immediate sense of having to expend additional effort. As this additional effort is made, the demand for oxygenated blood supply increases and to deliver that there is an automatic increase in respiration rate and a parallel increase in heart rate. There is, in addition, an increase in heat energy output and typically a reflex response of increased sweating in order to increase the rate of heat loss from the body. All these changes can be sensed by the person undergoing the physical task. Thus apart from the sense of effort there is feedback about physiological changes that are needed to support that effort. As physical workload increases even further, there comes a point where the work requirement approaches the upper limit of muscular output of which the person is capable. In this region the sense of effort required increases significantly and the emerging fatigue in muscle tissue is experienced not just as fatigue but as an aversive, even painful, condition, making it even more difficult to sustain the effort. Attempts to increase or even sustain the workload are self-limiting: The muscles are simply unable to work at the required level and the accompanying oxygen debt leaves the individual winded and with pounding heart. Immediate cessation of the level of activity is then the only option.

The selection by an individual of a particular level of sustainable workload for a physical task will be determined by the goals of the task, perceived level of capability (possibly modified by human factor variables such as level of activation and level of fatigue), the level of effort the person is prepared to make and possibly a level of preferred workload that is characteristic of the individual (as represented in the distinction: She or he is or is not a 'hard worker').

Is there a similar system of sensitivity to mental workload (as one possible representation of driving task difficulty) that parallels that for physical workload? There is no question that one can be aware that different cognitive tasks demand different degrees of cognitive effort (see, e.g., Shugan, 1980; Payne et al., 1993) but there do not appear to be reliable and, more importantly, detectable physiological changes which underpin that effort which can provide additional feedback to the individual in the same manner as increased respiration, heart rate, temperature and sweating as in the case of muscular effort. Nevertheless, of course, there are rate and/or capacity limits in the cognitive processes of information uptake, working memory storage and processing. As mental workload or task difficulty increase, there comes a point where the cognitive requirement approaches these upper limits. At this stage, just as with dynamic physical work, the sense of effort required will increase significantly, there may also be a sense of mental fatigue, the condition may even feel aversive, but there does not appear to be an equivalent sense of pain (although this possibility was once amusingly portrayed in a *Monty Python* sketch in which the intellectually challenged Mr. Gumby complained 'my brain hurts').

As indicated in Fig. 10.6 and just as in the case for a physical task, the selection of a sustainable workload for a cognitive task (i.e., task difficulty) will be determined by the goals of the task, perceived level of capability, the level of effort the person is prepared to make and again possibly a level of preferred workload that is characteristic of the individual. But without the physical changes which feed information back to the individual in physical work, how is a particular level of work or task difficulty detected and controlled? One possibility relates to the goals of the driving task.

The immediate goals of the driving task are twofold: To achieve a journey and to maintain control. Control is the primary element here because without control the journey cannot be completed. So perhaps we can rephrase the question as 'how is control represented in the system and what information provides feedback regarding the status of control?'

We might speculate that the representation of being in a state of control includes the ability to make progress, the ability to make avoidance responses where necessary (e.g., of objects or other road users), the maintenance of adhesion to the road surface, having access to critical information, such as the requirement for an avoidance response and a rate of flow of information and rate of response requirement that are within the individual's capability. All of these seem self-evident because control would be lost if any of them were absent. Imagine a vehicle with no accelerator, no brake, no steering and no forward vision or a vehicle with all of these but travelling at such a speed that the vehicle had no directional control or the rate of flow of information exceeded information processing limits or critical information arrived so late that there was no time opportunity to respond to it. Now given that the ability to accelerate, brake, steer and have forward vision is relatively stable characteristics of driving, the critical variables representing control become maintenance of contact with the road surface, rate of flow of information and available response time.

How might a human metacognitive system monitor adhesion, rate of flow of information and available response time in order to determine whether or not they are within acceptable limits? Is there a TOTE (test–operate–test–exit) mechanism (Miller et al., 1960) evaluating the status of each variable through a continuous, recursive control loop, against a set of tolerance criteria, triggering adjustment responses before the next test and so on? Is there a mechanism that recognises a decoupling when, say, information arrives at such a rate or arrives so late that it cannot drive output (see, e.g., the discussion of augmented cognition by Young et al., 2004)?

In the context of driving, one further possibility is that if the value of any of these variables exceeds the upper limits of tolerance it may trigger feelings of an impending loss of control and, given the potential punishing consequences of this, anxiety and fear. Such a process would clearly have an adaptive function in terms of motivating the individual to keep within safe boundaries of operation. Thus is there some critical loss of adhesion (and therefore directional control) or critical rate of information flow or response requirement which triggers feelings of anxiety and fear? Our evidence of the close association between feelings of risk and level of task difficulty is certainly highly consistent with such a suggestion and, as mentioned earlier, one researcher who has strongly advocated the role of feelings in decision making is Damasio (1994, 2003).

10.2.5 The Somatic-Marker Hypothesis

Although normal language usage regards emotion as a type of feeling, Damasio (2003) reserves the term 'emotion' for underlying body states (perhaps triggered by some precipitating event) and the term 'feeling' for the experience of these states (rather akin to the James–Lange theory of emotion). He concludes that emotions provide a natural means for the brain and mind 'to evaluate the environment within and around the organism and respond accordingly and adaptively' (p. 54). Whether or not one is paying attention, Damasio suggests that emotionally competent stimuli (i.e., stimuli with which some feeling is associated) can be detected and that attention and thought can then be diverted to those stimuli, thereby enhancing the quality of reasoning and decision making (an orienting role for emotion, earlier suggested by Zajonc, 1980). Emotional signals 'mark options and outcomes with a positive or negative signal that narrows the decision-space and increases the probability that the action will conform to past experience' (p. 148). The emotional signal has an auxiliary role that increases the efficiency of the reasoning process

FIGURE 10.8. An example of a potential 'emotionally competent' stimulus, linked to a somatic marker of anxiety or fear.

but is not necessarily a substitute for it. However, when we immediately reject an option that would lead to certain disaster, reasoning may be 'almost superfluous'. Because emotional signals are body-related, Damasio labelled this set of ideas 'the somatic marker hypothesis'. Slovic et al. (2002) refer to a similar set of ideas as 'the affect heuristic'. Through learning, somatic markers become linked to stimuli and patterns of stimuli. When a negative somatic marker is linked to an image of a future outcome, it sounds an alarm (see an example in Fig. 10.8).

What is compelling about the somatic marker hypothesis and the affect heuristic is the evidence cited in their support. Certain types of brain lesion specifically exclude access to feelings associated with objects, events and scenarios. At the same time they degrade decision performance: 'The powers of reason and the experience of emotion decline together and their impairment stands out in a neuropsychological profile within which basic attention, memory, intelligence and language appear so intact that they could never be invoked to explain the patients' failures in judgement' (Damasio, 1994, pp. 53–54). Damasio (2003) has also outlined a plausible and coherent neurological model which could sustain this entire process. In addition, Slovic et al. (2002) and Loewenstein et al. (2001) cite a number of experimental studies of decision making in normal individuals which clearly demonstrate the interplay between emotion and reason, with the clear conclusion that affect is essential to rational action.

In one such study cited by Slovic et al., participants were asked to rate the attractiveness of purchasing new equipment for use in the event of an airliner crash-landing. It was hypothesised that saving 150 lives was a somewhat diffuse positive outcome and would have a relatively weak positive effect. On the other hand, saving 98% of something would be more convincingly good and would have a much stronger positive effect. In one condition, participants were told that the equipment would save 150 lives, which would otherwise be at risk. In a second condition, they were told that the equipment would make it possible to save 98% of the 150 lives, which would otherwise be at risk. It was found that support for the purchase of the life-saving equipment was significantly higher in the 98% of 150 condition than in the 150 condition. Support for the purchase was also higher than in the 150 condition in a third situation in which participants were told the equipment would make it possible to save 85% of the 150 lives that would otherwise be at risk.

Now it might be suggested that explanation in terms of the somatic marker hypothesis simply brings us right back to the threat-avoidance model, as proposed in 1984 (Fuller, 1984), but with the concept of 'threat' being unpacked in terms of its associated negative, punishing feelings. Damasio (1994) argues that somatic markers are acquired through experience, under the control of an internal preference system and under the influence of an external set of circumstances. The internal preference system consists of 'mostly innate regulatory dispositions, posed (poised?) to ensure survival of the organism' (p. 179). The external set of circumstances includes

> 'events relative to which individuals must act; possible options for action; possible future outcomes for those actions; and the punishment or reward that accompanies a certain option, both immediately and in deferred time, as outcomes of the opted action unfold... The interaction between an internal preference system and sets of external circumstances extends the repertory of stimuli that will become automatically marked' (p. 179).

This sounds remarkably like the description of an affect-conditioning history. And indeed Damasio goes on to state: 'When the choice of option X, which leads to bad outcome Y, is followed by punishment and thus painful body states, the somatic marker system acquires the hidden, dispositional representation of this experience-driven, noninherited, arbitrary connection' (p. 180). However the somatic marker hypothesis goes beyond this learning process. It asserts that affective responses to presenting and anticipated stimuli not only inform response choice (as in reinforcement theory) but also capture attention to pertinent stimuli and prioritise their processing. In other words, affective responses have a direct effect on cognitive operations.

10.2.5.1 Predictions and Speculations from the Somatic-Marker Hypothesis

One prediction from this hypothesis is that somatic marker strength should have an impact on the distribution of attention over the traffic scene ahead of the driver. The affective profile of the visual scene should be matched by the profile of attention distributed over that scene. This selectivity might be operationalised in terms of prioritisation and dwell time for particular stimuli in the environment, reflected, for example, in patterns of visual fixations. In a field study of patterns of visual fixations by novice and experienced drivers, Underwood et al. (2003) have shown that on rural roads, two-fixation transitions by novices typically terminated in just one zone, the road far ahead, whereas fixations by experienced drivers terminated in five different parts of the scene. On a dual-carriageway, experienced drivers also showed more extensive scanning, particularly in the horizontal plane. Underwood et al. interpreted this as evidence for greater sensitivity of experienced drivers to prevailing traffic conditions. They concluded that the monitoring of other road users is learned through experience and thus novices have relatively little ability to switch the focus of their attention as potential hazards appear. The somatic marker hypothesis offers the possibility that these learned differences in visual scanning between novice and experienced drivers may be the result of learned affective responses to events on the roadway, such as fast-moving vehicles merging from both left and right in the dual-carriageway situation (Fuller, 2005b). Consistent with this is the speculation by Loewenstein et al. (2001), who suggest that age-related differences in risk-taking may be 'affectively mediated', in particular, perhaps, by differences in the vividness of mental simulations of consequences at the moment of decision making.

Although linking of somatic markers to images is suggested to arise from a process of learning, it is possible that affective responses to some events may be unlearned reflex responses or that they are associated with a 'learning readiness'. Put another way, it may be that there are universal somatically-marked stimuli. Recognition of impending loss of control of a threatening situation might be one such event that is, of course, highly pertinent to driver behaviour. Information overload or an impossible response requirement may contribute substantially to this recognition. Other unlearned but relevant affective responses, which might at the same time also contribute to a feeling of loss of control, include the responses to a looming stimulus (rapid expansion of the retinal image of an object, approaching collision; see, e.g., Schiff et al., 1962; Bottomore, 1999; Franconeri and Simons, 2003), to intense vestibular stimulation or *g* forces (e.g., Moro reflex; see, e.g., Goddard-Blythe, 1995) and to unexpected events (e.g., orienting reflex). There may even be the equivalent of an inverse square law of affect intensity in driving, with feeling intensity growing in proportion to the inverse square root (or some other expression) of the time-to-line crossing or to collision, for example.

A further prediction from the somatic marker hypothesis is that individual differences in the affective response to particular scenarios should be associated with different decisions in relation to those scenarios. Thus if we take speed choice as an operationalisation of decision making, drivers who are more emotionally reactive to road scenarios representing various degrees of threat (or impending loss of control) should opt for lower speeds than drivers who are less reactive. If there are stable individual differences in emotional reactivity (Larsen and Diener, 1987), this could mean that the same situation would ring alarm bells somewhat differently for different individuals. Some may be relatively so 'deaf' that an impending hazard has to be right on top of them before they are able to hear it, so to speak. These persons would unwittingly be in a condition of delayed avoidance

(Fuller, 1984). Fujita et al. (1991) have shown that women experience negative and positive affect more intensely than men. They asked 100 students to complete the affect intensity measure (Larsen and Diener, 1987), which consists of 40 items that measure how intensely participants feel emotions, yielding both a positive and negative affect intensity score. Females scored higher on both positive and negative affect intensity. Is it the case, then, that male–female differences in risk taking are mediated by differences in emotional reactions to potentially hazardous situations? Perhaps males crash more because they feel less.

Another individual difference factor that may be relevant in this discussion is the tendency to seek enhanced external stimulation. Personality traits of extraversion and sensation seeking are both considered to be constitutional characteristics of the individual (Zuckerman, 1979) and both are associated with a preference for enhanced levels of stimulation. Does this then mean that individuals with such traits may be more likely to accept higher levels of somatic arousal and tolerate more readily a driving situation where task demand is very close to capability, in other words tolerate smaller safety margins? Research on individual differences and accident involvement tends to support this prediction (Loo, 1979). Individuals high in sensation seeking are more likely to speed, overtake and adopt shorter headways. They are also over-represented in traffic crashes (Jonah, 1997). Furthermore, Dahlen et al. (2005) have reported that degree of sensation seeking predicts dangerous driving.

If the somatic marker hypothesis is correct in its implications for attention capture by competent stimuli, the possibility presents itself that emotional responses arising from the unfolding road and traffic scenario may be drowned out by or misattributed to other emotions or indeed, may even be suppressed or extinguished (see concept of 'desensitisation' in Summala, 1986). For example, feelings of anger may overwhelm the somatic marker indications, which would otherwise inform decision making. Indeed is this the effect we are referring to when we talk about rage being 'blind'? Deffenbacher et al. (2003) have shown that high anger drivers are between 1.5 and 2.0 times more likely to engage in risky driving, such as exceeding the speed limit and not wearing a seatbelt. Dahlen et al. (2005), in a questionnaire study of 224 undergraduate drivers, found that the propensity to become angry while driving predicted risky driving, minor losses of vehicle control and loss of concentration. Levelt (2001) has reported that drivers who say they are often irritated when driving also say that speeding is often the consequence and Carbonell et al. (1997) found that anxiety combined with time pressures can lead to engaging in dangerous manoeuvres (see review by Mesken, 2003).

10.3 Conclusions

Thus it is suggested here, albeit speculatively, that feelings of risk in driving may arise from a sensitivity to changes which signal an impending loss of control and that these feelings inform the driver's experience of task difficulty or workload.

They (or in Damasio's sense, their underlying emotional substrates) may arise naturally and spontaneously or through a process of learned association. They have the power to direct attention to pertinent stimuli and to determine priorities amongst response options. In short, they are integral to driver decision making, even where they are so weak they are equivalent to what Slovic et al. (2002) call 'whispers of affect'. If we reinterpret the hypothesis of task-difficulty homeostasis in terms of feelings of risk, the implication would be that drivers drive in such a way as to keep feelings of risk below some threshold level (which may even be zero). If the behaviour of other road users or the driver's own behaviour (such as an increase in speed) should stimulate an increase in feelings of risk above this threshold level, then the driver will take action to bring the level of felt risk back down, such as by reducing speed. Only if the rewards of any supra-threshold feelings of risk are compensated for by rewarding consequences of one sort or another will the driver intentionally tolerate any increase above threshold. Nevertheless, increases in risk may not be felt because of the swamping effect of other feelings or if felt they may be attributed to events other than those related to the driving task. And experience may not have provided sufficient learning opportunities to link particular potential hazard scenarios to feelings of risk, that is, to provide the link to a somatic marker. If we can accept all this as a working hypothesis and the evidence continues to support it, then a whole new agenda for driver behaviour research emerges (see Fuller, 2005b).

From the forgoing discussion it can be seen that the somatic marker hypothesis has the potential to provide a unifying explanation for a diverse set of empirical findings in the domain of driver behaviour, including our finding that feelings of risk track ratings of driving task difficulty and speed almost perfectly. It also raises a number of new questions regarding the role of affect and emotional conditioning in attention and decision making. This makes the experimental evaluation of the somatic marker hypothesis of some importance in the contemporary research agenda. It may be noted that one author has already begun to develop a model of driver decision making based fundamentally on the somatic marker hypothesis (Vaa, 2004, and this volume) and that Summala has proposed a thesis along similar lines (Summala, 2005, and this volume). The implication is that if we want to understand driver decision making more clearly, we need to take into account not just thinking but also feeling. Perhaps this is in part why decision making in safety-sensitive industries, such as commercial aviation, has moved away from individual decision making (reliance on somatic markers?) towards standard operating procedures (SOPs): Prescriptive rules for dealing with each contingency experienced. In areas such as aircraft maintenance, where the affective consequences of inappropriate actions must be relatively weak, a reliance on SOPs must be especially important for maintaining system safety. In this context any deviation from SOPs in decision making is a matter of very serious concern (McDonald et al., 1999). Work in this area also highlights the importance of avoiding conflict between SOPs and what is perceived by the operative to be a better procedure – avoiding the tension between formal and normal ways of working (Ward, 2005).

References

Ajzen, I. (1991). The theory of planned behavior. *Organizational Behavior and Human Decision Processes*, 50, 179–211.

Armitage, C.J. and Conner, M. (2001). Efficacy of the theory of planned behavior: A meta-analytic review. *British Journal of Social Psychology*, 40, 471–499.

Bem, S. and de Jong, H.L. (2006). *Theoretical issues in psychology* (2nd ed.). Sage Publications, London.

Bottomore, S. (1999). The panicking audience? Early cinema and the 'train effect'. *Historical Journal of Film, Radio and Television*, 19(2), 177–216.

Carbonell, E.J., Banuls, R., Chisvert, M., Monteagudo, M.J. and Pastor, G. (1997). A comparative study of anxiety responses in traffic situations as predictors of accident rates in professional drivers. *Proceedings of the Second Seminar in Human Factors in Road Traffic*, Universidade do Minho, Braga.

Dahlen, E.R., Martin, R.C., Ragan, K. and Kuhlman, M.M. (2005). Driving anger, sensation seeking, impulsiveness, and boredom proneness in the prediction of unsafe driving. *Accident Analysis and Prevention*, 37, 341–348.

Damasio, A.R. (1994). *Descartes' error: Emotion, reason and the human brain*. Putnam, New York.

Damasio, A.R. (2003). *Looking for spinoza: Joy, sorrow and the feeling brain*. Heinemann, London.

Deery, H.A. (1999). Hazard and risk perception among young novice drivers. *Journal of Safety Research*, 30(4), 225–236.

Deffenbacher, J.L., Lynch, R.S., Filetti, L.B., Dahlen, E.R. and Oetting, E.R. (2003). Anger, aggression, risky behavior, and crash-related outcomes in three groups of drivers. *Behaviour Research and Therapy*, 41, 333–349.

de Waard, D. (2002). Mental workload. In R. Fuller and J.A. Santos (Eds.), *Human factors for highway engineers*. Pergamon, Oxford, pp. 161–176.

Elliott, M.A., Armitage, C.J. and Baughan, C.J. (2003). Drivers' compliance with speed limits: An application of the theory of planned behavior. *Journal of Applied Psychology*, 88(5), 964–972.

Evans, L. (1991) *Traffic safety and the driver*. Van Nostrand Reinhold, New York.

Franconeri, S.L. and Simons, D.J. (2003). Moving and looming stimuli capture attention. *Perception and Psychophysics*, 65(7), 999–1010.

Fujita, F., Diener, E. and Sandvik, E. (1991). Gender differences in negative affect and well-being: The case for emotional intensity. *Journal of Personality and Social Psychology*, 61, 427–434.

Fuller, R. (1984). A conceptualisation of driving behaviour as threat avoidance, *Ergonomics*, 27, 1139–1155.

Fuller, R. (1991a). The modification of individual road user behaviour. In M.J. Koornstra and J. Christensen (Eds.). *Enforcement and rewarding: Strategies and effects*. SWOV Institute for Road Safety Research, Leidschendam, pp. 33–40.

Fuller, R. (1991b). Behaviour analysis and unsafe driving: Warning – Learning trap ahead! *Journal of Applied Behaviour Analysis*, 24, 73–75.

Fuller, R. (2000). The task–capability interface model of the driving process. *Recherche Transports Sécurité*, 66, 47–59.

Fuller, R. (2002). Learning to drive. In P. Barjonet (Ed.), *Traffic psychology today*. Kluwer Academic Publishers, Dordrecht, pp. 105–118.

Fuller, R. (2005a). Towards a general theory of driver behaviour. *Accident Analysis and Prevention*, 37, 461–472.

Fuller, R. (2005b). Driving by the seat of your pants: A new agenda for research. In *Behavioural research in road safety 2005*. Department for Transport, London, pp. 85–93.

Fuller, R. and Farrell, E. (2001). *Operation lifesaver assessment*. RS 459. Project OLA, NRA, Dublin.

Fuller, R. and Santos, J.A. (2002). Psychology and the highway engineer. In R. Fuller and J.A. Santos (Eds.), *Human factors for highway engineers*. Pergamon, Oxford, pp. 1–10.

Fuller, R., McHugh, C. and Pender, S. (2006). Task difficulty and risk in the determination of driver behaviour. *European Review of Applied Psychology*. In press.

Geller, E.S. (1998). *Applications of behavior analysis to prevent injuries from vehicle crashes*. Behavior monographs: Cambridge Center for Behavioral Studies, Cambridge.

Goddard-Blythe, S. (1995). The role of primitive survival reflexes in the development of the visual system. *Journal of Behavioural Optometry*, 6, 31–35.

Harrison, W.A. (2005). A demonstration of avoidance learning in turning decisions at intersections. *Transportation Research Part F: Traffic Psychology and Behaviour*, 8F, 4–5, pp. 341–354.

Hart, S.G. and Wickens, C.D. (1990). Workload assessment and prediction. In H.R. Booher (Ed.). *MANPRINT: An emerging technology. Advanced concepts for integrating people, machines and organizations*. Van Nostrand Reinhold, New York, pp. 257–300.

Hutton, K.A., Sibley, C.G., Harper, D.N. and Hunt, M. (2001). Modifying driver behaviour with passenger feedback. *Transportation Research Part F: Traffic Psychology and Behaviour*, 4F, 4, 271–278.

Janssen, W.H. and Tenkink, E. (1988). Considerations on speed selection and risk homeostasis in driving. *Accident Analysis and Prevention*, 20, 137–142.

Jonah B.A. (1997). Sensation seeking and risky driving: A review and synthesis of the literature. *Accident Analysis and Prevention*, 29, 651–665.

Larsen, R.J. and Diener, E. (1987). Affect intensity as an individual difference characteristic: A review. *Journal of Research in Personality*, 21, 1–39.

Levelt, P.B.M. (2001). *Emoties bij vrachtautochauffers*. R-2001-14, SWOV Institute for Road Safety Research, Leidschendam, The Netherlands.

Loewenstein, G.F., Weber, E.U., Hsee, C.K. and Welch, N. (2001). Risk as feelings. *Psychological Bulletin*, 127(2), 267–286.

Loo, R. (1979). Role of primary personality factors in the perception of traffic signs and driver violations and accidents. *Accident Analysis and Prevention*, 11, 125–127.

Ludwig, T.D. and Geller, E.S. (2000). Intervening to improve the safety of delivery drivers: A systematic behavioral approach. *Journal of Organizational Behavior Management*, 19(4), 1–124.

MacCorquodale, K. and Meehl, P.E. (1948). On a distinction between hypothetical constructs and intervening variables. *Psychological Review*, 55, 95–107.

Mäkinen, T., Biecheler-Fretel, M.M., Cardoso, J., Fuller, R., Goldenbeld, C., Hakkert, S., Sanchez Martin, M.C., Skladana, P., Vaa T. and Zaidel D. (1999). *Legal measures and enforcement*. GADGET WP-5-Report, VTI, Espoo.

McDonald, N., Daly, C., Corrigan, S., Cromie, S. and Ward, M. (1999). *Human-centred management guide for aircraft maintenance*. APRG, Trinity College, Dublin.

Mesken, J. (2003). *The role of emotions and moods in traffic*. D-2003-8, SWOV Institute for Road Safety Research, Leidschendam, The Netherlands.

Michon, J.A. (1989). Explanatory pitfalls and rule-based driver models. *Accident Analysis and Prevention*, 21(4), 341–353.

Miller, G.A., Galanter, E. and Pribram, K.H. (1960). *Plans and the structure of behavior*. Holt, Rinehart and Winston, New York.

Näätänen, R. and Summala, H. (1976). *Road user behaviour and traffic accidents*. North Holland/Elsevier, Amsterdam and New York.

Oborne, D.J. (1995). *Ergonomics at work* (3rd ed.). Wiley, Chichester.

OECD – Road Transport Research (1990). *Behavioural adaptation to changes in the road transport system*. OECD, Paris.

Payne, J.W., Bettman, J.R. and Johnson, E.J. (1993). *The adaptive decision maker*. Cambridge University Press, Cambridge.

Ranney, T.A. (1994). Models of driving behavior: A review of their evolution. *Accident Analysis and Prevention*, 26(6), pp. 733–750.

Reinhardt-Rutland, A.H. (2001). Seat-belts and behavioural adaptation: The loss of looming as a negative reinforcer. *Safety Science*, 39, 3, 145–156.

Rumar, K., Berggrund, U., Jernberg, P. and Ytterbom, U. (1976). Driver reaction to a technical measure: Studded tyres. *Human Factors*, 18, 433–454.

Schiff, W., Caviness, J.A. and Gibson, J.J. (1962). Persistent fear responses in rhesus monkeys to the optical stimulus of "looming." *Science*, 136, 982–983.

Shugan, S.M. (1980). The cost of thinking. *Journal of Consumer Research*, 7, 99–111.

Slovic, P., Finucane, M.L., Peters, E. and MacGregor, D.G. (2002). Risk as analysis and risk as feelings. Some thoughts about affect, reason, risk and rationality. *Paper presented at the Annual Meeting of the Society for Risk Analysis*. New Orleans, Louisiana, 10 December, 2002.

Slovic, P., Fischoff, B., Lichtenstein, S., Corrigan, B. and Coombs, B. (1977). Preference for insuring against probably small losses: Insurance implications. *Journal of Risk and Insurance*, 44, 237–258.

Summala, H. (1986). *Risk control is not risk adjustment: The zero-risk theory of driver behavior and its implications*. Reports 11: 1986. University of Helsinki Traffic Research Unit, Helsinki.

Summala, H. (1997). Hierarchical model of behavioural adaptation and traffic accidents. In T. Rothengatter and E. Carbonell Vaya (Eds.). *Traffic and transport psychology: Theory and application*. Elsevier Science, Oxford, pp. 41–52.

Summala, H. (2005). Towards understanding driving behaviour and safety efforts. In L. Macchi, C. Re and P.C. Cacciabue (Eds.), *Proceedings of the International Workshop on Modelling Driver Behaviour in Automotive Environments*. European Commission, Joint Research Centre, Ispra, Italy, 25–27 May, 2005. Office for Official Publication of the European Communities, Luxembourg, pp. 205–214.

Taylor, D.H. (1964). Drivers' galvanic skin response and the risk of accident. *Ergonomics*, 7, 439–451.

Underwood, G., Chapman, P., Brocklehurst, N., Underwood, J. and Crundall, D. (2003). Visual attention while driving: Sequences of eye fixations made by experienced and novice drivers. *Ergonomics*, 46, pp. 629–646.

Vaa, T. (2003). *Survival or deviance? A model for driver behaviour*. TOI Report 666/2003, Institute of Transport Economics, Oslo.

Ward, M. (2005). *Contributions to human factors from three case studies in aircraft maintenance*. Unpublished PhD thesis, University of Dublin, Trinity College.

Wilde, G.J.S. (2001). *Target risk 2: A new psychology of safety and health: What works? What doesn't? and why*? PDE Publications, Toronto.

Young, P.M., Clegg, B.A. and Smith, C.A.P. (2004). Dynamic models of augmented cognition. *International Journal of Human–Computer Interaction*, 17(2), 259–273.

Zajonc, R.B. (1980). Feeling and thinking: Preferences need no inferences. *American Psychologist*, 35, 151–175.

Zuckerman, M. (1979). *Sensation seeking: Beyond the optimal level of arousal*. Lawrence Erlbaum Associates, Hillsdale, New Jersey.

11 Towards Understanding Motivational and Emotional Factors in Driver Behaviour: Comfort Through Satisficing[1]

HEIKKI SUMMALA

11.1 Introduction

The early 'skill models' of driver behaviour and safety posited that the safety of a driver is mainly determined by the level of his or her perceptual and motor skills in relation to the task demands: a crash – a failure in driver performance – occurs when task demands exceed driver capabilities (e.g., Blumenthal, 1968). Consequently, improving driver skills and reducing task demands would make traffic safer. Obviously, however, this early concept was too simple. A good piece of counterevidence, among others, came from Williams and O'Neill (1974), who showed that classified U.S. race drivers have more crashes per exposure than average drivers – and also more speeding tickets. At least the advanced skills which make those drivers competitive in race track did not save them from crashes, as they obviously traded skills for speed on ordinary roads, too. Theorists and road safety people indeed forgot that driving is a self-paced task and drivers themselves do determine their task demands to a large extent (Näätänen and Summala, 1974). The behavioural adaptation concept is now one of basic tenets in traffic psychology, here defined by Summala (1996): 'the driver is inclined to react to changes in the traffic system, whether they be in the vehicle, in the road environment, in road and weather conditions, or in his/her own skills or states, and that this reaction occurs in accordance with his/her motives'.

The safe completion of the trip is usually taken for granted by drivers. Therefore, time goals, conservation of effort, maintenance of speed and progress, pleasure of driving, all what Näätänen and Summala (1976) called extra motives, gain ground in driver behaviour and cannot be forgotten anymore: they tend to push drivers towards hazards primarily in terms of higher speed and shorter safety margins. But what are the mechanisms which shelter us of crashes, of going too close to hazards, and of exposing us to hazards?

---

[1]This is an extension of the author's earlier paper presented in the symposium on traffic psychology theories in the 3rd International Congress of Traffic and Transport Psychology (see Summala, 2005).

11.2 Emotional Tension and 'Risk Monitor'

One line of thinking attempted to find one single motivational measure which could explain driver behaviour, even including the moment-to-moment speed control. It started from the work of Taylor (1964). In two on-road studies he measured galvanic skin responses in drivers who were driving in a wide range of roads and road conditions. He found that GSR activity varied substantially by conditions but, when controlled for speed, it was quite evenly distributed in time. He concluded that it is the level of emotional tension or anxiety which guides the driver: 'Driving is a self-paced task governed by the level of emotional tension or anxiety which the driver wishes to tolerate'. Interestingly, Taylor probably interpreted his results at least partly wrongly. Variation in speed and GSR activity in Taylor's data correlated with road type and road conditions such that lower speed and higher GSR activity occurred on road sections with more side turnings and more other traffic (Taylor, 1964). It can be assumed therefore that an important source of GSR was motor activity rather than anxiety (see also Näätänen and Summala, 1976, p. 191). However, Taylor's conclusion was quite influential on later theoretical work.

Wilde (1982), in his well-known and much debated model, proposed that drivers tend to target a certain level of risk. The actual model is a simple homeostatic (thermostatic) system with a traditional optimising decision model included in it, but the model is best known from its safety prediction: Should any changes be made in the traffic system, road users tend to maintain a certain target level of risk and, therefore, safety level keeps approximately constant. It is obvious that this is not the case, as already predicted by Smeed (1949) and confirmed by many big successes in safety developments (see, e.g., Evans, 1991; Robertson and Pless, 2002). The feedback loop from accident statistics (the knowledge of crash risk in a given jurisdiction) in Wilde's model also seems quite inefficient to guide drivers' daily task control and choices. Fuller (2000, 2004, 2005, see also Chapter 10 in this book) incorporates the concept of the target into his task–capability interface model. He claims that drivers are sensitive to task difficulty and try to keep experienced difficulty within a certain margin in a homeostatic loop. Vaa (2004, see also Chapter 12 in this book) lists several candidates for drivers' targets. Drivers may target for a certain arousal level, in all of its varieties, and sensation, pleasure, security, workload, avoiding violations or even non-compliance of the rules. Finally, while applying Damasio's model of emotions and feelings, he proposes that the pacing factor is target feeling or best feeling, and the body is the risk monitor (Damasio, 1994).

But to what degree dynamic driver behaviour can be explained with one 'motivational', *targeted* control measure which drivers tend to adjust? And, could it be possible to operationalise such a measure to test it adequately, and to apply in automotive and transportation research and development?

Näätänen and Summala (1974, 1976) adopted quite a different position. In line with Taylor (1964), they claimed that driving is a self-paced task. They proposed that the task difficulty level is determined by the drivers according to their motives. Drivers are not only able to compensate for changes in the degree of difficulty of

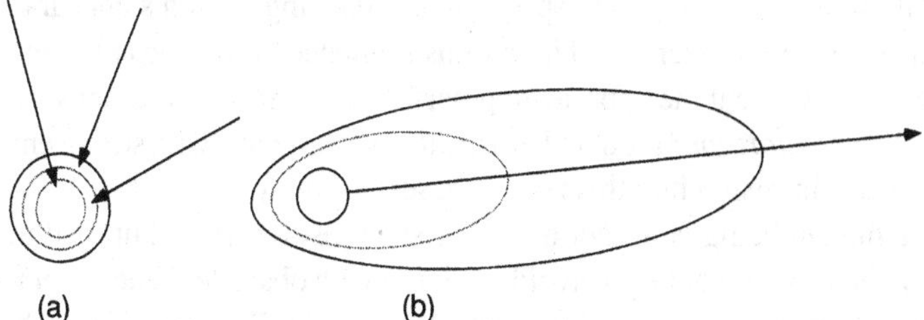

FIGURE 11.1. (a) Humans can be seen as having different zones (intimate, personal, social) around them (Hall, 1966), with thresholds which trigger approach or avoidance response, depending on the approaching person (or animal or object). (b) When in motion, more space is needed in front to avoid collisions with objects. The safety zone (Gibson and Crooks, 1938), whether in motion or not, can also be seen as a comfort zone, with no threat, risk, or discomfort felt (cf. 'zero-risk model', Näätänen and Summala, 1976; Summala, 1988).

traffic situations by modifying their efforts (attention, vigilance), but they also determine the nature and degree of the difficulty of these various situations and their current task (Näätänen and Summala, 1976, p. 35). This is the prerequisite for the fact that many safety measures have not led to expected results.

In sharp contrast to Taylor's and Wilde's models, they proposed a threshold model with three major starting points:

(1) 'Subjective risk monitor' for present or anticipated fear is the major inhibitory, limiting mechanism in driver behaviour.
(2) Drivers' goals and excitatory motives push them towards the limits, e.g., towards higher speed if not otherwise restricted.
(3) Safety margins are in a key position in driver's task control (see the next section).

In their control flow model, Näätänen and Summala (1974) postulated a motivation module which produces desired actions or tends to keep pace (to maintain progress). Action is continuously monitored by the subjective risk monitor which, given a certain threshold is exceeded or anticipated, alerts and takes a role in decisions. Drivers' goals and so-called extra motives, either arisen in traffic or brought from outside it, got an important role in Näätänen and Summala model.

11.3 Safety Margins and Safety Zone

Another line of thinking comes from two sources, from the so-called proxemics approach (Hall, 1966) and from an early work of Gibson and Crooks (1938) on safety zone (see Fig 11.1).

Hall (1966) described people having different zones around them, depending on who is approaching. The intimate zone, with full contact, is reserved only for closest people – family members and best friends – while personal, social and public zones are applied for less familiar people and social situations. These zones translate to critical distances, thresholds which trigger approach or avoidance response, or flight or fight response. In public space an approaching person's appearance and his or her perceived or interpreted intentions influence on feelings of comfort and safety, that is, the threat the approaching person represents. In that sense, humans have safety or *comfort zone* around them in all environments, with strong emotional characteristics: intrusion into this zone arouses discomfort.

When a human being is in motion, he or she must reserve additional margins, especially ahead of him or her, to avoid colliding with obstacles: The faster the self-motion the more space is needed in front. As noted by Rumar (1988), a Swedish engineer Sylwan (1919) already described the physical and psychological space which different traffic units require on streets, from a slowly moving pedestrian to a fast car. Two decades later, Gibson and Crooks (1938), in their excellent analysis and series of drawings, demonstrate how roadway, obstacles and other road users modify this space – safety zone. They also implied that safety zone – and stopping distance within it – is an objectively measurable concept:

> Phenomenally, it is a sort of tongue protruding forward along the road. Its boundaries are chiefly determined by objects or features of the terrain with a negative 'valence' in perception. It is not, however, merely a subjective experience of the driver. It exists objectively as the actual field within which the car can safely operate, whether or not the driver is aware of it. It shifts and changes continually, bending and twisting with the road, and also elongating and contracting, widening and narrowing, according as obstacles encroach on it and limits its boundaries. (Gibson and Crooks, 1938, p. 121)

The safety zone, or safety margins which road users must keep around them, can be expressed, measured, and are functional in both space and time. We have to drive a car through gaps, in space or time, and to keep distance to other vehicles and to pedestrians, bicyclists and road-side obstacles. This *distance from crash* is essential metrics in everyday control of safety. On a two-lane road, for example, an almost certain death lurks at a distance of 2 to 3 m when one meets a heavy vehicle (even a car) and every driver must take care of keeping a sufficient margin. If the distance – safety margin – is not wide enough, we feel uncomfortable.

However, car control is also extensively based on time margins such as time-to-collision and time-to-line-crossing. Therefore, keeping the car in a lane is not a simple tracking task nulling the error from the mid of the lane or the intended trajectory (cf. Donges, 1978). The latter model might be relevant in 'active driving', with all attention focussed on driving and optimal lane control. In normal everyday driving, instead, a lane should rather be conceived as a tube with a lot of tolerance and time to correct path within it. As proposed by Godthelp et al. (1984), time-to-line-crossing is a relevant measure, referring to the time until the car drifts out of the lane if not corrected through steering. It is the measure which sets the time limit – the threshold – for drivers' path correcting.

Time-to-collision or time-to-contact is a central control measure when we continuously adjust distance to a braking vehicle in front of us (Lee, 1976), or start braking when approaching an obstacle or a stop line at a crossing (van der Horst, 1990). It defines time distance to a crash, or to the moment that braking must be started to avoid the crash. As proposed by Lee (1976), the optical variable τ alone gives a direct approximation of the time to collision, and its first-time derivative (tau dot) provides a feasible strategy to control braking when kept within a certain range. There is indeed a lot of evidence that the human perceptual system is well equipped to accurately estimate time to collision, at short distances at least when optic resolution of the looming object is sufficient. This means that at any moment we know when we will crash with a car or an obstacle we are approaching to. However, this information does not yet reveal whether we are able to stop before the obstacle, or when we should start braking to avoid the crash.

Quite recently, Fajen (2005) showed that performance in stopping in front of an obstacle also depends on global optic flow and edge rate (providing speed information), and that information is needed (along with tau) to tell whether stopping is possible with available braking force. In other words, this information – open to continuous calibration of maximum deceleration level – provides us with an estimate of the *action boundary*, that is, the limit above which stopping is no more possible. Fajen (2005) also returns to Gibson and Crooks (1938): it was already in their paper that, in defining the safety zone, they made a distinction between trajectories which are available and the ones which not. It was a beginning of the later development of Gibson's concept of affordance – what the environment affords to the human.

It should be added that (mainly vision-based) space and time margins are not of course the only ones to determine and to set limits for driver behaviour. For example, while time-to-line-crossing has a role when approaching a bend, lateral acceleration is a marked factor and a marked source of proprioceptive and kinesthetic information in curves and steering manoeuvres (Reymond et al., 2001). Available friction in a curve can also be seen as a safety margin measure (Rumar et al., 1976; Summala and Merisalo, 1980; Wong and Nicholson, 1992), indicating a distance to a loss of grip and control. At low friction and low speed in a steep off-ramp drivers typically drive close to the threshold of loss of control, in terms of available friction, while safety margins grow with friction (when slipperiness decreases) and speed (Summala and Merisalo, 1980). It suggests that available friction margin is far from a simple distance measure. Drivers may misperceive the slipperiness at approach phase – in wintertime lower volume ramps are often more slippery than motorway lanes – but they may also accept a smaller margin to grip loss at slow speed when the chances to regain control are bigger (cf. Brown, 1980) and consequences of loss of control and running off the road smaller. Some drivers – young men especially – may also intentionally make their car skidding in more or less good control.

11.4 Available Time, Workload and Multilevel Task Control

It is essential to note that time safety margins have an important feature: they imply a *concept of available time*. Available time determines brake reaction latencies as well as time sharing while driving, among other things. The timing of brake response in front of an unavoidable obstacle therefore depends on the time-to-collision (or on time to the moment that braking is to be started to provide a smooth and comfortable stopping). Therefore, the brake reaction time of unalerted drivers in real-life conditions depends on the urgency of the situation, however such that there is a substantial variation due to drivers' attentiveness, age and individual response style among others (Summala and Koivisto, 1990; Summala, 2000).

For an experienced driver, especially in routine open road driving, time is an abundant resource which can be used for many kinds of in-car activities. As expected, in terms of time-to-line-crossing, a wider road means more time and, accordingly, drivers allow longer glances and more time for subsidiary tasks (Wikman et al., 1998; Wikman and Summala, 2005). Similarly, less time is available – and used – for an additional task at curves and at higher speeds, when more time is needed to update position information, to predict the course, and even to plan the next step in a subsidiary task (Wikman et al., 1997). On a curvy road at high speed drivers have to attend to the road and steering entirely, and subsidiary tasks typically drop out or slow down when available time (and spare capacity; see, e.g., Harms, 1991) diminishes.

The concept of available time is closely related to workload felt by drivers. It is the other side of task complexity, the information to be processed in a time unit. The more complex the task (e.g., traffic environment), given same speed, the higher the workload. By adjusting speed, however, the drivers can reduce the information processing rate and provide themselves with more time, make their task more controllable and less loading, simply speaking, less difficult.

Among many dimensions of workload (e.g., Hart and Staveland, 1988), time and time pressure are critical always when a human is in motion, and especially at speeds of vehicular traffic. This is in line with Hancock and Caird's model, which predicted that mental load grows as effective time for action decreases (Hancock and Caird, 1993). On the other side, sufficient time and adequate time margins imply the feeling of control, comfort and safety. This is also the essence of the expertise which practice brings for drivers during the first tens of thousands of kilometres, when car control skills get more automated and require less attention, and improved anticipatory traffic control skills allow more time to prepare for potential hazards.

Accordingly, the hierarchical model of behavioural adaptation (Summala, 1997) predicts that available time and related workload mediate between operational and tactical, even strategic levels of driving. Figure 11.2, outlining the role of time in traffic behaviour, proposes that mobility and other goals of driving influence on trip decisions and target speed planned to complete the trip. This target (desired) speed further affects on safety margins and modifies and generates manoeuvres, for example, overtaking a slower vehicle on highway or weaving in and out for a faster lane and progress in city.

A control loop from operational to upper levels is assumed on the basis of safety margins and available time. Given a certain speed and certain complexity of the environment, if a driver cannot complete all operational subtasks (in the control

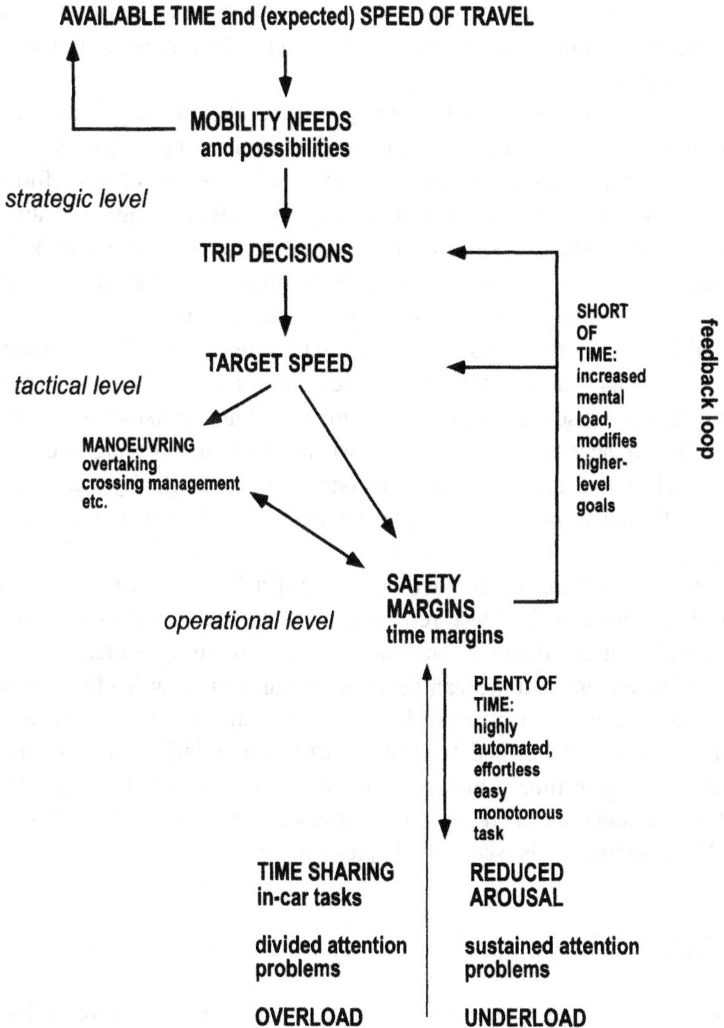

FIGURE 11.2. The role of time is essential when a human is in motion and making travel decisions. Time margins and available time for action, through mental load, also mediate between different levels of driving (adapted from Summala, 1997).

of car and traffic) at this speed, within available time margins, he or she feels high mental load and

either slows down to get more time, to reach the feeling of control and an acceptable (or comfortable) level of workload; or

continues in the unstable zone, feels increased mental load, and may experience sudden overload problems.

However, if a driver repeatedly or continuously experiences certain conditions too loading, pressing, or difficult, he or she starts to avoid them. For example, elderly drivers with slower performance (and lower contrast sensitivity and increased glare discomfort) start to avoid driving in the dark, in heavy traffic and in winter time, etc.

On the other side, if a driver has plenty of time, like on a high-standard road with a fairly low speed limit, he/she is inclined to perform secondary tasks; or is at risk of getting bored and tired, both of which mean unstable performance of the driver/vehicle system. Secondary tasks, while driving, require reliable time and attention sharing and easily lead to delayed detection of relevant information, overload, and increased risk. Underload and lowered arousal level also result in delayed responses and attention lapses, if not falling asleep.

Available time incorporates many essential features like task (environment) complexity, mental load and stress. It is, by definition, always a factor when humans are in motion. It is also a factor when road users are doing decisions while stopped in traffic, in gap acceptance for example, when drivers are crossing or entering a priority road. In that case the traffic flow on a main road actually means making a selection from a number of closing time margins, and the situation may be very loading.

The key issue in the model is that time margins (in the meaning of distance from crash or from the normal or 'last' response threshold) are very basic measures for humans, with a strong affective component if certain limits are violated. Available time in turn defines what we can do in each situation, how loading we feel a situation, and therefore it provides both cognitive and affective mechanism for control. Hollnagel (2002) and Hollnagel and Woods (2005) similarly gave the concept of available time a marked position in their Extended Control Model, such that time and control are closely intertwined and mediate between different hierarchical control levels (see also Chapter 4 in this volume).

11.5 Safety Margins, Affordances and Skills

We see that time (and space) margins have a double role in driver behaviour determination. On one hand, they set (and show) the limits to how close to a hazard we can go and, on the other hand, they provide (and show) us with opportunities to promote our goals and motives.

Time and space are actually resources which the traffic system affords, and we more or less actively look for time and space (or, to be more accurate, spatiotemporal) slots to promote mobility and progress. We look for sufficient – affordable, safe, comfortable – gaps in main road flow to cross the road, in the oncoming flow to afford overtaking a slower vehicle, in an adjacent lane to change lane, and empty (or faster) lanes to promote progress in city. Time and space slots can be seen as opportunities which dynamic traffic environment affords – affordances in Gibson's terminology (Gibson, 1979).

It is important to note that what the environment affords is necessarily related to one's abilities, skills and physical characteristics (e.g., Greeno, 1994). Warren (1984) nicely showed that 'climbability' of stairs of different height is directly dependent on the length of the knee, and Warren and Whang (1987) showed that an affordable aperture for walking through without body rotation depends on shoulder width. Available space in relation to the shoulder width therefore determines the action which is most *comfortable and efficient*, as well as the transition point between two choices, unrotated and rotated pass. The affordances of the car/driver system are similarly related to the 'body size' of the vehicle, but also on the driver's ability to estimate car dimensions relative to the available gap and to steer through it. Similarly, a gap between vehicles in the oncoming flow is sufficient or not for overtaking a slower vehicle in front, depending on its size, vehicles' speeds, the own car's acceleration and the driver's estimation skills. Therefore, the skills acquired during the driving career essentially affect on what is affordable. This is also the essence of the process where novice drivers extend the realm of the possible operations they will attempt while learning to know dynamic, spatiotemporal limits of the driver-car unit amid of traffic:

> Every decision made, every action taken, every traffic situation one is exposed to, provides some kind of feedback to the driver. It is presumably this feedback that is the really efficient driving teacher. As to the aspect of the safety of different actions, decisions and situations, the related feedback is presumably received in the form of subjective time and space separating the driver from an accident; hence the driver can test different kinds of operations, driving manners, etc. against these subjective dimensions and thus finally develop rather permanent criteria for different kinds of actions, decisions and traffic situations. It is proposed that these criteria are subject to a continuous back-and-forth change, at least to a minor extent, through the whole driving career. (Näätänen and Summala, 1976, pp. 87–88)

Among recent conceptualisations of the driver's choices between options, Groeger (2000), in his differential analysis, gives a detailed model of how drivers manage with implied goal interruptions, appraising them, and planning and implementing actions to handle them, along with a multitude of factors that explain interindividual variance in these performances. Goodrich et al. (2000) first defined a skill as a learned sequence of human activities, whether it be simple or complex, and then proposed that humans map environmental cues for a given task, and implement a skill when appropriate. Goodrich et al. fix affordances to skills such that the (cognitive) skills provide affordances for rational behaviour, with different attractive and repulsive potentials (p. 94): 'Skills whose affordances are compatible with top-down goals induce an attractive potential commensurate with their likely usefulness. ... However, in addition to task specific goals there are also context-dependent constraints on the efficiency of these skills, and these constraints induce a repulsive potential commensurate with their likely inefficiency.' The choice of an option then depends on the trade-off between its attractive and repulsive potentials (benefits and costs): this comparison defines whether the *option is satisficing*.

We see here again a certain resemblance with Gibson and Crooks (1938), who joined *negative valences* to those trajectories which are *not available* for a driver, and *positive valences* to the ones which are available. In Damasio's (1994) terms, we could say that in the potentially hostile road environment the options on the road obviously are tagged with either negative (risky) or positive (goal-directed) somatic markers. These markers then precede rational evaluation and facilitate and speed up the choice. In dynamic time-limited situations like driving, fast affective heuristics must have a big role (Finucane et al., 2000). We could even say that safety margins have such a role (see already in Summala, 1988), telling what choices are affordable and what are not, and when the situation is going out of the control and needs an appropriate reaction. In line with Näätänen and Summala's model, given certain environmental information through perception and expectancies it triggers, motives feed desired actions while 'risk monitor' blocks implementation if fired through perceived or anticipated threat.

11.6 Towards Unifying Emotional Concepts in Routine Driving

Emotional tension, task difficulty, or best feeling has been proposed (see above) as critical motivational or affective control measures which guide driving. Rather than a single (affective) control measure, there are many processes involved, and a unifying concept is sought here which should cover all major determinants of driving. It is also an attempt to outline what might be the role of weak emotions in driving. Although traffic psychologists have mostly considered strong emotions such as anger or fear, however, weaker, less aroused emotions may have a much bigger role in everyday driving, and highly probably even in everyday crashes.

Safety margins (and safety zone) are necessarily the primary and very basic control measures in on-road driving and, as proposed above, both continuous task control and choices at tactical and strategic levels can be defined using them. They both set the limits to how close to a hazard we can go and provide us with opportunities to promote our goals and motives. As proposed above, time margins also provide a mechanism for explaining mental load while in move.

In explaining driver behaviour we also have to conceptualise motives and goals which push drivers towards hazards – towards shorter safety margins. This is not enough yet however. We have to incorporate rules, social norms, vehicle and road system (in so far as not already included in the control of safety margins, in what is affordable on a certain road with a certain car). I recently proposed what I called 'multiple comfort zone model' to incorporate all relevant factors into one general framework (Summala, 2005).

This is not one-dimensional target model. Instead, a few functional control variables are defined (not exhaustively) which drivers are assumed to keep within an acceptable range, in the 'comfort zone', such that this process determines not only, say, the speed level in normal routine driving or a decision whether to overtake a slower car, but also results in a general 'comfortable' or 'best feeling' state. It may be seen as a target state, given a certain trip and conditions, but it is rather an output of many cognitively definable processes all of which can be included under the shared umbrella concept of *comfort*.

The factors to be kept within the 'comfort zone', to exemplify normal driving situations, are proposed below, both including inhibitory and excitatory ones. Note that for each main factor, there are specific models to explain cognitive processes involved.

11.6.1 Safety Margins – To Control and Survive

The 'comfort zone' implies sufficient space and time margins around the driver, that is, to road edges, obstacles, other vehicles and, finally, to a crash. Safety margins are understood as being the major tool for survival and the major control variable, and they also provide efficient feedback in the learning phase. Sufficient margins are needed by drivers to feel safe and comfortable while driving, with no excessive mental load, also implying that they feel able to manage with all subtasks within available time.

A threshold model for safety margin management is assumed. It is assumed that drivers normally feel full control over the task and no risk while driving. At certain (inherent and learned) thresholds of safety margins, corrective steering and speed adjustment is triggered. Too short time or space distances make drivers to feel uncomfortable, and they do not tolerate it at least without a very strong motive to continue.

It is to be noted that the ordinary language use of 'comfort' also corresponds very well to the essence of safety margins: a person may be *too close* to a danger (or cliff edge, road edge, a truck, etc.) *for comfort*. Several researchers have indeed used the comfort criterion or scale in their experimental research while assessing a limit for normal, comfortable, acceptable driving. A close connection of safety margins to the concept of comfort was already shown by Godthelp (1988), who instructed drivers in open road driving to correct their path only at the moment when it could still be corrected comfortably to prevent a crossing of the lane boundary. This resulted in a constant time distance (time-to-line crossing) at the moment of decision over a broad range of speeds. Ohta (1993) asked drivers to follow a car under four instructions in his on-road study, including, 'follow at a distance which you feel most comfortable; 'approach until you begin to feel the distance dangerous'; 'follow at the minimum safe distance'; and 'follow at a distance which you feel to be neither too far not too close'. On the basis of his data and Hall's (1966) proxemics concept, he defined a danger zone (headway up to 0.6 s), critical zone (up to 1.1 s), and comfortable zone (1.1 to 1.7 s, mean 1.4 s). Interestingly (cf. below), he concluded that longer headways, rather considered as pursuit distances, are uncomfortable for steady state following because they are against the social norm. For other relevant studies, see also, for example, van Winsum and Heino (1995), De Vos et al. (1997), Taieb-Maimon and Shinar (2001).

Other things being equal, motives typically push drivers towards the safety margins threshold but, typically, they keep at a comfortable margin from it. A violation of the safety/comfort zone alarms, and a sudden unexpected violation frightens: this is the affective 'subjective risk' monitor proposed by Näätänen and Summala (1974, 1976).

11.6.2 Vehicle/Road System – To Provide Smooth and Comfortable Travel

The modern cars are silent and go smoothly at speeds normally used. Poorly balanced tires make the car shaking at high speeds, however, and gravel, snow or ice on road makes control much less confident and comfortable. Thermal comfort, seat comfort and vibration are a widely studied area with advanced models on what is comfortable (e.g., Jiang et al., 2001; Gameiro da Silva, 2002). Glare discomfort has long been used as a criterion in vehicle headlight studies (Olson and Sivak, 1984; Sivak et al., 1991; Theeuwes et al., 2002), while visual comfort is a general concept (and scale) for texts, pictures and visual display units (see, e.g., Roufs and Boschman, 1997).

Drivers also appear to have certain thresholds for stopping deceleration, indicative of discomfort. Thus, while approaching a signalised intersection, drivers tend to pass through if the required deceleration exceeds 3 to 3.5 ms^{-2} at the time of yellow onset (Baguley, 1988; Niittymäki and Pursula, 1994; van der Horst and Wilmink, 1986). The motion change (jerks or the acceleration's time derivative) has been used as a passenger's comfort metrics in public transportation, with the threshold of 2 ms^{-3} (Canudas-de-Wit et al., 2005).

11.6.3 Rule Following – To Avoid Sanctions

Rule following is a major pacing factor when the speed limits restrict speed rather than the infrastructure. The 'comfort zone' implies no concern of getting fined. This is a simple mechanism which incorporates speed limits into speed adjustment by drivers. The cognitive analysis may indeed include optimisation with estimates of police enforcement, for example. However, strictly keeping to speed limits or to the announced sanction limit or 'driving with others' are those simple strategies which guarantee comfortable mood. Compliance with rules means not only the law but also social norms, which may differ a lot from what is defined in the law. Therefore, actual speed level on the road affects drivers' target speeds beyond speed limit (e.g., Haglund and Åberg, 2000), while drivers' perception of other people's speed may be biased and tend to amplify the social norm effect (Connolly andÅberg, 1993).

Some drivers appear to have a rather consistent intention to speed, also related to higher crash risk, which however seems to indicate general social deviance rather than, for example, underestimation of consequences (Lawton et al., 1997). A bulk of research has focused on analysing interindividual factors behind rule breaking in the context of Theory of Planned Action (Ajzen, 1991). However, in daily choices and ordinary driving, habit seems to be a stronger determinant of behaviour than intention (Ouellette and Wood, 1998; Verplanken et al., 1998).

11.6.4 Good (or Expected) Progress of Trip – Mobility and Pace/Progress

Good progress of the trip is a major mobility factor. Keeping in the 'comfort zone' implies that travel progresses as expected, while tendency to maintain progress – speed and fluent progress – may grow a strong motivational force such that deceleration is felt punishing and keeping the speed and pace represent the 'comfort zone'. Sensory and cognitive adaptation even tends to move the current speed upwards little by little. Therefore, these mobility-related goals should be conceived as excitatory ones. They push drivers towards rule breaking and critical safety margin thresholds.

11.7 Comfort Through Satisficing

A few major factors were listed above, relevant for a driver when he or she controls a car in traffic in normal everyday driving. It is hypothesised that drivers normally keep each of them within a certain range (or above certain threshold), in a 'comfort zone'. This mechanism results in a comfortable state, or best feeling in the sense of Damasio (1994) and Vaa (2004). The process can be called satisficing, in contrast to optimising, according to the well-known principle of Simon (1955), who proposed that the option is chosen which first fulfils a certain aspiration level on a few criteria.

Emotions can be practically located on two dimensions, pleasure and intensity. Comfort is here thought as a general mood, or emotion which is pleasant but not especially aroused, tense, or activated. Fig. 11.3 illustrates 'driving moods' in a schematic map of core affects (Russell and Barrett, 1999). Routine, daily, comfortable driving ranges from contended to relaxed or calm, while reduced arousal level (task induced, circadian or sleep deprived) makes driving drowsy and unpleasant.

Comfort is pleasant, by definition, and indeed riding comfort is sometimes equalled to pleasure (e.g., Canudas-de-Wit et al., 2005). A driver can experience pleasurable feelings in normal, safe, rule-following driving, for example, due to feeling of control, and when travel goes on fluently, without jams, delays or extra decelerations due to slow drivers ahead. Ride comfort of the car undoubtedly affects to such feelings. At best, very normal safe driving provides a flow experience of optimal control.

Hedonistic motives and pleasure indeed have long acknowledged as important determinants of driving (e.g., Black, 1966; Näätänen and Summala, 1976; Rothengatter, 1988) which, however, easily slip to hazardous behaviour. Speed tends to grow, and even normal comfortable driving may have negative effects on safety. Keeping the pace tends to elevate the threshold of slowing down for safety, and higher speed even forces to selective visual search which ignores less probable risks (e.g., Räsänen and Summala, 2000; Summala and Räsänen, 2000). Driving for pleasure may mean sensation seeking and 'high' from speed, acceleration, and close margins, and competitive tendencies. Other extra motives, additional to pure

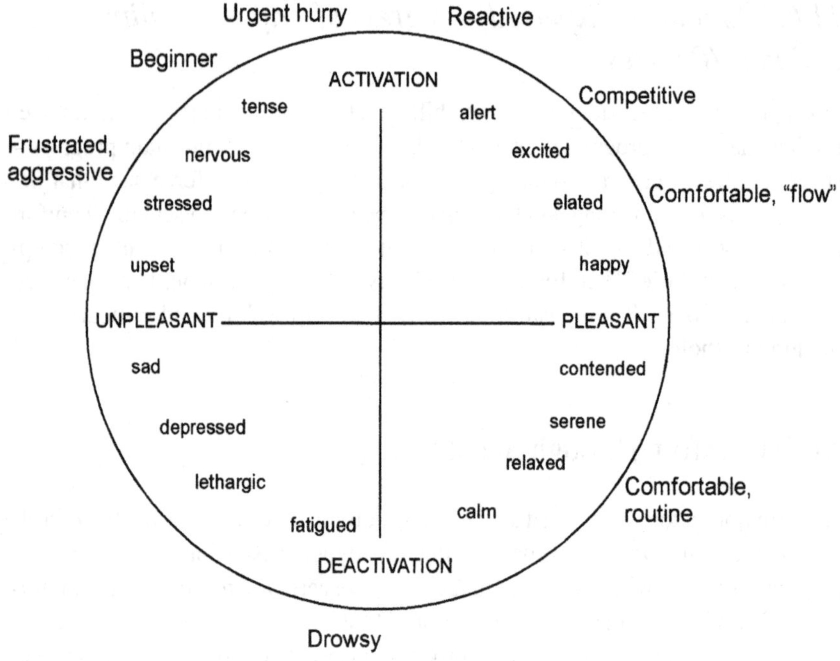

FIGURE 11.3. Driving moods as projected on the two-dimensional schematic map of core affects (Russell and Feldman Barrett, 1999). Routine, daily, comfortable driving ranges from contended to relaxed or calm.

mobility goals, such as hurry, social pressure (in car and by other drivers), self-enhancement, competition, thrill seeking, may also take control. Stronger emotions arise when driving becomes competitive, or reactive in heavy traffic, while hurry and frustrated aggressive driving exemplifies aroused (activated) emotions on the side of displeasure (Fig. 11.3). Even a thought that the roadway might be slippery due to black ice makes driving tense and unpleasant, at least for a while.

However, it is claimed here that normal everyday driving is largely habitual activity, aiming at keeping within comfortable limits, with no feelings of risk, or anxiety, or discomfort. The output is, then, a fairly stable emotional state (which, unfortunately, every now and then is disturbed by hurry, frustration, aggression and other strong effects). Our cognitive system provides fairly good information on where the limits of 'safety zone' are (even if it often tends to be biased) while the emotional system essentially contributes and warns about 'wrong' choices or when limits are being approached. This is well in line with weak emotional signals proposed by Damasio (1994; for more detail, see also Chapters 10 and 12 in this volume).

It is interesting to see how strongly emotions have now intruded into modelling human (risky) choices. Damasio's (1994) book and subsequent experimental work (e.g., Bechara et al., 1997) has attracted much enthusiasm. Also the long tradition of *risk perception* research, in the meaning of evaluating risks of different activities (e.g., Fischhoff et al., 1978) – has now more explicitly welcome the emotional component in risky decisions, 'risk as feeling' (e.g., Slovic et al., 2004). However, early 'risk theories' in driver behaviour already assumed a marked emotional component in driver task control. Taylor (1964) indeed launched the 'emotional tension' as a critical measure, and Näätänen and Summala (1976), while describing the function of 'risk monitor', considered risk as feeling:

> Hence, the general view of the road users' behavioral dynamics was advanced that his behavior is continuously pushed by his (other-than-safety) motives in their direction. For example, a driver in a hurry wants more and more speed, but that somewhere along this shift toward those behavioral forms which give more and more satisfaction to his (excitatory) motives (which, simultaneously, are also in general more dangerous), the 'Subjective Risk Monitor' becomes activated and this development is usually soon stopped. It was suggested that under 'normal', 'relaxed' driving motivation, only those decisions are made which are not associated with subjective risk (at the moment of decision) and that when subjective risk is felt in some actual driving situation, the behavior is changed so as to eliminate the source of this feeling. (Näätänen and Summala, 1976, p. 221)

11.8 'Go to the Road': Need of On-Road Research

However, it is not time to carry away the cognitive basis of driver task and risk control, but rather to remind that the cognitive and emotional systems cooperate closely intertwined. Much confusion has originated from the misunderstanding of their roles in interpreting different kinds of evidence in driver behavior analysis. Risk estimates 'from arm chair' (see McKenna, 1982; Summala, 1985), while filling questionnaires, pushing buttons in laboratory experiments, or even while driving in simulators, do not grasp real emotional contents of on-road driving. Even Fuller (2005, Fig. 5; and this volume) appears to misinterpret the results from his recent laboratory experiment in which participants looked at videoclips taken from a highway at different speeds. 'Estimated task difficulty' and (conscious, rational) 'risk experience' indeed correlated perfectly in his data – even to the degree that they seemed to be inseparable and semantically confused measures drawn from rational evaluation. However, when the presentation speed increased, the threshold where the estimated crash risk deviated from zero obviously equalled to the threshold for not being able to manage at higher speed: '95% of the sample would be uncomfortable driving at a speed at which there was some estimated risk of crashing' (Fuller, 2005, p. 469). Even if only based on a cognitive evaluation of the task in a laboratory and obviously not capable of triggering any emotional response (with no true hazard, no game or no social pressure included), this result appears to support the threshold model. We have indeed to assume that mobility-related and other excitatory motives push drivers towards a threshold such that the task difficulty grows and task demands follow capabilities at a certain margin.

Finally, when the role of motives and emotions in driver behavior is now generally acknowledged, theorising needs testable hypotheses and their tests in real-life driving.

References

Ajzen, I. (1991). The theory of planned action. *Organizational Behavior and Human Deision Processes*, 50, 179–211.

Baguley, C.J. (1988). 'Running the red' at signals on high-speed roads. *Traffic Engineering and Control*, 29, 415–420.

Bechara, A., Damasio, H., Tranel, D. and Damasio, A.R. (1997). Deciding advantageously before knowing the advantageous strategy. *Science*, 275(5304), 1293–1295.

Black, S. (1966). *Man and motor cars*. Seeker & Warburg, London.

Blumenthal, M. (1968). Dimensions of the traffic safety problem. *Traffic Safety Research Review*, 12, 7–12.

Brown, I.D. (1980). Error-correction probability as a determinant of drivers' subjective risk. In D.J. Oborne and J.A. Levis (Eds.). *Human factors in transport research* (Vol. 2, pp. 311–319). Academic Press, London.

Canudas-de-Wit, C., Bechart, H., Claeys, X., Dolcini, P. and Martinez, J.J. (2005). Fun-to-drive by feedback. *European Journal of Control*, 11(4/5), 353–383.

Connolly, T. and Åberg, L. (1993). Some contagion models of speeding. *Accident Analysis and Prevention*, 25(1), 57–66.

Damasio, A.R. (1994). *Descartes' error: Emotion, reason, and the human brain*. G. P. Putnam's Sons, New York.

De Vos, A.P., Theeuwes, J., Hoekstra, W. and Coëmet, M.J. (1997). Behavioral aspects of automatic vehicle guidance. Relationship between headway and driver comfort. *Transportation Research Record*, 1573, 17–22.

Donges, E. (1978). A two-level model of driver steering behavior. *Human Factors*, 20, 691–707.

Evans, L. (1991). *Traffic safety and the driver*. Van Nostrand Reinhold, New York.

Fajen, B.R. (2005). Calibration, information, and control strategies for braking to avoid a collision. *Journal of Experimental Psychology – Human Perception and Performance*, 31(3), 480–501.

Finucane, M.L., Alhakami, A., Slovic, P. and Johnson, S.M. (2000). The affect heuristic in judgments of risks and benefits. *Journal of Behavioral Decision Making*, 13(1), 1–17.

Fischhoff, B., Slovic, P., Lichtenstein, S., Read, S. and Combs, B. (1978). How safe is safe enough? A psychometric study of attitudes towards technological risks and benefits. *Policy Sciences*, 9, 127–152.

Fuller, R. (2000). The task–capability interface model of the driving process. *Journal Recherche-Transport-Sécurité (RTS)*, 66, 47–59.

Fuller, R. (2004). Zero risk versus target risk: Can they both be right? Paper presented at the *3rd International Conference on Traffic and Transport Psychology 2004, Symposium on Traffic Psychology Theories*. Nottingham, UK.

Fuller, R. (2005). Towards a general theory of driver behaviour. *Accident Analysis and Prevention*, 37, 461–472.

Gameiro da Silva, M.C. (2002). Measurements of comfort in vehicles. *Measurement Science and Technology*, 13, R41–R60.

Gibson, J.J. (1979). *The ecological approach to visual perception*. Houghton Mifflin, Boston.

Gibson, J.J. and Crooks, L.E. (1938). A theoretical field-analysis of automobile driving. *American Journal of Psychology*, 51, 453–471.

Godthelp, H. (1988). The limits of path error-neglecting in straight lane driving. *Ergonomics*, 31, 609–619.

Godthelp, H., Milgram, P. and Blaauw, G.J. (1984). The development of a time-related measure to describe driving strategy. *Human Factors*, 26, 257–268.

Goodrich, M.A., Stirling, W.C. and Boer, E.R. (2000). Satisficing revisited. *Minds and Machines*, 10(1), 79–110.

Greeno, J.G. (1994). Gibson's Affordances. *Psychological Review*, 101(2), 336–342.

Groeger, J. (2000). *Understanding Driving*. Psychology Press, Hove.

Haglund, M. and Åberg, L. (2000). Speed choice in relation to speed limit and influences from other drivers. *Transportation Research Part F: Traffic Psychology and Behaviour*, 3(1), 39–51.

Hall, E.T. (1966). *The hidden dimension*. Doubleday, Garden City.

Hancock, P.A. and Caird, J.K. (1993). Experimental evaluation of a model of mental workload. *Human Factors*, 35, 413–429.

Hancock, P.A. and Warm, J.S. (1989). A dynamic model of stress and sustained attention. *Human Factors*, 31, 519–537.

Harms, L. (1991). Variation in drivers' cognitive load: Effects of driving through village areas and rural junctions. *Ergonomics*, 34, 151–160.

Hart, S.G. and Staveland, L.E. (1988). Development of the NASA-TLX (Task Load Index): Results of empirical and theoretical research. In P.A. Hancock and N. Meshkati (Eds.). *Human mental workload* (pp. 139–183). Elsevier, Amsterdam.

Hollnagel, E. (2002). Time and time again. *Theoretical Issues in Ergonomics Science*, 3(2), 143–158.

Hollnagel, E. and Woods, D.D. (2005). *Joint cognitive systems*. CRC Press, Boca Raton, FL.

Jiang, Z.Y., Streit, D.A. and El-Gindy, M. (2001). Heavy vehicle ride comfort: Literature survey. *Heavy Vehicle Systems – International Journal of Vehicle Design*, 8(3/4), 258–284.

Lawton, R., Parker, D., Stradling, S.G. and Manstead, A.S.R. (1997). Predicting road traffic accidents: The role of social deviance and violations. *British Journal of Psychology*, 88, 249–262.

Lee, D.N. (1976). A theory of visual control of braking based on information about time-to-collision. *Perception*, 5, 437–459.

McKenna, F.P. (1982). The human factor in driving accidents: An overview of approaches and problems. *Ergonomics*, 25, 867–877.

Näätänen, R. and Summala, H. (1974). A model for the role of motivational factors in drivers' decision-making. *Accident Analysis and Prevention*, 6, 243–261.

Näätänen, R. and Summala, H. (1976). *Road-user behavior and traffic accidents*. North-Holland/American Elsevier, Amsterdam/New York.

Niittymäki, J. and Pursula, M. (1994). *Valo-ohjattujen liittymien simulointi ja ajodynamiikka (Simulation of signalized intersections and driving dynamics)* (Publication No. 81). Helsinki University of Technology, Transportation Engineering.

Ohta, H. (1993). Individual differences in driving distance headway. In A.G. Gale et al. (Eds.). *Vision in vehicles* (Vol. 4, pp. 91–100). Elsevier, Amsterdam.

Olson, P.L. and Sivak, M. (1984). Discomfort glare from automobile headlights. *Journal of the Illuminating Engineering Society*, 13, 296–303.

Ouellette, J.A. and Wood, W. (1998). Habit and intention in everyday life: The multiple processes by which past behavior predicts future behavior. *Psychological Bulletin*, 124, 54–74.

Räsänen, M. and Summala, H. (2000). Car drivers' adjustments to cyclists at roundabouts. *Transportation Human Factors*, 2, 1–17.

Reymond, G., Kemeny, A., Droulez, J. and Berthoz, A. (2001). Role of lateral acceleration in curve driving: Driver model and experiments on a real vehicle and a driving simulator. *Human Factors*, 43(3), 483–495.

Robertson, L.S. and Pless, I.B. (2002). For and against: Does risk homoeostasis theory have implications for road safety. *British Medical Journal*, 324, 1151–1152.

Rothengatter, T. (1988). Risk and the absence of pleasure: A motivational approach to modelling road user behaviour. *Ergonomics*, 31, 599–607.

Roufs, J.A.J. and Boschman, M.C. (1997). Text quality metrics for visual display units .1. Methodological aspects. *Displays*, 18(1), 37–43.

Rumar, K. (1988). Collective risk but individual safety. *Ergonomics*, 31, 507–518.

Rumar, K., Berggrund, U., Jernberg, P. and Ytterbom, U. (1976). Driver reaction to a technical safety measure: Studded tires. *Human Factors*, 18, 443–454.

Russell, J.A. and Barrett, L.F. (1999). Core affect, prototypical emotional episodes, and other things called emotion: Dissecting the elephant. *Journal of Personality and Social Psychology*, 76(5), 805–819.

Simon, H. (1955). A behavioral model of rational choice. *Quarterly Journal of Economics*, 69, 99–118.

Sivak, M., Flannagan, M., Ensing, M. and Simmons, C.J. (1991). Discomfort glare is task dependent. *International Journal of Vehicle Design*, 12, 152–159.

Slovic, P., Finucane, M.L., Peters, E. and MacGregor, D.G. (2004). Risk as analysis and risk as feelings: Some thoughts about affect, reason, risk, and rationality. *Risk Analysis*, 24(2), 311–322.

Smeed, R.J. (1949). Some statistical aspects of road safety research. *Journal of the Royal Statistical Society, Series A (General)*, 112, 1–34.

Summala, H. (1985). Modeling driver task: A pessimistic prediction? In L. Evans and R.C. Schwing (Eds.). *Human behavior and traffic safety* (pp. 43–65). Plenum, New York.

Summala, H. (1988). Risk control is not risk adjustment: The zero-risk theory of driver behaviour and its implications. *Ergonomics*, 31, 491–506.

Summala, H. (1996). Accident risk and driver behaviour. *Safety Science*, 22, 103–117.

Summala, H. (1997). Hierarchical model of behavioural adaptation and traffic accidents. In T. Rothengatter and E. Carbonell Vaya (Eds.). *Traffic and transport psychology* (pp. 41–52). Pergamon, Amsterdam.

Summala, H. (2000). Brake reaction times and driver behavior analysis. *Transportation Human Factors*, 2, 217–226.

Summala, H. (2005). Traffic psychology theories: Towards understanding driving behaviour and safety efforts. In G. Underwood (Ed.). *Traffic and transport psychology* (pp. 383–394). Elsevier, Oxford.

Summala, H. and Koivisto, I. (1990). Unalerted drivers' brake reaction times: Older drivers compensate their slower reactions by driving more slowly. In T. Benjamin (Ed.). *Driving behaviour in a social context* (pp. 680–683). Paradigme, Caen.

Summala, H. and Merisalo, A. (1980). A psychophysical method for determining the effect of studded tires on safety. *Scandinavian Journal of Psychology*, 21, 193–199.

Summala, H. and Räsänen, M. (2000). Top-down and bottom-up processes in driver behavior at roundabouts and crossroads. *Transportation Human Factors*, 2, 29–37.

Sylwan, C. (1919). Trafiksäkerheten på gata och landsväg (Traffic safety on streets and highways). *Industritidningen i Norden* (No. 50), 357–364.

Taieb-Maimon, M. and Shinar, D. (2001). Minimum and comfortable driving headways: Reality versus perception. *Human Factors*, 43(1), 159–172.

Taylor, D.H. (1964). Drivers' galvanic skin response and the risk of accident. *Ergonomics*, 7, 253–262.

Theeuwes, J., Alferdinck, J. and Perel, M. (2002). Relation between glare and driving performance. *Human Factors*, 44(1), 95–107.

Vaa, T. (2004). Developing a driver behaviour model based on emotions and feelings: Proposing building blocks and interrelationships. Paper presented at the *3rd International Conference on Traffic and Transport Psychology 2004, Symposium on Traffic Psychology Theories*. Nottingham, UK.

Van der Horst, R. and Wilmink, A. (1986). Drivers' decision making at signalized intersections: An optimization of the yellow timing. *Traffic Engineering & Control*, 27, 615–622.

Van der Horst, A.R.A. (1990). *A Time-Based Analysis of Road User Behaviour in Normal and Critical Encounters*. TNO Institute for Perception, Soesterberg.

Verplanken, B., Aarts, H., van Knippenberg, A. and Moonen, A. (1998). Habit versus planned behaviour: A field experiment. *British Journal of Social Psychology*, 37, 111–128.

Warren, W.H. (1984). Perceiving affordances – Visual guidance of stair climbing. *Journal of Experimental Psychology – Human Perception and Performance*, 10(5), 683–703.

Warren, W.H. and Whang, S. (1987). Visual guidance of walking through Apertures – Body-scaled information for affordances. *Journal of Experimental Psychology – Human Perception and Performance*, 13(3), 371–383.

Wikman, A.-S., Laakso, M. and Summala, H. (1997). Time sharing of car drivers as a function of driving speed and task eccentricity. In *The 13th Triennial Congress of International Ergonomics Association*. Tampere, Finland, June 29–July 4, 1997.

Wikman, A.S., Nieminen, T. and Summala, H. (1998). Driving experience and time-sharing during in-car tasks on roads of different width. *Ergonomics*, 41(3), 358–372.

Wikman, A.S. and Summala, H. (2005). Aging and time-sharing in highway driving. *Optometry and Vision Science*, 82(8), 716–723.

Wilde, G.J.S. (1982). The theory of risk homeostasis: Implications for safety and health. *Risk Analysis*, 2, 209–225.

van Winsum, W. and Heino, A. (1996). Choice of time-headway in car-following and the role of time-to-collision information in braking. *Ergonomics*, 39(4), 579–592.

Williams, A.F. and O'Neill, B. (1974). On-the-road driving records of licensed race drivers. *Accident Analysis and Prevention*, 6, 263–270.

Wong, Y.D. and Nicholson, A. (1992). Driver behavior at horizontal curves – risk compensation and the margin of safety. *Accident Analysis and Prevention*, 24(4), 425–436.

12 Modelling Driver Behaviour on Basis of Emotions and Feelings: Intelligent Transport Systems and Behavioural Adaptations

TRULS VAA

12.1 Introduction

Intelligent transport system (ITS) is a generic concept, which covers a wide range of systems. In this context the concept is applied on automotive systems and comprises systems generally defined as (advanced) driver assistance systems (ADAS/DAS), in-vehicle information systems (IVIS) and roadside telematics (RT). The present text focuses on anti-locking brake systems (ABS), which is used as an illustrative example of an ITS, mainly because evaluation studies have shown unintended effects that call for explanations. ABS, which aims to maintain the steering capacity during (heavy) braking by preventing the wheels from locking, is considered a driver assistance system (DAS). ABS has become an increasingly standard equipment of new car makes and has been around for more than 20 years. Several studies have evaluated the effects of ABS on behaviour and accidents and the system is a case of special interest for several reasons: One is the demonstration of risk compensation associated with ABS and other reasons are contra-intuitive and even detrimental effects on traffic safety. With ABS as an illustrative example, several key issues can be discussed when considering ITS in a more generic sense. Further, to better understand and predict effects of ITS, a theoretical driver behaviour model based on emotions and feelings is presented. Behavioural adaptation and risk compensation are regarded as core problems, which have to be addressed in terms of traffic safety. One of the very aims of the proposed driver behaviour model is to explain and predict risk compensation that might be associated with a given ITS.

12.2 Defining Motivation

Motives can be defined as 'factors, which give behaviour energy and direction' (Atkinson et al., 1996). Then, motives are factors, which initiate and govern behaviour. The energy component of the definition shows that a motive basically also is a drive. The direction component implicitly presupposes repulsion or attraction, that is, a movement away from something or attraction to something, which again implies that the repulsive or attractive object has to be loaded with some emotional quality. Otherwise, there would be no energy and no direction (Overskeid, 2000). A neutral object is neither repulsive nor attractive. Hence, the emotional dimension of motives is then a core aspect of motivation.

A second feature of the definition is that it does not say anything about cognition, that is, whether motives are rooted in consciousness or in the unconscious. It may seem self-evident as the role of the unconscious in psychoanalysis and psychodynamic theory is well known, but I nevertheless regard this issue as a significant point, for two reasons:

1. the role of the unconscious has seldom been made explicit in prevailing driver behaviour models, and
2. the phenomenon of risk compensation cannot reach any satisfactory explanation, without including and addressing unconscious processes.

A central concept in biological psychology is the principle of homeostasis, that is, when basic physiological needs are regulated by a homeostatic mechanism as with body temperature, thirst, hunger, sleep, etc. When deviances become larger than the body can regulate internally, the organism will be motivated for a given (external) behaviour resulting in a restored (internal) homeostatic state. Common to psychoanalytic and homeostatic theories on motivation is the way they look upon behaviour as initiated by states of tension in the organism, which in turn leads to specific, purposeful acts when the state of tension exceeds a given threshold. The behavioural goal is then to satisfy the need in order to reduce tension.

12.3 Motivational Aspects in Driver Behaviour Models

One can hardly say that the task of modelling driver behaviour has reached consensus. There is no breakthrough or 'great unified theory' within the field of traffic safety research regarding modelling of driver behaviour (Vaa, 2001a). Models address diverging aspects, several 'favourite' issues and/or concepts are pursued, discussions and disagreement prevail. The listing below includes some of the most predominant theories and models that have been applied to explain and predict driver behaviour and which have motivational aspects as a key factor. The history of models starts in 1938 when Gibson and Crooks' presented their theoretical field-analysis of automobile driving (motivational aspects or motivational processes are stated in short for each of the models):

- 'Field of safe travel' (Gibson and Crooks, 1938)
- 'Driving as a self-paced task governed by tension/anxiety' (Taylor, 1964)
- 'Zero-risk model' (Näätänen and Summala, 1974)
- 'Target level of risk' (Wilde, 1982)
- 'The threat-avoidance model' (Fuller, 1984)
- 'Theory of planned behaviour' (Aijzen, 1985)
- 'The role of pleasure' (Rothengatter, 1988)

- 'Sensation seeking' (Zuckerman, 1994)
- 'Task difficulty' (Fuller, 2000).

The above listing is by no means a complete list of theories and driver behaviour models, the purpose of presenting it is to focus on the main motivational aspects which have been proposed, applied and discussed within traffic safety research. It can be argued that a common denominator for most of the models is emotion: 'Safe travel' (Gibson and Crooks, 1938), 'tension/anxiety' (Taylor, 1964), 'zero risk' (Näätänen and Summala, 1974), 'target risk' (Wilde, 1982), 'threat-avoidance' (Fuller, 1984), 'pleasure' (Rothengatter, 1988) and 'difficulty' (Fuller, 2000). Wilde's RHT, which has been heavily debated since it was launched, represents something different, because the target level of risk is understood and defined as a number, that is, as a number > 0 (Vaa, 2001a), not as an emotion or a feeling. On the other hand, Wilde's RHT is inescapable regarding the discussion of models because of its reliance on central concepts as homeostasis and risk compensation. There is a need, however, for a reorientation of RHT, because the debate somehow has resulted in a deadlock for the development of driver behaviour models. Such a reorientation is also strongly needed because risk compensation is still not fully understood and accounted for in a satisfactory way.

One may get the impression that models have been too focused on cognitive aspects as determinants of driver behaviour, as in theory of reasoned action (TRA) (Aijzen and Fishbein, 1980) and theory of planned behaviour (TPB) (Aijzen, 1985). One could even say that the focus on cognitive models has been predominant to such an extent that the role of the unconscious has more or less been neglected. Extending this assertion, I would argue that there is no common understanding of driver behaviour that is based on recent achievements in cognitive psychology and neurobiology. In fact, Taylor's early work of 1964 may be more in line with recent achievements in neurobiology than any other of the models listed above (Damasio, 1994; Bechara et al., 1997). No deep understanding of risk compensation will emerge unless recent developments in cognitive psychology and neurobiology are integrated in the modelling of driver behaviour (Vaa, 2001a).

The hypothesis which is proposed is that the role of the unconscious is significant as a motivating force also when it comes to driver behaviour. Hence, there is a need for a deeper and more considerate elaboration of the role of the unconscious. This is made a predominant point in the present discussion, which aims at a deeper understanding of the phenomenon of risk compensation.

12.4 Behavioural Adaptation and Risk Compensation

All living organisms have to adapt to their environments in order to survive. We adapt continuosly to changing characteristics of the environments. Road traffic is a specific case of environment, which calls for continous adaptations to reach our destinations without being involved in accidents. This is self-evident. However, behavioural adaptations have certain meanings when it comes to road traffic, especially for drivers, which call for specific definitions. Behavioural adaptation and risk compensation are concepts which sometimes are used interchangeably, but here a distinction between them is proposed. Behavioural adaptation is naturally the widely used generic concept and this meaning remains. However, as our perspective is road traffic and especially driver behaviour, I will limit *behavioural adaptation* to *strategic* decisions, that is, to conscious decision making. Strategic decision making may take place outside as well as inside the road traffic system. One example is driving in darkness, when the number of elderly drivers and women (all ages), increases as a function of road lighting on a given stretch of road, because these specific driver groups feel more secure when a road is lit up by road lighting (Assum et al., 1999). A second example is when you decide to drive faster because you are out of time or you decide to take an alternative route because you are stuck in traffic, these are, likewise, also strategic decisions.

Risk compensation also represents behavioural adaptation, but I regard it as a special case of adaptation, that is, adaptations which predominantly occur without involving consciousness. Hence, this concept is used only for decisions made on an unconscious level, as when the driving speeds are increased (Aschenbrenner et al., 1987) or when time headways are reduced (Sagberg et al., 1997), for drivers driving cars equipped with ABS compared to a control group of drivers with cars without ABS. This distinction is deliberately made because these kinds of decisions origin in bodily reactions, that is the hypothesis, which drivers do not necessarily experience at a conscious level. This type of process is named risk compensation, because, when a given, supposed risk-reducing measure is introduced in the road traffic system (here: Cars with ABS), the risk-reducing effects, which are expected, are compensated by certain behaviour changes, most predominantly by increased driving speeds or by changes of levels of attention (Elvik and Vaa, 2004).

It should be added that the 'hierarchical' categorisation strategic–tactic–operational introduced by Michon (1985) is not adopted here, behaviour is rather seen as belonging to a continuum ranging from highly conscious to completely unconscious as end points, i.e. not as separate and distinct categories in itself (Vaa, 2003a). The degree of conscious/unconscious information processing and decision making is then understood as going back and forth along the continuum, thus illustrating the dynamics and integration of cognitive processes, bodily reactions and emotions and feelings.

12.5 Wilde's Risk Homeostasis Theory (RHT)

Why considering Wilde's theory of risk homeostasis in more depth than other driver behaviour models? There are several reasons for this: (1) It has been central for years and it has been at the core of heavy debates since it was first published, (2) it addresses risk compensation which certainly exists and remains as an unsolved and not fully understood problem in traffic safety work, (3) in its radical form it represents a deadlock theoretically speaking, as it is not suitable for testing,

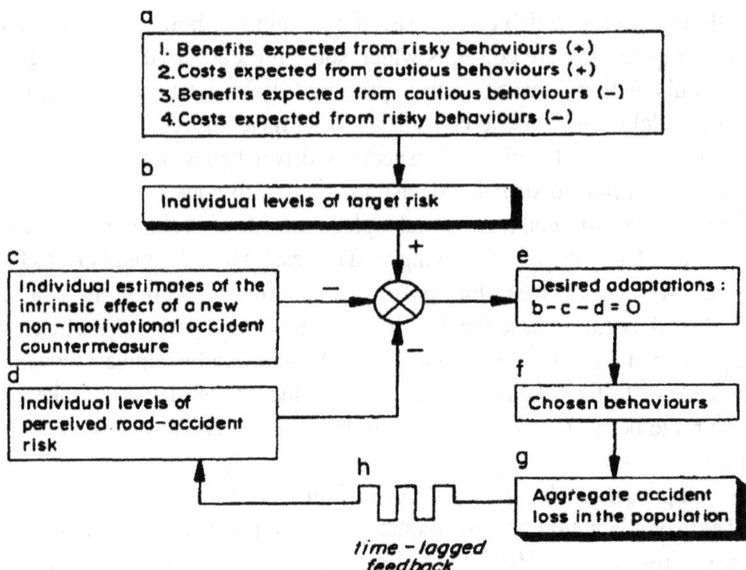

FIGURE 12.1. Wilde's model of risk homeostasis (after Wilde, 1982, 1988).

and finally (4) RHT is inescapable, it addresses a core problem in driver decision making, there is an essence in it, which I will try to extract by contrasting Näätänen and Summala's 'zero-risk'-model with Wilde's RHT.

While Näätänen and Summala (1974) postulate that drivers try to avoid risk by regulating their behaviour according to a perception of zero risk, Wilde postulates the opposite by stating that drivers *seek* a certain risk level – 'a target risk level' – a risk level that must be perceived as a number > 0 presumed to be defined by a measure of exposure, that is, as number of accidents per kilometres driven, a certain unit of time or the like (Vaa, 2001a). This target risk level varies between drivers, it seems partly to have idiosyncratic origins, partly to be a regulator in a homeostatic system: When the driver is confronted with certain changes in the road environment, he or she will meet these changes with adaptations that secures that the level of target risk is sustained. Wilde postulates further that the target level of risk can be increased when expected benefits from risky behaviour or expected costs from cautious behaviour, increases. And finally, it can be reduced when expected benefit from cautious behaviour or expected costs from risky behaviour, increases.

Wilde's RHT model contains one explicit element called a comparator. This is a place, a function, a process where three input factors are put together and compared: b, c and d (Fig. 12.1) resulting in one output factor e, where:

b = Individual levels of target risk
c = Individual estimate of the intrinsic effect of a new, non-motivational road safety measure
d = Individual levels of perceived road-accident risk
e = Desired adaptation satisfying the formula: $b - c - d = 0$

According to Wilde, the three input factors are 'weighed together' in the comparator. This is a *bound* weighing: RHT predicts that the end result should be *zero*. All three input factors must be comprehended as numbers where the values of b, c and d have the property that

$$b - c - d = 0 \qquad \text{(I)}$$

Translated into words, it means that the output from the comparator, the result of the weighing procedure, must be chosen in such a way that the property (I) is fulfilled. Translated to behaviour, it means that the output factor must be regarded as *the desired adaptation of the individual driver*, which is such that the risk homeostasis is sustained on an individual basis.

A problem with RHT, which in my opinion must be read according to the above, is that all input factors and the predicted output factor, are comprehended as numbers. And, as such, they should be confirmed to exist by individual drivers. Are they? I have never seen any such numbers or calculating procedures being confirmed by drivers and I have no such numbers or comparing in myself. If they exist, the prediction must take place unconsciously. The prediction would hence be impossible to test, as the entities are impossible to observe and impossible to measure.

Looking more closely at the factor d, individual levels of perceived road-accident risk, d seem to be the time-lagged feedback product (h) of a preceding aggregate accident loss in the population (g). I guess we all have a perception of an 'aggregate accident loss', but it is not very accurate. It may be uttered in terms of 'speeds are increasing', 'traffic is getting worse' or 'traffic seem to improve now', but such terms are very crude and not based on any kind of calculation or unbiased knowledge of the situation. We may remember certain accidents, because of their magnitude or some other characteristic, but we may have forgot all the ones with minor injuries or damage. Tversky and Kahneman (1974) show that people put much weight into their own experiences. The properties of one small sample may, independent of its size, be considered as being representative of a much larger population. Tversky and Kahneman are, however, not referred to in Wilde (1982, 1988). There seem to be no trace in the literature of the asserted weighing procedure between b, c and d, that is, between target level of risk (b), individual estimates of effects (c) and individual levels of perceived risk (d) constituting the desired adaptations $b - c - d = 0$. Not even on a strategic level of driver behaviour, that is, thinking supposed to take place in a highly conscious and rational manner, does it seem possible to observe these kinds of cognitive operations.

As a conclusion, a target level of risk cannot be a number, a thought or an imagination that I bring with me consciously and which I put into some weighing procedure when I decide what speed I should choose or what kind of acts I should perform as was it a constant, predominant thought or imagination in the dynamics of my thinking. And that is exactly my critique against Wilde: The RHT model does not grasp or mimic the varied dynamics of thinking and feeling, 'the streams of consciousness', the fluctuations of automated states mixed with thoughts coming and going so characteristic of everyday driving. The RHT model somehow assumes

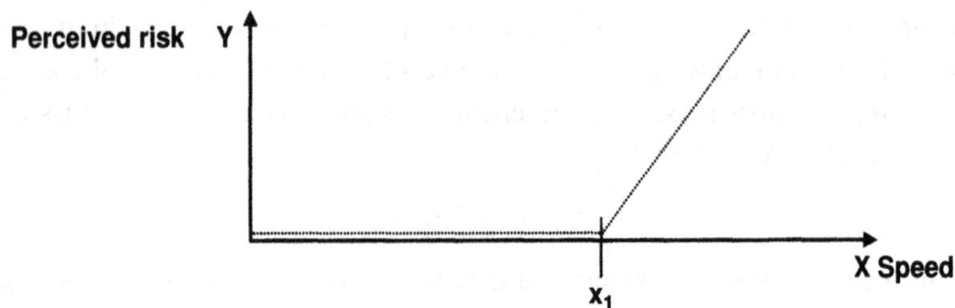

FIGURE 12.2. Hypothetical distribution of perceived risk according to driving speed.

a powerful, hidden, unconscious force that forces us to act in such a way that the target level of risk is sustained individually for everyone as well as for everybody else. Such a powerful force somehow resembles the cosmological anti-gravity force, 'dark matter', 'dark energy' or whatever: The force is there, it makes the universe accelerate in its expansion, but we cannot observe it (Vaa, 2001a).

12.5.1 Target Risk or Target Feeling?

So what is in Wilde's RHT? Let me start with the 'zero-risk' model of Näätänen and Summala (1974). An experience of 'zero risk' will be fulfilled at several driving speeds, in fact any number in the interval $[0, x_1]$ may satisfy the experience of a zero risk (Fig. 12.2):

Why stop at x_1 as the chosen speed? Why not choose any speed $< x_1$? Why exactly x_1? In my view, Näätänen and Summala do not answer this question directly. But let us see what happens if we loosen Wilde's tight and rigid presupposition of regarding the target level of risk as a certain number or level that the individual driver seeks to achieve or sustain. Let us suppose that this target is of another nature. Let us instead presume that drivers are searching for a certain *feeling*, a certain way of driving that suits him or her well, that gives the driver 'a best feeling'. This is exactly what I would characterise as Wilde's contribution by his RHT, the introduction of the *target*. However, the target should not be regarded as a number, but as a certain kind of *feeling*. Furthermore, a fulfilment of a 'zero-risk' is not sufficient, there has to be another dimension added to it as well. A dimension, an experience, a feeling, that is achieved at the exact speed of x_1, but not at speeds $<x_1$ (Vaa, 2001a). This is then my hypothesis, which could be stated more generally:

Assertion: In addition to avoid accidents, drivers seek a certain 'target feeling'. This feeling is not the same in all drivers, all drives have a unique target feeling, which is not necessarily experienced consciously. Targets can be defined and characterised by an emotional dimension, either positively or negatively.

Candidates for target feelings are as follows:

- Tolerable tension/anxiety
- Vigilant, attentive, highly aware ('arousal')
- Sensation (seeking)

- Joy/pleasure
- Relaxed, secure
- Threat-avoidance
- Avoiding/reducing difficulties
- Compliance/rule-based driving: Avoid violations, no errors, 'always behave correctly'
- Non-compliance

It is worth noting that several of the driver behaviour models mentioned previously do have inherent emotional aspects, but, with the exception of Taylor (1964) and Näätänen and Summala (1974) none of the models view emotions and feelings as a governing principle in a general way i.e. only in a specific way, they somehow isolate single feeling dimensions as their key variable as with threat-avoidance (Fuller, 1984), joy/pleasure (Rothengatter, 1988) and sensation seeking (Zuckerman, 1994). Three other feeling dimensions as motivating forces are also suggested: 'Arousal' (being vigilant, attentive), compliance/rule-based driving and non-compliance. The idea is to make the picture complete by not singling out one specific feeling, but rather try to grasp a more complete variety of feelings that may govern driver behaviour. Drivers are different, some feelings might be more predominant than others. The predominance of certain feelings are likely to be associated with personality traits, as suggested by Ulleberg (2002).

Not all drivers enjoy driving, so the 'best feeling' that can be achieved or sustained may be negatively defined, as an optimal choice where unpleasantness, difficulties, etc., are reduced to their minimum in any given situation. It is proposed that such choices are at least two-dimensional. Avoiding accidents, 'zero risk', is not the full answer. A certain emotional experience has to be added. Car driving is characterised by constantly solving problems, problems that involve thinking, choosing and deciding between different alternatives. All alternatives, scenarios, acts, can be characterised by an outcome that has an emotional dimension attached to it. In fact, that emotional dimension is the very variable that enables drivers or any other in any other situation, to evaluate and choose between alternatives. If there is no feeling, there is no possibility for evaluating the outcomes (Damasio, 1994; Overskeid, 2000). There is no such thing as thinking and reasoning without an emotional dimension.

12.6 Effects of ABS: An Illustrative Example of ITS

A German field study addressing the effects of antilocking brake systems (ABS) on behaviour and accidents has become a classic study of risk compensation (Aschenbrenner et al., 1987). Aschenbrenner et al. applied Wilde's risk homeostasis theory (RHT) to predict that risk compensation might be seen among drivers using cars equipped with ABS. As a conseqeunce, the suggested safety potential inherent in ABS, might be reduced or even cancelled out. To test this hypothesis Aschenbrenner et al. designed an experiment with a taxi company in Munich. The taxi company had some of their cars equipped with ABS, while others were without ABS. The two groups were similar; the only difference was the fitting with and without ABS. The drivers were randomly assigned to the groups and they were all told, which kind of brakes their taxi had. Driver behaviour was recorded by observers camouflaged as passengers. They all asked the taxi drivers to drive exactly the same trip. Data from a total of 113 trips were recorded, evenly distributed between taxis with and without ABS.

Driver behaviour data were collected for 18 variables. Of these, statistically significant differences were observed for four variables (Aschenbrenner et al., 1987). These were as follows:

- Drivers of taxis equipped with ABS were more often outside their lane than drivers of taxis without ABS.
- Drivers with ABS 'cut corners' more often than drivers without ABS.
- Drivers with ABS predicted the traffic ahead to a lesser degree than drivers without ABS.
- Drivers with ABS were more often involved in conflicts with other road users than drivers without ABS.

Driving speeds were measured at four sites along the fixed route. By one of these, in a 60 km/h speed zone, driving speeds were measured. The driving speeds of ABS drivers were significantly higher than among drivers without ABS.

Accidents were also recorded and analysed. The number of accidents was controlled for mileage and also for seasonal variations. It turned out that cars with ABS were involved in as many accidents as cars without ABS. Aschenbrenner et al. conclude that driving behaviour of the ABS-taxis has been less cautious as no effect of ABS on the number of accidents was recorded (Aschenbrenner et al., 1987).

What happens to drivers who drive vehicles equipped with ABS? What lie behind the behavioural differences? Is it a matter of thinking differently than drivers of vehicles without ABS? Do they feel differently? Do the differences in driver behaviour have their origin in conscious processes, in unconscious processes or both? Is it to be explained by vehicle characteristics, driver characteristics or both? Aschenbrenner et al. The study of is not the only one confirming behavioural differences between drivers of ABS-vehicles and drivers of vehicles without ABS. Sagberg et al. (1997) found that taxis with ABS had significantly shorter headways than taxis without ABS, but they found no relationships with driving speeds, possibly because dense traffic at the observation site may have prevented drivers from driving at their preferred speeds. No other behavioural differences for drivers with cars with and without airbags were found.

Broughton and Baugha (2002) found in a postal survey that ABS does have the potential of reducing the number of accidents, but also that many drivers have little or no knowledge of ABS and its effects. They found an overall accident reduction tendency of 3% (insignificant at confidence level of 90%), a tendency of increased number of accidents by 10% (insignificant) among men aged 56+, a 16% accident reduction among men aged 17–55 (significant) and a tendency among women of

TABLE 12.1. Effects of ABS on accidents. Percentage change in the number of accidents. Results from meta-analysis (from Elvik and Vaa, 2004).

	Percentage change in the number of accidents		
Level of injury	Accident types that are affected	Best estimate	95% CI
ABS – Brakes on personal cars			
All vehicles	All	−3.5	(−44; −2.6)
Injury accidents	All	−5	(−8; −2)
Fatal accidents	All	+6	(+1; +12)
Effects on specific types of accident			
Unspecified (All)	Overturning accidents	+22	(+11; +34)
Unspecified (All)	Single acc. without overturning	+15	(+9; +22)
Unspecified (All)	Intersection accidents	−2	(−5, +1)
Unspecified (All)	Rear-end collisions	−1	(−5; +3)
Unspecified (All)	Collision with fixed objects	+14	(+11; +18)
Unspecified (All)	Collision with turning vehicles	−8	(−14; −1)
Unspecified (All)	Pedestrians/cyclists/animals	−27	(−40; −12)

The meta-analysis is based on the following evaluation studies: Aschenbrenner et al. (1987), Kahane (1993 and 1994), HLDI (1995), Hertz et al. (1995A and 1995B), and Evans and Gerrish (1996).

increased number of accidents by 18% (insignificant). One reason why there is a tendency of an increased number of accidents among women as well as among men aged 56+, may be that some drivers have little or no knowledge of ABS and its effects. One hypothesis is that the way in which some women and older men use the ABS may tend to increase their risk of accidents (Broughton and Baugha, 2002).

In a comprehensive meta-analysis of accident studies on ABS, it was found that the overall effect of ABS for personal cars was a marginal, although statistically significant accident reduction of 3.5% (Elvik and Vaa, 2004). However, the effect on fatal accidents went in the opposite direction as they were increased by 6%, also statistically significant (Table 12.1).

Even more compelling are the effects on different accident types. On the one hand, ABS seems to reduce collisions with turning vehicles and accidents with pedestrians, cyclists and animals. A reduction of accidents with moving objects is what would be expected, as an effect of ABS is the ability to maintain steering capability during braking. On the other hand, however, the number of overturning accidents, single accidents without overturning and collision with fixed objects, are all accident types that were significantly increased. The effects on intersection accidents and rear-end collisions, were practically zero, no changes in the number of accidents regarding these accident types were documented (Elvik and Vaa, 2004).

ABS also reduces stop lengths on most road surfaces. Personal cars with ABS on all wheels have considerably shorter stop lengths on wet surfaces than personal cars without ABS (Robinson and Duffin, 1993). ABS may reduce stop lengths by 20% at speeds over 80 kmh and with maintenance of stability. But doubts have been raised that ABS may have failed or lost its effect in critical situations. American traffic police have addressed this question (Brandt, 1994). The situation they wanted to investigate would probably be rare for the common driver, but more prevalent for police patrols during an alarm, chasing a criminal or the like. Suspicions arose among traffic police forces to the extent that they decided to investigate and measure stop lengths in critical avoidance manoeuvres. The suspicions were confirmed, stop lengths did increase when police drivers were braking in avoidance manoeuvres. The explanation to this phenomenon is uncertain, but consider the difference between braking with ABS and with ordinary brakes: Heavy braking with ordinary brakes in a critical situation would lock the wheels; that is, all friction will be used to reduce speed to the disadvantage of loosing steering control, while the braking forces with ABS would be split between reducing speed and maintaing steering capacity. In other words, some of the friction forces between wheel and road surface is utilised for steering, resulting in less friction for reducing the speed of the car (Brandt, 1994).

12.7 Issues Raised by the Example of ABS: The Relevance for ITS

Why describe a system like ABS to such detail? Is it of relevance for ITS in a more general sense? Indeed it is. Several issues can be extracted from this special case of ABS:

1. Drivers with ABS cars seem to behave differently than drivers in cars without ABS. ABS seems to affect speed choice, headways, lateral position and conflicts with other road users. ABS seems 'to do something' with drivers, it affects the driver in certain ways. What is this 'something', what exactly does ABS do with the drivers?
2. The findings of Broughton and Baugha indicate that drivers' knowledge of the system or rather lack of knowledge affects the way drivers understand and use ABS. Anecdotal evidence suggests that some drivers, when imposing all their powers on the brake pedal in an emergency, have experienced that the pedal 'kicks back', the brake pedal 'shakes'. This kickback is a property of the ABS when sensors shall prevent the wheels from locking, but some drivers may experience this kickback from the pedal as 'something is wrong' (with the brakes or other), which in turn may make drivers lift their pressure off the pedal, then reducing the braking powers and the result may be an accident.
3. The third issue to be discussed is the Brandt hypothesis; that is, that stop lengths may be increased because steering in critical avoidance manoeuvres may lead to less friction for reducing the speed of the car. This could then be a case of which the engineers who developed the ABS technology in the first place, did not foresee every possible outcome of the effect of the system, which in turn suggests that the initial risk analysis of the system has been insufficient.

With ABS as an illustrative example, these three issues could be of relevance in a more basic and generic sense, that is, of relevance for ITS in more general terms as five hypotheses can be extracted from the issues 1–3 above:

(a) The suggested effects of ITS may be counteracted and compensated by behavioural changes among drives. If so: Why do (some) drivers change their behaviours as a function of a given ITS?
(b) What kind of properties elicit behaviour changes among drivers?
(c) Improper or insufficient knowledge of a given system may lead to a reduction of the potential effect of ITS or even to detrimental effects.
(d) The scenarios incorporated in the risk analysis preceding the development of a given ITS may be incomplete; that is, some outcomes of an ITS may be unforeseen. Given the large variation of driving situations, driving tasks and drivers, (some) drivers will hit the occasions where the effects are reduced, unforeseen and/or detrimental.
(e) Technology can be defined, at least in some cases, as an extension of the human organism, which can bring humans to situations in which the organism is poorly suited for mastering. In principle, any ITS could have the potential of 'transporting' a driver to situations which are difficult to master.

12.8 Adaptation – Mismatch Between Technology and Human Capability

Human beings try to adapt to whatever environment he or she is exposed to. Adaptation is a necessary prerequisite for survival; it is an integral part of the survival mechanism of the human organism. Survival is regarded as the most basic motive of human beings (Damasio, 1994). Piaget has at times simply defined intelligence as the ability to adapt (Hoff, 2002). A driver will adapt to whatever car he or she wishes to use. A car represents a technology with a potential of transporting a driver to situations he or she would not have been exposed to without using the car. A car somehow *extends* the organism, the car has the potential of eliciting propensities in humans that may otherwise have been hidden, repressed, not seen, unless he or she had been 'extended by the car'. Driver aggression and eliciting hostility towards other road users is one example; the feeling of status is another, the transition from powerlessness to status/power is a third. Some drivers are even tempted to frighten people: Várhelyi (1996) has shown that some one in 6 drivers accelerates when they see a pedestrian entering a pedestrian crossing. There are numerous cases of drivers using the car as weapon and as a means to injure or even kill people (Vaa, 2000). As humans beings we carry abilities and propensities developed by evolution processes over a time span of some 2,000,000 years or so, propensities are brought into situations and environments by means of technologies, which have not been part of the evolution history of the human organism. The ability to monitor risk for avoiding accidents in traffic is the very one our forefathers used to spot and escape predators. The risk of being killed by a predator some 30,000 years ago has been estimated to have been 1 in 10.

It follows that the inherent propensities and the behavioural repertoire of the human organism may have limitations regarding the ability to cope with situations created and provided by today's technology, which also means that we might be misguided, misled and not adequately warned, when we enter situations brought to us by technology, because the ability to monitor and judge risk is not adapted to situations into which technology has 'transported' us. The expansion of the window of opportunities is not fully accompanied with the tools the organism needs for coping adequately with the dangers, which are provided by the technology of the car. Given the enormous death tolls and personal injuries, the car is probably the most unprecedented example of the mismatch and maladjustment between humans and technology of any time.

Who is responsible for the mismatch between man and technology? Should we demand that human beings, by their ability to think, of being conscious of what he or she is doing, should detect, stop and refrain from situations, which he or she is at danger? Should we demand that the human organism, with its inherent, but limited ability to monitor and assess risk, should detect any danger in situations created by the technological expansion of the window of opportunities?

12.9 ITS Technology May Enhance As Well As Reduce the Window of Opportunities

It is obvious that a car 'do something' with drivers in terms of compensation mechanisms by bringing the driver into situations, which are difficult to handle. There is a difference between a VW 1200 1974-model which accelerate from 0 to 100 km/h in some 30 s and a 2004-model Mercedes 200 SLK Kompressor which accelerates from 0 to 100 km/h in some 7.5 s. The Mercedes sports car can realise potentials of overtaking and speeding behaviours that are impossible to realise in a 1974 VW. It follows that the basic entity to be studied should not be the driver as such, but rather 'the-driver-in-a-car', because a car represents different limitations as well as potentials of behavioural opportunities. In a generic way, IT-systems do have potentials of counteracting or limiting dangerous driver behaviour by improving risk monitoring in situations where the human organism is at enhanced risk either because of the organism's limited ability to assess risk or by preventing drivers from entering those dangerous situations, but the opposite is also an option, as shown with ABS.

Electronic stability control (ESC) is a relatively new system, which is installed in cars to prevent the vehicle from spinning, especially on slippery surfaces. It seems to have very promising effects on accidents (Dang, 2004; Farmer, 2004; Lie et al., 2004). Accident reductions from 30% to 67% have been reported (fatal accidents with personal cars and single accidents with SUVs, respectively (Dang, 2004)).

It is a paradox that ESC seems to have unambiguously positive effects on accidents, which, as shown, was not the case with ABS. It is seemingly a paradox, because ESC and ABS utilises technologies which are almost identical: Both systems use sensors to monitor the speed of each of the wheels, but, in addition, ESC cars also have instruments which measure yaw rate and lateral acceleration. If the discrepancy between yaw rate and lateral acceleration is increasing, individual wheels are brought to brake in order to reduce the rotation of the vehicle. To explain the difference of effects between ABS and ESC, one hypothesis is that the effects of ESC cannot be compensated, while ABS can, that is, by increased driving speeds and reduced headways. Another way of stating this hypothesis, considering for example driving speeds in curves, is that ABS may 'invite' you to higher driving speeds, while this opportunity is denied when the car is equipped with ESC. The same driver may experience an enlarged window of opportunities with an ABS car, but a reduction of the same window with an ESC car. It is the equipage that matters, the 'driver-in-the-car', it is the driver behaviour potentials that differ, because of the dependency of the technology of the car. The general question to be asked, when considering ITS, is again whether a given ITS will enhance or limit behavioural opportunities.

Keeping in mind the examples of ABS and ESC above, several issues are essential when considering effects of ITS on driving behaviour:

- How will drivers adapt to ITS?
- To what extent can behavioural adaptations of ITS be predicted?
- To what extent will predicted effects of ITS be counteracted and/or compensated by behavioural changes among drives?
- To what extent is a given ITS based on a model of driver behaviour?

The scope here is not to answer all these issues, but rather to present a model of driver behaviour that may have a potential of understanding and predicting behavioural effects of a given ITS.

12.10 Damasio and the Somatic Marker Hypothesis

A disadvantage with previous driver behaviour models is that most of them do not include aspects of physiology and neurology. Only Taylor, by proposing GSR-constancy as a governing principle, includes such an aspect (Taylor, 1964). Damasio and the neurobiological perspective he elaborates in his book, *Descartes' Error: Emotion, Reason and the Human Brain* (Damasio, 1994), provides a more basic understanding of humans that may serve well as a basis for developing a model of driver behaviour. A new aspect in the development of the present model compared to previous driver behaviour models is its theoretical foundation on neurobiology, where concepts as emotions, feelings and the relationship and interplay between unconscious and conscious process are central. The base for what subsequently shall be labelled 'the monitor model' is three simple statements, which all are extracted from Damasio:

- *Axiom*: Man's deepest and most fundamental motive is *survival.*
- *Deductions*: Humans must possess a specialised ability to detect and avoid dangers that threatens his or her survival. Hence, humans must possess an organ that provides the monitoring of potential threats.
- *Assertion*: The body is the monitor.

It follows axiomatically from the assumption that man's deepest motive is survival, that the organism must have an instrument, an organ, enabling it to monitor its surroundings and the situations in which it acts. This organ is the organism itself, the complete body and its inherent physiology developed by evolution through the history of man where observation and identification of dangers have been of vital importance. The organism taken as a whole is considered as a monitor, an organ for surveillance whose prime task is to monitor the interior, that is, the state of the body and the exterior, that is, the environment and other actors with which the organism interact.

Damasio postulates a relationship between internal states and external behaviour when the human organism is exposed to certain strain and emotional stress, which forms:

.... a set of alterations [which] defines a profile of departures from a range of average states corresponding to a functional balance or homeostasis, within which the organism's economy probably operates at its best, with lesser expenditure and simpler and faster adjustments. (Damasio, 1994)

A central concept in the above citation is the *functional balance*. This functional balance is defined as the *target feeling*, which was discussed previously. This target feeling is a kind of state that drivers are seeking to achieve and/or maintain while driving. The drive to achieve a functional balance is regarded as a central, predominantly unconscious knowledge, which the organism possesses about itself and which the organism is actively seeking to maintain or to restore.

Damasio states his model by saying that something important happens before thinking and reasoning. If, for example, a situation seems to develop into something threatening or dangerous, a feeling of unpleasantness will enter the body, an unpleasant 'gut feeling' may be under way. Because this emotion is knit to the body, Damasio labels it *somatic* ('soma' is Greek for 'body') and *marker* because the emotion marks the picture or the scenario. Damasio describes the consequence of this *somatic-marker* in the following way:

[A somatic marker]....forces attention on the negative outcome to which a given action may lead and functions as an automated alarm signal which says: Beware of danger ahead if you choose the option which leads to this outcome....

.... The automated signal protects you against future losses, without further ado and then allows you to choose from among fewer alternatives. (Damasio 1994, p. 173)

Damasio separates between emotion and feeling and limits the concept of *emotion* to what goes on in the body of the organism, that is, the myriads of changes in the state of the body that is induced autonomously in all its parts and organs when the organism is exposed to a given external event. Damasio points out that a lot of the changes in the body state, as changes in skin colour, body position, facial expressions etc., are also visible to others. The etymological meaning of the word *emotion* relates to the direction of the changes in body state as *e-motion* means '*movement out*' (Vaa, 2001b).

Damasio distinguishes specifically between emotions and feelings and limits *feeling* to processes of consciously experience, consciously sensing, the changes of the body and the mental states. Damasio distinguishes between several levels and defines emotions and feeling as follows:

- *Primary emotions*: Emotions that are innate and unconscious, corresponds to the neurobiological apparatus of the newborn infant.
- *Secondary emotions*: Emotions that are learnt and based on individual experiences, accumulated by the individual – that is, as they develop into 'the emotions of the adult'. Predominantly unconscious or pre-conscious.
- *Feelings*: The process of 'feeling an emotion', the process of 'making an emotion conscious', to feel and transform changes in body states into conscious experiences.

This is, in short, what I will label as 'The Damasio model'. Damasio is explicitly aware that his definitions are 'unorthodox' (Damasio, 1994). Personally I adopt his definitions as I consider them as fruitful definitions that facilitate an understanding of – say – driver behaviour and also fruitful for an elaboration of a model for driver behaviour.

While primary emotions are exclusively sub-cortical and directed towards the body, secondary emotions also include activation of numerous prefrontal cortices, which means that secondary emotions, in addition to the sub-cortical responses of primary emotions, also include cortical, but still unconscious responses activated by the external stimuli. It is assumed that the cortical loop in prefrontal cortices that is involved in secondary emotions may give access to schemas formed and accumulated by the learning history of the individual and that this loop enables the body to react without involving conscious processes. And furthermore, it is this 'loop of secondary emotions' that enables the organism to act automatically in behaviours that are 'over-learnt' – as often experienced by drivers in driving tasks (Vaa, 2001b).

Finally, to feel an emotion, it is necessary, but not sufficient, that neural signals from the viscera, muscles, joints, neurotransmitter nuclei, that is, all body organs that are emotionally activated, are redirected towards the neo-cortex and certain sub-cortical nuclei. The signals from the body back to cortex go through endocrine and other chemical routes and reach the central nervous system via the bloodstream. The feelings, that is, the conscious experience of body states impinged by external stimuli, then establish an association between an external object, say a given situation in traffic and an emotional body state. Hence, by the processes of feeling and emotion, the individual is able to evaluate, consider and choose between alternative acts in a situation that demands action. The consciousness needs a continuous update of 'here-and-now', of what the body does and what it experiences. Feelings are then the conscious experience of what the body does – by representations of emotional body states or, as Damasio puts it,

> That process of continuous monitoring, that experience of what your body is doing while thoughts about specific contents roll by, is the essence of what I call a feeling. (Damasio 1994, p. 145).

12.11 The Monitor Model

The introduction of a monitor is justified by the Damasio model and his assertion that emotions and feelings are fundamental mechanisms which are involved in the organism's perception and evaluation of dangers. The concept is also adopted from Näätänen and Summala's 'zero-risk model' (1974). Hence, the monitor is then both a concept and a principle, as well as a model for organising processes that influence sensing, processing of information and decision making that will affect factors outside the organism. Figure 12.3 presents the basic structure of the monitor model:

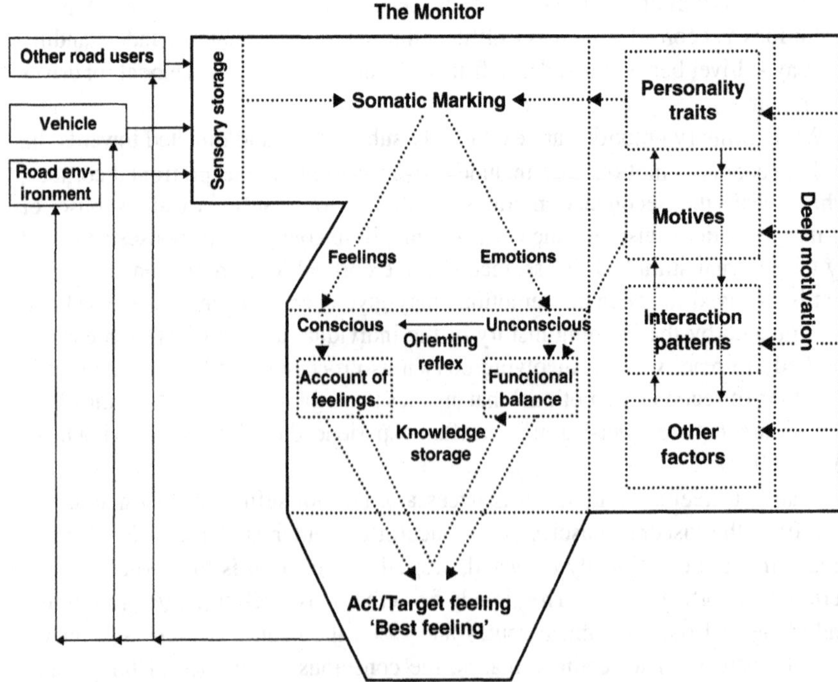

FIGURE 12.3. Basic structure of the monitor model (from Vaa 2003).

The monitor is nothing less than the whole of the body, the whole organism. The boundaries of the monitor (solid line) correspond to the boundary of the body. The internal components are all elements and processes surrounded by the solid line: Somatic marking, personality traits, motives, interaction patterns and a residual of other factors. Deep motivation serves as a base and will influence other components through personality traits and motives. Personality traits influence motives and dispose for idiosyncratic interaction patterns. The interaction patterns of the individual driver can in turn elicit new, latent motives as a consequence of other road users' responses on the initial act(s) of the driver. Feedback loops through characteristics of the vehicle, of the road environment and of the interactions with other road users are indicated; that is, the figure of the model is an excerpt of a certain, instantaneous time window, which is constantly changing by new, upcoming information fed back to the organism by feedback-loops.

A second central concept of the model, that is, in addition to *target feeling*, is the *account of feelings*, a concept which is used to describe an internal, conscious process in which one is imagining two or more alternative actions or 'inner scenarios', as when considering what to do in a given situation. It is a process of cognitive 'weighting' or 'cost–benefit analysis' of conscious, internal scenarios against each other (Damasio, 1994; Overskeid, 2000). The point is that given alternatives/scenarios must have a dimension of feeling, say of being attractive or repulsive, pleasant or unpleasant or the like, that are weighed together in order to come up with a decision of what would be the best solution in a given situation. It is this process of weighing the alternatives together that is proposed to result in some 'account of feelings' on which a given decision is based.

In the monitor model (Fig. 12.3) the organism is, in principle, by adopting Damasio's concept, always 'somatically marked' as it always will be filled with sensory stimuli from the external world (sensory storage) and with internal stimuli from somatic marking and the knowledge storage (a concept used here equivalently with Damasio's 'secondary emotions'). Two routes or modes of information processing and decision making are suggested.

1. *One predominantly conscious*: From the 'marking of the body' in a given situation through feelings to the account of feelings (if more than one alternative has to be considered) and finally resulting in a certain *target feeling* (a 'best feeling' may also be used as a proper label of the target of the act). The result of the decision, that is, the act itself, is fed back to the organism, through and by the effects it might have on the vehicle, on other road users and the road environment.
2. *The other route or mode is predominantly unconscious*: The organism is (unconsciously) seeking a functional balance, which is achieved by restoring or maintaining a target feeling. The organism will constantly seek to maintain this functional balance by appropriate behaviours. As long as the functional balance is maintained in an automated mode, there is no need for involving consciousness. Automated mode may prevail as long as the functional balance is maintained.

The two modes of information processing and decision making described above are naturally stylised and simplified. In real driving, there is no deliberate decision to 'drive in automated mode', this should be looked upon as an unconscious decision of the organism itself and understood as a decision which is adequate because the driving environment is recognised as so simple and familiar that no conscious appraisals seem necessary. Both modes aim at maintaining or restoring a functional balance of the organism, which is achieved by the act that realises the target feeling, either by the conscious route or by the automated route. Two connections or 'bridges' between the unconscious and the conscious modes of information processing are indicated. One is represented by the orienting reflex; that is, the ability to be oriented towards certain objects by a light, a sound or a smell, which bridges the gap from automated mode to conscious mode and further to account of feelings if necessary. The second connection is the bridge between the boxes of 'functional balance' and 'account of feelings'. The latter bridge is suggested for describing an upcoming situation in which the driver is confronted with a conflict, a consideration of overtaking, of choosing between certain routes, of changing driving speeds, etc. Simply stated, that is what consciousness or working memory is there for, as an instrument for conscious appraisals when needed. The organism will prefer and seek to be governed by an automated mode if possible, as this mode is less costly, that is, the organism wants to economise with its cognitive (mental) resources (Reason, 1990; Damasio, 1994). However, the organism does not decide (consciously) to go to automated mode, this 'decision' should rather be regarded as a property of the organism itself, that is, a 'decision' to be governed by automated mode whenever possible.

The direction of the links or bridges between the unconscious and the conscious is from the former to the latter, not the other way around. One predominant logic of the model is to maintain or restore functional balance by seeking a *target* or *best* feeling, also indicated by the arrow directly from 'motives' to 'functional balance' and finally to 'target feeling'. During automated behaviour, there is identity between target feeling and functional balance (Vaa, 2003a).

It is an assertion that this unconscious quest for functional balance becomes the steering principle in the model, which also may constitute a base for a deeper understanding of risk compensation. This view is presented as an alternative to Wilde's RHT and especially also to his concept 'target risk' (Wilde 1982); that is, drivers are not seeking a certain risk level other than zero, as in Näätänen and Summala's 'Zero-Risk Model'(1974). In conclusion, drivers are seeking a target *feeling* rather than a target *risk.*

Finally, some limitations of the monitor model should be mentioned. Naturally, there are a lot of states that may jeopardise risk monitoring, some might be covered up under 'deep motivation', other in the residual of 'other factors'. What the model considers is basically an average driver, of average age, average health and with an average composition of personality traits, etc., that is, general states where the monitoring of risk should operate optimally. We know, however, that a variety of states increase risk. Drink driving is by far the most dangerous of conditions: A blood alcohol concentration (BAC) of 0.05%–0.1% has a relative risk of 10 compared to sober drivers (Vaa, 2003). The risk monitoring function is definitely distorted in a drunken driver. To be affected by other substances also increase risk levels, but not in the same magnitude as alcohol: Benzodiazepines, cannabis and opiates all increase the risk of accidents as they have relative risks of 1.54, 1.70 and 1.83, respectively. Other examples are mental disorders, neurological disorders and sleep apnoea with relative risks of 1.72, 1.75 and 3.71. Some, but not all, of these states may be addressed and counteracted by adequate ITS solutions, as with AlcoLock in the case of drink driving.

12.12 The Monitor Model and Prediction of Effects of ITS

It is remarkable that humans' inherent ability to handle risks is as effective and safe as it is in road traffic. According to the most recent estimates of accident risks in Norway (Bjørnskau, 2003), the risk of a personal injury accident among drivers is 0.18 accidents per million kilometres; that is, one driver must drive some 5.5 million km before he or she, on the average, would be injured in an accident. Let us suppose that a driver drives from 18 to 83 years of age, that is, for 65 years. The Norwegian average driving distance is ca 14,000 km per year. One driver will then drive a total of approx 910,000 km in 65 years. Hence, it takes $5.5/0.910 \approx$ nearly 400 years or a group of six drivers of which only one, on the average, will experience one injury accident during a lifelong carrier as a car driver. Then, individually speaking, it is quite safe to drive. Furthermore, it illustrates the relative success of risk monitoring of drivers, which is remarkable taking into account that the ability to monitor risk has been developed for a different time and for different environments, than for the road traffic system.

One basic question to be asked is whether a given ITS would alter the functional balance of the driver. Obviously, ABS has done just that, as shown by ABS drivers driving faster and with shorter headways than drivers driving cars without ABS. A second question would be whether a given ITS addresses aspects where the organism's ability to monitor risk is weak or inadequate. No doubt, drivers' ability to monitor risk is far from perfect. The risk monitoring ability of the human organism is not an infallible machine, and it has weaknesses regarding monitoring of dangers. Some important examples of monitor weaknesses that theoretically could be improved by ITS would be:

- Prevention of excessive speeds, especially among young, inexperienced drivers who underestimate the dangers of high driving speeds. Cars fitted with electronic stability control (ESC) and intelligent speed adaptation (ISA) should be beneficial especially for young drivers as inexperienced drivers are especially susceptible to risk of accidents, because they lack 'the warnings' provided by the schemes or secondary emotions, which accumulate in the organism as a function of being repeatedly exposed to potentially dangerous situations.
- The ability to detect speed changes of the car in front seem to have been poorly developed in the human organism. The assertion is that no evolutionary selection

on the ability 'to-detect-dangers-when-following-after-a-leader-in-a-queue' has been necessary, because risk monitoring could be said, that is my hypothesis, to be considered to be the responsibility of the leader. Hence, as this may be classified as a real weakness of the inherent ability to monitor risk, alarm systems that warn drivers of speed changes and/or changes of time headways should be beneficial in terms of detecting dangers and thereby preventing accidents.

- In cases of considering overtaking, the looks for other drivers in the rear view and side view mirrors will leave the driver with a 'dead angle'. This is definitely a weak point in drivers' monitoring ability regarding perception, information processing and decision making. Alarming drivers attempting to overtake when there is a moving object in the dead angle of the mirrors should likewise be beneficial, then applying analogous reasoning as with car following.
- Questions could likewise by raised regarding drivers' perception of motorcyclists and pedestrians, that is, that the human organism in the role of a driver might have inherent, weaknesses in detecting motorcyclists and cyclists in certain situations. Some drivers fail to spot 2-wheeled road users on a crossing course, especially in left turns. A Norwegian study found that MCs are overrepresented by a factor of eight to one in collisions between a car and a motorcyclist on a crossing course (Glad, 2001). One hypothesis predicted by the monitor model is that drivers 'look for dangers'; that is, drivers look primarily for other cars, as motorcyclists do not represent a danger in the same meaning as other cars do. Then drivers seem to overlook a motorcyclist, they sometimes might 'look without seeing'. The same phenomenon is also seen in conflicts with cyclists.
- Ordinary marked pedestrian crossings increase the number of accidents by some 28% (95% CI: +39; +19) (Elvik and Vaa, 2004). Whatever cause, it must have something to do with a perceptual weakness or inattentiveness by the driver, by the pedestrian or by both. An ITS-solution which reliably could detect and warn the driver of pedestrians should work in a beneficial way.
- An ITS which warns drivers of crossing vehicles at junctions should have a potential of reducing accidents, especially among elderly drivers who are over-represented in accidents at junctions.
- Sleep apnoea and fatigue increase accident risk considerably and much more than being influenced drugs as benzodiazepines, anti-depressant, cannabis and opiates (Vaa, 2003b). Drivers' appraisal of their ability to stay awake while driving seems very insufficient. Hence, systems that monitor and warn drivers of attention failures and incidents of falling asleep should, in principle, be beneficial in terms of traffic safety. It seems, however, to be quite difficult to develop reliable algorithms that could warn drivers of falling asleep, probably because the markers of sleepiness and fatigue vary considerably between drivers as well as within an individual driver. Hence, with reference to the EU projects AWAKE and SENSATION, a high frequency of false alarms might probably be expected.

The above group of IT-system ideas would generally, as they all address the primary task of driving, be labelled driver assistance systems (DAS) or advanced driver assistance systems (ADAS), although the difference between these two groups of systems is not well defined. The examples address situations and conflicts where drivers may have difficulties with inattention and/or in perceiving the presence of other road users. The main objective is then to provide the driver with devices that increase attention by warning him or her of upcoming dangers. The general issue considered here regarding (A)DAS is the one of risk compensation, that is, whether or not a given ITS will enable the driver to seek a better feeling by increasing the speed, changing the time headway and/or the level of attention. Risk compensation has been documented to be present with ABS, but not with ESC. For other ITS in this group of driver assistance systems the question remains if or how they will influence the monitoring of risk by compensatory mechanisms.

12.13 Summary and Conclusions

As documented previously, the average and experienced driver perform quite well regarding risk monitoring as it must be regarded as normal to have a lifelong career of driving without a single personal injury accident. The introduction of new ITS in cars would then face an issue of trust, that is, whether or not the driver would perceive a given system as reliable. Consequently, it is suggested that a given ITS must perform better than the driver, because the driver generally will regard him or herself as competent and skilled in handling the dangers of everyday driving. It is a matter of driver confidence and reliance of a system. ITS must prove its relevance and its reliability. If false alarms occur too often, it will create mistrust and subsequently the driver will probably abandon the system.

Initially, an attempt to categorise and define different subgroups of ITS was made. In the present discussion only (A)DAS have been considered, while IVIS (in-vehicle-information-systems) deliberately have been left out of consideration. The main reason for this deliberate exclusion has been that the IVIS group is more obscure than the (A)DAS-group. While (A)DAS generally could be said to address primary driving tasks, especially by providing information about and warnings of dangers, IVIS may address primary as well as secondary driving tasks. Nomadic systems, as mobile phones and portable route guidance systems belong to the IVIS group. Hence, IVIS may represent distractions and increased workload and thereby threats to risk monitoring, more than provisions of information about upcoming dangers. One example is the use of mobile phones, which increases the risk of accidents. In a study conducted by Sagberg, the relative risk of using a mobile phone while driving was estimated to 1.72; that is, mobile phone use increases the risk of accidents by some 72% (Sagberg, 2001). It follows that drivers may misjudge their ability to monitor risk while operating systems which do not address primary driving tasks. By incorporating systems that impose distractions and increased workload, the monitoring of risk may be hampered to such an extent that the safety of driving is jeopardised.

If, or rather when, mobile phone manufacturers succeed in integrating functions as Word, Excel, Internet, GPS, route guidance, MP3, TV/video and the like and thereby reduce the need for other nomadic systems, it will provide the driver with an enormous amount of information that is irrelevant for driving a car. Such a scenario should be regarded as a major threat to future road safety, because it represents possibilities of more distraction and increases in workload. So far, no driver behaviour model seems to have adequately integrated both risk monitoring and driver workload as their prime dimension. The monitor model predicts that IT systems which address inherent weaknesses of risk monitoring in the human organism may succeed in preventing road accidents. The broader picture of behavioural with adaptations with which drivers will meet current and future implementation of ITS in cars and the road system is still to a large extent unknown. More evaluation studies are needed. Some predictions of ITS are suggested, but more elaborate driver behaviour models seem likewise to be needed in order to provide better predictions of the effects of IT systems.

References

Aijzen, I. and Fishbein, M. (1980). *Understanding attitudes and predicting social behaviour*. Prentice-Hall, Englewood Cliffs, NJ.

Aijzen, I. (1985). From intentions to actions: A theory of planned behaviour. In J. Kuhl and Beckmann (Eds.). *Action control. From cognition to behaviour*. Springer Verlag, Berlin, pp. 11–40.

Aschenbrenner, K.M., Biehl, B. and Wurm, G.W. (1987). Einfluß Der Risikokompensation auf die Wirkung von Verkehrsicherheitsmassnahmen am Beispiel ABS. *Schriftenreihe Unfall- und Sicherheitsforschung Straßenverkehr*. Heft 63 Bergisch Gladbach, Bundesanstalt für Strassenwesen (BASt), pp. 65–70.

Assum, T., Bjørnskau, T., Fosser, S. and Sagberg, F. (1999). Risk compenasation – The case of road lighting. *Accident Analysis and Prevention*, 31, 545–533.

Atkinson, R.L., Atkinson, R.C., Smith, E.E., Bem, D.J. and Nolen-Hoeksema, S. (1996). *Hilgard's introduction to psychology* (12th ed.). Hartcourt Brace College Publishers, Fortworth, TH.

Bechara, A., Damasio, H., Tranel, D. and Damasio, A.R. (1997). Deciding advantageously before knowing the advantageous strategy. *Science,* 275, 1293–1295.

Bjørnskau, T. (2003). *Risk in road traffic 2001/2002*. Oslo, Institute of Transport Economics. TØI report no 694/2003. (In Norwegian, with summary in English).

Brandt, B. (1994). ABS increases stopping distances in braking/evasive manoeuvre. *Accident Reconstruction Journal*, 41–42.

Broughton, J. and Baugha, C. (2002). The effectiveness of antilock braking systems in reducing accidents in Great Britain. *Accident Analysis and Prevention*, 34, 347–355.

Damasio, A.R. (1994). *Descartes' error: Emotion, reason and the human brain*. G.P. Putnam's and Sons, New York.

Dang, J.N. (2004). *Preliminary results analyzing the effectiveness of electronic stability control (ESC) systems*. Report no. DOT-HS-809-790. U.S. Department of Transportation, Washington, DC.

Elvik, R. and Vaa, T. (2004). *The handbook of road safety measures*. Elsevier, Oxford.

Evans, L. and Gerrish, P.H. (1996). Antilock brakes and risk of front and rear impact in two-vehicle crashes. *Accident Analysis and Prevention*, 28, 315–323.

Farmer, C. (2004). *Effect of electronic stability control on automobile crash risk.* Insurance Institute for Highway Safety, USA Traffic Injury Prevention.

Fuller, R. (1984). A conceptualization of driving behaviour as threat avoidance. *Ergonomics*, 27, 1139–1155.

Fuller, F. (2000). The task–capability interface model of the driving process, *Recherche Transports Sécurité*, 66, 47–59.

Gibson, J.J. and Crooks, L.E. (1938). A theoretical field-analysis of automobile-driving. *The American Journal of Psychology*, 51(3), 453–471.

Glad, A. (2001). *Glare effects of high beam on motorcycles in daylight.* Oslo, Institute of Transport Economics. TØI-report 521/2001. (In Norwegian with summary in English).

Hertz, E., Hilton, J. and Johnson, D.M. (1995A). *An analysis of the crash experience of light trucks equipped with antilock braking systems*. Report DOT HS 808 278. U.S. Department of Transportation, National Highway traffic Safety Administration, Washington, DC.

Hertz, E., Hilton, J. and Johnson, D.M. (1995B). *An analysis of the crash experience of passenger cars equipped with antilock braking systems*. Report DOT HS 808 279. U.S. Department of Transportation, National Highway traffic Safety Administration Washington, DC. (USA, smaller lorries and multi-purpose vehicles).

HLDI – Highway Loss Data Institute (1995). *Three years on-the-road experience with antilock brakes*. HLDI Special Report A-47. Highway Loss Data Institute Arlington, Va, (USA, cars).

Hoff, T. (2002). *Mind design: Steps into an ecology of human–machine systems*. Dr. Polit. Dissertation. Trondheim, Department of Psychology and Department of Product Design Engineering, Norwegian University of Science and Technology.

Kahane, C.J. (1993). *Preliminary evaluation of the effectiveness of rear-wheel antilock brake systems for light trucks*. Draft Report December 1993. US Department of Transportation, National Highway Traffic Safety Administration, Washington, DC.

Kahane, C.J. (1994). *Preliminary evaluation of the effectiveness of antilock brake systems for passenger cars*. Report DOT HS 808 206. US Department of Transportation, National Highway Traffic Safety Administration, Washington, DC.

Lie, A., Tingvall, C., Krafft, M. and Kullgren, A. (2004). The effectiveness of ESP (electronic stability programme) in reducing real life accidents. *Traffic Injury Prevention*, 5, 37–41.

Michon, J.A. (1985). A critical view of driver behavior models: What do we know, what should we do? In L. Evans and R.C. Schwing (Eds.). *Human behaviour and traffic safety*. Plenum Press, New York.

Näätänen, R. and Summala, H. (1974). A model for the role of motivational factors in drivers' decision-making. *Accident Analysis and Prevention*, 6, 243–261.

Overskeid, G. (2000). The slave of the passions: Experiencing problems and selecting solutions. *Review of General Psychology*, 4, 284–309.

Reason, J. (1990). *Human error*. Cambridge University Press, Cambridge.

Robinson, B.J. and Duffin, A.R. (1993). The performance and reliability of anti-lock braking systems. Braking of road vehicles. *Proceedings of the Institution of Mechanical Engineers, 23-24 March 1993*. Institution of Mechanical Engineers (IMechE), Birdcage Walk, London. Published by Mechanical Engineers Publications Limited, pp. 115–126.

Rothengatter, T. (1988). Risk and the absence of pleasure: A motivational approach to modelling road user behaviour. *Ergonomics*, 31, 599–607.

Sagberg, F., Fosser, S. and Saetermo, I.A.F. (1997). An investigation of behavioural adaptation to airbags and antilock brakes among taxi drivers. *Accident Analysis and Prevention*, 29, 293–302.

Sagberg, F. (2001). Accident risk of car drivers during mobile telephone use. *International Journal of Vehicle Design*, 26(1), 57–69.

Taylor, D.H. (1964). Driver's galvanic skin response and the risk of accidents. *Ergonomics*, 7, 439–451.

Tversky, A. and Kahneman, D. (1974). Judgement under uncertainty: Heuristics and biases. *Science*, 185, 1124–1131.

Ulleberg, P. (2002). Personality subtypes of young drivers. Relationship to risk-taking preferences, accident involvement and response to a traffic safety campaign. *Transportation Research Part F*, 4, 279–297.

Vaa, T. (2000). A comment on the definition of aggression and aggressive driving behaviour. *Proceedings of the Conference 'Road Safety on three Continents' Pretoria*. South Africa, September 2000, pp. 20–22.

Vaa, T. (2001a). Cognition and emotion in driver behaviour models: Some critical viewpoints. *Proceedings of the 14th ICTCT Workshop*. Caserta 2001 (www.ictct.org).

Vaa, T. (2001b). Driver behaviour models and monitoring of risk: Damasio and the role of emotions. *Proceedings from VTI-Conference Traffic Safety on Three Continents*. Moscow 19–21 September 2001.

Vaa, T. (2003a). *Survival or deviance? A Model for Driver Behaviour*. Final report. Oslo, Institute of Transport Economics. TØI-report no. 666/2003 (In Norwegian with summary in English).

Vaa, T. (2003b). *Impairments, diseases, age and their relative risks of accident involvement: Results from meta-analysis*. Deliverable R1.1 of EU-project IMMORTAL. Oslo, Institute of Transport Economics, TØI report no. 690/2003.

Várhelyi, A. (1996). *Dynamic speed adaptation based on information technology: A theoretical background*. Department of Traffic Planning and Engineering, Lund Institute of Technology, University of Lund, Bulletin 142.

Wilde, G.J.S. (1982). The theory of risk homeostasis: Implications for safety and health. *Risk Analysis*, 2, 209–225.

Wilde, G.J.S. (1988). Risk homeostasis theory and traffic accidents: Propositions, deductions and discussion of dissension in recent reactions. *Ergonomics*, 31(4), 441–468.

Zuckerman, M. (1994). *Behavioural expressions and biosocial bases of sensation seeking*. Cambridge University Press, Cambridge.

V
Modelling Risk and Errors

13 Time-Related Measures for Modelling Risk in Driver Behaviour

Richard van der Horst

13.1 Introduction

Accident statistics have an important general safety monitoring function and form a basis for detecting specific traffic safety problems. However, the resulting information is inadequate for analysing and diagnosing, defining remedial measures and evaluating their effects. Systematic observations of driver behaviour, combined with knowledge of human information-processing capabilities and limitations, offer wider perspectives in understanding the causes of safety problems and modelling driver behaviour in both normal and critical situations. Renewed interest results from the need to develop, test, assess and evaluate driver support systems in terms of drivers' behaviour, performance and acceptance.

The processes that result in near-accidents or traffic conflicts have much in common with the processes preceding actual collisions (Hydén, 1987); only the final outcome is different. The frequency of traffic conflicts is relatively high, and they offer a rich information source on causal relationships since the preceding process can be systematically observed. In this approach, traffic situations are ranked along a continuum ranging from normal situations, via conflicts to actual collisions. A pyramidal representation of this continuum was introduced by Hydén (1987), clearly visualising the relative rate of occurrence of the different events (Fig. 13.1). The analysis of driver behaviour in critical encounters may not only offer a better understanding of the processes that ultimately result in accidents, but, perhaps even more efficient in the long run, also provide us with knowledge on drivers' abilities of turning a critical situation into a controllable one.

A general conceptual description of the driving task as commonly used in traffic psychonomics, with time-to-line crossing (TLC) and time-to-collision (TTC) as a measure for describing the lateral and longitudinal driving task will be used to distinguish normal from critical behaviour. That may serve as realistic criterion settings for in-car warning systems such as forward collision warning and intersection collision avoidance warning systems.

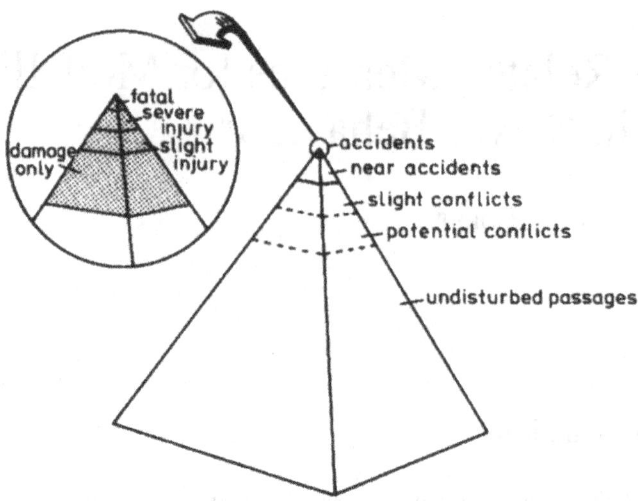

FIGURE 13.1. The continuum of traffic events from undisturbed passages to fatal accidents (from Hydén, 1987).

13.2 The Driving Task

In the literature the task analysis for driving a car is well documented. A frequently used conceptual model of the driving task consists of three hierarchically ordered levels, navigation, guidance and control (Allen et al., 1971). In other publications these levels are also referred to as strategic, manoeuvring and control. Tasks at the navigation level refer to the activities related to planning and executing a trip from origin to destination. The need for processing information only occurs occasionally, with intervals ranging from a few minutes to hours. The guidance level refers to tasks dealing with the interaction with both environment (roadway, traffic signs, traffic signals) and other road users. Activity is required rather frequently with intervals of a few seconds to a few minutes. At the control level the motion of the vehicle is controlled in longitudinal and lateral direction. Information has to be frequently processed, ranging from intermittent activities every few seconds to almost continuous control. Alexander and Lunenfeld (1986) visualised the relationship between the levels by a set of nested triangles (Fig. 13.2), hierarchically ordered from a low level to a high level with an increasing complexity and from high to low with an increasing urgency (primacy). For example, a flat tire or suddenly being confronted with a heavy wind gust will immediately interrupt activities at

FIGURE 13.2. The three hierarchical levels of the driving task (according to Alexander and Lunenfeld, 1986).

FIGURE 13.3. The driving task in three dimensions (according to Theeuwes, 1993).

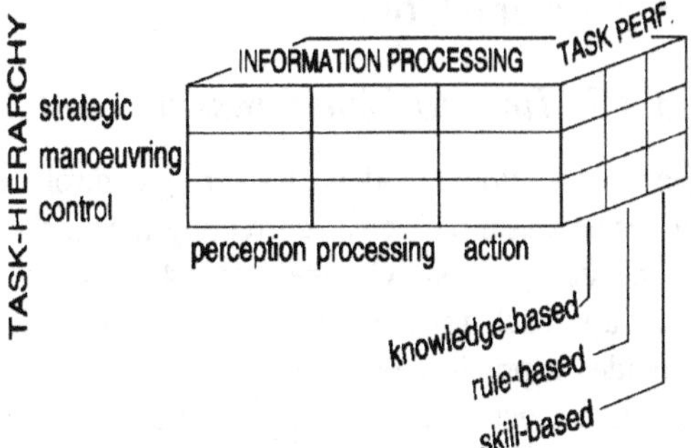

the navigation level and put all attention to the control level, since getting lost has less severe consequences than running off the road.

At each level of the driving task successive steps of information processing; that is, perception, processing and decision making, and action take place. Moreover, the way a driver performs these steps strongly depends on the routine one has developed in task performance. Rasmussen (1985) distinguishes three levels of task performance: knowledge-based, rule-based and skill-based. The highest level (knowledge-based) refers frequently to new situations (e.g., finding the best route to a new destination) or situations that occur frequently in itself, but in which the driver still has little experience. The choice of behaviour depends on interpretation and deductive reasoning. When a situation occurs frequently, then after some time a rule develops how to deal with that situation and recognising that situation leads to appropriate behaviour without a 'need' to understand exactly what is going on. Skill-based tasks are conducted automatically, incoming information automatically results in behaviour without any cognitive control. Theeuwes (1993) introduced a nice three-dimensional representation of the driving task as is given in Fig. 13.3.

It is obvious that also other aspects of the driver such as his intentions, attitudes, emotions and subjective norms play a role in modelling driver behaviour. One possible representation of this is given in Fig. 13.4 (van der Horst, 1998).

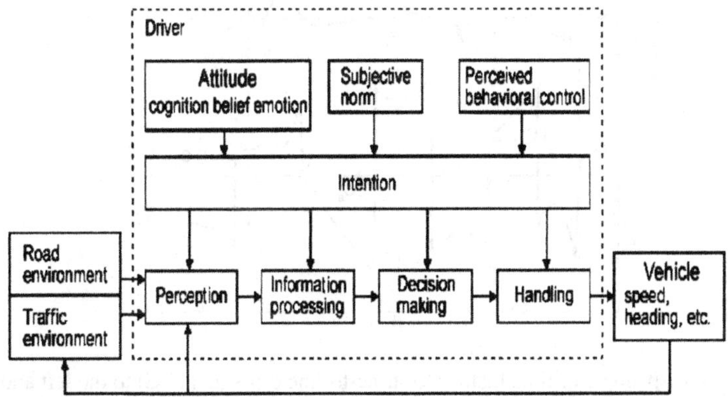

FIGURE 13.4. A driver behaviour model according to van der Horst (1998).

13.3 Lateral Control

13.3.1 Time-to-Line Crossing (TLC)

Several traditional models on steering control are based on the assumption that the driver acts as a path error-correcting mechanism continually allocating attention to the steering task. Godthelp (1984) and Godthelp et al. (1985) developed the TLC approach for describing the driving task merely as a supervisory task. It provides a preview predictor model for time periods; for example, path errors can be neglected. TLC can be calculated on the basis of lateral position, heading angle, speed, and commanded steering angle, and quantifies the time needed by the vehicle to reach either edge of the lane. Figure 13.5 shows an example from an experiment on straight lane keeping with driver's self-paced occlusion times (T_{occ}). Subjects made a series of runs (with a given speed of 20, 40, ..., 120 km/h) on the right lane of a motorway closed for other traffic with a voluntary occlusion wearing the PLATO spectacles (Milgram and van der Horst, 1984; van der Horst, 2004). In its normal state, the occlusion device occluded the visual field completely. On command of the driver (by pressing the horn lever) the device switched to the open mode for 0.55 s. The study showed a very good correlation between TLC and the T_{occ} as voluntarily chosen by the subjects. Figure 13.6 indicates that drivers use a

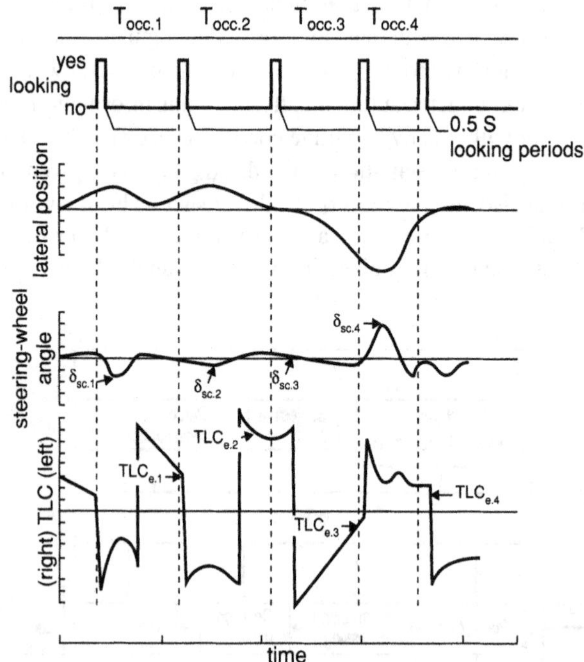

FIGURE 13.5. Example of time history for time-to-line crossing (TLC) to the left and right lane marking at the moment of looking (from Godthelp 1984).

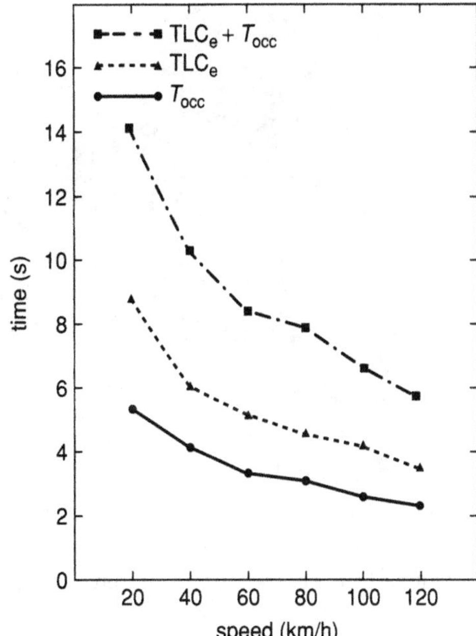

FIGURE 13.6. Speed dependency of median T_{occ}, and TLC$_e$ (from Godthelp et al., 1985).

rather consistent internal representation of the time available to neglect path errors dependent of speed with a T_{occ} at about 40% of the totally available time.

Since then, many studies illustrated the value of the TLC approach for describing drivers' steering strategy and performance (a.o. Godthelp, 1988; Godthelp and Kaeppler, 1988; Van Winsum et al., 2000).

13.3.2 Lateral Distance When Passing

High speeds are an important contributing factor of accidents on rural 80 km/h roads where about 50% of all people killed in traffic in The Netherlands occurs. An experimental project in Drenthe (one of the provinces in The Netherlands) was aimed at the development of measures that effectively reduce speed without significantly reducing driving comfort up to speeds of 80 km/h. First, several options were tested in a driving simulator study (van der Horst and Hoekstra, 1994) resulting in the recommendation of a reduced lane width of smooth asphalt of 2.25 m, a 0.30-m central chipping strip marking, and a 0.60-m wide edge strip of 4 m long blocks of chippings with a pacing of 4 m (see Fig. 13.7). Some concerns arose with respect to the lateral placement of drivers due to the wide edge strip. The question was whether drivers would choose a lateral position in the traffic lane closer to the middle of the road with, as a consequence, a higher risk of head-on collisions. To quantify the effects of the measures on the lateral placement of vehicles, the driving behaviour at one experimental location was compared with that at a conventional 80 km/h road (lane width 2.75 m and standard road delineation of a 0.10-m centre line and edge lines) by means of a quantitative analysis of video recordings

FIGURE 13.7. Speed-reducing measures as tested in Drenthe (van der Horst, 1996).

(van der Horst, 1996) (see Fig. 13.8). The analysis of cumulative distributions of the lateral placement of free-driving vehicles (both passenger cars and trucks) at both sites reveals that the package of speed-reducing measures does not result in a lateral placement more to the middle of the road. On the contrary, the 0.30-m central chipping strip marking (instead of the 0.10-m conventional central marking) even results in a lateral placement of minimally 0.10 m further away from the centre of the road (see Fig. 13.9). Drivers mainly seem to focus on the most nearby side of the central marking. At the moment oncoming traffic is passing, drivers seem to focus on the other vehicle. The mutual distance between two passing vehicles does not differ at all between the experimental and control location (see Fig. 13.10).

13.4 Longitudinal Control

13.4.1 Time-to-Collision (TTC)

In research on traffic conflicts techniques, Hayward (1972) initiated a search for objective measures to describe the danger of a conflict situation. He concluded that TTC is a dominant one, being 'the time required for two vehicles to collide if they continue at their present speed and on the same path'. TTC at the onset of braking (TTC_{br}) represents the available manoeuvring space at the moment an evasive action starts. The minimum TTC (TTC_{min}) as reached during the approach process of two vehicles is taken as an indicator for the severity of an encounter; in principle, the lower the TTC_{min} the higher the risk of a collision. As an example, Fig. 13.11 indicates what happens when a car approaches a stationary object. Usually, the concave shape of the TTC curves does not show up so clearly since

FIGURE 13.8. Quantification of lateral placement from video at a control location with conventional markings (top) and at an experimental location in Drenthe (bottom).

in more complex interactions between two moving road users the collision course is often ended before point B is reached. But even then, TTC_{min} indicates how imminent an actual collision has been. Details of the calculation of TTC can be found in van der Horst (1990). He evaluated the TTC measure in normal and more critical encounters between road users in several empirical observation studies. In one study he analysed all encounters with a collision course between intersecting

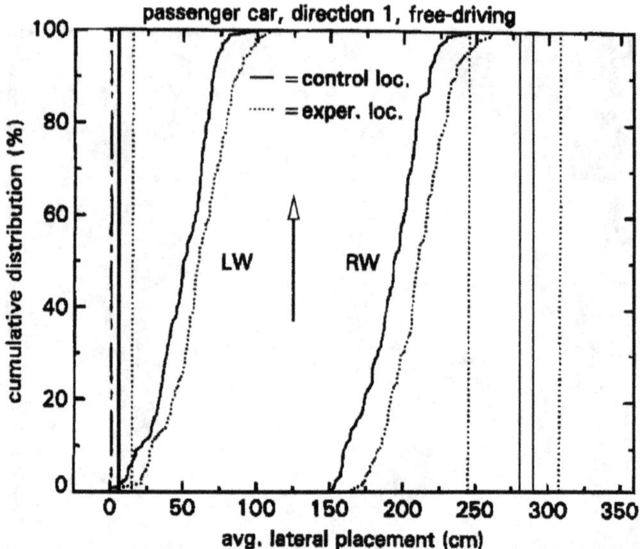

FIGURE 13.9. Cumulative distributions of the left (LW) and right (RW) wheel of free-driving passenger cars at experimental and control location relative to the middle of the road (0 cm).

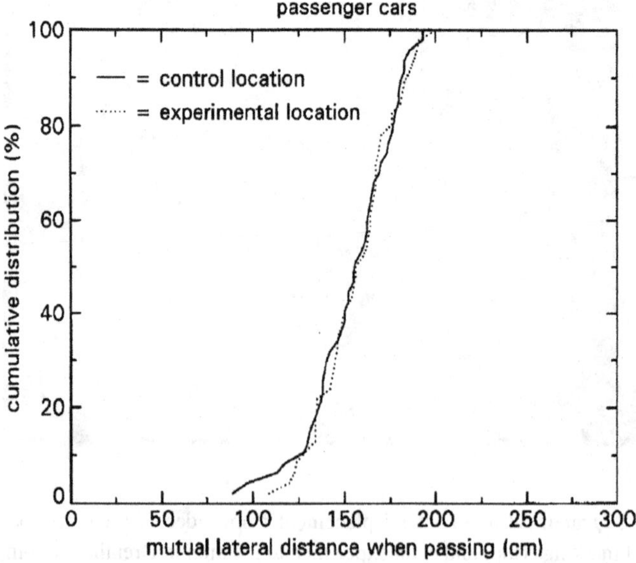

FIGURE 13.10. Cumulative distributions of the mutual distance between passenger cars at the moment of passing at experimental and control locations.

road users (at a priority intersection and a general rule intersection) for a given time period. Figure 13.12 gives the distribution of all encounters with a collision course (van der Horst, 1991a). Only 1.6% of the 373 encounters with a collision course displayed a TTC_{min} of less than 1.5 s. Figure 13.13 combines these results

FIGURE 13.11. Time histories of braking by a car approaching a stationary object; DIST, distance to object; *V*, velocity; ACC, acceleration and TTC, time-to-collision based on constancy of speed and heading angle. Point A indicates TTC_{br} and point B TTC_{min}.

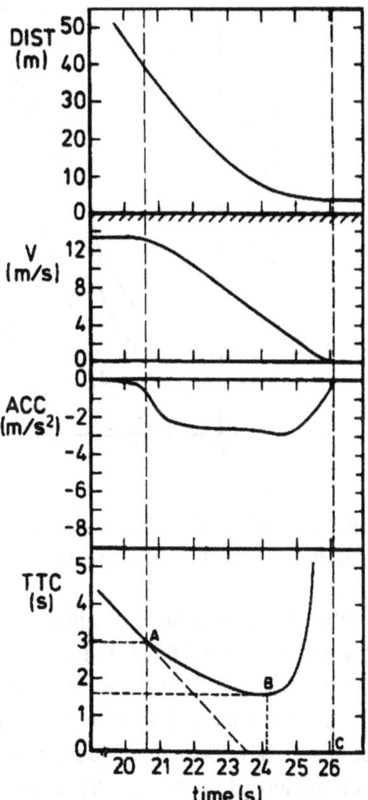

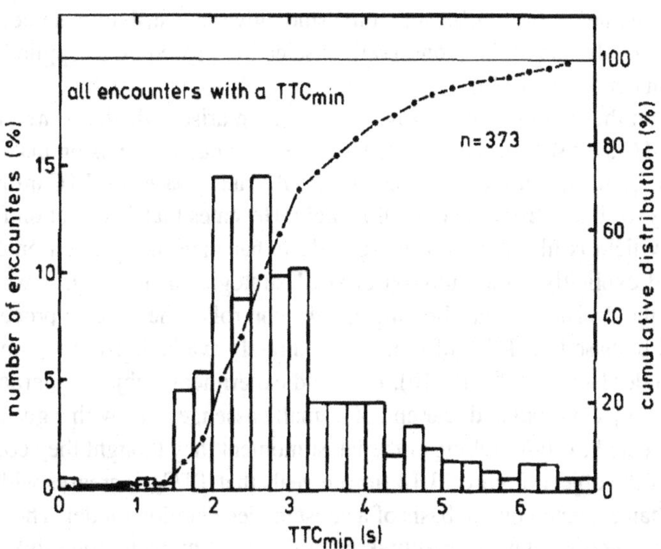

FIGURE 13.12. TTC_{min} distribution of all encounters displaying a collision course at two intersections. The scale at right relates to the cumulative distribution (from van der Horst, 1991a).

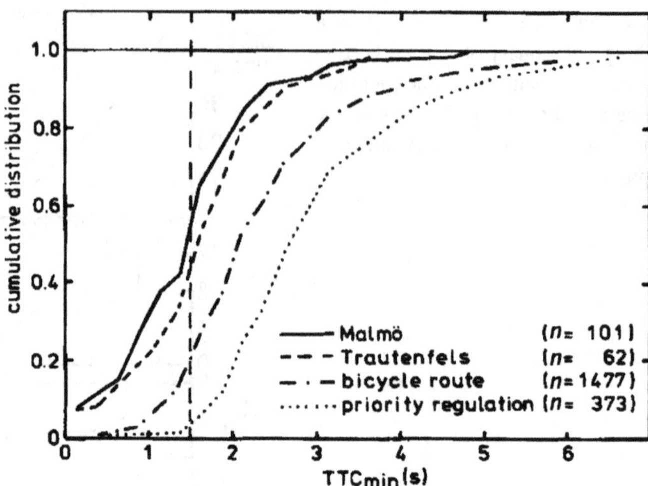

FIGURE 13.13. TTC_{min} distributions of conflicts from the Malmö and Trautenfels calibration studies, of encounters at intersections with bicycle tracks, and of the study from Fig. 13.12.

with the outcome of two calibration studies on traffic conflicts techniques under the auspices of the ICTCT (now International Co-operation on Theories and Concepts in Traffic Safety). In these studies, one in Malmö and one in Trautenfels, the conflicts as scored by traffic conflict observation teams from eight different countries have been analysed quantitatively in terms of TTC. Obviously, the interactions scored as conflicts by conflict observer teams in the field, have much lower TTC_{min} values than all encounters with a collision course that occur at a yield and general rule intersection. A bicycle route study gives a distribution somewhere in between, mainly due to the (conservative) selection procedure as applied for that study (van der Horst, 1990).

Based on these empirical findings, the question arises whether time measures such as TTC are used directly by the road user as a cue for decision making. Lee (1976) suggested that drivers are able to control braking based on TTC information as directly available from the optic flow field. He states that information from the optic flow field is likely to be used directly rather than information on distance and speed explicitly. In a study on drivers' strategies of braking, it was found that both the decision to start braking and the control of the braking process itself may well be based on TTC information as directly available from the optic flow field (van der Horst, 1990, 1991b). In a field experiment, subjects approaching a stationary object (simulated rear end of a small passenger car) with a given speed, were instructed to start braking at the latest moment they thought they could stop in front of the object. Figure 13.14 (top) reveals that TTC_{br} increases with speed, but less than expected on the basis of a constant deceleration model. The effect of braking instruction (start normal braking at the latest moment you think you can stop safely versus hard braking at the latest moment you think you are able to stop in front of the object) indicates that subjects are able to apply the given instruction well, independent of approach speed. The minimum TTC as reached during the

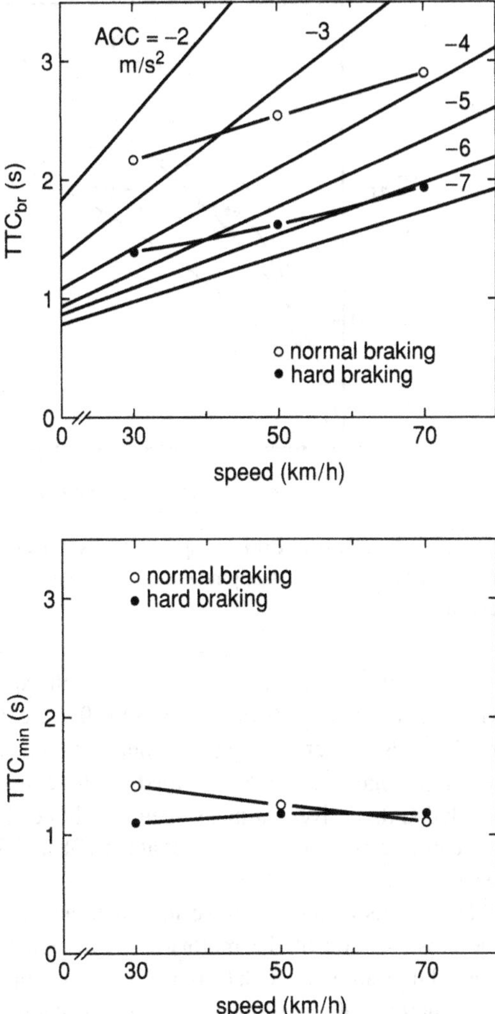

FIGURE 13.14. TTC_{br} (top) and TTC_{min} (bottom) as a function of approach speed and braking instruction (from van der Horst and Hogema, 1994).

approach appears to be independent of approach speed and normal or hard braking instruction and reaches a mean value of about 1.1 s (Fig. 13.14 bottom).

In a study on the evaluation of a fog detection and signalling system, Hogema and van der Horst (1994) analysed a huge amount of inductive loop data on an individual vehicle-by-vehicle basis together with visibility measurements from a nearby scatter type visibility sensor. Figure 13.15 shows the mean-free driving speed (free driving defined as having a headway of >5 s) as a function of visibility range on a motorway (speed limit 120 km/h) that served as a control location for the fog warning system itself on the A16 nearby. Two lines are added that indicate the (maximum) initial speed possible as a function of the required stopping distance, the left for a rather extreme case of a short reaction time (1 s) and hard braking (acceleration -5 m/s^2 with no safety margin left). The right line corresponds to a more moderate reaction time and deceleration and a margin of 5 m left after

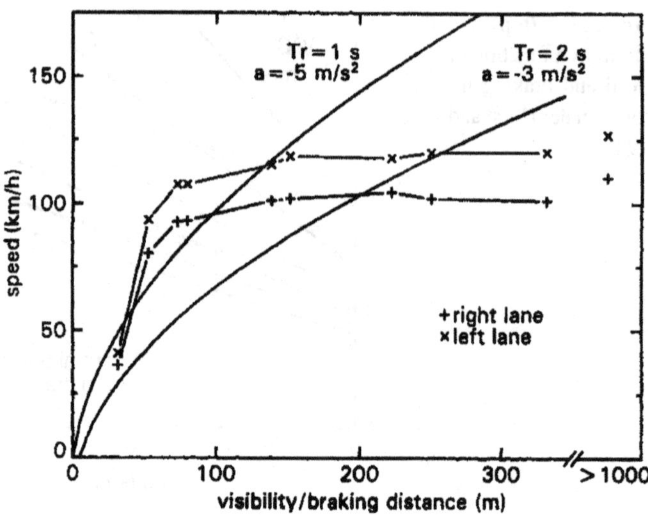

FIGURE 13.15. Mean free driving speed and visibility on the A59 motorway and initial speed possible as a function of stopping distance given reaction time T_r and required deceleration level a.

stopping. Even in the more extreme case, the speeds of the free driving vehicles with a visibility range between 40 and 120 m are too high to avoid a collision when the driver is suddenly being confronted with a stationary object (e.g., a stopped vehicle). Hogema and van der Horst (1994) computed other scenarios as well and concluded that drivers at mean speed might be able to slow down in time for lead vehicles that drive with a speed of at least 38 and 53 km/h in the right and left lane, respectively.

The results of the inductive loop data analysis only refer to the behaviour at one cross section of the motorway. Although this approach has the advantage that a huge amount of data is available on road user behaviour in real traffic, the dynamics of car-following behaviour cannot be studied this way. To study car-following behaviour of drivers over time and to have full control over the experimental conditions, a driving simulator study has been conducted on car-following behaviour in both good and adverse visibility conditions (day/night, fog) (Hogema and van der Horst, 1994). Visibility distances were 40, 80, 120 and 600 m, according to the standard definition for the meteorological visual range (MVR) (White and Jeffery, 1980). Since at night, the rear lights of a vehicle are visible over a larger distance than the contour or the road outline following the definition of MVR, the rear lights of the lead vehicle were made visible over a larger distance according to the results of Heiss (1976). In each run, subjects were partly free driving (i.e., no lead cars) and partly in car-following situations with varying speeds. To prevent overtaking, the left lane of the freeway was closed by means of diagonally striped work-zone panels.

The free driving speeds as found in the simulator experiment reveal a good resemblance with real-world data in good and very poor visibility. In moderate

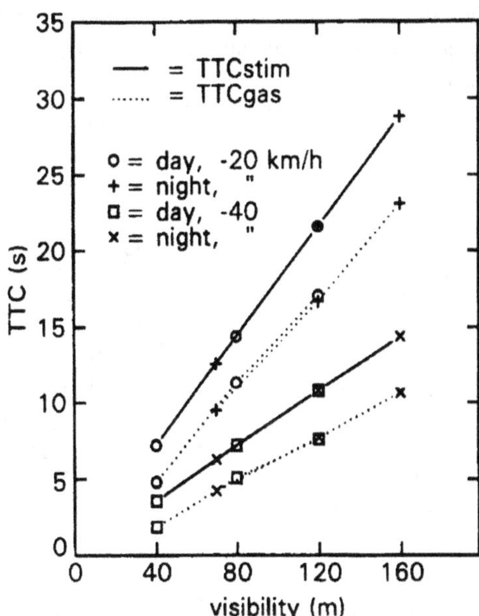

FIGURE 13.16. TTC_{gas} as compared to TTC_{stim} as a function of visibility, light condition, and relative speed.

visibility, speeds in the simulator appear to be somewhat lower. Driver's high expectancy of the presence of a lead vehicle in the simulator and the absence of overtaking possibilities due to the working zone situation may well explain this difference. The relevant cue in approaching a lead vehicle is TTC: in the simulator the lead vehicles would become visible at the pre-determined visibility distance, whereas the speed difference was either 20 or 40 km/h. TTC_{stim} represents the corresponding TTC values. In the night conditions, TTC_{stim} values were larger since, with an equal speed difference, the visibility distance (of the rear lights) was larger. Figure 13.16 gives a comparison of TTC_{stim} and TTC_{gas}, being the TTC at the moment the subject fully releases the gas pedal for the first time after the lead car has become visible.

The finding that the TTC_{gas} curves in the night condition coincide with the day-time curves when taking into account the different visibility distances for vehicle contours and rear lights, indicates that, at night, subjects already react to the lead vehicle before its contour becomes visible. Their first reaction is based on the extra visibility range provided by the rear lights. Apparently, TTC_{gas} is mainly determined by whatever is visible first.

The relationship between TTC_{gas} and TTC_{stim} can be described by a linear regression line ($r = 0.97$, $p < 0.0001$) of the following form (Fig. 13.17).

$$TTC_{gas} = -1.15 + 0.83 \times TTC_{stim} \tag{1}$$

Similar results were obtained for TTC_{min}, the minimum TTC value as reached during the whole approach phase (Hogema and van der Horst, 1994). Equation (2) gives the linear relationship between TTC_{min} and TTC_{stim} ($r = 0.92$, $p < 0.0001$).

$$TTC_{min} = -2.58 + 0.80 \times TTC_{stim} \tag{2}$$

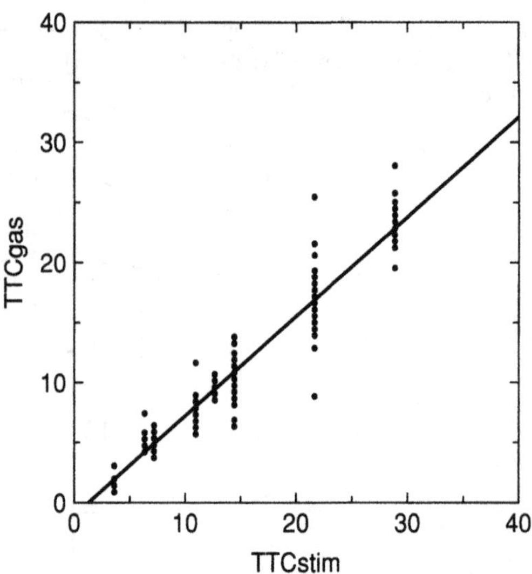

FIGURE 13.17. TTC_{gas} as a function of TTC_{stim} according to Eq. (1).

13.4.1.1 TTC and Collision Avoidance Systems (CAS)

The study conducted by van der Horst (1990) provided values for minimum TTC values that should be avoided in normal traffic conditions. Together with a 1.5-s reaction time (including the time needed for moving the foot from the gas to the brake pedal), an average TTC_{br} of 2.5 s would result in a TTC-criterion of at least 4-s for activating a collision avoidance system (CAS). The first tests with various CASs reveal that a CAS with this 4-s TTC-criterion in combination with a system action to the driver via an active gas pedal reduces the percentage of small headways considerably without having contra-productive effects on other behavioural measures (Janssen and Thomas, 1997). Apparently, a criterion based on TTC seems most in line with what drivers expect to get from a CAS. The question arises whether it would be worthwhile to try other TTC-criterion values as well. For determining an appropriate criterion setting for a CAS, it would be of interest to combine these relationships with earlier findings of critical TTC_{min} values. A TTC_{min} value of 1.1 s as found in the study on TTC and driver's decision making in braking, and the 1.5 s TTC_{min} to distinguish critical from normal behaviour in Traffic Conflicts studies (van der Horst, 1990). By applying Eq. (2), it would result in a TTC criterion for activating a CAS of about 4.5 and 5 s, respectively (van der Horst and Hogema, 1994).

13.4.2 Time-to-Intersection (TTI)

van der Horst (1990) describes a study in which encounters between vehicles approaching from the minor road and traffic from the left on the main road were analysed quantitatively on the basis of video recordings at a yield intersection. Figure 13.18 gives the individual time-to-intersection (TTI) curves (TTI defined by the distance to the edge of the main road divided by the speed at any given time

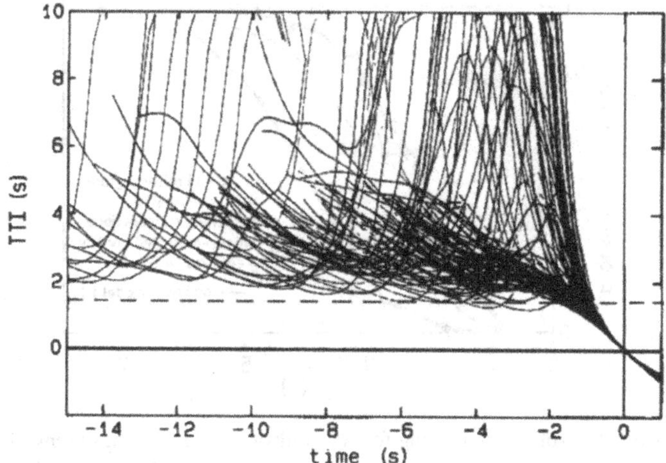

FIGURE 13.18. Individual TTI curves of straight-going cars from the minor road at a yield intersection involved in an encounter with traffic from the left.

moment) of straight-going cars from the minor road. An approach and negotiation of the intersection with a constant speed would result in a TTI curve linearly decreasing with time.

By decelerating gradually, it is possible to reduce the decrease of TTI, to keep TTI constant for a while or even to increase TTI. A complete stop would result in a minimum TTI value (TTI_{min}) followed by TTI increasing to infinity. Again, it is striking that hardly any encounter results in a $TTI_{min} < 1.5$ s (Fig. 13.18). This indicates that drivers from the minor road display rather consistent behaviour in an encounter with another road user and that they may use a time-related measure such as TTI directly for controlling the braking process relative to the intersection geometry.

13.4.3 Time-to-Stop-Line (TTS)

A description of drivers' decision making in terms of a time-related measure such as time-to-stop-line (TTS) has been successfully applied in studies on driver behaviour at signalised intersections and railway grade crossings. It accounts for the individual approach speeds of vehicles (van der Horst and Wilmink, 1986; Tenkink and van der Horst, 1990). Figure 13.19 shows that the willingness to stop at AKI railway grade crossings (controlled by automatic signal control and bell sound, no gates) is higher than at signalised intersections. Also the type of intersection control has its influence on drivers' decision making. At vehicle-actuated control the occasion where a driver is able to run a red light is much lower than at fixed-time controlled intersections. However, the willingness to stop in case of being confronted with the onset of yellow appears to be lower. Drivers have certain expectations about the functioning of the vehicle-actuated control system and act accordingly.

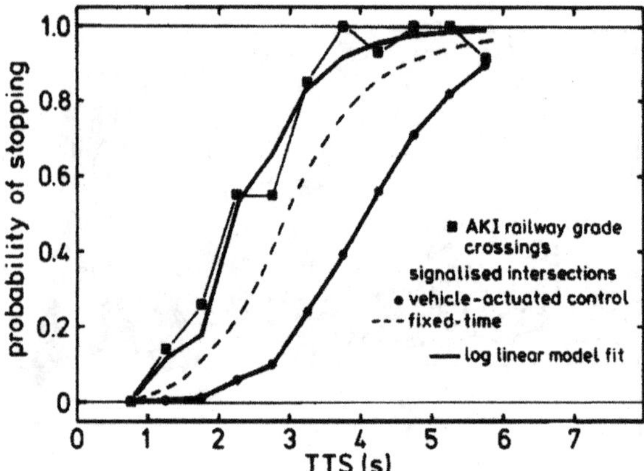

FIGURE 13.19. Probability of stopping for AKI railway grade crossings (Tenkink and van der Horst, 1990) versus vehicle-actuated controlled and fixed-time control intersections (van der Horst and Wilmink, 1986, and Williams, 1977, respectively).

13.5 Conclusions

On the basis of the described studies, it can be concluded that one can learn a lot from systematic behavioural observations in real traffic to come up with measures for improving both safety and efficiency. These studies also point to the direct use of time-related measures such as TTC and TLC as a direct cue for decision making in longitudinal and lateral control of the vehicle. Time-related measures such as TTI and TTS serve as appropriate measures for modelling driver behaviour when negotiating intersections.

These time-related measures provide a framework for modelling driving as a supervisory control task. Driving is considered to be a time-management task in which two related measures at the different levels of the driving task are comparable and may serve as a uniform decision criterion when to switch among subtasks.

One example for modelling driver behaviour for automotive applications is an appropriate criterion for activating a CAS (collision avoidance (warning) system) based on the TTC approach, together with results of studies on driving behaviour in adverse visibility conditions resulting in TTC criterion settings in the range of 4.5–5 s. For driving in fog as an important application area of CASs, special attention should be given to a distance range of 40–120 m.

References

Alexander, G.J. and Lunenfeld, H. (1986). *Driver expectancy in highway design and traffic operations* (Report No. FHWA-TO-86). Federal Highway Administration, Washington, DC.

Allen, T.M., Lunenfeld, H. and Alexander, G.J. (1971). Driver information needs. *Highway Research Record*, 366, 102–115.

Godthelp, J. (1984). *Studies on human vehicle control.* Ph.D. Thesis, Delft University of Technology, Delft.

Godthelp, J. (1988). The limits of path error neglecting in straight lane driving. *Ergonomics*, 31, 609–619.

Godthelp, J. and Kaeppler, W.D. (1988). Effects of vehicle handling characteristics on driving strategy. *Human Factors*, 30, 219–229.

Godthelp, J., Milgram. P. and Blaauw, G.J. (1985). The development of a time-related measure to describe driving strategy. *Human Factors*, 26, 257–268.

Hayward, J.C. (1972). *Near miss determination through use of a scale of danger* (Report no. TTSC 7115). The Pennsylvania State University, Pennsylvania.

Heiss, W.H. (1976). *Highway fog visibility measures and guidance systems* (NCHRP Report 171). Transportation Research Board, Washington, DC.

Hogema, J.H. and Horst, A.R.A. van der (1994). Driving behaviour under adverse visibility conditions. In ERTICO (Ed.). *Towards an intelligent transport system: Proceedings of the First World Congress on Applications of Transport Telematics and Intelligent Vehicle–Highway Systems* (pp. 1623–1630). Artech House, Boston London.

Horst, A.R.A. van der (1990). *A time-based analysis of road user behaviour in normal and critical encounters.* Ph.D. Thesis, Delft University of Technology, Delft.

Horst, A.R.A. van der (1991a). Video analysis of road user behaviour at intersections. In T.W. van der Schaaf, D.A. Lucas and A.R. Hale (Eds.). *Near miss reporting as a safety tool* (pp. 93–109). Butterworth-Heinemann Ltd, Oxford.

Horst, A.R.A. van der (1991b). Time-to-collision as a cue for decision-making in braking. In A.G. Gale et al. (Eds.). *Vision in vehicles III* (pp. 19–26). Elsevier, Amsterdam.

Horst, A.R.A. van der (1996). Speed-reducing measures for 80 km/h roads. In *Proceedings of the 9th ICTCT Workshop in Zagreb* (pp. 84–95). University of Lund, Lund, October 1996.

Horst, A.R.A. van der (1998). *Factors influencing drivers' speed behaviour and adaptation* (TNO-Report TM-98-D006). TNO Human Factors, Soesterberg.

Horst, R. van der (2004). Occlusion as a measure for visual workload: An overview of TNO occlusion research in car driving. *Applied Ergonomics*, 35, 189–196.

Horst, A.R.A. van der and Hoekstra, W. (1994). Testing speed reduction designs for 80 kilometer per hour roads with simulator. In *Transportation Research Record 1464* (pp. 63–68). Transportation Research Board, Washington, DC.

Horst, A.R.A. van der and Hogema, J.H. (1994). Time-to-collision and collision avoidance systems. In *Proceedings 6th ICTCT Workshop* (pp. 109–121). Salzburg. Kuratorium für Verkehrssicherheit, Salzburg, October 27–29, 1993.

Horst, A.R.A. van der and Wilmink, A. (1986). Drivers' decision-making at signalised intersections: An optimisation of the yellow timing. *Traffic Engineering and Control*, 27(12), 615–622.

Hydén, C. (1987). *The development of a method for traffic safety evaluation: The Swedish Traffic Conflicts Technique* (Bulletin 70). University of Lund, Lund Institute of Technology, Department of Traffic Planning and Engineering, Lund.

Janssen, W.H. and Thomas, H. (1997). In-vehicle collision avoidance support under adverse visibility conditions. In I. Noy (Ed.). *Ergonomics and safety of intelligent driver interfaces* (pp. 221–229). Lawrence Erlbaum, Mahwah, NJ.

Lee, D.N. (1976). A theory of visual control of braking based on information about time-to-collision. *Perception*, 5, 437–459.

Milgram, P. and Horst, R. van der (1984). Field-sequential colour stereoscopy with liquid crystal spectacles. In *Proceedings Fourth International Display Research Conference*. Societe des electriciens, des electroniciens et des radio-electroniciens, Paris.

Rasmussen, J. (1985). Trends in human reliability analysis. *Ergonomics*, 28(8), 1185–1195.

Tenkink, E. and Horst, A.R.A. van der (1990). Car driver behavior at flashing light railroad grade crossings. *Accident Analysis and Prevention*, 22(3), 229–239.

Theeuwes, J. (1993). Visual attention and driving behaviour. In *Proceedings of the International Seminar Human Factors in Road Traffic*. 5–6 April 1993. Universidade do Minho, Braga, Portugal.

White, M.E. and Jeffery, D.J. (1980). *Some aspects of motorway traffic behaviour in fog* (TRRL laboratory report 958). Transport and Road Research Laboratory, Crowthorne.

Williams, W.L. (1977). Driver behavior during the yellow interval. In *Transportation Research Record 644* (pp. 75–78). Transportation Research Board, Washington, DC.

Winsum, W. van, Brookhuis, K.A. and Waard, D. de (2000). A comparison of different ways to approximate time-to-line crossing (TLC) during car driving. *Accident Analysis and Prevention*, 32, 47–56.

14
Situation Awareness and Driving: A Cognitive Model

M. BAUMANN AND J. F. KREMS

14.1 Introduction

One of the major preconditions of safe driving is that drivers correctly perceive and interpret the relevant objects and elements of the current traffic situation and that they consider these elements in planning and controlling their behaviour. Such elements may be other drivers, the condition of the street or traffic signs. For each of these elements drivers do not just have to perceive them but they must understand them according to their relevance to their goals. In addition, drivers must also make assumptions about the future actions or states of these elements. For example, perceiving a car coming from the right when entering a crossroads is far from being enough in order to react accordingly. The driver must interpret this car according to its relevance to his own goal, that is, safely passing the crossroads. He has to take into account whether he or the car from the right has to give way. But even this is not enough to select the appropriate action. If the other car has to give way, the driver will try to assess from the speed of the car whether the other car will indeed stop. A concept that has recently become rather popular in aviation psychology and that aims at describing and integrating these different cognitive processes is called *situation awareness*.

14.2 Situation Awareness

According to Endsley (1995b), situation awareness comprises a state of knowledge, that is, knowing what is going on. She uses the term synonymously with *situation model*, defining situation awareness as 'the perception of the elements in the environment within a span of time and space, the comprehension of their meaning and the projection of their status in the near future' (p. 36). According to this definition, three levels of situation awareness can be distinguished. Level I involves perception of the status, attributes and dynamics of the relevant situation elements. Level II, the comprehension level, involves integrating the different situation elements into a holistic picture of the situation, resulting in the comprehension of the meaning of the different elements. Level III, situation assessment, involves the generation of assumptions about the future behaviour of the elements on the basis of the comprehension of the situation. Situation assessment encompasses the processes of achieving, acquiring and maintaining situation awareness and is distinct from it.

Situation awareness as a state of knowledge and situation assessment as the processes that lead to this state of knowledge are highly interdependent. Adams et al. (1995) describe this interdependence, using Neisser's (1976) perception-action cycle. Perceived changes in the task environment may lead to a change in the comprehension of the current situation, that is, to a change in situation awareness. This updated situation awareness will trigger certain actions that might lead to the perception of new pieces of information, that is, because these actions change the task environment or because they comprise the sampling of new pieces of information. In either case the perception of these new pieces of information will again change the current situation model. This will again trigger new actions and so on. This is in line with Klein's (2000) proposal that constructing situation awareness is an active process of guided information seeking rather than a passive receipt and storage of information. Klein points out that situation awareness is determined not only by the current situation but also by the person's actions.

14.2.1 An Algorithmic Description of Situation Awareness

Endsley's (1995b) model of situation awareness is certainly one of the most influential models of situation awareness to date. A number of studies on situation awareness as well as efforts in modelling focus on different aspects of situation awareness. Most of them stay within the scope and constraints of Endsley's model (Rousseau et al., 2005). However, despite the remarkable influence of the model, it also has some shortcomings. Endsley's model is a descriptive model of situation awareness; that is, it aims at describing situation awareness in terms of the processes that serve it. According to Marr (1982) and Dawson (1998), an information processing system can be analysed at three levels: Computational, algorithmic and implementational. The level of concern for descriptive models of situation awareness is the algorithmic level. At this level of analysis an information-processing system is described in terms of information-processing steps and a functional architecture. In the end the goal at this level is to identify the connection between the functional description of the information processor and its implementational description. This is achieved when the computational steps an information processing system takes can be described in terms of primitive functions that are implemented in the system's hardware. In this sense the three levels of situation awareness in Endsley's model can be viewed as different functions of situation awareness (McGuinnes and Foy, 2000, cited in Rousseau et al., 2005). Yet even when Endsley (1995b) describes some more primitive mechanisms of how these functions are performed, these mechanisms are far too abstract to be part of the functional architecture. The goal of this paper is to move the algorithmic analysis and description of situation awareness a step further, to a description in terms of the functional architecture and therefore to come closer to a more complete algorithmic analysis of situation awareness. To this end, we propose a model that describes how situation awareness is (1) constructed, (2) maintained and used as a basis for (3) action selection in terms of primitive functions.

The present model views the construction and maintenance of situation awareness as a comprehension process. The model proposes in detail a mechanism of how the comprehension of the situation, that is, how Level II situation awareness is achieved. Essentially it assumes that the comprehension process for understanding the meaning of different elements in a situation is comparable to the comprehension process for understanding language or discourse. In both cases an integrated mental representation of the perceived and processed pieces of information is constructed. This representation reflects the understanding of these elements. Fundamental to our approach is Kintsch's (1998) Construction-integration theory of text comprehension. As was explained above, situation awareness is a dynamic representation that is influenced by both the situation and the actions of the person. Therefore, for a model of situation awareness to be complete it has to specify how situation awareness is translated into action. As for the construction of situation awareness we believe that cognitive psychology already offers a theory that can be used for this purpose. The theory we use here is Norman and Shallice's (1986) theory of action selection. Groeger (2000) described how this theory can be applied within the driving context to explain the selection and execution of driving manoeuvres. In this paper we will describe how this theory can be combined with Kintsch's construction–integration theory to provide a comprehension based model of situation awareness. With the combination of these two theories it is possible to describe in more detail than in Endsley's model how situation awareness is constructed, maintained and used as a basis for action selection.

14.2.1.1 The Construction of the Situation Model: Comprehending the Situation

How is the situation model built according to the construction–integration theory? According to Kintsch (1998), comprehending new pieces of information involves two phases. In the first phase, the construction phase, the perception of new pieces of information activates knowledge structures in long-term memory, such as propositions and schemata that are associated with these pieces of information. This activation process is undirected and follows learned associations among these different pieces of knowledge. The result of this automatic activation process is a rather unstructured activation of knowledge in long-term memory. This activated knowledge then becomes integrated in a following step, the integration phase. Integration is accomplished through inhibitory and excitatory processes: Knowledge that has become activated in the first phase and is compatible to already activated knowledge (i.e., to the existing situation model) will remain activated and at the same time activate other knowledge compatible with it. Simultaneously, incompatible pieces of knowledge inhibit each other. For example, if an event such as a traffic light turning yellow triggers two incompatible interpretations, 'I have to decelerate to stop before the traffic light' and 'I have to accelerate to pass the crossroads before the traffic light turns red', these two interpretations will inhibit each other. At the same time, these two interpretations are also activated or inhibited by other knowledge. For example, if the driver knows that the police monitor this crossroads, that knowledge will inhibit the acceleration interpretation. However, being a short distance from the traffic light will activate the acceleration interpretation. In the end, the 'winning' interpretation will be the one that receives the most activation from other activated knowledge.

The result of these two phases is an episodic memory representation. Despite being a unitary representation, Kintsch (1998) distinguishes between two components of the episodic memory representation: The text base and the situation model. The text base consists of information that is directly derived from the text. The situation model results from the connection between the text representation and the comprehender's world knowledge. Translating into the domain of driving and situation awareness, we propose that the episodic memory representation similarly consists of two components: A situation-specific representation (analogous to the text base model) and the situation model. The situation-specific representation consists of information that is directly perceived from the environment. This mainly includes the situation elements the driver perceives and information about the status of these elements that can be directly perceived, such as one's own speed. It also might include inferences that can be directly made from the perception of the situation elements and their status, such as that one's own speed is greater than the speed of the lead vehicle. This representation might reflect what Endsley (1995b) terms Level I situation awareness. The situation model then results from the connection between this situation-specific representation and the driver's world knowledge. Through this connection the perceived configuration of situation elements becomes connected to prior experienced situations with similar configurations of elements. This connection provides an interpretation of the current situation, partly depending on the outcome of similar prior situations. This mechanism might at least in part explain the advantage of experienced drivers compared to novice drivers in hazard perception (Chapman and Underwood, 1998; Groeger, 2000; McKenna and Crick, 1994). Experienced drivers have a much greater chance of having stored in long-term memory the relevant information that identifies the current situation as dangerous because their database of experienced traffic situations is much greater than that of novices. But the situation model does not only provide interpretations of the current situation, such as whether it is dangerous or not. It also contains expectations about the future development of the situation and the future behaviour of the situation elements. These expectations are also derived from prior experienced situations that get connected to the situation-specific representation. For example, an experienced driver will know how long it will take a yellow light to turn red and perceiving a traffic light turning yellow will automatically activate this expectation. The situation model therefore might reflect Endsley's Level II and Level III situation awareness.

To summarise, this model proposes that the different levels of situation awareness are highly interconnected as they are part of an unitary episodic memory representation. By using Kintsch's (1998) construction–integration theory of text comprehension, the model also specifies a mechanism of how this representation is constructed beginning with the perception of elements of the current situation. It is accomplished by a two-phase process. The first phase consists of an unstructured activation process, the second phase of a constraint–satisfaction process. This constraint–satisfaction process keeps the representation of the current situation coherent through the reciprocal activation of compatible knowledge and inhibition of incompatible knowledge.

14.2.1.2 Selection of Actions and the Control of Behaviour

The selection of situation-appropriate actions can also be integrated seamlessly into this comprehension-based model of situation awareness. During the construction of the situation representation, not only knowledge relevant to the interpretation of the situation and its future development get activated, but also actions that are appropriate in the current situation. According to the framework of Norman (1981) and Norman and Shallice (1986), actions are represented as schemata. These schemata are programmes for the control of routine tasks. Each schema is part of a hierarchy of schemata and is connected to superordinate and subordinate schemata. For example, the schema 'stop at a red traffic light' is subordinate to a general driving schema and it is superordinate to other schemata, such as 'push the brake pedal to decelerate'. Besides these hierarchical connections there are also connections to functionally related schemata or to schemata that are incompatible. The connections are either excitatory, like the connections from a superordinate schema to its subordinates, or inhibitory if the schemata are incompatible with each other, such as accelerating or decelerating when facing a yellow traffic light. Each schema is connected with certain trigger conditions that activate the schema if present in the current situation representation. In our example, detecting a yellow traffic light activates both the acceleration and deceleration schemata. In this way, the activation of situation-appropriate actions becomes part of the construction of the situation representation. One possibility of how these trigger conditions become connected to action schemata is through prior experience. Successfully performing an action in a given situation will establish excitatory links between relevant elements of the situation and this action schema. These elements will then become the trigger conditions for this schema. A failure in performing this action in this situation may reduce the strength of already existing excitatory connections or might even establish inhibitory links between relevant situation elements and the action schema. If more than one schema is activated, as in the above example, a selection has to be made. Norman and Shallice (1986) propose a mechanism called *contention scheduling*, which operates on two processes: *Competition*, the different action schemata compete with one another for their activation value, and *selection*, which takes place on the basis of the activation alone. In the traffic light example, the yellow traffic light triggers two possible action sequences, decelerating and accelerating. Both schemata receive activation as their trigger conditions are satisfied. At the same time, other elements in the situation may be present such as a leading car that is already decelerating. This additional element will activate the deceleration schema further. Because of the inhibitory link between the deceleration and acceleration schema, both schemata inhibit each other. As the deceleration schema becomes more activated than the acceleration schema, the acceleration schema will be more strongly inhibited. As a result, the deceleration schema is more highly activated than the acceleration schema and the deceleration schema takes over the control of action. In sum, contention scheduling is sufficient to control well-learned, simple action sequences. It resolves competition for selection, prevents competitive use of common resources and negotiates cooperative use of common resources when possible.

In cases where a schema is not available or when the task is novel or complex, another control structure is necessary. *Norman* and Shallice (1986) call this structure the *Supervisory Attentional System (SAS)*. The SAS allows for voluntary, attentional control of performance. The SAS is basically an attentional system that influences the selection of schemata in the contention scheduling process by providing additional activation and/or inhibition to schemata in order to bias their selection. The selection process itself is always based on the highest activation values of the competing schemata. This system allows for top-down influences in the action selection process. For example, if a physician on the way to an emergency call sees the traffic light turning yellow, he will not stop. Instead he will try to proceed even if the light is red because of his goal to get to the patient as quickly as possible. In this case the deceleration schema receives greater inhibition from the output of the SAS and is unlikely to be selected by the contention scheduling process.

To summarise, we described two well-established theories, Kintsch's (1998) construction-integration theory of text comprehension and Norman and Shallice's (1986) theory of action selection. Both theories possess a firm empirical foundation and describe their assumptions in detail. In addition, Norman and Shallice's theory was already applied to the driving context as a framework to describe the selection and execution of driving manoeuvres (Groeger, 2000). What we believe is new and fruitful is the combination of these two theories as a framework for situation awareness. We proposed to combine these two theories into a comprehension-based model of situation awareness. By this it is possible to make much more detailed assumptions about the processes that are involved in the construction and maintenance of situation awareness and its use as a basis for action selection in driving.

14.3 Errors and the Comprehension Based-Model of Situation Awareness

Driver distraction is a major cause for errors in driving. Distraction can stem from different sources, such as other occupants, objects outside the car or in-vehicle tasks. The distraction can be visual, as when the driver looks at an in-vehicle display while driving; psychomotor, for example when the driver removes a hand from the wheel to adjust the heat; auditory, such as when the radio obfuscates auditory signals from other vehicles; or cognitive, for example, when the driver's mind is preoccupied with a conversation. The comprehension-based model of situation awareness addresses especially the last kind of distraction, cognitive distraction. Next we will demonstrate how certain errors in driving can be explained within the framework of this model.

An error that is called 'inattention blindness' or 'looked-but-did-not-see' describes the phenomenon that the distracted driver was actually looking at the relevant situation element (e.g., the red traffic light), but did not react accordingly. How can this be explained in terms of our model? The comprehension-based model of situation awareness implicitly assigns working memory a key role in the processes of situation awareness construction, maintenance, updating and action selection. Working memory resources are necessary for associating perceived elements in the environment with knowledge stored in long-term memory, for integrating these new elements in the current situation model, for removing irrelevant elements from the situation model, for keeping the information in the situation model available for the selection of appropriate actions, for monitoring the selection and execution of actions and so on. In the case of cognitive distraction, some of these resources may not be available because they are assigned to other tasks, such as entering the destination into a navigation system or talking to the passenger. The remaining working memory capacity might be too reduced to ensure that the perceived situation elements get fully connected to the relevant knowledge in long-term memory. The comprehension process stops prematurely and some relevant implications of the perceived situation element do not become activated and therefore are not available in the situation representation to trigger the relevant action schemata. In addition, the impoverished processing of a perceived situation element may lead to a shallow memory trace for this element, which then rapidly decays and is lost from the situation representation. Again, this situation element is not considered in the action selection process.

Cognitive distraction may not only impair the comprehension of situation elements, but it can also impair action selection directly. As explained above, actions are controlled by action schemata that compete for the highest activation value. The activation of each schema is partly determined by the match between its trigger conditions and the current situation and by the SAS. The SAS preactivates those schemata that are compatible with the current task goal and inhibits those that are incompatible. Yet as an attentional system the SAS depends on the availability of the respective cognitive resources. If these are not available because the driver is preoccupied with a demanding in-vehicle task or engaged in a conversation, action selection may be primarily determined by the match between the schemata's trigger conditions and the current situation. In such a case the driver often exhibits the behaviour that is most strongly connected to the current situation even if it is not compatible with the current task goal. As an example, imagine someone driving along a very familiar road. At a certain crossroads the driver is used to turning right, in the direction of the workplace. But on this day the driver wants to go to the supermarket, requiring a left turn. The driver is very busy with thinking about what to buy for dinner and automatically turns right, towards the workplace, instead of to the supermarket. In this case the resources of the SAS were so occupied with reasoning about what to buy that it could not no longer control behaviour. That is, preactivation of the less common action schema for this situation ('turn left') failed in order to prevent the most highly connected action schema to this situation ('turn right') from taking over control.

14.4 Situation Awareness and In-Vehicle Information System Tasks

One of the major concerns connected to the on-board use of information and driver assistance systems is related to this kind of driver distraction and the errors that follow from impaired situation awareness. Safe driving requires uninterrupted surveillance of one's vehicle and awareness of the traffic situation and changes in environmental conditions. Interacting with an in-vehicle information system can lead to distraction, increased cognitive workload and a rise in the probability of accidents. Therefore, within the ITS domain there is a need for a procedure to measure the effects of IVIS tasks on the driver's situation awareness (European Commision, 2000).

The theory outlined above emphasises the importance of working memory processes for the construction and maintenance of the situation representation while driving. It immediately follows that IVIS tasks that are associated with high working memory load should clearly impair the construction and maintenance of a proper situation representation.

14.4.1 A Measurement Procedure: Context-Dependent Choice Reaction Task

How can the effect of IVIS tasks on situation awareness be measured? One possible way is to have drivers perform these IVIS tasks while driving and use some measure to determine their effect. However, up to now most of the available procedures for the measurement of situation awareness were developed for use in the aviation domain. Situation Awareness Global Assessment Technique (SAGAT; Endsley, 1995a) was developed for investigating pilots' situation awareness. Hauß and Eyferth (2001) developed SALSA, a similar technique used in air-traffic control studies. Only recently have procedures for studying the driving task begun to be developed. For example, Bailly et al. (2003) propose a methodology that uses video to analyze drivers' situation awareness.

Both SAGAT and SALSA are so-called 'freezing techniques'. Domain experts, such as pilots, perform the relevant task in a simulator. While working on the task (e.g. a flight mission), the simulation is halted and the experts are asked several questions regarding relevant parameters of the current task situation. The proportion of questions answered correctly is used as an indicator of the pilot's situation awareness. The advantage of these procedures is that they directly measure the availability of relevant parameters of the current task. However, these techniques require, as a prerequisite, a detailed task analysis that can be used to formulate the questions asked during the task interruption. These techniques are content based in so far as they compare the content of the operator's situation awareness with the obligatory content derived from the task analysis. Given the diversity of driving tasks and driving situations as well as the dynamics of the driving task, such a task analysis is very difficult to perform within the driving domain. Furthermore, it is difficult to draw conclusions about the causes of degraded situation awareness using these procedures.

The focus of the measurement approach we propose is on the processes that serve to maintain situation awareness in terms of the comprehension-based model of situation awareness. Therefore this approach could be characterised as a process-based approach of situation awareness measurement. The basic idea is to measure the degree of interference between the processes involved in the construction and maintenance of situation awareness and those that are involved in performing IVIS tasks. In terms of our model of situation awareness, both visual attention and working memory play a key role for situation awareness. Therefore, our procedure uses a dual-task technique to measure the visual attention and working memory demands of different IVIS tasks. IVIS tasks are performed in the laboratory and regarded as the primary task. A secondary task is used to measure the residual visual attention and working memory resources not utilised by the primary IVIS task. As mentioned above, the underlying assumption is that IVIS tasks that demonstrate high demands for visual attention and working memory interfere with the construction and maintenance of a proper situation representation in memory and therefore will lead to degraded situation awareness.

This secondary task is a choice reaction task where the appropriate reactions to the different stimuli are context-dependent. It combines a visual perception task with a memory task. The perceptual component of the task consists of presenting one of two possible visual stimuli at 23° of visual angle, either to the right or to the left of the participant at a distance of 2.25 m. The stimuli are presented with interstimulus intervals varying between 1 and 3 s. The participant's task is to respond with a button press. This component of the task is similar to a laboratory variant of the peripheral detection task (PDT). Winsum et al. (1999) developed the PDT on the basis of Miura (1986) and Williams (1985, 1995). Miura (1986) found that reaction times to spots of light presented at different horizontal eccentricities on the windscreen while driving increased with traffic density, thereby reflecting demands of the driving task. Williams (1985, 1995) showed that with increasing foveal load the accuracy of responses to stimuli presented peripherally decreased. Within the advanced driver attention metrics (ADAM) project (Baumann et al., 2003; Breuer et al., 2003), we developed a version of the PDT that is applicable under laboratory conditions. It has been shown that this version is a valid measure of the visual demand of IVIS tasks (Baumann et al., 2003).

But contrary to the PDT the procedure used in this project to measure the visual and the cognitive demand of IVIS task requires a choice reaction not only a detection reaction. The participants have to press a different button depending on the stimulus presented. But the correct response depends not only from the presented stimulus but also from the current context. For example in context A, the participant presses the right button if stimulus 1 appears and the left button if stimulus 2 appears. In context B the stimulus-button pairing is reversed. The current context is signalled by acoustic signals, a high- and a low-frequency tone. Every three to five visual stimuli a new context signal is presented that can indicate either a new context or the same as before. Remembering the current context and updating the context define the memory part of this task.

This task yields two measures that are intended to allow the independent assessment of visual and working memory demands of the primary task. First, one can look at the proportion of visual stimuli responded to, not differentiating whether the response was correct or not according to the respective context. This detection rate is used as a measure of the visual demand of the primary task. If the primary task is highly visually demanding, the participant will simply miss more of the visual stimuli than if the primary task is of low visual demand. The proportion of correct reactions from all *given* reactions is used as a measure of working memory demands of the primary task. If the task is highly demanding in terms of working memory, the participants may often forget the current context or may frequently fail to update the context after a new context signal was presented. This leads to more erroneous responses to the visual stimuli.

14.4.2 Evaluation of the Context-Dependent Choice Reaction Task

In a current project the validity of the context-dependent choice reaction task is evaluated. The first step consists of evaluating differently visually and cognitively demanding tasks with this procedure. The aim is to examine whether the detection rate and the correct response rate are sensitive to visual and working memory demands of IVIS tasks. Specifically, we wanted to know whether the simple detection rate is sensitive primarily to the visual demand of the IVIS task and whether the correct response rate is sensitive primarily to the memory demands of the IVIS task. The second step of the project consists of comparing these evaluations of visual and working memory demands of IVIS tasks with the effects of these IVIS tasks on situation awareness while driving. In this paper we will summarise results of the first experiment.

In this experiment, 23 participants had to perform either a demanding visual search task or a demanding working memory task as primary tasks. The visual search task consisted of finding a target letter among 160 distractor letters. The working memory task consisted of a one-back task. In this task participants were shown a series of letters, one at a time. Each time a new letter was presented participants had to name the letter that was presented just before. Simultaneously to these tasks, participants performed the context-dependent choice reaction task. As a baseline condition participants performed the context-dependent choice reaction task also alone. We expected that the simple detection rate of the secondary task would be lower when the visual search task was the primary task,

TABLE 14.1. Detection and correct response rate in the baseline, visual and working memory condition.

	Detection rate		Correct response rate	
	Mean	SD	Mean	SD
Baseline	0.98	0.05	0.87	0.20
Visual	0.81	0.13	0.81	0.13
Working memory	0.89	0.09	0.78	0.11

than when the working memory task was the primary task. The reverse pattern was expected for the correct response rate. Table 14.1 presents the mean detection and correct response rates in the baseline, visual and working memory condition. The rates are based on the responses to the first stimulus after a context change.

As predicted, the results show that the detection rate is clearly lower when the visual search task is the primary task than for the working memory task, $Z = -2.516$, $p = 0.012$. This indicates that the detection rate is sensitive to the visual demand of the primary task, confirming the results of Baumann et al. (2003). The correct response rate was only slightly lower for the working memory task than with the visual search task, indicating that the correct response rate is not very sensitive to the working memory demands of the primary task. The difference was not significant, $Z = -0.608$, $p = 0.543$. We assume that the failure to find a significant difference in the correct response rate between the visual and working memory condition is due to the too small working memory demands of the context-dependent choice reaction task. Therefore, in a second experiment we will increase the working memory demand of the task be increasing the frequency of the context changes.

14.5 Conclusions

The goal of our approach is to establish the cognitive basis of situation awareness in order to be able to apply it to the driving task. We assume, similar to Adams et al. (1995), that the construction of situation awareness is basically a comprehension process that yields a mental representation of the meaning of the different elements of a traffic situation and the situation as whole, that is, the situation representation. This situation representation serves as a basis for planning future behaviour that in turn alters the situation representation again. According to this perspective, driver knowledge plays a key role in determining the significance of events and elements in a traffic situation. Viewing situation awareness as a comprehension process also highlights the role of working memory in the process of constructing and maintaining situation awareness. The processes necessary to interpret new pieces of information, to determine their consequences for the current situation model, to integrate new pieces of information into the situation model and to remove irrelevant information from the situation model must take place in working memory. If the resources of working memory are occupied by other tasks, for example IVIS tasks, these processes will be impaired leading to a degraded situation awareness. This process model of situation awareness is used to develop a procedure that should allow the evaluation of visual and working memory demands of IVIS tasks. The idea is that knowing the visual and working memory demands of IVIS tasks allows to make predictions about the effects of these IVIS tasks on situation awareness.

References

Adams, M.J., Tenney, Y.J. and Pew, R.W. (1995). Situation awareness and the cognitive management of complex systems. *Human Factors*, 37(1), 85–104.

Bailly, B., Bellet, T. and Goupil, C. (2003). Driver's mental representations: Experimental study and training perspectives. In L. Dorn (Ed.). *Driver behavior and training*. Aldershot, UK, Ashgate.

Baumann, M., Rösler, D., Jahn, G. and Krems, J.F. (2003). Assessing driver distraction using occlusion method and peripheral detection task. In H. Strasser, K. Kluth, H. Rausch and H. Bubb (Eds.) *Quality of work and products in enterprises of the future*. Ergonomia Verlag, Stuttgart, pp. 53–56.

Breuer, J., Bengler, K., Heinrich, C. and Reichelt, W. (2003). Development of advanced driver attention metrics (ADAM). In H. Strasser, K. Kluth, H. Rausch and H. Bubb (Eds.). *Quality of work and products in enterprises of the future*. Ergonomia Verlag, Stuttgart, pp. 37–39.

Chapman, P.R. and Underwood, G. (1998). Visual search of driving situations: Danger and experience. *Perception*, 27(8), 951–964.

Dawson, M.R.W. (1998). *Understanding cognitive science*. Blackwell, Malden.

Endsley, M.R. (1995a). Measurement of situation awareness in dynamic systems. *Human Factors*, 37(1), 65–84.

Endsley, M.R. (1995b). Towards a theory of situation awareness in dynamic systems. *Human Factors*, 37(1), 32–64.

European Commission (2000). Recommendation of 21st December 1999 on safe and efficient in-vehicle information and communication systems: A European statement of principles on human machine interface. *Official Journal*, 2000/53/EC.

Groeger, J. (2000). *Understanding driving*. Psychology Press, Hove.

Hauß, Y. and Eyferth, K. (2001). The evaluation of a multi-sector-planner concept: SALSA – A new approach to measure situation awareness in ATC. *Fourth International Air Traffic Management R&D Seminar ATM-2001*. (http://atm2001.eurocontrol.fr./finalpapers/pap136.pdf).

Kintsch, W. (1998). *Comprehension: A paradigm for cognition*. Cambridge University Press, New York.

Klein, G. (2000). Cognitive task analysis of teams. In J.M. Schraagen, S.F. Chipman and T.D. Shalin (Eds.). *Cognitive task analysis*. Lawrence Erlbaum Associates, Mahwah, pp. 417–430.

Marr, D. (1982). *Vision*. Freeman, San Francisco.

McKenna, F.P. and Crick, J.L. (1994). *Hazard perception in drivers: A methodology for testing and training*. Transport Research Laboratory (Contractor Report 313), pp. 1–29.

Miura, T. (1986). Coping with situational demands: A study of eye movements and peripherial vision performance. In A.G. Gale, I.D. Brown, C.M. Haselgrave, P. Smith and S.H. Taylor (Eds.). *Vision in vehicles–II*. Elsevier, Amsterdam.

Neisser, U. (1976). *Cognition and reality: Principles and implications of cognitive psychology*. Freeman, San Francisco.

Norman, D.A. (1981). Categorization of action slips. *Psychological Review*, 88(1), 1–15.

Norman, D.A. and Shallice, T. (1986). Attention to action: Willed and automatic control of behavior. In R.J. Davidson, G.E. Schwartz and D. Shapiro (Eds.). *Consciousness and self-regulation* (Vol. 4). Plenum Press, New York, pp. 1–18.

Rousseau, R., Tremblay, S. and Breton, R. (2005). Defining and modeling situation awareness: A critical review. In S. Banbury and S. Tremblay (Eds.). *A cognitive approach to situation awareness: Theory and application*. Ashgate, Hampshire Burlington, pp. 3–21.

Williams, L.J. (1985). Tunnel vision induced by a foveal load manipulation. *Human Factors*, 27, 221–227.

Williams, L.J. (1995). Peripheral target recognition and visual field narrowing in aviators and nonaviators. *International Journal of Aviation Psychology*, 5(2), 215–232.

Winsum, W. van, Martens, M.H. and Herland, L. (1999). *The effects of speech versus tactile driver support messages on workload, driver behaviour and user acceptance (Report No. TM-99-C043). TNO Human Factors*. Soesterberg, the Netherlands.

15
Driver Error and Crashes

DIANNE PARKER

15.1 Slips, Lapses and Mistakes

The first distinction to be considered is between slips/lapses and mistakes. Reason (1990) defined *error* as 'the failure of planned actions to achieve their desired ends – without the intervention of some unforeseeable event'. In these terms, while a slip represents a problem with the execution of a good plan, a mistake involves an inappropriate or incorrect plan that is correctly executed. Slips and mistakes map directly onto Rasmussen's (1974, 1990) differentiation of three levels of human performance. According to Rasmussen's model, the cognitive mode in which people operate changes as the task performed becomes more familiar, from the knowledge-based through the rule-based to the skill-based level. The three levels are not mutually exclusive, but represent a progression, leading to skilled performance. *Knowledge-based performance*, which involves consciously thinking the task through, is relevant when the task faced is novel and conscious effort must be made to construct a plan of action from stored knowledge. Knowledge-based performance is necessary if you are planning to drive to a destination never previously visited. Errors at this level of performance are mistakes, arising from incorrect knowledge or from the limitations of cognitive resources. Moreover, decision making itself is subject to a range of biases (Parker and Lawton, 2003). For example, Kahneman and Tverskys' classic laboratory experiments identified the availability bias, referring to the fact that probability judgements (e.g., judgements of the likelihood of having a car accident) are strongly influenced by the ease with which past cases can be recalled (Tversky and Kahneman, 1974).

Rule-based performance occurs when we already have some familiarity with the task, and can perform it by drawing on a set of stored mental if–then rules. For example, a learner driver may have learned the appropriate routine for negotiating a roundabout, but will still probably have to give the task full concentration, retrieving the rules and applying them appropriately. Errors at this level are also mistakes, involving the misapplication of a rule, for example misremembering the correct lane to be taken when turning right at a roundabout. At the *skill-based level of performance* tasks are familiar and actions occur without conscious thought. For example, experienced drivers give little thought to changing gear, steering or using the brakes and are able to combine these tasks with others such as talking to a passenger or monitoring hazards on the road ahead. At this level of performance, errors come in the form of slips and lapses. For example, driving towards work when you intend to go to the supermarket on a Saturday because you were distracted by the children at the point on the route where a different turning was required.

15.2 Errors and Violations

Having established the distinction between slips/lapses and mistakes, a second distinction has been made between these types of error and violations. The unifying characteristic of slips, lapses and mistakes is that they are all unintentional. These different types of error all arise from information-processing problems, their occurrence can be understood in relation to the cognitive processes of a single individual, and their frequency can be reduced by skills training, improving knowledge, workplace information and redesign.

In contrast, violations often have nothing to do with knowledge or skills and much more to do with motivation. The chief characteristic of a violation is that it represents a deliberate deviation from normal or recommended practice: it is, at least in part, intentional. The frequency of violations cannot usually be reduced by competence assessment or training, because violations reflect what the individual decides to do, rather than what he or she *can* do. A reduction in violations can be best achieved with attention to aspects of the organisation such as morale, attitudes, beliefs, norms and organisational safety culture (Reason et al., 1989).

Violations represent deviations from formal or informal rules that supposedly describe the best/safest way of performing a task, for example a railwayman who steps on and off a moving shunting engine in order to save time. In this case, although the action was intended, the occasionally bad consequences were not. For the most part, violations go unpunished but occasionally and often in combination with an error, the results can be catastrophic. Violations are of particular interest in an organisational context where rules, guidelines, policies and protocols are often developed to control practice (Johnson and Gill, 1993) and prevent mistakes.

Violations can also be sub-divided into types (Lawton, 1998; Reason et al., 1998). Routine violations occur when an individual believes themselves to have sufficient skill and experience to violate rules habitually, for example, where failure to wear a safety helmet is widespread throughout a workforce. Situational violations occur when the local situation makes following the rules difficult or impossible. Continuing with the safety helmet example, if an insufficient number of safety helmets were provided by management, then failing to wear one would be a situational violation. Optimising violations serve the needs of the violator to express mastery and skill and may be the province of the very experienced staff member. Some individuals might choose not to wear a safety helmet perceiving them to be uncomfortable and embarrassing to wear. Finally, the exceptional violation occurs when a novel situation arises which cannot be dealt with in accordance to existing rules. For example, a safety helmet may restrict movement and so become a safety hazard in a confined area.

15.3 The Manchester Driver Behaviour Questionnaire

Our programme of work has identified three basic types of bad driving, initially using a 50-item self-report questionnaire, the Manchester Driver Behaviour Questionnaire (DBQ) (Reason et al., 1990). The DBQ was administered to a national sample of 520 drivers, who were asked how often each of the behaviours happened to them in the course of their normal driving, using a simple frequency response scale, where 0 = never and 5 = nearly all the time. Factor analysis of their responses revealed three strong underlying dimensions, reflecting distinct types of bad driving that were statistically as well as conceptually, different. The questionnaire was streamlined to 24 items, to include the eight top loading errors, lapses and violations. In a further study, the revised measure was completed by almost 1600 drivers, and the three factors were confirmed.

The first type, true errors, are mistakes and slips, such as misjudging the speed of oncoming traffic when attempting to overtake, attempting to overtake a vehicle you had not noticed was signalling a right turn, and failing to notice a Give Way sign at a junction. This type of behaviour is potentially dangerous, for the driver and other road users. The second group of behaviours, which we called lapses, are usually harmless but irritating. They include turning on the windscreen wipers when you mean to turn on the indicator, forgetting where you have left your car in a car park, and realising you have no clear recollection of the road you have just driven along. The focus of this paper is on the third group of behaviours, which we called violations, includes speeding, tail gating and overtaking on the inside. These behaviours differ from mistakes, slips and lapses in that they are committed, at least in part, intentionally and in the knowledge that one is engaging in potentially dangerous and often illegal behaviour.

Incidentally, this tripartite typology, of violation, error, and lapse has been replicated in studies carried out by other researchers in Britain, and in the Netherlands, Finland, Sweden, Brazil, Spain, Germany, Australia and China. In particular, Lars Aberg in Sweden and Timo Lajunen in Turkey have worked with the DBQ extensively (e.g., Lajunen et al., 2004). While the factor structure uncovered varies slightly from time to time, there is now clear evidence that this is a robust and meaningful instrument.

15.4 The DBQ and Road Traffic Accidents

The distinction between error and violation on the road is important because they are related differently to *crash involvement* (Parker et al., 1995a). For each of our sample of 1600 we had access to their driving histories during a specified 3-year period. We regressed crash rate onto several predictor variables, including the three

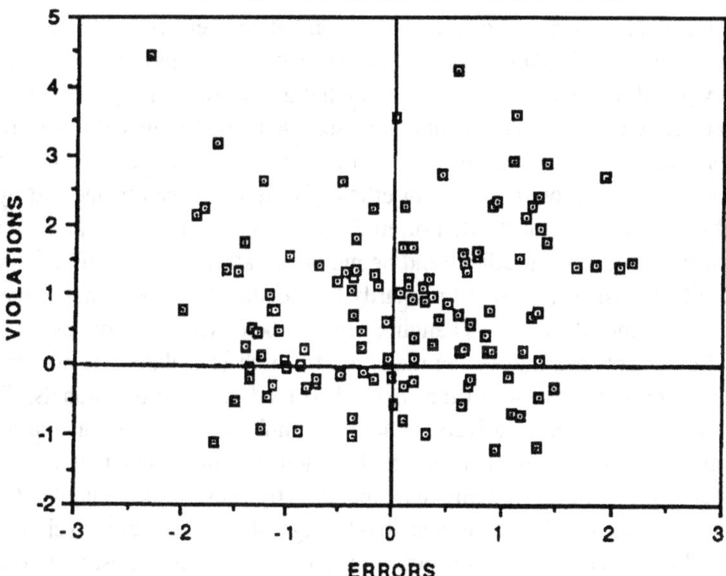

FIGURE 15.1. The error and violation factor scores of 185 crash-involved drivers (from Reason et al., 1989).

DBQ factor scores, and demographic information about the drivers, including their annual mileage, and age and sex, as these are all known to be associated with crash involvement.

Annual mileage driven, age and sex were all predictive of crash involvement, in predictable ways. Those who drove more had more crashes, older drivers had fewer crashes, and males had more crashes than females. However, even after statistically controlling for the effects of mileage, age and sex, adding DBQ factor scores to the equation resulted in a significant improvement in explained variance. The violations factor score was significantly predictive of crash rates. Equally significantly, scores on the error factor were not predictive of crash rate. Moreover, this predictive relationship was found in a subsequent prospective study (Parker et al., 1995b) to hold good for crash involvement in the 3-year period after the DBQ measure was used, showing that the measure is truly predictive.

The relationship is shown in Fig. 15.1, which plots almost 200 high crash-involvement survey respondents (i.e., those who had had two or more crashes in the previous 3 years) in terms of their scores on the DBQ violation and error factors. Factor scores, by their nature, have a mean value of 0 and a standard deviation of 1. Therefore, a negative score indicates a higher than average number of reported errors or violations, and a negative score indicates a lower than average number. It is evident from Fig. 15.1 that these respondents were characterised by high mean scores on the violation factor, but not by high mean scores on the error factor. In the equivalent plot for those respondents who had had only one crash, error and violation scores are equally distributed around the means on both factors.

The practical importance of this distinction between errors, on the one hand, and violations, on the other, is that they have very different psychological origins and they therefore have very different remedial implications. Errors are based on perceptual, attentional, or judgmental processes, so if crashes are caused primarily by errors, we should try to improve the situation by training people to use their cognitive resources more carefully or efficiently. So errors can be tackled by the type of driver training most often offered. Violations, on the other hand, would seem to be based on attitudinal and/or motivational factors. So, if there were evidence that crashes are caused primarily by violations, it would make sense to try to improve the situation by changing people's beliefs and/or motives.

It is well established that young males are the highest violators. However, that piece of information is not all that helpful to road safety professionals. There will always be young male drivers on the roads, unless some fairly radical policy decisions are taken. Moreover, no one could seriously argue that there is something about being young or about being male that directly causes risk-taking behaviour behind the wheel. It is far more plausible to suggest that there are psychological factors, which are correlated with youth and maleness, that predispose some drivers to commit violations. This suggestion is supported by the fact that not all young males are high violators, and not all high violators are young males.

The crucial characteristic of high violators is that they are choosing to take risks. The commission of a driving violation is a matter of choice. We do not simply find ourselves overtaking on the inside, or gesturing to another road user, or shooting through traffic lights as they turn red. While many drivers stopped by the police plead that they were unaware that they were breaking the speed limit, it can be argued that at some level we are well aware of the speed we are travelling. If that were not the case the presence of a police vehicle would not have such an immediate impact on traffic speeds. High violators are choosing to drive in a way that is unacceptable to society, and the way to reduce the level of violating on the roads is to change the attitudes of the violators. Put simply, we need to find ways to persuade them not to do it. The threat of sanctions, in the form of penalty points, fines or a driving ban, are powerful persuaders. Monitoring in the form of increased police presence and speed cameras also play an important part. However, the level of enforcement that would be necessary to eliminate the commission of driving violations would be practically impossible as well as politically unpopular. It is my contention that stable and enduring reductions in the level of violating are more likely to be realised through attitude change. While attempting to change the attitudes of existing drivers is a difficult process, fostering desirable attitudes among young people who do not yet have a driving licence may be more fruitful in the long term. Unfortunately, at least in England, to my knowledge little or no effort is made to impress upon young people that being a good driver is about being a responsible and courteous driver as well as having the right skills.

Emphasising the predictive link between violations and crashes does not imply that errors are not important in crash causation. It is obviously necessary for all drivers to have the basic level of driving skill that training of novices provides. But it is a truism that to err is human. Every driver makes mistakes behind the wheel, and usually, thanks to good fortune and the efforts of engineers in designing primary and secondary safety features into vehicles and road environments our errors escape punishment. However, if a driver makes an error while committing a violation, or if any other road user in the vicinity does, the consequences are more likely to be disastrous.

The commission of violations takes the driver closer to the limits of his or her abilities, into a situation where an error of their own, or of anyone else, is far more likely to be punished, with dreadful results. Therefore, alongside the continuing efforts to prevent, and recover from, driver error, there must be continuing research to understand and explain driver violations.

15.5 Aggressive Violations

Having made the initial distinction, we have continued to refine the Manchester DBQ. For example, in a study focusing on the behaviour of drivers under 40 (Lawton et al., 1997), factor analysis of the DBQ produced a split in the violations factor. Inspection of the items loading onto each factor showed that the interpersonally aggressive violations included in the scale had separated from what we called the 'normal' or Highway Code violations. In other words, those violations that in some sense were committed 'against' a specific other road user (racing, chasing, etc.) appeared to be different from those with no immediately obvious victim (speeding, drink-driving, etc.). To investigate this distinction further, we produced a 12-item version of the violations scale, that included six interpersonally aggressive, and six normal violations. Table 15.1 shows the wording of these violation items.

This scale has since been used in a number of DBQ studies (e.g., Parker et al., 2002; Lajunen et al., 2004) and the distinction between the two scales broadly supported. There is also some suggestion that the interpersonally aggressive violations consist of two further sub-types. The first sub-type of aggressive violation is related to anger/hostility and may reflect a general personality characteristic. Lajunen and Parker's (2001) study of personality aggression, anger while driving and propensity to commit violations provided some support for the idea that aggressive driving may be seen as a learned problem-solving strategy.

The second sub-type of aggressive violations is to do with gaining advantage over other road users and maintaining progress. These violations are more likely to occur in areas of high traffic density, where the motorist comes across unexpected hold-ups and delays. In our research (Lajunen et al., 1999), traffic obstructions like traffic jams or road constructions did not seem to provoke anger among British drivers, a finding supported by Underwood et al.'s (1999) diary study. These kinds of impediments may be so common in today's traffic in Britain that drivers can expect them to occur and therefore do not become unduly frustrated. Hence, the frustration–aggression hypothesis (Dollard et al., 1939) might be more applicable

TABLE 15.1. Wording of the extended DBQ violation items.

Violation type	Item wording
Normal	Disregard the speed limit on a motorway.
Aggressive	Drive especially close to the car in front as a signal to its driver to go faster or get out of the way.
Normal	Disregard the speed limit on a residential road.
Normal	Overtake a slow driver on the inside.
Aggressive	Have an aversion to a particular class of road user and indicate your hostility by whatever means you can.
Aggressive	Become angered by another driver's behaviour, and give chase with the intention of giving him or her a piece of your mind.
Aggressive	Sound your horn to indicate your annoyance to another road user.
Normal	Drive even though you realise that you may be over the legal blood–alcohol limit.
Normal	Cross a junction knowing that the traffic lights have already turned against you.
Aggressive	Pull out of a junction so far that the driver with right of way has to stop and let you out.
Aggressive	Stay in a motorway lane that you know will be closed ahead until the last minute before forcing your way into the other lane.
Aggressive	Get involved in unofficial 'races' with other drivers.

in situations where drivers' goals are dramatically blocked by a sudden and unexpected event.

15.6 Anger-Provoking Situations

Analysis of data from over 2500 drivers from Finland, the Netherlands and Britain identified five broad types of situation that provoke anger and/or aggression in drivers (Parker et al., 2002). Each of the factors identified formed reliable scales (alpha reliability coefficients 0.73–0.86). The first situation that typically can generate anger most frequently was one involving a perceived lack of consideration, or discourtesy, such as when an oncoming driver fails to dip their headlights. The second most anger-provoking type of situation was when others are putting you in danger by their driving style, maybe weaving in and out of lanes of slow traffic. The typical thought response to this might be 'How come he's allowed to get away with it?' Interestingly, this was the only type of driving that provoked more anger among older, than among younger respondents, perhaps because it represents a real threat to your physical safety. The third type of anger-provoking situation involves a challenge to your personal competence as a driver. You are on the receiving end of gestures, verbal abuse or a blast of the horn. This threatens your self-identity as a better than average driver (and nearly everyone thinks they are a better than average driver). You feel insulted and challenged. The fourth type of situation occurs when your progress is impeded by another driver's hesitance or sluggishness. You feel thwarted, impeded and may be tempted to believe that the other driver is doing it purposely, just to inconvenience you. The fifth type of anger-provoking driver to emerge reflected impatience on the part of the other driver. It is typified by the situation when someone nips in and takes the parking space you had been waiting for.

15.7 Conclusions

Several aspects of human error have been outlined in this paper. It is clear that intelligent systems can help in some of types of error, for example by reminding drivers not to dazzle with their lights, or by warning them in advance about unexpected problems on their route and suggesting alternatives to prevent or minimise delay. However, our studies suggest that the reduction of other types of aberrant driving, that is, driving violations, will also require attention to the social and motivational aspects of driving. It is crucial to acknowledge that driving is a motivated behaviour that involves emotions as well as rational decisions.

When drivers know what to expect, they usually cope relatively well. When something unexpected crops up, that is going to impede their progress, they are likely to become stressed, react with anger, and begin to take risks, committing aggressive violations in order to gain advantage over other road users and maintain progress. The provision of information may help to prevent these aggressive violations. At first it may appear that intelligent systems can have their greatest impact in error reduction. However, it may be that, provided the social aspects of driver behaviour are taken into account, such systems have an important role to play in preventing the commission of at least some types of driving violation.

References

Dollard, J., Miller, N.E., Doob, L.W., Mowrer, O.H. and Sears, R.R. (1939). *Frustration and aggression*. Yale University Press, New Haven, CT.

Johnson, P. and Gill, J. (1993). *Management control and organizational behaviour*. Paul Chapman, London.

Tversky, A. and Kahneman, D. (1974). Judgements under uncertainty. *Science* 185, 1124–1131.

Lajunen, T. and Parker, D. (2001). Are aggressive people aggressive drivers? A study of the relationship between self-reported general aggressiveness, driver anger and aggressive driving. *Accident Analysis and Prevention*, 33, 243–255.

Lajunen, T., Parker, D. and Summala, H. (1999). Does traffic congestion increase driver aggression? *Transportation Research Part F*, 2, 225–236.

Lawton, R. (1998). Not working to rule: Understanding procedural violations at work. *Safety Science*, 28, 77–95.

Lawton, R.L., Parker, D., Stradling, S.G. and Manstead, A.S.R. (1997). The role of affect in predicting social behaviors: The case of road traffic violations. *Journal of Applied Social Psychology*, 27, 1258–1276.

Lajunen, T., Parker, D. and Summala, H. (2004). The Manchester Driver Behaviour Questionnaire: A cross-cultural study. *Accident Analysis and Prevention*, 36(2), 231–238.

Parker, D. and Lawton, R. (2003). A psychological contribution to the understanding of adverse events in healthcare. *Quality and Safety in Healthcare*, 12, 453–457.

Parker, D., Reason, J.T., Manstead, A.S.R. and Stradling, S.G. (1995a). Driving errors, driving violations and accident involvement. *Ergonomics*, 38, 1036–1048.

Parker, D., West, R.W., Stradling, S.G. and Manstead, A.S.R. (1995b). Behavioural characteristics and involvement in different types of road traffic accident. *Accident Analysis and Prevention*, 27, 571–581.

Parker, D., Lajunen, T. and Summala H. (2002). Anger and aggression among drivers in three European countries. *Accident Analysis and Prevention*, 34(2), 229–235.

Rasmussen, J. (1990). Human error and the problem of causality in analysis of accidents. *Philosophical Transactions of the Royal Society B: Biological Sciences*, 327, 449–460.

Rasmussen, J. and Jensen, A. (1974). Mental procedures in real-life tasks: A case study of electronic troubleshooting. *Ergonomics*, 17, 293–307.

Reason, J. (1990). *Human error*. Open University Press, Cambridge.

Reason, J., Parker, D. and Lawton, R. (1998). The varieties of rule-related behaviour. *Journal of Organisational and Occupational Psychology*, 71, 289–304.

Reason, J.T., Manstead, A., Stradling, S., Baxter, J.S., Parker, D. and Kelemen, D. (1989). A report to the TRRL on Research Contract 9885/35. *The social and cognitive determinants of aberrant driver behaviour*. Unpublished report.

Reason, J.T., Manstead, A., Stradling, S., Baxter, James, S. and Campbell, K. (1990). Errors and violations on the roads: A real distinction? *Ergonomics*, 33(10/11), 1315–1332.

Underwood, G., Chapman, P., Wright, S. and Crundall, D. (1999). Anger while driving. *Transportation Research Part F: Traffic Psychology and Behaviour*, 2F(1), 55–68.

VI
Control Theory Models of Driver Behaviour

16
Control Theory Models of the Driver

THOMAS JÜRGENSOHN

16.1 Introduction

From the viewpoint of modelling theory, modelling human behaviour is one of the most interesting and challenging issues. In this overview, the term 'model' refers to something 'formal', which can be calculated or simulated. The models described in the following reflect behaviour of a human during a special task, the car driving, formalised by means of control theory.

Control theory is a mathematical discipline, which was developed for describing technical controllers. As a consequence, the application area of control theory is in modelling the human as a controller. Interestingly, the car driving task is only to a small extent a controlling task. Driving a car is much more constituted by observing, deciding, estimating, etc. However, keeping the car on the street and keeping the distance to the heading car are typically controlling tasks and therefore they seem predetermined to be described by means of the mathematics of control theory. After an introduction of different approaches of modelling the human controlling behaviour in general, the focus in this paper will be on models of controlling the vehicle path. In the last part, I will shortly discuss modelling speed control and distance control.

16.2 Modelling Human Controlling Behaviour

Mathematical modelling and subsequent simulation of the human as a machine operator are very well investigated and elaborated topics within the field of modelling human action in dynamical environments. Often the term 'operator model' is used synonymously for such models of the human as a controller.

16.2.1 The Tustin-Model: Linear Part + Remnant

Tustin (1947) is considered to have published the first article describing human behaviour by means of mathematical models outside the military field. He investigates the behaviour of an operator controlling the rotational speed of a flight

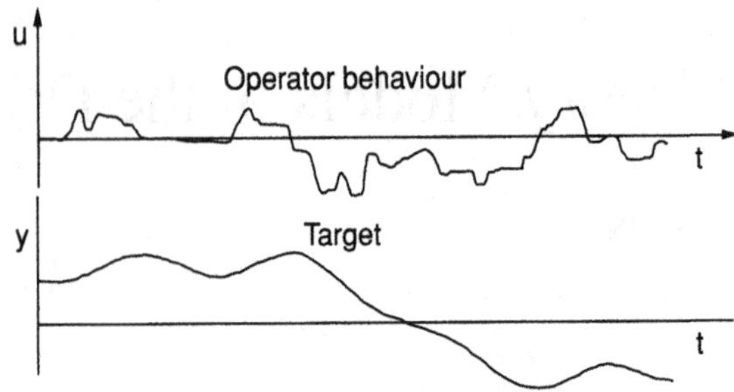

FIGURE 16.1. Behaviour of an operator controlling the rotational speed of a flight defence cannon via a hand gear (modified from Tustin, 1947).

defence cannon via a hand gear. This is a typical tracking task where the human has to compensate a deviation. Tustin observed the behaviour of the controllers (Fig. 16.1), which is fundamentally different from a technical controller: *a jerky curve with 'flats'* (Tustin, 1947, p. 119).

Tustin tries to approximate the human controller behaviour by means of a linear system. The remaining difference u_r between approximation u_t and real controller behaviour u he denotes as the *remnant* (Fig. 16.2).

Both terms of the operator model together, the linear part H(s) and the remnant U_r, are not an approximation of human behaviour, but describe it completely. The idea of Tustin was to find a description of the remnant properties which is independent from the experiment set-up, for example, in a stochastic sense. For special cases, this is indeed possible (Elkind and Dorlex, 1963; McRuer and Krendel, 1974). But mostly the remnant has to be considered as an error signal, which has no special traits, and which cannot be described by means of simple mathematical methods. However, the remnant part of the operator's output is often

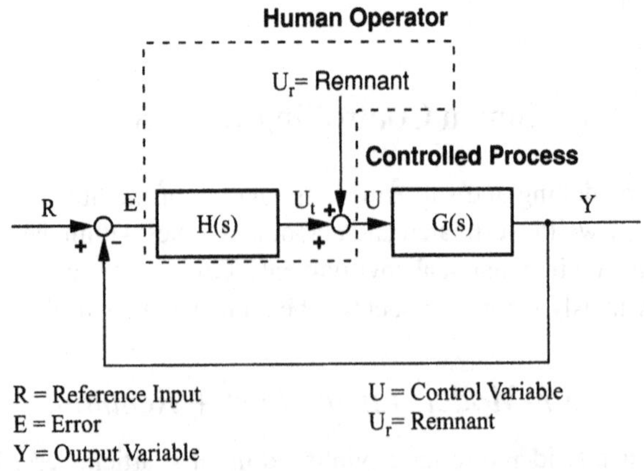

FIGURE 16.2. Control theoretic model of the controlling human in the Laplace domain (from Tustin, 1947).

small, so the linear part characterises most of the control activity. The models of the human as a controller, which were set up in the following, still contain the remnant, but this item is usually neglected. In some applications, remnant models can be useful. But in general, modelling non-linear parts of human behaviour by assuming a remnant in terms of stochastics is not appropriate for many applications.

The existence of the remnant in the controller models of the human is an example of an adoption of paradigms from the technical–physical modelling, which is not appropriate. The successful method for improving the model quality applied in the technical sector, that is, adding nonlinear parts to the model modelling approach (e.g., Böcker et al., 1986) does not resolve the problem of modelling human behaviour. Human behaviour is variable to such an extent that the refinement using nonlinear terms only seems to produce a more accurate model.

16.2.2 Laboratory Research, Stochastic Input, Quasi-Linear Model

After Tustin it became clear very quickly that human control behaviour cannot be reproduced at large by means of mathematical and system theoretic methods. Especially the facts that humans not only behave fundamentally differently with different plants, but that behaviour also depends on the type of input and that there are vast inter-individual differences as well as intra-individual variations interfere with a well-defined model.

For sinusoidal reference input signals it can be observed that the human can follow this signal without phase shift. Such behaviour cannot be explained within the frame of a causal linear system only for special cases. Figure 16.3 shows the tracking behaviour of a test person for reference input signals that show a certain pattern. Contrary to the assumption that models humans as a controller, the operator does not evaluate the actual control deviation, but reproduces the reference pattern by means of a motion sequence which is synchronised at discrete times with the reference signal. This capability to memorise and reproduce the pattern or the *gestalt* in certain behaviour cannot be modelled by means of differential equations.

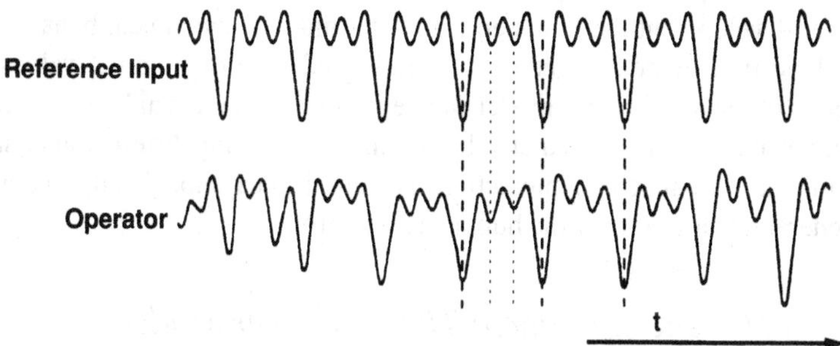

FIGURE 16.3. Tracking behaviour of an operator following reference signals with a pattern (modified from Vossius, 1964).

TABLE 16.1. Meaning of the parameters of the quasi-linear model.

τ	Reaction time
T_N	Neuromuscular delay
K, T_L, T_I	Adaptation to the controlled plant

In order to come to practical assertions in spite of the strong dependency of human behaviour from all kind of environmental conditions, researchers in the engineering area choose the same method as the psychologists: they go to the laboratory and reduce both tasks and boundary conditions, until reproducible experiment results allow unambiguous modelling.

The task is reduced to pure tracking on a screen and input signals are constrained to stationary stochastic signals. This assumption will be dropped later and models are also set up for deterministic input signals, but limited to few cases such as step function, ramp or sine wave. From the preparatory work done by Krendel (1951) and Elkind (1956), this research direction was completed in the 1950s and summarised by McRuer and Krendel (1959), who formulated the quasi-linear model (Eq. 1).

$$\text{Quasi-linearModel: } H(s) = \frac{K \cdot (T_L s + 1)}{(T_I s + 1)(T_N s + 1)} e^{-\tau s} \tag{1}$$

The quasi-linear model describes the human by means of a linear second-order differential equation with dead time. Differences in the task environment and in operator properties are described by means of five free parameters. τ (dead time = reaction time) and T_N (neuromuscular delay time) are considered as physiological parameters independent from the task. The parameters K, T_L und T_I (Table 16.1) depend on the control plant and the type of stochastic input signal. This is the reason for the prefix 'quasi', as the model is only linear in the considered context. The dependency on the input value is in contradiction with the property of linearity. In addition, the term $\exp(-\tau s)$ in the model makes it transcendental, rather than linear.

For the different combinations, a catalogue set-up to be used for the model could be established (McRuer and Krendel, 1974).

In a practical application to predict operator behaviour in machine environments still under development the first step is to determine the dynamical behaviour of the machine in a model. Together with estimated type of nominal values, the parameters of the quasi-linear model can be looked up in the catalogue. Then the operator behaviour can be calculated by solving the resulting differential equation describing the man–machine interaction. The quasi-linear model is up to now the most general linear model of the human as a controller.

16.2.3 A Holistic Approach: The Crossover Model

The quasi-linear model is unsatisfactory, because the parameters can only be determined very roughly beforehand. However, already in one of the first systematic studies which were conducted by Elkind (1956) and Ekind and Forgie (1959) dependencies between the parameters could be noticed. The operator adapts his behaviour in such a way that the overall system behaviour remains approximately constant in spite of different nominal values. A similar assertion is formulated by McRuer und Krendel (1962) in their *crossover-model*. Experimentally measured frequency responses of the total system exhibit a common property under different conditions. If the open-loop linear transfer function $L(s)$, which describes human and machine together, is calculated from the observed closed-loop behaviour, then the behaviour can be very well approximated by an integrator and an additional phase correction by means of a dead time for all task environments in the region of the crossover frequency, ω_c ($L(j\omega) = 0$ dB). The crossover model requires only two parameters, that is, the crossover frequency ω_c and the dead time τ, which is not identical with the dead time of the quasi-linear model.

$$\text{Crossover model: } L(s) = \frac{\omega_c}{s} e^{-\tau s} \tag{2}$$

The interesting point of this model is that human and machine are not modelled separately as successive connected structures, but as *one system*. The focus is not on how humans manage to adapt to different environments, but this is assumed to be the case. Only total system behaviour is considered. It should be noted that the crossover model is not a rough approximation with very few parameters, but in many cases a very precise description.

In a certain way the crossover model already contains the element of goal-oriented action which dominated in recent approaches. The great similarities in the frequency responses of the man–machine system for various types of control plants are manifestations of the operator will. The operator wants to minimise the control error and achieve a certain overall system behaviour, a goal that is indeed accomplished for very different types of control plants. The behaviour of the operator is different, but the overall system behaviour is approximately identical.

Although the crossover model contains internal goals of the operator implicitly and is therefore more suitable to predict human control behaviour within unknown control plants than the quasi-linear model, the parameters of the crossover model depend on the type of the input function, too. Therefore, the description of the influence of boundary conditions on goal achievement is still only possible a posteriori or via a catalogue. McRuer and Krendel (1974) and other authors established comprehensive collections of crossover model parameters for different system environments and nominal signal types. As these parameters are not related to other invariant human properties, the validity of the crossover model for predicting operator behaviour in unknown environments is also limited.

16.2.4 Nonlinear Approaches: Improved Reproduction of Measured Behaviour

The crossover model is the most compact quantitative description of human dynamical behaviour. But it is still a linear model and has – as the quasi-linear

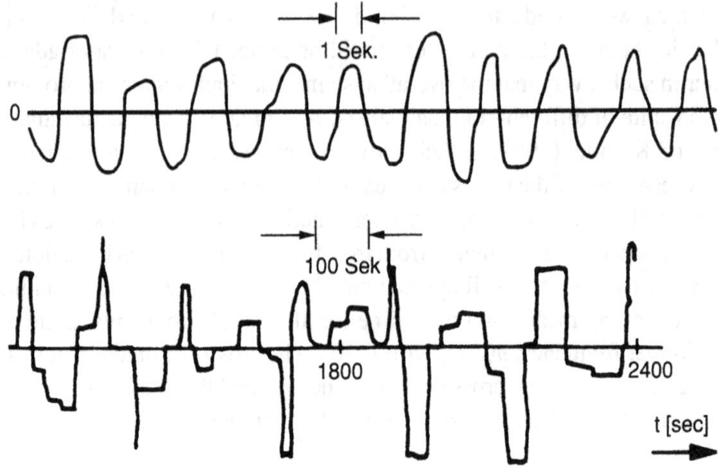

FIGURE 16.4. (Top) Control action of a double integrating control plant by a very well-trained pilot (from McRuer et al., 1968). (Bottom) Steering motion of a helmsman on a ship (from Veldhuyzen and Stassen, 1976).

model – only limited capabilities to describe non-stationary behaviour. Non-stationary behaviour is distinguished by discontinuities with a change between action and hold phases (Fig. 16.4).

In the 1960s and 1970s, diversification of the approaches and experimenting with the evolving methods of control theoretic was prevailing in the research work within the field 'human controller': the models developed included sample and hold models for discontinuous behaviour, bang–bang controllers for time optimal behaviour, state space models for multidimensional sensors and Kalman filters for disturbed estimation processes (extensively described in Johannsen, 1980). Due to the great part of special system theory mathematics, the operator modelling was almost entirely advanced by engineers.

Due to space restrictions, it is impossible to go into details of all the many approaches that were put forward. It is important that the different models can reproduce human behaviour for the investigated experiments, but that the prediction quality for other boundary conditions or other tasks is quite poor. The paradigm of describing dynamic behaviour by means of differential equations remains unquestioned. The main issue is just to find the right differential equation, be it linear or nonlinear.

Similar to the psychological theories of that time, who – while competing for truth – were caught in their specific framework of possible explanations in the sense of a falsification process according to Popper and were only able to explain certain aspects in a satisfactory way, the applicability of the different model approaches of the human controller were limited to the respective aspects of behaviour.

The recourse to the complex control theoretic method stock was based on the hope to model complex human behaviour better than by means of simple linear differential equations. On the other hand, the choice of the method is often also due to the attraction of a 'modern' tool. Conceptional reasons are often given only ex post. An example is the BBN model by Baron and Kleinman (1969), which is a linear model based on an optimal filter approach. Retrospectively, this model was often praised as especially appropriate, because it contains elements, which can be interpreted as 'internal model'. In another example the advantage of models containing adaptive control approaches is deduced from the adaptivity of human behaviour. The suitability of modelling approaches thus is justified with resemblances of the model to observed characteristics of human behaviour.

16.3 Driver Models for Vehicle Design

For the majority of automotive vehicle engineers the term *driver model* means a dynamic driver model, combined with models of lateral vehicle dynamics. These driver models were developed to obtain information on how a design change influences the handling quality. Allen (1983) has called this kind of driver model 'design driver'. As the vehicle behaviour is generally described by means of differential equations, driver models are usually formulated in this way, too. Especially for stability investigation of the complete system, it is useful to employ the method of linear control theory. Although there are alternative models, up to now the models using differential equations are most popular. Not until the seventies algorithmic models, models with decision-making structures, models using fuzzy decision or fuzzy control or artificial neural networks have been established.

Linear driver models have already been reviewed in detail (see, e.g., Hoffmann, 1975; Billing, 1977; Reid, 1983; Reichelt, 1990; Guo and Guan, 1993; Willumeit and Jürgensohn, 1997; Jürgensohn, 1997). Most driver models developed heretofore model the driver as a *controller* of lateral vehicle dynamics. These models are adapted from the so-called tracking-models in which the human manipulates a machine according to an externally set value (Fig. 16.5). The prevalent descriptions that are used are linear differential equations or difference equations.

These driver models were developed to anticipate influences of design on the handling quality. As the vehicle behaviour is generally described by means of differential equations, driver models are also usually formulated in this way. Especially for stability analysis of the complete system, it seems to be useful to employ methods of linear control theory.

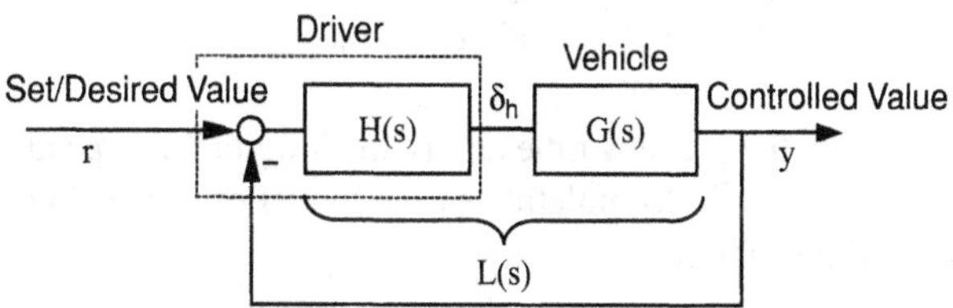

FIGURE 16.5. The driver as a controller.

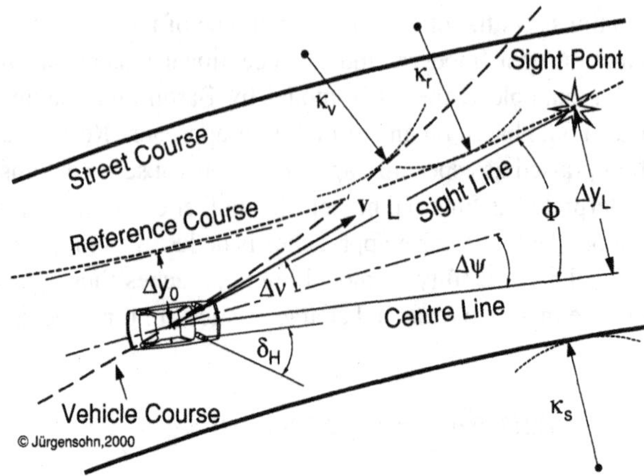

FIGURE 16.6. 'Shaft model' of driver's control strategy. Copyright, Jürgensohn (2000).

The lateral control driver models were initiated in Japan. In 1953, Kondo (1953) developed two different models for driver behaviour due to side wind disturbance and calculated the behaviour of the whole system on a straight path with constant speed by means of a single-track model. Both models already show the general structure of the majority of models to be published for the following 35 years.

In the first model, Kondo assumes that the driver always steers in a way that an imaginary point within a certain preview distance L, the *sight point* or *aim point*, is on a predetermined course (Fig. 16.6). In terms of control theory this would mean that the driver minimises the lateral offset Δy_L of the vehicle's projected centreline from the desired course within the preview distance L in front of the vehicle.

His assumption was inspired by a situation after an accident in which his car was towed with a very short rope. For this reason the model is often called the *shaft model*. He was also inspired by an experience by driving bicycle in the narrow streets of Japanese cities: *In a narrow lane it is easier to hold the bicycle steady looking to the exit of the lane*. This linear prediction model has been adopted by many authors, especially in Japan and later in Germany (Fiala, 1967).

The model *depicted* in Fig. 16.6 can be described in control theoretic terms in three different ways. First of all Δy_L can be taken as a prediction of $\Delta y_0$with a prediction time T_p. For a simple P-controller it follows that

$$\delta_H(s) = K \cdot e^{T_p s} \Delta y_0(s) \tag{3}$$

where $Tp = L/v_0$ are the preview time and v_0 the longitudinal speed.

Another control theoretic formulation of the model of Fig. 16.6 can be found for small values of the sight angle Φ.

$$\delta_H(s) = K \cdot (\Delta y_0(s) + L \cdot \Delta\psi(s)) \tag{4}$$

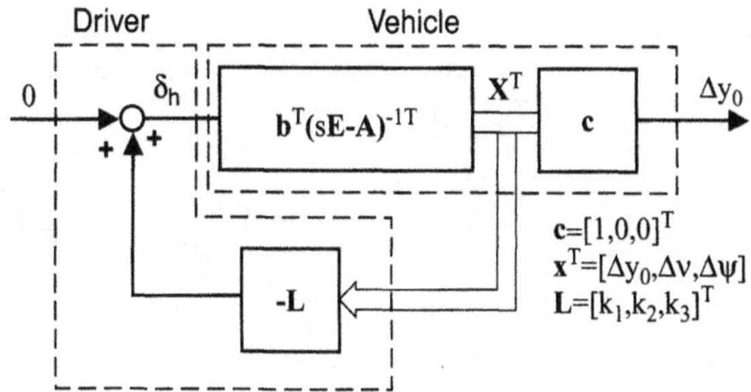

FIGURE 16.7. Model of driver's control strategy as state-variable controller (Kondo, 1953).

With this transformation the model is reduced to a control of the centre of gravity. For small steering angles, we can write:

$$\Delta \dot{y}_0 = \Delta \psi \cdot v_0 \tag{5}$$

and the following simple preview predictor model results:

$$\delta_H(s) = K \cdot (T_p s + 1) \cdot \Delta y_0 \tag{6}$$

The latter equation is in fact a linearisation of Eq. (3): A lead term as an approximation of a time-preview term.

Kondo's second model from 1953 assumes that the steering angle is a linear combination of yaw angle error ($\Delta \psi$), heading angle error (Δv) and lateral position error in the gravity centre (Δy_0). In control theoretic manner this can be described as a linear state variable controller (Fig. 16.7). This second model is modified and used in many other models, too (e.g., Donges, 1978; Reid et al., 1981).

In another kind of graphical representation, this model has the following form (Fig. 16.8).

Another well-known model is the so-called 'STI'-model. Systems Technology Inc. dominated the research in the USA with already mentioned scientists such as McRuer, Weir, Klein and others. They developed a model (Fig. 16.9), which was derived from tracking models and pilot models. Besides the model class of preview predictor models and linear state control models invented by Kondo, the STI model can be seen as another model class.

A 'translation' of this cybernetic view of the model into a control theoretic version (Fig. 16.10) shows the similarity to the model of Kondo.

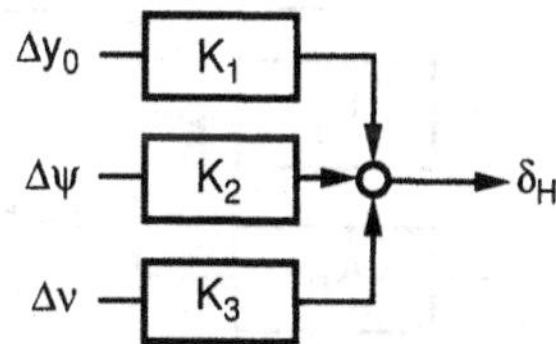

FIGURE 16.8. Linear state control model of the driver (Kondo, 1953).

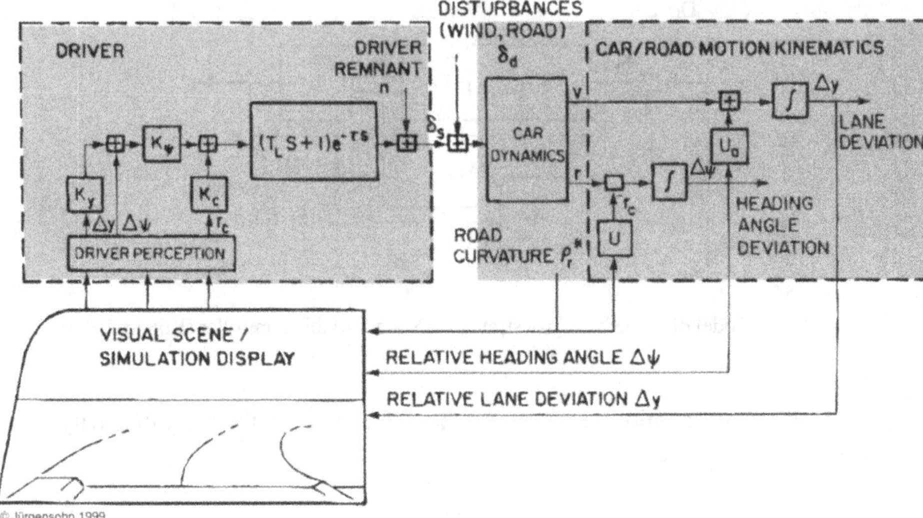

FIGURE 16.9. 'STI'-model (McRuer et al., 1977).

A noteworthy difference to the approach of Kondo is the existence of the time-delay term τ. The purpose of this term is to reflect the reaction time of the driver (usually a few seconds). We know this term from many models published in the early 1950s to represent human behaviour when controlling an aircraft. In contrast to car driving, the control task in an aircraft was, in the 50s, dominated by compensating disturbances. Car driving, in opposite, is more dominated by following a curved band, which can be seen far ahead. So, during normal driving conditions, the driver has no reaction time with respect to the task 'following the street'. The STI model was derived from the classical models of human compensatory behaviour, whilst Kondo started as a mechanical engineer from the stretch without preconceived notion.

Besides these two main concepts we can find a third basic idea in many control theoretic driver models: the concept of anticipatory open-loop control. According to this approach, the driver does not react to variables of the vehicle only, but to

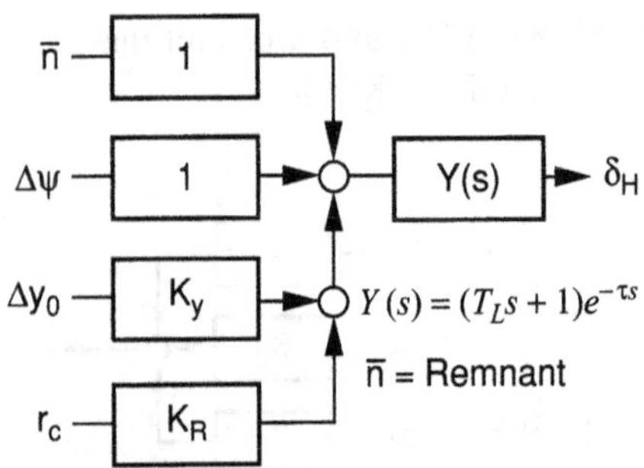

FIGURE 16.10. Block diagram of the 'STI' model.

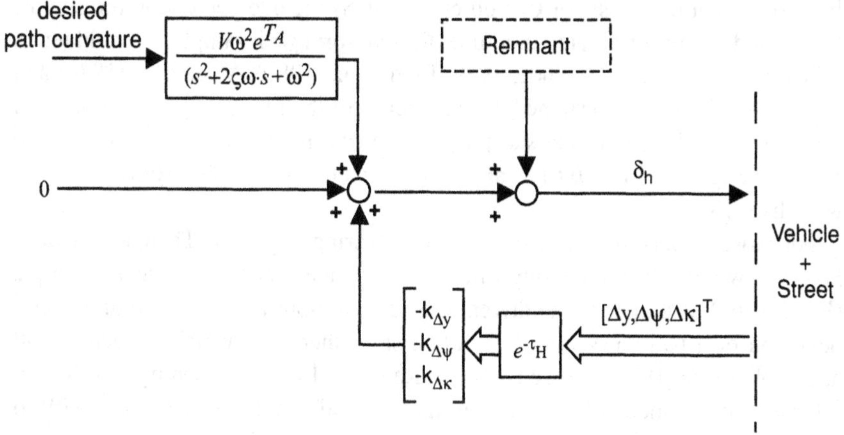

FIGURE 16.11. Two-level model of Donges (1978).

street variables, too. This type of driver model was published first by Fiala (1967) and Ohno (1966). It assumes that part of the steering angle is determined from lane curvature κ (see Fig. 16.11) at a particular heading distance. This is open-loop control, because the lane curvature is independent from vehicle motion. Fiala called this 'Scheinwerferorientierung' (head light orientation), whereas Ohno talks about *programmed action* and *intuitive steering*. In Fig. 16.10, the structure of one of the most renowned models with an anticipatory open-loop part, the 'two-level model' by Donges (1978) is shown. It is a combination of the state variable controller in the closed-loop as shown in Fig. 16.7 and an open-loop term, assumed as a linear system with time prediction having 2 df. The reaction time τ_H of the driver is modelled by a time delay term. The remnant is an additional source of unknown influences (driver noise) – also adopted from the old pilot models.

The idea of a compensatory closed-loop control model with an additional open loop part has found many imitators (Horn, 1986; Mitschke, 1977; Reid et al., 1980). Yet another step further ahead are the models by Bösch (1991) and Plöchl and Lugner (1994), who introduce a third additive scope of control, the so-called 'local control' (correction of the instantaneous path deviation) besides compensatory control and anticipatory control.

Moreover, there are models, which are capable to change their structure during simulation, for example the *dual mode model* (Mc Ruer et al., 1977) which can switch between open-loop and closed-loop behaviour. This model has been realised in DRIVEM (Lieberman and Goldblatt, 1981). This kind of modelling can also be found in adaptive models which link sudden changes in the environment, for example, sudden appearance of black ice (Reichelt, 1990; Nagai, 1983; Nagai and Mitschke, 1987), with changes in the model.

Besides these four types of driver models there are some variations, which are distinguished by dead times, the kind of input or output parameters or by non-linear elements. For example Baxter and Harrison (1979) include non-linearities by assuming a hysteresis or Carson et al. (1978) include perception thresholds. Some models are formulated in a time discrete form with sample and hold terms (Crossman et al. 1966; Hayhoe, 1979; Reid et al., 1980). MacAdam (1980) and Blaauw et al. (1984) determined the parameters of their model by an optimisation criterion. Included in this class of preview models are also models, which choose the *sight angle* Φ (Fig. 16.6) as an input parameter (Baxter and Harrison, 1979; Mitschke, 1977).

For most models the driver output is the steering angle δ_H. There are models, however, which take the steering wheel rate (Hayhoe, 1979) or the steering torque (Fiala, 1967) as output of the driver. The desired input is usually a future lateral deviation or a path curvature. Very often still other state variables such as roll angle (Niemann, 1972) are used as input. Reichelt (1990) can identify 21 different information parameters for the driver, from attitude angle rate (Braess, 1970) to the third derivative of the reference curvature (Fiala, 1967).

These early examples of driver models briefly reviewed here represent the majority of all known models of driver's lateral control activity. Their structure is very similar to mechanical systems plus a controller applied to such systems. The advantage of this modelling method is, as mentioned before, that we are able to describe and examine the whole system with a well-known mathematical apparatus.

An example for a commercial driver model currently used in real-time vehicle dynamics simulations is the ve-DYNA® advanced driver controller. This model guides the vehicle along a given trajectory, especially near the driving limits at high speeds, for example, for race line optimisation. Other application fields are virtual driving tests like double lane change for handling investigation, comfort studies, as well as various tests for electronic control units like ESP, active body control, etc. (software-in-the-loop and hardware-in-the-loop).

Most electronic vehicle controllers are designed to support the driver in mastering difficult driving manoeuvres, typically caused by driving errors. To test these support functions, critical driving situations have to be realised, for example, driving through curves at high speed near the driving limits. For reasonable testing of controller behaviour in the vehicle environment, it is therefore desirable that the virtual driver, that is, the driver model also exhibits non-perfect driving behaviour, like ordinary human drivers do.

The driver model is therefore realised as a technical controller considering some human characteristics. Different from technical controllers, a human driver does not simply follow a given trajectory, but sets the target course within given constraints (i.e., road width or lane width). This is reflected in a two-level structure of the driver model, consisting of guidance and stabilisation (see Fig. 16.12).

At the guidance level, the time-dependent target position, target speed, target direction and target path curvature are determined. These values serve as nominal values for the stabilisation level which is basically a position controller based on the theory of nonlinear system decoupling and control supplemented by a model for perception of vehicle state information (e.g., side slip angle).

The position controller at the stabilisation level keeps the vehicle as near as possible to the target point moving along the given track, as illustrated in Fig 16.13.

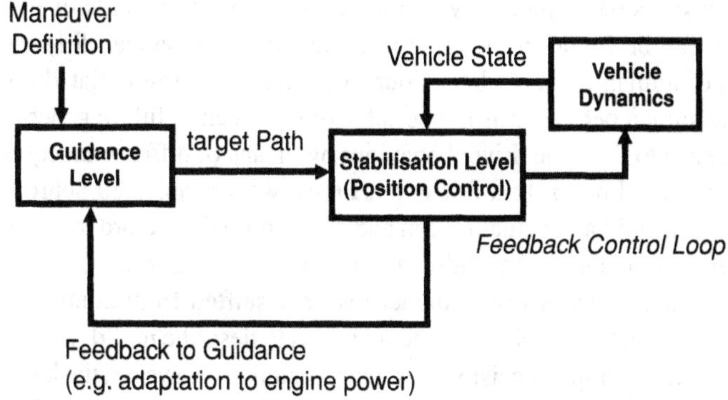

FIGURE 16.12. Structure of the advanced driver (TESIS GmbH, München).

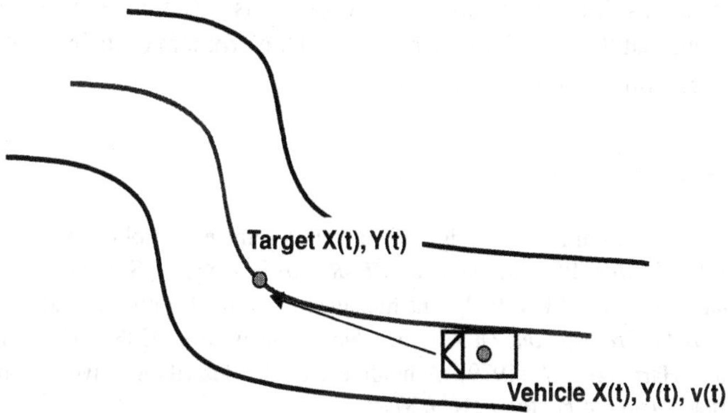

FIGURE 16.13. Target trajectory tracking and position control.

The distance between target point and vehicle is not fixed. One could imagine an elastic linkage between the vehicle and the moving target point towing the vehicle: The more the vehicle deviates from the target, the harder it will be pulled towards the target. In the ideal case the driver will keep the vehicle just atop the target at any time.

Individual driving behaviour like differences in risk-taking and driving expertise, as well as typical driver errors can be reproduced by means of parameters of the driver controller, for example, the preview distance, delay times for steering response, etc., and by influencing the target course (Irmscher and Ehmann, 2004).

16.4 Summary and Future Prospects

This short presentation of examples for models of the car driver shows that the control theoretic core of the models has not changed much from the beginnings in the 1950s up to now. Although much time was spent for iterative improvements, there was just a small, 'model evolution' as in many other fields of modelling. The reason can be found in the large inter- und intra-individual differences and deviations of human dynamic behaviour. A precise and differentiated modelling of dynamic human behaviour is not possible or not meaningful. In general, it does not make sense to describe driver behaviour by means of differential equations of higher than second order. In a few applications, well-established neuromuscular models for arm and hand actuation can add an additional third order. Such models can be useful, for example, in studying steering characteristics.

Therefore, the focus of driver model research shifted from control theory to other modelling methods, which are better suited to describe non-dynamic aspects of behaviour, for example, decision making or planning. However, the last example (cf. Fig. 16.13) illustrated that for the description of dynamic steering characteristics of the driver control theory is still the most appropriate means. However, the incorporation into an algorithmic environment is the central point here. Summing up, it can be said sufficient research on driver models based on control theory has been done, but that there are still open issues on the problem of its integration into a 'hybrid modelling' (Jürgensohn, 1997).

References

Allen, R.W. (1983). Defining the design driver from a vehicle control point-of-view. *62nd Annual TRB Meeting, Washington, USA, STI-Report, No. 83327*, S. 1–11.

Baron, S. and Kleinman, D.L. (1969). The human as an optimal controller and information processor. *IEEE Transactions on Man–Machine Systems*, Vol. MMS-10(1), 9–17.

Baxter, J. and Harrison, J.Y. (1979). A nonlinear model describing driver behaviour on straight roads. *Human Factors*, 21(1), 87–97.

Billing, A.M. (1977). Modelling driver steering in normal and severe manoeuvres. In J.E. Bernard (Ed.), *An overview of simulation in highway transportation, Part II*. Bosten: Simulation Councels, Inc. (S. 151–165).

Blaauw, G.J., Godthelp, H. and Milgram, P. (1984). Optimal control model applications and field measurements with respect to car driving. *Vehicle System Dynamics,* 13, 93–111.

Böcker, J., Hartmann, I. and Zwanzig, Ch. (1986). *Nichtlineare und adaptive Regelsysteme*. Springer-Verlag, Berlin.

Bösch, P. (1991). *Der Fahrer als Regler* (the driver considered as a control element). Dissertation, TU, Wien.

Braess, H.-H. (1970). Untersuchung des Seitenwindverhaltens des Systems Fahrzeug – Fahrer (investigation of side gust behaviour of the driver–vehicle system). *Deutsche Kraftfahrtforschung und Straßenverkehrstechnik, Heft.* 206, 5–32.

Carson, J.M., Wierwille, W.W. and Eastman, C. (1978). Development of a strategy model of the driver in lane keeping. *Vehicle System Dynamics,* 7(4), 233–253.

Crossman, E.R.F.W., Szostak, H. and Cesa, T.L. (1966). Steering performance of automobile drivers in real and contact-analog simulated tasks. *Human Factors Society 10th Annual Meeting*. Anaheim, California.

Donges, E. (1978). A two-level model of driver steering behaviour. *Human Factors*, 20(6), 691–707.

Elkind, J.I. (1956). *Characteristics of simple manual control systems*. M.I.T. Lincoln Laboratories, Lexington, Massachusetts., Technical Report, No. 111.

Elkind, J.I. and Forgie, C.D. (1959). Characteristics of the human operator in simple manual control systems. *IRE Transactions on Automatic Control*, 4(1), 44–55.

Elkind, J.I. and Dorlex, D.L. (1963). The normality of signals and describing function measurement of simple manual control systems. *IEEE Transactions on Human Factors in Electronics*, 52–55.

Fiala, E. (1967). Die Wechselwirkung zwischen Fahrzeug und Fahrer (Interaction between vehicle and driver). *Automobiltechnische Zeitschrift*, 69(10), 345–348.

Guo, K. and Guan, H. (1993). Modelling of driver/vehicle directional control system. *Vehicle System Dynamics*, 22, 141–184.

Hayhoe, G.E. (1979). A driver model based on the cerebellar model articulation controller. *Vehicle System Dynamics*, 8, 49–72.

Hoffmann, E.R. (1975). Human control of road vehicles. *Vehicle System Dynamics*, 5, 105–126.

Horn, A. (1986). *Fahrer-Fahrzeug-Kurvenfahrt auf trockener Straße* (driver–vehicle curve driving on dry road). Dissertation, TU, Braunschweig.

Irmscher, M. and Ehmann, M. (2004). *Driver Classification using ve-DYNA Advanced Driver*, SAE paper 2004-1-0451.

Johannsen, G. (1980). *Manuelle Regelung in Mensch-Maschine-Systemen*. Habilitation RWTH Aachen.

Jürgensohn, T. (1997). *Hybride Fahrermodelle* (Hybrid driver models, ZMMS-Spektrum, Band 4). Sinzheim: Pro Universitate Verlag.

Kondo, M. (1953). Directional stability (when steering is added). *Journal of the Society of Automotive Engineers of Japan (JSAE), Jidosha-gijutsu*, 7(5/6) (in Japanese). Tokyo, 104–106, 109, 123, 136–140.

Krendel, E.S. (1951). *A preliminary study of the power-spectrum approach to the analysis of perceptual-motor performance*. Wright Air Development Center, Wright-Patterson Air Force Base, Dayton, Ohio, Technical Report, No. 6723.

Lieberman, E.B. and Goldblatt, R.A. (1981). *A review of the driver–vehicle effectiveness model.* Final Report under NHTSA Contract,DTNH22-80-C-07082 (DOT-HS 806110).

MacAdam, C.C. (1980). An optimal preview control for linear systems. *Journal of Dynamic Systems, Measurement, and Control*, 188–190.

McRuer, D.T. and Krendel, E.S. (1959). The human operator as a servo system element Part I + II. *Journal of The Franklin Institute*, 267(5/6), 381–403, 511–536.

McRuer, D.T. and Krendel, E.S. (1962). The man–machine concept. *Proceedings of the IRE*, 50, 1117–1123.

McRuer, D.T., Hofmann, L.G., Jex, H.R., Moore, G.P., Phatak, A.V., Weir, D.H. and Wolkovitch, J. (1968). *New Approaches to Human-Pilot/Vehicle Dynamic Analysis*. Air Force Flight Dynamics Laboratory, Technical Report, AFFDL-TR-67-150.

McRuer, D.T. and Krendel, E.S. (1974). Mathematical models of human pilot behavior. *Agardograph, No. 188*. Technical Editing and Reproduction Ltd., Harford House, London.

McRuer, D.T., Allen, W.R., Weir, D.H. and Klein, R.H. (1977). New results in driver steering control models. *Human Factors*, 19(4), 381–397.

Mitschke, M. (1977). Kraftfahrzeug-Fahrer-Aktive Sicherheit (Vehicle–driver–active safety). *Automobil-Industrie*, 3, 29–32.

Nagai, M. (1983). Adaptive behaviours of driver–car systems in critical situations. *Proceedings of the International AMSE Summer Conference "Modelling and Simulation"*. Nice, France.

Nagai, M. and Mitschke, M. (1987). An adaptive control model of a car–driver and computer simulation of the closed-loop system. In M. Apetaur (Ed.), *The Dynamics of Vehicles on Roads and on Tracks*. pp. 275–286.

Niemann, K. (1972). *Messungen und Berechnungen über das Regelverhalten von Autofahrern* (measurements and calculations of the control behaviour of drivers). Dissertation, TU, Braunschweig.

Ohno, T. (1966). Steering control on a curved course. *Journal of the Society of Automotive Engineers of Japan (JSAE), Jidosha-gijutsu*, 20(5) (in Japanese), 413–419.

Plöchl, M. and Lugner, P. (1994). Theoretical investigations of the interaction driver–Feedback–Controlled automobile. *Proceedings of the International Symposium on Advanced Vehicle Control 1994.*, SAE Paper, No. 9438006, pp. 42–48.

Reichelt, W. (1990). *Ein adaptives Fahrermodell zur Bewertung der Fahrdynamik von PKW in kritischen Situationen* (An adaptive driver model to evaluate vehicle dynamics in critical situations). Dissertation, TU, Braunschweig.

Reid, L.D. (1983). A survey of recent driver steering behaviour models suited to accident studies. *Accident Analysis and Prevention*, 15(1), 23–40.

Reid, L.D., Graf, W.O. and Billing, A.M. (1980). *The validation of a linear driver model.* University of Toronto, UTIAS Report, No. 245.

Reid, L.D., Solowka, E.N. and Billing, A.M. (1981). A systematic study of driver steering behaviour. *Ergonomics*, 24(6), 447–462.

Tustin, A. (1947). The nature of the operator's response in manual control and its implications for controller design. *IEEE Journal*, 94, Part II A2, 190–202.

Veldhuyzen, W. and Stassen, H.G. (1976). The internal model. What does it mean in human control? In T.B. Sheridan and G. Johannsen (Eds.), *Proceedings of Monitoring Behavior and Supervisory Control.*, Berchtesgaden, Germany, pp. 157–170.

Vossius, G. (1964). Die Vorhersageeigenschaften des Systems der Willkürbewegung. *Neuere Ergebnisse der Kybernetik*. München, Wien: Oldenbourg Verlag, pp. 196–209.

Willumeit, H.-P. and Jürgensohn, T. (1997). *Driver-models: A critical survey.* ATZ Worldwide, Vol. 99, Part 1 + 2 in No. 7 + 8. Wiesbaden: Vieweg, pp. 19–22/19–25.

17
Review of Control Theory Models for Directional and Speed Control

David H. Weir, PhD and Kevin C. Chao, MS

17.1 Introduction

Models of driver steering control in regulation tasks are well established and have been used in a number of studies of driver/vehicle response and performance, e.g. Weir (1973), Weir and McRuer (1968, 1973), Weir and DiMarco (1978), Weir et al. (1982) and McRuer et al. (1975, 1977). There is a large literature on this general topic, including the work of Hoffman (1975), Donges (1978), Sheridan and Ferrel (1981), Godthelp (1985), Levison and Cramer (1995), Allen et al. (1996) and the recent survey article (MacAdam, 2003), among many others.

The directional control models of interest here apply to straight or curving roadways, with approximately constant speed operation and steering to stay in the centre of the lane in the presence of a random (directional) yaw disturbance. The models can involve multiple loops or perceptual feedbacks. They are typically expressed in Laplace transform (transfer function) or differential equation form, in a classical control theory manner.

The driver model for speed control is similar in form to the model for directional control, but simpler. The model of interest here is for speed regulation, where the driver uses the accelerator pedal to maintain a specified constant speed in the presence of a perceived speed error. The speed error could result from a disturbance such as a headwind gust or could arise in a car-following situation. The more general topic of car following can involve a number of additional factors not addressed here, including nonlinear and deterministic behaviour, e.g. Brackstone and McDonald (1999), Brown et al. (2001) and Fancher and Baraket (1998). The speed regulation model described herein is a single-loop model. An additional driver output, and perhaps additional feedback loops, can be added for braking control.

Useful and simple forms of the driver control models are based on the 'crossover model' of the human operator, e.g. McRuer and Weir (1969) and McRuer and Krendel (1974). This model applies to a wide variety of manual control tasks, including driving a car or piloting an aircraft. It can be used to model single-loop activity such as speed control. It can also model the inner and outer loop control activity in multiple-loop tasks, as illustrated subsequently. The crossover model quantifies driver control behaviour, based on task variables, such as the vehicle dynamics and the disturbance and command inputs to the driver/vehicle system. It is both descriptive and predictive of driver control activity. Given a quantitative description of the task variables, it can be used to estimate and predict driver control behaviour by use of a describing function (transfer function-like, input/output relation).

The driver models can be quantified for a particular task using a driving simulator or a suitably equipped instrumented vehicle. A driving simulator, computer simulation, or analytical methods can be used to apply the models, e.g., in the analysis or optimisation of a vehicle control subsystem.

17.2 Basic Crossover Model of the Human Operator

The crossover model of the human operator was originally developed and applied in the 1960s (see McRuer and Krendel, 1974). This quasilinear model and its extensions have been used, subsequently in a wide variety of studies involving the prediction, analysis, and measurement of aircraft and ground vehicle control and performance. The crossover model underlies the more specific driver control models and embodies important manual control principles. It is a useful place to start.

The crossover model can be described using the simple single-loop system of Fig. 17.1. The system input (i) can be either a command to follow or a disturbance. The operator is the driver, and the controlled element is the vehicle dynamics, in the driving task.

The driver describing function has the form

$$Y_{\mathrm{p}} = K_{\mathrm{p}} e^{-\tau s} \frac{(T_{\mathrm{L}} s + 1)}{(T_{\mathrm{I}} s + 1)} \tag{1}$$

where K_{p} is the gain, adopted by the driver, τ is the driver's time delay, T_{L} is a lead element reflecting anticipation, T_{I} is a lag element reflecting smoothing and s is the Laplace transform variable.

These parameters are adjusted according to the model, and the values of T_{L} and T_{I} depend on the vehicle dynamics. The quasilinear model, Y_{p} is called a describing function, because it characterises only the linear part of the driver's

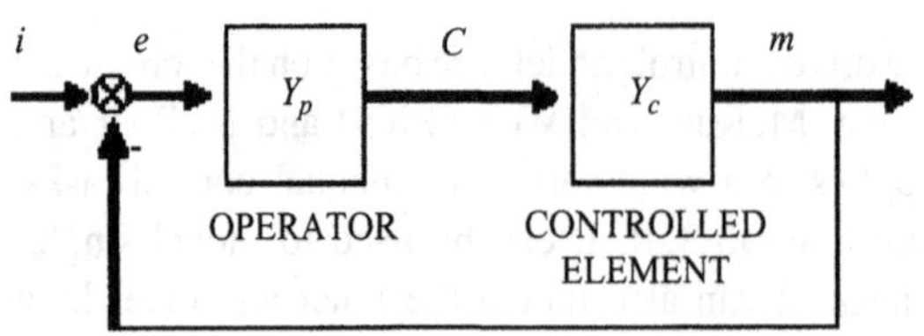

FIGURE 17.1. Single-loop manual control system.

input/output or control activity. The nonlinear part is called remnant, and it can be modelled as an additive noise (McRuer and Krendel, 1974). The linear part is the main topic here, and it typically accounts for most of the driver's control activity.

The model is applied by considering the open loop-properties of the driver/vehicle system ($Y_p Y_c$). The crossover model says that the driver adjusts the lead and lag terms (T_L and T_I) as necessary to achieve a K/s-like amplitude ratio characteristic in the frequency region of closed-loop control. This is the region of the crossover frequency (ω_c), where the closed-loop 0 dB value occurs, based on the driver's gain (K_p). For example, if the vehicle dynamics are K_c/s, then no lead or lag equalisation is needed, and the driver describing function is simply a gain plus a time delay. This is illustrated in the Bode (frequency response) plot of Fig. 17.2, which shows the amplitude and phase properties of $Y_p Y_c$ for $Y_c = K_c/s$, $T_L = T_I = 0$, and a time delay of 0.3 s. The amplitude ratio in Fig. 17.2 is seen to represent a K/s transfer characteristic (a slope of −20 dB/decade). The phase

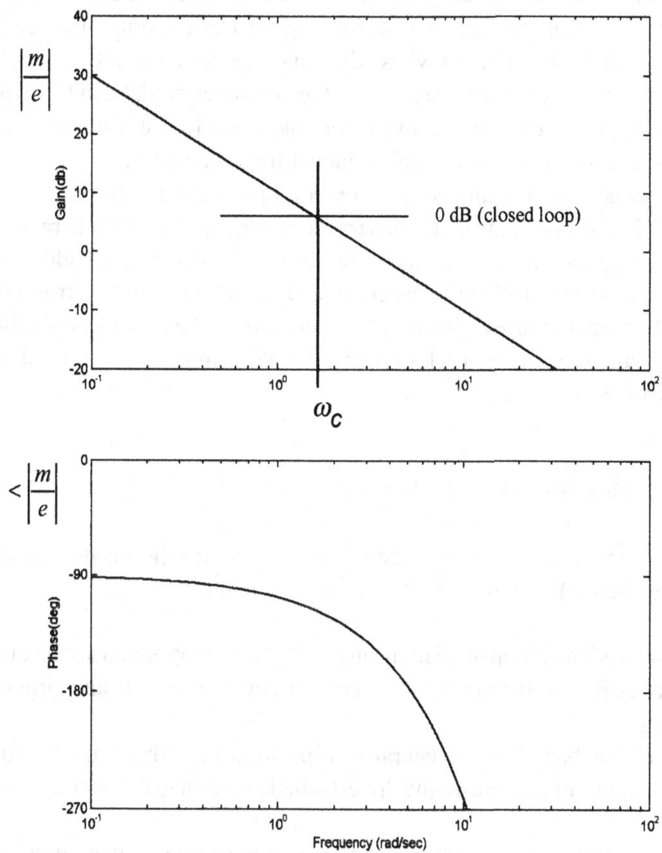

FIGURE 17.2. Open-loop driver/vehicle system bode plot.

angle plot shows 90° of phase lag at low frequency, corresponding to K/s. There is additional phase lag at mid and high frequency due to the driver's time delay (τ). Typical values of time delay in the continuous control tasks for which this model applies are typically in the range of 0.2 to 0.3 s and the values depend on the controlled element dynamics, input bandwidth, manipulator characteristics and driver factors such as skill and level of attention, among other things.

It should be noted that time delay values of the order of 0.3 s reported in the manual control literature often resulted from experiments with relatively simple and well-defined displays, lightweight manipulators and reasonably skilled subjects (engineers or pilots). As will be shown subsequently, more mature typical drivers using automobile controls can have larger values of time delay and correspondingly lower crossover frequencies. The phase margin values are similar, however, reflecting desirable damping and stability qualities.

The crossover model can be used to quantify and analyse such things as driver/vehicle system closed-loop stability, on-centre control characteristics, directional and speed disturbance regulation, path following and easy manoeuvres, the terminal control (residual error correcting) phases of abrupt manoeuvres, and driver behaviour with vehicles whose dynamics are augmented by a stability control system. As illustrated subsequently, the crossover model can be applied to a single-loop system, or to successive inner- and outer-loop closures of a multiple-loop system such as the driver/vehicle model for path control.

From a control standpoint, when an open-loop system has the properties shown in Fig. 17.2, it is a good system. The large low frequency amplitude ratio provides good error regulation. A comparatively high closed-loop bandwidth (ω_c) gives good performance in following the command input (i) and helps error regulation. The phase margin (phase angle at ω_c) is a measure of the closed-loop stability and damping, which can be set at a desired level by adjusting the operator's closed-loop gain (0 dB line).

17.3 Model for Driver Steering Control

Figure 17.3 shows a model structure for steering control (terms used in the figure are defined below). The model contains the following:

- An inner feedback loop of heading angle (ψ). This loop equalises the outer loop, and makes it easy for the driver to control lane position. It also provides path damping.
- An outer feedback loop of lateral lane position (y). This provides for lateral deviation control and causes the driver/vehicle system to follow the desired path input (y_c).
- A random appearing yaw rate disturbance input (r_d) that can be used to help define the driving task and as a basis for identifying the driver describing function components.

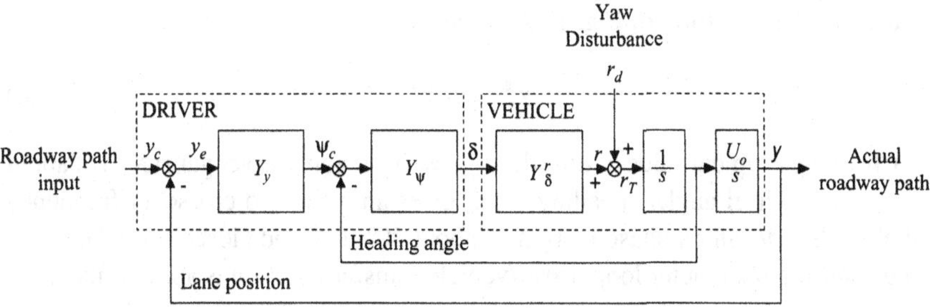

FIGURE 17.3. Model for directional control with steering.

An alternative and nearly equivalent inner loop candidate is path angle, which can be used if that is preferred. Path angle involves perceiving the total velocity vector or focus of expansion relative to the surround, whereas heading angle relates a position vector (line) in the vehicle to a geometric reference in the surround (e.g. a lane centreline or edge line). Other possible feedbacks such as sideslip and lateral acceleration are less good from a perceptual standpoint and less good in terms of desirable manual control qualities (path following, path damping, etc.). These feedbacks may play a supplementary role in some manoeuvres, such as near limit turns, which the model in Fig. 17.3 does not address.

Referring to Fig. 17.3, the dynamic model of the vehicle (Y_δ^r) is known or can be measured. The driver describing functions Y_y and Y_ψ can be predicted or estimated using a combination of the crossover model, control principles and empirical results from driving simulator or instrumented vehicle studies. The describing functions can also be measured using a driving simulator or test vehicle, and correlation or spectral analysis methods. The main driver model parameters are gains and a time delay (τ). Equalisation (lead or lag, anticipation or smoothing) can also be included, but this refinement is often not needed for contemporary passenger vehicles.

The specific forms of the driver describing function Y_ψ and Y_y can be estimated for an example typical passenger car by successive application of the crossover model. Consider the (inner) heading angle loop. The vehicle dynamics can be given by the transfer function relating yaw rate to steer angle which can be approximated by

$$Y_\delta^r = \frac{K_\delta^r}{(T_r s + 1)} = \frac{U_o/(a+b)}{(T_r s + 1)}. \tag{2}$$

Here, T_r is the vehicle's yaw rate time constant, which typically has a value of about 0.1 s for modern passenger cars at a typical highway speed. U_o is the speed and $a + b$ is the wheelbase. So, in the region of crossover for the inner loop in Fig. 17.3 (about 1 to 2 rad/s), Y_δ^r is approximately a gain and Y_δ^ψ is approximately K/s (heading angle is the integral of yaw rate). Therefore, applying the crossover model, it follows that the inner loop driver model in this case is

$$Y_\psi = K_\psi e^{-\tau s} \tag{3}$$

and $Y_\psi Y_\delta^\psi$ has the form of Fig. 17.2, where

$$Y_\delta^\psi = \frac{1}{s} Y_\delta^r. \tag{4}$$

Choosing a typical value of time delay, $\tau = 0.3$ s, and a driver gain (K_ψ) of about 0.25° front wheel angle/° heading error, gives an estimated crossover frequency of about 2 rad/s and a phase margin of about 40° for good closed-loop damping. The resulting open outer loop driver/vehicle transfer function is approximately

$$\frac{y}{y_e} = \frac{Y_y}{\left(\frac{1}{\omega_c}s + 1\right)(T_r s + 1)} \frac{U_o}{s} \tag{5}$$

and for a 10 ft wheelbase and a speed of 80 ft/s

$$\frac{y}{y_e} = Y_y \frac{80}{s\,(.5s + 1)(.1s + 1)}. \tag{6}$$

This open outer-loop driver/vehicle system has considerable low to mid frequency lag. Applying the crossover model, it is apparent that a considerable amount of low frequency driver lead in responding to the lateral position error would be needed or else the driver would use a relatively low outer loop gain (K_y) in order to achieve an outer loop closure in accordance with the model. Data from simulator and actual vehicle experiments show that drivers do the latter, i.e. use a relatively low outer loop gain and rely on the inner loop function to provide the needed lead equalisation or anticipation. Therefore, the outer loop describing function is simply a gain, that is

$$Y_y = K_y. \tag{7}$$

An example value of K_y for the assumed vehicle is about 0.2° heading command/ft of path error (1 rad/300 ft), or an outer loop crossover frequency $K_y U_o$ of about 0.27 rad/s. If the vehicle dynamic properties are other than these typical passenger car examples, driver lead or lag equalisation can be used in the inner loop to obtain the desired characteristics according to the crossover model.

17.3.1 Equivalent Single-Loop System for Steering Control

For measurement and data analysis purposes, since a useful form of the driver model for directional control with steering is known, it is possible to identify the parameters in the multiple-loop model in Fig. 17.3, using the single yaw disturbance. The system in Fig. 17.3 can be expressed as an equivalent single-loop system by using block diagram algebra on Fig. 17.3, resulting in the expression

$$\frac{r_T}{r_d} = \frac{1}{1 + \frac{Y_\psi Y_\delta^r}{s^2}\left(Y_y U_o + s\right)}, \tag{8}$$

where the terms are defined above and in Fig. 17.3. This expression was originally published in (McRuer et al., 1975).

FIGURE 17.4. Equivalent single-loop system.

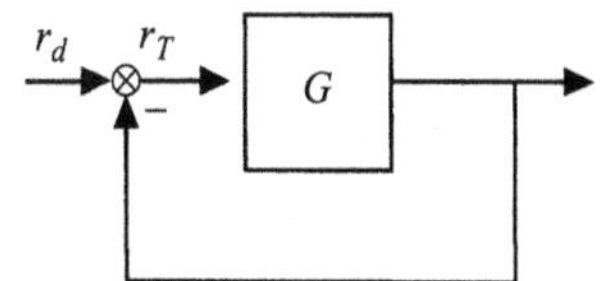

An equivalent form of Eq. (8) can be written as

$$\frac{r_T}{r_d} = \frac{1}{1+G} \tag{9}$$

which corresponds to Fig. 17.4, and where

$$G = \frac{Y_\psi Y_\delta^r}{s^2}\left(Y_y U_o + s\right) \tag{10}$$

and for s or ω small

$$G = \frac{Y_\psi Y_y U_o}{s^2} Y_\delta^r \tag{11}$$

while for ω large

$$G = \frac{Y_\psi y_\delta^r}{s} = Y_\psi Y_\delta^\psi . \tag{12}$$

The resulting combined driver/vehicle open-loop system, Eq. (10) is shown in the Bode plot of Fig. 17.5. The following are interesting things to note in Fig. 17.5:

- The outer loop driver gain (K_y) defines a low frequency break point in the amplitude ratio. This also results in an increasing phase lag at low frequency.
- The crossover frequency (ω_c) defines the closed-loop 0 dB line, and this becomes the closed-loop bandwidth of the heading control loop. The crossover frequency is equivalent to $K_\psi K_\delta^r$.
- The time delay term ($e^{-\tau s}$) results in a progressively increasing phase lag.
- The vehicle yaw time constant (T_r) appears as an additional high frequency lag term.

These features of this example model application are shown subsequently in the data for actual drivers.

17.4 Model for Speed Control with Accelerator Pedal

The driver model for speed control is similar to the model for directional control, above, but simpler. The model of interest is for speed regulation, where the driver uses the accelerator pedal to maintain a specified constant speed in the presence of a speed disturbance. This model assumes that the driver perceives and operates only on forward velocity. A possible multiple loop alternative could include an inner loop of longitudinal acceleration, for situations where that cue can be usefully

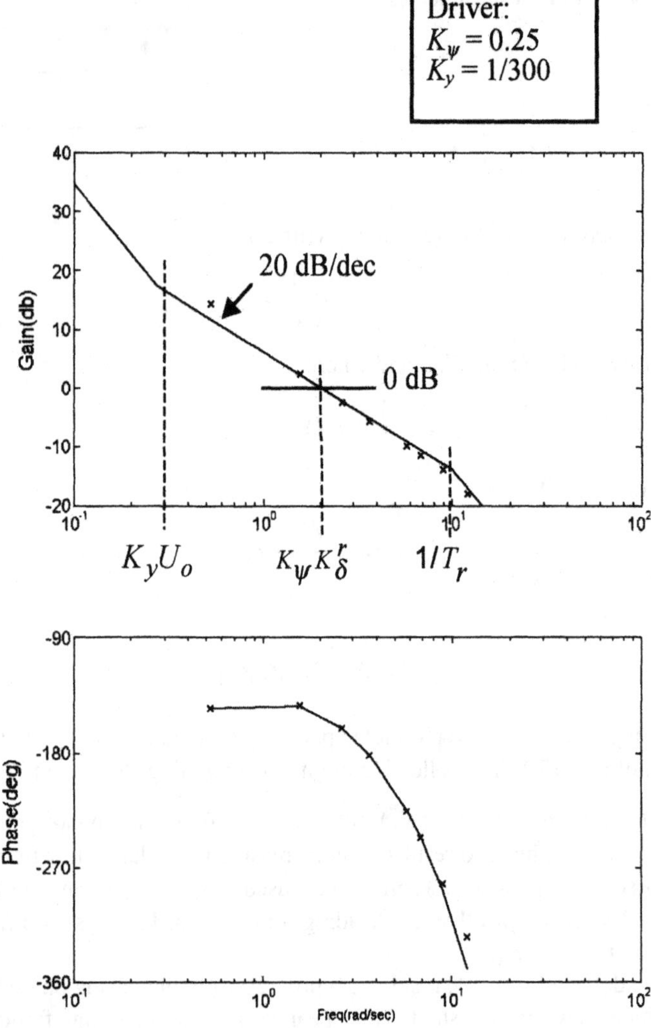

FIGURE 17.5. Open-loop combined driver/vehicle system bode plot for steering control.

perceived. The additional model for speed control of braking is beyond the scope of this paper.

The speed control model is shown in Fig. 17.6. It has only a single loop with one driver describing function element (Y_u). The speed disturbance (U_d) helps define the driving task, and can be used to experimentally identify describing function parameters. The dynamic model of the vehicle (Y_δ^u) is assumed to be known. The driver describing function can be estimated as discussed below.

The first step in applying the crossover model is to examine the controlled element (vehicle) transfer function. The transfer function relating forward speed

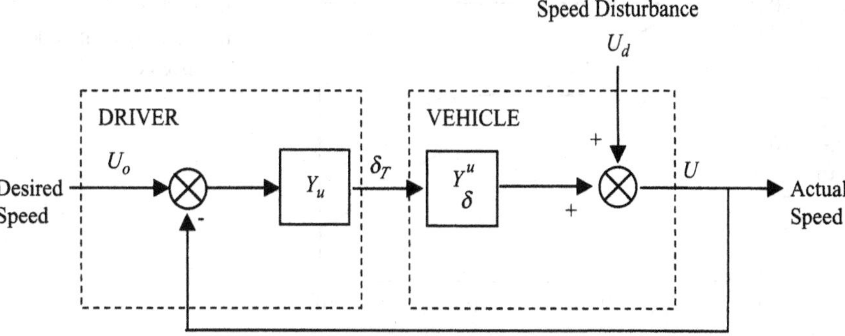

FIGURE 17.6. Model for speed control with accelerator pedal.

to accelerator pedal position can be approximated by

$$Y^u_\delta = \frac{K^u_\delta}{(T_u s + 1)}, \tag{13}$$

where T_u is the time constant associated with a change in vehicle speed.

This linear representation assumes (for simplicity) that positive and negative changes in speed result from corresponding equivalent changes in pedal position. Representative values in Eq. (13) for a passenger car at 50 mph are

$$K^u_\delta = 1 \text{ ft/s per \% pedal travel} \tag{14}$$

$$T_u = 10\,\text{s}. \tag{15}$$

So, Eq. (13) for this example is

$$Y^u_\delta = \frac{1}{(10\,s + 1)}. \tag{16}$$

Applying the crossover model and related manual control principles, a corresponding form of the driver model is

$$\begin{aligned} Y_u &= K_u \left(\frac{1}{s} + T_L\right) e^{-\tau s} \\ &= K_u \frac{(T_L s + 1)}{s} e^{-\tau s}. \end{aligned} \tag{17}$$

This involves proportional plus integral (trim) response, which reflects the lack of very low frequency gain in the open-loop vehicle characteristic in Eq. (16) (it is not K/s-like at very low frequency). A representative set of driver model parameters for this speed control task is

$K_u = 0.3$ % pedal travel/ft/s
$T_L = 12$ s
$\tau = 1.7$ s

The drivers lead T_L approximately cancels the vehicle lag T_u. The result is a relatively low bandwidth driver/vehicle system for speed control, with a relatively

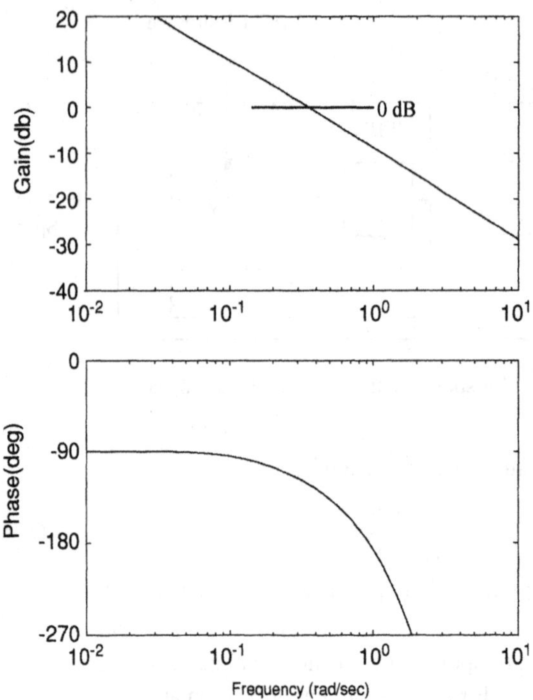

FIGURE 17.7. Open-loop driver/vehicle system bode plot for speed control.

large time delay and a crossover frequency of about 0.3 rad/s, as shown in Fig. 17.7.

Interestingly, the earlier literature and data involving the crossover model do not address the low frequency integration form of Eq. (17). Therefore, the values shown above are taken from more recent driving simulator studies involving this particular control task, the large time delay in particular. More data examples are given subsequently.

17.5 Experimental Data

Driver behaviour studies using both the DRI Driving Simulator and an actual test vehicle provide example driver describing function data for a variety of driving tasks.

17.5.1 Driving Simulator Measurements

The DRI Driving Simulator has been used extensively in studies of driver behaviour and driver/vehicle interaction. Operational since 1993, it is a large-scale research grade simulator, which features an automobile cab with instrumented controls and displays, an electromechanical steering loader, computer-generated graphics roadway scenes with a 180° field of view using three projectors as well as visual scene graphics and animation accomplished on an SG ONYX IR using proprietary

FIGURE 17.8. DRI Driving Simulator.

DRI software. Motion cues are provided by a large hexapod motion system, with a secondary 4DF seat motion system to provide road vibration and other ride cues (see Fig. 17.8).

A driving simulator is useful for driver behaviour studies because it is easy to study a range of conditions, the conditions are well defined and repeatable, it is easy to change tasks and parameters, experimental measures are easy to obtain, and a simulator is efficient and has low risk compared to studies using actual vehicles.

17.5.1.1 Steering Control

Driving simulator study results are available for the 10 typical but more mature driver subjects listed in Table 17.1. The task was to maintain the vehicle in the centre of the lane on a straight road in the presence of a random appearing lateral disturbance. Similar to crosswind gustiness, the disturbance consisted of a sum of non-harmonically related sinewaves to facilitate the describing function measurements. The drivers were also controlling speed in the presence of a random appearing longitudinal disturbance. Each run lasted about 2 min, including startup, and 60 s of steady-state driver/vehicle response data from the middle of the run were analysed. The subjects were doing only this primary driving task.

The resulting describing function parameters for the 10 subjects are shown in Table 17.2. Two runs are shown for each subject. The average values over

TABLE 17.1. Driver subjects in an example steering control study.

Subject	Occupation	Gender	Age
1	Engineer	M	46
2	Ship captain	F	51
3	Small businessman	M	55
4	Publisher	M	44
5	Homemaker	F	48
6	Administrator	M	47
7	Retired police officer	M	57
8	Postal supervisor	F	54
9	Insurance agent	M	55
10	Insurance agent	F	54

the 20 runs are in the bottom row. The data were analysed using the equivalent single-loop method described in Fig. 17.5. The first data column is the crossover frequency (ω_c). The second column (ω_{180}) is the frequency where the open-loop driver/vehicle phase angle is –180°. The next column is the phase margin (ϕ_m), which is a measure of closed-loop stability and damping. Combining ω_c and ϕ_m gives an estimate of the driver time delay (τ) and this is shown in the next column. Note that the driver time delay shown is the result of subtracting the 0.1 s yaw time constant, and an additional 0.07 s simulator graphics delay, from the total measured driver/vehicle system delay. The final column is the linear coherence (ro2), which is the ratio of the driver's control action which is linearly correlated with the disturbance input to the driver's total steering control activity. The parameter values in the table illustrate both the within-subject and between-subject variability for typical driver subjects.

The previous literature on the crossover model, and its occasional application to driving, typically show values that differ somewhat from those in Table 17.2. In particular, the example data for mature (age 44 to 57) typical drivers in Table 17.2 show somewhat lower crossover frequencies (gains) and larger time delays. In addition to possible age effects, these differences may reflect the effect of such things as multiple tasking (speed regulation at the same time), use of a steering wheel (increasing the arm-hand closed-loop neuromuscular delay), and lower levels of skill (compared to pilot subjects, for example). Note that the main difference is a difference in the time delay (τ). To the extent that the subjects use the same phase margin, the crossover frequency is a consequence of the time delay, as expressed in the crossover model. Note also that Subject 1, who is an engineer and a pilot, had larger ω_c and lower τ. These contemporary data and others like it, reflecting more mature drivers and typical driving tasks, may be pertinent to future applications of the driver models in addition to the values used in the past.

17.5.1.2 Speed Control

Limited describing function measures for speed control area also available, and example data for two subjects are given in Table 17.3. The characteristics for

TABLE 17.2. Example describing function parameters for steering control.

Subjects	ω_c (rad/s)	$\omega180$ (rad/s)	ϕ_m (deg)	τ (s)	ro2
1	1.6	3.6	29	0.51	0.57
1	1.4	3.4	41	0.44	0.52
2	1.2	3.1	50	0.42	0.53
2	1.0	2.7	29	0.95	0.48
3	0.9	4.5	43	0.79	0.20
3	0.7	3.8	29	1.36	0.65
4	1.1	2.9	34	0.72	0.66
4	0.9	3.3	35	0.95	0.76
5	1.2	3.8	33	0.67	0.66
5	1.1	3.6	30	0.79	0.69
6	1.5	5.6	40	0.40	0.63
6	0.8	4.1	37	0.96	0.70
7	0.8	3.5	50	0.73	0.60
7	0.7	3.8	44	1.04	0.65
8	1.3	4.0	49	0.37	0.34
8	0.6	3.6	50	0.98	0.6
9	1.0	3.7	31	0.92	0.59
9	0.8	3.7	43	0.81	0.56
10	1.1	3.4	52	0.44	0.65
10	1.0	3.6	52	0.49	0.60
Average	1.0	3.7	40	0.74	0.58

Subject 1 are in Table 17.1. Subject 11 was a 33-year-old female business administrator. The task was similar to that described above for the steering control data. A random appearing longitudinal disturbance consisting of a sum of sinewaves was used to define the task and facilitate the describing function measures. The describing function calculations were made over an interval of 48 s imbedded in a 2-min run.

The columns in Table 17.3 are similar to those of Table 17.2. Analysed in terms of the crossover model, and compared to typical results for other tasks in the manual control literature, the example results for speed control show relatively low crossover frequencies, large time delays, and large stability margins, for reasons previously noted. Note that data for Subject 1 appear in both Tables 17.2 and 17.3, which provides an interesting direct comparison of control activity in the two simultaneous control tasks. Although more data would be useful, the data of

TABLE 17.3. Example describing function parameters for speed control.

Subjects	ω_c (rad/s)	$\omega180$ (rad/s)	ϕ_m (deg)	τ (s)
1	.35	1.0	65	1.7
11	.3	0.8	50	2.3

TABLE 17.4. Comparison of steering control describing function measures in driving simulator and actual vehicle, Subject 1.

Method	Run length (s)	ω_c (rad/s)	ω180 (rad/s)	ϕ_m (deg)	τ (s)
Driving simulator	60	2.2	4.1	36	.43
Actual vehicle	40	2.8	5.9	53	.23

Table 17.3, representing typical drivers in this task, may provide guidance in future applications of the model.

17.5.2 Actual Vehicle Measurements

Data are also available from an actual vehicle configured for the input of a yaw disturbance, similar to the disturbance used in the driving simulator studies described above. For comparison purposes, the same random appearing directional disturbance signal was used.

Example steering control describing function data for Subject 1 are shown in Table 17.4. The driving simulator values shown are the average of 7 runs, 60 s each. The actual vehicle values are the average of 2 runs, 40 s each. These limited and preliminary example data show an interesting comparison between driving simulator and actual vehicle, in that the measured time delay is less in the latter case. The vehicle dynamics (yaw time constants) were approximately the same in the two cases. The measured simulator τ can be reduced by the 0.07 s graphics lag, as noted previously, which reduces 0.43 to about 0.36. The remaining difference of about 0.1 s can probably be attributed to the fact that these particular simulator runs were made fixed base (motion turned off), while the actual car runs had motion. The observed difference of 0.1 s is consistent with previously reported effects of motion versus no motion in simulator studies (e.g. Stapleford et al., 1969). Note, also, that the describing function parameters for this subject in the simulator in Table 17.4 show smaller τ and larger crossover frequency, than did the average of the typical subjects in Table 17.2. Again, this probably reflects a higher level of skill on the part of Subject 1. The data of Table 17.4 also serve as an interesting further confirmation of the DRI simulator's validity, as has been demonstrated repeatedly in the past.

17.6 Example Directional Control Application

An example application of the steering control model in Fig. 17.3 can be given by the analysis of a hypothetical high-speed driver/vehicle stability problem. Consider an inappropriately overloaded large sports-utility-type vehicle with the following hypothetical example values for cg location (wheelbase), mass, yaw moment of inertia and front and rear tire cornering stiffness, respectively:

$a = 3.5$ ft (1.1 m)
$b = 5.5$ ft (1.7 m)
$m = 185$ slugs (2700 kg)
$I = 4000$ slug/ft^2 (5400 kgm^2)
$Y_1 = 4000$ lb/rad (18 kN/rad)
$Y_2 = 5000$ lb/rad (22.4 kN/rad)

A simple set of 2° of freedom lateral-directional equations for the vehicle is given by

$$\begin{bmatrix} s - y_v & U_o - Y_r \\ -N_v & s - N_r \end{bmatrix} \begin{bmatrix} v \\ r \end{bmatrix} = \begin{bmatrix} Y_\delta \\ N_\delta \end{bmatrix} \delta, \tag{18}$$

where v is the lateral velocity, r is the yaw rate, δ is the steer angle, U_o is the forward velocity, s is the Laplace transfer variable and the coefficients are

$$Y_v = \frac{-2}{mU_o}(Y_1 + Y_2)$$
$$Y_r = \frac{2}{mU_o}(bY_2 - aY_1)$$
$$N_v = \frac{2}{IU_o}(bY_2 - aY_1)$$
$$N_r = \frac{-2}{IU_o}\left(a^2Y_1 + b^2Y_2\right)$$
$$Y_\delta = \frac{2}{m}Y_1$$
$$N_\delta = \frac{2a}{I}Y_1.$$

Assume a speed of 120 ft/s (130 km/h). The result is a relatively poor handling example vehicle, with the assumed excessive load and inadequate tires, but it can serve to illustrate the analytical use of the driver model. Entering the numerical parameters listed into the equations above gives the following vehicle transfer function for heading control (from Eq. 4):

$$Y_\delta^\psi = \frac{7\,(s + 1.16)}{s\left[s^2 + 2\,(.3)\,(2.7)\,s + (2.7)^2\right]}. \tag{19}$$

The damping ratio is 0.3 and the undamped natural frequency is 2.7 rad/s in the characteristic equation, represented by the complex conjugate pair. While the Eq. (2) vehicle approximation for yaw rate was a simple high frequency lag, the slightly more complete form of Eq. (19) replaces that with a lead-double lag combination. The equivalent yaw time constant, T_r, and phase lag contribution for frequencies less than 2.7, would now be about 0.22 s, instead of the 0.1 s example used with Eq. (2). The driver/vehicle open-loop response properties (see Fig. 17.3) for this example become

$$Y_p Y_c = K_\psi e^{-\tau s} Y_\delta^\psi, \tag{20}$$

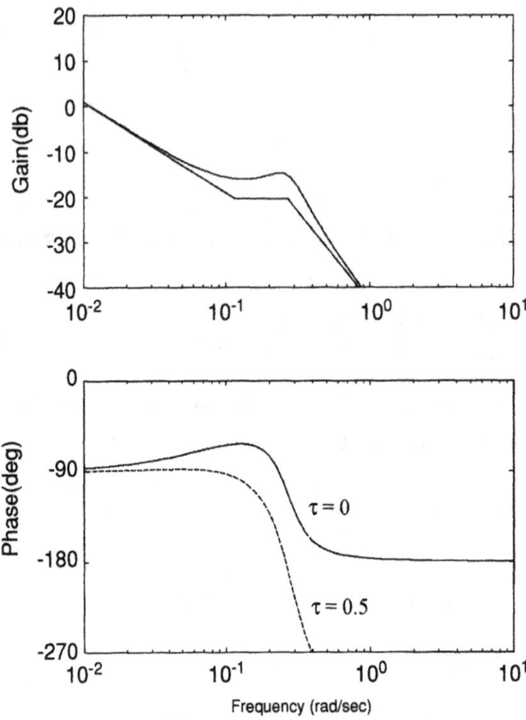

FIGURE 17.9. Example driver/vehicle system bode plot for heading control.

where Y_{δ}^{ψ} is given by Eq. (19). The corresponding frequency response plot for Eq. (20) is shown in Fig. 17.9, in the manner of Fig. 17.2. A driver time delay of 0.5 s is used in this example, and its effect is shown by the lower phase angle curve.

The next step is to estimate the driver gain K_{ψ}. Fig. 17.9 shows that the driver gain is limited by the lightly damped second order made at 2.7 rad/s. If the driver's gain is increased so that the closed-loop 0dB line intersects the peak in the amplitude ratio plot at $\omega = 2.7$ rad/s, the closed-loop driver/vehicle system becomes unstable. Therefore, a lower driver gain has to be used resulting in relatively low values of closed-loop bandwidth and directional stability. This is illustrated, alternatively, in the corresponding root locus plot of Fig. 17.10. The branch of the locus from the quadratic pole moves into the right half plane and becomes neutrally stable or unstable for a relatively low level of driver gain K_{ψ}. This value of gain would cause the vehicle to move back and forth in the lane. Figs. 17.9 and 17.10 both show that this oscillatory behaviour for this hypothetical vehicle configuration is due to the driver's time delay. The resulting phase lag causes the closed-loop poles to move towards a region of instability as the driver's gain is increased (as the driver tries harder and makes larger control inputs). This type of system response has sometimes been characterised as a 'driver induced oscillation'. Note that there is little point in analysing the outer path loop, since adding that feedback would

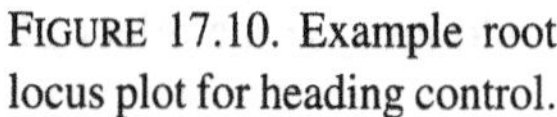

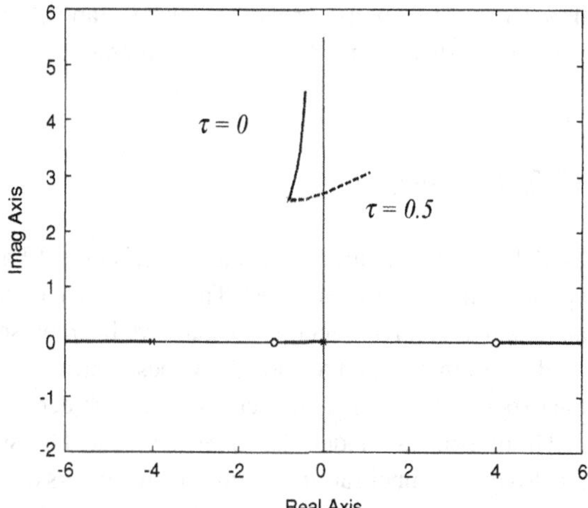

FIGURE 17.10. Example root locus plot for heading control.

have little effect on the vehicle's behaviour and lane-keeping performance in this example.

A more detailed analysis would show that lag equalisation might improve the closed-loop bandwidth in Fig. 17.9 a small amount. But, for the purposes of this example, it assumed that the driver does not provide such smoothing. For this hypothetical poor vehicle configuration, corrections of heading errors by the modelled driver can only be done using small steering inputs. Aggressive or large amplitude steer corrections would tend to result in oscillatory directional behaviour, as noted above. In other words, the quasilinear model says that if the driver tries harder it only worsens the stability, in this case. The driver could perhaps adapt a nonlinear control behaviour, wherein the frequency of the oscillatory response of the vehicle is recognised and the driver makes a properly timed and predicted discrete steering correction to reduce the oscillation, in effect reducing or eliminating the effect of his or her time delay. Another possibility is to hold the steering wheel approximately fixed and let the directional oscillations damp out if the vehicle alone has positive path damping.

It should be emphasised that this hypothetical high speed vehicle example is only to illustrate a possible use of the model. If the vehicle were to slow down the damping would improve. In addition, or alternatively, the example vehicle configuration could be readily changed to eliminate the undesirable effect shown, by reducing the mass and inertia (the load), or by increasing the tire cornering stiffness characteristics (more suitable, higher performance tires).

This example shows how driver/vehicle response properties can be predicted analytically. This type of comparatively simple and robust model and analysis can assist the understanding of a problem or issue. Such analysis also shows the contribution of the several driver and vehicle parameters to the resulting response, and it suggests how sensitivity analyses can be performed to improve or optimise driver/vehicle response properties. For instance, one could analyse the effect of varying the driver time delay in this example.

17.7 Discussion

Models for driver directional and speed control have been presented, and their application has been illustrated. These are based on models in the classic literature and manual control principles. Data have been presented for typical values of the model parameters and to show how these parameters vary depending on the task, the experimental venue and across driver subjects.

The quasilinear models described herein are best suited to regulation tasks where the driver is compensating and minimising errors on straight and gradually curving roads at an approximately constant speed, and these conditions represent a large percentage of driving. Other models that are available for other driving tasks such as rapid manoeuvres, obstacle avoidance, near limit turning and/or braking manoeuvres, etc., are beyond the scope of this paper.

Driver models of the sort described herein have a wide variety of applications. For example, they can be used to characterise the driver element in R&D-related studies of vehicles, of devices-in-the-vehicle, or vehicles augmented by devices. The models can be used to interpret driver behaviour or driver/vehicle response and performance data. They can be used to represent the driver or driver/vehicle system in simulations involving one vehicle or multiple vehicles. Perhaps most usefully, they serve to quantify driver behaviour and driver/vehicle response and performance in engineering terms, and in a way that both predicts what the driver will do and quantifies data resulting from what the driver has done.

References

Allen, R.W., Rosenthal, T.J. and Hogue, J.R. (1996). Modelling and Simulation of Driver/Vehicle Interaction. SAE Paper 960177.

Brackstone, M. and McDonald, M. (1999). Car following: A historical overview. *Transportation Research Part F*, 2, 181–196.

Brown, T.L., Lee, J.D. and McGehee, D.V. (2001). Human performance models and rear-end collision avoidance algorithms. *Human Factors*, 43, 462–482.

Donges, E. (1978). A two-level model of driver steering behaviour. *Human Factors*, 20, 691–707.

Fancher, P.S. and Baraket, Z. (1998). Evolving model for studying driver-vehicle system performance in longitudinal control of headway. *Transportation Research Record No. 1631* (pp. 13–19).

Godthelp, J. (1985). Precognitive control: Open- and closed-loop steering in a lane change maneuver. *Ergonomics*, 28, 1419–1438.

Hoffman, E.R. (1975). Manual control of road vehicles. *Vehicle System Dynamics*, 5, 1–2.

Levison, W. and Cramer, N. (1995). Description of the integrated driver model. Report FHWA-RD-94-092. FHWA, US DOT.

MacAdam, C.C. (2003). Understanding and modelling the human driver. *Vehicle System Dynamics*, 40, 101–134.

McRuer, D.T. and Weir, D.H. (1969). Theory of manual vehicular control. *IEEE Transactions*, MMS-10(4). (Also *Ergonomics*, 12 (5), 1969.)

McRuer, D.T. and Krendel, E.S. (1974). Mathematical models of human pilot behaviour. AGARDograph No. 188. NATO Advisory Group for Aerospace Research and Development.

McRuer, D.T., Weir, D.H., Jex, H.R., Magdaleno, R.E. and Allen, R.W. (1975). Measurement of driver/vehicle multiloop response properties with a single disturbance input. *IEEE Transactions*, SMC-5(5).

McRuer, D.T., Allen, R.W., Weir, D.H. and Klein, R.H. (1977). New results in driver steering control models. *Human Factors*, 19(4), 381–397.

Sheridan, T.B. and Ferrell, W.R. (1981). *Man–Machine Systems, Information, Control, and Decision Models of Human Performance*. MIT Press, Cambridge, MA.

Stapleford, R.L., Peters, R.A. and Alex, F.R. (1969). Experiments and a model for pilot dynamics with visual and motion inputs. NASA CR-1325.

Weir, D.H. and McRuer, D.T. (1968). A theory for driver steering control of motor vehicles. *Highway Research Record*, 247, 7-39.

Weir, D.H. and McRuer, D.T. (1973). Measurement and interpretation of driver/vehicle system dynamic response. *Human Factors*, 15(4), 367–378.

Weir, D.H. (1973). Driver/vehicle response and performance in the presence of aerodynamic disturbances from large commercial vehicles. In First International Conference on Driver Behaviour, Zurich, Switzerland.

Weir, D.H. and DiMarco, R.J. (1978). Correlation and evaluation of driver/vehicle directional handling data. SAE Paper 780010.

Weir, D.H., Klein, R.H. and Zellner, J.W. (1982). Crosswind response and stability of car plus utility trailer combinations. SAE Paper 820137.

VII
Simulation of Driver Behaviour

18 Cognitive Modelling and Computational Simulation of Drivers Mental Activities

THIERRY BELLET, BÉATRICE BAILLY, PIERRE MAYENOBE AND OLIVIER GEORGEON

18.1 Introduction: A Brief Historical Overview on Driver Modelling

Several car driver models are available in the literature. From an historical point of view, it is possible to identify three main phases, for the last 40 years, in this research area. The works of Mc Knight and Adams (1970), centred on *task analysis*, are typically representative of the studies carried out during the 1970s. The authors proposed a taxonomy of the main driving tasks (e.g. accelerating, steering, overtaking, lane changing) organised in nine categories (e.g. basic control tasks, tasks related to traffic condition). This work closely parallels the research of Allen et al. (1970), who divided the driving task in three levels: the *microperformance*, the *situational performance* and the *macroperformance*. These levels differ both according to their time scale and with regard to the kind of cognitive activity required. At the *microperformance* level, most of the actions are automated skills. Steering and speed control are the main subtasks. Feedback loops, concerning driving action implemented at this level, are very short (on the order of seconds). The *macroperformance* concerns the trip planning and the route finding during the trip. It corresponds to slow conscious processes requiring cognitive resources. The time scale can be hours at this level. Between these two levels, *situational performance* corresponds to the analysis of the road environment and to the selection of relevant behaviour in the current situation and traffic conditions. Performance at this level is determined by the driver's perception and understanding of the driving context.

These types of studies are descriptive in nature and aim to propose an exhaustive taxonomy of the different kinds of driving subtasks. This approach provides an interesting framework to analyse driving behaviours, but is poor in terms of mental activities study. It provides models of the driving task more than model of the drivers. During the 1980s, the main paradigm was the *human information processing* approach. Several models were developed in order to explain accidents. Most of them are focused on the notion of *risk*: the *risk threshold model* of Näätänen and Summala (1976), Wilde's *risk homeostatis* model (1982) and Fuller's *threat avoidance* model (1984). These models describe drivers activity as a regulation task in order to maintain a subjective (i.e. estimated) level of risk underneath of a given target level (i.e. accepted risk). Consequently, they more particularly insist on the driver's motivations and risk assessment. One of the most interesting model developed during this decade is the *hierarchical risk model* of Van der Molen and Bötticher (1988). This model aims to provide '*a structural framework permitting the description of perception, judgement and decision processes at every level of the task*'. Based on Michon's works (1985), the model is hierarchically structured with a *strategic*, a *tactical* and an *operational* level. This three-level hierarchy parallels the skill–rule–knowledge (SRK) model of human information processing proposed by Rasmussen (1983). It also evokes the division of driving tasks proposed by Allen et al. (above-mentioned). Nevertheless, by contrast with King approach, the *hierarchical risk model* is not focused on the *driving task* itself, but on the drivers' mental activities (as SRK). The model describes several cognitive mechanisms such as the formulation of a *risk judgement*, *expectations* or *decision making*. However, each of these processes is only modelling via really simplified equations. Moreover, information processing is strongly sequential in this model, and it seems not appropriate to describe the functioning of the human cognitive system. Lastly, while insisting on the role of *internal representations* in decision-making processes, the authors do not describe these mental structures, and the cognitive processes involved in these mental models construction are also not defined. Therefore, we will see that COSMODRIVE (cognitive simulation model of the driver) has been more particularly developed in order to modelling these cognitive mechanisms.

During the 1990s, a third generation of models was introduced with the aim to provide computer simulation of the driver. It is possible to identify at least two types of simulation models: *models* of *performance* (Levison, 1993) and *cognitive simulation models* (Wierda and Aasman, 1992; Salvucci et al., 2001; Krajzewicz et al., 2004). Except that they both propose computational models, these two approaches are different in their theoretical foundations as well as in their application areas. The firsts one are essentially focused on human behaviour, with the aim to simulate it and predict performances (i.e. *predictive models*) and not the internal processes implemented behind behaviour. By contrast, the main objective of the cognitive simulation models (or *explicative models*) is to describe and simulate internal states and cognitive processes carried out during driving. Some of these models can be also used as predictive models of human performance, even though it is not their main goal. This distinction between *predictive* versus *explicative* models is very important in terms of epistemology (Thom, 1991). It determines the computational modelling phase: for a performance model, what is the most important is the final result, irrespective of how the processes are implemented. These models are generally limited to one (or more) black box(es) whose *inputs* correspond to information coming from the road environment, while the *outputs* correspond to performances. The implementation choices, at the level of the 'black box', are essentially determined by technical criteria (e.g. calculation time), without considering the real nature of the processes involved in the human cognitive system. Only the matching of the model's prediction (predicted behaviour) and the facts observed in the real world (effective behaviour) is considered. This kind of model is more appropriate in the framework of a behavioural approach. On the other hand, cognitive simulation models are not just focused on the probability of occurrence between a situational context (the characteristics of a traffic situation) and driving behaviour. The way the processes are implemented leads to an homomorphism with the human cognitive processes. This approach is heavier in terms of human modelling, but allows a better understanding of the cause–effect relationships between behaviour and the driving conditions.

The purpose of this paper is not to judge these two approaches in terms of correctness. Both of them are relevant, but can differ in their goals. Performance models are more appropriate if the aim is only to predict behaviour. In our case, the goal is to evaluate theoretical approach and experimental results concerning cognitive processing in the driving context, with the aim to provide a deep understanding of driver's cognition. From this point of view, the explicative modelling approach was needed.

18.2 COSMODRIVE Model

COSMODRIVE is based on several empirical data coming from drivers' activities analysis in real driving situations (Bellet, 1998) or from lab experiment results (Bailly et al., 2003). Empirical data are focused on the activity of turning left at an urban road junction. Two series of observations were carried out: on-site observations (outside the car) and on-board observations (on an experimental car equipped with sensors a video cameras), followed by interviews with the drivers (based on the video film recorded during the trip). Lab experiments are based on video film and the main results obtained are described in Section 18.4.

18.2.1 Cognitive Architecture of COSMODRIVE

From a fundamental point of view, COSMODRIVE's cognitive architecture distinguishes two main types of *information processing and storage structures* (Fig. 18.1): the long-term memory (LTM), modelling as *knowledge bases* that hold driver's knowledge, and the working memory (WM), modelling as *blackboards* that contain *mental models* of the driving situation. Several cognitive processes (or *agents*) are in charge (a) to activate (retrieval) or store (acquisition) knowledge in the LTM, (b) to process information coming from the road environment and integrate it in the WM, (c) to carry out reasoning (e.g. decision, anticipation, action planning) and (d) to manage cognitive resources. Mental representations build in the WM play a central role in the driver's cognitive activity. They correspond to the driver's understanding of the driving situation and provide *mental models* that are more or less true to reality. It is on the basis of this 'representation of the world' that the driver takes decisions when driving. COSMODRIVE endeavours to simulate all the processes involved in generating and using these mental models.

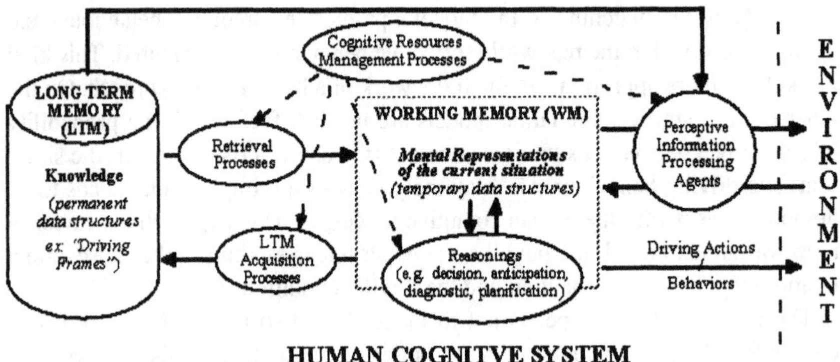

FIGURE 18.1. Simplified view of the cognitive architecture of COSMODRIVE.

In terms of level of control, COSMODRIVE's architecture is based on Michon (1985) and Van der Molen and Bötticher (1988) approaches. The model distinguishes a *strategic module*, a *tactical module*, an *operational module* and an *emergency management module* (the latter two modules being part of the risk hierarchy model). Three other modules complete this basic framework: *perception*, *execution* and *control and management* modules.

The *strategic module* includes trip planning and route finding activities and integrates travel constraints (e.g. to reach the destination at a given time) and global goals (e.g. to find a service station). The initial plan can change during the trip, if new goals are integrated (e.g. to find a restaurant, if I am hungry). The results of reasoning carried out at the strategic level are given to the tactical module in the form of *local goals* to be reached at varying times. The *tactical module* can be considered as a generator of mental models of the current driving situation. Driving actions (e.g. overtaking a car, crossing an intersection) are also planned and decided at this level. This module includes several cognitive processes such as decision making, driving context categorisation, place recognition or anticipation. The tactical module also has an anticipation process that generates anticipated representations (ARs) from the current state of the world. Each AR corresponds to a possible evolution of the current situation. These anticipations play a decisive role in choosing the driving actions to be implemented. Once they have been selected, the actions are transmitted to the *operational* module. The *operational module* is built as a multi-agent system with a set of autonomous *operational units*, specialised in implementing elementary driving subtasks (steering control, speed control and distance maintaining between vehicles). From a cognitive point of view, mental computation are generally sub-symbolic at this level, by contrast to the strategic and the tactical reasoning based on symbolic computation. In any case, operational units cooperate in order to define the precise action plan of driving decision determined at the tactical level. Then, driving behaviour will be carried out by the *execution* module, via vehicle controls (pedals, steering wheel, etc.), in order to progress on the road infrastructure. Another function of the operational module is to assess the risk of accident. Specific reasoning is in charge to identify a danger and, if necessary, to activate (sending a message) the *emergency management module*. In this case, tactical and strategic modules are 'disactivated', until an emergency reaction has been selected in memory and the problem solved. Once the driving situation is under control, the emergency module sends a message to the *control and management* module in order to reactivate the tactical and strategic modules. Then, the emergency management becomes inactive until the occurrence of a new incident. COSMODRIVE also integrates two other modules. The *perception module* is the interface between the road environment and the model. It simulates information processing of sensorial data before integration in the tactical module (i.e. in the mental model of the driving situation). Two modes of information processing are implemented. The first one is 'data-driven' (bottom–up procedure based on a set of filters) and allows cognitive integration of unexpected information. The second one is 'knowledge-driven' (top–down mechanism) and is implemented via a *perceptive exploration* agent in order to examine the road environment according to the perceptive expectations included in the tactical representation or requested by operational level agents. From a computational point of view, *perception* is in charge to manage the *perceptive queries* (request for information to be obtained) coming from the different cognitive processes active at a given time. At this level, the aim is to determine the order of priority of these queries and, on this basis, to specify the perceptive exploration strategies for exploring the road scene. Information collected is then transmitted to the querying cognitive processes. A detailed description of this module is available in Mayenobe (2004). Lastly, the *control and management module* is in charge to simulate the management mechanisms of cognitive resources. Like the human driver, COSMODRIVE is limited in his attentional capacities. The main task of control and management is to share cognitive resources between the different cognitive processes implemented at a given time. Schematically, the resource allocation procedure starts with the demand, from each active process, for a quantity of resources necessary to perform its current task. This 'demand' occurs by sending a query to control and management. This module analyses all the demands and the allocation is done, in return, via the parameterisation of the demanding process. Control and management also manages the transition between the 'abnormal situation'/'normal situation' modes: as soon as a danger is detected, all cognitive resources are allocated to the emergency module, and the tactical and the strategic modules must wait the solving of the critical situation to have cognitive resources. The central module of COMODRIVE in the field of this chapter is the tactical module.

18.2.2 The Tactical Module

Driver's behaviour is not directly based on the objective state of the world, but on a mental model (internal representation) of the driving situation. This mental model is built in a working memory from perceptive information extracted from the road scene and from permanent knowledge stored in the long-term memory. At the tactical level, this mental model provides a meaningful and self-oriented understanding of the reality, including anticipations of potential evolutions in the current driving situation. From this point of view, it corresponds to the driver's *situation awareness*, according to Endsley's definition of this concept: 'the perception of the elements in the environment within a volume of time and space, the comprehension of their meaning, and the projection of their status in the near future' (Endsley, 1995). Moreover, this mental representation is 'action-oriented' (i.e. the driver does not passively observe the road scene as a 'spectator', but as an 'actor'). It constitutes an *operative image* (i.e. a functionally deformed view of the reality; cf. Ochanine, 1977), a 'goal driven' model of the road environment. Once built, these mental models generate perceptive expectations, guide the road environment exploration and the new information processing, orientate decision making and lastly, determine all driving behaviours carried out by the driver. From this point of view, tactical representations are a key element of the driver's cognition, and an erroneous representation means, potentially, decision-making errors and unsafe driving actions. The central objective of COSMODRIVE is the computational simulation of the cognitive processes involved in this mental model building.

18.2.2.1 Driving Frames: A Framework for Modelling Mental Models

In order to study mental model, drivers' activity observations have been done during a specific task: 'turning left at a urban crossroads with traffic lights' (Bellet, 1998). Several data have been collected and analysed (driver's visual strategies, actions performed, vehicle position and speed). All these data have been considered taking into account the traffic conditions (other vehicles positions and manoeuvres). Moreover, driver interviews were conducted after this driving task (based on the video film collected during the trip) with the aim to collect drivers' opinion concerning their behaviours, their strategies, the perceptive information used, and the knowledge involved for decision making. As a result, it appears that the drivers use a *functional representation* of the road environment to drive the car and to adapt their behaviour according to the traffic conditions. A specific formalism – based on the *frame theory* of Minsky – has been defined at LESCOT for these mental representations modelling (Bellet et al., 1999). *Frame* refers to psychological concepts such as 'schema' (Bartlett) or 'scheme' (Piaget). In a classic paper, Minsky (1975) defines frames as complex data-structures for representing situation knowledge stored in human memory. The main advantage of the frame formalism is the possibility to integrate, in the same structure, *declarative* and *procedural* knowledge. Consequently, frames can describe objects, situations, events, sequences of events, actions and sequences of actions. Moreover, frames act like models of the world that guide the interpretation of sensorial inputs and the perceptive explorations of the environment. Frame approach has been used in different type of human operators model, more particularly in the industrial control process area (e.g. Cacciabue et al., 1992).

Driver's mental model has been described in COSMODRIVE as *driving frames*. A driving frame is a mental representation of the road scene, functionally structured according to the goal pursued in this particular infrastructure. Figure 18.2 presents

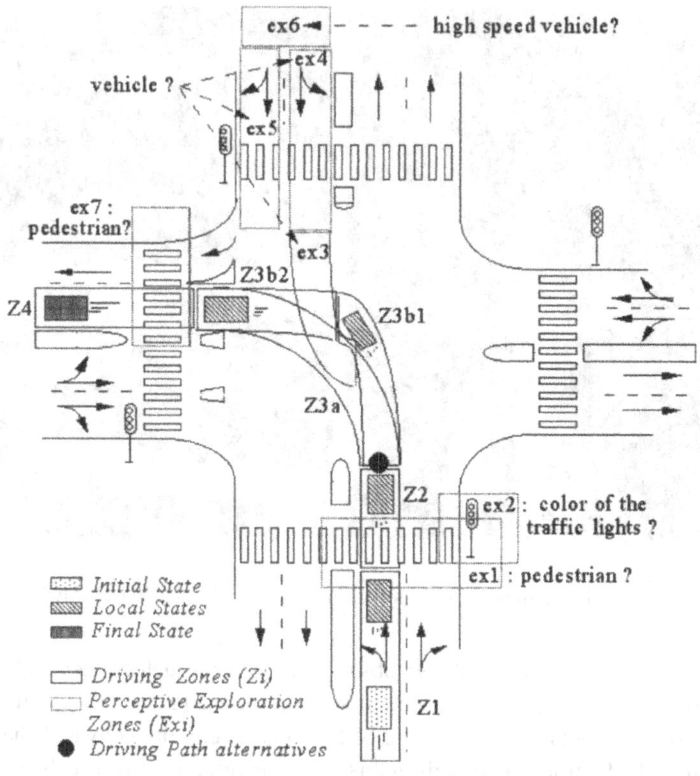

FIGURE 18.2. Driving frame of an urban crossroad with traffic lights.

the generic driving frame (i.e. driving knowledge) of an urban crossroad with the goal 'turn on the left' (this frame must be instantiated with event occurrences to provide a mental model of a particular driving situation). A frame is defined by a *global initial state*, a *global final state*, a set of *perceptive exploration zones* and a *driving path*. A *state* corresponds to the vehicle position and speed at a given time. The *global initial state* corresponds to the initial position and speed of the car when the driver approaches the intersection. The *global final state* corresponds to the final position of the driver when he or she leaves the junction. Reaching this last position constitutes the global goal of the driver in this crossroad. The *driving path* is composed of a sequence of *driving zones*. It allows the driver to pass from the initial to the final state. Each driving zone is described by three elements: a *local initial state*, and a set of *local final states* and a set of *actions*. An action allows the driver to pass from the local initial state to one of the local final states. In concrete terms, if we consider the Fig. 18.2, the road infrastructure is described as a set of two kinds of zones: the *driving zones* (Zi) and the *perceptive exploration zones* (Exi). The sequences of driving zones constitute the driving paths. In this particular case, two driving paths are possible: Z1, Z2, Z3a, Z4 and Z1, Z2, Z3b1, Z3b2, Z4. The perceptive exploration zones correspond to the part

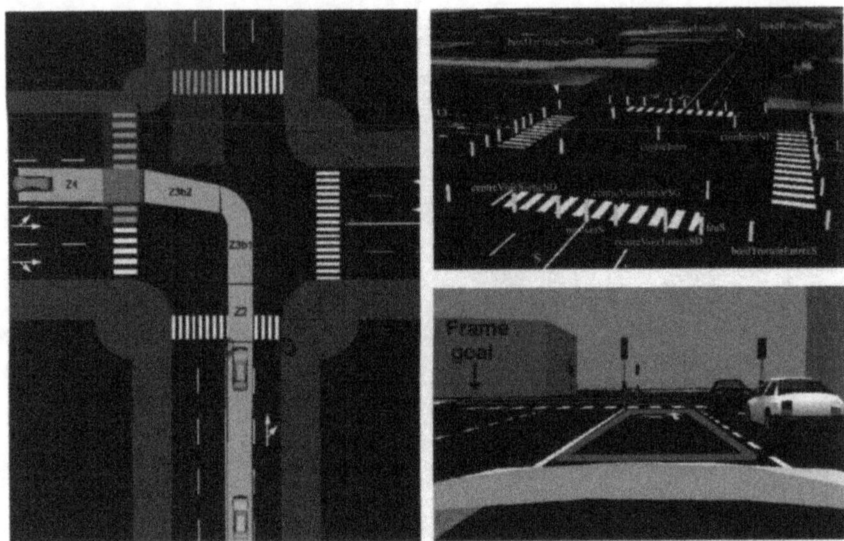

FIGURE 18.3. Three-dimensional modelling of driving frames in COSMODRIVE.

of the environment that the driver observes in order to detect *events*. An event corresponds to an object occurrence in a specific zone (e.g. a vehicle in ex3) or to identify a particular characteristic of this object (e.g. the colour of the traffic lights in ex1). In order to turn left in this infrastructure, the driver realises several consecutive steps: at the beginning of Z1 (global initial state), he observes the colour of the traffic lights. If the traffic lights are green, he then proceeds to Z2 with the same speed. If not, he stops the car at the end of Z1. In Z2, the driver checks for vehicle presence in the opposite lanes near the crossroads (ex3, ex4 or ex5 zones), and the presence of any high-speed vehicle in ex6 zone. If there is no vehicle, the driver goes to Z3a. Else, he stops the car at the end of Z3b1, and waits until there is no vehicle in the ex4 and ex5 zones. In Z3a or Z3b2, the driver looks for any pedestrian in the ex7 zone. If a pedestrian is present, he stops at the end of Z3a or Z3b2 while the pedestrian crosses the street. And then, he continues his path in Z4, towards the global final state of the frame. From a computational point of view (Bellet and Tattegrain-Veste, 1999, 2003), driving frames has been modelled in COSMODRIVE with the object-oriented modelling technique of Rumbaugh et al. (1991) and have been implemented in SmallTalk language. In a more recent work (Mayenobe et al., 2002, 2003; Mayenobe, 2004), a three-dimensional (3-D) version of *driving frames* has been also developed, allowing dynamic simulation of drivers' mental models (Fig. 18.3).

In terms of human cognition, these 3-D models correspond to visuo-spatial representations of the road scene, mentally used by the driver for decision taking and action planning at the tactical level. Content of these mental models depends on several things, like the current driver's goal, driving experience, attention sharing problem, age and so on. Experimental results will be presented in the next part of this chapter to illustrate the potential impact of a secondary task or driving

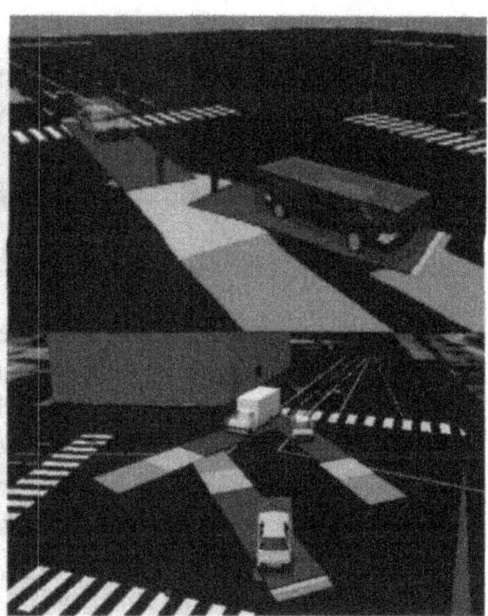

FIGURE 18.4. The 'relative zones' and COSMODRIVE simulation of vehicles' interaction management.

experience effect on driver's situation awareness. In any case, these 3-D models provide simulation of the driver's understanding of the road environment, including infrastructure and events perceived from the pilot point of view. They also integrate *relative zones* around the driver's own car (Fig. 18.4). These relative zones correspond to the part of the space that drivers must to keep around their car to avoid collision or to comfortably interact with other road user. From a theoretical point of view, the *relative zone* approach is partly based on Hall's concept of *proximity bubbles* (Hall, 1966), which concerns social interactions between humans. In driving context, a same idea has been also proposed with the concept of *safety margin* (Gibson and Crooks, 1938). Nevertheless, COSMODRIVE three-relative-zones model is more particularly based on Kontaratos' work (Kontaratos, 1974) and distinguishes the *danger*, the *threat* and the *safety* zones. These zones are called 'relative' because they are dependent on the car speed and position. They correspond to the portion of space to be occupied by the future trajectory of the vehicle. The lengths of these "relative zones" depend of the car speed, and correspond to the distance covered by the vehicle during this period of time. According to Otha's results (1993), the reserved values of the coefficients are, respectively, 0.6, 1.1 and 1.7 s for the zones of danger, threat and safety. However, inter-vehicular distance regulation may vary according to the context, the driving strategies and the traffic density.

Moreover, 3-D mental models also integrate a set of*remarkable points* (i.e. restricted set of points corresponding to specific landmarks, like corners of the roads or intersection centre; cf. see Fig. 18.3) needed to geometrically match the mental model and the road infrastructure (i.e. objective reality as perceived by the driver). Once a driving frame is matched with reality (Fig. 18.5), the driver

FIGURE 18.5. From reality (left) to mental model simulated with COSMODRIVE (right).

can mentally use the *driving path* of the frame to mentally simulate trajectories of vehicles, according to its own trajectory. This mental simulation mechanism provides anticipations, which correspond to drivers' expectations.

Lastly, at a lower level (which corresponds to the *operational* and the *execution* modules of COSMODRIVE) driving frames are implemented through the method of *pure-pursuit point* developed for automatic car driving (Amidi, 1990) and used by Sukthankar (1997) for drivers' situation awareness simulation (Fig. 18.6). A *pure-pursuit point* is defined to be the intersection of the desired vehicle trajectory and a circle of radius (l), centred at the vehicle's rear axle midpoint (assuming front wheel steer). Intuitively, this point describes the steering curvature that would bring the vehicle to the desired lateral offset after travelling a distance of approximately l. Thus the position of the pure-pursuit point maps directly onto a recommended steering curvature: $k = -2x/l$, where k is the curvature (reciprocal of steering radius), x is the relative lateral offset to the pure-pursuit point in vehicle coordinates and l is a parameter known as the look-ahead distance.

18.2.2.2 Architecture of the Tactical Module

The whole activity of the tactical module of COSMODRIVE is dedicated to the elaboration and the handling of these driving frames, as mental models of the current driving situation. Computationally, the tactical module is implemented as a *multi-agent system* based on a *blackboard architecture*: different processes or *cognitive agents* process the information in parallel and exchange data (read/write) via

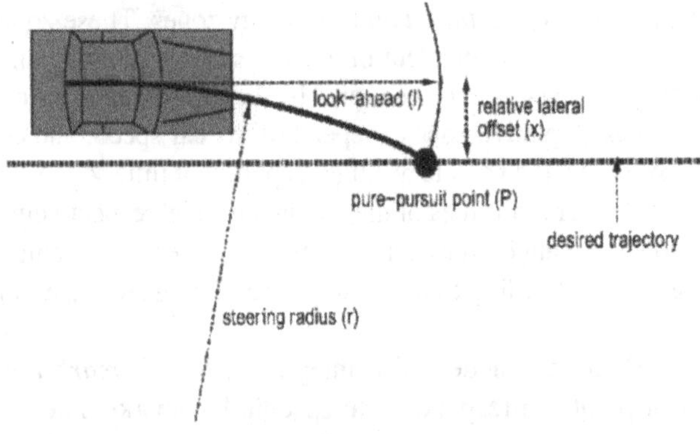

FIGURE 18.6. The pure-pursuit method.

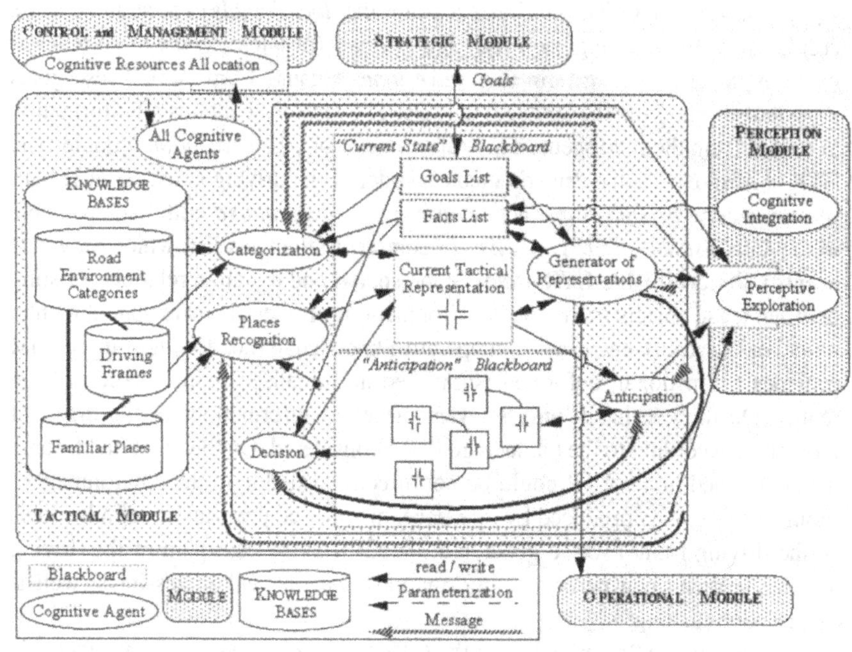

FIGURE 18.7. General architecture of the tactical module.

common storage structures: the *blackboards*. Consequently, problem solving (e.g. what driving action to take?) is distributed, resulting from the cooperation between several agents: each cognitive agent has only a part of the required expertise to find the solution. As the solving procedure progresses, the product of each agent reasoning is written in the blackboard. It then becomes available to the other agents sharing this blackboard, and they can then use these results to furthering their own reasoning. They can also modify the content of the blackboard and thus contribute to the collective solving of the problem. Communication between the cognitive agents of the tactical module can also be done via *message* sending. Lastly, the complexity and speed of the processes performed are dependent on the cognitive resources allocated to the solving agent by the *control and management* module. The quantity of resources allocated can change according to the number of active processes and their respective needs. A lower quantity of resources can slow down the agent computation, change the solving strategy or momentarily interrupt the process underway. Synthetically (Fig. 18.7), the tactical module is composed of two *blackboards*, three *knowledge bases* and five *cognitive agents*.

18.2.2.3 The Blackboards of the Tactical Module

The tactical module has two blackboards: the *current state blackboard* (CSB) and the *anticipation blackboard* (AB). The CSB contains all information related to the current driving situation. It includes a *goals list*, a *facts list* and a *current tactical representation* (CTR). The *goals list* contains the *'local' goals* to be attained in the current infrastructure (e.g. *turn left*) and *'global'* (or latent) *goals* to be reached in the more or less long term (e.g. *save time,* because I am late). These goals essentially come from the strategic module. The *facts list* contains all information extracted from the road scene. This data comes from the *perception* module. The CTR corresponds to the driver's mental model of the driving situation. It is built from a generic *driving frame* activated in LTM, *instantiated* with data available in the *facts list* and in the *goals list.* In contrast to the facts list, which only lists events individually, the CTR specifies the spatial and dynamic relations existing between these objects in the road environment. It provides a visuo-spatial mental model of the road scene. Based on operative knowledge (i.e. driving frame), CTR provides a functional, deformed, simplified and finalised representation of the reality. On the one hand, only relevant pieces of information for the driver at moment *t*, according to the pursued goal, are considered. On the other hand, some data contained in the CTR could be not directly available in the environment at moment *t* (e.g. data produced by inference, memorised previously, default values of the driving frame). Once generated, the CTR provides a plan of the driving activity. It orients new perceptive information collection and processing as well as the decision making.

The AB holds ARs derived from the CTR by the *anticipation* agent. Each AR constitutes a possible evolution of the current driving situation. ARs are organised in a tree, whose *root* corresponds to the CTR, *nodes* correspond to the potential future state of this situation (AR) and *links* between AR correspond to the *actions* to be carried out and/or the *conditions* to be complied with to go from one AR to the next one. Each AR is associated with two parameters indicating the *potential risk* and the *time saving* to pass from the previous AR to this new one. In some cases, these parameters come from default values (e.g. starting to cross the junction when the lights are amber presents systematically more risk than stopping, but allow the driver to save time). But generally, they depend on the current driving conditions (e.g. according to visibility, the configuration of the crossroads and the traffic conditions, the risk will be more or less important). *Anticipation* agent is in charge to assess the value of these parameters for each new temporal derivation (i.e. AR generation). This assessment is partly based on the *relative zone* conflicts between the own driver's car, on the one hand, and other road users, on the other (see Fig. 18.4). Furthermore, as the elaboration of the AR-tree progresses, *anticipation* computes the overall value of these two parameters for the whole branch that integrate the new derived AR (the whole sequence of AR starting from the RTC-root). These 'local' (from one AR to another one) or 'global' values (for the whole branch) will be then used by the *decision* agent to select the best action (or sequence of elementary actions) in the current context.

18.2.2.4 The Knowledge Bases (KB) of the Tactical Module

Several research carried out at INRETS (e.g. Van Elslande, 1992; Dubois et al., 1993; Bellet, 1998) on drivers knowledge modelling have permitted to identify two major types of driving knowledge: *declarative knowledge* describing the road context and *operative schemas* including procedural knowledge (i.e. practical know-how) required to drive the car in the road environment. Regarding COSMODRIVE, three specific KB are implemented at the tactical level: the *road environment categories* KB, the *familiar place* KB and the *driving frame* KB. These different knowledge bases are not independent from each other. Strongly interconnected, they constitute a global network handled by two cognitive agents specialised in information retrieval: *categorisation* and *place recognition*. The *road environment categories* KB is a typology of the different types of driving environment likely to be encountered by the driver. This KB is hierarchically structured (Bellet, 1998). At the top of the hierarchy can be found very generic categories corresponding to classes of *driving contexts* (urban, country, highway). On descending the hierarchy, the knowledge becomes more and more specialised (e.g. urban junction, access lane), until reaching precise categorisations of the driving context (e.g. 'crossroads with traffic lights in city centre'). The *familiar places* KB holds specific knowledge of the road sites familiar to the driver. This KB is a direct extension of the environment categories base: each familiar place constitutes a specific *instance* of one of the *classes* represented by the road categories. Lastly, the *driving frame* KB holds the driver's operative knowledge, as described earlier in this paper. Once activated and instantiated with reality (matching with objective characteristics of the infrastructure and integration of dynamic events), the driving frame becomes the CTR, and this mental model will be used for driving the car.

18.2.2.5 The Cognitive Processes of the Tactical Module

The central aim of this module is to simulate mental model of a road scene (CTR) elaboration in the human cognitive system. As mentioned above, this representation is built by matching a driving frame with perceptive information extracted from the driving environment. Integration of the perceptive information can be done according to two distinct modes. Either the information is actively sought by the driver (e.g. expectations of the probable event occurrence in such area of space), or the information is particularly salient and catches driver's attention (like a red light at night, on a deserted road). The first type of information integration is called *top–down* and is performed in COSMODRIVE by the *perceptive exploration* process. Indeed, this agent receives all the perceptive exploration queries from all the model's cognitive agents. According to their level of priority, perceptive exploration defines the visual strategies permitting the best response to these queries, then it positions the glance at the road scene. This leads to a change in the buffers of the perception module, and as soon as the information sought is found, it is sent to the requesting process(es). The second type of information integration is *bottom–up* and performed by the *cognitive integration* process. This can be likened to an array of filters that allows only the information of the perception module having greater physical magnitudes than certain thresholds (e.g. size, speed of movement, colour, shape, etc.) to pass into the tactical representation. The filters used as detection thresholds can vary according to the spatial position of the object in relation to a fixed point (e.g. distance, eccentricity), the characteristics of the environment (e.g. ambient luminosity) or those of the sensorial receivers (e.g. visual pathologies). These mechanisms, and the whole Perception module, are described in Mayenobe et al. (2004). Beyond perception module, five *cognitive agents* co-operate at the tactical level: (1) *categorisation*, (2) *place recognition*, (3) *tactical representation generator*, (4) *anticipation* and (5) *decision*. These agents run in parallel and they are potential users of cognitive resources.

18.2.2.5.1 Categorisation

The main function of this process is to provide a more or less precise categorisation of the road environment into which the driver is going. Furthermore, this agent simulates the retrieval processing of a relevant driving frame for car driving. To do this, *categorisation* attempts to match, on the one hand, the information contained in the hierarchy of *road environment categories* KB and, on the other, the data available in the fact list of the CSB. If the facts list does not contain any of the discriminatory criteria permitting the selection of a category, *categorisation* sends a queries to the *perceptive exploration* agent (perception module) in order to extract new data from the road scene. As soon as a category of road environments is identified, *categorisation* considers the list of goals to be attained, then it activates one of the frames (permitting to reach this goal) linked with this category (driving frame KB). The chosen frame is then transferred in the CSB, in place of the previous CTR.

18.2.2.5.2 The Place Recognition Process

As *categorisation*, the place recognition (PR) agent intervenes in recovering a driving frame from LTM. In this perspective, PR examines the CSB and attempts to match the facts it contains with the characteristics of one of the many places stored in the familiar places KB. As soon as a familiar place has been identified, PR examines the goals list, selects one of the driving frames associated with this familiar place, then it assures its transfer in the CSB. The tactical representation generator (TRG) agent can then use this representation 'as is' with the aim of orienting the driving activity in this particular place. Although the generic knowledge recovered by *categorisation* requires adaptation in order for it to fit with reality, the familiar place frames are very specific from the outset. Instantiation procedure implemented by TRG is therefore reduced (limited to only dynamic events) and its cognitive cost decreased.

18.2.2.5.3 The Tactical Representations Generator Process

This agent is the 'orchestral conductor' of the tactical module. The main cognitive tasks carried out by TRG are (1) the driving frame instantiation by integration of the current situation characteristics, (2) integration and interpretation of new data coming from the *perception* module, (3) to verify the CTR validity (e.g. has the situation changed; is the goal pursued still valid?) and, if necessary, participate in changing it, (4) activation the *decision* agent in order to determine what driving

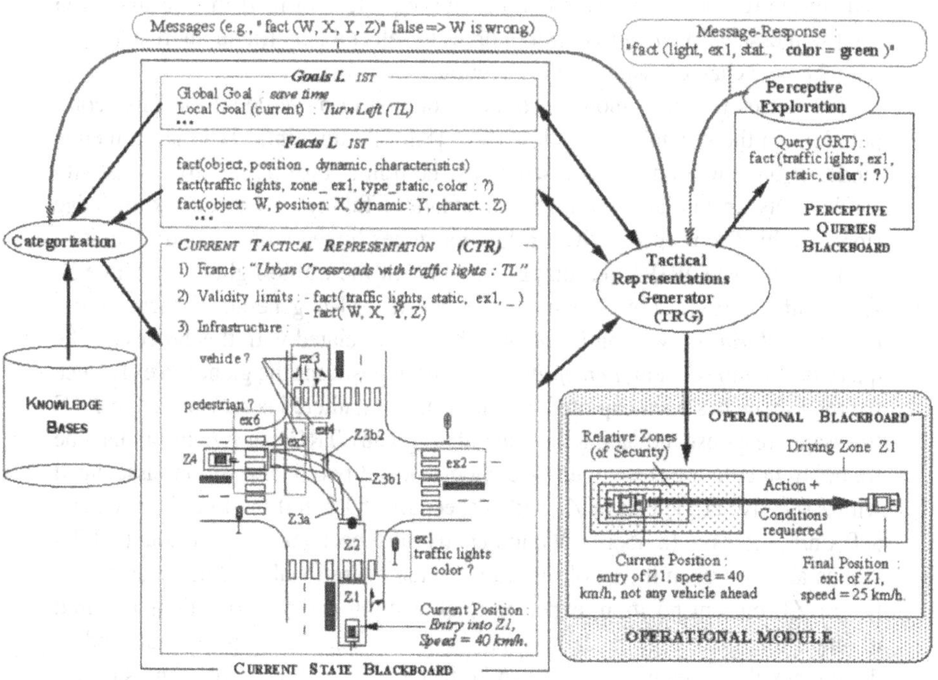

FIGURE 18.8. The TRG agent (tactical representations generator).

action should be taken, (5) sending this action to the operational module for its effective implementation and (6) checking that the chosen action provides the expected effects. Figure 18.8 illustrates the general activity of TRG in the turn left (TL) situation at an urban crossroads as observed on a real site. At moment *t0*, the driver enters the junction (initial state of Z1, speed 40 km/h). During the seconds preceding *t0*, the *categorisation* agent has selected a generic driving *frame 'crossroads with traffic lights: turn-on-the-left'*, then it transfers this frame to the CS Blackboard. From this time, TRG task is to instantiate this frame with reality. At this level, TRG must match the generic infrastructure contained in the frame with the real road environment. Dynamic objects present in the road scene are then integrated in the frame. At the end of this instantiation procedure, COSMODRIVE has a CTR corresponding to its own mental model of the world at this time *t0*. If nothing contradicts it, this CTR will guide the driver's actions until the frame is totally performed (exit of crossroads at Z4), according to some updating in order (a) to integrate new facts (TRG constantly consults the *facts list* for this purpose) and (b) take into account the progression of the vehicle's current position as it moves. Furthermore, a TRG verification procedure is in charge to assess the CRT validity. To carry this out, TRG verify if the changes observed in the *facts list* do not contradict the frame's validity limits (e.g. what has initially been identified as a traffic light is in fact a shop sign). It will also ensure that the goal pursued can actually be reached (e.g. diversion, prohibiting a left turn). If this occurs, TRG sends a message to *categorisation* in order to select a new frame, more adequate with the new characteristics of the situation.

Now, let us return to moment *t0*, and examine in more detail the TRG computations in the seconds that follow (Fig. 18.8). At this time, TRG has a mental model of the environment represented by the frame 'turn left at crossroads with traffic lights' instantiated with the real situation. Taking into account knowledge stored in this frame (perceptive exploration zones linked with the entry into Z1), the first COSMODRIVE reasoning will concern the traffic lights colour in ex1. As the information is not available in the facts list, TRG generates a query to *perceptive exploration* (writing in the blackboard associated with this process). The query taken into account, *perceptive exploration* positions the glance in ex1. Once the road scene has been explored, the information gathered is transmitted to TRG (message–response indicating that the light is green). TRG can then instantiate the frame (light colour ex1 = green) and choose one of two final positions associated with Z1: arrive at the exit of Z1 with a speed of 25 km/h if the light is green and at 0 km/h if it is red (amber light although has also been taken into account). TRG is thus able to transmit part of the frame to the operational module (characteristics of Z1, current position, expected final position and the conditions required to attain this goal, e.g. the light remains green). Then, the operational module determines the elementary actions to be taken (e.g. on the peddles and steering wheel) to change from 40 to 25 km/h along the Z1 straight length. This procedure only partially describes COSMODRIVE reasoning for decision making. In fact it is also equipped with anticipatory capacities: TRG usually does not need to take decision itself, but only validates the decisions previously taken by *anticipation* and *decision* agents.

18.2.2.5.4 The Anticipation Process

This agent's task is to predict changes in the current situation so as to orient driving behaviour. Anticipation mechanism is essential in order to overpass the reactive mode generally proposed by behavioural models. From a cognitive point of view, anticipation permits the human drivers to project themselves into the future. It is therefore possible to predict events and, more generally, to self prepare for any situational change before it occurs. Mental simulation is also used to assess the potential effects of an action and, on this basis, to compare this action with some of its alternatives in view to determining the most relevant behaviour in the current context. Anticipation is particularly essential in a dynamic situation. Without any capacity for anticipation, the driver's chances of survival should be limited! The greater the pressure of time becomes, the less time there is to act *in situation*, and the more anticipation plays a decisive role. At the level of COSMODRIVE, the anticipation process has the task of deriving, on the basis of the CTR, possible future states in the driving environment. Each derived state constitutes an AR. All the ARs generated are organised in the form of a tree whose nodes are constituted by different ARs and whose inter-AR links correspond to actions to be taken and/or conditions required to go from one AR to the next. The anticipation procedure starts by the transfer of the CTR in the AB. This will constitute the root of the ARs tree. Once this transfer has been performed, *anticipation* successively examines the different movement zones composing the driving path of the frame. It should be recalled that a movement zone is characterised by an *initial state* (the vehicle's position and speed when entering the zone), by a *goal state* (position and speed when leaving the zone), and by an *elementary action* to be taken to reach this goal state (on the tactical level, this action is limited to the command, 'attain goal state in this zone' which will be intimated to the operational module). This action is associated with *conditions* that cover events liable to occur in certain sections of the road environment (movement zones and perceptive exploration zones). During this examination, *anticipation* 'virtually executes' the frame. This amounts to 'taking stock': each zone is considered, the goal states are defined and the necessary conditions are explored (transmission of queries to *perceptive exploration* in order to check the facts corresponding to these conditions). Nonetheless, this 'deployment' of the frame can be so costly in cognitive terms that, according to the available time and resources, it will not be possible to derive all the ARs. In this context, *anticipation* will give priority to the movement zone(s) immediately consecutive to the current zone. Beyond these, the *decision* agent determines the better derivation strategy according to its own requirements.

18.2.2.5.5 The Decision Process

This agent's task consists in examining the different ARs contained in the AB, in making a selection from among these and in instantiating the CTR of the CSB as a consequence. The TRG agent then transfers the actions associated with these different ARs to the operational module, in order to implement them. More specifically, the decision-making process supposes (1) to consider the AB with the aim to determine what branch of the AR tree is most adapted to the present context, (2) to select the first AR of the branch (that immediately succeeding the current zone already taken in hand by the operational module), (3) to instantiate the corresponding movement zone of the CTR contained in the AB, (4) to wait for the message from TRG indicating that this solution has been transmitted to the operational module, (5) to restart the same procedure for the following zone and (6) so forth until reaching the last zone of the frame. Furthermore, the *decision* agent does not simply wait for solutions proposed by *anticipation*. It also plays an active role in the AR derivation procedure. *Decision* permanently supervises the work done by *anticipation*: Each new derived AR is examined with respect to decision-making criteria (such as *risk* run and saving or loss of *time*) and, according to whether these criteria are satisfied or not, *decision* determines the best derivation strategy to be adopted. Insofar as the criteria of the moment are conformed to, an 'in-depth first' research strategy will be given priority in order to result in one of the frame goal states as soon as possible. Inversely, if the derived AR proves itself to be incompatible with the decision-making criteria taken into account at this moment (risk judged too high, for example), *decision* will choose a 'wide first' strategy in order to examine other ARs liable to offer a more appropriate solution.

18.3 Methodology to Study Driver's Situation Awareness

As previously described, COSMODRIVE provides a theoretical framework to analyse and simulate the cognitive processes involved in drivers' mental model elaboration. This part of the chapter presents a specific methodology developed at LESCOT (Bailly et al., 2003; Bailly, 2004) in order to experimentally study the 'quality' of these internal models (adequacy with the reality), according to several sources of variation like driver's experience (experienced *versus* novice drivers comparison) and the quantity of cognitive resources available and/or the attention sharing effect due to the impact of a secondary task of mental arithmetic. Beyond these fundamental objectives, the aim was also to design a tool able to raise drivers' awareness of a secondary task impact on driving performance.

18.3.1 Main Hypothesis

Two main hypotheses have been investigated in this part of the research program. The first one suggests a better performance for experienced drivers (EDs) than for novices due to the benefit given by driving knowledge. The second one postulates a negative impact of a secondary task on the experiment performance. Concerning the potential impact of driving experience, several studies have shown better performances of EDs in terms of visual search, information processing, mental model elaboration and driving situation understanding (Mourant and Rockwell, 1972; Chapman and Underwood, 1998; Bellet, 1998; Crundall et al., 1999). According to the COSMODRIVE framework, it is expected that the driving frames used by expert drivers allow them to have better perceptive explorations of the road scene (i.e. focused on the most relevant information), increase information processing performances and, consequently, provide a more adequate mental model of the current driving situation (i.e. better understanding and awareness of what is happening on the road). Concerning the potential effect of a secondary task, several studies have shown that parallel activities while driving (e.g. telephoning) have a negative impact in terms of reaction time, visual strategies, situation awareness and, more generally, risk of accident (Lamble et al., 1999; Recarte and Nunes, 2000). From this point of view, it is expected that participants' mental model will be potentially impaired by the mental arithmetic task. Beyond that this research aims to determine more precisely the nature of this effect on the CTR (as described in COSMODRIVE model). Two main questions will be more particularly considered: Which kind of information is more 'robust' in terms of lack of cognitive resources impact (event occurrences *versus* infrastructure components like road signs)? Are there any differences according to the distance of the element considered (e.g. is far *versus* nearby information more or less impaired by the secondary task)? The last aspect of this experiment is focused on potential links between these two sources of variation (driving experience, on one side, and secondary task impact, on the other side). This research aims also to compare the accuracy of the CTR, according to a combined effect of these two dimensions.

18.3.2 Methodology

A specific methodology has been developed in order to study these questions (Bailly et al., 2003; Bailly, 2004). The experimental plan comprises 40 video sequences of driving situations. Participants are invited to look at these video films on a TV screen. At the end of each sequence, the video suddenly stops. Then, the last picture of the video film appears on the TV and subjects have (a) to determine if something has changed or not and (b) to indicate the nature and the location of the detected modification(s). Modifications can occur on events (e.g. add or suppress car) or on road infrastructure components (e.g. add or suppress road signs or change traffic lights colours). Forty participants (20 novices and 20 EDs) took part in this study. During the first phase of the experience, the subjects' task is limited to looking at 20 video sequences (*simple task* condition). During the second phase, video observation is done with an additional task (mental arithmetic; *dual task* condition). At this level, the aim is to analyse the impact of a secondary task on the tactical representation content and the attention sharing strategies required through lack of cognitive resources. Note that the 40 video sequences have been divided into two series. According to a turning experimental plan, each of the two series has been equally used in the simple task (ST) and in the dual task (DT) conditions.

18.3.3 Main Results

Results obtained reveal several things. Firstly, the modification detection is strongly dependent on the driving experience. Indeed, if we consider the global performance (including both experimental conditions, ST and DT), EDs obtained better results than novices (68.2% versus 50.6% of right detection) (Fig. 18.9). If we consider driving experience effect for, respectively, each of the two experimental conditions, this difference is significant for the ST (74.9% for ED versus 58.5% for novices) as well as for the DT condition (61.5% versus 42.7%). From another point of view, the lack of cognitive resources has a negative effect on the detection performance. For EDs, the detection performance decreases from 74.9% (ST) to 61.5% (DT) if cognitive resources are allocated to an additional task. The same effect is observed for novice drivers (58.5% versus 42.7%). These results clearly demonstrate that cognitive resources are required to build a reliable mental model of the driving situation: The DT negative impact on mental model quality is systematically significant and concerns all drivers.

Concerning driving experience and DT effects, according to the nature of modifications (events versus infrastructure), Fig. 18.10 shows that EDs are always better than novices of detecting all types of modification (for *infrastructure* as well as *event*).

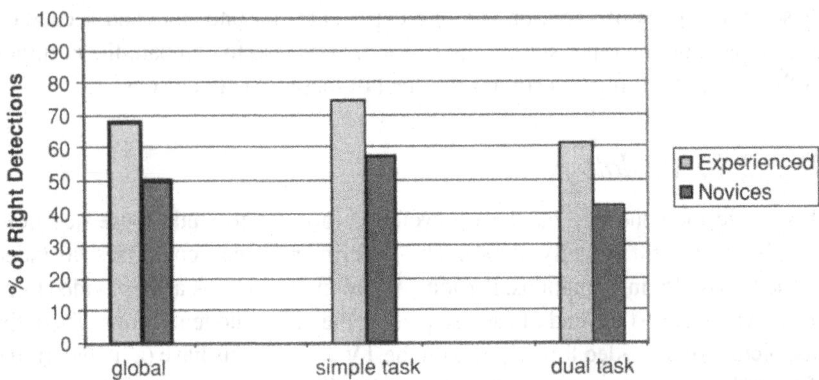

FIGURE 18.9. Percentage of right detection according to the experimental conditions (ST versus DT).

For the ST condition, EDs detected 79.1% of the road infrastructure component modifications, whereas novices detected only 60.9%. Concerning event modifications, EDs obtained 70% of right detection, whereas novices obtained only 55.8%. The same tendency is observed for the DT condition. EDs detected 57.3% of road infrastructure modifications, whereas novices detected only 36.4%. For events modifications, EDs' performance is 66.3% and novices' performance is 50%. If we consider, for each population of drivers (ED *versus* novices), the secondary task impact according to the nature of modifications, the results reveals a difference between event versus infrastructure. On the one hand, the secondary task has a significant effect on the infrastructure modification detection for all

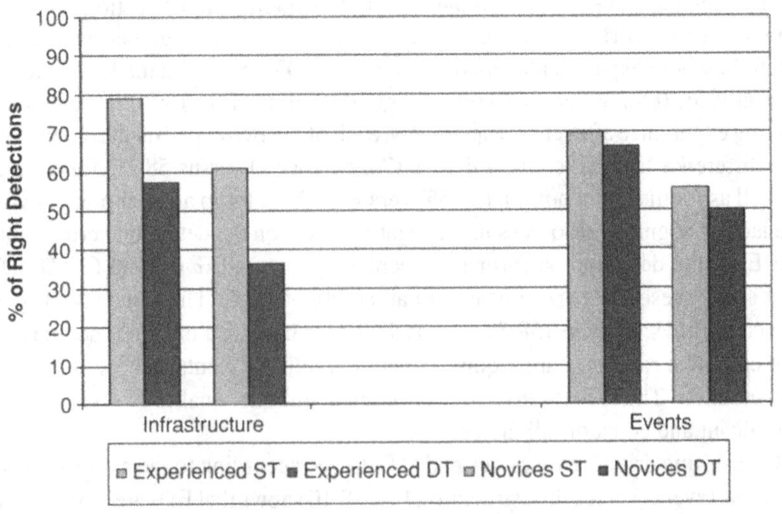

FIGURE 18.10. Percentage of right detection according to the nature of the modification.

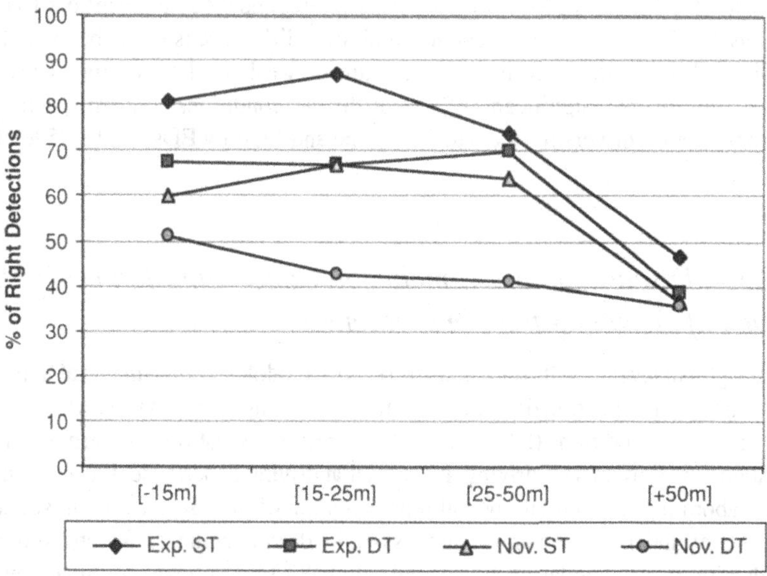

FIGURE 18.11. Percentage of right detection according to the distance of modifications.

the drivers (respectively, 79.1% versus 57.3% for ED and 60.9% versus 36.4 for novice drivers). On the other hand, no significant effect was found concerning event modifications according to the ST versus DT condition (even if the performance is globally better for ST condition). The result is the same for EDs (70% in ST versus 66.3% in DT, but $khi_2 = 0.594$, $p = 0.441$) and for novice drivers (55.8% in ST versus 50% in DT, but $khi_2 = 1.278$, $p = 0.258$). In other words, event modification detection is clearly more 'robust' (i.e. lesser effect of the DT condition) than infrastructure components modification detection.

The last comparison presented herein concerns the distance of the modified component. Four distances have been defined: 0 to 15 m (*nearby zone*), 15 to 25, 25 to 50, and beyond 50 m (*far zone*). Performances for each distance are compared according to the drivers' experience and to the secondary task effect (Fig. 18.11). In ST conditions, EDs obtain better results than novices for modifications concerning the nearby zone (81.3% versus 60%) and also for modifications in the 15 to 25 m zone (87.1% versus 67.1%). Beyond 25 m, differences between ED and novices are not significant. For the DT conditions, differences between experts and novices are significant for three of the four distances considered. Performances are, respectively, 67.5% (expert) versus 51.3% (novices) for the nearby zone (0 to 15 m), 67.1% versus 42.9% for the 15 to 25 m zone, and 70% versus 41.4% for the 25 to 50 m zone. No significant effect is found for the far zone. If we now consider, for each population of drivers, the secondary task impact according to the distance of modifications, the results reveal some relevant differences. For EDs, a DT significant effect occurs in the nearby zone (81.3% versus 67.5%) and for the 15 to 25 m zone (87.1% *versus* 67.1%). However, for novices drivers, DT impact concerns the 15 to 25 m zone (67.1% *versus* 42.9%) and the 25 to 50 m zone (64.3% *versus* 41.4%). For all the drivers, no significant difference is found beyond 50 m, probably because the performances were already weak in ST conditions. The other main relevant 'non-significant' effects of the DT conditions concern specifically (a) only novice drivers for the 0 to 15 m zone and (b) only EDs for the 25 to 50 m zone.

18.3.4 Discussion and Conclusion Concerning Experimental Study of Drivers Situation Awareness

At the global level, results obtained with this methodology confirm initial hypotheses. Firstly, modification detection is better for EDs than for novices, whatever the experimental conditions (ST and DT). Insofar as modifications concern only relevant information for safe driving, it means that driving experience is a key element for elaborating an accurate mental representation of the current driving situation (i.e. better understanding and awareness of the driving context). Secondly, the introduction of a secondary task (mental arithmetic) has a negative impact on the mental model elaboration. This effect is significant for all drivers (novices as well as EDs). Fundamentally, to carry out a mental arithmetic task, cognitive resources are required. Consequently, other mental activities that require cognitive resources (i.e. involving controlled processes) will be affected (i.e. cognitive resources and attention sharing between the primary and the secondary task) (Schneider and Schiffrin, 1977; Schneider and Chein, 2003). On the contrary, the DT does not have impact on automatic processing. From this theoretical point of view, results obtained in this experiment reveal several things. Firstly, mental model tactical representation elaboration partly requires cognitive resources (i.e. mental model building is not only based on automatic processing). Moreover, the DT effect is proportionately more important for novices than for EDs. It means that driving experience also has a positive effect in managing a secondary task and in sharing attention during driving. Lastly, the DT impact allows us to reveal the level of priority of information collected in the environment and integrated in the drivers' mental model. Indeed, the DT condition considerably reduces the quantity of cognitive resources available. Consequently, only the most relevant and salient pieces of information will be taken into account. In terms of experimental test performances, it means that the secondary task effects are inversely proportional to the level of relevance and/or salience of information. In other words, 'non-significant effects' of the DT condition (compared to the ST condition) will indicate a high level of relevance and/or salience of this specific information. Concerning this aspect, an interesting result has been obtain according to the distance, via the specific 'no significant effects' found, respectively, for each population of drivers. For EDs, DT does not impact detection performance for the 25 to 50 m zone, whereas for novices, DT have no effect for the nearby zone (0 to 15 m). This result reveals a difference between novices and EDs concerning the main 'focal point' used for visual scanning of the driving scene. For novices, perceptive explorations are first and foremost focused on the nearby environment of the vehicle. For EDs, the focal point is between 25 and 50 m ahead the car (between 2 and 3.5 s).

18.4 Some Experimental Results Simulation with Cosmodrive

By considering this type of experimental results, it is possible to use COSMODRIVE simulation to visualise drivers' mental models of the road scene at different times. Figures 18.12 to 18.14 give some examples of mental models content, according to driving experience and attention sharing (i.e. lack of cognitive resources) effects.

Figure 18.12 typically illustrates mental model differences between experienced *versus* novice drivers, in ST conditions (i.e. all driver's attention is focused on the road). At this time of the driving situation, main dynamic significant events (salient and close) have been perceived and integrated by all the drivers in their mental representation. Nevertheless, only EDs have generally take into account the car coming in front of us, with the future aim to turn on the left. According to COSMODRIVE model, it is possible to explain this result by *anticipation* agent reasoning through the turning-left frame *deployment* (i.e. mental simulation of the driving situation evolution). An event is more particularly significant if its trajectory interferes with our own driver's trajectory. From this point of view, the opposite car will be particularly important in the future. Nevertheless, novices' attention is essentially focused on interactions with nearest events. Consequently, they generally neglect this long-term event at this time. On the contrary, anticipation abilities of EDs allow them to anticipate the future 'turning-left' phase (i.e. mental examination of the driving frame 'Z3' zone) for adequately planning their behaviour. As a result, the majority of EDs are generally aware, since the approaching phase (Z1) of this incoming car occurrence and of the potential conflicts with it in the future.

Figure 18.13 illustrates the potential impact of attention sharing on mental models. For novice drivers, the lack of cognitive resources involves an attention focalisation on the nearby zone (i.e. vehicles behaviours on the left side), but nothing

FIGURE 18.12. Novice (view) versus experienced drivers (right) mental model in a ST condition.

FIGURE 18.13. Novice (left) versus experienced (right) drivers' mental model in dual-task condition.

is observe and known concerning the traffic flow in the intersection itself. On the contrary, EDs focused as a priority the residual attention on the 25 to 50 m zone. If some secondary events are potentially missing, experienced drivers have generally integrated at this time the most significant events (i.e. car coming from the opposite direction) in relation with their own "left-turn" goal.

Lastly, Fig. 18.14 illustrates the COSMODRIVE simulation interest in order to dynamically visualise mental models evolution, during the whole approaching phase of the crossroad. If we consider, for example, the previous novices' mental model in DT condition, drivers' attention will gradually be focused on the area ahead as they progress on the road and the traffic flow will be finally considered (and partly integrated) a few seconds latter.

FIGURE 18.14. Example of simulation of a novices' mental model evolution during the whole crossroad approaching phase (zone Z1 of the driving frame).

18.5 Conclusion and Perspectives: From Behaviours to Mental Model

Several recent researches, carried out at INRETS-LESCOT, have been presented in this paper. The common point of these works is the drivers' mental model study (i.e. internal representation of the current driving situation), with the aim to simulate this cognitive component on computer. The central part of this human modelling program is the COSMODRIVE described in the third part, by considering (a) its cognitive architecture, (b) the formalism used to represent driving knowledge and simulate mental models and (c) the cognitive processes involved at the tactical level of the driving activity. The fourth part of the paper focused on a specific methodology developed at LESCOT in order to experimentally study the 'quality' of these mental models (i.e. its adequacy with the information available in the road scene), according to several sources of variation (driver's experience and cognitive resources available). We would like to conclude this paper by a short presentation of a starting research in the field of Humanist Network of Excellence, with the aim to define a theoretical and methodological framework to carry out a cognitive analysis of the car driving activity. From a practical point of view, the goal is to develop models, methods and cognitive engineering tools for 'ecological' data (collected in real driving conditions) processing and analysis in order to infer driver's situation awareness (i.e. mental model) from driving activity 'traces'. Concerning drivers behaviour modelling, the research will use the 'driving frame' approach defined at LESCOT. Indeed, *driving frames* formalism can be used for modelling the driving activity as well as the driver's mental models. This new research will aim to define methods and develop computational tools in order to 'abstract' the driving frames from objective data including (a) driver's behaviours, (b) vehicle state and (c) environmental conditions.

Concerning artificial intelligence and cognitive engineering tools, the research will use the MUSETTE (*modelling uses and tasks for tracing experience*) methods (Fig. 18.15) developed at LIRIS (Champin et al., 2004). Figure 18.16 illustrates

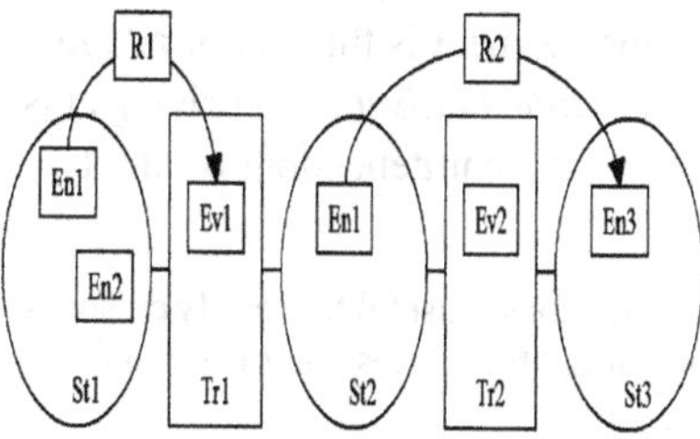

FIGURE 18.15. 'Primitive trace' encoding.[1]

[1] The MUSETTE theory provides a method for encoding traces of human behaviours. The first level of trace, called rough trace, is made up of a succession of observables, called objects of interest (OI). The second level of trace, called primitive trace, is a succession of states and transitions embedding the OIs. OIs are of three kinds: 'entities' (static facts) allowing description of states, 'events' allowing description of transitions and 'relations' from entities or events to each other. In Fig. 18.15, states are represented by circles, transitions by rectangles, entities are labelled En, events are labelled Ev and

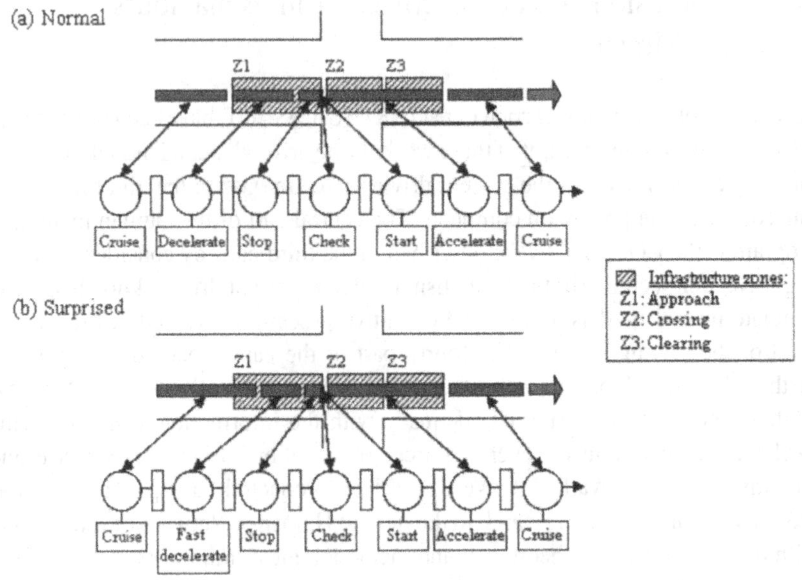

FIGURE 18.16. Normal versus surprised operational sub-schema.[2]

how it is possible to connect a low-level *trace* of the driving activity (i.e. *operational sub-schemas*) to the upper descriptive level embodied by the *tactical driving frames*. This work falls under the LESCOT's effort to better understand the car driving activity. Within this new framework, the possibility of automatically assess the driver's situation awareness from driving behaviours could have multiple uses such as to get a better understanding of the accidents or to identify needs or possibilities of assistance. In a long-term perspective, it could also be a first step towards *adaptive technologies* based on a mental model sharing between, on one side, the human driver and, on the other, driving aids (Bellet et al., 2003).

Providing assistance that is adapted to the current driver's needs and to the specific characteristics of the driving situation of the moment is the aim of adaptive technologies. The objective is to head towards the *contextualisation* of driving aids. It is easy to imagine that driver's needs may be different depending on the type

---

relations are labelled R. The cutting into states and transitions is useful to identify episodes, which consist of passing from one state to another through a succession of intermediate states.

[2] The creation of the primitive traces led us to widen a tactical driving frame to a finer granularity level. This level is called operational sub-schema. This representation allows us to describe tiny differences between situations. Figure 18.16 shows how we can represent a 'surprised driver' sub-schema that is characterised by an initial 'Cruise' state that encroaches on the approach zone (Z1) of the infrastructure, followed by a 'strongly decelerate' state characterised by a value of deceleration higher than in the normal sub-schema. From future developments we want to implement search functionalities, which enable us to find patterns in the primitive trace likely to match with a tactical driving frame, according to specified criteria (Georgeon et al., 2005).

of the driving task (e.g. monotonous driving on motorways, going through roads junctions in urban areas, overtaking), depending on the driving conditions (e.g. traffic density, weather conditions), or depending on the driver's permanent (e.g. age) or momentary capacities (e.g. cognitive resources available, state of stress, fatigue). *Contextualising aid* involves developing technologies that are 'open to the world', that is to say capable to assess – in real time – the driver's activities and all the requirements dictated by driving conditions. This must all be done to (a) determine if it is necessary or not to assist the driver in the present situation and (b) identify the kind of aid required in this specific context and the form it should take (giving information to the driver, warning him of a danger, or taking control of the vehicle). We can also imagine using this kind of analysis capacity for diagnosing human errors: Is the driver's behaviour appropriate according to the characteristics of the driving situation? Alternatively, does the driver's behaviour present certain risks not taken into account by human awareness? Several researches have been done at LESCOT concerning adaptive technologies (see Bellet et al., 2003), with the aim to manage on-board information or to design cooperative collision avoidance system. Nevertheless the previous works were based on behavioural analysis methods, but not on a cognitive simulation model. This new research will explore this possibility by using some part of COSMODRIVE model. It could be a first step to bring man–machine cooperation closer to man–man cooperation situations in which two human agents (the driver and the co-driver) co-ordinate their efforts to carry out the driving task together. In this context, each partner mentally imagines the activities of the other partner (i.e. activities he does and those of which he is in charge) and uses this internal model for interacting with him in an appropriate way. In terms of man–machine cooperation, this means 'symetrising' the man–machine relationship (Amalberti and Deblon, 1992) and developing technology capable to represent itself the human partner activity (by using a more or less complex internal model) like the human partner imagines (through a more or less true *mental model*) the technological system in charge to assist him or her (i.e. what it is supposed to do, what it really does and, if needs be, the way it goes about doing it).

References

Allen, T.M., Lunenfield, H. and Alexander, G.J. (1971). Driver information needs. *Highway Research Record*, 366, 102–115.

Amalberti, R. and Deblon, F. (1992). Cognitive modelling of fighter aircraft's control process: A step towards intelligent onboard assistance system. *International Journal of Man–Machine Studies*, 36, 639–671.

Amidi, O. (1990). Integrated mobile robot control. Technical Report CMU-RI-TR-90-17. Carnegie Mellon University Robotics Institute.

Bailly, B. (2004). *Conscience de la situation des conducteurs: Aspects fondamentaux, méthodes, et applications pour la formation des conducteurs*. PhD Thesis, Université Lyon 2.

Bailly, B., Bellet, T. and Goupil, C. (2003). Driver's mental representations: Experimental study and training perspectives. In *Proceedings of the 1st International Conference on Driver Behaviour and Training*, Stratford-upon-Avon, England. CD-ROM, 8 pp.

Bellet, T. (1998). *Modélisation et simulation cognitive de l'opérateur humain: une application à la conduite automobile*. PhD Thesis, Université Paris V.

Bellet, T. and Tattegrain-Veste, H. (1999). A framework for representing driving knowledge. *Intenational Journal of Cognitive Ergonomics*, 3(1), 37–49.

Bellet, T. and Tattegrain-Veste, H. (2003). COSMODRIVE: un modèle de simulation cognitive du conducteur automobile. In J.C. Spérandio and M. Wolf (Eds.). *Formalismes de modélisation pour l'analyse du travail et l'ergonomie* (pp. 77–110). Presses Universitaires de France, Paris.

Bellet, T., Tattegrain-Veste, H., Chapon, A., Bruyas, M.P., Pachiaudi, G., Deleurence, P. and Guilhon, V. (2003). Ingénierie cognitive dans le contexte de l'assistance à la conduite automobile. In G. Boy (Ed.). *L'Ingénierie Cognitive: IHM et Cognition*. Hermès, Paris.

Cacciabue, P.C., Decortis, F., Drozdowicz, B., Masson, M. and Nordvik, J.P. (1992). COSIMO: A cognitive simulation model of human decision making and behaviour in accident management of complex plants. *IEEE Transaction on Systems, Man and Cybernetics, IEEE-SMC*, 22(5), 1058–1074.

Champin, P.-A., Prie, Y. and Mille, A. (2004). Musette: A framework for knowledge capture from experience. In *Proceedings of EGC04*, Clermont Ferrand, France.

Chapman, P.R. and Underwood, G. (1998). Visual search of dynamic scenes: Event types and the role of experience in viewing driving simulation. In G. Underwood (Ed.). *Eye Guidance in Reading and Scene Perception*. Elsevier, North Holland.

Crundall, D., Underwood, G. and Chapman, P. (1999). Driving experience and the functional field of view. *Perception*, 28, 1075–1087.

Dubois, D., Fleury, D. and Mazet, C. (1993). Représentations catégorielles: perception et/ou action? Contribution à partir d'une analyse des situations routières. In A. Weill-Fassina, P. Rabardel and D. Dubois (Eds.). *Représentations pour l'action* (pp. 79–93). Octares Editions, Toulouse.

Endsley, M.R. (1995). Toward a theory of situation awareness in dynamic systems. *Human Factors*, 37(1), 32–64.

Georgeon, O., Bellet, T., Mille, A., Lettisserand, D. and Martin, R. (2005). Driver behaviour modelling and cognitive tools development in order to assess driver situation awareness. In *Proceedings of HUMANIST Workshop on Driver Modelling*, Ispra, Italy, 25–27 May 2005.

Gibson, J.J. and Crooks, L.E. (1938). A theoretical field-analysis of automobile driving. *American Journal of Psychology*, 51, 453–471.

Hall, E.T. (1966). *The Hidden Dimension*. Doubleday, Garden City.

Fuller, R.A. (1984). Conceptualization of driving behaviour as threat avoidance. *Ergonomics*, 27(11), 1139–1155.

Kontaratos, N.A. (1974). A system analysis of the problem of road causalities in the United State. *Accident Analysis and Prevention*, 6, 223–241.

Krajzewicz, D., Hühne, R.D. and Wagner, P. (2004). A car driver cognition model. In *Proceedings of ITS Safety and Security 2004*, Miami Beach, FL, 24–25 March 2004.

Lamble, D., Kauranen, T., Laakso, M. and Summala, H. (1999). Cognitive load and detection thresolds in car following situations: Safety implications for using mobile (cellular) telephones while driving. *Accident Analysis and Prevention*, 31, 617–623.

Levison, W.H. (1993). A simulation model for driver's use of in-vehicle information systems. *Transportation Research Record*, 1403, 7–13.

Mayenobe, P. (2004). *Perception de l'environnement pour une gestion contextualisée de la coopération Homme-Machine*. PhD Thesis, University Blaise Pascal de Clermont-Ferrand.

Mayenobe, P., Blanc, C., Trassoudaine, L., Bellet, T. and TattegrainVeste, H. (2003). Active perception tasks driven by a cognitive simulation model. In *Proceedings of the IEEE Intelligent Vehicles Symposium: IV-2003*, Columbus, OH (pp. 378–382).

Mayenobe, P., Trassoudaine, L., Bellet, T. and TattegrainVeste, H. (2002). Cognitive simulation of the driver and cooperative driving assistances. In *Proceedings of the IEEE Intelligent Vehicles Symposium: IV-2002*, Versailles, June 17–21, 2002 (pp. 265–271).

Mc Knight, A.J. and Adams, B.B. (1970). *Driver Education Task Analysis. Vol. I: Task Descriptions.* Human Resources Research Organisation HumRRO, Alexandria.

Mourant, R.R. and Rockwell, T.H. (1972). Strategies of visual search by novices and experiences drivers. *Human Factors*, 14(4), 325–335.

Michon, J.A. (1985). A critical view of driver behavior model: What do we know, what should we do? In Evans and R.C. Schwing (Eds.). *Human Behavior and Traffic Safety* (pp. 485–520). Plenum Press, New York.

Minsky, M. (1975). A framework for representing knowledge. In P. Winston (Ed.). *The Psychology of computer vision* (pp. 211–281). McGraw-Hill, New York.

Näätänen, R. and Summala, H. (1976). A model for the role of motivational factors in driver's decision-making. *Accident Analysis and Prevention*, 6, 243–261.

Ochanine, V.A. (1977). Concept of operative image in engineering and general psychology. In B.F. Lomov, V.F. Rubakhin and V.F. Venda (Eds.). *Engineering Psychology*. Science Publisher, Moscow.

Otha, H. (1993). Individual differences in driving distance headway. In A.G. Gale (Ed.). *Vision in Vehicles IV*. Elsevier, Netherlands.

Rasmussen, J. (1983). Skills, rules and knowledge; Signals, signs and symbols and other distinctions in human performance models. *IEEE Transaction on Systems, Man and Cybernetics*, 13(3), 257–266.

Recarte, M.A. and Nunes, L.M. (2000). Effect of verbal and spatial-imagery task on eye fixations while driving. *Journal of Experimental Psychology: Applied*, 6, 31–43.

Rumbaugh, J., Blaha, J., Eddy, F., Lorensen, W. and Premerlani, W. (1991). *Object Oriented Modeling and Design*. Prentice Hall, Londres.

Salvucci, D.D., Boer, E.R. and Liu, A. (2001). Toward an integrated model of driver behavior in a cognitive architecture. *Transportation Research Record*, 1779, 9–16.

Schneider, W. and Schiffrin, R.M. (1977). Controlled and automatic human information processing I: Detection, search, and attention. *Psychological Review*, 84(1), 1–66.

Schneider, W. and Chein J.M. (2003). Controlled and automatic processing: Behavior, theory, and biological mechanisms. *Cognitive Science*, 27, 525–559.

Sukthankar, R. (1997). *Situation Awareness for Tactical Driving*. PhD Thesis, Carnegie Mellon University.

Thom, R. (1991). *Prédire n'est pas expliquer*. Eshel, Paris.

Van der Molen, H.H. and Bötticher, M.T. (1988). A hierarchical risk model for traffic participants. *Ergonomics*, 31(4), 537–555.

Van Elslande, P. (1992). Les erreurs d'interprétation en conduite automobile: mauvaise catégorisation ou activation erronée de schémas? *Intellectica*, 15(3), 125–149.

Wierda, M. and Aasman, J. (1992). Seeing and driving: Computation, algorithms and implementation. Traffic Research Centre, University of Groningen, Netherlands, Haren: Verkeerskundig Studiecentrum, VK91-06.

Wilde, G.J.S. (1982). Critical issues in risk homeostasis theory. *Risk Analysis*, 2(4), 249–258.

19
Simple Simulation of Driver Performance for Prediction and Design Analysis

P. C. CACCIABUE, C. RE, AND L. MACCHI

19.1 Introduction

19.1.1 Modelling Human Behaviour in Modern Technology

The ability to model and predict Human–Machine Interaction (HMI) with consistent approaches is a crucial aspect of modern technological systems, where the consideration for the presence of humans in control of systems is necessary at design level as well as during production and implementation processes. A reliable and realistic approach that enables to anticipate what will be "done" at different levels of cognition and behaviour by a human being, enables the prevention of erroneous or risky behaviour, as well the implementation of means of intervention exploiting the power of modern technologies and the decision making skill of humans.

The literature of the last decades is rich with methods that focus on this subject. A comprehensive and short review of methodological approaches and theoretical constructs has been given by Moray (1997), covering the last 30 years of research and development in the field of human factors applied to different domains and industrial settings.

In modern systems, modelling human behaviour entails considering primarily cognitive processes and system dynamic evolution, i.e., mental activities, resulting from the time-dependent interaction of humans and machines. In this sense, a model of human behaviour cannot be developed in total isolation and abstraction, but it must be coupled and linked to a model of plant performance in order to develop the simulation of a 'joint' human–machine system, also called 'Joint Cognitive System' (Hollnagel and Woods, 1983; Hollnagel, 1993). Therefore any model of human behaviour comes necessarily framed in a clear interaction context with the associated technological system.

The formulation of models of HMI is an evolutionary process whose origin lies in the cybernetic paradigm of Wiener (1948), who developed the analogy between the human operator and the servomechanism, and in the similarities between computers and brains pointed out by von Neumann (1958). These analogies have increased the awareness of the closed-loop nature of HMI, with the specific goal-oriented behaviour of the human controller. However, the most substantial theories on human behaviour derived from these first paradigms did not consider the predictive nature of human behaviour, as all relevant human activities were practically associated with manual control and direct interaction with physical phenomena. The inclusion of the human element in the control loop of a process was thus a simple exercise of mathematical consideration of action delays and parameters estimation.

The progress of technology towards supervisory control and automation required the formulation of much more complex models of human reasoning and decision making processes, able to account primarily for cognitive rather than manual activities. The need of simulating the *man-plus-the-controlled-element* was then enunciated in the 1960s by McRuer and colleagues (1965). Other pioneering research in this area, combined with the development of computer technologies, inspired the first formulations of theoretical models of cognition (Neisser, 1967) and, in the early 1970s, the metaphor of the operator as *Information Processing System* (Newell and Simon, 1972).

Since then, a variety of paradigms of human behaviour have been developed (Rouse, 1980; Rasmussen, 1983; Stassen et al., 1990; Sheridan, 1992; Wickens, 1984, 2002), which aim to cover different levels of complexity and depth in representing mental processes, cognitive functions as well as behavioural performances. These models vary quite substantially for many reasons. Certain models focus on a specific domain of application. Other models pay attention primarily to cognitive functions, such as decision making or diagnostic processes. Certain models concentrate on the role of operators and their interactions, such as supervisory control process and teamwork.

This variety of models offers the analysts and designers of joint cognitive systems the possibility to choose the most suitable approach and paradigm to apply for specific applications. However, in order to make the best selection in relation to the problem at hand, the scope of application of the available methods and models must be recognised. The existence of conceptual frameworks that enable to identify boundaries and areas of consideration for modelling human behaviour is discussed in detail in Chapter 2 of this book.

19.1.2 Modelling Drivers in the Automotive Context

Focusing on the problems associated with modelling driver behaviour, it is important to realise that what may seem a simple domain to account for is instead much more complex and varied than other similar environments with high levels of automation and complexity. The major peculiarities of the automotive environment are associated with five specific aspects, namely: the *Users* of vehicles; the *Temporal Aspects* of the HMI; the driving *Working Context*; the *Social Environment* in which driving occurs; and finally, the type and mode of *System Integration* that occurs with respect to the actual technical systems made available by different manufacturers.

- *Users*
  A large variety of people can obtain a driver license. These include teenagers, elderly and disabled persons. In other domains, the types of users are much less

variable. Moreover, drivers receive minimal initial training, often little or no refresher training at all, and no training with specific new vehicles or devices. In contrast, the users of plants and systems in other domains (e.g. pilots, air traffic controllers, control room operators, medical staff, technicians and so forth) may be highly selected, relatively homogenous, well trained and supervised or monitored.

- *Temporal Demands*
  The temporal demands for in-vehicle warning practises are typically much more time-critical than for other applications. For a potential crash situation, there may be only a second or two between the recognition of conflict and the moment of the impact. In contrast, emergency situations in other contexts may be measured in tens of seconds or even minutes.
- *Working Context*
  Most technological domains are based on specific and dedicated workplace environments. This is not the case for automotive domain. This difference has many implications in terms of acceptability of constraints and practices and assumptions about the user. As an example, the acceptable level of intrusiveness or annoyance and tolerance for false alarms in a car may be quite different than in an aeroplane cockpit. In addition to this context 'internal' to the vehicle, there is also a context that is 'external' to it, namely the roads and traffic. This is also a very specific peculiarity of road transportation, as it represents a domain where there is an extremely high density of traffic and the rules for traffic management are almost completely left to the decision of drivers rather than a specific traffic management authority.
- *Social Context*
  There is a social context in driving that is substantially different than other environments. The presence of other passengers in the vehicle means that various driver warnings may be public. Consumer acceptance of an in-vehicle-warning device, or behavioural reactions to the warning, can be influenced in various ways by the social context (e.g. embarrassments, feelings of competence, need to appear daring or competent to peers). Social context is also present in other domains, such as aviation, air traffic control, train driving, etc. However, in these other environments, human behaviour is more affected by organisational factors and national cultures than the local social context.
- *System Integration*
  In many applications and domains, the workplace is designed as an integrated system so that the system requirements can be well defined from the beginning. For vehicle applications many devices may be aftermarket add-ons, not integrated into the original design of the vehicle. Then the environment is evolving and it is not fully predictable, neither consistent from vehicle to vehicle.

This overall picture is further complicated by the massive presence, in modern vehicles, of Advanced Driver Support Systems (ADAS) and In-Vehicle Information Systems (IVIS), which add another level of complexity. For all these reasons, the development of a model of driver behaviour is a very complex and difficult endeavour. However, the implementation of a model and associated simulation is a necessary step forward for the improvement of the effectiveness of all new means and systems that are designed and implemented in modern vehicles.

19.1.3 Use and Applications of Driver Models

The models of drivers and operators in general can be utilised for many different purposes. The goals of the users of models are the means for selecting amongst the variety of proposed paradigms that can be found in the literature. The key for choosing is therefore a set of criteria on which to compare the different paradigms and approaches. One way to compare is to consider models ability to describe performance or to evaluate motivational aspects. Another assessment perspective is the capability to account for actual performances versus risk taking and perception. A very important way to compare models is to consider their ability to describe the dynamic interaction and predictive power versus their capability to describe real-time behaviour in a realistic and coherent way.

In general, it is not possible to identify an architecture or a structure that is the best in absolute, unless the generality of the approach is so wide that it looses site of potential applications. What is instead very important is that the users of models have a clear picture of the goals and objectives of the applications so as to select in the range of paradigms the one that best suits their aims (Carsten, 2007, this volume).

In this paper, we focus on the development of a model and associated simulation with the primary objective to be a predictive tool for studying possible Driver–Vehicle–Environment (DVE) interactions dedicated to design and safety analyses. Such type of tool is normally associated and compared with real-time applications that can be utilised on board of vehicles, as they are usually integrated and streamlined version of the former model. This is considered an evolutionary process that firstly realises a tool that is able to reproduce reasonable and verified behaviours for design studies. These simulations are very useful for predicting behaviour and DVE interactions that enable the designer and safety analysts to evaluate potential applications, drawbacks and advantages of new systems and design solutions, without spending too much time and effort in performing field tests on expensive prototypes and lengthy experiments. With a valuable model and simulation, it is possible to assess potential errors and mishaps derived from various aspects of a new tool, such as type of interface, location on board, effects on driver attitudes and behaviour with respect to other systems, etc. Once such a simulation is tested and validated, it is then possible that a simplified or streamlined version is developed that can be utilised on board of vehicles for anticipating behaviour and avoiding errors or improving information management by on-board communication tools.

The simulation described in this paper concentrates on the first part of such a development. It aims therefore at predicting DVE interactions in a sufficiently accurate fashion to be utilised by designers and safety analysts for studies and preliminary evaluations of HMIs. The evolution of this approach into a real-time tool is a natural follow up of the development, but is not discussed here.

19.1.4 Content of the Paper

In this paper, we will primarily describe the modelling architecture from the simulation perspective. We will concentrate on the algorithms that have been selected to represent the driver behaviour in a form that can be implemented in a computerised expression. Secondly, we will describe the different numerical formalisms and the mathematical expressions utilised for simulating the dynamic interactions with the vehicle and environment. We will then present a series of sample cases of predictive interactions between drivers, vehicles and environments, which can be used for design and safety assessment purposes. Finally, we will conclude with some speculative consideration of the possible extension of this simulation in a streamlined version that may be considered for real-time representation of driver behaviour for in-vehicle systems implementation.

19.2 Simple Simulation of Driver Behaviour

19.2.1 Paradigm of Reference

The criteria for selection of the paradigm of reference for the development of this simulation of driver behaviour have been the following:

1. The model must enable rapid assessments of DVE interactions with different configurations so as to evaluate prototypes of different conceptual nature.
2. The dynamic interactions between driver, vehicle and environment need to be included in the simulation. The vehicle and environment should offer dynamic changing situations and interactivity with driver actions.
3. Cognitive aspects of behaviour and 'joint modelling' between humans and vehicle–environment must be considered.
4. The model needs to account for behavioural adaptation to different types of ADASs and possible emotional/attitudinal aspects.
5. The model should enable to consider possible driver errors, in addition to normative behaviour, in different traffic conditions. Error-generation mechanism needs to be included in the model.
6. The overall model and simulation should be developed in such a configuration to facilitate the evolution towards a 'real-time' simulation approach of the DVE system.

The first two requirements concentrate on the specific objective of generating a simulation tool for design and safety assessment, which is able to predict driver behaviour and interactions with the vehicle and environment in dynamic conditions.

The next three requirements focus on the model of the driver and, in particular, concentrate on the need to consider cognitive aspects of behaviour, in addition to manifestations and performances, when modelling the integrated DVE system. In addition, adaptive behaviour and emotional and attitudinal aspects are also identified as necessary peculiarities that need to be included in the simulation since they are essential components of behaviour. Modelling human error is also essential for evaluating mishaps and inadequate performance.

The last requirement is specific to the perspective application of the simulation. Indeed, even if the primary objective lies in the ability to support designers in predictive assessments, it is equally relevant to identify how to adapt a predictive model and simulation of this nature to more direct implementation in vehicles for real-time application.

According to these requirements, the simulation should not necessarily 'run' faster than real time. However, the ability to perform predictive studies of DVE for safety purposes demands that many simulations are performed with different behavioural characteristics and traffic/vehicle conditions. A balance between these two requirements is therefore needed. Moreover, the consideration for errors and dynamic aspects enhance quite considerably the need to enable the performance of several simulation runs, even for single traffic configurations. Therefore, the overall simulation has to present the basic characteristic of being *predictive, simple* and *fast running*, accounting for *dynamic interactions, human errors* and *adaptive behaviour.*

Amongst the variety of paradigms that enable to describe the DVE interactions, those described in Chapter 2 of this book cover the vast majority of architectures that have been proposed and are sufficiently developed to represent driver's interaction in modern automotive systems and traffic contexts. The specific requirements of the simulation discussed here favour the selection of the paradigm described by Carsten (2007), in this volume, as it offers the possibility to represent a simple DVE interaction, based on a quite normative type of approach to describe 'normative' and task oriented behaviour. At the same time it depicts the framework to consider cognitive and adaptive behaviour by means of a limited number of *parameters* and offers the possibility to account for *human error* on the basis of these same parameters. The specificity of dynamic interaction is also permitted, even if these aspects are not actually discussed at modelling level. Also the characteristics of real time and fast running are not reviewed, even if they are very relevant features when transforming a paradigm into a running tool, at simulation level.

The simulation that has been developed on the basis of this paradigm is called '*Simple Simulation of Driver Performance*' (SSDRIVE). The specific characteristics of the SSDRIVE will now be briefly described by discussing primarily the way to represent normative behaviour, followed by the description of the algorithm by which to consider cognitive aspects, behavioural adaptation and errors, and finally by considering the dynamic interaction of the SSDRIVE within the overall DVE simulation.

19.2.2 Simulation Approach for Normative Behaviour

19.2.2.1 Task Analysis

The most suitable model for representing driver behaviour during the performance of normative activities, both at primary and secondary levels, is to apply a simple Task Analysis (TA) approach. The detail of accuracy of the analysis and description of the tasks that are performed by the driver defines also the *granularity* of the simulation (Michon, 1985).

By carrying out a driving TA, the performance of a driver can be formalised and structured in a sequence of goals and actions that are carried out during the interaction with the vehicle and environment. Commonly used task analysis techniques such as Hierarchical Task Analysis (HTA) or Time Line Analysis (TLA) (Kirwan and Ainsworth, 1992) are best suited to represent tasks that are associated with procedures or routines in industrial environments. Driving on the other hand is not suitable to a description following the principles of a traditional task analysis, but rather requires a method that can cope with the irregularity of the driving situation. Driving can be easily seen as a set of interconnected and dynamically linked set of goals, where the top goal is getting to the destination, while several series of lower or simpler tasks are associated with local traffic situations. From this a set of subgoals, corresponding means can be derived. Consequently, instead of proposing a hierarchical structure of goals and subgoals, the functional dependencies among goals are analysed and described. From this basis, a goals-means structure can be instantiated for any given situation and set of conditions. While a HTA tend to generate a single, typical task, a goals-means analysis produces a description of a set of possible tasks. Therefore, the approach selected for the SSDRIVE simulation to describe 'normative' driver behaviour is based on the rationale that identifies the Goals-Means Task Analysis (GMTA) approach (Hollnagel, 1993).

In order to represent the set of Tasks that are carried during driving, a certain differentiation has been defined according to the complexity associated with the actual activity described by a Tasks. The following three basic elements have been identified:

- **Elementary Functions**, which represent the basic activity that cannot be further subdivided into simpler components.
- **Elementary Task**, which is a task made of elementary functions only.
- **Complex Task**, which is a task made of a combination of elementary tasks and elementary functions.

The first step to perform is to define the correlations between what has been called '*task*' and individual 'Elementary Functions'. Table 19.1 contains a set of *Elementary Functions* that can be accounted for in order to describe the basic actions of a driver. As an example, the *Elementary Function* 'Receive Perceptual Input' is associated with visual, aural or haptic perception.

Table 19.2 shows a sample of correlations that are defined between tasks and elementary functions. Several *tasks* have been developed for implementing the simulation, such as 'Attain higher speed', 'Attain lower speed', 'Stop vehicle', 'Reverse vehicle', 'Turn left', 'Turn right', 'Change lane', 'Pass Vehicle', 'Overtake', 'Keep lateral safety margins', 'Keep longitudinal safety margins', 'Maintain speed', 'Give way at intersection', 'Emergency manoeuvre', etc.

19.2.2.2 Dynamic Logical Simulation of Tasks

Each *task* is represented in the simulation as a 'frame' (Minsky, 1975), which is associated with attributes or *pre-condition*, which in turn enable the frame to be initiated, and *post-conditions*, which are applied for 'closing' the frame.

TABLE 19.1. Sets of elementary functions.

ELEMENTARY FUNCTIONS	
Receive Perceptual Input	• *Perceive phone ringing* • *Perceive warnings* • *Perceive indicators* • ...
Elementary checking actions (primary task – vehicle controls)	• *Check mirrors* • *Check speedometer* • *Check road signals* • *Check signals for direction* • *Scan road side* • ....
Elementary control actions (primary task – vehicle controls)	• *Accelerate* • *Brake* • *Steer* • *Change gear* • *Set indicator (right/left)* • ...
Elementary control actions (primary task – vehicle ADAS)	• *Adaptive Cruise Control (ACC):* √ *Headway* √ *Check distance to lead vehicle* √ *Check ACC is enabled* √ *Select speed*

The *tasks*, or *frames*, are simulated implementing the associated procedure and sequence of elementary tasks/functions by means of sequences of rules and actions described through object oriented programming languages. Attributes (pre- and post-conditions) are correlated according to rules and entity-attribute matrices.

The logical dynamic sequence of tasks is defined according to a hierarchy derived from the satisfaction of the pre- and post-conditions, coupled with a model based on *decision making* and definition of *intentions.* This model is crucial for the entire dynamic evolution of the DVE interaction. A simple model of this nature is described in next section and may be associated with the maximum allowed speed and on specific road and traffic conditions.

Another fundamental characteristic of the SSDRIVE simulation is the consideration for the *permanent* or *automatic tasks.* These tasks are identified by the fact that they are permanently carried out during a DVE interaction and do not require specific pre-conditions to be launched. These are stereotypes of what may be called 'skill-based behaviour' in a very 'classical' modelling architecture based on a skill–rule–knowledge type behaviour that has been the most known implementation of the information processing paradigm proposed in the early 1980s for describing human behaviour (Rasmussen, 1983). Two *permanent tasks* are considered in the present simulation approach, namely 'keep lateral safety margins' and 'keep longitudinal safety margins'.

The concept of permanent tasks is quite straightforward, as it is associated with the fact that drivers 'normally' keep their vehicle within lane margins and at a reasonable safety distance with preceding vehicles or obstacles, without specific

TABLE 19.2. Examples of correlations between tasks and elementary functions.

Goal/task	Task/elementary functions involved	Pre-conditions
Attain higher speed (complex task) Goal/Post-condition: **Reach the selected speed**	*1. Accelerate* *2. Check speedometer* **3. Maintain speed**	**1. No ahead vehicle with lower speed** 2. All Preconditions of *Elementary Tasks*
Attain lower speed (complex task) Goal/Post-condition: **Reach the selected speed**	*1. Brake* *2. (Change gear)* *3. Check speedometer* **4. Maintain speed**	1. Check all Preconditions of *Elementary Tasks* **2. Ahead vehicle with lower speed** **3. Presence of give way signals**
Stop vehicle (elementary task) Goal/Post-condition: **Vehicle speed equal to zero**	*1. Brake* *2. Change gear*	**1. Presence of Red traffic light or** **2. Presence of an obstacle on the carriageway** **3. Car incoming from the main road**
Keep longitudinal safety margins (complex task) Goal/Post-condition: **Maintain safe distance from leading vehicle**	*1. Scan road forward* *2. Check speedometer* *3.* (**Attain lower speed–emergency manoeuvre**)	***Permanent task***
Maintain speed (elementary task) Goal/Post-condition: **Have the previous time-step speed**	*1. (Accelerate/ Brake)*	**1. No ahead vehicle with lower speed or obstacle on road** **2. No red/yellow traffic light** **3. No speed limitations signals** **4. No give way at intersection**

Entries in Italics indicate elementary function; entries in bold indicate task; entries within parenthesis indicate conditional activity (function/task).
Elementary task = task made of elementary functions only. Complex task = task made of a combination of elementary tasks and elementary functions.

effort and cognitive demand. Consequently, these two tasks are permanently active in the DVE loop and are always performed every time the driver simulation is activated. This simulation requirement, associated with the fact that there is no cognitive load in performing these 'simple vehicle control' tasks, in normal conditions, has generated the choice of a classical (optimal) control modelling approach (Weir and Chao, 2007, this volume) for their simulation in the DVE loop.

In practice, every time the driver simulation is activated in the DVE loop, the *permanent tasks* are performed first, unless a human error is underway. They aim at keeping the vehicle under control with respect to longitudinal and lateral coordinated of the driving environment (road and traffic) (Fig. 19.1). The other tasks are then performed according to the model of decision making and intentions described above.

19.2.3 Algorithms for Cognition, Behavioural Adaptation and Errors

The basic assumption made for the development of the driver model is that the driver is essentially performing a set of actions on the vehicle commands and

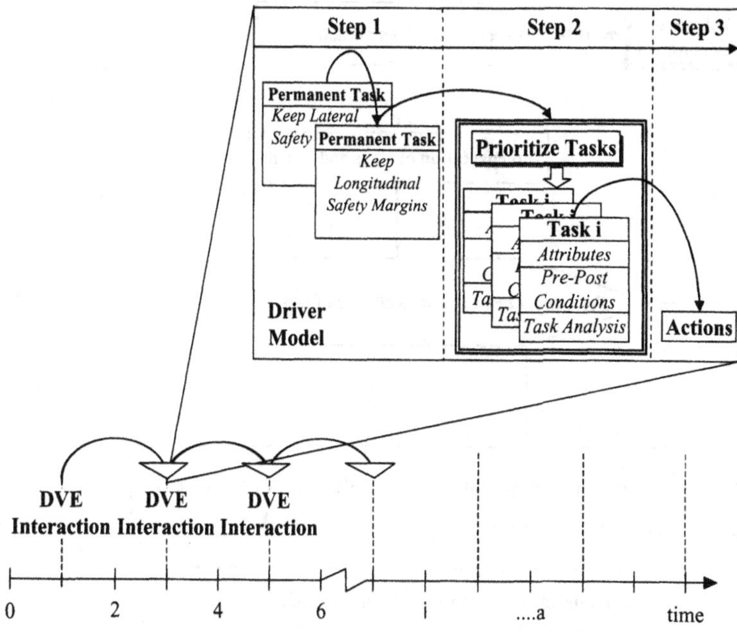

FIGURE 19.1. Dynamic-Logical Task sequence.

controls that are known and, in many cases, familiar, according to experience. As the driving process is very dynamic, these actions are continuously selected or developed from the knowledge base of the driver. However, prior to this activity a process of information management and formulation of goals and tasks is necessary.

Consequently, independently of the specific model selected for describing the driver behaviour, the following four steps of cognitive and behavioural interactions must be considered:

1. Perception of signals from vehicle and environment.;
2. Interpretation of information.
3. Formulation of goals and intentions and selection of tasks to be carried out.
4. Performance of actions on control panel and on vehicle commands.

This is a typical formulation of a model based on the paradigm called 'Information Processing System' (IPS), which has been applied in almost all fields to account for human interaction with technology at different levels of automation (Cacciabue, 2004). The important characteristic of this approach is that it allows considering the behavioural as well as the cognitive aspects of human performance. This paradigm is the reference model for the SSDRIVE simulation.

The way in which the various cognitive functions of the model are implemented in the simulation is quite simple and straightforward and depends on two possible types of modelling architecture: the simple and linear *normative driver behaviour* or the complex and more realistic *descriptive driver behaviour.* These two types of simulation are now described in some detail.

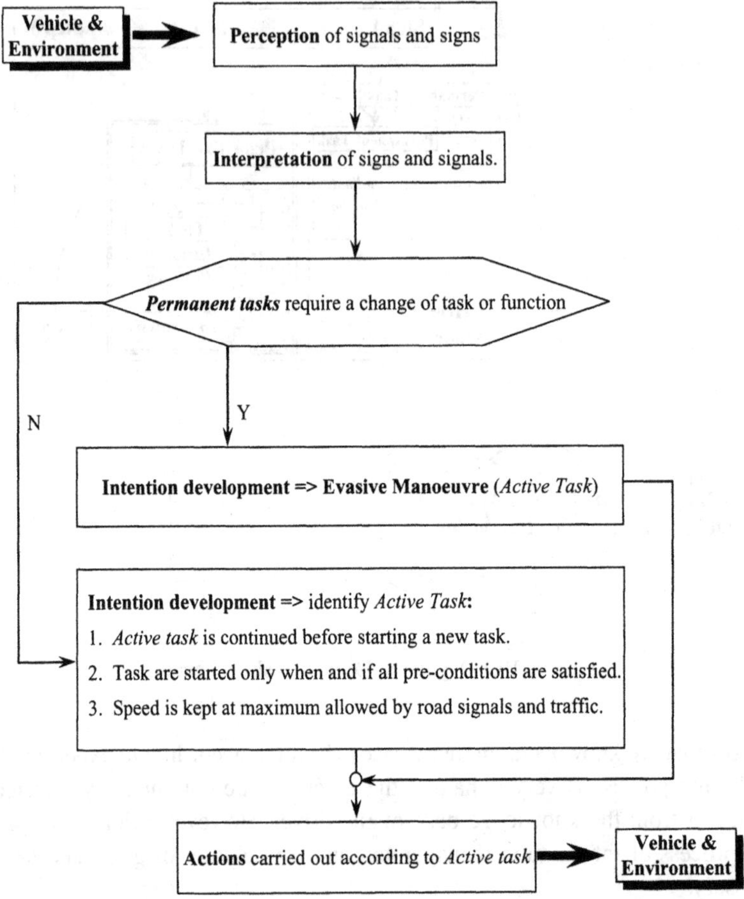

FIGURE 19.2. Flowchart of the simulation of *normative driver behaviour*.

19.2.3.1 Normative Driver Behaviour

In *normal conditions*, i.e., when the driver has a very low or zero level of impairment and no behavioural adaptation occurs, the simulation covers what may be called *normative driver behaviour*. This is a merely theoretical condition not reflected in realistic behaviours. However, from the simulation point of view it is necessary that these formal aspects of driver behaviour are represented and stored in the overall simulation tool.

The following sequence of steps is performed (Fig. 19.2):

1. All signals and signs that are produced inside and outside the vehicle are perceived.
2. Interpretation is conforming to the meaning associated with signs and signals.

3. Intentions are formulated in relation to the ongoing task and information perceived and interpreted. A task is then either continued or newly started. This task is called *active task.*
4. Actions are carried out according to the *active task.*

The key step in normative behaviour is the process of formulation of intentions. In the simulation, a very simple approach has been selected based on cost/benefit rule for prioritising tasks. The rule implies that the driver minimises cognitive efforts and time for reaching indented location. Therefore the following principles apply:

1. Assess whether *permanent tasks* require a change of task or function (conditional activity).
   a. In the case of conditional activity, then adapt to demands of permanent task.
   b. Otherwise continue the process.
2. The ongoing task is terminated before starting a new task.
3. Tasks are started only when and if all pre-conditions are satisfied.
4. Speed is kept at maximum allowed by road signals and traffic.

19.2.3.2 Descriptive Driver Behaviour

In *non-normal conditions*, i.e., when a certain impairment and 'error' may occur, or when behavioural adaptation becomes a relevant factor, then the simulation covers what is called *descriptive driver behaviour.* In this case, the sequence of steps remains unchanged as far as the information processing is concerned. However, before entering the IPS loop, the *parameters* governing adaptation and error must be evaluated. This may lead to modifying some of the cognitive functions, including the performance of actions. The latter represents the manifestation of adaptive or erroneous behaviour. Task selection and performance is also affected by behavioural adaptation. This type of simulation is much more realistic with respect to actual driver behaviour. However, the level of complexity from the simulation viewpoint is much higher and requires some degree of simplification and linearisation.

In essence, descriptive driver behaviour is identified by a number of *parameters* that enable to modify and adapt the way in which the more cognitive functions are carried out, namely the perception and interpretation of signs and signals and the generation of intentions. Moreover, the *parameters* are essential for the definition of the actions that are performed.

According to the selected model, the following five parameters can be identified for considering descriptive and adaptive behaviour:

- *Attitudes/personality* (ATT): static parameter associated with each driver.
- *Experience/competence* (EXP): static parameter associated with each driver.
- *Task demand* (TD): objective dynamic parameter resulting from DVE interaction.
- *Driver State* (DS): subjective dynamic parameter resulting from DVE interaction.
- *Situation Awareness/Alertness* (SA): subjective dynamic parameter resulting from DVE interaction.

TABLE 19.3. Identified correlations between parameters and measurable or observable variables or the DVE evolution.

Parameters	Definition	Measurable Variables
Experience	The accumulation of knowledge or skills that result from direct participation in the driving activity.	1. No of kilometres per year 2. Number of years with driving license
Attitudes	A complex mental state involving beliefs and feelings and values and dispositions to act in certain ways. *Sensation Seeking* and *Locus of Control* have been identified as personality based predictors of accident involvement.	1. Speed 2. Lane keeping 3. Overtaking 4. Headway
Task demand	The demands of the process of achieving a specific and measurable goal using a prescribed method. When Task Demand is focused only on driving, then Task Demand = Driving Demand.	1. Traffic complexity 2. Weather 3. Light 4. Speed 5. Driving direction
Driver state	Driver physical and mental ability to drive (fatigue, sleepiness...). A set of dynamic parameters representing aspects of the driver relevant for the human–machine interaction.	1. Lane keeping; headway control 2. Duration of driving; time-on-task 3. Weather; Road conditions 4. Traffic complexity 5. Speed
Situation awareness	Perception of the elements in the environment within a volume of time and space, the comprehension of their meaning and the projection of their status in the near future.	1. Distraction 2. Driver State 3. Task Demand

The discussion on the reasons for selecting these parameters accounting for descriptive driver behaviour goes beyond the scope of this paper and can be found in Carsten (2007, this volume). The definitions that are associated with each *parameter* are shown in Table 19.3. However, it is primarily noticeable that the two static parameters of Attitude/personality and Experience/competence enable the definition of some initial characteristics of behaviour that affect all decision making processes and performances throughout the simulation. On the other side, the dynamic parameters enable to account for the variability of conditions and environmental changes that are encountered during a typical journey. In this sense, both types of parameters are very important and may play a crucial role in the simulation of DVE interactions. Naturally, this implies that the model and associated simulation are sufficiently powerful to incorporate all these effects.

It is important to note here that the parameter *Task Demand* is in most cases equivalent to *Driving Demand.* However, as the objective of the correlations between parameters and behaviour covers all potential aspects affecting driver performance, it is preferable to retain in this parameter also the factors associated with secondary task performance, including social and personal demands derived from the overall vehicle context.

The set of variables that govern the dynamic driver model is directly correlated with the ability of the model to account for the above functions at different levels of depth. The crucial open issues that remain to be resolved with respect to the DVE parameters are of three types:

1. *Correlation of parameters with respect to measurable variables.* This involves two aspects:
   - Which are the actual measurable variables that affect the *parameters.*
   - How these variables influence the change of value of the *parameters.*
2. *Intentions/goals.* The dynamic process of decision making and interaction with the Vehicle–Environment is regulated by the development of intentions, such as 'intention to overtake a vehicle in front', 'increase speed', etc.
3. *Correlation of parameters with respect to driver behaviour.* How the parameters combine in affecting driver behaviour and/or performance.

19.2.3.3 Parameters and Measurable Variables

The next issue that needs to be resolved in order to progress with the development of a simulation is the identification of the way in which parameters affect driver behaviour. This issue, as stated above, involves two aspects: the definition of which measurable variables are associated to each parameter and how such variables affect parameters.

Since we are here interested in the implementation of the SSDRIVE from the simulation perspective, the theoretical discussion associated with the first part of the problem is of less interest. Consequently, we will not discuss the reasons and scientific findings about the selection of the variables that are associated to each parameter. The reader should refer to the specific literature in this area and in particular to Chapter 2 for a more specific treatment of this subject. Table 19.3 contains a set of variables that can be measured, or evaluated in the case of a simulation, which enable the estimation of the dynamic values associated to each parameter.

The problem of interest in the case of the development of a simulation is the numerical or analytical expressions that are applied for the evaluation of the parameters on the basis of the calculated values from the dynamic simulations of the vehicle, of the environment, and also from the driver itself.

The initial values associated to the *Attitude/personality* and *Experience/competence* do not change over time, as they are static parameters and are simply input data for the SSDRIVE simulation. Static parameters influence, together with the dynamic values associated with the other three parameters, driver decision making and behavioural aspects, as it will be discussed in next section.

Focusing on the dynamic parameters and on possible forms of correlations between them and measurable variables, the most generic representation that can be formulated, according to the quantities identified in Table 19.3, are as follows:

Task demand: *TD = f (Traffic Complexity, Weather, etc.)*
Driver state: *DS = g (Lane Keeping, Duration of Drive, Weather, etc.)*
Situation awareness: *SA = l (Driver State, Distraction, Task Demand, etc.)*

The forms that these functions may take are numerical or logical expressions. In the SSDRIVE approach, the choice of utilising *fuzzy* descriptions has been made. Consequently, during the simulation, each (independent) variable of interest is evaluated by a numerical correlation and then associated to a fuzzy value. Subsequently, the estimation of the (fuzzy) value of each parameter requires the application of typical fuzzy rules that combine the (fuzzy) values of the associated independent variables.

In practice, the five *parameters* that govern the SSDRIVE are fixed. A set of *default correlations* between parameters and measurable independent variables is available. These require in input only the limits for each independent measurable variable to structure the fuzzy correlations. The fuzzy rules that define the values of the parameters are fixed, while screening on the fuzzy correlations associated to each independent variable is possible via input data to the simulation tool.

On the other side, if the user of the simulations intends to study and apply new functions and rules, then the input requires the definition of new independent variables, to be selected amongst those calculated by the three modules of the DVE simulation, and the formulation and programming of new correlations that replace the default ones. This is a very flexible aspect of the simulation tool that is based on a 'modular' structure. However, this requires programming ability and detailed knowledge of the simulation software.

The correlations adopted as default for each dynamic parameter will now be briefly discussed.

19.2.3.3.1 Task Demand

The default fuzzy correlations and the rule for the evaluation of *Task Demand* are (Fig. 19.3) as follows:

1. *Task Demand (TD)* is assumed to be a fuzzy function with values *High, Acceptable,* and *Low*, and is correlated only to visible level of traffic and environment (*Visibility*), and to the number of vehicles present on the road (*Complexity of traffic, CoT*):
   - *TD = f (Visibility CoT)*
2. *Visibility* is measured in terms of distance and is considered
   - *Good*, when the driver can see at a distance of more than 100 metres;
   - *Acceptable*, for distances of clear vision between 70 and 100 metres;
   - *Bad*, for less than 70 metres of clear vision.
3. *Complexity of traffic* (*CoT*) is measured in terms of vehicles per kilometre on the road:
   - *Good*, when the density of vehicles is less than 100 per kilometre;

Task Demand (TD)	***Variables* (v)**	***Fuzzy Values***		
	Visibility (*Vis*)	*Good*	*Acceptable*	*Bad*
	Complexity of traffic (*CoT*)	*Good*	*Acceptable*	*Bad*

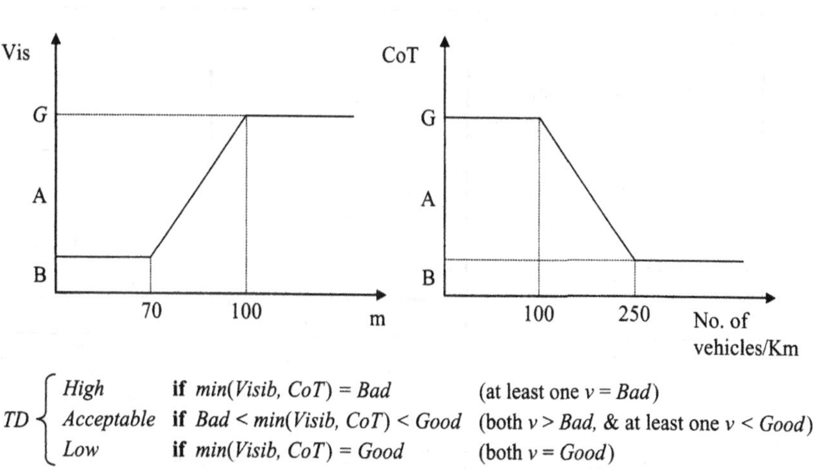

FIGURE 19.3. Example of fuzzy correlations and fuzzy rule between *Task Demand versus Complexity of traffic and Weather Conditions (Visibility).*

- *Acceptable*, when the density of vehicles is between 100 and 250 per kilometre; and
- *Bad*, when the density of vehicles is greater than 250 per kilometre.

4. The fuzzy rule applied to calculate the fuzzy value of *task demand* is
   - *TD = High* if *min (Visibility, CoT) = Bad*;
   - *TD = Medium* if *min (Visibility, CoT) = Acceptable*;
   - *TD = Low* if *min (Visibility, CoT) = Good.*

   This means that the less favourable value is associated with TD between the two fuzzy values of *Visibility* and *Complexity of traffic*.

19.2.3.3.2 Driver State

The default fuzzy correlations and rule for the evaluation of *Driver State* are shown in Fig. 19.4.

1. *Driver State (DS)* is assumed to be a fuzzy function with values *Bad, Acceptable*, and *Good*, and is correlated simply to the time dedicated to driving (*Duration of Driving, DoD*), and to the *Speed change* ($|\Delta Speed|$) and *Steering* ($|\Delta\varphi|$), over a period of driving of 10 minutes:
   - $DS = f(DoD, |\Delta Speed|, |\Delta\varphi|)$
2. *Duration of Driving (DoD)* is measured in terms of overall driving time and is considered
   - *Low*, when the driver has been driving for less than 60 minutes;
   - *Acceptable*, for a driving time between 60 and 180 minutes;
   - *High*, for more than 180 minutes of driving time.

Driver State (DS)	*Variables (v)*	*Fuzzy Values*		
	Duration of Drive (*DoD*)	*Low - L*	*Acceptable - A*	*High - H*
	$\lvert \Delta Speed \rvert_{10'}$	*Low - L*	*Medium - A*	*High - H*
	$\lvert \Delta\varphi \rvert_{10'}$	*Low - L*	*Medium - A*	*High - H*

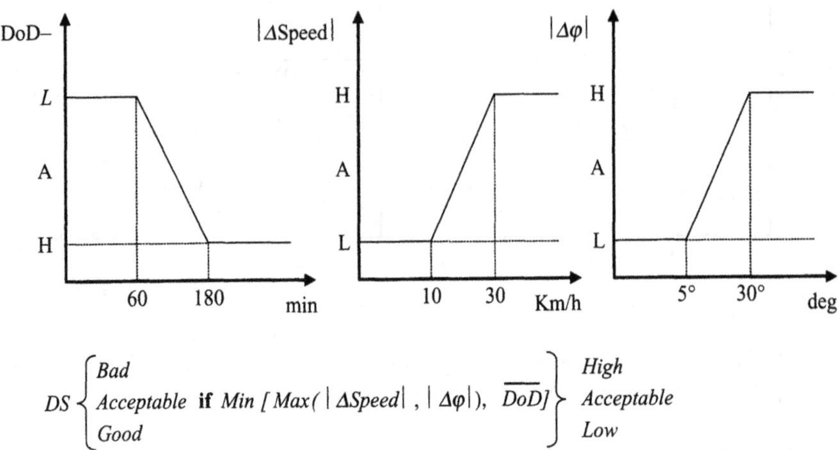

FIGURE 19.4. Example of fuzzy correlations and fuzzy rule between *Driver State versus Duration of Drive, Speed change and Steering.*

3. Variation of steering ($|\Delta\varphi|$) is associated to the road geometry and not to the yaw disturbance. Variation of speed ($|\Delta Speed|$) is associated to the traffic conditions and road type/geometry. Therefore, it is assumed that in the case of roads with constant geometry (straight roads or small bends and curves, e.g., highways) very little change of steering and speed occurs. These are causes of possible drowsiness in drivers. Changing either of them, over a period of 10 min, is considered sufficient to retain an acceptable level of vigilance. They are therefore combined in defining a fuzzy measure of Driver State. The fuzzy correlations for the variation of speed and steering (for a period of driving $\Delta t =$ *10 minutes*) are as follows:
   - *Low*, when $|\Delta Speed| < 10$ *km/h* or $|\Delta\varphi| < 5°$.
   - *Medium/Acceptable*, when $10 \leq |\Delta Speed| \leq 30$ *km/h* or $5° \leq |\Delta\varphi| \leq 30°$.
   - *High*, when $|\Delta Speed| > 30$ *km/h* or $|\Delta\varphi| > 30°$.
4. The fuzzy rule applied to calculate the fuzzy value of *Driver State* is as follows:
   - *DS = Bad* if = *Low*
   - *DS = Acceptable* if *min [max(*$|\Delta Speed|$, $|\Delta\varphi|$*), DoD] = Acceptable*
   - *DS = Good* if = *High*

   This means that the less favourable value is associated with DS between the fuzzy values of *Duration of Driving* and the combination of *Speed change* and *Steering*.

Situation Awareness	Variables (v)	Fuzzy Values		
	Distraction (**Dis**)	Low	Medium	High
	Task Demand (**TD**)	Low	Acceptable	High
	Driver State (**DS**)	Good	Acceptable	Bad

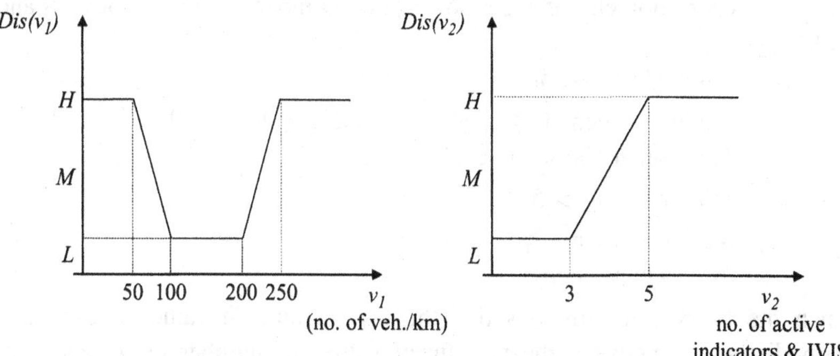

$Dis = f$[no. of veh./km (v_1), no. of active indicators & IVIS (v_2)]

$$Dis \begin{cases} High & \textbf{if} \ \ max\,(v_1, v_2) = High & \text{(least one } v = High\text{)} \\ Medium & \textbf{if} \ \ Low < max\,(v_1, v_2) < High & \text{(both } v < High, \text{ \& at least one } v > Low\text{)} \\ Low & \textbf{if} \ \ max\,(v_1, v_2) = Low & \text{(when both } v = Low\text{)} \end{cases}$$

$SA = f_1(TD)$

$$\mathbf{SA} \begin{cases} Bad & \textbf{if} \ \ TD = Low \\ Good & \textbf{if} \ \ TD = Medium \\ Bad & \textbf{if} \ \ TD = High \end{cases}$$

$SA = f_2(DS)$

$$\mathbf{SA} \begin{cases} Bad & \textbf{if} \ \ DS = Bad \\ Acceptable & \textbf{if} \ \ DS = Acceptable \\ Good & \textbf{if} \ \ DS = Good \end{cases}$$

$SA = f_3(Dis)$

$$\mathbf{SA} \begin{cases} Bad & \textbf{if} \ \ Dis = High \\ Acceptable & \textbf{if} \ \ Dis = Medium \\ Good & \textbf{if} \ \ Dis = Low \end{cases}$$

$\boldsymbol{SA = f(Dis, TD, DS)}$

$$\mathbf{SA} \begin{cases} Bad & \textbf{if} \ \ min\,[f_1(TD), f_2(DS), f_3(Dis)] = Bad \\ Acceptable & \textbf{if} \ \ min[f_1(TD), f_2(DS), f_3(Dis)] = Acceptable \\ Good & \textbf{if} \ \ min[f_1(TD), f_2(DS), f_3(Dis)] = Good \end{cases}$$

FIGURE 19.5. Example of fuzzy correlations and fuzzy rules between *Situation Awareness* versus *Driver State, Task Demand* and *Distraction*.

19.2.3.3.3 Situation Awareness

Finally, default fuzzy correlations and rules for the evaluation of *Situation Awareness* are shown in Fig. 19.5.

1. *Situation Awareness (SA)* is assumed to be a fuzzy function with values *Bad, Acceptable*, and *Good* and is correlated to *Task Demand (TD), Driver State (DS)*, and *Distraction (Dis)*:

- $SA = f(TD, DS, Dis)$

2. *Task Demand (TD)* and *Driver State (DS)* are measured according to the two fuzzy rules and functions described above.
3. *Distraction (Dis)* is a fuzzy rule, associated to two fuzzy functions, i.e., number of vehicles per kilometre on the road (v_1) and number of active indicators and IVIS (v_2):
   - Dis_{v1}: *High* when $v_1 < 50$ *or* $v_1 > 250$
     Medium, when $50 \leq v_1 \leq 100$ *and* $200 \leq v_1 \leq 250$
     Low, when $100 < v_1 < 200$
   - Dis_{v2}: *High* when $v_2 > 5$
     Medium, when $3 \leq v_2 \leq 5$
     Low, when $3 < v_2$

   Then the fuzzy rules imposes that the less favourable value is associated with distraction between the two fuzzy values of number of vehicles per kilometre on the road (v_1) and number of active indicators and IVIS (v_2): $Dis = Max\,(Dis_{v1}, Dis_{v2})$
4. The fuzzy rules that combine *SA* with each variable *TD, DS* and *Dis* are as follows:
   - $f_1\,(TD) = SA\,(TD)$

SA (TD) = Bad	if	*TD = Low*
SA (TD) = Good	if	*TD = Medium*
SA (TD) = Bad	if	*TD = High*

   - $f_2\,(DS) = SA\,(DS)$

SA (DS) = Bad	if	*DS = Bad*
SA (DS) = Acceptable	if	*DS = Acceptable*
SA (DS) = Good	if	*DS = Good.*

   - $f_3\,(Dis) = SA\,(Dis)$

SA (Dis) = Bad	if	*Dis = High*
SA (Dis) = Acceptable	if	*Dis = Medium*
SA (Dis) = Good	if	*Dis = Low*

5. Finally, SA is evaluated according to the following fuzzy rule:
   - *SA = Bad* if $min\,[f_1(TD), f_2(DS), f_3(Dis)] = Bad$
   - *SA = Acceptable* if $min\,[f_1(TD), f_2(DS), f_3(Dis)] = Acceptable$
   - *SA = Good* if $min\,[f_1(TD), f_2(DS), f_3(Dis)] = Good$

   This means that the less favourable value between the three fuzzy values of *Task Demand, Driver State,* and *Distraction* is associated to SA.

The complete set of fuzzy correlations and fuzzy rules that govern the SS-DRIVE simulation is quite complex and requires a considerable effort of data input and data definition. This is not surprising as the actual combinations of variables, parameters and effects are distributed and cannot be oversimplified with the risk of undermining the overall effort of modelling carried out at theoretical level.

The actual formulation of the parameters that govern the model of the driver is obviously critical for the overall DVE modelling. For this reason, the implementation of the correlations linking all static and dynamic *parameters*, i.e., *EXP, ATT, DS, TD,* and *SA*, and *measurable variables* is kept wide open in the simulation approach of SSDRIVE. This means that the users have two main options:

1. To utilise the set of *default correlations*, i.e., those that are described in this paper, and adapt simply their boundary conditions and limits by input data. This alternative is obviously easy and simple.
2. To apply a set of *specific correlations*, by developing appropriate programming routines that will then be interfaced with the main SSDRIVE simulation. This makes the input process more complicated and time consuming. However, in this way, the flexibility of the overall simulation is widely improved and makes possible to test different formulations and combinations of (fuzzy) functions and rules that combine parameters and variables.

19.2.3.4 Intentions, Decision Making and Human Error

The overall simulation is governed by the dynamic (time dependent) unfolding of intentions and decisions of the driver model. This is another crucial aspect of the model, from the theoretical viewpoint, as it impacts on the validity of the overall approach and relies on the enormous amount of research in this area, in association with humans attitudes, characteristics, personality, individual and social aspects, etc. Many of these issues are discussed in various papers of this book. The literature on this matter dates back several decades and is rich of many different theoretical stands and formulations.

From a simulation perspective, the choice that has been made in the development of SSDRIVE is to keep maximum flexibility, as it has been done in the case of the definition of the *parameters* and *measurable variables.* The user will retain the possibility either to apply a set of default options or to separately develop parts of the SSDRIVE so as to modify the default settings. As in the case of parameters and measurable variables:

1. the default settings are kept as simple as possible in order to make the development of standard cases relatively easy and fast and
2. the development and implementation in the simulation of new algorithms will require a more complex definition of the input and deeper knowledge of the simulation architecture and programming languages.

The set of defaults conditions existing in the simulation are now briefly discussed. These are simple correlations that govern primarily development of *intentions and decision making*, and *error generation*.

19.2.3.4.1 Intentions and Decision Making

The generation of intentions is simulated by means of a very simple correlation that enables the dynamic simulation of tasks and elementary functions and new intentions and goals, as the overall DVE interaction progresses and new traffic conditions are met.

At the default level, the correlation that has been chosen is very simple and it is based on the driver assessment of the cost-benefit of the minimum time to reach the objective, i.e., going from the starting point of the journey to its destination in the minimum allowable time. In other words, the vehicle is driven at the highest 'intended' speed, depending on driver characteristics, traffic and maximum allowed speed. The static parameters of experience and attitude will affect the highest intended speed in a very simple manner. The decision making process based on the two parameters *EXP* and *ATT* would give a constant and thus static value of highest intended speed with respect to the maximum allowed speed.

In order to introduce a dynamic contribution to this decision making process, two other parameters are introduced in the correlation, namely, *Task Demand* (*TD*) and *Road condition/geometry*. The overall correlation that is set as default for the intended speed ($Speed_{intended}$) is

$$Speed_{intended} = \{1 + 0.2[f(EXP, ATT) + g(TD)] + 0.2\psi(Road_{cond.})\}^{*} Speed_{max\text{-}allowed}.$$

The following data and functions apply:

ATT has three possible fuzzy input values
1. ATT = 0, for Low-Risk-Taker
2. *ATT = 1,* for Moderate-Risk-Taker
3. ATT = 2, for High-Risk-Taker

EXP has also three possible input data
1. EXP = 0, for Low-Experience
2. *EXP = 1,* for Moderate-Experience
3. *EXP = 2,* for High-Experience

$f(EXP, ATT) = (ATT - EXP + 1) \quad -1 \leq f \leq 3$

and

- *if* $TD = High \rightarrow g(TD) = -1$
- *if* $TD = Medium \rightarrow g(TD) = 0$
- *if* $TD = Low \rightarrow g(TD) = 1$

and

- *if* $Road_{cond} = Bad \rightarrow \psi(Road_{cond.}) = -1$
- *if* $Road_{cond} = Acceptable \rightarrow \psi(Road_{cond.}) = 0$
- *if* $Road_{cond} = Good \rightarrow \psi(Road_{cond.}) = 1.$

In this way, the intended speed may vary between the two following maximum and minimum values:

$Max\ Speed_{intended} = 2 * Speed_{max\text{-}allowed}$

and

$Min\ Speed_{intended} = 0.4 * Speed_{max\text{-}allowed}$

The consequent dynamic unfolding of tasks, such as overtaking of slower vehicles and avoiding obstacles, depends on this simple process of decision making associated with the intention of the driver to select and maintain the intended speed ($Speed_{intended}$), as the limits change along the road. As discussed earlier, also in this case, the possibility for the user to utilise different and more complex correlations is granted by the specific type of simulation.

19.2.3.4.2 Error Generation

The last open issue concerns the correlation of the five basic *parameters* with driver behaviour and performance with respect to error generation. As in the previous cases, the user will have the possibility to apply different and complex correlations by exploiting the flexibility of the simulation tool.

At the default level, very simple assumptions are made, associated with the dynamic evolution of the DVE interaction. The mechanism that has been devised to describe driver error and behaviour in relation to the basic parameters is called Model of Basic Indicators of Driver Operational Navigation (BIDON). To provide a first attempt of evaluation of dynamic change of DVE conditions, it is assumed that the variables affecting the driver behaviour, i.e., the subjective dynamic parameters *DS* and *SA* and the objective dynamic parameter *TD*, are represented by 'containers' with thresholds/levels, which change from a driver to another and enable to define the overall state/performance-ability of the driver, as the DVE interaction evolves. The static parameters *Experience/competence* and *Attitudes/personality* are evaluated at the beginning of a simulation and remain constant. They also contribute to the initial 'filling' of the 'containers' and can therefore be associated to the starting levels of *Situation Awareness* (SA_0), *Driver State* (DS_0) and *Task Demand* (TD_0).

Every time a relevant event happens, the level of both subjective and objective conditions will change, affecting the efficiency and performance of the driver behaviour. This will contribute to the dynamic process of progressive 'filling' or 'draining' of the 'containers' of the BIDON model.

The error-generation mechanism that is implemented in the SSDRIVE is as simple as the other correlations that have been discussed above. The same rule of flexibility applies, whereby the user of the simulation tool is able to make use of more complex error making functions by means of more complicated formulations from input data setting and definition of specific programs that may be interfaced with the main simulation. At default level, the error-generation process is essentially associated to a single parameter called Driver Impairment Level (DIL). The DIL depends essentially on the static and dynamic parameters.

The values of *Experience/competence, Attitudes/personality, Situation Awareness* (SA_0), *Driver State* (DS_0) and *Task Demand* (TD_0) are user input. The DIL or error-generation mechanism is associated to the following correlations:

$$DIL_t = f(SA_t, DS_t, TD_t, EXP, ATT) \quad 0 \leq DIL \leq 1.$$

The following logics and fuzzy correlations are implemented as default:

1. An error occurs when $DIL = 1$.
2. $DIL = 1$, *if*
   - all three dynamic parameters reach their most negative conditions at the same time, i.e., $SA_t = Bad, TD_t = High, DS_t = Bad$; *or*
   - anyone of the three dynamic parameters reaches and remains at its most negative condition for at least N consecutive minutes (Δt_{DIL}). Δt_{DIL} depends on the *age* of the driver and on the parameters *EXP* and *ATT*. The following fuzzy rule applies:

     $$\Delta t_{DIL} = N + f(EXP, ATT) + g(AGE),$$

     where $N = 4$ (default value)

     $$f \begin{cases} -2 & \textbf{if} \quad min(\overline{EXP}, ATT) = High \\ 0 & \textbf{if} \quad Moderate < min(\overline{EXP}, ATT) < High \\ 1 & \textbf{if} \quad min(\overline{EXP}, ATT) = Low \end{cases}$$

     and

     $$g \begin{cases} -1 & \textbf{if} \quad AGE \geq 50 \\ 0.5 & \textbf{if} \quad 35 < AGE < 50 \\ 0 & \textbf{if} \quad AGE \leq 35 \end{cases}$$

   - In this way, the maximum and minimum time intervals for error making when one of the critical parameters is at its most negative condition are

     $$Max\ \Delta t_{\mathrm{DIL}} = 5\ minutes$$
     $$Min\ \Delta t_{\mathrm{DIL}} = 1\ minute$$

When an error occurs, then the types and modes of errors are associated with the ongoing activity being carried out by the driver at the time of the error. The types and modes of errors are also defined through the input data system. However, the simulation is able to combine different errors, situations and solutions.

Moreover, the whole variety of potential errors (types and modes) that may occur when the $DIL = 1$ needs to be studied in order to enable the evaluation of the largest variety of DVE dynamic interactions. This concept is described in the example shown in Fig. 19.6, where the first error occurs in time-step 6 ($SA_{t=6} = Bad$, $DS_{t=6} = Bad$ and $TD_{t=6} = High$). In this case, two possible types/modes of errors have been identified by input data and consequently, three sequences are generated: one with no error; one with the first type/mode of error; and the third one with the second type/mode of error. This generates a very complex spectrum of possible sequences and requires a very accurate analysis tool for screening, the selection of relevant results, and outcome of the simulation.

19.2.4 Simulation of Control Actions

The overall DVE and SSDRIVE simulation processes are shown in Fig. 19.7 and Fig. 19.8. In particular, at each time interval, the *driver model* receives the *'real'*

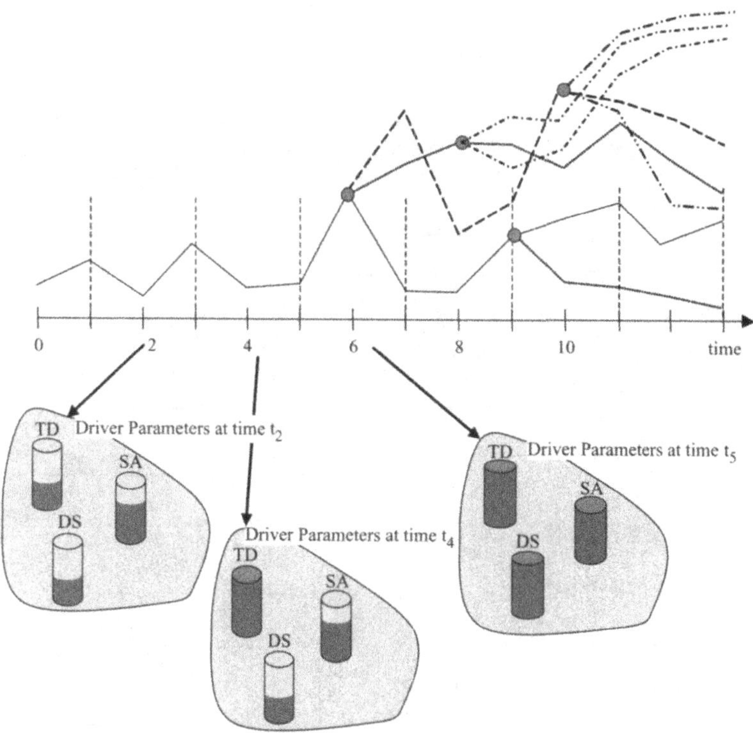

FIGURE 19.6. Error mechanism and dynamic sequences generation.

vehicle and environment conditions, i.e., the dynamic variables calculated at previous time steps, and evaluates the new actions that are carried out on the vehicle controls (Fig. 19.7, upper part). These are essentially the settings of indicators, ADAS, IVIS etc., and the basic vehicle control actions of steering and accelerating/braking in order to obtain to the desired position and speed. The cognitive processes and behavioural adaptation that lead to decisions have been discussed in the previous sections. In the following, the implementation of control actions is discussed in some details.

19.2.4.1 Normal Driving

In order to implement the performance of tasks and actions on the vehicle controls, few robust driver control theory models have been chosen. The first model is the Crossover Model (McRuer and Krendel, 1974; see also Chapter 17 of this volume), which is described in terms of steering control and acceleration pedal. The second model is the Shaft Model of driver's control strategy (Kondo, 1953). A control theory based approach is an efficient and low cost way to perform simulations of DVE interactions. In particular, it allows to account for perturbations associated with behavioural aspects such as noise on steering control, delay in trajectory planning, and delay and loss of recognition of target information.

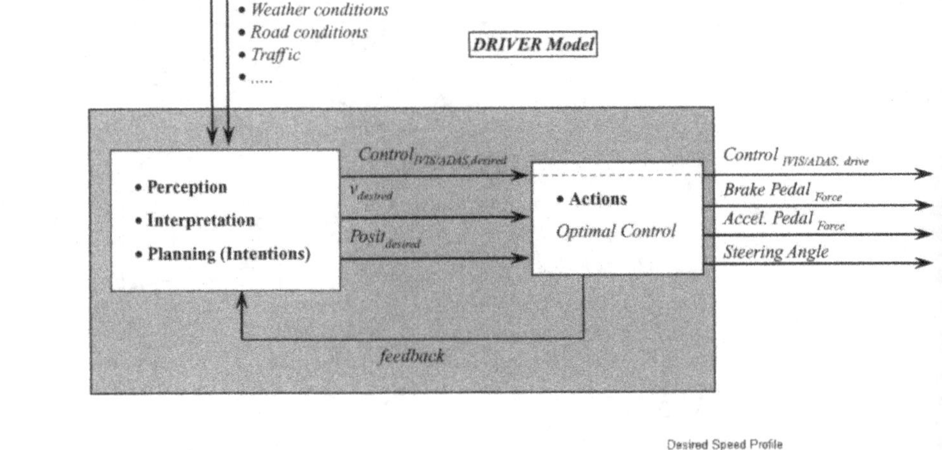

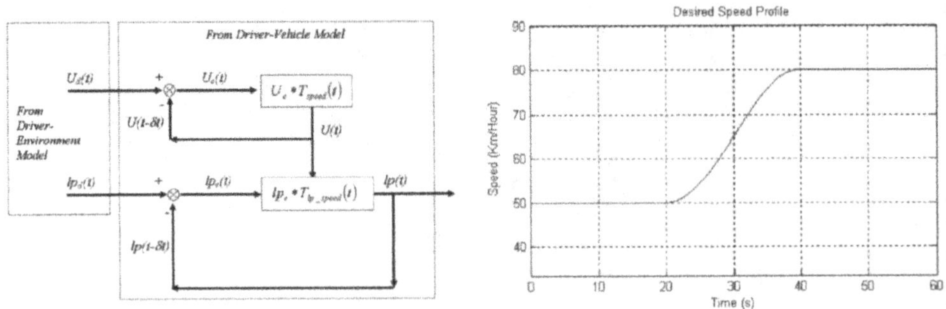

FIGURE 19.7. Control theory model of the SSDRIVE simulation and desired speed profile during transition from 50 to 80 km/h with a τ_{style} of 20 s.

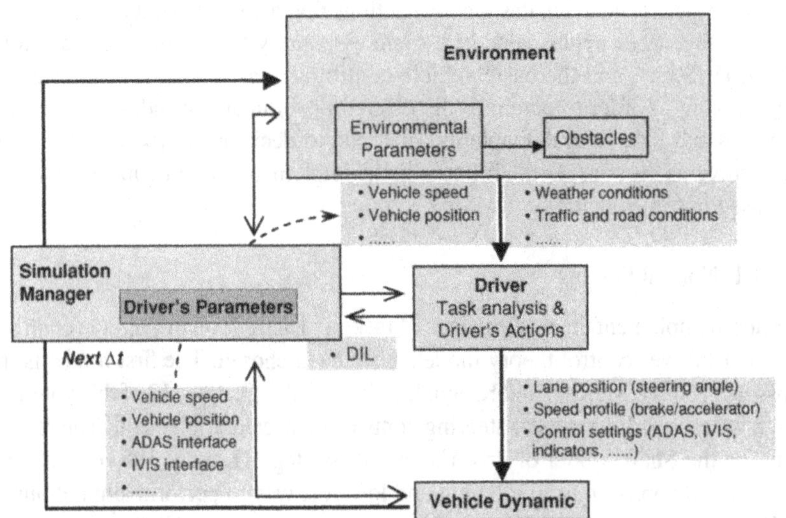

FIGURE 19.8. Overall dynamic DVE interaction process.

The detailed description of the control theory model applied within the SS-DRIVE simulation goes beyond the scope of the present chapter and can be found elsewhere (Re and Carusi, 2005). In brief, the simplified driver behaviour rules applied in the simulation are associated to the desired lane position (lp_d) and desired speed profile (U_d) (Fig. 19.7). These quantities are evaluated according to the following rules:

- Desired Lane Position (lp_d): the car maintains the centre of the lane.
- Desired Speed Profile (U_d): while the rule for desired lane position is regulated also in terms of driving good practice, to define the ideal speed profile is not equally simple. Taken into account the rule of minimising travel time according to driving at the maximum allowed speed (which means that after the transition U_d is almost constant in a highway), the desired driver speed profile is obtained by means of a smooth profile. This allows to increase or decrease speed after the decision of attaining higher or lower speeds taken by the more cognitive part of the simulation.

During the transition from a speed limit to the successive speed limit, U_d is modelled as $U_{Transition}$:

$$U_{Transition}\left(\tilde{t}\right) = \Delta V\left(\frac{1+\sin(\omega\tilde{t}-\pi/2)}{2}\right),$$

where $\omega = \pi/\tau_{style}$ and $\tilde{t} = 0 \div \tau_{style}$. The outcome of the optimal control process is then transformed into steering angle and actions on accelerator/brakes. The optimal control model does not affect the positions of controls and indicators of ADAS/IVIS and other settings, as these are evaluated by the cognitive part of the simulation.

The overall dynamic interaction within the DVE simulation of the SSDRIVE is finally summarised in Fig. 19.8. In particular, at each time step of the simulation, the *driver model* calculates the implementation of tasks and actions and generates profiles of steering angle and actions on the break or the accelerator, in order to accommodate for the desired lane position and speed profile.

The *Simulation Manager* is the governing module of the simulation, which receives input from all three main DVE components and evaluates the overall error-generation mechanism by means of the DIL and keeps account of the synchronisation of the simulation. The effect of ADAS and IVIS, if contained by the vehicle simulation, is also fed to the simulation manager.

19.2.4.2 Error in Control Actions

In the case of the SSDRIVE, moving from a control theory model extracted from assessed real data and designed in the continuous time domain to the implementation in discrete time domain without real mechanical constraints required some mathematical manipulations. In this way, it was possible to ensure the consistency between the cross-over model evaluated on test and the simulation. First of all the formulas were all merged from the Laplace S Transform to the time

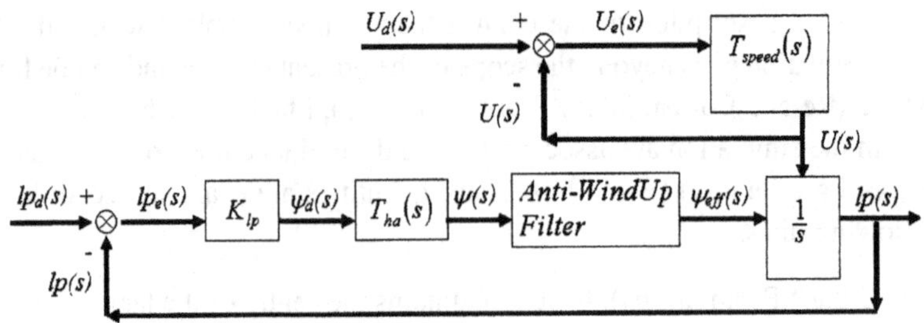

FIGURE 19.9. *Control model* in terms of the equivalent inner open loop Laplace transfer function of heading angle control.

domain. Following the Astrom–Wittenmark book, an anti-windup regulator has been added. This filter was proven necessary in order to avoid unrealistic output in certain condition, e.g., discontinuity due to U turns.

The actual formulation of the Open Loop Transfer Function for Speed Regulation, $T_{speed}(t)$, for Lane Position and Speed Control, $T_{lp\_speed}(t)$, for Lane Position Regulation with constant speed, $T_{lp\_const\_speed}(t)$, and the Closed Loop Transfer Function for Heading Angle Regulation, $T_{ha}(t)$, are shown in Fig. 19.9.

In order to simulate inadequate driver behaviour, the available variables are associated with the output of the *driver model*, namely actions on the vehicle controls, brake/accelerator pedals and steering angle (Fig. 19.7). The error types are defined at *modelling level.* While the actual modes, i.e., the actual magnitude of the errors, are defined in terms of amount of inappropriate steering, speed selection (brake/accelerator), IVIS/ADAS setting, etc., are defined at *input level* of the simulation. These quantities are implemented in the simulation through the control model by either inhibiting the appropriate feedback loop or by setting erroneous desired speed and vehicle positions.

The following are typical examples of errors that can be simulated and are defined in input:

- Incorrect settings of ADAS/IVIS.
- Improper acceleration/braking (ΔU_d).
- Insufficient or excessive steering (Δlp_d).

Discrete values of these quantities must be assigned in input in order to allow the simulation of limited sets of sequences of events.

An example of improper steering, due to driver distraction or other causes, is shown in Fig. 19.10, where a driver is simulated and will not correct the heading angle by means of the steer controller and will not decrease the speed for a certain time ($\tau_{distraction}$). This type of approach has also been attempted by Salvucci (2001). However, the SSDRIVE approach offers a wider variety of inadequate actions and causes as well as permitting the application of novel and diversified correlations of human error generation.

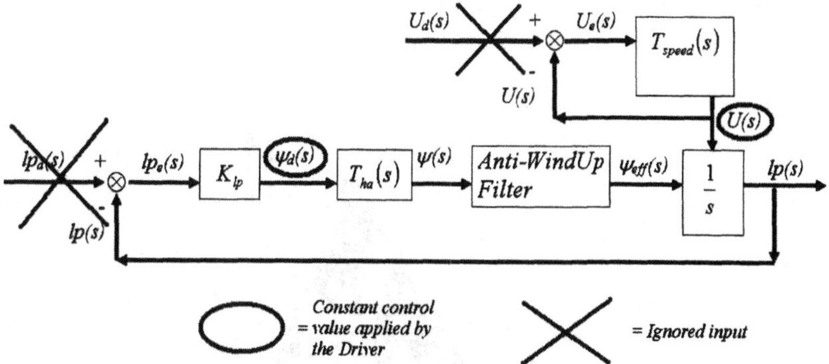

FIGURE 19.10. Simulation algorithms of inappropriate steering and speed control.

19.3 Sample Cases of Predictive DVE Interactions

The two sample cases discussed hereafter have the only objective to demonstrate the functionality of the simulation, rather than discussing detailed applications of predictions of DVE interactions according to well-defined scenarios and dynamic situations. The reason for such type of approach is dual: firstly, it would be too long to discuss in detail an application that attempts to predict DVE interactions, as the overall scenarios setting and DVE correlations would require an extended discussion and a accurate scientific justification. Secondly, the results of the simulation runs should also be analysed for their implications on the design and associated safety issues.

However, these issues go beyond the objectives of this paper, which is focused at demonstrating the availability of a DVE simulation tool, centred on the driver behaviour modelling, and at showing its potentialities in terms of diversity of behavioural adaptation, error generation and parametrical correlations. For these reasons, the following two sample cases discuss rather simple situations and highly theoretical situations that stress the computational power of the simulation rather than representing realistic behaviours of drivers in similar situations.

19.3.1 Case 1

The first sample case discussed here is based on a simple path considering a series of round turns and multiple lanes roundabouts trajectories. The lateral and angular deviations have been evaluated. The path is composed of two turns, one anticlockwise and one clockwise, and several times lane change on a three-lanes roundabout. No human error or inadequate behaviour is considered. The driver simulation follows the normative behaviour. The desired and actual paths calculated by the driver lane control model are illustrated in Fig. 19.11. It is clear that the desired path and the actual position of the vehicle are almost completely overlapping, even in the presence of a rather complex trajectory.

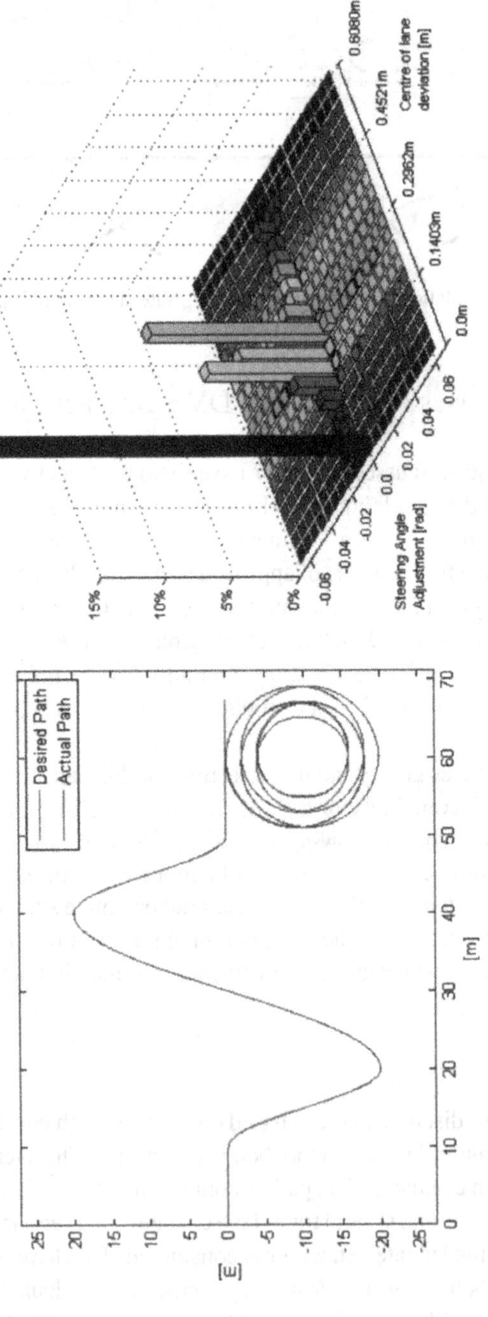

FIGURE 19.11. Study Case 1: Vehicle path analysis and centre lane deviation against steering angle adjustment.

As the speed profile was chosen constant, the effect of the adjustments of steering angle versus lateral deviation from the desired centre of lane could be evaluated. Negative values of steering angle correspond to steers in the right direction. As shown in Fig. 19.11, there are no particular trends in terms of steering angle adjustment and centre of lane lateral deviation. The histogram contains the distribution of the samples. The peak (20%) is around position (0.0; 0.0) and represents the samples coming from straight sections of the path. Most of the samples (>90%) are concentrated in the angular adjustment interval −0.01 to +0.01 radiant and more than 95% of samples have a centre of lane lateral deviation less than 0.29 m.

19.3.2 Case 2

The second sample case discussed here is the performance of the same paths simulated in the first sample case, where the difference is introduced in terms of a loss of control. We will not discuss here the reasons for such human error since the goal of the case study is to demonstrate the power of the simulation to represent the consequences of erroneous behaviour. The simulation of loss of control is performed by modelling the error as a freezing of steering control. As a consequence, no further adjustment of the steering angle occurs in order to follow the road centre lane.

As in the previous case, the desired and actual paths calculated by the driver lane control model are reported in Fig. 19.12. It is clear that at a certain instant, the desired path and the actual position of the vehicle separate completely and, unless a recovery action takes place, the vehicle is actually driven off the road. In

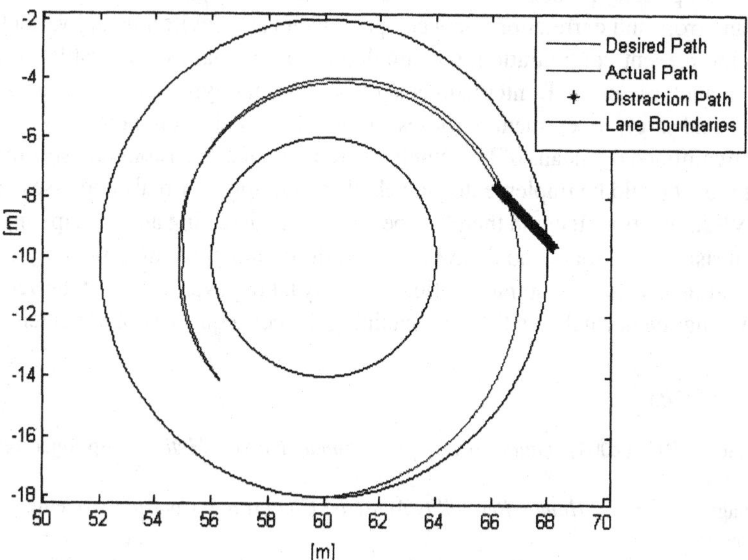

FIGURE 19.12. Study Case 2: Vehicle path analysis in the case of erroneous steering.

this case, no recovery action was simulated and the overall DVE interaction was stopped at the time of expected vehicle loss of control.

19.4 Conclusions

In this paper, we have described the SSDRIVE. While the governing model and the basic theoretical considerations are derived from a specific paradigm described in *refer to the paper* (Carsten, 2007), in this paper we have discussed the set of default correlations and algorithms that are implemented in the simulation. The overall architecture of the SSDRIVE simulation has been conceived with the objective of maximum flexibly from the user point of view. In other words, the simulation is based on a modular structure and the user is able to include in the simulation different models and modules describing specific driver support and information systems, in accordance to specific needs or design options.

Following a set of preliminary tests, the model can be considered stable and reliable. The development of the model and simulation will continue in terms of deviation analysis during control delay and control freezing conditions. In particular, the analysis of a variety of IVIS and ADAS interventions will be gradually included in the simulation, following the same principle of maximum flexibly for the user. In this way, the core features of the SSDRIVE simulation will remain unchanged, in terms of basic modelling architecture and fundamental principles, such as the consideration for task analysis process, normative versus descriptive driver behaviour, number of *parameters* that govern driver behaviour and basic DVE interactions. At the same time, thanks to the modularity of the simulation approach adopted, the users of SSDRIVE will be able to test specific configurations, typical proprietary models of ADAS and IVIS, as well as particular algorithms for human errors and correlations between parameters and environmental variables.

In the present configuration, the simulation tool is mainly applicable for predictive analyses of DVE interactions and for studying hypothetical scenarios for design and safety assessment purposes. However, once the simulation is validated and streamlined by means of fast running parametrical expressions and specific algorithms, it could be implemented in vehicle technology for real-time assessment of DVE interaction. It could therefore be applied for detecting and anticipating potential risky behaviours and dangerous conditions, and preventing them by either suggesting possible driver intervention and/or by taking over control of the vehicle, recovering the normal situation or containing the consequences of a incident.

References

Cacciabue, P.C. (2004). *Guide to Applying Human Factors Methods.* Springer-Verlag, London.

Hollnagel, E. (1993). *Human Reliability Analysis: Context and Control.* Academic Press, London.

Hollnagel, E. and Woods, D.D. (1983). Cognitive Systems Engineering: New wine in new bottles. *International Journal of Man-Machine Studies*, 18, 583–606.

Kirwan, B. and Ainsworth, L.K. (1992). *Guide to Task Analysis.* Taylor and Francis, London.

Kondo, M. (1953). Directional stability (when steering is added). *Journal of the Society of Automotive Engineers of Japan,* 7(5/6), 104–106, 109, 123, 136–140. (In Japanese.)

McRuer, D.T., Allen, R.W., Weir, D.H. and Klein, R.H. (1977). New results in driver steering control. *Human Factors,* 19, 381–397.

McRuer, D.T., Graham, D., Kredel, E. and Reisener, W. (1965). Human pilot dynamics in compensatory systems – theory, models and experiments with controlled elements and forcing function variations. Report AFFDL-TR65-15. Wright Patterson AFB, OH.

McRuer, D.T. and Krendel, E.S. (1974). Mathematical models of human pilot behavior. AGARDograph No. 188. NATO Advisory Group for Aerospace Research and Development.

Michon, J.A. (1985). A critical review of driver behaviour models: What do we know? What should we do? In L.A. Evans and R.C. Schwing (Eds.). *Human Behaviour and Traffic Safety* (pp. 487–525). Plenum Press, New York.

Minsky, M. (1975). A framework for representing knowledge. In P. Winston (Ed.). *The Psychology of Computer Vision.* McGraw-Hill, New York.

Moray, N. (1997). Human factors in process control. In G. Salvendi (Ed.). *Handbook of Human Factors and Ergonomics* (pp. 1945–1971). Wiley, New York.

Neisser, U. (1967). *Cognitive Psychology.* Appleton-Century-Crofts, New York.

Newell, A. and Simon, H.A. (1972). *Human Problem Solving.* Prentice-Hall, Englewood Cliffs, NY.

Rasmussen, J. (1983). Skills, rules and knowledge: Signals, signs and symbols; and other distinctions in human performance model. *IEEE Transactions on Systems, Man, and Cybernetics,* 13(3), 257–267.

Re, C. and Carusi, E. (2005). Driving stability correlated with automated in-vehicle systems. In *24th Annual European Conference on Human Decision Making,* Athens.

Rouse, W.B. (1980). *Systems Engineering Models of Human-Machine Interaction.* North Holland, Oxford.

Salvucci, D.D. (2001) Predicting the effects of in-car interface use on driver performance: An integrated model approach. *International Journal of Human-Computer Studies,* 55, 85–107.

Stassen, H.G., Johannsen, G. and Moray, N. (1990). Internal representation, internal model, human performance model and mental workload. *Automatica,* 26(4), 811–820.

Sheridan, T.B. (1992). *Telerobotics, Automation and Human Supervisory Control.* The MIT Press, Cambridge, MA.

von Neumann, J. (1958). *The Computer and the Brain.* Yale University Press, New Haven, CT.

Wiener, N. (1948). *Cybernetics.* MIT Press, Cambridge, MA.

Wickens, C.D. (1984). *Engineering Psychology and Human Performance.* Merrill, Columbus, OH.

Wickens, C.D. (2002). Multiple resources and performance prediction. *Theoretical Issues in Ergonomics Science,* 3, 159–177.

Weir, D.H. and Chao, K.C. (2007). Review of control theory models for directional and speed control. In P.C. Cacciabue (Ed.). *Modelling Driver Behaviour in Automotive Environments.* Springer, London.

VIII
Simulation of Traffic and Real Situations

20
Real-Time Traffic and Environment Risk Estimation for the Optimisation of Human–Machine Interaction

ANGELOS AMDITIS, ARIS POLYCHRONOPOULOS AND E. BEKIARIS

20.1 Introduction

The development of next generation driver–vehicle interaction systems should be focused towards obtaining a safe and sustainable mobility, with the aim to half the number of road accidents as proposed by the European Commission (2001). Mobility should be promoted in the future towards 'intermodality' in order to reduce traffic congestion and to optimise travel planning; however, towards this aim there is an increasing demand for on-board information systems. These needs together with the demand for new on-vehicle support and services and the need of the users to be connected to their own information cell (mobile phone, PDA, etc.) will unavoidably increase the number of interaction of the driver with the vehicle thus raising the potential risk of driver's distraction and fatigue, which are among the main causes of road accidents.

While conventional vehicle safety measures (seatbelts and airbags) have contributed significantly to the reduction of fatalities in the last decades, their safety contribution is reaching its limits and currently further improvement is difficult to be achieved at a reasonable cost. Today, the development of new advanced driver assistance systems (ADAS, e.g. collision avoidance, lane-keeping aid and vision enhancement systems) offers great potential for further improving road safety, in particular by means of mitigating driver errors. In addition, the number of in-vehicle information systems (IVIS) increases rapidly in today's vehicles. These systems have the potential to greatly enhance mobility and comfort (e.g. navigation aids and traffic information systems, media players, web browsers, etc.), but at the same time increase the risk for excessive and dangerous levels of inattention to the vehicle control task. Furthermore, many IVIS functions are today featured on portable computing systems, such as PDAs or advanced mobile phones, which are generally not designed for use while driving. In the near future, many of these functions could be expected to be easily downloadable from a remote service centre, directly to the vehicle or the nomadic device.

This variety of systems and functions that interact with the driver in one way or another leads to a number of challenges, both technical and human factors related, for the designer of the future automotive HMIs. These challenges include the HMI design for the individual systems as well as the question as to how to integrate a range of different systems into a functioning whole with respect to their interaction with the driver. Another challenge concerns how to best exploit the technological possibilities of adaptive interfaces in the automotive domain.

The latter is the main proposition that the paper deals with. It primarily addresses the adaptivity features of human–machine interaction related to the external traffic and environmental conditions. In particular, the environment is modelled and risks are calculated based on the current macroscopic driver's behaviour. A real-time supervision system is being developed and presented, which detects, analyses and assesses the environment. The outcome is a calculated level of risk on several driving scenarios or states of the environment. According to the risk level, a message can be presented to the driver or not, enabling the aforementioned adaptivity features of integrated HMI systems.

In the sequel, two different use cases are presented that represent two different systems and concepts: the AWAKE system, in which the traffic and environment supervision is used to adapt a safety application to the environment – an adaptive hypovigilance driver warning system (DWS) – and the AIDE system that offers an adaptive integrated HMI solution for conflicts between on-board messages that compete in order to be presented to the driver. AWAKE was the first attempt to calculate an overall level of traffic risk, whereas AIDE proposes a complete algorithm that covers most of the critical traffic scenarios.

20.2 The AWAKE Use Case – Adaptation of a Driver Hypovigilance Warning System

20.2.1 AWAKE System Overview

Recent research indicates that driver hypovigilance is a major cause of road accidents (Horne and Rayner, 1999). Accidents related to hypovigilance are generally more serious than accidents related to other causes (alcohol, speeding, right of way refusal) because a drowsy driver is not likely to take an evasive action prior to a collision. If a cruise control is used, the vehicle may keep its speed until a major impact. Reduction of collisions due to driver hypovigilance may contribute significantly to a reduction of traffic crash losses. Drowsiness-related accidents usually occur during late-night hours, with a smaller peak in the mid-afternoon. Young drivers have no increased risk during the afternoon, while drivers over 45 have fewer night time crashes, and are more likely to have such crashes during the mid-afternoon. It is also estimated that drivers younger than 30 years (constituting one fourth of licensed drivers) account for almost two thirds of drowsy driving crashes. These research results led to the need for the development of a system for monitoring the driver's state: the AWAKE system (www.awake-eu.org).

Additionally, apart from normal drowsiness, the problem might be also directly related to the introduction of various ADAS in the next years in the market. Automated or even assistive driving systems may also induce fatigue and stress to the driver caused by prolonged driving under monotonous driving conditions. Stress due to overload of information may also lead to fatigue. Therefore, the occurrence of driver hypovigilance might well increase due to the introduction of ADAS. However, at the same time ADAS technology may as well provide solutions to this problem.

The objective of the AWAKE project was the development of an unobtrusive and reliable in-vehicle system to monitor the driver and the environment, for real-time detection of hypovigilance, based on multiple parameters. Continuous, instead of discrete, event-related driver monitoring, effective system personalisation based on driver characteristics, and consideration of the actual traffic situation enhances the reliability of the system and minimises the false alarm rate. In case of hypovigilance, the system provides an adequate warning to the driver. Several warning levels were used, depending on the estimated level of driver's hypovigilance and the estimated level of traffic risk. The system was designed for highway driving and should operate reliably and effectively in all highway scenarios. The system consists of the following modular components (Amditis et al., 2002b):

- Hypovigilance diagnosis module (HDM) that detects and diagnoses driver hypovigilance in real time. Based on an artificial intelligence algorithm this module fuses data from on-board driver monitoring sensors (eyelid and steering grip data) and data regarding the driver's behaviour (lane tracking, gas/brake and steering position data).
- A traffic risk estimation module (TRE) that assesses the traffic situation and the involved risks. It matches, following a deterministic approach, data from an enhanced digital navigational map, a positioning system, anti-collision radar, the odometer and a driver's gaze direction sensor. This module is not designed as a complete new system to estimate traffic risk, but rather as an expert combination of existing ADAS technology. The output of this module was used by the HDM to re-assess the state of the driver and by the DWS to determine the adequate level of warning.
- A DWS that uses acoustic, visual and/or haptic means. The module uses inputs from the HDM and the TRE to determine the adequate warning level for a certain situation.

20.2.2 Traffic Risk Estimation in AWAKE System

The purpose of a TRE module is to assess the traffic situation around the vehicle and thus, the involved risks for the driver and passengers. The information computed by TRE is communicated with a number named RLI (risk-level index), in which there is information about the severity of the situation, deriving from the situation itself. In on-board system architecture, the TRE module can be regarded as part of the on-board information system. The TRE module generates useful information to adequately prioritise the information flow towards the driver in view of the surrounding traffic situation. Moreover, the computation of a general risk level can also be used for other applications, e.g. for tuning of the warning strategies to the specific situation. In the AWAKE project, the evaluation of a general risk index is used as input to the warning system. In summary, risk is a function of

- the state of the vehicle (its dynamic condition described by speed, acceleration, etc.);
- road scenario (type of road: motorways, urban roads, etc.);
- traffic scenario (complexity, speed, density);
- environment (weather conditions, visibility);
- driver conditions (perception of the surrounding environment, distraction).

A complete and integrated TRE system would be very complex and was far from an industrial exploitation phase in AWAKE. It was not an objective of the AWAKE project to develop new sensors to create such advanced system. However, the concept of the TRE system is modular and can therefore be easily adapted to the sensor system of the vehicle in which it is installed. TRE module consists of four main blocks (Damiani et al., 2003). The first unit, sensors, includes both the sensors that are standard available in the car, and which are shared with other on-board functions (ABS, etc.), and specific sensors added to the vehicle for the TRE module. The second unit, scenario assessment (SA), integrates all information coming from the sensors. The third unit, warning strategies, identifies discrete risks and their risk level, while the fourth unit, risk-level assessment (RLA), integrates the discrete risks into a unique overall RLI.

20.2.3 The Scenario-Assessment Unit

The goal of an SA unit is to collect and process information from all sensors and to make this information available to other units. In particular, it collects, synchronises, filters and integrates the raw data from the sensors. Moreover, it provides additional information derived from integration of sensor information and combination with previous information (e.g., the gaze sensor provides angles, from which may be calculated what the driver is actually looking at; the vehicle trajectory is calculated from current position – calculated from sensor inputs – in combination with previous positions) and describes the situation (scenario). Different sensors have different sample frequencies and may not be synchronised. The module has to manage these time and frequency differences in the flow of incoming data, to match and translate the data into a flow of descriptions (pictures) of the situation around the vehicle, and of the (dynamic) situation of the vehicle itself, with a typical update rate of 10 Hz. The unit has an open and modular structure, which allows both different combinations of sensors, according to the sensor availability in the vehicle in which the TRE module is installed, as well as easier future addition of newly installed sensors.

20.2.4 The Warning Strategies Unit

The warning strategies unit receives a high-level situation description in terms of environment identification and physical data. It produces a set of warning levels

TABLE 20.1. Definition of warning level index.

Warning level	Situation
WL1	No danger (normal situation)
WL2	Attention required (cautionary)
WL3	Danger (imminent risk)

that represent the risk level for each single event. The warning strategies unit employs several algorithms that implement the specific warning criteria. As output, a warning level index is generated as described in Table 20.1.

20.2.5 The Risk-Level Assessment Unit

The RLA unit receives a set of warning levels (one for each warning event that is taken into consideration) and computes the final RLI. This value describes the risk level of the overall situation and is also an output of the TRE (as are the warning levels of the warning strategies unit). The RLI implicitly contains information about the time factor of a dangerous situation and about the severity of the potential damage. As mentioned before, the RLA unit receives a set of warning levels (one for each warning event that is taken into consideration) and computes the composite RLI. This value describes the risk level of the overall situation and it is an output of the TRE module as well.

At the actual stage of work progresses, a scale for the TRE module output is defined and proposed in which four levels of risk are distinguished, as described in the previous table. Based on a survey of the state of the art of these topics (e.g. Montanari et al., 2002), the messages to be given to the driver were divided into four main groups depending on their priority level. This approach to assign four levels of priority to the messages has been the starting point for defining the four levels of risk as output from the RLA unit. According to Table 20.2, there is a normal situation when no risks are identified and the corresponding risk level is given the value of 1. The cautionary case is divided in two distinct levels, slight cautionary and severe cautionary. Because of this distinction four (instead of three) risk-levels emerge. Risk level 4, the imminent case, represents the most dangerous situation and corresponds to a red alarm. This requires an immediate driver reaction. A special problem is how to assess the overall traffic risk, i.e. how to reduce different

TABLE 20.2. Level of risk.

Risk level index	Description	Associated colour
1	Normal situation (no risk estimated, scenario identified, factor detected)	Green
2	Slight cautionary case (single scenario or factor)	Yellow
3	Severe cautionary case (combination of scenarios and factors)	Orange
4	Imminent case (highest risk)	Red

traffic risks to the same denominator. For this purpose, a method was proposed by Damiani et al. (2003) for the classification of critical traffic scenarios according to the associated level of risk. The more promising approach seems to be a mix of a simple rule-based system with a weighted sum approach, which assigns a pre-defined value to each single warning originating from a specific function. In particular, the proposed rules are as follows:

Normal situation – If the levels of warning coming out from the different functions are all at their own minimum value, then the output will be always 1.

Intermediate cases – In order to distinguish between levels 2 and 3, the criteria are based on a sum of weighed values (a particular pre-defined value is assigned to a warning level originating from a specific function).

Imminent case – As soon as a maximum level of warning is provided by one of the functions, the output will be always 4.

20.3 The AIDE Use Case – Optimisation of the In-Vehicle Human–Machine Interaction

The general objective of the AIDE (adaptive integrated driver–vehicle interface) project (www.aide-eu.org and Engström et al., 2004) is to address these challenges by means of tightly integrated interdisciplinary work, involving leading human factors as well as technical expertise. Following are the specific topics addressed by the project:

- The development of a detailed understanding of the behavioural effects of interacting with different types of in-vehicle functions.
- The design of human–machine interaction (HMI) strategies for ADAS that maximises the safety potential of the systems.
- The design of HMI strategies for IVIS that minimise the added workload and distraction to the driving task.
- The development of strategies for integrating multiple in-vehicle functions into a coherent interface towards the driver.
- The development of technological solutions, e.g. multimodal input–output devices, driver–vehicle–environment monitoring techniques and an underlying software architecture that supports this.
- The development of solutions for the safe integration of nomadic devices into the driving environment.
- The development of valid and cost-efficient methods for in-vehicle HMI evaluation with respect to safety and usability.

In the above context, driver–vehicle–environment (DVE) is modelled in order (a) to understand driver behaviour in presence of ADAS and IVIS and (b) to estimate in real time the current state of the DVE components. While (a) is not under the scope of the paper, (b) is the main focus of the presented work. DVE real-time modelling includes the development of a perception system that extends existing or under development frameworks for safety of comfort applications, e.g. Tatschke et al. (2006) in order to include driver's information to the perception architecture. The DVE module estimates the state of the DVE individual components and calculates level of risks as higher levels of abstraction for direct exploitation from the HMI component. The following components are included:

(a) Traffic and environment risk estimation (vehicle, traffic, environment and their relationships) – TERA
(b) Cockpit activity assessment (driver's activities not related to the driving task) – CAA
(c) Driver availability estimation (driver's activities related to the driving task) – DAE
(d) Driver state degradation (driver's physical ability) – DSD
(e) Driver characteristics (driver's individual behaviour and preferences) – DC

The (a) component is a successor of TRE module, namely the TERA module and it is described in details in this paper.

20.3.1 Overview

Traffic and environment risk assessment (TERA) in AIDE monitors and measures activities outside the vehicle in order to assess the external contributors to the environmental and traffic context and also to predict the driver's intention for lateral manoeuvre. Existing sensors used by collision-warning (long-range radars), lane departure warning (cameras), blind spot warning (cameras), maps and positioning systems combined with a table of corresponding roadway characteristics and vehicle inertial sensors could be used to help understand the environment outside the vehicle and adapt the HMI accordingly. The supervision algorithms collect all available raw (e.g. radar signals) and processed data (e.g. tracked object list). The role of TERA is threefold:

- to calculate in real time a total level of risk related to traffic and environmental parameters;
- to calculate environmental and traffic parameters according to the requirements of the other DVE modules and/or warnings if a function is absent in the vehicle (e.g. the collision warning function could be produced from TERA if a radar is available);
- to estimate the drivers' intention (e.g. for manoeuvre of a possible lane change).

The above analysis is applicable to all possible parameters:

- time to collision in longitudinal control systems;
- predicted minimum distance and time to go in dynamic systems;
- speed when approaching a curve;
- environmental profile;
- road profile.

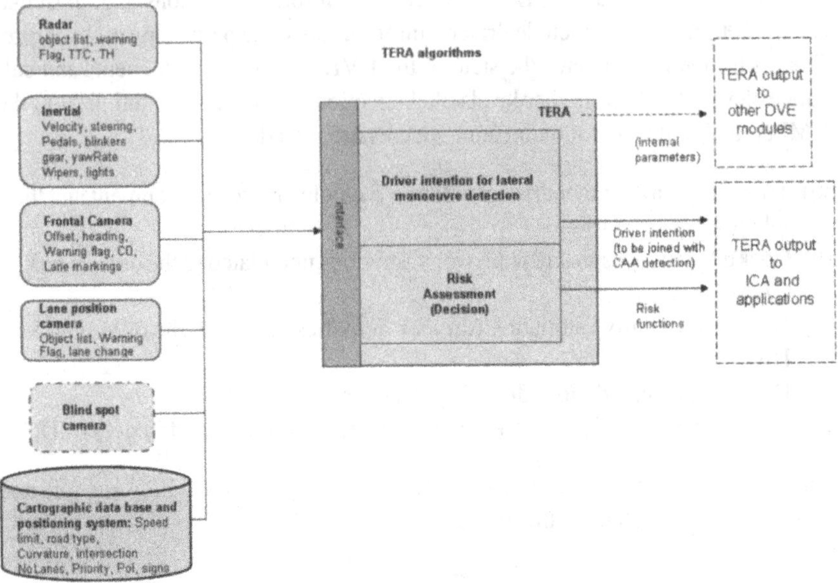

FIGURE 20.1. TERA module functional architecture.

20.3.2 Architecture

The role of TERA is represented by the two physical blocks, namely the risk assessment and the intention detection. In Fig. 20.1, the connections with the other components are indicated in the vehicle environment. The physical interfaces are out of the scope of this document (CAN, TCP, etc.). An adequate software module is under development, to combine all different pieces of information from the various subsystems in a coherent whole, running on an on-board computer.

Input sensor array includes input control sensors (e.g. steering wheel angle sensor, pedal position sensor), environment sensors (radar, laser, IR, etc., but also GPS and digital maps) and vehicle dynamic state sensors (speed sensors, accelerometers, yaw rate sensors).

20.3.2.1 Relevance to the AIDE Use Cases

Starting from the AIDE design scenarios, a scheme for adapting a vehicle HMI to a high traffic or environment risk situation is presented. Two different cases (in terms of the cause and not of the proposed solution) of HMI adaptation are considered accordingly to TERA module's outputs:

- *High traffic risk situations* – High traffic risk value should signify a quite dangerous situation where a warning might have already been generated or the possibility to be generated is high. In those cases, adaptation can only have the meaning of a stricter prioritisation by the ICA in order to let only warnings to be presented (and even only one warning in order to minimise possible distraction effects from other messages in a difficult driving situation). Thus, high traffic risk value affects only output messages' scheduling (delay or cancel).

- *High environment risk situations* – High environment risk value signifies an increased workload situation where the reaction time of the driver might be reduced due to road characteristics or bad weather conditions and thus we propose to present important information or warnings earlier or with greater intensity. A modality adaptation could also be the case if a recommended alternative modality is available for an output message. In a heavy rain situation, where the audio messages are not so well received due to the surrounding noise, a modality alteration to visual could occur. Thus, high environment risk value can affect the presentation of both warnings and important output messages.

In addition, to the two former subcategories of TERA-detected conditions, there is also a third output of this module which will affect the AIDE HMI. This is the detection of the driver intention to perform a lateral manoeuvre.

- *Lateral manoeuvring intent* – In the envisioned HMI adaptation functionality, is generally of interest that the intention detection will be able to discriminate between a simple manoeuvre and a high-demanding manoeuvre in order to treat accordingly low- and high-priority information scheduling. Finally, it can be noted that in the general envisioned HMI functionality, detecting on-going manoeuvres, is considered a case of driving demand detection. The intention detection is presented in Section 20.3.4.

20.3.2.2 Description of Environment

The challenge in recent years is the environment recognition all around the subject vehicle so as to be able to prevent risks (collision, lane/road departure, etc.) in the longitudinal, rear and lateral field. Traffic and environment risk within AIDE is perceived as a major contributor to the driver's workload. The elements that describe the scenario that is assessed through the TERA module are as follows:

(a) the road infrastructure consisting of the lanes, the road borders and the infrastructure elements (e.g. speed limit, traffic signs);
(b) the subject vehicle and its dynamics;
(c) the moving and stationary obstacles;
(d) the traffic flow representing the number of obstacles ahead or/and their distances from the ego-vehicle;
(e) environmental parameters.

Using the vehicle data (e.g. yaw-rate sensor) and the data coming from 'external sensors' (radar and possibly camera), it is possible to compute and assess the subject vehicle's trajectory. The method that is used within AIDE TERA module is the scenario representation by analysing the following state elements (Polychronopoulos et al., 2005):

(a) Object State = the dynamics of the objects in the longitudinal field.
(b) Subject State = the dynamics of the subject-vehicle.
(c) Road State = the geometry of the lanes and road borders.

The vehicle's present curvature (C_0) is represented by the following formula: $C_0 = \Omega/v$, where Ω is the yaw-rate value, v is the vehicle speed and C_0 is the inverse of the radius of the curvature covered by the vehicle ($C_0 = 1/R$). The more sophisticated is the model that is used, the more precise the vehicle motion assessment will be. All elements in the proposed approach can be mathematically represented by a state vector and are briefly described below:

(a) The road borders and lanes are described by a clothoid model (Kirchner and Heinrich, 1998): $y(x) = c_0\frac{x^2}{2} + c_1\frac{x^3}{6} + y_0$, where y_0 is the offset from the ego-vehicle's position, c_0 is the road curvature andy_{0l} the rate of the curvature. Different offsets y_{0l} and y_{0r} represent the left and the right border locations. Thus, the following state vector can describe the road (or the lane): $\hat{x}_{RB} = (c_0\ c_1\ y_{0l}\ y_{0r})^T$. The measurement space includes higher level parameters from a camera (and its image processing unit for lane detection), map and positioning data and inertial sensors (odometer, yaw rate sensor).
(b) The state of the subject vehicle (SV) contains kinematics, attributes and properties. A typical state vector of the former case is $\hat{x}_{SV} = (V\ a\ \omega\ \theta)^T$, where V is the velocity, $\alpha\alpha$s the tangential acceleration, θ is the heading and ω the yaw rate.
(c) The state of the obstacles contains also kinematics, attributes and properties such as: $\hat{x}_o = (x\ y\ V_x\ V_y\ a_x\ a_y\ w\ h)^T$. Here, (x, y) are the Cartesian coordinates in a local coordinate system (i.e. the subject's vehicle coordinate system) and V, and α is the relative velocity and acceleration respectively in the two axis. W and h refer to the properties of the tracked obstacles.

The measurement space is produced by the radar signals corresponding to moving obstacles due to the Doppler effect. Other signals coming from the vehicle bus (CAN bus – controller area network) or from the map database assist to the correct interpretation of the scenario. These signals are raw data communicated through the vehicle network:

(a) *Road data* – Type of road context (country, urban, peri-urban, highway, urban highway), priority level of the road, number of lane, speed limit, presence of school, etc.
(a) *Vehicle data* – Blinkers status, wipers' position and light position.

20.3.3 Algorithm for Risk Assessment

20.3.3.1 Rule-Based System Employed for TERA Algorithms

TERA module expected condition detection involves detection of the following conditions:

- *Driver is approaching a dangerous curve with high speed* – A prediction of the risk involved in terms of the vehicle leaving its lane, or road, in the curve due to over speeding with respect to the road's curvature.
- *Risk of frontal/lateral collision* – Frontal and lateral obstacles presence, and distance and acceleration estimation should lead to a decision on the potential unsafe driving situation with respect to the ego-vehicle's path against surrounding vehicles' estimated path.
- *Risk of road/lane exit* – Risk involved with respect to the lateral position of the vehicle in comparison with the road/lane limits.

On the basis of these three basic conditions, TERA risk assessment produces a set of traffic risk functions that take into consideration not only this detection of discrete dangerous situations around the subject vehicle but also the traffic and the environment context where these situations occur. However, in order to ensure the correct system's output in case of a dangerous situation, this conditions' correlation with the traffic and environment context takes place only when the basic conditions are not classified as imminent.

In the following, *the rule-based approach* adopted for TERA algorithms is illustrated explaining the functions' derivation. In each of the TERA functions, the *first coefficient* reflects the *main condition to be detected*, where the *second coefficient* reflects the *risk contributor* derived from specific characteristics (parameters) of the current driving scenario. Each coefficient inside the second coefficient represents a sub-condition (subsidiary condition) and is multiplied with a number w between 0 and 1 (confidence weight) where $\sum_m w_i = 1$ and m is the amount of selected sub-conditions (if main condition NOT imminent):

$$TERA\,Function = (\text{main-condition})\times\{[(\text{sub\_condition1})\times w_1]+[(\text{sub\_condition2})\times w_2]+\ldots\ [(\text{sub-condition})\times w_m]\}$$

where (float) *TERAFunction* $\in [0,1]$ and each of the main conditions and their corresponding sub-conditions can either have deterministic (wipers status) or fuzzy (TTC) values. In the first case, variables that are involved in the conditions or sub-conditions' derivation are modelled by membership functions (trapezoidal or Gaussian) and thus, the operations among variables are replaced from operations among fuzzy sets. In the second case, relevant variables have scalar or Boolean values. In addition, a sub-condition can also be the logical output of two or more conditions following the binary aggregation according to the Boole algebra. Weights give the possibility to externally control system's outputs. Moreover each condition can influence in a different way each function which gives the system a more realistic-intelligent overview of the current scenario.

Thus, the enhanced rule-based approach adopted for each of the TERA traffic risk functions is based on estimating one main condition (high level situation description), which is then modulated by a factor representing the confidence assigned to the main condition detection. This factor consists of a weighted sum of the sub-conditions considered to influence the specific main condition. Such sub-conditions may involve consideration of the data coming from the vehicle inertial sensors (including environmental information) and the data coming from the map and positioning system combined with a table of corresponding roadway characteristics in order to create a more global picture of the environment outside the vehicle within the current driving scenario. However, it should be noted once again that this approach is valid only if the main condition has not been classified as imminent.

The main conditions to be detected lead to the three following traffic risk functions:

- Risk of approaching a curve with high speed (DangCurveAppr).
- Risk of frontal/lateral collision (RiskLFColl).
- Risk of road/lane exit (RiskRLExit).

First weights will be defined from experts' opinions and previous experience in the field (Bekiaris and Portouli, 1999; Damiani et al., 2003). TERA function concerning environment risk assessment will be similar to the way that traffic risk is calculated.

In the second step, an overall risk assessment function associates these higher level functions with each other and eventually produces the two risk functions required by the ICA in order to adapt the system's HMI with respect to traffic and environment risk estimation. This association of the individual higher level risk functions adopts a weighted-aggregation approach based on experts' opinions and TERA team's previous experience in the field.

The final overall traffic risk function (TrRisk) can be thus derived using a weighted sum of the three internal risk functions:

$$\text{TrRisk} = (\text{DangCurveAppr} > \text{thres1}) \times w_1 + (\text{RiskLFColl} > \text{thres2}) \times w_2 + (\text{RiskRLExit} > \text{thres3}) \times \text{w3}$$

First weights will be defined from experts' opinions and previous experience in the field and modulated in accordance with real data sets tests.

20.3.3.2 Main Traffic Risk Condition Detection

The risk assessment supervision algorithms collect all available raw (e.g. radar signals) and processed data (e.g. tracked object list) from the sensors in terms of the traffic and the environment parameters. The risk assessment produces a set of basic risk functions representing an interpretation of the current driving scenario in terms of discrete dangers around the vehicle. The types of possible situations are frontal (lateral/blind spot) collision, lane/road departure and dangerous curve approaching situation. The functions used to evaluate each of the above situations are based on deterministic consideration of the road scenario. The risk value is extracted by comparing the value of relevant parameters with pre-defined fixed or adaptive thresholds. For each function, three modalities are defined: information and imminent and an intermediate cautionary case.

20.3.3.2.1 Risk of Frontal/(Lateral) Collision

The frontal/lateral collision risk function has the aim to evaluate the risk due to an obstacle present on the host-vehicle trajectory. Such a function uses a long-range radar to assess the distance, the velocity and the angular position of the objects ahead or aside. The fundamental point is to understand if one (or more) object(s) detected by the radar in front of the vehicle is dangerous, and in case it becomes an obstacle, or not. In order to assess this event, the object has to be inside the driving path (a path wide 1.5 to 2 m, more or less the same width of an ordinary sedan): If this is the case, it is considered as a potentially dangerous obstacle. In the method used by conventional ACC systems, one main assumption is made about the motion of the objects (deterministic method which ignores the time parameter): The host-vehicle obstacle is regarded as moving with constant speed (straight uniform motion).

20.3.3.2.2 Criteria of Assigning the Level of Risk

The common measurements concerning safety distance are calculated according to the criteria of 'time-to-collision (TTC)' and 'headway':

- TTC is the time that results from the distance Δx (between leading and rear bumper) from a leading car ($\text{car}_{\text{leading}}$) to the own car ($\text{car}_{\text{system}}$), divided by the difference of velocity ($v_{\text{system}} - v_{\text{leading}}$) between both of them

$$t_{\text{TTC}} = \left| \frac{\Delta x}{v_{\text{system}} - v_{\text{leading}}} \right| .$$

- Headway is the time that results from the above-named distance Δx and the velocity v_{system} of the system car

$$t_{\text{Headway}} = \frac{\Delta x}{v_{\text{system}}} .$$

The corresponding warning distances are calculated with a predetermined time (t_{TTC} and t_{Headway}) for several dangerous situations (cautionary and imminent). The larger calculated warning distance is defined as criterion of the system activation. The determination of the specific thresholds of TTC and headway for both dangerous situations is accomplished deriving from NHTSA (see below). The imminent case applies to

- TTC between 3 and 5 s or less;
- headway between 1 and 1.5 s or less.

The cautionary case applies to

- TTC is larger than in the imminent case but not larger than 10 to 14 s (5 s $\leq$ TTC $\leq$ 10 to 14 s);
- headway is larger than in the imminent case but not larger than 2 to 3 s (1.5 s $\leq$ headway $\leq$ 2 to 3 s).

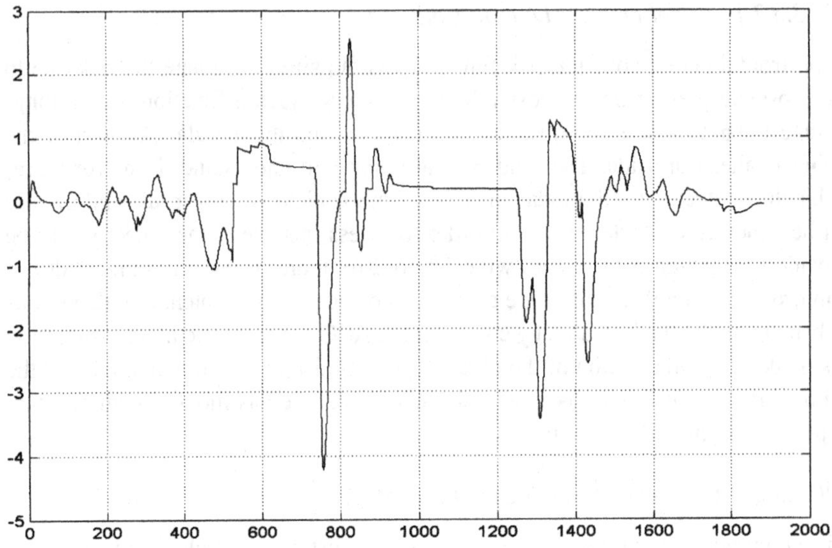

FIGURE 20.2. Lateral velocity (m/s) evolution in time in a given scenario.

20.3.3.2.3 Risk of Lane/Road Departure

The lane/road risk function evaluates the risk due to unintentional lane departure or in a more general way the risk due to a wrong lateral behaviour of the driver in the road (i.e. travelling between two lanes). The frontal camera is the main sensor for this function but information about speed and use of indicators are also considered.

The strategy that seems to be the nearest to driver's needs (to have a proper and constant reaction time) is 'Time to Line Cross': when the time to cross the line decreases under a threshold time, a warning is issued. These computations take into account the lateral speed of the vehicle. If the lateral speed is low, the car is lined up to the road. Even though the car is close to the border, this condition is not dangerous; when the lateral speed increases quickly, the situation becomes critical. Thus, detected condition follows the conjunction:

if (lod > threshold) then activate warning, where lod = left offset derivative

In order to guarantee a suitable driver's decision and action time, the system can be perceived as too strict, increasing its risk level before the line is crossed. In order to guarantee a good comfort level of driving the time to line cross parameter is set very low so that the risk level becomes imminent very close to the marker. Threshold definition is subject to the experimental procedure where real data values (plots of input data) will be compared with what was really happening in the driving field (real time video data). In Fig. 20.2, the deviation of left lateral velocity is presented indicatively taking data from an image-processing unit.

20.3.3.2.4 Risk of Approaching a Dangerous Curve Too Fast

The dangerous curve approaching risk function has the aim to evaluate the risk in case the driver is approaching a curve too fast. The followed approach is similar to the frontal/lateral risk function one, but in this case the obstacle ahead is the curve, which is static and so only the motion of the subject vehicle must be taken into account.

The goal of this method is to arrive at a certain time with a determined velocity (the right one to route into the bend). This could be considered a reference speed, depending, of course, on the type of vehicle and curve (and in particular on its curvature). Using formulas, the reference speed (v_f) is $v_f = \sqrt{a_{\text{lat}} \times R}$, where a_{lat} = maximum lateral acceleration requested for the vehicle and $R = \frac{1}{C_0}$, with C_0 = the curvature of the bend.

In this context, lateral acceleration values (for cautionary and imminent warning) are stated by proper experimental phase, deriving the reference speed, which is compared with the current one of the host vehicle. If $v_f \geq v_v$, then the (longitudinal) deceleration value to arrive at a certain distance d_{warning} from the curve with the right velocity (namely the reference speed) is computed. If it is over a defined threshold, the risk level is modulated accordingly. Thresholds' definition will be subjects of experimental procedure. Other possible methodologies to compute the curvature (however, not treated in this approach) are the B-Spline and the Bezier methods.

20.3.4 Algorithm for Estimating the Intention of the Driver

The intention detection is carrying out a complementary task, which is the prediction of the intention of the driver based on possible overtaking or lane change manoeuvre. To detect a manoeuvre is rather simple by monitoring the steering angle or the lateral behaviour of the vehicle. For example, if the derivative of the lateral offset is estimated by a Kalman filter and it is compared with a threshold then the manoeuvre estimator will detect all steering and corrective actions of the driver. In Fig. 20.3, 600 successive system scans are plotted for such a detector (0 – no manoeuvre, 1 left manoeuvre, −1 right manoeuvre); in this scenario only one overtake between scans 690 and 830 takes place.

TERA module with its assessment properties uses a decision fusion system (versus any other conventional rule based system) in order to detect lane changes within a critical time before they occur. Thus, in order to solve the problem of diagnosing a lane change, evidence theory of Dempster–Shafer (D-S) is applied to realise the information fusion of multi-parameter in determining lane changes.

In the D-S theory (Shafer, 1976), the set of all possible outcomes in a random experiments is called the frame of discernment (FOD), usually denoted by θ. The (2) subsets of θ are called propositions, and probability masses are assigned to propositions, i.e. to subsets of θ. The interpretation to be given to the probability mass assigned to a subset of θ is that the mass is free to move to any element of the subset. Under this interpretation, the probability mass assigned to θ represents ignorance, since this mass may move to any element of the entire FOD. When a source of

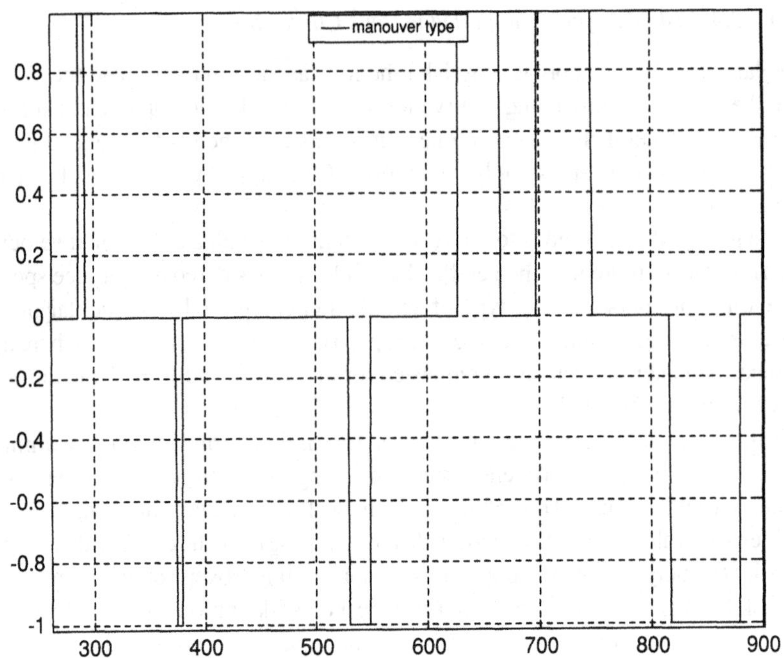

FIGURE 20.3. Manoeuvre detection.

evidence assigns probability masses to the propositions represented by subsets of q, the resulting function is called a basic probability assignment (BPA). Formally, a BPA is function m: $2^{\theta} \rightarrow [0, 1]$, where $m(\emptyset) = 0$ and $\sum_{A \subseteq \Theta} m(A) = 1$. Subsets of θ that are assigned non-zero probability mass are said to be focal elements of m. The core of m is the union of its focal elements. A belief function, Bel (A), over θ is defined by $\text{Bel}(A) = \sum_{B \subseteq A} m(B)$.

In the case of TERA, the FOD is $\theta = \{\text{lane change, no lane change}\}$. It is critical to determine a basic probability assignment when we use the D-S model to match the information. Generally, the basic probability assignment is closely relative to the data type and special objective. When we established the basic probability assignment, we acquired knowledge from experts who got more useful information ADAS systems. The source of evidence selected is

1. time to lane crossing (TLC);
2. lateral offset (lateral position of the vehicle with respect to the middle of the lane);
3. derivative of the lateral offset (lateral velocity);
4. the difference between the curvature of the road and the curvature that the vehicle is following, i.e. $C_0 - \omega/V$, where ω is the yaw rate, C_0 is the road curvature and V the velocity of the vehicle;
5. the product of the curvature of the road and the curvature that the vehicle is following $C_0 \cdot \frac{\omega}{V}$; if the product is negative, then this is an evidence of a lane change;
6. The gaze of the driver, if the driver is looking at the side mirrors of the car.

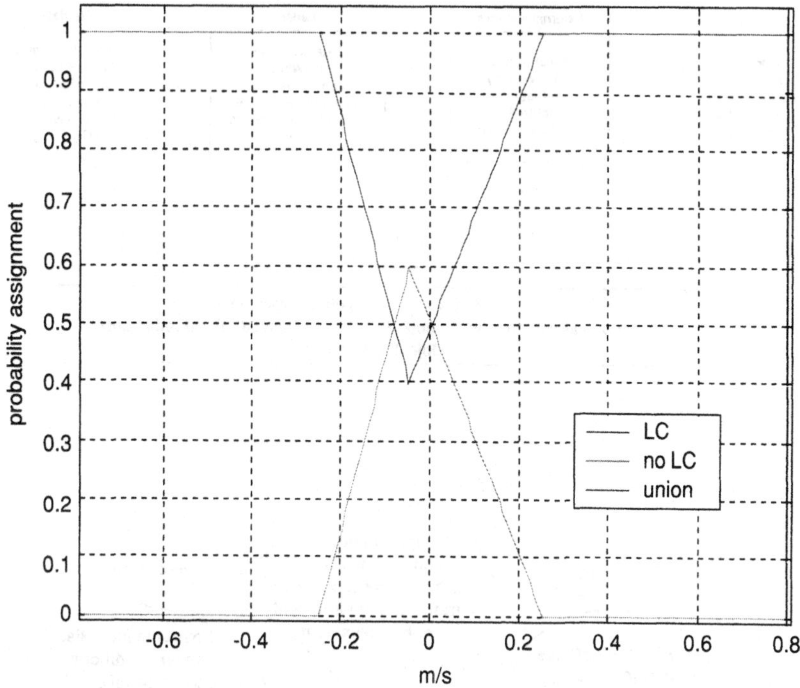

FIGURE 20.4. BPA for the derivative of the lateral offset.

The basic probability assignment, for each evidence, is calculated through proper trapezoidal fuzzy membership functions. An example is given in the following figure for the derivative of the lateral offset. The figure shows that if the value of the derivative is 0.2 m/s then 0.9 is the BPA assigned for the lane change and 0.1 for its negation (Fig. 20.4).

Assume that belief function Bel(i) are assigned to independent sources of evidence in same frame of discernment and the relevant basic probability assignment is m_1, m_2, etc. Then according to Dempster's rule of combination, the new belief function Bel(A) and basic probability assignment $m(A)$ may be yielded via

$$m(A) = \frac{\sum_{\substack{i,j \\ A_i \cap B_j = A}} m_1(A_i) m_2(B_j)}{1 - \sum_{\substack{i,j \\ A_i \cap B_j}} m_1(A_i) m_2(B_j)}.$$

20.3.5 TERA Implementation

Fig. 20.5 illustrates the process of input data, categorised in four categories, exploitation by the traffic and environment risk supervision algorithm, whilst Fig. 20.6 shows a more detailed data mapping into the three TERA traffic risk functions.

CAN
velocity
yaw rate filtered
steering angle
wiper position
(head lamps)

External sensors
ObjectNumber
radial velocity
ObjDistance
ObjAngle
(ObjClass, ObjID)

Lanes
LateralOffeset
LaneWindth
Lanecurvature
LaneCurvatureRate
Type of Lane marking
(neighbour lanes)

Map data
NumberSegments
NumberLanes
CurveRadious
Type of Road
DistIntersection/
DistTrafficSign

Raw data + processed data + tracking →
functions already ready: ObjectPath(), ObjectClosest(), PathPrediction(),
ObjectSynthesis()

Figuring out the
algorithm which will
provide the envisioned
traffic and environment
risk assessment

traffic
OverallTrafficRisk=
f(DangCurveAppr,
RiskFLColl,
RiskRoLExit)

environment
Environmental Risk=
f(weather conditions, type
of road), to be reflected in two
separate conditions:
- LowVisibility
- Low Audiblity in the Cockpit
(due to different HMI adaptation
requested)

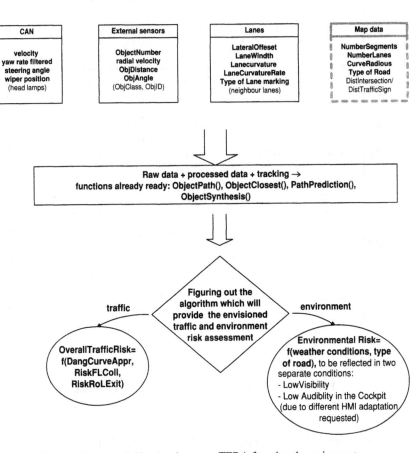

FIGURE 20.5. Available signals versus TERA functional requirements.

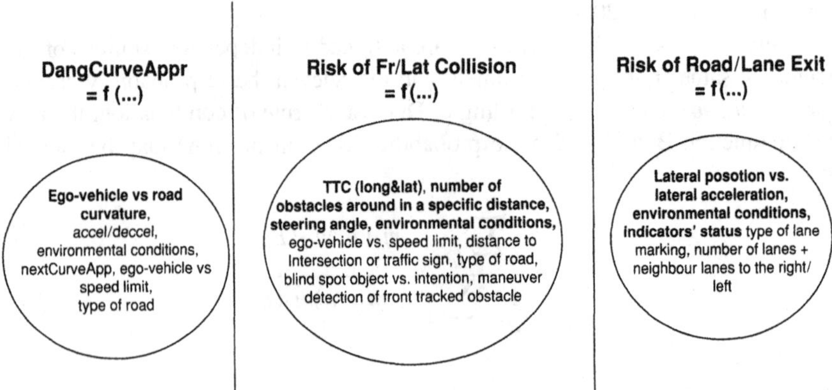

FIGURE 20.6. Available signals mapped onto TERA traffic risk functions.

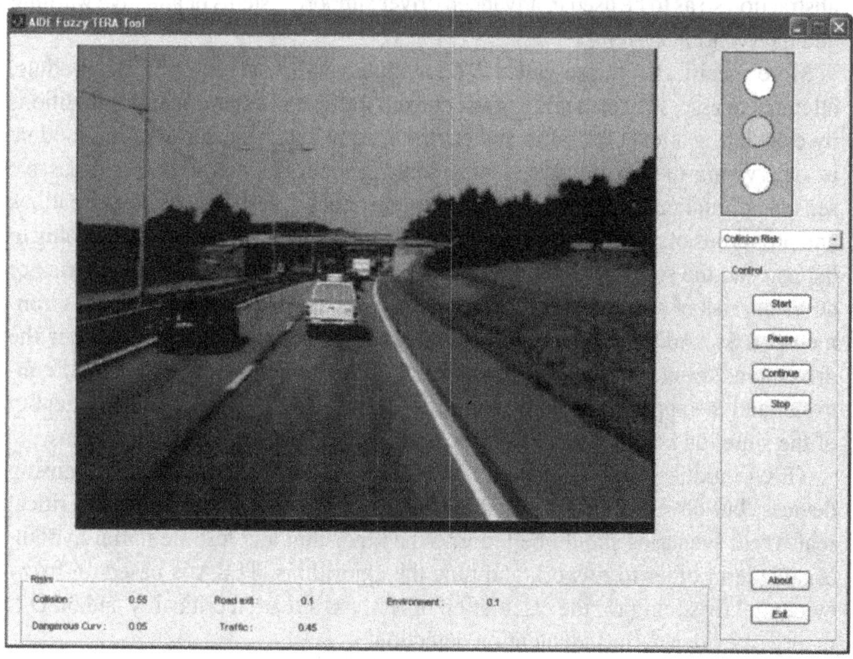

FIGURE 20.7. A screenshot from 'Fuzzy TERA development tool 1.0' laboratory tool.

The algorithms both for risk assessment and driver intention have been implemented in MATLAB and C++. A tool (fuzzy TERA development tool 1.0) has been developed that loads data sequences and video files in a playback mode, synchronises data, runs off-line the TERA algorithm and displays results in a graphical user interface. The tool works both with real (recorded from test cars and trucks) and simulated data and it is developed for evaluation purposes. The tool (Fig. 20.7) shows internal traffic risk conditions' values, video and marks whether the driver is considered to be in high traffic risk situation (three detection levels). The TERA traffic risk conditions' thresholds are manually tuned by varying several thresholds and weights and comparing the algorithm with recorded videos of real driving. The algorithm for the detection of possible manoeuvres is integrated in the same GUI. The C++ version is integrated in an automotive processing unit and will run in AIDE demonstrator vehicles.

20.4 Conclusions

The paper presented a novel approach on the real-time assessment of the traffic and environmental situation with respect to the risk that the driver is exposed to. The work focuses on the description of the relevant risk in a higher level of abstraction so as to be used in advanced driver support systems or adaptive warning and intervention systems.

More specifically, the so-called TRE module, and its successor TERA module, attempts to assess the criticality of the current traffic and environmental conditions by calculating a level of traffic and environmental risk, respectively. The module is supervising the surroundings using sensing input devices (active and passive sensors, digital maps, etc.), establishes a view of activities, manoeuvres, locations and properties of road elements, and from it assesses what is happening or going to happen and the severity which events will occur. These events include the risk of collision, risk of road/lane exit, risk of dangerous approaching curve and environmental risks. Additionally, TERA, starting from surround sensors, estimates the driver's intention for lateral manoeuvres. Therefore, TERA allows the HMI controller and the applications to be adapted to the driving demand and the criticality of the situation both in terms of traffic and external environmental conditions.

TERA module is developed as a first prototype by using a limited set of sensing devices, but covering major possible causes of critical driving demand. Critical real-world scenarios should be fed into the algorithm and test the initial hypothesis made in order to re-work and tune the algorithms. TERA is based on fuzzy evidential reasoning for the calculation of risk and situation criticality and on D-S theory of evidence for the intention detection.

References

Amditis, A., Polychronopoulos, A., Belotti, F. and Montanari R. (2002a). Strategy plan definition for the management of the information flow through an HMI unit inside a car. In *e-Safety Conference Proceedings*, Lyon.

Amditis, A., Polychronopoulos, A., Bekiaris, E. and Antonello, C. (2002b). System architecture of a driver's monitoring and hypovigilance warning system. In *IEEE Intelligent Vehicle Symposium Versailles*, France.

Bekiaris, E. and Portouli, E. (1999). Driver warning strategies Internal Deliverable ID4.1. IN-ARTE Project TR4014.

Damiani, S., Antonello, C., Tango, F. and Saroldi, A. (2003). Functional specification and architecture for the traffic risk estimation module. In *Proceedings SICICA 2003*, Aveiro, Portugal.

Engström, J., Cacciabue, C., Janssen, W., Amditis, A., Andreone, L., Bengler, K., Eschler, J. and Nathan, F. (2004). The AIDE integrated project: An overview. In *Proceedings of ITS Congress*, Budapest.

European Commission. (2001). White Paper on European Transport Policy for 2010: Time to decide.

Horne, J. and Reyner, L. (1999). Vehicle accidents related to sleep: A review. *Occupational and Environmental Medicine*, 56, 289–294.

Kirchner, A. and Heinrich, T. (1998). Model based detection of road boundaries with a laser scanner. In *Proceedings of IEEE International Conference on Intelligent Vehicles*, Vol. 1, Stuttgart, Germany, 1998, 93–98.

Montanari, R. et al. (2002). COMUNICAR: Integrated on-vehicle human machine interface designed to avoid driver information overload. In *ITS Conference*, Chicago, ILO.

Polychronopoulos, A., Andreone, L. and Amditis A. (2005). Real time environmental and traffic supervision for adaptive interfaces in intelligent vehicles. In *IFAC congress*. Prague.

Shafer, G. (1976). *A Mathematical Theory of Evidence*. Princeton University Press, Princeton, NJ.

Tatschke et al. (2006). ProFusion2: Towards a modular, robust and reliable fusion architecture for automotive environment perception. In V. Jürgen and G. Wolfgang (Eds.). *Advanced Microsystems for Automotive Applications 2006* (pp. 451–470). Springer, New York.

21
Present and Future of Simulation Traffic Models

FABIO TANGO, ROBERTO MONTANARI AND STEFANO MARZANI

21.1 Introduction

In transportation research, simulation technologies have acquired a huge relevance since they permit to reproduce, under controllable conditions, different scenarios with a growing degree of complexity. In this sense, a general trend can be anticipated here since it represents one of the backbone of this paper. The simulators of traffic scenario are enlarging the numbers of factors to be considered, from the sole link between vehicles and driving environment to a joint scenario in which drivers' intentions, autonomous behaviours of different vehicles and adaptive technologies (providing ad-hoc reactions according to specific driving conditions) are all together considered and computed. Therefore, the more the complexity grows, the more the network of factors influencing the reliability of these scenarios becomes articulated.

Proposing different working cases (some of them still under research), this paper tries to describe the main technological features of the traffic simulator model, the corresponding design approaches and the uses that these simulators offer towards the research community.

According to the results of the surveys done while writing this paper, a key point in which a reliable simulation is not yet completely achieved (even if many benchmark initiatives are acquiring promising results) is a study of drivers' behaviours and prediction of drivers' status, especially in terms of workload. This is a crucial challenge since once the level of workload will be properly and in real time monitored, the researchers will have the chance to actually improve safe systems, reducing the number (still too high[1]) of vehicles' related fatalities. Since the rationale behind a workload monitoring system seems to be mainly heuristically detected (Balaban et al., 2004; Dixon et al., 2005; Recarte and Nunes, 2003; Schvaneveldt et al., 1998; Zhang et al., 2004; Zhang et al., 2004), simulation plays a decisive role in their assessment and in the evaluation of the most suitable

[1] From many accident statistics carried out at European project level (PREVENT, AIDE, etc.), each year there are around 1,400,000 accidents, out of which 40,000 are fatalities.

counteractions (e.g. a delayed delivery of low priority information (low priority delivering in case the driving situation is critical).

This paper is organised as follows: In the first part, an overview of the main types of traffic simulators, including their relevant computing components and technological solutions, is reported. Later, many use cases are described and discussed. The use cases depict the transition from the standard model of traffic simulators to the complex ones where driver, vehicle and environment models are joined and embedded. The last part is dedicated to the integration between the traffic simulator complex models, the paradigm of distributed intelligence and multi-agent systems approach.

21.2 Traffic Simulator

21.2.1 General Overview: A Survey of Road Traffic Simulations

Hundreds of traffic simulation models are available nowadays. Some of them are quite effective and widely applied by the transportation research community for research in different domains, from human factors to advanced engineering and from road traffic to driver's training.

Recent studies on the competences and facilities of a sample of 34 human–machine interaction R&D laboratories and companies throughout Europe found that most of them (c.a. 45% of the sample) have adopted a driving simulator to conduct specific tests on driver behaviour. For example, TNO (http://www.tno.nl) is set up with a simulation platform reproducing a BMW or a DAF truck cabin with a 120° visual scene and six DOF motion. The Competence Centre Virtual Environment of Fraunhofer Institute (www.ve.iao.fhg.de) is equipped with three simulators, from low to high fidelity driving environment's definition. Many other research institutes and firms, such as Renault (France), Cidaut (Spain), ICCS I-SENSE (Greece), have embraced these kind of technology (Ferrarini, 2005; Minin, 2005).

Among the others, the topic of representing traffic congestion in virtual simulation has a particular relevance since it is one of the causes of lost productivity and decreasing standard of living in urban settings, including of course safety. However, limited by some constraints, especially the computational power availability, current traffic simulators are not still completely realistic, which is the eternal goal of simulation (Champion et al., 1999).

The traffic simulation deals with dynamic problems in complex environment that cannot be easily described analytically (Lieberman and Rathi, 1997). These problems derive from the interaction of several components of the system (namely its entities), which aim at reproducing (and in a certain way at 'mimicking') the behaviour and the interactions between the real traffic actors (cars, trucks, etc.) as accurately as possible. The simulation produces both statistical results and a visual rendering. The statistical results are numerical, i.e. they give quantitative and qualitative information referring to the evolution of the simulation. With this knowledge background, a visual representation is created, and it provides an idea regarding the state of the simulated environment. The main fields of applications for a road traffic simulator are the following:

- Design and improvement of car equipment, where the simulator can be a powerful tool for the on-board system evaluation. In fact, it allows to save time (and thus money) among the different phases of a product, from the concept to the series development, in particular between the validation with the proof of concept and the sign off with the begin of production. In the evaluation of innovative steering devices, the driving simulator has been used (e.g. in Toffin et al., 2003) to investigate different torque feedbacks in the steering wheel. Results indicate that drivers on the simulator can control their vehicles in curves with quite different torque feedback strategies, either linear or nonlinear. However, zero torque or inverted torque feedback makes driving almost impossible. These observations, which cannot be implemented in real driving conditions, confirm the essential role of coherent haptic information for driving real cars and simulators and also suggest the existence of driver adaptation mechanisms in steering control. Finally, simulators are used in the context of speech-controlled driver information systems. Manstetten et al. (2001) studied how drivers interact with such a system if it allows for natural-language communication in simulation environment. The present contribution to the book on driver's model is more focused on this point. The other concepts that are also considered as follows:
- *Training* – real-time simulator is increasingly used to educate and train professional drivers (trucks, buses, etc.) and dedicated personnel (i.e. traffic control centre) (Dols et al., 2002).
- *Testing new structure* – to quantify performances according to different design options before the works start or before the commitment of resource for construction.
- *Security and environment* – with some applications in this area dealing with studies on intelligent highways and vehicles (Sukthankar et al., 1996; 1998), impact of road signs and infrastructure towards the driving tasks (Fitzpatrick, 2000; Horberry et al., 2004; Horberry and May, 1994; Horberry et al., 2005), driver's behaviour analysis in critical scenarios (Pentland et al., 1999; Salvucci et al., 2001), accident reconstruction, as well as researches on emissions and pollution.
- *Studies on drivers' distraction* – Karlson (2004) studied driver distraction and its countermeasures in driving simulator evaluating the gaze direction. Lansdown et al. (2004) investigated the impact of multiple in-vehicle information systems on the driver, undertaken using a high fidelity driving simulator. Martens and Winsum (2000) investigated driver's distraction in simulator using the peripheral detection task (PDT,[2] Olsson and Burns, 2000), that is a very sensitive method of measuring peaks in workload, induced by either a critical scenario or messages

[2] Peripheral detection task.

provided by a driver support system. The more demanding the task, the more cues will be missed and the longer the response times to the PDT.

- *Rehabilitation of driving skills for persons with neurological compromise* – Rizzo et al. (2002) performed a study of 54 individuals (21 with traumatic brain injury, 13 with stroke and 20 healthy controls) who were administered a driving evaluation using the driving simulator (mainly based on virtual reality technologies).
- *Basic research* – traffic simulation is used for mathematical and statistical studies, with the aim to improve traffic flow models, analyse interesting aspects, such as emergent collective behaviour, swarm intelligence topics and so on (Leonardi et al., 2004).

As next section describes, simulators can be classified according to different factors, depending on the selected methods, on the chosen applications and on the present constraints. In general terms and as described in Ni and Feng (2002), there are three main actors in a simulator: traffic and environment, vehicle and driver.

21.2.2 Types of Simulator

Since the most of traffic simulator describe dynamic systems (and on the other hand this is their most interesting application), time is always the basic independent variable. There are two types of models: *discrete* and *continuous*. We will pay particular attention to the discrete ones since these represent real-world systems with enough precision and at the same time with a computational complexity sufficiently low.

According to the level of details requested by a simulation, there are generally three approaches in traffic simulation: *macroscopic*, *mesoscopic* and *microscopic*.

Macroscopic approach treats traffic as one-dimensional compressible fluid and emphasises the general behaviour of traffic such as speed, flow, density, etc. This means that entities, actions and interactions are described at (very) low level of detail. Traffic stream may be represented in some aggregate manner or by scalar values of flow rate and density. For example, individual lane changes are not represented since the model provides global quantitative or qualitative information (Helbing and Treiber, 1998).

The *microscopic* approach concerns the interactions between pairs of vehicles and emphasises the individual behaviour of traffic such as car-following and lane-changing; that is, most entities and their interactions are described at a high level of detail. In this context, a lane change could invoke a car-following law with respect to its current leader, then with respect to its putative leader and follower in the target lane (Sukthankar et al., 1998). An example is represented by the simulator developed in the project PELOPS (Neunzig et al., 2002; www.pelops.de), where the traffic flow in motorways is simulated with a specific view of vehicles affair. The basic idea is a combination of high-detailed vehicle and traffic technical models; this permits an investigation concerning the longitudinal dynamics of vehicles as well as the analysis of the course of traffic (traffic flow). The advantage is the opportunity to take into account all the interactions occurring among vehicle, driver and traffic (that is, the environment). Another practical example is called simulated highways for intelligent vehicle algorithms (SHIVA): a tool for simulation, design and development of tactical driving algorithms (for more details, see Sukthankar et al. (1995)).

Finally, the *mesoscopic* approach lies somewhat in between. It captures some microscopic behaviour of traffic such as car-following, but with this approach the general characteristics of traffic (i.e. speed, flow and density, etc.) are examined. In other words, mesoscopic model generally represents most entities at a high level of detail, but describes their activities and interactions at a lower level. For example, lane change manoeuvres are represented but could be performed as an instantaneous event (Kemeny, 1993).

Another classification of simulators groups them into two sets: *deterministic* and *stochastic*. Deterministic simulators have no random variables; all entities interactions are defined through exact relationships (mathematical or logical). On the contrary, stochastic simulators include probability functions. Deterministic models are well suited to experiments wherein scenarios are intended to be completely reproducible. On the other hand, the vehicle behaviour may appear too mechanical and monotonous, thus realism is somehow lessened (Champion et al., 1999).

A relevant role in the traffic simulator is represented by the programming methodology that should be used to create the traffic scenario. This can be programmed in a *sequential way*[3], as for some macroscopic simulators. On the contrary, this can be also designed according to object-oriented principles, as for many microscopic simulators. Starting from this approach, some relevant breakthroughs have been achieved in the last 10 years, thanks to the development of the so-called 'distributing artificial intelligent' (Brodie and Ceri, 1992). In particular, the most recent and widely used of these innovations is the *agent-oriented method*. The traffic generator mentioned in Champion et al. (1999) has been designed using an object-oriented method where several software agents are embedded (detailed in the next section).

Concerning the way to compute and reproduce the driving task, three are the main relevant levels: *strategic*, *tactical* and *operational* (Michon, 1985). At the highest (strategic) level, a route is planned and goals are determined; at the intermediate (tactical) level, manoeuvres are selected to achieve short-term objectives (i.e. deciding whether to pass a blocking vehicle); eventually, at the lowest level, these manoeuvres are translated into control operations.

Consider the typical scenario depicted in Fig. 21.1: In the figure, the host-vehicle[4] (A) is in the right lane of a divided highway, approaching the chosen exit. Unfortunately, a slow car (B) blocks the lane, preventing (A) from moving at its preferred velocity. If A desires to overtake (pass) the slower car, a conflict can arise with the necessity of not missing the exit. The correct decision in this case

[3] That is, each program has a beginning, an execution sequence, and an end. At any given time during the runtime of the program, there is a single point of execution.

[4] With host-vehicle, it is meant the vehicle considered, i.e. the one under evaluation.

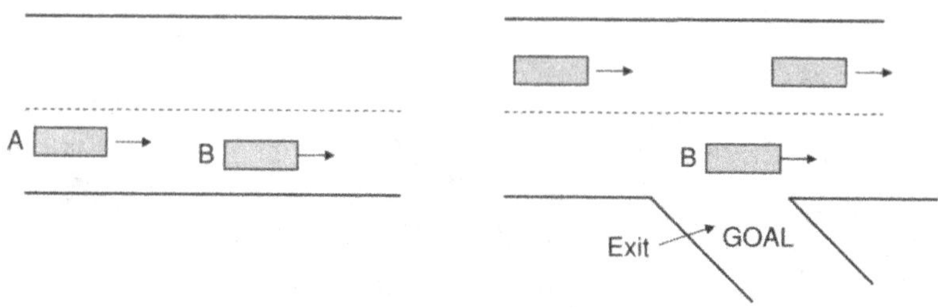

FIGURE 21.1. Typical scenario for a simulator, requiring a possible tactical decision.

depends not only on the distance to the exit, but also on the traffic configuration in the area. Even if the distance to the exit is sufficient for a pass, there may be no suitable gaps in the right lane ahead before the exit. Thus tactical level reasoning combines high-level goals with real-time sensor constraints in an uncertain environment. Simulation is essential in developing such systems because testing new algorithms in real traffic is risky and potentially disastrous. For example, SHIVA not only models the elements of the driving domain most useful to designers but also provides tools to rapidly prototype and test algorithms in challenging traffic situations.

Following are some other examples: PHAROS (Reece and Shafer, 1988), SMARTPATH (Michon, 1985) and SMARTAHS (Gollu, 1995). *PHAROS* focused on important perceptual issues and directed SHIVAs early development. *SMARTPATH* is well suited to modelling the PATH AHS concept (even with large numbers of vehicles) and it uses SGI[5] animation package for visualisation tools (Sukthankar et al., 1995). SMARTAHS is an object-oriented simulator, which stores its evolution state in a persistent DBMS[6].

As discussed above, the most recent advances in distributed artificial intelligence have allowed to study systems characterised by autonomous entities, such as a navigation by autonomous agents for intersection management is investigated in Dresner and Stone (2004), where multi-agent systems (MAS) is the sub-field of artificial intelligent (AI) aiming at providing both principles for construction of complex systems involving multiple agents and mechanism for coordination of independent behaviour of agents. In Stone and Veloso (2000), a MAS-approach is used to alleviate traffic congestion, basically at intersections.

21.2.3 Case Studies of Traffic Simulator

In this section, cases studies of traffic simulator are discussed. Particular attention is paid to SCANeR© II simulator[7] (more details on SCANeR II features specifications can be found at www.scaner2.com and www.oktal.fr). The main idea

[5] Silicon Graphic, Inc.
[6] Database management system.
[7] SCANER(c)II is a co-branded software between OKTAL and RENAULT

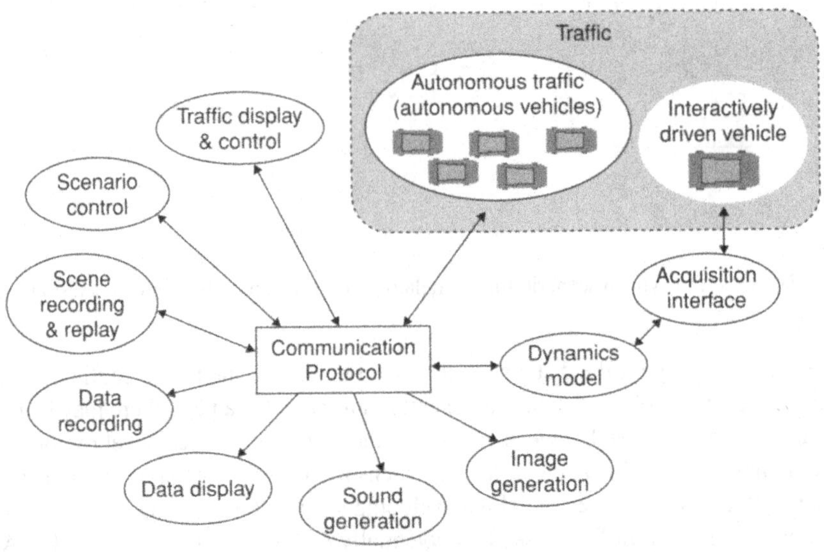

FIGURE 21.2. SW architecture of SCANER II.

behind this simulator is that *the traffic is the union of the driven vehicle and the autonomous traffic, which interact mutually*. The main design features are:

- road geometry is 3D;
- highway and urban scenarios are both included;
- vehicle types include cars, trucks, motorcycle and bikes, pedestrians, tram, etc;
- the development methodology is object-oriented and based on C++ language (with the possibility of 2D and 3D visualisation).

With reference to the classifications disscused in the previous section, the model implemented is microscopic with discrete time (possible to set, default value is 20 Hz) and stochastic. The architectural scheme is detailed in Champion et al. (1999) and illustrated in Fig. 21.2. This architecture allows the parallel execution of different traffic generation modules within the limits of the network capacity, if an experiment requires a relatively high-density of traffic (few hundred vehicles). Each module is supported by a different machine and manages a subset of vehicles.

Regarding the *simulator environment*, there are two fundamental elements: the road network and signs (RNS) and vehicle model properties, used for the description of the autonomous vehicles in the simulator. We will now discuss RNS, whereas vehicle model properties is described in the next section.

RNS is used by the autonomous vehicles to drive on the terrain; it is defined by a set of roads connected to each other through road nodes. Each road can have the following features: Width, different lanes for one or two directions, road markings, speed limits, road authorisations (for pedestrians, no trucks, bus only and so on), road signs (stop, traffic lights, yield, pedestrian ways, etc.), barriers, etc.

RNS has two objects: on the road side, to order list of points, minimum two, usually placed at the centre of an actual road; on the nodes side, this is a point placed to connect two or more roads. Each road must be connected with two nodes: one at the beginning and one at the ending. A road cannot be connected to the same node. Moreover, each rode can have the following attributes: width, category, length, list of lanes. Then, each lane can be defined by offset relative to the middle of the road, initial and final width, direction relative to the road (same or opposite direction), driving rules like speed limits, left or right markings, vehicle categories enabled for the lane, etc.

In each point of a road, it is possible to place one or more signs, which refer to a lane. Road surface database is used to compute tyre contact with the road and consequent reactions. Usually users can set some parameters such as adherence factor (to be used by dynamic models), spatial noise factor (how bumpy is the road), road type (normal road, sidewalk, car park, etc.), and road nature (asphalt, snow, concrete, etc.). Road surface and user defined information are queried by the simulation and enter in the vehicle model to compute the behaviour of the system, the reaction of the vehicle itself and possible feedbacks to the user. Finally, environment objects are embedded in boxes named *collision boxes* used in order to detect collision between the driving vehicle and the environment.

21.2.4 Vehicle Model Properties

As described in several research papers (Champion et al., 1999; Sukthankar et al., 1995) all vehicles constituting the intelligent autonomous vehicles in the simulation can be regarded, by a functional point of view, as consisting of three subsystems: *perception, cognition* and *control*.

The architecture presented in Fig. 21.1 has the advantage to describe both these autonomous objects and the host-vehicle in interactive way. Hence, vehicles can perceive each others, use available resources (such as lanes, roads, etc.), interact mutually and with the simulated world. This situation is illustrated in Fig. 21.3. As a general view, this structure recalls what is stated in Panou et al. (2005) about drivers and their modelling. There, the basic assumption is that drivers are essentially performing a set of actions that are well known and familiar, according to their experience. As the driving process is very dynamic, these actions are continuously selected from a vast repository of knowledge by a diagnostic process, which – together with the interpretation of information acquired – becomes crucial for the dynamic sequencing of driver's activity.

In the case study considered here, the model of the driver adopted is based on a very simple approach, which assumes that behaviour derives from a cyclical sequence of four cognitive functions called *PIPE*: *perception*, *interpretation*, *planning* and *execution* (Cacciabue, 2004).

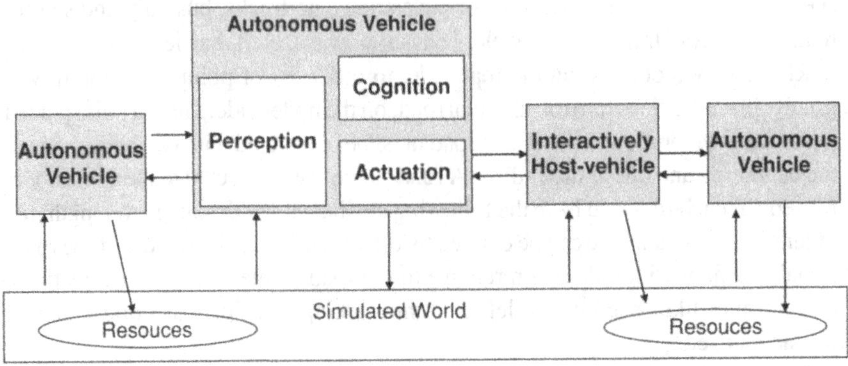

FIGURE 21.3. Structure of the vehicles constituting traffic flow.

This model is not sequential; this may result from several iterations (cyclical) of the other functions. Moreover, in agreement with the initial hypothesis, the planning function is usually bypassed by the 'automatic' selection of familiar frames of knowledge that are associated with procedures or sets of several actions aiming at the fulfilment of the goal of a frame. This function is however important as it becomes effective in unknown situations or in the case of novice drivers, when 'simpler' frames, based on single actions or on a limited sequence of very simple/familiar actions, are used to deal with the (new) situation.

These four cognitive functions can be associated to either sensorial or cognitive processes and are activated according to certain rules or conditions (see Table 21.1).

Comparing the PIPE framework with the Fig. 21.3, it is possible to say that:

- the first topic, *perception*, is common to both architecture;
- *interpretation* and *planning* of *PIPE* are grouped in the *cognition* issue;
- eventually, *execution* corresponds to the *control* item in the autonomous vehicle structure.

TABLE 21.1. Driver's model and rules for implementation.

PIPE framework	Type of process	Rules/governing assumption
Perception (of signals)	Sensorial	Haptic Visual Aural
Interpretation	Cognitive	Similarity matching Frequency gambling
Planning	Cognitive	Inference Reasoning
Execution	Behavioural	Performance of selected actions Interactions

In the next section, more details on the three aforementioned elements are pointed out.

21.2.4.1 Perception Topics

Perception remains one of the most complicated tasks for humans[8] and difficult problems in implementation for simulator. In fact, control algorithms making unrealistic perceptual assumptions can remain unimplementable on real systems. On the other hand, perfectly modelled realistic sensors are infeasible since the simulated world cannot match the complexity of real life as whole. Simulator designers must therefore balance these alternative issues, selecting an appropriate level of detail for their task. In the tactical driving domain, items such as occlusion, ambiguity and obstacle-to-lane mapping are important. Moreover, autonomous vehicle acquires knowledge of the surrounding world in two stages: The first stage consists in scanning the road ahead to detect the possible changes in driving conditions (traffic lights and signs, pedestrian crossing, barriers, etc.), while the second stage relates to the perception of the other vehicles.

The two simulators discussed so far (SCANeR II© and the SHIVA) support a variety of sensors and perception routines that enables cognition algorithms to gather information about their surroundings in a realistic manner. A typical vehicle configuration contains the following sensors:

- Positioning: Dead-reckoning and/or global positioning system (GPS).
- Lane tracking: Possibly with exit ramp counting features.
- Car tracking modules or rangefinders.
- Vehicles' self-state: Odometer, speedometer.
- Potential communication system towards other equipped vehicles.

The outputs of the sensors can be corrupted by noise if desired. Some sensors are explored in greater depth, e.g. vehicle detection in particular, since it is of critical importance at the tactical level.

In SCANeR© II, perception is based on the road network since it is used for trajectory calculations and acquisition of information. The road network designer should pay attention to the fact that the information has to be available to the vehicles (road sections, signs positioning); moreover, two vehicles have to know each other's status (position, speed, acceleration and direction). Autonomous vehicles also use the knowledge of the future route of the other vehicles to foresee their behaviour when approaching an intersection. Furthermore, designers may select

---

[8] Drivers rely on their experience with the driving task and perceiving the road environment relies on top–down expectations (Theeuwes, 2002). For example, Theeuwes and Hagenzieker (1993) have shown that drivers expect that objects that are likely to appear in a given scene should occupy specific positions in that scene. Results from their study also showed that errors in perceiving objects occurred when road users had wrong expectations regarding the location of particular target objects. Therefore, extremely dangerous situations may occur when the design of the traffic environment induces incorrect expectations regarding the spatial arrangement of the object in that scene.

different types of vehicle sensors or a more abstract vehicle sensor that can be used to prototype reasoning schemes. Once the useful information is obtained (road curve, signs and marking, position and trajectory relative to the perceived vehicles, etc.), a vehicle goes into the cognition phase. This phase corresponds to the reasoning and to the decision-making processes (see also next section).

21.2.4.2 Cognition Topics

Situational awareness is the key to achieve an effective navigation in traffic; in fact, intelligent (autonomous) vehicles should assess the outcomes of various actions and balance the desires of higher-level goals (such as taking a specified exit) with sensor driven constraints (observed vehicles). Moreover, these algorithms should be tested under a variety of situations (among which the critical and dangerous ones).

So and as aforementioned, the three cognitive processes relative to the driving task can be characterised by decision taken at *strategic, tactical* and *operational* levels. These are represented by a specific task-analysis, whose purpose is to describe tasks and to characterise the fundamental features of a specific activity or set of these. According to literature (Drury et al., 1987; Fuller, 2005; Lansdown et al., 2004; Spillers, 2003), task analysis can be defined as the study of what an operator (or a team of operators) is required to do, in terms of actions and/or cognitive processes, in order to achieve a given objective. In this context, a goal that a vehicle must reach is associated to each one of the aforementioned levels and its realisation implies a choice to achieve (see Table 21.2).

For example, considering as the strategic goal the route of a vehicle driving on a highway, it can take the next exit towards a 'service area'. In order to fulfil its choice, the selected road, if we suppose that the vehicle is on the left lane, it has to take the tactical decision to pass through the other lanes before the intersection.

Each choice is then implemented while being based on the lower decision level and according to the constraints related to the vehicle's environment. So, at highest level, autonomous vehicles have to follow their route by taking into account the fixed and further constraints.

The tactical level corresponds to the choice of short-term objectives combining the high level goals (route to achieve) and the constraints imposed by the lower level (physical characteristics of the road layout, dynamics of the vehicle, traffic flow and status). These objectives are mainly lane changes, performed in order to optimise the route between intersections. For example, recalling again Fig. 21.1, if vehicle (A) has to take the next exit and vehicle (B) strongly reduces its speed,

TABLE 21.2. Autonomous vehicles driving task characterised as decision levels.

Level	Goal	Choice
Strategic	Planning a route	Road
Tactical	Selecting a (appropriate) manoeuvre	Lane
Operational	Executing the manoeuvre	Speed and lateral offset

TABLE 21.3. Example of GMTA to a driving vehicle environment model.

Goal/tasks	Task/elementary functions involved	Pre-conditions
Attain higher speed (Complex task)	*1. Accelerate* *2. Check speedometer* *3. Maintain speed*	Check all conditions for elementary tasks
Change lane (Elementary task)	*1. Check road signals* *2. Check mirrors* *3. Scan road side* *4. Scan road forward/backward* *5. Set indicators (right/left)* *6. Steer*	- Lane free - No incoming faster vehicles - Change lane allowed - Visibility

Text in italics indicate elementary function and text in bold indicate tasks.

then vehicle (A) has to decide whether it can change lane to overtake vehicle (B) and take exits or simply to follow (B) and wait for the same exit. It is worth to note that tactical-level is of great importance for the feeling of realism of a simulator and thus designers should pay particular attention to this issue.

Finally, at the operational level, if (A) decides to overtake (B), then it has to compute the speed and the relative lateral offset appropriate with the execution of the lane-change manoeuvre.

Always focusing on task-analysis another example is the so-called 'goals-means task analysis' (GMTA), (see also Hollnagel (1993), where more details are provided). In this context, Table 21.3 shows a general instance for its application.

All in all, one of the major difficulties is the hand-tuning of the reasoning/deciding object parameters. Thereby, a careful investigation of learning techniques is one of the main activities to carry out in order to make this task automated. Potential solutions are described in Baluja (1994).

21.2.4.3 Actuation/Control Topics

This part provides the actuation of what has been decided by the cognition subsystem, the operational level. Acceleration and wheel angle are computed so that the autonomous vehicles can move. Then, vehicles can get also the status of other objects in the environment and thus performing their task while trying to avoid accidents (unless they have to be simulated, i.e. due to a high driver's impairment level).

21.2.4.4 Implementation of Vehicle Model

Several kinds of vehicles can be represented, such as cars, tractors, pedestrian, motorcycle, etc., each one with a specific set of parameters (e.g. type, dimensions, weight, including loaded and unloaded status, position and length of axles, driver's eye position, wheel radius and tyre categories, engine category, maximum speed, wheel angle amplitude, acceleration, brake and inertia factor). The car model used

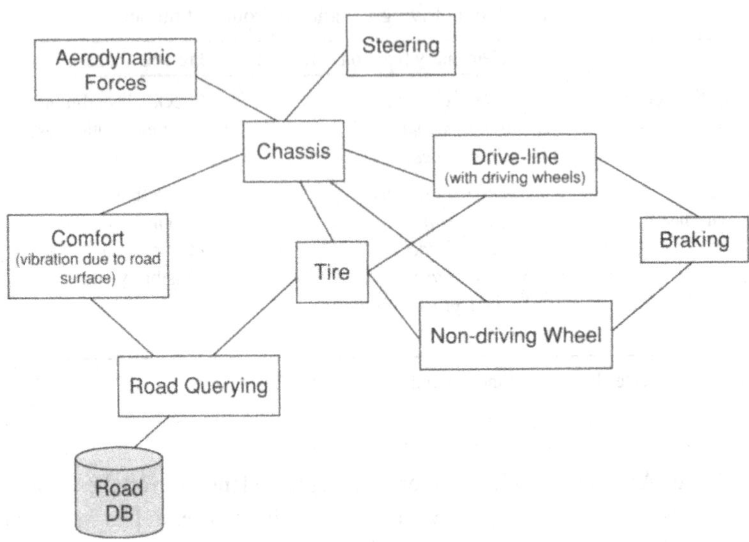

FIGURE 21.4. Scheme of sub-models for the dynamic vehicle module.

is a simplified dynamic model, constituting of a set of sub-models, as illustrated in Fig. 21.4.

Concerning the dynamic behaviour, the various models involved in the simulations are elaborated in real-time with a defined refresh-time (100 Hz), which is often called *simulation step*. At every simulation step the simulation considers: Vehicle configuration as defined by the driving scenario; all the kinematics variables; external inputs such those coming from the driver or environmental conditions; eventually, type and topography of the road under the tyres, as defined by the SCANeR© II RNS.

21.2.5 Two Examples of Applications with Traffic Simulator

In this paper, two examples of applications of traffic simulator are illustrated. One is surveyed by literature and in particular it is derived by an activity carried out at University of Michigan, in which a study is performed about the evaluation of adaptive cruise control (ACC) and collision warning (CW) using a longitudinal driver's model. In this context, only an overview is given on the microscopic traffic simulator used, but more details can be found in Lee (2004).

The other example is a case of a simulator which is recently installed within a laboratory on Mechatronics named MECTRON and placed in Reggio Emilia (North of Italy)[9]. The simulator is used for human factors and human machine

[9] The MECTRON Laboratory (www.mectron.org) re-enters within the projects of regional laboratories of the district for the HIgh MECHanical technology (HI-MECH). The project is financed through the regional program for the industrial research, the innovation and the technology transfer (PRRIITT) of the Emilia-Romagna region. The goal of Mectron is

interfaces studies, including both innovative devices for primary and secondary task. The simulator and the corresponding research activities are carried out by the Human Machine Interaction Group of University of Modena and Reggio Emilia[10].

21.2.5.1 The University of Michigan Microscopic Traffic Simulator

A microscopic simulator, developed at University of Michigan and called UM-ACCSIM, was used to evaluate the performance of ACC and CW systems. This tool has the possibility to simulate and record the motion of each vehicle operating on a two lane circular track (as in SHIVA simulator) and to produce many microscopic and macroscopic outputs. Because there are two lanes, lane change behaviour is one of the major source of speed variation for the leading vehicle; therefore, the implemented lane change algorithms take into account both the intention and the safety factors. The first one is the period of time during which the host-vehicle is driven below its desired speed due to the slower lead-vehicle; when it becomes higher than a certain threshold, the host-vehicle decides to make a lane-change (this choice should depend on the driver's model implemented). For the second, the host-vehicle looks at the nearest adjacent lane vehicles, front and rear, in order to determine if a lane-change can be safely executed. When both these factors are satisfied, a lane change manoeuvre occurs.

Concerning the driver's model that has been used, two main ones have been taken into account (for more details, see Lee (2004)): The first is by Liang and Peng (2000), where the dynamic speed control behaviour of human-driven vehicles is represented, but where a linear-follow-the-leader model is used, with the same parameters for all vehicles; the second model is the modified Gipps model, where the model itself and the parameters are identified from real human driving data and thus all aspects of longitudinal human driver's model in controlling vehicle motions are based on statistical driver's behaviour data (for more details, see Gipps (1981)). Preliminary results showed that the best one (fittest and more robust) was the second and thus the Gipps model was used and since human driving behaviour is unstable and this model with its set of parameters is not guaranteed to be stable either, emergency collision avoidance algorithms were implemented. Here it is worth to note that, if all behavioural models describe human-controlled vehicles with enough fidelity, the whole simulator can be expected to demonstrate many characteristics exhibited by human drivers.

When the traffic density is low, no shock wave is observed in the simulations and lane changes can occur. When the traffic density is high, lane changes become rare, since safe empty spots available for such a manoeuvre are harder to access. In this sense, the behaviour is more similar to the one of a single lane. Initially, no wave propagation behaviour is observed, but because of the fact that all vehicles

to design, prototype, test and develop innovative solutions for mechatronic systems, such as control by-wire applications, human factors for mechatronics' systems (e.g. Ergonomic by-wire steering-wheels), the study of fluid power for mechatronics and advanced materials.
[10] www.hmi.unimore.it.

have their own desired speed, some vehicles move closer and thus begin to interact with each other. As this type of interactions increases, deceleration and acceleration waves are propagated upstream. On the other hand, if traffic is string-stable, these waves would be attenuated. Therefore, traffic density is expected to be a fundamental factor in wave propagation velocity, with average speed that monotonically decreases as density increases. In high-density case, emergency braking algorithms are used with much greater frequency.

In this section only a general and brief overview of the main results achieved by a microscopic traffic simulator have been presented, in order to evaluate the characteristics of the longitudinal driver's model. More details on this research are available in Lee (2004). All in all, a modified Gipps model has been used to describe the longitudinal human driving behaviour (and so the 'personality' of each vehicle-entity in the simulator). Traffic flow simulations for several traffic densities were carried out: the resulting traffic flow and the average velocity results agree with real traffic data. This means that the modified Gipps model and all the related parameters can represent in a satisfactory way the macroscopic traffic characteristics, such as traffic flow rate and average velocity with respect to traffic density. The impact of intelligent transportation systems in this context is expected to be high and to influence the traffic rate as well as the speed of shockwave propagation.

21.2.5.2 The MECTRON-HMI Group at University of Modena and Reggio Emilia Driving Simulator used in Human factors and Human – Machine Interfaces Studies.

This section presents a research carried out by the Human Factors Laboratory of the MECTRON project (details on MECTRON are reported above). As previously introduced, the Human Factors Laboratory is led by the HMI Group of University of Modena and Reggio Emilia.

The main objective of this research is to develop specifications and requirements of a steer-by-wire device, which has the peculiarity to give primary importance to the human factors and ergonomics aspects (a so-called ergonomic steer-by-wire, i.e. ESBW). In particular, this is illustrated and investigated in terms of driving quality and performances, vehicle controllability[11] and human cognitive functionalities (such as mental workload and situational awareness). Here, only the experimental set-up concerning the use of traffic and environment simulation is pointed out, where the main scenarios are described.

At the moment, the experiments are in course. The basic idea of this work is that a by-wire device is able to support properly the driving task only if the drivers' perception in the usage of this system remains the same of a traditional steering wheel.

---

[11] This concept is used as within the EU Integrated Project PREVENT (and particularly it sub-project RESPONSE 3). For more information, see the web site www.prevent-ip.org/en/prevent_subprojects/horizontal_activities/response_3.

FIGURE 21.5. Driving scenario in OKTAL simulator.

In this context, the simulated environment is based on SCANeR© II and it presents the following characteristics: operative scenarios for the single external scene (highways, rural roads, etc.) combined with simple manoeuvres (such as rural roads plus lane change, highway plus lane keeping, etc.). An example of this driving scenario is illustrated in Fig. 21.5. The simulator allows joining different technologies and devices, in order to:

- reconstruct the driving scenario (route, weather conditions, traffic density) in a reliable way and in real-time;
- project the scenarios on the dedicated screen;
- perform (and promote) the interaction between user and system, by means of a reproduction of the automobile cockpit, the use of steering wheel, accelerator and brake pedals, with force feedbacks and feed forward (to reproduce the same feeling and dynamics of a car).

In the aforementioned experiment by this tool, the rules describing the behaviour of the force-feedback and force-feed forward actuator in the ESBW are under investigation. To perform such analysis, a previous benchmark on the different types of steering devices and reactive torque algorithms was evaluated. The analysis focused on two different kinds of force-feedback; one concerning reactive torque algorithms based on vehicle behaviour (e.g. lateral acceleration, yaw rate, sideslip angle), the other one based only on steering-wheel dynamic behaviour (e.g. steering angle, steering rate). In literature, both were investigated from a human factor point of view, that is the results of tests of driver performances in different driving scenarios (e.g. lane change, car following, highway, rural road) under primary and/or secondary tasks. The comparison among these results allowed to define the best user-centred algorithms, then to design different solutions of an ergonomic steer-by-wire featuring several force-feedback models. Finally, these prototypes are in course of implementation on the steering wheel of the driving simulator; the aim is to evaluate, during driving tests, the most performing algorithm in terms of driver response. These assessments are performed comparing the following dependant variables:

- Driver's performances in driving task.
- Mental workload, situational assessment and safety level of the user in executing the primary and secondary tasks using both subjective scale, as rating scale mental effort (RSME[12], (Zijlstra, 1993)) and objective evaluation, as peripheral detection task (PDT).
- Subjective evaluation of the driving device, on the basis of scale of preference and driving quality as driver opinion scale (DOS) and driving quality scale (DQS; Nilsson (1995).
- Factor analysis of driver's distraction in well-defined driving contexts/scenarios.
- Error analysis on determined scenarios, due to the introduction of new actuators and devices.

At the moment, experiments are in progress and it is not possible to anticipate any results. Nevertheless, the simulator will be used not only as an assessment tool but also to observe how the ESBW can become a supportive system aimed at improving drivers' situation awareness in specific conditions (e.g. via the implementation of proactive supportive actions as a major resistance of the steering-wheel in case the drivers is trying to change the lane, risking a collision with a vehicles which is already occupying the adjacent lane). These studies will be carried out in the late phase of MECTRON project, once the ESBW assessment will be properly completed.

Traffic simulators aim at investigating the impact of these adaptive interfaces[13] with reference to drivers' reactions and expectations; this can represent a valuable perspective for these tools. Nevertheless, the only simulation, based on traffic, could not be enough: thus a mutual interaction with environment, drivers' models and vehicles is needed, as described in details in the next section (introducing another relevant case study of AIDE project) and regained in the conclusions.

---

[12] Rating scale mental effort.

[13] According to Hoedemaeker et al., 'by an *adaptive support* it is meant a system that in some way takes into account the momentary state of the driver, in particular his present level of workload, in determining the appropriate timing and the content of the supporting message or intervening activity the system will produce. This should thus prevent the driver from becoming overloaded or distracted because of the impending multitude of information. These are based on an analysis of potential bottlenecks, including risk estimates derived from the prevailing traffic situation, so that it can be determined what types of support messages are allowed in a particular situation'. This involves both primary (as an adaptive steering wheel able to warn the driver in case of potential collision) and secondary tasks (as vehicular phone which stopped an incoming call in case of critical driving condition).

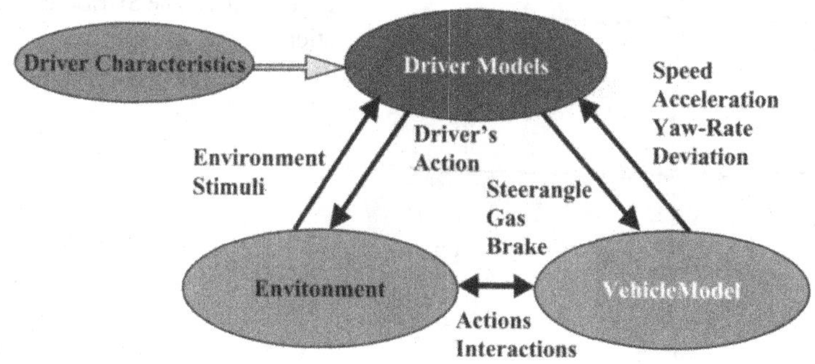

FIGURE 21.6. Closed-loop scheme for DVE simulation.

21.2.6 Integration of Driver, Vehicle and Environment in a Closed-Loop System: The AIDE Project

The European Integrated Project AIDE[14] has been explicitly planned to develop concepts for safe and efficient human-machine interaction as a key step towards the realisation of intelligent road vehicles with higher safety and value-added services, as pointed out in the e-safety report (European Commission, 2002). In particular, one of the main sub-goals of the AIDE integrated project is to perform theoretical analyses and field studies aimed at predicting human behaviour and error, specifically related to the interaction with advanced driver assistant systems (ADAS) and in-vehicle information systems (IVIS).

In order to achieve these goals, the simulation model should include a mutual interaction among the driver, the vehicle and the environment. This is a precise approach named driver–vehicle–environment (DVE) and the corresponding model and simulation is expected to retain the essential correlations between the fundamental independent variables, predicting the driver's behaviour in dynamic and rapidly changing conditions. Therefore, the DVE can be seen as closed-loop system as shown in Fig. 21.6.

Such a system can work as follows: the intelligent driver sub-model collects information related to its driving task. The information comes from three sources: Environment stimuli, vehicle feedbacks and driver characteristics. Some pieces of the information may need to be 'fuzzyfied'. A possibility is to use a neural network, which is capable of associating input patterns with their corresponding output patterns, just as human beings have the ability to deal with unknown situation, based on his/her knowledge and past experience. According to the information fed in, the neural network suggests the corresponding control strategies, i.e. gas, brake and steering angle (more details on this point are reported in the conclusive discussion).

---

[14] AIDE stand adaptive integrated driver–vehicle interface - IST-1-507674-IP).

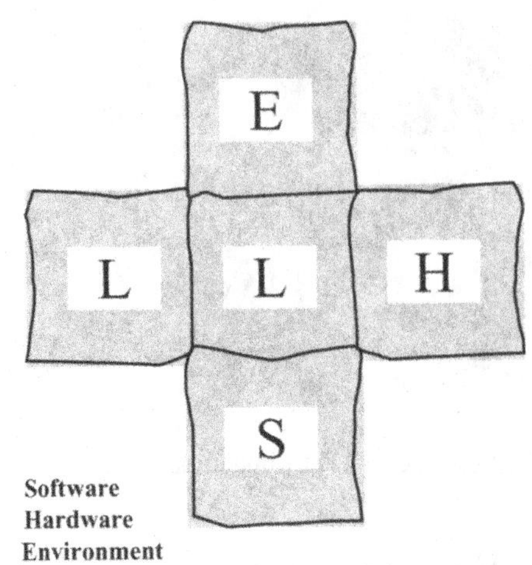

FIGURE 21.7. The SHELL configuration.

21.2.6.1 General DVE Architecture

Inside the AIDE project (and particularly in the sub-project which is taking care of the simulation related topics, i.e. the sub-project 1[15]), the development of the architecture adopted to represent the interactions between driver, vehicle and environment is framed in a generic architecture describing the way in which humans interact with the world and systems around them (Panou et al., 2005). This is called SHELL (Edwards, 1988), whose structure describes the connections existing between humans, defined *Liveware* (L), and the other elements of the working environments (driving, in this case), as described in the following list and in Fig. 21.7:

1. The physical sources, such as equipment, systems, interfaces and machines, which may be termed *Hardware (H)*: Corresponding interaction between *Hardware* and *Liveware* are mentioned as *L-H interactions.*
2. Rules, regulations, laws, procedures, customs, practices and habits governing the way in which a plant or a machine are operated, called *Software (S)*: *L-S interactions.*
3. Social, physical and technical aspects of working contexts, which may be called *Environment (E)*: *L-E interactions.*
4. Direct communications and exchange of information of the driver with other human beings, such as passengers or other drivers in different vehicles, which is termed *Liveware (L)*: *L-L interactions.*

The model focuses on the way in which a process of interaction is influenced and can be simulated with respect to a single journey. The model intends to deal

[15] More details in www.aide-eu.org.

with dynamic and adaptive characteristics of a driver, driving environment and vehicle; in principle, it can be continuously updated and modified.

Hence, the SHELL architecture can be used to represent the different variables that affect the DVE model. Moreover, in order to capture the crucial dimension time, affecting the process of driving in different conditions and situations, a further sub-division can be considered; in particular, three discrete time levels are envisaged:

- *Static variables*, which account for variables that do not change over the journey (examples of these are age of driver, gender, personality, procedures, etc.).
- *Quasi-Static variables*, which account for the phenomena and interactions that may change during a journey even though these changes are slow and foreseeable (examples of quasi-static variables are attitudes, behavioural adaptation, etc.).
- *Dynamic variables*, which account for the events and phenomena that occur during a journey and may be affected by the evolution of the DVE interaction itself or may not be anticipated (examples of dynamic variables are workload, stress, traffic conditions, type of roads, weather conditions, traffic situations, etc.).

The next section details the time-frame concept.

21.2.6.2 Time Frame for DVE Model

The time distribution of the model takes into consideration a single time-step prediction system which is continuously updated by real data, resulting for the actual behaviour of the overall DVE environment. Thereby, for each time step of the simulation ($t = t_i$), the overall contribution of the three components of the DVE model is evaluated by extracting the variables that influence an index namely *driver impairment level (DIL)*. This index is evaluated on the basis of several variables, both subjective (risk-taking, complacency, etc.) and objective (such as risk-level and performance limitations), as well as their linear combination (for more details, see Panou et al., 2005). Moreover, the error generation mechanism is related to the DIL index, to the dynamic interaction process of the three elements of the DVE model and to the 'failure mode and effect analysis' (FMEA) process carried out by the component, which manages the DVE simulation. So, the simulation manager firstly performs the FMEA and identifies whether the driver is able to continue the ongoing activity, that is DIL is over a defined threshold ($0 \leq DIL(t = t_i) \leq DIL_1$) or if driver performs inadequately or if he/she is impaired ($DIL > DIL_1$). In particular, the effect analysis selects the actual effect that should be shaping the activity in the following time step. Fig. 21.8 shows the dynamic DVE architecture in AIDE.

Such a process of FMEA discussed for the Diver model can be replicated for the models of the vehicle and environment in the case of a full simulation of the DVE interaction, thus generating possible inadequate or improper performances of the vehicle or risky situation associated with the environment. In a real situation the

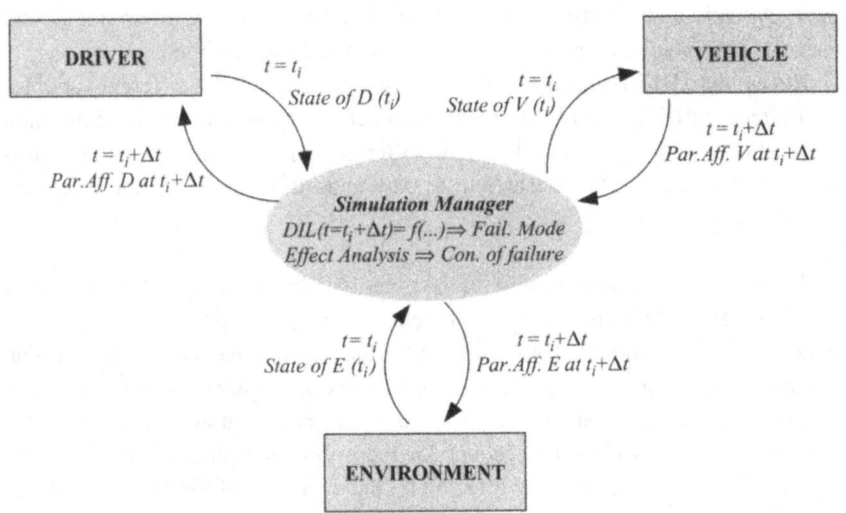

FIGURE 21.8. Architecture of time-evolution DVE model.

dynamic evolution of both vehicle and environment can be recorded and compared to the simulated data (or derived by them).

All in all, the activity on DVE model simulator is still in progress and therefore current formulation may be not cover a number of variables and cases which then could become very important. This will be clarified by the experiments envisaged inside the project AIDE, particular in the topic-related subproject.

However, the overview provided in this section is enough to describe the main idea and objective of the DVE simulator and the rationale of a promising perspective for the traffic simulator: An integration of the three main actors involved in the driving scenario that is the driver, the vehicle and the environment. In this case, the main topic is not the development (at least, not only) of a specific algorithm for the simulation of traffic/environment or the implementation of a new driver's model, but to point out the interaction of these three elements, in an integrated approach.

21.3 Conclusions and Further Steps

In simulator experiments, different needs and different situations must be considered, as well as specific conditions have to be reproduced, such as insertion on highways, accidents, reduction of the number of lanes, etc. In these cases, conflicts between vehicles may appear and the flow stops even if in real world such conditions would not cause congestions. In order to deal with this trouble, activity carried out in distributed artificial intelligent (DAI) and multi-agent systems (MAS) are taken into consideration for the traffic simulation. We will now into details about these advanced works.

21.3.1 Towards a Multi-Agent Approach

As aforementioned, DAI is the area of computer science coping with a set of entities aimed at imitating the human intelligent behaviour. Road traffic belongs to this field, as described in Ossowski et al. (2004). A MAS is a set of software which coordinate beliefs, desires and intentions, knowledge, goals and plans of human entities, so as to act or solve problems, including the coordination among agents themselves. To be regarded as 'intelligent', these entities have to show behaviours that are rational, autonomous and capable of communication and actions. In the real environment, a vehicle and its driver is an agent; in simulator, an autonomous vehicle (including the driver as well) and an 'inter-actively driven vehicle' are agents. Anyway, both in real and in simulated situations, the traffic is constituted of multi-agent systems and entities. In case this view is missing—due to an absence of communication, for example—an individualistic behaviour appears. The consequence is a penalty of a part or of the whole traffic stream; vehicles, in fact, are able to move but not to coordinate their knowledge and goals to get deal with some of the illustrated drawbacks.

21.3.2 New Developments and Prospective

New possible developments concern each of the three main actors described in our approach, that is the driver, the vehicle and the environment, presented as following. The general statement is that traffic is composed by autonomous entity with (basically) the capacity of perceiving their local environment and communicating each other.

The first entity is to model the *driver–vehicle* control-loop system. Starting from the vehicle, a description of possible configuration and architecture has been provided; this is of course one of the possible different approaches. For example, if a four-wheels vehicle model is considered rather a two-wheels, this can vary the realism of object behaviour and thus of the simulation. Furthermore, by a physical point of view, 2D dynamics accuracy might not impair real-time performances, such as engine and gearbox. The other fundamental aspect is the drivers and their behavioural and cognitive model (i.e. psychological security distance, average latency at cross-sections and so on). In this sense, one of the more advanced projects dealing with these topics is still AIDE, as discussed earlier, where we have addressed a specific model of human behaviour enabling to predict actions and sufficiently adaptive to individual characteristics, in order to personalise the interface between driver and technological system. For example, based upon data gathered over long periods of driving and under different conditions, driver's reaction time is estimated and clustered into four levels: very slow, (i.e. above 1.3 s), slow (above 1 s), average (0.8–1 s) and quick (below 0.8 s). Driver's average lane position and change (based upon time to line crossing (TLC) measurements) are also estimated. Other preferences, such as provision of navigation and route guidance by map, will be estimated by monitoring the driver's own selections through a series of system usages.

All these three items can be handled by two different agents. Initially, a *user's profile configuration agent* will support different 'types of users', with some preferences selected by the users themselves. Then, a *customisation agent* will monitor the user's driving behaviour and preferences/actions, by keeping and processing the user's driving record, i.e. average position in the lane, average headway, typical speeding and braking pattern, preferred seating position, average use of radio and mobile phone, other services, like navigation, requested often, etc. The self-built user profile will be always possible to be reviewed and changed by the user.

The Java agent development framework (JADE) is the basis for building interoperable agents FIPA[16] compliant. Such a framework ensures that agents' aspects (message transport, encoding, parsing, agent life cycle, etc.) are dealt. Data will be stored in a driver smart card (for example), in order to be used in other equipped cars. This personalisation can help to better estimate the DIL, because it considers also the effects due to the differences between different driver's typology (recalling the PIPE framework, at the *execution* level, as pointed out by the AIDE project).

Furthermore, also taking into account the effects produced by the use of ADAS and IVIS applications can be included in the human model (i.e. in terms of behavioural adaptation), thus enlarging the applicative scenarios of use of the simulation.

All these aspects can contribute to make easier and more realistic the creation and implementation of driver–vehicle systems as autonomous agents, in order to deal with a wide variety of traffic conditions and applicative scenarios.

The other item to be considered is the *environment*, which is closely related to the local perception in simulated world. We have already described the so-called RNS framework, where the road network has to be apprehended according to the local environment of the agent (vehicles ahead, road type, road layout, etc.). In order to fulfil this perception issue, it is necessary to take into consideration the interaction between the driven vehicle (that is, the vehicle with more sophisticated human model and specific system on-board) and the other autonomous agents. The study and the implementation of the environment model is one of the main tasks for a traffic simulator, since it could not be too different from real scenarios, but on the other side a complete imitation of real world is not possible. Therefore several approaches are used, both considering particular aspects of the traffic management (as in Dresner et al. (2004) and Qi (1997)), investigating specific types of on-board systems as collision warning, adaptive cruise control, etc. (Christen and Neunzig, 2002; Miller and Huang, 2002; Özgüner et al., 2004). The ambitious goal of joint-DVE approach is point towards the merging of these works, including the impact of ADAS/IVIS applications with a traffic model.

21.3.3 Open Points and Future Steps

In all simulators the main goal is to achieve a realistic behaviour of each entity, that is DVE in its design and its evaluation. The basic idea pointed out in this

[16] Foundation for intelligent physical agent.

paper has been about the perception issue: even if data are sometimes insufficient (as quantity) or erroneous (as in real life), a perception based on (simulated) visual information can alone enable the vehicles to communicate each other their objectives. For example, if a simulated scenario involves a motorway network, an insertion has to be simulated (maybe with a congestion caused by an accident occurred downstream) and vehicles should be able to perceive surrounding entities intentions and to accord with (for example, entering the motorway, changing lane manoeuvre, etc.). In other words, it is necessary to implement a structure that enables an agent to apprehend and answer any request concerning a resource access: If it is common and shared, agents have to cooperate in order to coordinate their actions. In case vehicles do not have this capacity and even if they observe the highway code, a vehicle wishing to access the highway does not have any priority and thus it risks staying stuck on the access-ramp.

Many architectures nowadays do not allow a cooperative behaviour immediately. As pointed out, several aspects have to be considered and merged together, concerning the perception, the cognition and the interaction. They need to be implemented following a DAI/MAS approach. Whilst the agents have only a reactive behaviour, it is possible to note a multi-agents coordination: in the example previously shown, flow of vehicle is strongly slowed down, which is normal, but it is not stopped. In other words, it can be said that an *emergent behaviour* arises and different research works can be carried out on this item.

To sum up, considering traffic as a multi-agent system allows to simulate a more realistic but simulated environment, with which also (more) complex scenarios can be analysed, by starting a coordination of traffic entities. This environment model can be coherent with a homogenous integration of the interactively driven vehicles, using a joint approach of user's behavioural and personalisation model (including the presence of driving supporting systems on-board). This is the actual area of research and work of some projects, such as AIDE. In this context, the environment model is built by considering driving behavior from the point of view of how drivers perceive, attend and memorize environmental conditions to make choices and take proper actions to those conditions.

One of the possible future activities is to model how these conditions are related to risk factors, in order to determine which are the most critical scenarios. Therefore, the DVE model should include all those parameters from the environment which drivers indicate as the most attention demanding. This type of environment model is synthesised into a preliminary joint DVE model, as illustrated before.

Another one, and related to the previous by a certain viewpoint, concerns the evaluation and assessment of predictive models of driver's workload, in different contexts and using specific hap-tic devices (such as the steer-by-wire prototype, as aforementioned).

It is worth to add, however, that a DAS/MAS approach cannot be regarded as a *panacea* for each problem in simulation, because drawbacks and shortcomings exist in this case as well; in fact, possible criticism could be related to the use of neural networks performance as a decision-making framework, since sometimes revealed limits when applied in real-time systems due to the time spent in learning phase if any and/or in the evaluation of proper solution among a list of alternatives.

Therefore, the activities on these topics are continuously running. Some suggestions to overcome possible difficulties of tuning the reasoning object parameters concern the investigation of learning techniques, such as in Baluja (1994), where an abstraction of the basic genetic algorithm, the equilibrium genetic algorithm (EGA), is reconsidered within the framework of competitive learning. This paper explores population-based incremental learning (PBIL), a method of combining the mechanisms of a generational genetic algorithm with simple competitive learning. Moreover, an empirical analysis is presented, with a description of a class of problems in which a genetic algorithm approach may be able to perform better. Among the cases discussed in this document, the DVE simulator could be a possible field of application, especially the part concerning the traffic and environment agents, based on a training data set constituted by real road data from several driving session performed by different drivers in different scenarios.

References

Balaban, C.D., Cohn, J.V., Redfern, M.S., Prinkey, J., Stripling, R. and Hoffer, M. (2004). Postural control as a probe for cognitive state: Exploiting human information processing to enhance performance. *International Journal of Human–Computer Interaction*, 17, 275–286.

Baluja, S. (1994). Population-based incremental learning: A method for integrating genetic search based function optimisation and competitive learning. Technical Report CMU-CS-94-163. Cornegie Mellow University, Pittsburgh, PA, USA.

Bertacchini, A., Minin, L., Pavan, P. and Montanari, R. (2006). Ergonomic steer by wire: Caratteristiche e modalità funzionale. Deliverable R5.1, MECTRON Laboratory, Reggio Emilia, Italy.

Brodie, M.L. and Ceri, S. (1992). On intelligent and cooperative information systems: A workshop summary. *International Journal of Intelligent and Cooperative Information Systems*, 1(2), 249–289.

Cacciabue, P.C. (2004). *Guide to Applying Human Factors Methods—Reference Model of Cognition Chapter*, Springer, Berlin.

Champion, A., Mandiau, R., Kolski, C., Heidet, A. and Kemeny, A. (1999). Traffic generation with the SCANeR© II simulator: Towards a multi-agent architecture. In *Proceedings of DSC'99*, Paris, France, pp. 311–324.

Christen, F. and Neunzig, D. (2002). Analysis of ACC and stop and go using the simulation tool PELOPS. Final Technical Report IKA.

Dixon, K.R., Lippitt, C.E. and Forsythe, J.C. (2005). Modelling human recognition of vehicle-driving situations as a supervised machine learning task. In *Proceedings of the 11th Conference on Human–Computer Interaction*.

Dols, J., Pardo, J., Breker, S., Arno, P., Bekiaris, E., Ruspa, C. and Francone, N. (2002). The TRAINER project: Experimental validation of a simulator for driver training. In *Driving Simulation Conference*, Paris, France.

Dresner, K. and Stone, P. (2004). Multiagent traffic management: A reservation-based intersection control mechanism. In *The Third International Joint Conference on Autonomous Agents and Multiagent Systems*, New York, USA.

Drury, C.G., Paramore, B., Van Cott, H.P., Grey, S.M. and Corlett, E.N. (1987). Task analysis. In G. Salvendy (Ed.). *Handbook of Human Factors*. J Wiley, New York, pp. 370–401.

Edwards, E. (1988). Introductory overview. In E.L. Wiener, and D.C. Nagel (Eds.). *Human Factors in Aviation*. Academic Press, San Diego, CA, pp. 3–25.

European Commission (2002). Final report of the esafety working group on road safety. Information Society Technologies, Bruxelles.

Ferrarini, C. (2005). Analisi comparata dell'usabilità di un software per la supervisione e il controllo dei processi industriali: il caso Moviconx. MS Thesis, University of Modena and Reggio Emilia.

Fitzpatrick, K. (2000). Alternative design consistency rating methods for two-lane rural highways. FHWA Report RD-99-172.

Fuller, R. (2005). Towards a general theory of driver behavior. *Accident Analysis and Prevention*, 37(3), 461–472.

Gipps, P.G. (1981). A behavioural car-following model for computer simulation. *Transportation Research*, 15B, 105–111.

Gollu, A. (1995). *Object Management Systems*. PhD Thesis.

Helbing, D. and Treiber, M. (1998). Jams, Waves and Clusters. *Science*, 282, 200–201.

Hoedemaeker, M., De Ridder, S. and Jahnsenn, W. (2002). Review of European human factors research on adaptive interface technologies for automobiles. TNO Report, TM-02-C031.

Hollnagel, E. (1993). *Human Reliability Analysis: Context and Control*. Academic Press, London.

Horberry, T., Anderson, J., Regan, M. and Tomasevic, N. (2004). A driving simulator evaluation of enhanced road markings. In *Proceedings of the Road Safety Research, Policing and Education Conference*, Perth, Australia. Peer reviewed paper.

Horberry, T. and May, J. (1994). *SpaD Human Factors Study: Directory of Relevant Literature*. Applied Vision Research Unit. University of Derby. UK

Horberry, T., Regan, M. and Anderson, J. (2005). The possible safety benefits of enhanced road markings: A driving simulator evaluation. *Transportation Research Part F*, 9, 77–87.

Kangwon, L.J. (2004). *Longitudinal Driver Model and Collision Warning and Avoidance Algorithms Based on Human Driving Database*. PhD Thesis. UMI 2004.

Karlson, R. (2004). Evaluating driver distraction countermeasures. Master Thesis in Cognitive Science, Cognitive Science Study Program, Linköpings universitet, Sweden.

Kemeny A (1993) A cooperative driving simulator. In *Proceedings of the International Training Equipment Conference and Exhibition Conference (ITEC)*, London, pp. 67–71.

Lansdown, T.C., Brook-Carter, N. and Kersloot, T. (2004). Distraction from multiple in-vehicle secondary tasks: Vehicle performance and mental workload implications. *Ergonomics*, 47, 91–104.

Leonardi, L., Mamei, M. and Zambonelli, F. (2004). Co-fields: Towards a unifying model for swarm intelligence. In *Engineering Societies in the Agents World III: Third International Workshop* (Vol. 2577, pp. 68–81). *Lecture Notes in Artificial Intelligence*. Springer-Verlag, Berlin.

Liang, C.Y. and Peng, H. (2000). String stability analysis of adaptive cruise controlled vehicles. *JSME International Journal Series C*. 43(3), 671–677.

Lieberman, E. and Rathi, A.K. (1997). Traffic simulation. InN.H. Gartner , C.J. Messer and A. Rathi (Eds.). *Traffic Flow Theory* (chapter 10). Federal Highway Administration and Oak Ridge National Laboratory.

Manstetten, D., Krautter, W., Grothkopp, B., Steffens, F. and Geutner, P. (2001). Using a driving simulator to perform a wizard-of-oz experiment on speech-controlled driver information systems. In *Proceedings of the Human Centered Transportation Simulation Conference (HCTSC 2001)*, Iowa City.

Martens, M.H. and van Winsum, W. (2000). Martens, M. H. and van Winsum, W. (1999). *Measuring distraction: The peripheral detection task.* Online paper. Available at www.nrd.nhtsa.dot..gov/departments/nrd-13/driver-distraction/welcome.htm.

Michon, J.A. (1985). A critical view of driver behaviour models: What do we know, what should we do? In L. Evans and R. Schwing (Eds.). *Human Behaviour and Traffic Safety.* Plenum Press, New York, pp. 485–520.

Miller, R. and Huang, Q. (2002). An adaptive peer-to-peer collision warning systems. *IEEE Vehicular Technology Conference (VTC).* Birmingham, AL, USA.

Minin, L. (2005). Prototipazione virtuale nell'interazione uomo-macchina: Benchmark analysis e testcomparati per supportare la scelta dei software di prototipazione virtuale più adeguati a differenti tipologie di interfacce utente. MS Thesis, University of Modena and Reggio Emilia.

Neunzig, D., Breuer, K. and Ehmanns, D. (2002). Traffic and vehicle technologies. Assessment with simulator PELOPS. *ISSE Conference.*

Ni, D. and Feng, C. (2002). A two-dimensional traffic simulation model. In *Proceedings of the 7th Driving Simulation Conference.*

Nilsson, L. (1995). Safety effects of adaptive cruise controls in critical traffic situations. In *Proceedings of The Second World Congress on Intelligent Transport Systems.* pp. 1254–1259.

Olsson, S. and Burns, P. (2000). *Measuring distraction with a peripheral detection task.* The National Highway Traffic Safety Administration Driver Distraction Internet Forum, on-line paper, available at http://www-nrd.nhtsa.dot.gov/departments/nrd-13/driver-distraction/Papers20006.htm#A6

Ossowski, S., Fernández, A., Serrano, J.M., Pérez-de-la-Cruz, J.L., Belmonte, M.V., Hernández, J.Z., García-Serrano, A. and Maseda, J.M. (2004). Designing multiagent decision support system—The case of transportation management. *Third International Joint Conference on Autonomous Agents and Multiagent Systems (AAMAS 2004)*, New York, pp. 1470–1471.

Özgüner, F., Özgüner, U., Takeshita, O., Redmill, K., Liu, Y., Korkmaz, G., Dogan, A., Tokuda, K., Nakabayashi, S. and Shimizu, T. (2004). A simulation study of an intersection collision warning system. In *Proceedings of the International workshop on ITS Telecommunications*, Singapore.

Panou, M., Cacciabue, N., Cacciabue, P.C. and Bekiaris, A. (2005). From driver modelling to human machine interface personalisation. *IFAC 16th World Congress*, Prague, Czech Republic.

Pentland, A. and Liu, A. (1999). Modelling and prediction of human behavior. *Neural Computation*, 11, 229–242.

Qi, Y. (1997). *A Simulation Laboratory for Evaluation of Dynamic Traffic Management Systems.* PhD Thesis at Massachusetts Institute of Technology, Boston, MA, USA.

Recarte, M.A. and Nunes, L.M. (2003). Mental workload while driving: Effects on visual search, discrimination, and decision making. *Journal of Experimental Psychology: Applied*, 9, 119–137.

Reece, D.A. and Shafer, S.A. (1988). An overview of the PHAROS traffic simulator. In Rothengater, J.A. and De Bruin, R.A. (Eds.). *Road User Behavior: Theory and Practice.* Van Gorcum, Assen.

Regan, M.A. and Horberry, T. (2004). A driving simulator evaluation of enhanced road markings. In *Proceedings of Australasian Road Safety Research, Policing and Education Conference*, Australia.

Rizzo, M., Jermeland, J. and Severson, J. (2002). Instrumented vehicles and driving simulators. *Gerontechnology*, 1(4), 291–296.

Salvucci, D.D., Boer, E.R. and Liu, A. (2001). Toward an integrated model of driver behavior in a cognitive architecture. *Tranportation Research Record No.* 1779, pp. 9–16.

Schvaneveldt, R.W., Reid, G.B., Gomez, R.L. and Rice, S. (1998). Modelling mental workload. *Cognitive Technology*, 3, 19–31.

Spillers, F. (2003). Task analysis through cognitive archaeology. In D. Diaper, N. Stanton (Eds.). *The Handbook of Task Analysis for HCI*. Laurence Erlbaum Associates, Mahwah, NJ.

Stone, P. and Veloso, M. (2000). Multiagent systems: A survey from machine learning perspective. *Autonomous Robots,* 8(3), 345–383.

Sukthankar, R., Hancock, J., Pomerleau, D. and Thorpe, C. (1996). A simulation and design system for tactical driving algorithms. In *Proceedings of AI, Simulation and Planning in High Autonomy Systems.*

Sukthankar, R., Hancock, J. and Thorpe, C. (1998). Tactical level simulation for intelligent transportation systems. *Journal on Mathematical and Computer Modelling, Special Issue on ITS*, 27(9/11), 228–242.

Sukthankar, R., Pomerleau, D. and Thorpe, C. (1995). SHIVA: Simulated highways for intelligent vehicle algorithms. In *Proceedings of IEEE Intelligent Vehicles.*

Theeuwes, J. (2002). Sampling information form the road environment. In R. Fuller, J.A. Santos (Eds.). *Human Factors for Highway Engineers*. Elsevier, Amsterdam.

Theeuwes, J. and Hagenzieker, M.P. (1993). Visual search of traffic scenes: On the effect of location expectations. In A. Gale, I.D. Brown, C.M. Haslegrave and S.P. Taylor (Eds.). *Vision in Vehicles* (Vol. 4, pp. 149–158). Amsterdam, The Netherlands.

Toffin, D., Reymond, G., Kemeny, A. and Droulez, J. (2003). Influence of steering wheel torque feedback in a dynamic driving simulator. In *Proceedings of the Driving Simulation Conference*, North America, Deaborn.

Zhang, Y., Owechko, Y. and Zhang, J. (2004). Driver cognitive workload estimation: A data-driven perspective. In *Proceedings of 77th International IEEE Conference on Intelligent Transportation Systems*, Washington, DC.

Zhang, Y., Owechko, Y. and Zhang, J. (2004). Learning-based driver workload estimation. In *Proceedings of 7th International Symposium on Advanced Vehicle Control*, Arnhem, The Netherlands.

Zijlstra, F.R.H. (1993). *Efficiency in Work Behaviour: A Design Approach for Modern Tools.* Delft University Press, Delft.

Index

E

J

K

L

S

T

U

V